WHAT THE E
ABOUT THIS BOO

"If you're fantasizing about living or retiring in Costa Rica, Christopher Howard is the go-to guy.

—Sara Davidson, *Oprah Magazine*

"Chris is *the* expert on relocating to Costa Rica — that's clear within a few minutes of reading his book or spending any time with him. For someone with his boundless knowledge and experience, he's also incredibly down to earth. For the neophyte, he really boils things down and takes care in answering your questions and introducing you to every major facet of life in this beautiful country. There's no better way to get introduced, settled and assimilated in Costa Rica than to have Chris as your point man."

—Peronet Despeignes, *Fortune Magazine*

"It's **FULL** of **VALUABLE** information, paints a **CLEAR** picture of what life is like for foreigners living there and is very **DOWN-TO-EARTH**."

—*USA TODAY*

"Another **SPLENDID** comprehensive guide to making the break. The **BEST** of several books geared to would-be residents. It leaves **NO** stone unturned.

—**Christopher Baker,** ***Costa Rica Handbook***

"Mr. Howard makes it **EASY** for anyone to leave the 'rat race.' This is by far the **BEST** guidebook on the subject."

—***Los Angeles Times***

"This book is **PACKED** with **PRACTICAL** information for both retirees and tourists."

—***Chicago Tribune***

"Potential residents of Costa Rica, shouldn't leave home **WITHOUT** this guide."

—***Dallas Morning News***

"*The New Golden Door to Retirement and Living in Costa Rica* offers **LOADS** of **USEFUL** information for the permanent resident."

—**Jack Reber,** ***San Diego Union-Tribune***

THIS IS WHAT OUR READERS HAVE SAID ABOUT THE BOOK

"**FANTASTIC BOOK!** Great, useful information for first-time visitors. A real VALUE at any price." —**Cory Brey, Siesta Key Florida**

"Your book is the most **COMPREHENSIVE,** informative help I could find, you have done a fine job." —**Niki Lesko**

"I just read your book and hope to run into you someday so you can sign it! Don't get me wrong, I'm not a typical autograph hunter, you may remember that I'm in corporate aviation? Thanks to the owner of the airplane and his circle of friends, we fly the likes of Don Henly, Ann Richards, etc. around. **NEVER** have I asked them to sign anything; you're the first, my man! —**Hank Guichelaar**

"I picked up your book about a year ago. I have found it very useful. Thanks for providing a good **INSIGHT** into Costa Rica." —**William Baio**

I received a copy of the "14th edition" from the library and was so impressed that I have been telling everyone I know that they **MUST** own this book!!. —**William F. Wessely**

"I have read your excellent book — the **BEST** I have read yet on the subject. I am returning to Costa Rica after a 25-year absence and consider your book an invaluable reference tool." —**Thomas Marino**

"NEVER before have I been so thoroughly prepared for moving to a new location as I was after reading — "The New Golden Door to Retirement and Living in Costa Rica"—. In fact, after arriving here, I was utterly and continuously amazed at how much **VALUABLE** knowledge I had previously obtained through reading this book. Furthermore, I find it **INDISPENSABLE** as a constant reference source for day-to-day operations. Subsequently I had purchased two similar, popular guide books and after several attempts at trying to read them, I find that they are incapable of holding my attention." —**Steve Stickles, Heredia, Costa Rica**

"I just picked up your book (The New Golden Door to Retirement and Living in Costa Rica) and I **LOVE** it. My wife and I have had a long time dream to someday retire (young) in paradise. It sounds like we have found our future destination. Your book has been very **HELPFUL**." —**Dan Graham**

THE NEW GOLDEN DOOR TO RETIREMENT AND LIVING IN COSTA RICA

A GUIDE TO INEXPENSIVE LIVING, MAKING MONEY AND FINDING LOVE IN A PEACEFUL TROPICAL PARADISE

WRITTEN BY
CHRISTOPHER HOWARD
WITH THE HELP OF RYAN PIERCY
OF THE ASSOCIATION OF RESIDENTS OF COSTA RICA

THE NEW GOLDEN DOOR TO RETIREMENT AND LIVING IN COSTA RICA

By Christopher Howard

Sixteenth Edition

Printed in China

ISBN 978-1-881233-66-4

Costa Rica Books
Suite 1 SJO 981
P.O. Box 025216
Miami, FL 33102-5216

www.costaricabooks.com
www.liveincostarica.com
www.amazon.com

"If there be any splendor in peace, let it rest in a country like this..."

Lambert James

"Costa Rica is a proud example of a free people practicing the principals of democracy. And you have done so in good times and in bad, when it was easier and when it required great courage."

Ronald Reagan, 1982

Christopher Howard with Costa Rica's Presidents

Former Costa Rican President, Luis Alberto Monge, receives a copy of Christopher's Bestseller.

Christopher Howard meets with Oscar Arias, Costa Rica's Nobel Peace Prize Winning President

BIBLIOGRAPHY

One-of-a-kind books written and published by Christopher Howard

1. **"Costa Rican Spanish Survival Course"** (1986)
2. **BEST SELLER "Christopher Howard's The New Golden Door to Retirement and Living in Costa Rica"** (1988-2010) 16 editions
3. **"Driving the Pan-American Highway to Mexico and Central America"** (1996)
4. **BESTSELLER "Christopher Howard's Living and Investing in the New Cuba** (1997, 2000, 2009) three editions
5. **BEST SELLER "Christopher Howard's Living and Investing in Nicaragua"** (2002, 2005, 2009) three editions
6. **BEST SELLER "Christopher Howard's Living and Investing in Panama"** (2005 and 2009) Two editions
7. **BEST SELLER "Christopher Howard's Guide to Costa Rican Spanish"** (2005, 2010) two editions
8. **BESTSELLER "Christopher Howard's Official Guide to Spanish in Panama"** (2009) first edition
9. **BESTSELLER "Christopher Howard's Official Guide to Cuban Spanish"** (2009) first edition
10. **"Christopher Howard's Official Guide to Mexican Spanish"** (2009) first edition
11. **"Christopher Howard's Official Guide to Nicaraguan Spanish"** (2009) first edition
12. **BLOCKBUSTER "Christopher Howard's Guide to Real Estate in Costa Rica"** June of 2009
13. **"Christopher Howard's Official Guide to the Costa Rican Legal System"** to be published in 2011
14. **"Christopher Howard's Guide to Living and retiring in Colombia"** to be published in 2011
15. **"Christopher Howard's Official Guide to Colombian Spanish"** to be published in 2012
16. **"Christopher Howard's Guide to Living and Retiring in South America"** to be published in 2012

Christopher Howard is interviewed on the NBC Today Show in April 2006

Media Attention and Accolades for Christopher Howard's Costa Rica Retirement Tours

Christopher Howard appears on the International Herald Tribune and CNBC World News in June of 2006

ACKNOWLEDGEMENTS

This edition would not have become a reality without the invaluable help of many people.

I would first like to thank my graphic designers, William "El Mago" Morales and Gabriela Watson, for their hard work and patience.

I am also very grateful to Pam and Mary at Blue Jewel Travel.

A special thanks to the following local writers and Costa Rican residents for their contributions to this edition: Martha Bennett, Landy Blank, Lair Davis, Annie Drake, Arnoldo Fournier, David Garrett, Rob Hodel, Guillermo Jiménez, Eric Liljenstrope, Randall Linder, Rudy Mathews, Charles Mills, Loyd Newton, Roger Petersen, Jacqueline Passey, Michael Pierpont, Ryan Piercy, Carlos Morton, Les Nuñez, Martin Rice, Todd Staley, Jo Stuart, the late Jay Trettien, John Vickery, John Williams, Meg Yamamoto and Abby Danielle of the *Tico Times* and all of the people at Costa Rica Living.

I am also indebted to all the critics whose many favorable reviews made my previous editions a success.

I would like to acknowledge all of the help I have received from the Publishers Marketing Association's and Amazon.com's programs for independent publishers. Thanks to them, this book is now available in the U.S., Canada and the rest of the world. A special thanks to my Costa Rican distributor, 7th Street Books, for a job well done.

Finally, I would like to express my eternal gratitude to members of my family, especially my late mother and wife, for their constant support when I needed it the most.

Christopher Howard
San José, Costa Rica

MORE ABOUT THE AUTHOR

Christopher Howard has lived, worked and played in one of the most magical places on earth for more than 30 years. His love for Costa Rica is so great that he became a citizen.

During this time, he has had the opportunity to gather a plethora of information about living, investing and retiring in Costa Rica. It is not surprising that he has first-hand knowledge and insight into all aspects of Costa Rica's culture and its people. Because of his expertise, he is a frequent lecturer at numerous investment seminars.

Mr. Howard has an extensive foreign language background, having earned a Bachelor of Arts in Latin American studies and a Master's of Arts (M.A.) degree in Spanish from the University of California. He also has credentials to teach Spanish at all levels from California State University, San Francisco.

He was the recipient of scholarships for graduate study at the University of the Americas in Puebla, Mexico and the Jesuit University of Guadalajara, Mexico in conjunction with the University of San Diego, California. In 1985, he founded a successful language institute in San José, Costa Rica. Mr. Howard has written five foreign language books including the best-selling, one-of-a-kind *Christopher Howard's Guide to Costa Rican Spanish* It is the only Spanish book that teaches Costa Rican style Spanish.

The author lives full-time in Heredia, Costa Rica

His other Spanish guides include *The Official Guide to Panamanian Spanish*, *The Official Guide to Cuban Spanish*, *The Official Guide to Mexican Spanish* and *The Official Guide to Nicaraguan Spanish.*

Chris Howard has worked as a paid consultant for *National Geographic Magazine*, published articles and columns in *Costa Rica Today*, *Escape Artist.com*, *Costa Rica Outdoors*, *Inside Costa Rica*, *AM Costa Rica*, the real estate publication *Casa Galeria*, and for various newsletter about living abroad. He is presently working on a feature action movie script to be filmed in Central America (the author also studied movie production at U.C.L.A's Motion Picture Department and his father was in the business).

Mr. Howard has also served as an officer on the Board of Directors of the Association of Residents of Costa Rica (ARCR) and is a lecturer at their monthly seminar.

He also has written and published a series of books for those who want to live and retire in the region including 16 editions of the perennial best-selling *New Golden Door to Retirement and Living in Costa Rica*, *Living and Investing in Panama* (2nd edition 2009), *Living and Investing in the New Nicaragua* (3rd edition 2009), the visionary *Living and Investing in Cuba* (4th edition 2009) and his most recent blockbuster the 550-page *Christopher Howard's Guide to Real Estate in Costa Rica* (2009).

His forthcoming guidebooks are, *Christopher Howard's Official Guide to the Costa Rican Legal System* , *Christopher Howard's Living and Investing in South America* and *Christopher Howard's Living and Investing in Colombia.* Like all of Mr. Howard's guidebooks, they promise to be the definitive books on their respective subjects.

Due to a multitude of requests from the readers of this guidebook, Christopher Howard began to offer relocation and retirement tours to Costa Rica starting in 1997. Since then he has personally introduced thousands of people to Costa Rica through his one-of-a-kind licensed monthly tours, seminars and private consultation services. Please see **www.liveincostarica.com** for more information about his unique tours.

–The Publisher

CONTENTS

FOREWORD

Why live in Costa Rica?

Recently I led a group of prospective residents on a trip around Costa Rica. After a week of traveling and attending a series of informative seminars, most of my clients decided they would like to live here for at least part of the year. Some of them even wanted to invest in real estate. It comes as little surprise that they felt this way. Costa Rica has more Americans per capita than any other country outside the United States.

Why do so many people want to live here?

The most obvious reason is the climate. People are tired of freezing winters, scorching summers and the high utility bills that go with them. In Costa Rica they can enjoy one of the best year-round climates in the world (72 degrees average in the Central Valley.) We have only two seasons here, dry and rainy, both with an abundance of sunshine. We rarely need air conditioning and never need heat. Costa Rica has more winter sunshine than Hawaii or Florida and fewer people.

Costa Rica is called "the Switzerland of the Americas" by many due to its neutral political status and magestic mountains. From the huge, curling waves of the Pacific coast, to the sight of spectacular volcanoes and verdant rain forests, Costa Rica's natural beauty has something for everyone. This unique little country offers a real paradise for the nature lover, fishing enthusiast and water sports fanatic as well as the retiree.

Many come here for the lifestyle. Costa Rica fits the bill for anyone sick of the hustle and bustle, seeking a more laid-back way of life. One of the tour participants remarked, "Costa Rica reminds me of the U.S. about 40 years ago when everything was unspoiled, unhurried and less crowded." A famous travel writer summed up the country in a recent article by stating, "This whole country is kind of a post-hippie paradise, the most laid-back place I've ever seen"

Costa Rica will also appeal to people of all ages seeking to move to a new and exotic land outside the States and Canada, as well as the energetic entrepreneur, the burned-out baby boomer, those sick of long rush-hour commutes and anyone seeking an alternative way of life.

Costa Rica is a place for people seeking economic opportunities and for those who believe and are willing to seek something better in this world and their lives. A country that offers health care for the poorest of its people, while providing free education for every child. A place where where there is abundant health, peace, prosperity and a country populated by the "happiest people in the world." As one resident says, "I now live in a freer country now than I ever have. I can remodel my house and not need as many permits, keep chickens in my backyard and have the freedom to live with low taxes, be an entrepreneur and create a business in a culture where there is less competition than in my homeland. You don't have to be rich to have a maid, a gardener or employees."

You can even live longer by moving to Costa Rica. Recently, *NBC Prime Time World News* had a special about a group of centenarians who live in an area located in Costa Rica's Nicoya Peninsula. In fact, the country boasts over 900 centenarians. Costa Ricans who reach the age of eighty have the longest longevity rate in the world beyond that age. This is mostly due to the lifestyle here. Many a foreigner who has moved here claims that "they have added years to their lives and life to their years." Perhaps the country will do the same for you?

This beautiful country is so appealing because it has the warmth and flavor of Mexico, without anti-Americanism or fear of government expropriations; the physical beauty of Guatemala without a large military presence; and the sophistication of Brazil without the abject poverty and with far less crime.

One travel brochure summed up the whole Costa Rica experience by stating, "Costa Rica, so small yet so big."

Is there a downside?

Yes, Costa Rica does have a few warts. The bureaucracy is slow moving and people get frustrated. There is crime but nothing like what is found in some cities in the U.S. or Mexico, El Salvador, Guatemala and other places in the region. Traffic is bad in San José and some of the other urban areas of the Central Valley. However, as a whole the many positives far outweigh the few negatives.

But isn't it expensive?

Although much has been written about the high cost of living here, what you spend depends on your lifestyle. If you must have a luxurious home, drive a late model car and buy imported goods, you will spend as much or more than you would in North America. But if you live more like the locals and are careful with your money, you will spend considerably less.

Many Americans living below the poverty line in the United States can live in moderate luxury on a modest retirement or investment income in Costa Rica.

The favorable exchange rate and low rate of inflation let you stretch your dollars here. The cost of food, utilities and entertainment are all substantially lower than in the United States.

Costa Rica's affordable medical care is among the best anywhere. The quality of health care is comparable to North America but the prices are one half or less. Considered by many to be the healthiest country south of Canada, Costa Rica has a longer life-expectancy than the United States (76.3 for men, 79.8 for women), and is rumored to be the third longest in the world.

In most areas housing costs are less than what you would be accustomed to paying in the United States. A few years ago I purchased a new three-bedroom 2000-foot home in San Francisco de Heredia, about five miles from downtown San José, for $85,000. It has a cathedral ceiling, sits on a 270-square-meter lot and is very comfortable for three people and a dog. I have a 15-year mortgage and pay $600 monthly including insurance, with a nine percent loan from a Costa Rican state bank.

Besides our home, I have two cars and a maid. Household help makes life easier. (You can hire a full-time maid for as little as $200 per month or a couple of dollars per hour.) My son goes to one of the best private universities in the country. I eat out a few times a week and enjoy various types of entertainment. We spend a week at the beach during Easter and go to the United States every Christmas. Our monthly expenses are about $3,000.

Costa Rica's inexpensive medical care, affordable housing, excellent transportation and communication networks, and abundance of activities with which to stay busy and happy, all contribute to the country's appeal and place it at the top of the list of retirement and expatriate havens.

According to a survey of potential foreign retirement areas in the *Robb Report*, due to the high quality of life Costa Rica surpasses all countries, including Mexico, Puerto Rico, Spain, Portugal, Australia, the Caribbean Islands and Greece.

What sets Costa Rica apart from its neighbors?

Nicaragua, Belize, Honduras and Guatemala have lower living costs, but you get what you pay for. The quality of life and lack of infrastructure in those countries leave a lot to be desired. Safety is a concern, especially where paramilitary police have power or where police are corrupt, as in Mexico. Costa Rica is politically stable and is unique in having no army. Although theft occurs, violent crime is minimal.

So to the person who is wondering about retiring to Costa Rica because it is more expensive than the other countries in the region, I would say research more than just economics because other components are more important.

What about Panama and Nicaragua?

Here is a foreigner's take on Panama," Panama City has very little access to the ocean, for a city right on the water. Most hotels own right to the water's edge. Panama City's harbor reeks of pollution at low tide. The causeway that passes by the ocean is usually noisy and choked with traffic. The weather is uncomfortably hot and humid (those who live on Costa Rica's coast will find this untrue, but those who prefer the moderate climate of the Central Valley will relate). As a result, you live constantly inside, with closed windows and air conditioning."

"According to the most recent polls forty-seven percent of all Panamanians view crime as the most pressing problem. The number of homicides has increased the last couple of years: 444 in 2007, 593 in 2008 and at the rate things are going the latter number will be topped. Forty-two percent of the murders have to do with drugs and fighting among local gangs."

"Poverty is another issue in Panama. The country has one of the worst distributions of wealth in Latin American which helps explain why nearly 30 percent of the population is living in poverty."

"Up in the mountain above David (the northern part of Panama, including Boquete), the climate is like the Costa Rica's Central Valley. Nice.

No crime. Friendly people who have not yet learned that an foreigner's pockets are a good way to accelerate one's retirement plan. But there's not much to do there. It reminds me of what I hear Costa Rica was like 20 years ago."

"Those who love Panama refer to the more efficient government, the good roads and road signs that make one think he is in a real country, and not a pueblo. They mention the cheaper prices (which are lower if you buy goods produced in Panama, but otherwise are fairly comparable to prices in Costa Rica). Yes, there is a police presence, but supposedly they are there to protect the foreign tourist, and not to favor the nationals, as happens reportedly in Costa Rica. They mention the government's tax breaks for foreigners (but neglect to mention that these are an endangered species, since the government has twice tried to remove them, and eventually will succeed)."

"What I did not like about Panama: Cops of various kinds are everywhere, constantly stopping people randomly to check your credentials etc. We had a scary run-in with an immigration cop who threatened us and extracted a bribe from us (Long story but we basically just made an innocent mistake and the guy took advantage of that to mess with us.) The nature (parks, forests) there is more "tucked away" in parks as opposed to being visible everywhere like in Costa Rica People didn't seem as friendly as in Costa Rica."

"Rather than live in Panama City, I'd go for Miami at today's lower real estate prices, better access to beaches and better sales at stores."

Here is another report about Panama: "I have decided to leave Panama City. One of the reasons is that my wife is afraid to leave the house because of the rapidly rising crime rates, especially the murders and killings that saturate the television stations every night. It has been said that the largest number of assassinations never make it to the news room because the government is covering up in order to protect the image of Panama as a retirement paradise. Another is the incredible deterioration in the quality of life in the capital city in the last five years. I have neighbors who are extremely inconsiderate of their co-owners and insist on making life difficult for others in their pursuit of self satisfaction.

" It gets tiring after a while to have to be fighting the service providers such as the banks, cable companies, phone companies to keep them from abusing their customers with incompetent service. It is almost as if it were a national obligation to stick it to the other guy lest you be considered. Everyday you are fighting tooth and nail to exercise one upmanship on all with whom you come in contact throughout the day to day dealings that are required. This is especially true when you see the maniacs driving on the roadways of the capital."

"The country beginning with the government from the highest to lowest level is totally corrupt. The business sector probably less so. That isn't to say that there are no honest people, there are but they have no power to make changes. It isn't hard to imagine that if improvements are not made in reducing corruption, the consequences of political upheaval will make living here more unbearable. Most anglos do not follow the news because they are incompetent in Spanish and are not aware of what is going on. I, fortunately, am fluent in the language, read it and therefore do notice the ongoing cover ups."

On the other hand, here is what resident says about Costa Rica. "Costa Rica has one of the most pacifist cultures in the world. Think of it: it has been almost 60 years since Costa Rica outlawed the army. This is the reason that I always return to Costa Rica its lack of an army. When I first arrived here in 1978, they used to boast that they had more teachers than policemen. I don't know if that is still true but they still put more emphasis on education and health than any other Central American country, not to mention the States and many European countries.

As for Nicaragua, is the second poorest country in the western hemisphere after Haiti. Hundreds of thousands of Nicaraguans have fled to Costa Rica to seek employment opportunities that don't exists in their own country where the average income is under $100 per month. Unfortunately, Mother Nature has raised havoc with the country in the form of a devastating earthquake which leveled Managua in the 1970s and Hurricane Mitch in the 1980s. Combine this with a who string of unscrupulous leaders like Ortega and Alemán who have stolen millions form the impoverished country and constant political squabbles and you have country immersed in a quagmire from which it may never emerge.

Home ownership is also in question in Nicaragua since the Sandinistas of the 1980s confiscated many properties. To this day this problem has not been resolved.

Crime has been on the upswing in Nicaragua, according to the U.S. State Department. The State Department also warned that U.S. citizens "are increasingly targeted shortly after arriving in the country by criminals posing as Nicaraguan police officers who pull their vehicles — including those operated by reputable hotels — over for inspection. In each case, the incidents happened after dark and involved gun-wielding assailants who robbed passengers of all valuables and drove them to remote locations where they were left to fend for themselves.

A place to invest

Costa Rica is a place for people seeking economic opportunities for those who believe in and are willing to seek something better in this world and in their lives. Costa Rica has a myriad of business opportunities awaiting creative, hard-working individuals. You can run a global business from here by using Internet access, fax machines and cell phones. It is also relatively easy to start a small business on a shoestring. Tax incentives and a government that encourages investments and affords investors the same rights as citizens contribute to a propitious business climate. Many countries either do not permit non-citizens to own property or they place restrictions on foreign-owned real estate, but this is not the case in Costa Rica. Anyone may buy real estate with all the legal rights of citizens. Actually, an investment in Costa Rica today is much better than an investment in California real estate was 30 years ago.

What gets people excited about Costa Rica is that it offers some of the best real estate on the planet at affordable prices. Prices will eventually go up as the rest of the world catches on. There's only so much beautiful beachfront and prime real estate left in the world. When you consider that almost every bit of coastline in the United States is becoming overcrowded and overpriced, Costa Rica seems like a bargain.

Passive investors will find CDs, second mortgages or other investments that offer a high interest rate in *colones* annually. These returns are good when you consider that a million dollars invested in the United States at a standard two to four percent annual rate will generate only$25,000 to $40,000 a year if you are lucky in today's economy.

A burgeoning global economy and the Internet communications revolution have created unlimited possibilities for doing business in Central and South America. Furthermore, trade pacts between Costa Rica, the United States, Mexico and South America are becoming a reality. These free-trade treaties promise to link all of the nations in the hemisphere in to one trading block.

Costa Rica's current prosperity is being fueled by the immigration of affluent baby boomers from around the world seeking their own piece of paradise and the same engine that has fueled the growth in California for the last 30 years, technology. When Intel decided it needed more capacity, they looked all over the western hemisphere and chose Costa Rica for the very same reasons you will.

Word is getting out about Costa Rica. And that's why now is such a good time to invest.

The adventure of starting over

Some move here to start over and seek adventure in an exotic land. They are tired of dead-end jobs or the rat race and want new challenges, a chance to pursue their dreams and achieve greater personal growth. As a foreigner, you have the challenge of immersing yourself in a new culture and, if you choose, the rewards of learning a foreign language.

Newcomers can make friends easily because foreigners gravitate towards one another. One transplant from Florida told us he had lived in Florida for 20 years and hardly ever had contact with his neighbors. He claims not to be the most sociable person in the world, nevertheless he has made more than a hundred friends in Costa Rica. He proudly says, "Everywhere I go I bump into people I know."

As strange as it may seem moving to Costa Rica has helped thousands of Americans improve their lives. Unplugging from their past and moving to a foreign country can make you feel rejuvenated and change your whole outlook on life. By living better with less as you can do in Costa Rica, people find their lives do change for the better. Scores of people adopt a simpler and less complicated Latin lifestyle. You just get a sense by looking at many of the ex-pats here that they have experienced personal growth by immersing themselves in all that Costa Rica has to offer. You would probably have to live here for a while to understand this, but the signs of renewed energy and vitality can be seen on most everyone's face who makes the move.

Why do some people choose to live overseas?

Most citizens of the United States and Canada feel comfortable living where they have always resided. Some are lucky enough to have invested in property and have good retirement programs, affordable health insurance, stocks, bonds or IRAs to ensure a good quality of life during their retirement years.

Others may not be so fortunate. They realize that they may have not planned well and may be a little short on money to maintain their present lifestyle. A simple solution is to try to lower their standard of living and be more frugal in their own country to compensate for poor financial planning and/or bad investments. They can downsize to a smaller home, move to a more affordable but less suitable area, give up their yearly vacations, fire the gardener and cut back on other areas of their life to just scrape by. But what if they could move to another country with the same amount of income and improve their lifestyle dramatically instead of reducing it?

Ernst & Young reported last year that three out of five (60%) middle class retirees would outlive their financial assets if they didn't cut back on spending significantly. Please stop and think about this for a minute. Can you imagine a life in retirement where every day you worry that you will live longer than your money lasts? What would you do? How would you allocate your precious resources? Would you cut back on, food or medicine? Both perhaps? The thoughts of a life like this are just plain frightening.

The math gets ugly when it comes to gaining back a loss. (Note: a 50% drop requires a 100% gain to break even) The S & P has decreased considerably and continues to be volatile. It's going to take a lot of earnings to justify a big rally.

The other major source of funding that people have planned on for retirement is the equity built up in their homes. Many retirees expected to sell their appreciated home asset and use those funds for a new acquisition in a warmer climate and then bank the rest for additional income in the golden years. We all know what has happened to the value of most homes in North America. Retirees planning to free up cash for a retirement purchase will likely find the numbers lacking

The bottom line is that we don't have to leave our future in the hands of the uncertain and volatile real estate and stock markets. There are concrete things that we can do to take control and assure a higher quality of life in retirement (or anytime) for less cost.

Living in the right country outside the United States can make all the difference in the world between just subsisting and maintaining the lifestyle to which you are accustomed. Costa Rica offers a viable alternative.

The idea of living overseas is not new. The huge number of Americans due to retire is staggering. Currently almost 40 percent of the population of the United States is over 50. By 2020, half the U.S. population will be over 50. Most Americans ages 41 to 59 say they will move when they retire.

Adjusting and keeping busy

Adjustment to a new way of life can take many months. However, an open mind, a positive attitude and a willingness to seek out new experiences can make the transition relatively painless.

Costa Rica has come a long way in the last decade. Satellite and DirecTV (called Sky here), private mail service and the Internet make it easier to stay in touch with family and friends in the United States and keep up with what is going on all over the world. If you don't own a computer, you can go to an Internet café.

Costa Rica's modern technology has made life easy for foreign residents. In most areas of the country you can get cash at a local ATM, manage your investments online and read almost any major newspaper in the world the day it comes out.

A friend of mine, a 20-year resident of Costa Rica, said, " My days are so filled with exciting activities and interesting experiences that each day seems like a whole lifetime. I really feel that I have discovered the fountain of youth."

Single men are attracted to the country because it has the reputation of having the most beautiful, flirtatious and accessible women in Latin America. It comes as no surprise that Costa Rican women are highly sought as companions by foreign men of all ages. Single men will have no problem finding love, romance and a second chance in life with a devoted Costa Rican woman.

You will never be bored here unless you choose to be. Costa Rica has something for everyone. In *The Tico Times*, the weekly English-language newspaper, you can find hundreds of interesting activities: movies in English, support groups, computer and bridge clubs — you name it, Costa Rica has it.

Living in Costa Rica can open the door to a new and exciting life. Who knows? You may never want to return home.

One expatriate's experience

Michael Pierpont, the founder of Sunburst Coffee, fell in love with Costa Rica a few years ago and knew right away that this was where he wanted to live. You, too, may find that you want to spend more than just a few weeks every year in this delightful country.

"People ask me all the time why I chose Costa Rica," says Michael. "I like this country for several reasons. First, it is a spectacularly beautiful place. Along the Pacific coast you will find rocky outcrops and pounding surf. The beaches look just like those in California, which is where I am from. But you can buy here for one-tenth the cost of California. Inland you'll find a lush jungle Lake Arenal, the Irazú Volcano and coffee plantations and the most beautiful rain forests in the world. In the northwest you will find white-sand beaches, many that are declared turtle reserves, one of the numerous areas in this country that is set aside for wildlife research and preservation.

"Second, and important to me, is the cost of living. I can live well in this country on as little as $2,500 per month. You can rent a comfortable house in San José, where I chose to settle, for $700 per month. You can employ a full-time maid for $185 monthly. You will spend $300 per month on groceries, $65 per month on electricity. You can see a movie for $4 and have a nice dinner with drinks for $25.

" Third, I was smitten by the people. Costa Ricans are good-natured and kind, trusting and friendly and extremely beautiful. I knew I'd be happy living and making friends here."

"A few more notes on why I came to Costa Rica: the weather is great, the Spanish colonial history and architecture is delightful, the small expatriate community is welcoming and an extremely interesting bunch. Everyone's got a story. And best of all the taxes are low and easy to deal with. "

Another view of the country

One resident remarked, "There are many reasons why people come to Costa Rica, but here are the reasons I personally hear most frequently:

1. The sweetest people in the world. The *ticos* welcome foreigners and, are affectionate, and sunny.
2. One of the world's best climates. Even in the rainy season, it beats almost anywhere else.
3. Still affordable prices: you can build a simple but pleasant home here for $65 per square foot.
4. A government that allows you to retire here with a modest pension.
5. Almost any part of Costa Rica is cheaper than most parts of the United States and Europe. Exceptions might be Florida, Texas and other southern states.
6. Medical care is excellent and inexpensive.
7. The people here are generally handsome and well-groomed. Many ladies I emphasize lady, please are pretty, slender and appealing. We do not encourage, however, exploitation, although it sometimes happens.
8. There are micro-climates for all tastes. I personally like the higher elevations and mountainous areas where it is cooler and fresher. Others crave beaches, which are hotter and more humid. There are literally dozens of climates, and you can pick an area that is comfortable for you.
9. This is both a rustic, primitive country, and an upcoming economy with many amenities, Internet, movies and shopping malls - you can have the best of all worlds.
10. Although there is considerable petty pilfering here, it is also a gun-free country for the most part, and people feel safer here than in equivalent areas in the United States and abroad. The worst thing that might happen to you is that someone takes your T.V. because they think they need it more than you do."

Actually, Costa Rica is a lot like the United States

Thirtyish expatriate Jacqueline Passy stated in her blog, I've lived in San José for six months and I've found I can get almost anything here that I could get in the United States. I live in a house with all the same services I had in the United States: electricity, hot water to all my sinks and showers, flush toilets, cable television with US programming, high-speed Internet service, etc. The main difference is that I don't have or need air conditioning or heating and we are able to leave our windows open year-round.

I go shopping at supermarkets, pharmacies, malls, and other stores that are very similar to the ones in the United States. They close earlier, but stock almost all the same stuff.

Más x Menos and AutoMercado are very similar to U.S. supermarkets, except some of the foods are different and the cash registers and sales displays are actually more advanced than the ones I've seen in the US. I can also buy liquor in the grocery store which is a nice change from my home state of Washington.

The pharmacies here are well stocked and you can buy many more drugs without a prescription than you can in North America; just tell the pharmacist what is wrong with you, and he or she will hook you up.

Hipermás is bigger than any Wal-Mart I've ever been in. PriceSmart is very similar to Costco or Sam's Club. There are Office Depots here.

The malls here are very much like the malls in the United States, except the VIP theaters in Terra Mall in Cartago are far superior to any movie theater I've been to in the United States.

Cars and gas are more expensive than in the United States but are becoming more common as rising middle-class incomes allow people other than the rich to buy them. There are new car dealerships, used car dealerships, private party sales, etc. just like in the United States.

I have yet to find a service that I used in the United States that isn't available here. Not only are services widely available, they are much cheaper than in the United States. A general rule of thumb is services are cheaper and physical things (especially imports) are more expensive.

I said I have been able to find "almost" everything here. Here are the few things that I have not been able to find (yet):

- Christmas cookie cutters.
- Bubble tea.
- Foundation and powder in my skin tone (very pale).
- The selection of English-language books is not very big.

- Occasionally the brand of shampoo I use is sold out in all the stores at the same time.
- The Sci-Fi Channel is not available on cable here, but all I wanted to watch was Battlestar Galactica and I discovered that I could buy and download the episodes from iTunes.

Other than the above I have had no problem obtaining the goods and services necessary to lead an "American lifestyle", for significantly less money than it would cost me to live a similar lifestyle in the US.

Yes, there are some significant differences between the United States and Costa Rica, but these have to do with culture, language, politics, economics and climate — not with the availability of material things. So the people who tell you that you can't live the same sort of lifestyle here as you can in the United States are either a) lying (and who knows what their motives are), b) living way out in the country, or c) very poor.

Why the author chose Costa Rica

About 35 years ago I spent a year as an exchange student in Puebla, Mexico. It proved to be the best experience I ever had and the turning point of my life. I truly became enamored with the Latin culture and decided I really wanted to live in a Spanish-speaking country.

I was barely 20 years old and still had to finish my last year of undergraduate work at UCLA. Nevertheless, I did not give up on my dream. After graduating, I obtained a teaching credential so I would have three months of vacation each year to explore Mexico and the rest of Latin America.

My journey began with Guatemala. Every country I visited in Central and South America had something to offer. But as a whole Costa Rica was by far the leader of the pack. Brazil had Rio and its vibrant culture. Argentina had cosmopolitan Buenos Aires, Mendoza, the Pampas, Patagonia and Bariloche. Chile had its Switzerland-like lake region in the south and Santiago in the center of the country set against the backdrop of the Andes. Peru had Lake Titicaca, pre-colonial Cuzco and Machu Picchu with its rich Incan culture. Ecuador had the Galapagos Islands and colonial Quito. But none of these countries, including beautiful Mexico to the north, came close to Costa Rica as a whole. So, after extensive research and travel I decided the country where I really wanted to live was Costa Rica.

I began to return to Costa Rica every chance I had. My first trip was for two weeks. My next visit was for a month. Each time I found a way to protract my stay. I was living in the San Francisco Bay Area but found myself spending most of my time thinking about Costa Rica. I really felt more at home there than in the United States. Consequently, I decided to follow my heart and move to Costa Rica to pursue my dream. I did not want to wait until I was 65 years old and retired to make the move.

All of my friends and relatives said I was crazy to give up a secure teaching position and move abroad. They just couldn't understand why I would leave the comforts of the good old USA to move to a third world country. Some even asked me if there was a revolution going on in Costa Rica. Obviously they were confusing Costa Rica with Nicaragua and El Salvador of the 1980s.

Needless to say, I made my move twenty-nine years ago and have never looked back. I love the country, the culture and the people. My adopted country has been very good to me and I have found success and happiness here.

¡Pura vida!

INTRODUCTION

Welcome to beautiful Costa Rica

Costa Rica's friendly 4 million people, or ***ticos*** as they affectionately call themselves, invite you to come and experience their tranquil country, with its long and beautiful coastlines, alluring Caribbean and Pacific waters, pristine beaches and some of the most picturesque surroundings you have ever laid eyes on.

Many visitors say Costa Rica is even more beautiful than Hawaii, and, best of all, still unspoiled. In fact, Costa Rica took over Hawaii's place as best adventure destination last year, according to the publication *Pacific Business News.*

Travel Weekly selected Costa Rica as "the 2004 best destination for tourists traveling from the United States." — Costa Rica has Hawaii's weather, spectacular green mountains, and beaches without the high prices. The country offers more beauty and adventure per acre than any other place in the world.

In the heart of the Central Valley, surrounded by beautiful rolling mountains and volcanoes, sits San José, the capital and largest city in the country. Viewed from above, this area looks like some parts of Switzerland.

Downtown San José is always bustling with activity

San José is the center of the country's politics and cultural events. It has a mixture of modern and colonial architecture, yet remains charmingly quaint and retains a small-town feel despite being a fairly large city with a slightly international flavor. It feels more like a town that has grown in all directions, rather than a metropolis. Though San José and adjacent suburbs have a population of approximately 1 million, you get a small-town feeling because of the layout of the city. San José and Panama City are considered the most cosmopolitan cities in Central America.

In a 2004 survey by Mercer Human Resource Consulting, San José ranked 130 out of 140 cities world wide with respect to cost of living. Tokyo and London were at the head of the list. The British publication *The Economist* ranked San José as the second most affordable city in Latin America. The cost of living is only 45 percent of that of New York.

San José or *Chepe*, as the locals call it, is also the cultural and business center of the country and a mecca for North Americans. There is something here for everyone. The city and surrounding areas boast the three largest shopping malls in Central America, with lots of stores to which you are accustomed back home.

San José and its suburbs also offer a variety of night life, a wide range of hotels, restaurants serving international cuisine, casinos, quaint cafés, lovely parks, the old National Theater with a wonderful orchestra and lots of outside attractions on a regular basis. Also of interest are a zoo, art galleries, theaters, museums, parks, an English-language newspaper, places for people watching and much more. Virtually everything in a large U.S. city can be found here. Americans have no trouble feeling at home. It is very easy to find something to do to entertain yourself. At an altitude of just over 3,750 feet above sea level, San José adds year-round spring-like temperatures to its appeal.

The city is laid out in a grid. *Calles* (streets) run north and south and *avenidas* (avenues) run east and west. Avenues to the north of *Avenida Central* have odd numbers and those to the south even numbers. Streets to the east of *Calle Central* have odd numbers and those to the west even. There are a number of pedestrian closed to traffic streets which are idea for taking stroll and enjoying the sites.

San José's convenient central location makes any part of the country accessible in a matter of hours by automobile. We recommend you use San José as a gateway, starting point or home base while you explore Costa Rica and look for a permanent place to reside.

Because of the country's small size, it is possible to spend the morning at the beach, visit a volcano at noon and enjoy dinner at a mountain resort overlooking the Central Valley.

COSTA RICA
A country that lives up to its name
by Julie Campbe

"In my capacity as Fashion and Travel Editor of Sports Illustrated magazine, I've produced every one of the magazine's swimsuit issues from 1965 to 1996, thirty-two in all. My annual search for beautiful and unspoiled locations has led me to every continent except Antarctica, and I've walked literally hundreds of miles of beaches, mountain trails, deserts, and even glaciers in order to take our readers to some of the most exotic, and often overlooked, corners of our planet. Sometimes my choice was a resort so new that it could only be envisioned from an architect's blueprint; in other years I've settled on an island or a country or even an entire continent— Australia.

So what brought me to Dominical, Costa Rica? Looking at the map I was struck for the first time by how near a neighbor Central America was, and at the same time how little I knew about it. I had to know more, and when I discovered Costa Rica, the jewel of the Central American chain, and traveled its length and breadth, I knew I had found something very special—a country that truly lives up to its name.

Costa Rica means Coast of Abundance or richness of nature. Its rainforests comprise a virtual cornucopia of flowers, lush vegetation, birds and wildlife—all still unspoiled. Rising from the coastline at Dominical are the majestic green mountains with rushing clear streams leading to crystal waterfalls and swimable fresh-water pools.

Coming down from mountains that were often tucked behind mist and clouds I found myself in a beautiful and varied stretch of coast. One side of the country faces the Pacific and the other the Caribbean. For our shoot I chose the Pacific at a place called Dominical, where one beach is more lovely and dramatic than the next. The diversity was breathtaking. And on these immaculate beaches there is no one to step over you while sunning, and only the sound of tropical birds and rolling surf.

I came to Dominical to take gorgeous pictures of gorgeous models in a gorgeous setting, and indeed I was able to do that. But the real discovery was a small piece of God's Country that I'll want to revisit again and again—and on my own time!

**Courtesy of Sports Illustrated*

Costa Rica Love Song

Written by: Lair Davis

I love you, Costa Rica, my home. Let me count the ways.

I love the fact that I have no mailbox, which means I receive no junk mail. I do have a post office box, however. There is never any junk mail in it, either.

I love my neighborhood bar, where they welcomed me effusively and let me run a tab the first time they ever laid eyes on me. Each time I go to that happy place, you would think I am their most regular customer. I've been there three times in the past year.

I love being able to make monthly payments on something the full cost of which is $25.

I love the iguana that lives in the drainage ditch up the block, and that he has become so fat because all the neighbors feed him constantly.

I love never having to think about tomatoes (or other fruits and vegetables) being out of season.

I love the jugglers who entertain you at street intersections in San José while you wait for the light to change.

I love the police — wow! Never thought I'd say that! Costa Rican police really aren't law enforcers so much as peace-keepers and information-givers. They seem so much less full of themselves than police I've encountered elsewhere.

I love those wonderful massages given by the fully accredited physical therapist in my town. It costs $15 for a 90-minute treatment.

I love that the buses will stop to pick up and drop off people anywhere along the road between towns.

I love it that there is a shop where they only repair umbrellas. It costs about a dollar to have one fixed — while you wait.

I love receiving a discount from just about every store and business in the country simply because I smile and say *buenos días* to everyone when I enter. I enjoy watching other gringos in the same stores seriously "get right down to business," having not learned this little touch of Costa Rican social grace — and then watching them pay more everywhere every time. You think cultural differences do not matter? You feel that simple, basic courtesy doesn't pay?

I love the continued tradition in this country of doctors, lawyers and other professionals making "house calls."

I love watching a teenage boy holding hands with his mother while walking through the public park in the center of town in full view of all his friends.

I love never having seen a single child throw a fit in the grocery store. How have these children learned to behave so well in public places, I wonder.

I love never having to trim the fat off the beef.

I love knowing when the national soccer team scores without even watching the game. Everyone else is watching, though. With every goal, the whole community lets out a roar.

I love when I ask someone for directions and he or she completely stops what they are doing in order to escort me personally halfway across town, deliver me to the door, and proudly introduce me to the proprietor.

I love the politeness most teenagers display to people my age. Yesterday I watched a teenage boy leave his friends waiting while he went back across the street and assisted an elderly gentleman in making his way. No snide, smart-alecky remarks greeted the good Samaritan when he returned to his group of friends.

I love not knowing the weather forecast. Actually, I DO know the forecast. Everyone who lives in Costa Rica knows what the weather will be like today.

I love not having to decide what to wear today.

I love not being able to hear the televisions in so many places because of the sound of the rain falling on the tin roofs.

I love when the clouds suddenly roll in and hide that tremendous mountain across the valley, and then just as suddenly roll out again.

I love having sidewalks along country roads.

I love sunsets that take my breath away, and the necklaces of streetlights that sparkle at night up and down the mountains in the distance.

I love being awakened at dawn by the noisiest birds on the planet.

I love having a cup of java at the local coffee shop that is as good as any offered by Starbuck's — at one-fifth the price.

I love when a storekeeper informs me that I am the greatest living customer he has ever had the honor and privilege to humbly serve and that my presence in his establishment has surpassed any possible visit in the future by Her Majesty Queen Elizabeth II of England herself. (A slight exaggeration, I suppose but, hey, it worked — I'll be back!)

I love the smiles on the faces of the taxi drivers as they go about their daily work. I love the fact that tipping taxi drivers is not customary. I love that so many *taxistas* insist that I take back the change from my fare, even when it amounts to less than a nickel.

I love that I am coming to understand the joy of "now." Tomorrow will come — or not — but "now" is this moment's pleasure. *¡Pura vida!* Pure life!

** Printed with the author's permission.*

Costa Rica's National Anthem

(The country's beautiful National Anthem
is sung in Spanish. This translation is to help non-Spanish
speakers understand its meaning.)

Noble country, our lives are revered
in your flying flag;
For in peace, white and pure,
we live tranquil beneath the clear
limpid blue of your sky.

And their faces are ruddy with hard work,
In fields beneath the life giving sun.
Though are but farm workers, their labors eternal,
Esteem, renown and honor have won.

Hail, oh land of our birth!
Hail, oh gracious land we love!

If an enemy seeking to slander
you or harms your name,
then we will abandon our farms
and arise with fervor to take up arms.

Oh, sweet country, our refuge and shelter;
How fertile your life giving soil!
May your people contended and peaceful
unmolested continue their hard work.

Things to think about before moving to a new country or making foreign investments

- What is required to become a legal resident? Can I meet these requirements? What is the cost? How often does residency have to be renewed, what are the conditions of renewal and what is the cost?
- What is required to visit, or stay while I'm waiting for residency?
- What is the political situation? How stable is the country?
- Weather — Will I like the weather year-round?
- Income taxes — Will I be taxed on income brought into the country? — Am I allowed to earn income in the country? If yes, how is it taxed?
- Other taxes — Sales tax, import duties, exit taxes, vehicle taxes, etc.
- How much will it cost in fees, duties and import taxes to bring my personal possessions into the country— cars, boats, appliances, electronic equipment, etc.?
- Rental property — How much? Availability?
- Purchase property — property taxes, restrictions on foreign ownership of property, expropriation laws, building regulations, squatters rights, etc. Is there a capital gains tax?
- Communications — Are there reliable phone and fax lines, cellular phones, beepers, connections to Internet and other computer communication services? Is there good mail service between the country and the rest of the world? Are there private express mail services such as DHL, UPS and FedEx? Are there local newspapers, radio and TV in a language I will understand? Is cable or satellite TV available?
- Transportation — How are the roads? Are flights available to places I will want to go? How are the buses and taxis ? How costly is it to travel to and from other international destinations?
- Is it difficult for friends and family to visit?
- Shopping — Are replacement parts available for the items I have brought from home? If so, what are the costs? If not, how much will it cost to import what I need?
- Are the types of food to which I am accustomed readily available in both markets and restaurants?
- If I have hobbies, are clubs, supplies and assistance available?
- What cultural activities are available - (art, music, theater, museums, etc.)?

- What entertainment is available - (sports, movies, nightclubs, dancing, etc.)?
- What recreational facilities are available? (golf courses, tennis, health clubs, recreational centers, parks, etc.)?
- If I like the beach, are good beaches available? Can they be reached easily? What is the year round temperature of the water?
- What is the violent crime rate? Minor crime (theft, car and house break-ins)? What support can be expected from the police? Are the police helpful to foreign residents?
- How do local residents treat foreign visitors and residents?
- What are the local investment opportunities like? Is there any consumer or protective legislation for investors? What return can I expect from my investments?
- Is the banking system safe and reliable? Can banks transfer funds and convert foreign currency, checks, drafts, and transfers? Are checking, savings and other accounts available to foreigners? Is there banking confidentiality? Is there a favorable rate of exchange with the U.S. dollar?
- Are good lawyers, accountants, investment advisors and other professionals available?
- How difficult is it to start a business? What kinds of opportunities are there?
- How is the health care system? Is it affordable? Do they honor U.S. and Canadian health insurance? Are there any dangerous diseases, and if so, does the local health care system address the problem? What is the quality of hospitals, clinics, doctors and dentists? What is the availability of good specialists?
- How is the sanitation? Can I drink the water? Do the restaurants have good sanitation standards? Are pasteurized milk and other dairy products available? Do meat, fish and vegetable markets have satisfactory sanitary standards?
- If I am interested in domestic staff, what is the cost of cooks, housekeepers and gardeners, etc.? Is the local help reliable? What regulations are involved in hiring employees? What are employers' responsibilities to workers?
- What legislation is there to protect foreign residents? What rights do foreign residents have in comparison to citizens?
- What natural disasters are there — hurricanes, tornadoes, typhoons, earthquakes, droughts, floods?
- Can pets be brought into the country?
- Is there religious freedom?

**Courtesy of the Association of Residents of Costa Rica*

1

COSTA RICA'S LAND, HISTORY AND PEOPLE

The Lay of the Land

Costa Rica occupies a territory of about 20,000 square miles in the southern part of Central America, and includes several small islands, mostly on the Pacific side. It is much like the state of Florida with two long coastlines. The country is only about 200 miles long and 70 miles wide at its narrowest part.

Costa Rica is often compared to Switzerland and Hawaii because of its mountains and forests. The country's three mountain ranges create five geographically diverse areas, the Northern Central Plains, the Northwest Peninsula, the Tropical Lowlands on the Pacific and Caribbean coasts and the Central Valley where 70 percent of the population resides. The country is divided into seven provinces: Alajuela, Cartago, Guanacaste, Heredia, Puntarenas, Limón and San José.

Unlike many areas of Mexico, Central and South America, Costa Rica remains beautiful and warm year-round. This is partly because it borders the Pacific Ocean on the west, the Atlantic Ocean on the east, and has a string of towering volcanoes on the Central Plateau. Combine all this and you have a unique tropical paradise with 11 climatic zones.

COSTA RICA General Information

Capital	San José
Population	4,300,000
Size	19,730 square miles
Quality of Life	Excellent,(good weather, friendly people, affordable)
Official Language	Spanish (English is widely spoken)
Political System	Democracy
Currency	Colón
Investment Climate	Good-many opportunities
Per capita income	$4,288
Official Religion	Catholicism
Foreign Population (U.S., Canadian and European)	Over 50,000
Longevity	77.49 is almost as high the U.S.
Literacy	95%
Time	Central Standard (U.S.)

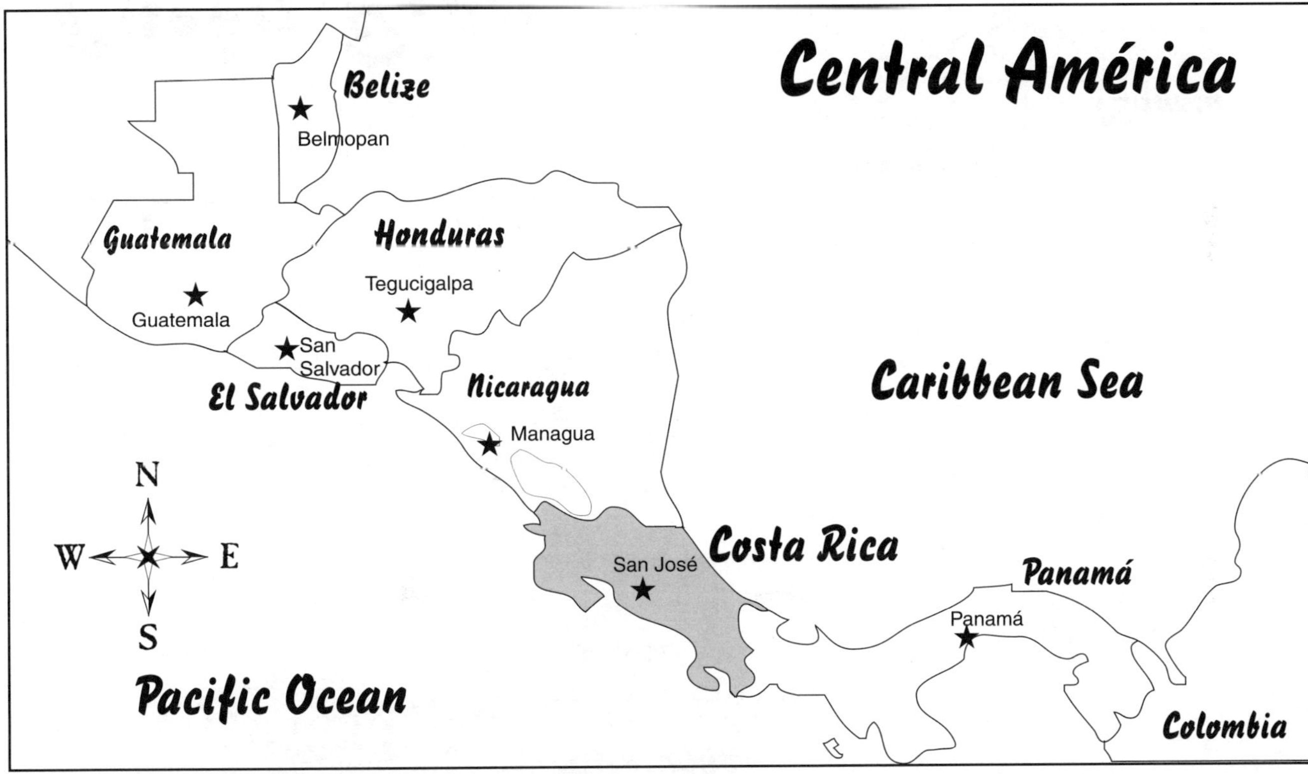
Central América
Belize
Belmopan
Guatemala
Guatemala
Honduras
Tegucigalpa
San Salvador
El Salvador
Nicaragua
Managua
Caribbean Sea
N
W
E
S
Costa Rica
San José
Panamá
Panamá
Pacific Ocean
Colombia

Nicaragua
ATLANTIC
OCEAN
PACIFIC
OCEAN
Panamá
Guanacaste
Alajuela
Heredia
San José
Cartago
Limón
Puntarenas
PEÑAS BLANCAS
LA CRUZ
SANTA CECILIA
LOS CHILES
UPALA
GOLFO DE PAPAGAYO
SAN RAFAEL
LIBERIA
SANTA ROSA
ARENAL
MUELLE
TORTUGUERO
EL COCO
FORTUNA
TILARAN
PUERTO VIEJO
CARIARI
CAÑAS
FLORENCIA
TAMARINDO
BELEN
SAN CARLOS
SANTA CRUZ
GUAPILES
JUNQUILLAL
NICOYA
MANSION
NARANJO
SIQUIRRES
PUERTO LIMON
CARMONA
PUNTARENAS
ESPARZA
ATENAS
SAN JOSE
TURRIALBA
NOSARA
SAMARA
OROTINA
CARTAGO
PAQUERA
SANTIAGO
SAN IGNACIO
TARCOLES
CAHUITA
MONTEZUMA
PUERTO VIEJO
JACO
SANTA MARIA
BIBRI
CABUYA
SIXAOLA
PARRITA
SAN GERARDO
GUABITO
QUEPOS
SAN ISIDRO DE EL GENERAL
DOMINICAL
BUENOS AIRES
N
W
E
S
PUERTO CORTES
PALMAR
PASO REAL
COTO BRUS
JABILLOBRUS
SAN VITO
GOLFITO
PUERTO JIMENEZ
PASO CANOAS
CARATE
Costa Rica

La Nacion newspaper's web site offers a great digital map of all cities in Costa Rica: http://lnmapas.nacion.co.cr/maps/index.shtml. Also try http://www.mapealo.com/mapealo/mapealo/index.php?idioma=esp&provincia=0

Weather

Costa Rica has a tropical climate since it lies so near the equator. In fact, the country is famous for having one of the best climates in the world. You dress in lightweight clothing year-round; a jacket may be necessary for higher elevations and cool nights. For the rainy season U.S.-style rain gear is too warm and cumbersome for the tropics.

Temperatures vary little from season to season and fluctuate with altitude. The higher you go, the colder it gets, and the lower you go the warmer it gets. In the Central Valley, spring-like daytime temperatures hover around 72 degrees all year, while lower elevations enjoy temperatures ranging from the upper 70s to the high 80s. Temperatures at sea level fluctuate between the high 80s and low 90s in summer with slightly more humidity than at higher elevations.

Like other tropical places, Costa Rica only has two seasons. The summer, or *verano,* is generally from late December to April with March and April being the warmest months of the year. The rainy season or *invierno*, runs from May to November. January is usually the coolest month. At times, there is an unseasonably dry spell or Indian summer either in July, August or September. The Costa Ricans call this pause in the rainy weather, *veranillo,* or "little summer." A relatively dry period at the end of July is referred to as *canícula* when there is a respite in the May to November rains. Light rains mixed with sunshine characterize this period, which can sometimes extend into August.

Unlike many of the world's tropical areas, almost all mornings are sunny and clear, with only a few hours of rain in the afternoons during the wet season. Since the temperature varies little, the wet months are usually as warm as the dry months. It is unusual to have two or three days of continuous rainy weather in most areas of the country. October is usually the rainiest month of the year. However, the Caribbean coast tends to be wet all year long. For this reason, many foreigners choose to live on the west coast of Costa Rica. This climate, along with a unique geography, is responsible for Costa Rica's lush vegetation and greenness at all elevations, especially during the rainy season.

Foreigners should not let the rain get them down, since there are a variety of indoor activities available. San José's many museums, theaters, malls, casinos, roller skating rinks, Internet cafés and other indoor activities will more than keep you busy when it rains.

Here are several good sites that offer information about Costa Rica's weather: **http://costa-rica-guide.com/Weather/WeatherMap.html**, **http://www.vacationscostarica.com/costa_rica_weather.htm**, **http://www.fallingrain.com/world/CS**, **www.planetario.ucr.ac.cr**, **www.imn.ac.cr/prono/prono.htm** weather for next five days, for 20 Costa Rican cities **www.worldweather.org/171/m171.htm** (for 20 cities in Costa Rica) and for sea weather **www.imn.ac.cr/marino/MARINO.htm**.

Costa Rica's Unique History in Brief

Traditionally Costa Rica has been a freedom-loving country living by democratic rules and respecting human rights.

According to archeologists, the northern part of Costa Rica was originally inhabited by the Chortegas, who got their name from an ancient place in Mexico called Cholula. Another group of pre-Columbian people migrated from northern South America. They were skilled gold artisans.

When Columbus set foot on the Atlantic coast at a place called Cariari (Puerto Limón) on September 18, 1502, he anticipated finding vast amounts of gold, so he named this area Costa Rica "rich coast" in Spanish. However, unlike Mexico and Peru, Costa Rica had neither advanced indigenous civilizations nor large deposits of gold. The small Indian population offered little resistance to the Spanish and was eventually wiped out by disease. Faced with no source of cheap labor, the Spanish colonists were forced to supply the labor themselves. Consequently, the people became quite independent and self-sufficient, and were basically very poor. Thus, a sort of democratic, equalitarian society developed with everyone doing their share of the work, and few becoming very rich or very poor.

For a couple of centuries Costa Rica was almost forgotten by Spain because it lacked trade and wealth. In fact, Costa Rica became so isolated and unimportant to the mother country that it didn't experience the same conquest and domination that took place in countries to the north and to the south. Costa Rica was so far removed from the mainstream that there was no War of Independence from Spain in the early 1800s, as there was in the rest of Latin America. Costa Ricans learned of their newly won independence from a letter that arrived one month after independence was officially granted in October of 1821. During this period, coffee became the leading export and the wealth it brought to the coffee growers allowed them to dominate politics.

In the mid-1800s the country experienced imperialism first-hand when an impish American, named William Walker, tried to establish himself as dictator in Central America. Costa Ricans rallied to defend their sovereignty and soundly beat Walker's mercenary army in a couple of battles. Walker was eventually executed in Honduras when he tried to conquer Central America again.

Coffee continued to be the mainstay of the economy and allowed the rich coffee growers to dominate politics for the rest of the 19th century.

During this time, construction on the railroad began on the Atlantic coast and was eventually finished in 1890.

Costa Rica's development continued well into the 20th century with only a few minor interruptions. In the 1940s Rafael Angel Calderón Guardia became president and initiated a series of reforms, including a labor code and social security system to protect the rights of workers and citizens. The most notable achievement was the abolition of the army forever in 1948 after a brief civil war. The same year, a new constitution was drafted that laid the groundwork for the most enduring democracy in Latin America. Women received the right to vote and all banks and insurance companies were nationalized. Presidential terms were also limited to prevent dictatorships.

Although the military has frequently threatened democratic institutions throughout the rest of turbulent Latin America, this is not the case in Costa Rica. Costa Rica has a 5,000-man, non-political National Guard or police force under control of the civilian government. Like the police in the United States, they concentrate on enforcing the law and controlling traffic.

Instead of devoting a large budget to maintain an army, Costa Rica has put its money into human development and has been able to establish one of the best all-encompassing social security systems in the world. It also developed an excellent public education system, hospitals, housing, modern communication systems and roads. Every school now has at least one computer. As a result, Costa Rica has the largest proportion of middle class citizens in Latin America and a literacy rate of over 90 percent. Furthermore, the prohibition of armed forces guarantees political stability and peace for future generations and reaffirms Costa Rica's dedication to respecting human rights.

Government

Costa Rica's government has been an outstanding example of an enduring democracy for over 50 years. This is quite an achievement when one looks at the rest of the world—particularly Latin America. In an area of the world noted for wars, political chaos and even dictatorships, Costa Rica stands out as a beacon of democratic tranquility.

The World Bank rates Costa Rica and Chile as having the best governments in Latin America and the highest degree of governability. According to the Konrad Adenauer Foundation Costa Rica and the annual Democratic Development Index Costa Rica is the country with the most democratic development. The country is also number one in the region in the number of citizens who love their democracy according to Latinobarómetro Corporation which did the study.

Costa Rica is compared to Switzerland because of its neutral political stance, with one exception: Costa Rica has no military. As mentioned earlier, in 1948 Costa Ricans did what no other modern nation has done — it formally abolished its army. That same year, the country limited the power of its presidents, began universal suffrage and dedicated its government to justice and equality for all, thus ending discrimination and making Costa Rica a truly unique nation. Consequently, in Costa Rica you do not see any of the racial tension so prevalent in the United States and some other parts of the world. Non-citizens have the same rights as Costa Ricans. Today there is even a growing women's - rights movement.

Costa Ricans set up the legislative, judicial and executive power structure to prevent any one person or group from gaining too much power in order to ensure the continuity of the democratic process. For example, to eliminate the possibility of a dictatorship, all presidents are limited to four-year non-consecutive terms. In April of 2003 the *Sala IV* constitutional court reinstated Article 132 enabling past heads of state to run for president again eight years after their term expired.

The members of the legislative assembly are limited to a single four-year term and cannot be re-elected. There are 57 seats in the national legislative assembly, elected by proportional representation from seven districts. Seats are allocated to districts by population: San José has 20, Alajuela has 11, Cartago has seven, Heredia, Limón and Puntarenas have five each, and Guanacaste has four.

Costa Rica's government is divided into four branches: the Executive (the president and two vice-presidents), the Legislative Branch (Legislative Assembly and 57 legislators), the Elections Tribunal and the Judicial Branch (the Supreme and lower courts).

The court is divided into four sections. The first court, called the *Sala Primera*, decides civil matters. The second court is called the *Sala Segunda*, and is the labor court. The third court, the *Sala Tercera*, is the criminal court. The fourth court is the Constitutional Court, called the *Sala Cuarta*, and by its name it is obvious that it decides constitutional issues. Its decisions can override laws made by any of the lower courts.

The country's two main political parties are the National Liberation Party and the Social Christian Unity Party.

The Costa Rican National Assembly has an Internet site (**www.asamblea.go.cr**) that you can visit to keep up with new laws and legislation and contact local legislators and politicians.

Since Costa Rica is such a small country, voters can participate more directly in the democratic process. Each vote carries more weight, so politicians are more accessible and have more contact with the people. Costa Ricans approach the presidential elections with such enthusiasm that they celebrate Election Day as if it were a big party or national holiday. People wearing party colors, honking car horns and, bands playing Latin music all contribute to the festive atmosphere. For the 2010 presidential election the turnout was about 90 percent— a figure that dwarfs that of the United States,' meager 50-percent turnout.

In Costa Rica people settle arguments at the ballot box, not on the battlefield. A group of American Quakers established a colony here because of this peaceful democratic tradition, and the University for Peace was established and still exists near San José.

In 2006, former president Oscar Arias Sánchez, who during his first presidency was awarded the Nobel Peace Prize in 1987 for his efforts to spread peace and democracy from Costa Rica to the rest of strife-torn Central America, was re-elected to the country's highest office. In 2009 Mr. Arias was considered the most popular president in Central America according to a CID Gallup poll.

Much has been made about corruption in Latin America. According to the *Transparency International Corruption Perceptions Index*, Costa Rica is ranked third in all of Latin America in a list of least corrupt countries. As a whole Costa Rica is considered the 40th least corrupt country in the world. This is a very favorable ranking since there is currently a worldwide corruption crisis.

All government services may be accessed at **Gobiernodigital.org**.

Economy

Presently, tourism and high technology have replaced coffee and bananas as the main income earners for the country. Costa Rica's reputation as the "the premier Latin American destination" has helped the economy.

According to an article that appeared in a June edition of *La República* (Costa Rica's Financial newspaper), Costa Rica will be one of the countries in Latin America whose economy will rebound starting in 2010. In addition, "Latin America in general, will experience a quicker recovery that the larger economies" according Nicolás Eyzaguirre Director of International Monetary Funds (IMF) for the Western Hemisphere.

Moody's considers the Costa Rican economy stable and sees improvement in the country's fiscal and debt positions despite ongoing global turbulence. Furthermore, according to The International Organization of Work (OIT), Costa Rica has the lowest unemployment rate in Latin America and the Caribbean.

According to Costa Rica's Central Bank, foreign investment in Costa Rica topped a $1 billion in 2007.

Tourism

Because of its endless beauty, natural wonders and peaceful atmosphere, Costa Rica has become very popular with nature lovers, adventurers and others.

Costa Rica's strategic location, political stability and adventure tourism, have all contributed to increased tourism development. Tourism is now the number-one source of income for Costa Rica. Since 1993 to the present the tourism industry has been the prime source of foreign capital. In 2004 Costa Rica's tourism industry had its best year ever, with an estimated 1.5 million foreign visitors. From December 2004 to May 2005 the occupancy rate of hotels was between 85 and 90 percent as compared to the same period in 2004 when it ranged between 75 percent and 90 percent. The average tourist spent $1,938, which is a 23 percent increase over the previous year. In 2005, 1.7 million tourists spent more than one billion dollars. In 2008 Costa Rica was the most visited nation in the Central American region.

With a $2.2 billion per year tourism industry, the 2 million foreign visitors in 2008 translates into a relatively high expenditure per tourist of $1,100 per trip. Most of these travelers arrived on an ever-increasing number of flights to the country. Approximately 310,000 came through the new Liberia airport.

In 2009 there was a drop in tourism due to the crisis in the United States. In the response to this drop, the Tourism Institute or ICT launched a massive campaign to promote tourism in the U.S. Locally they urged Costa Ricans to take trips within the country at discounted prices. Fifty to one hundred thousand more tourists are expected in 2010 according to Cantur (The national Chamber of Tourism).

The publication *Travel Weekly* rated Costa Rica as the best tourism destination in Latin America at the annual International Tourism Fair. *Forbes* rated the country as the fifth cleanest nation in the world only topped by Switzerland, Sweden, Norway and Finland.

In 2009 the *New York Times* called Costa Rica a Disneyland for ecotourism.

Interest in Costa Rica and development continues

Good news! The Walt Disney Company announced that Costa Rica would be the only country in Latin America selected for their new vacation program called **Adventures by Disney**. The only other countries selected in the world were the United States, Italy, Great Britain, Canada and France. Travelers will view Costa Rica's natural wonders on these highly specialized tours.

Costa Rica is now on the map for the rich and famous. A Saudi prince visited the country and met with the president. Celebrities like Bill Gates, Tiger Woods, Michael Jordan, Gwyneth Paltrow, Matthew McConaughey, Brad Pitt and Angelina Jolie, Charlie Sheen, Steven Seagal, Caroline Kennedy, Woody Harrelson, Tom Brady and his model wife Gisele Bundchen and other stars have visited the country in the last couple of years. Mel Gibson liked Costa Rica so much that he personally invested over $25,000,000 in real estate. More and more luminaries will visit Costa Rica as the word get out about all the country has to offer to both tourists and investors.

Real estate investment increased during the last few years. Big players Monroe Capital Corporation and Hyatt Regency Hotels are investing heavily in real estate projects. This activity is sure to boost investor confidence in Costa Rica.

Steve Case, co-founder of AOL and of Time Warner fame, spent millions on beach property to build an upscale resort in the Northwest Pacific area. Solarium is a $250 million dollar project being built right across from the Daniel Oduber Airport in Liberia. When finished it will be a virtual city with shops, a hotel, homes, a free trade zone, warehouses, a hospital, movie theaters and restaurants.

In 2007 Ritz Carlton announced the construction of a $250 million tourist complex at Playa Guacamaya. A one hundred fifty room hotel and 800 homes will be built in the complex. Plans also call for a marina with 250-slips.

The list of new multinational hotel groups includes:

- Ritz Carlton
- Hilton
- RIU
- St. Regis
- Aman
- Mandarin Oriental.

These large resort developers are helping to expand the Costa Rican economy. The following new projects have broke ground recently.

- The 310-room J.W. Marriott, will be built inside the Hacienda Pinilla beach resort community in Guanacaste.
- The 214-room Hyatt Azulera Resort formally broke ground in Playa Brasilito, Guanacaste.
- The Rosewood Hotel and Spa on 45-hectares (112 acres) of property fronting Playa Guachipelín in Guanacaste.Rosewood's Costa Carmel tent village, which is expected to be completed in 45 days, is not just about showing off the facilities of the 80-room hotel, rather it is part of an aggressive sales and marketing campaign.

Outsourcing, high-tech, bananas, pineapple, coffee, retirees, gambling and more

The most dynamic segment in the service sector in Costa Rica during the last few years has been call centers customer service: Customer service call centers require from its workforce the ability to speak English fluently. All of these companies find in Costa Rica's labor force the quality and the language skills that enable them to provide world-class service worldwide. Bank of America has 600 employees whose ages run from 18 to 25 working at their local call center.

The 2005 *Global Outsourcing Report* ranked Costa Rica third in outsourcing potential behind only India and China. This study takes such factors into consideration as cost, reliability and efficiency. My son works at Amazon.com's call center in Heredia.

Procter & Gamble has opened a facility in Costa Rica that showcases the possibilities and opportunities that this country has to offer. Other Shared Services operations include Chiquita Brands, GTC, Baxter Americas Services and British American Tobacco SSC. There are many other outsourcing operations of companies such as Hewlett Packard and IBM that have created a platform to serve their clients from their centers. Costa Rica also hosts regional offices and headquarters for several Fortune 1000 companies such as Motorola, Pfizer, Roche, 3M, Kimberly Clark, Cisco, Microsoft and Oracle, among others. Lastly, the availability of a very productive work force enables the operation of data processing centers in Costa Rica, such as the ones operated by Equifax and Maersk Americas.

According to the World Bank, Costa Rica is the number four exporter of high technology behind, the Philippines, Malaysia and Singapore. More than 13,000 Costa Ricans are employed by high-tech firms. U.S. high-tech firms are drawn by Costa Rica's lower costs, educated and bilingual workforce, political stability, tax breaks and proximity to the Unites States. Consequently, the electronic sector, led by multinational microchip manufacturer **Intel**, became one of the country's top foreign currency earners by the end of 1998.

Micro chips, the country's smallest export, continue to be its biggest moneymaker. The Intel plant has turned Costa Rica into a leading exporter of computer parts. It produces about one-third of the company's computer chips. In 1999, microchips exported by Intel continued to drive the Costa Rican economy and were responsible for about half of the country's booming 8.3 percent growth (GDP), which gave rise to some of the decade's best economic indicators. In 2009, Intel exported 75 million microprocessors and chips accounting for $2 billion in sales for the third consecutive year. Intel plans to invest $90million more in its Costa Rican facility to update its equipment. Hopefully this will lead to more foreign investment in this area.

Emerson is hiring 200 local employees for its new technical support center. The company has 265 offices around the world and over 140, 000 employees. **Digicel** plans to invest $350 million as a cell phone provider once the telecommunications market opens up.

Banana exports continue to be a major source of income. After Ecuador, Costa Rica is the second-largest banana exporter in the world. However, worldwide fluctuations in prices have affected this export in recent years. Pineapple could soon be the number one agricultural export. In the period between October of 2008 and September 2009 bananas generated $604 million while pineapples accounted for $574 million.

Ideal growing conditions have enabled Costa Rica to produce some of the world's best coffee for over a hundred years. Other exports include electrical components, sugar, cacao, papaya, macadamia nuts and ornamental household plants. Some of these non-traditional export items are beginning to rival traditional exports such as bananas, coffee and sugar.

Another surprising source of income for the country is its foreign residents. According to the November 14, 2005, edition of the *Wall Street Journal*, "Costa Rica's retirees contribute significantly to the $1.4 billion a year in direct spending by Americans according to the government. The multiple effects — salaries in health care, construction, retail and other services — could bring the total benefit to $4 billion , nearly 25 percent of Costa Rica's gross domestic product." The waves of almost 70 million baby boomers are sure to increase the figures as Costa Rica becomes even more popular as a retirement haven.

Surprisingly, sportsbooks contribute more than $100 million a year to the Costa Rican economy. More than 100 such firms are presently operating in the country. Local workers make good salaries in the online betting industry. Costa Rica is sometimes referred to as the "Las Vegas of the Internet" because of the number of sportsbooks that operate here. One wealthy sportsbook owner was recently featured on the cover of *Forbes* magazine.

Lately, new companies have invested in Costa Rica, which should help the domestic and export economy. The California-based wholesale shopping chain PriceSmart has opened five warehouse-style stores in the San José , Alajuela and Heredia areas in the last several years. The PriceSmart concept has revolutionized shopping in other Central American countries as well. In 2005 several big players made sizable investments in Costa Rica. Wal-Mart purchased a large portion of Supermercados Unidos and built five Hipermás mega-markets to rival PriceSmart. Western Union expanded its facility in Costa Rica and now employs 600 Costa Ricans.

The Swiss pharmaceutical giant Roche announced it would build its operations center in Costa Rica to service its plants in Central America and the Caribbean. U.S. health products manufacturer Several U.S. pharmaceutical companies also have opened plants here.

Many U.S. companies are setting up shop here

U.S. all-night diner franchise Denny's opened its first two restaurants and will open several more in coming years. The GNC nutritional chain has opened several stores in the San José area. Multinational tire manufacturer Bridgestone Firestone inaugurated a new plant in April of 1999, promising to double its exports. This wave of new foreign investment will create thousands of jobs for Costa Ricans. Baskin-Robbins and Dunkin' Donuts plan to open branches in Costa Rica in the near future; Cinnabon already has. Midas Shop plans to open franchises in the country within a year. They boast over 2,500 shops worldwide. Wendy's hamburger chain is expected to open 15 restaurants in Costa Rica over the next five years.

General Electric bought 50 percent of the stock in BAC San José, one of the country's best private banks. The largest US bank, Citigroup, purchased Grupo Financiero Uno, and Banco Cuzcatlán both of which had a presence in Central America. Shortly afterwards both banks were incorporated into Citibank. This acquisition follows earlier purchases of Corporación Interfín by Scotiabank of Canada, and the recent purchase of Banistmo de Panamá by HSBC of England.

Dependence on foreign loans and investment

Despite the new areas of investment and exports just mentioned, Costa Rica is still heavily dependent on foreign investment and loans to help fund its social programs and keep its economy afloat. However, the country no longer receives as much foreign aid as it used to and still has one of the highest per capita debts in the world. The government has, at times, been hard-pressed to meet loan payments from abroad, which take up most export earnings. Foreign debt has hindered economic development to some extent. Gradual currency devaluations have helped the country meet its obligations. Fortunately, these devaluations have been in small increments.

China is Costa Rica's new bedfellow and is providing a lot of money in exchange for trade privileges and other perks. The new state-of-the-art National Stadium in the Sabana Park is gift from China. They even provided the workers and all of the materials for this project. China is likely to keep money and investment flowing Costa Rica's way as long as it is feasible.

One problem is the number of people employed by the government's massive bureaucratic apparatus. About one of every seven Costa Rican employees works in some way or another for the government. Consequently, large parts of the country's resources go toward workers' salaries, benefits and operating expenses instead of toward pressing needs such as road repair. Some economists believe one way to help the country progress is to lay off all of the unnecessary government workers.

Hopefully the present growth in tourism and continued foreign investment will help the country's economic future. President Clinton's trip to Costa Rica in May 1997 set the wheels in motion for a free-trade treaty with the Central American countries. Costa Rica has voted to adopt the Central American Free-Trade Agreement (CAFTA), and it promises to be much like the NAFTA treaty between the U.S., Canada and Mexico.

The **Central America Free-Trade Agreement (CAFTA)** will help all of the Central American countries' economies. The most salient feature of the new trade pact calls for the partial opening of the government-run telecommunications monopoly. Costa Rican and foreign companies will be able to offer their telecommunication services, despite the seeming strangle hold of the *Instituto Costarricense de Electricidad*, commonly referred to by its acronym, ICE. Broadband Internet and cellular phone service will be affected by the opening up of telecommunications. The treaty also calls for the complete opening of the country's insurance monopoly or the *Instituto Nacional de Seguros* (INS) by 2011. Costa Rica must allow foreign companies to sell all types of insurance except mandatory policies.

Other sectors of the economy affected by the new treaty are rice, sugar, beef, chicken drumsticks, pork, oils, ethanol, dairy products, industrial goods, free zones, textiles and intellectual property.

In an effort to control inflation, the Central Bank of Costa Rica modified its system to establish the rate of exchange in October 2006, by switching from the mini-devaluation one to one in which the rate is allowed to fluctuate between two ranges. Mini-devaluations had been applied for 22 years and they consist basically in a gradual increase of the price of the U.S. dollar. In the past the dollar increased an average 13 cents of a *colón* a day.

According to the Central Bank, Costa Rica's inflation rate was an estimated 9.3 percent in 2007, 13.9 percent in 2008 and between 7 to 9 percent in 2009.

The Gross Domestic Product or PIB *(producto interno bruto)* in Spanish for the last couple of years: 4.2 percent in 2004, 5.8 percent in 2005, 8.7 percent in 2006 , 7.7 in 2007 and 2.9 percent in 2008 and 4.0 in 2009.

Central Bank economic indicators and other financial information are available (in Spanish) on the bank's web site: **www.bccr.fi.cr**.

The People

Besides its excellent weather and natural beauty, Costa Rica's unique people are probably the country's most important resource and one of the main factors in considering Costa Rica as a place to live or retire.

Costa Ricans are the happiest people in Latin America and thirteenth happiest people in the world according to a study by Leicester University in England. The Costa Ricans are also the most satisfied with their lives according to the Banco Interamericano de Desarrollo (BID) or Bank of Interamerican Development.

Costa Ricans proudly call themselves ***ticos.*** They affectionately and playfully use this nickname to set themselves apart from their neighbors. This practice is derived from their habit of adding the diminutive suffix *-"ico"* to words

Pura Vida and other *tico* greetings

by Guillermo Jiménez

Greetings in Costa Rica are always backed by a smile. If a *tico* doesn't feel like smiling he/she will say something other than a greeting, maybe equally dignifying. In the worst of cases and forced to say something a *tico* will use a greeting but qualify it somehow to avoid coming across as a liar, for instance: *Diay, pues estoy Pura Vida* (Hey, I'm kind of *Pura Vida*) is not by any means an unqualified *¿Pura Vida, mae, y vos?* (Pura Vida, buddy, and you?). Greetings are that important in the *tico* language.

You should know however that the ability of a Costa Rican to smile has very little to do with his or her personal situation. Even in the worst of moments a *tico* usually smiles and is eager to say `hi' but that doesn't really mean he is happy, only that he still keeps his hopes up and thinks he will come out on top of the situation.

When a *tico* is indeed happy however you can bet his greeting will be contagious and all of the features of his expression will tell you so. In fact when a *tico* is happy he purposely abandons all semblances of education and resorts to slang to express his mood. Of course, for the non-Spanish speaker this may be a problem, but don't

worry this is why I am writing this to begin with.

So you have heard of *Pura Vida*, but have you heard of *Pura Davi*? A common technique of people in the street is to flip Syllables in well-known greetings so that they come out funny. *Davi* is of course *vida*. You may have also heard *Tacuen* or *Cuenta* (tell) which we also use to start conversations as

in *¿Qué mae, que me tacuen/cuenta?* (What's up?).

Along side these more `proper' greetings you will also hear variations on *Pura Vida*, like *Pura Carnita* and *Puros Dieces*. These two phrases always bring a big smile to the receiver because they are intended to bring forward the reason why a word like *carnita* (diminutive of meat) and *dieces* (plural for 10) have any relevance in a greeting.

In my case *carnita* always reminds me of *tica* moms telling their kids to look for meat that has more meat than fat, or in the meat *tortas* (beef patties) they put in hamburgers. I know it sounds weird but that means that the higher the ratio ^to say it in *gringo*-speak˜of meat to straw/fat the better, hence `Pura Carnita,' in a circuitous kind of way comes to have a similar meaning than *Pura Vida* that is I'm full of life, 100% pure meat.

This is also true of *Dieces* or 10s. You see *Pepito* one of our favorite characters in jokes came back home to his mom really happy one day to tell her that he had scored *puros dieces* (all 10s) in all of the subjects in school. His mother got really happy, jumped up from the chair to hug her baby and congratulate him. Then Pepito said: "And that's nothing mom, many of my friends scored *Puros Cienes* (straight 100s)." Get it?

Back in the old days grades in schools were based on a 10 scale, where 10 was the equivalent of A+, but that was in Pepito's Mom's Youth. The new scale is based on 100 points and *Pepito* was supposed to score at least 65 to pass so in the end he came up with a clever way to break that news to his mom.

Pura Galleta' is another one of these strange word plays that *ticos* like to play a lot. *Galleta* means `Cookie' but it is not used as in the English `smart cookie'. Some 20 years ago Pozuelo, the big cookie making manufacturer here in Costa Rica came up with a new slogan: *Pozuelo es Muuuchaaaa Galleta* (Pozuelo is A lot of cookie) referring to their great assortment of products. Soon *Mucha Galleta* became synonymous with `Top of my game,' which then yielded sentences like *Es que vos sos mucha galleta* (That's because you are a lot of

cookie (figuratively). It didn't take long for the *Pura Galleta* phrase to be coined and to become the equivalent to *Pura Vida*.

Think of all the variations as slang of slang. *Pura Vida* is still the official *tico* greeting and it is in fact a bit more formal than the rest. The other sare considered *pachuco* (vulgar) and therefore their use is more restricted.

Have a *Pura Vida* day!

instead of "*ito,*" as is done in most Spanish-speaking countries. For example, instead of saying *un ratito* (a little while), *ticos* say *un ratico.*

Foreigners who have traveled in Mexico and other parts of Central America are quick to notice the racial and political differences between Costa Ricans and their neighbors.

Costa Ricans are mostly white and of Spanish origin, with a mixture of German, Italian, English and other Europeans who have settled in Costa Rica over the years. This makes Costa Ricans the most racially homogeneous of all the Central American peoples. More than 90 percent of the population is considered white or *mestizo.* Argentina and Uruguay are the only other countries in Latin America with similar racial compositions.

There is also a small black population of about two percent, living mainly on the Atlantic coast. Indigenous groups in the mountainous areas of the Central Plateau and along the southeastern coast account for one percent of the population. Costa Rica has never had a large indigenous population compared to other countries in the region.

In recent times, the country's stability and prosperity have made it a kind of melting pot for people from less stable Latin American countries, such as neighboring Nicaragua, Colombia, Cuba and Argentina. Many Colombians have sought refuge in Costa Rica because of the strife at home and similarities between the two countries' food, culture and language.

Nicaraguans make up 10 percent of the population. About 400,000 Nicaraguan immigrants make their home in Costa Rica. Economic hardship in their own country has caused them to flock to Costa Rica to find work. Most Nicaraguans work as domestics, in construction, picking coffee, cutting sugarcane and in other types of manual labor. As prosperity and opportunities have increased, fewer and fewer Costa Ricans will do this type of work.

Most of these new immigrants come to Costa Rica to seek a piece of the so-called, *sueño tico* or "Costa Rican dream," the Latin American equivalent of the American dream.

Unofficially there are about 50,000 North American English-speaking residents living in Costa Rica. Many more North Americans and Europeans live here illegally as tourists. Some are "snow birds" who spend only part of the year in the country.

Politically, Costa Ricans have always been more democratic than their neighbors—especially during the last 45 years. Indeed they should be congratulated for being the only people to make democracy work in such a troubled region.

National Geographic reported several years ago that, when asked why Costa Rica isn't plagued by political instability and wars like its neighbors, a Costa Rican replied, in typical *tico* humor, or *vacilón*, "We are too busy making love and have no time for wars or revolutions."

Because they have the largest middle class of any Central American nation, Costa Ricans love to boast that they have a classless society. Most people share the middle-class mindset and tend to be more upwardly mobile than in other countries of the region.

Although there is some poverty, most Costa Ricans are well-to-do when compared to the many destitute people found in neighboring countries.

Another thing setting Costa Ricans apart from other countries in the region is the cleanliness of its people. Costa Ricans take pride in their personal appearance and are very style-conscious. I know a *tico* of modest means who dresses so well he is often mistaken for a millionaire. Men, women and children all seem to be well-dressed. Above all, you don't see as many ragged beggars and panhandlers as in Mexico or in many other Latin American countries.

Costa Ricans are healthy people and have a life expectancy on par with most first-world countries — 76.3. In fact, they have the highest life expectancy in all of Latin America and just about the same as people in the United States. This is primarily due to the country's excellent Social Security System that provides "cradle-to-grave" health care.

The people of Costa Rica place great emphasis on education. Education has been compulsory in Costa Rica since 1869, and the federal government currently spends about 20 percent of its budget on education. Costa Rica's 95 percent literacy rate is among the highest in Latin America. A higher percentage of the population is enrolled in universities than in any other country in Latin America.

Costa Ricans are friendly and outgoing and will often go out of their way to help you even if you do not speak Spanish. They are also very pro-American and love anything American—music, TV, fashion and U.S. culture in general. Because of these close ties to the United States and just the right amount of American influence, Costa Ricans tend to be morelike North Americans than any other people in Latin America.

Much of the *ticos* disposable income is spent all at once, on clothes, entertainment, makeup, jewelry, or the latest gadgets on the market. *Ticos* are consumers and this mentality has led many of them to get deeply in debt with their credit cards.

Surprisingly, Costa Ricans, especially the young people of the country, seem to have more liberal attitudes in some areas. Costa Rican women are considered to be some of the most sexually liberated females in Latin America. Their liberation is due in part to the fact that the Catholic Church seems to have less of a foothold in Costa Rica than in some other Latin American countries.

However, you should not get the wrong idea from reading this. The vast majority of the people are Catholic and can be conservative when it comes to such issues as movie censorship. Also, Costa Ricans don't miss the chance to

Communicating with Costa Ricans

by Eric Liljenstrope

On many occasions I have been engaged in a conversation with a Costa Rican friend or acquaintance when a very basic conversational miscue occurs. I ask a question and my friend responds by saying yes. I assume that the yes I receive means an affirmative response, i.e. Yes, I'll be there, yes, I'll do it, or Yes you can dress like that in public without people laughing at you. However, my experience in Costa Rica and other Latin American countries has taught me a different meaning of the word yes of which I was not previously aware . Yes, can be merely an acknowledgement of the fact that I am talking, that the listener has heard me, or a reflection of what I want to hear. Yes does not necessarily mean an affirmative, positive response. The person may not show up, may not do what you thought they would do, and you may be dressed ridiculously and shouldn't be allowed to go out in public.

Costa Rican playwright Melvin Méndez from the book, *The Ticos*, expands on this point. He writes of his fellow Costa Ricans, "We beat around the bush to avoid saying 'No', a syllable which seems almost rude to us. And rather than hurt someone, we say one thing and do another." I had an experience recently that illustrates this point. I was supposed to meet a friend at a party and when I called him after arriving at the party he assured me that, yes, he'd be right over. When I called again, an hour later, he said, yes, he was almost ready and was just leaving the house. He never showed up. The truth was that he was waiting for a phone call from a girl that he wanted to go out with but didn't want to tell me that he was choosing her over me, so in order not to hurt my feelings he just told me what I wanted to hear. This was not the first time I had experienced such difficulties in basic communication, and experience has taught me to take such snubs in stride. No disrespect or injury was intended. My friend was doing the culturally acceptable, correct and polite thing by expressing to me that he wanted to be at the party with me and that he liked me. He was answering a different question than the one I was asking. I was literally asking, "Are you coming to the party?" But he was answering a question much like, "Would you like to come to the party with me if you could?"

So, how in the world can a person adjust to such conversational conundrums? Understanding the basic differences between the communication styles of indirect culture and direct culture can be helpful. A person from a culture with direct communication style values "putting all the cards on the table" and "cutting to the chase." Direct communicators do not place as much emphasis on context or on body language to get their point across. For direct communicators, if it is not verbally stated, it is not communicated. In contrast, indirect communicators place a heavy emphasis on context and often consider stating what appears to be obvious as insulting. It is assumed that an intelligent person will read the context and body language in communication, whereas direct communicators assume that if something is important then it will be stated clearly with no room for misinterpretation.

Perhaps you are left feeling a little overwhelmed at the prospect of having to reinterpret what people are saying to you with the added complexity of communication in a foreign language. The good news is that one gets better at interpreting indirect speech patterns as well as adjusting expectations appropriately. In the example above, I knew after the second phone call that my friend was not going to be coming. or at least I knew there was a strong possibility he wouldn't be there. Something in his tone of voice tipped me off. Of course, the ability to read those subtleties took years to develop, so one must have patience during the process.

What well-adapted Costa Rican residents know about adapting their communication style.

(1) Give people an option. Sometimes one doesn't know *ticos* are sincere until you give another option.
(2) Ask in another way, using qualified speech. You might try to say something like, "Is it difficult for you to come tonight?"
(3) Ask a third party. Sometimes a friend of a friend or someone else who is familiar with the situation is the only source for accurate information.
(4) Ask a Costa Rica. Costa Ricans will always be able to interpret their compatriots much better than foreigners.

celebrate the many religious holidays that occur throughout the year. (See Chapter 12 for a list of some of the most important holidays.)

Generally speaking, the people of Costa Rica love to have fun, to live with "gusto" and know how to enjoy themselves. One has only to go to any local dance hall on a weekend night to see *ticos* out having a good time, or observe entire families picnicking together on any given Sunday—the traditional family day in Costa Rica.

Soccer is king in Costa Rica

Soccer or *fútbol* is by far the most popular sport here. All of the locals have their favorite team. When there is an important game everything comes to a virtual standstill. The atmosphere is festive and beer flows freely. Things really heat up when the national soccer team (*la sele*) plays another country. The day of the game there is a sea of red white and blue soccer jerseys on the streets as the people show their support for the national team. If the national team wins the people party all through the night.

They say there are three important things in a Costa Rican man's life: soccer, beer and women — although not necessarily in that order.

The people of Costa Rica, no matter what their station in life, seem to enjoy themselves with less and do not give as much importance to materialism as do North Americans. Even people who can't afford to seem to be able to eat, drink, be merry and live for today.

Recent polls indicate that the majority of Costa Ricans are happy with their quality of life. Out of 162 countries polled, Costa Rica is in the top 40 when it comes to quality of life. More and more job opportunities, accessibility to education and a state-run health care system are cited as the prime reasons for the country's excellent quality of life.

Basic old-fashioned family values and unity are very important to Costa Ricans. Just as in the rest of Latin America, a strong family unit seems to be the most important element in Costa Rican society. Social life still centers around the home. Much of one's leisure time is usually spent with family. Mother's Day is one of the most important holidays. Parents and relatives go to almost any length to spoil and baby their children. Elderly family members are revered and generally treated better than their counterparts in the United States or Canada. Most are not sent to nursing homes as in North America. Young adult singles, especially women, tend to live with their families until they marry.

Costa Rican families help each other through hard economic times and in the face of poverty. Some foreigners complain that it is difficult to develop deep friendships with Costa Ricans because the family unit is so strong and predominant.

Generally speaking, most *ticos* live at home until they are married. This is especially true of young single females. When grown children get married, generally a room is built on to the family home to accommodate the young couple or a little house is built on the family property. Most of their disposable income is spent all at once, on clothes, entertainment, makeup, jewelry, or the latest gadgets on the market.

Nepotism, or using relatives and family connections to get ahead, is the way things work in business and government in Costa Rica. In many instances it doesn't matter what your qualifications are but who your family knows that helps you.

Despite all their admirable qualities, there is a negative side to the character of the Costa Rican people. While similar to North Americans in many ways and with a fondness for some aspects of *gringo* culture, Costa Ricans are distinctly Latin in their temperament. They suffer from many of the same problems common in Latin American societies.

Corruption and bribery are a way of life, bureaucratic ineptitude and red tape thrive, the concepts of punctuality and logical reasoning are almost non-existent by North American standards, and the "*Mañana* Syndrome"—leaving for tomorrow what can be done today—seems to be the norm rather than the exception.

Unfortunately, as in most Latin American countries, ***machismo*** (manliness) is prevalent to some degree among Costa Rican males. *Machismo* is the belief in the natural superiority of men in all fields of endeavor. It becomes the obsession and constant preoccupation of many Latin men to demonstrate they are *macho* in a variety of ways. Fortunately, the Costa Rican version of *machismo* is much milder than the type found in Mexico, but it nevertheless exists.

A tightly-knit Costa Rican family

There is no telling to what lengths some men will go to in order to demonstrate their virility. A man's virility is measured by the number of seductions or *conquistas* he makes. It is not unusual for married men to have a *querida* or lover. Many even have children with their mistresses. Since many married men do not want to risk having a lover, they sleep with prostitutes or loose women called *zorras*. For this reason many Costa Rican women prefer American men to Costa Rican men. As the *ticas* say, "Costa Rican men are *machista* and always have to prove it. You marry a Costa Rican man today and tomorrow he is out chasing other women and drinking."

Costa Rica is said to have the highest rate of alcoholism in Central America -- an estimated 20 percent of the population are problem drinkers. This should come as no surprise, since drinking is part of the *macho* mentality. Making love, drinking and flirting are the national pastimes of most Costa Rican men.

As discuss in Chapter 8, foreign women walking along the street will be alarmed by the flirtatious behavior and outrageous comments of some Costa Rican men. Many of these flirtations or *piropos*, as they are called in Spanish, may border on the obscene but are usually harmless forms of flattery to get a female's attention. Foreign women are wise to ignore this and any other manifestations of Costa Rican men's efforts to prove their manliness.

Sadly, many Costa Ricans have misconceptions about North Americans' wealth. A few people seem to think that all Americans and Canadians are millionaires. It is easy to understand why many *ticos* think this way because of the heavy influence of U.S. television and movies that depict North Americans as being very affluent. Also, the only contact many Costa Ricans have with Americans is primarily with tourists, who are usually living high on the hog and spending freely while on vacation.

It is therefore not surprising that some individuals will try to take advantage of foreigners by overcharging them for services and goods. Others will use very persuasive means to borrow amounts of money ranging from pocket change to larger sums of money, with no intention of ever repaying the debt. Please, take this advice: do not lend money to anyone, however convincing their sob story.

Another thing to be wary of is the "*regálame* mindset" of some Costa Ricans. Basically this term comes from the Spanish verb *regalar*, which means to give something as a gift with no intention of repayment. The verb *dar* is the correct verb to use when requesting something. People here use *regalar* in a figurative way in everyday conversation when asking for everything from small items in stores to ordering a beer in a bar. Unfortunately, too many people take this verb literally and expect something for nothing.

There have been many instances where foreigners have been overly generous to locals. As long as they continued their altruistic ways, they were liked. Once they got wise or decided to curtail their generosity, they were considered cheapskates. The bottom line is not to be too generous or spoil people here. Some people will take advantage of your generosity and misunderstandings inevitably will arise.

There have been cases of foreigners who have married Costa Rican women, being taken to the cleaners. Because family ties are so strong in Costa Rica, you can end up supporting your spouse's whole family. I talked to one retired American who could not live on his $2,000-a-month pension because he had to support not only his wife and stepchildren, but his wife's sister's children as well. Furthermore, he had to lend his father-in-law money to pay off a second mortgage because the bank was going to repossess the latter's house. This is an extreme example, and though I have heard many similar stories while living in Costa Rica not all Costa Rican families are like this one.

When doing business with Costa Ricans, you should exercise extreme caution. A few years ago, I had the pleasure of dining with a prominent Costa Rican banker who eventually became the country's Minister of the Interior. I mentioned that I wanted to start a business in Costa Rica. He replied, "Be very careful when doing business with Costa Ricans. This is not to say that all people are dishonest here. Just be cautious with whom you deal."

Do not dwell on these negatives but realize how difficult it is to generalize about a group of people. After you have resided in Costa Rica and experienced living with the people, you will be able to make your own judgments. The good qualities of the Costa Rican people far outweigh any shortcomings they may have.

One View of Living in Costa Rica

By Martha Bennett

Costa Rica is, quite naturally, very Latin. The *Ticos* are fatalistic and live for the moment. They have extended families which often supply most of their social life. By and large they are a happy people, accepting their lot in life and finding a bright side to dark issues. Music and laughter are common sounds everywhere. For me, these are the positives.

Ticos do things that amuse rather than irritate me, such as shoot off fireworks to celebrate a Virgin's Day. Do virgins like fireworks? On the negative side, I must tolerate what appears to be a total lack of planning. Things happen when they happen no matter what promise has been made. It is not a place where "to do" lists get done. Long lines are common in banks, telephone offices or almost everywhere.

Costa Rica is caught between the old world where oxen still pull *carretas* (carts) and the new world of TV and computers. Because of this, there is apt to be confusion about what North America is like, and problems with computers that don't compute because there is a lack of training of the user.

Ticos seem to have a love-hate relationship with the U.S. They want to be like it, but resent it at the same time. This sometimes produces jaded dealings with *Gringos*, i.e.: special prices for blue eyes. But it doesn't happen all of the time and sometimes they cheat each other too. I am a guest in their country and don't try to tell them how to run it.

Since I used to live in Michigan, I find the climate in Costa Rica perfect. It's the same all year round. The sun shines daily and the rain keeps everything green. The countryside is outrageously beautiful .

Ticos are paranoid about crime and all houses in the cities have bars. Yes there is crime here, but I feel safer here than I did in Detroit.

Driving here can be a nightmare. This combined with some bad roads can ruin your day. Buses are cheap and go everywhere.

The cost of living is low if you don't buy a lot of imported stuff. A three-bedroom house can be rented for under $700 in some areas like Heredia. Utilities are a bargain. Food is cheap. Fruits and vegetables are almost free. However, appliances cost almost double. Books are expensive, so bring reference books. Cars are twice the cost to buy or bring in. Group health insurance costs around $800 a year per person.

Spanish is important. It allows you to make many friends.

I have been living here ten years and never dream of returning to the States. But that's me. To know how it is for you, you'll have to try it.

2

Where to Live in Costa Rica

The Central Valley

The Central Valley, or *Meseta Central*, is the center of Costa Rica due to its geographical location, culture and economic activities. The valley lies at an altitude of 3,000 to 4,000 feet above sea level. It is surrounded by mountains and semi-active volcanoes such as Poás and Irazú. Its fertile volcanic soil makes it an ideal place for growing anything, including some of the world's best coffee. It is not surprising that more than 70 percent of the country's 4.5 million population lives in this region of the country because of its almost perfect year-round spring-like climate. The capital city of **San José** is located here as well.

The region covers large urban centers including San José, Cartago, Alajuela, and Heredia; rural villages dotting the hillsides and farmland; and medium-sized towns including Escazú, Santa Ana, Palmares, Naranjo, Grecia, Puriscal, Ciudad Colón, and San Ramón.

The Central Valley is also one of the most popular places for foreigners to live because of its lovely, eternal-spring-like climate and

Central Valley Map

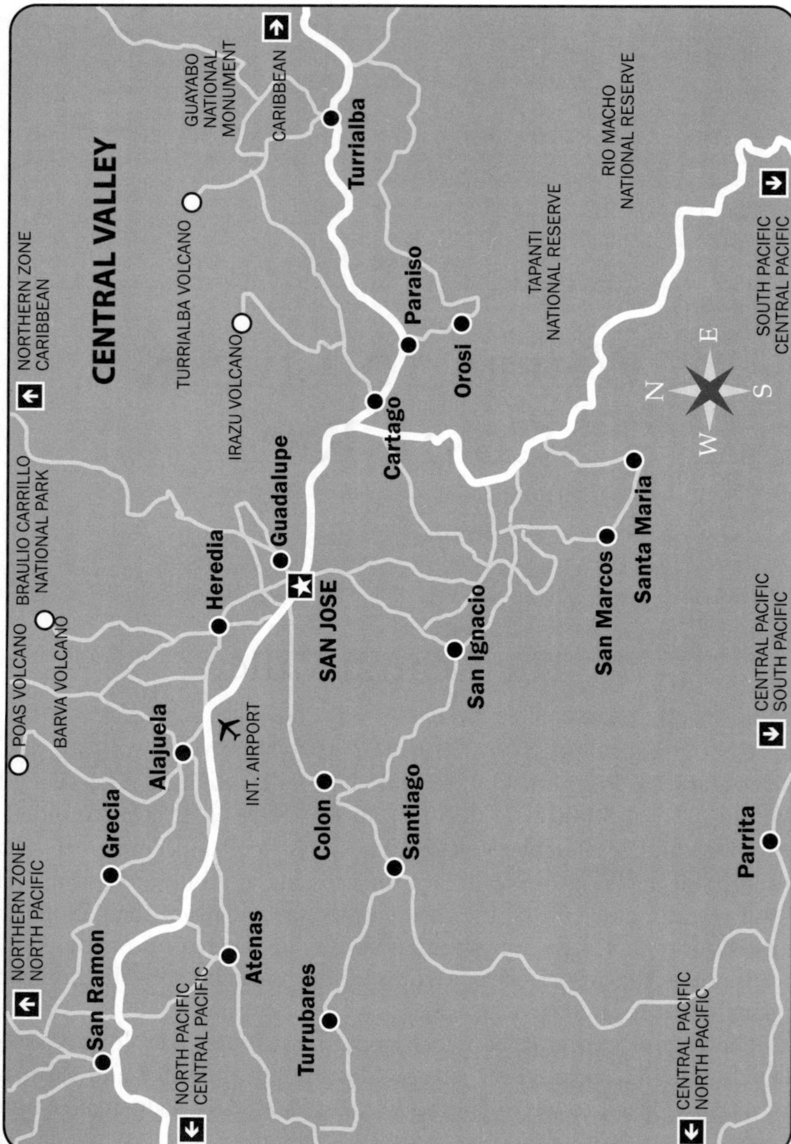

many other factors. But The region offers the best access to services and infrastructure in the country by far, including top-notch hospitals, an international airport, plenty of shopping and restaurants, Internet and cable connections, and public transportation. In addition to (or, more likely, because of) the preceding, the Central Valley is also the country's business center. It has a wide range of free trade zones and office parks, and many multinational corporations have their national or regional headquarters in the Central Valley.

The Central Valley – or more specifically, from Cartago west and north through San José to Santa Ana and Alajuela – is and always has been the focus of the country's government, business and industry. The supreme courts, the majority of the country's law firms, congress, the presidential house, the seats of all the ministries, and the headquarters of the major trade and agricultural associations are all located in San José and its surroundings, as are the aforementioned subsidiaries of the many multinational companies that have set up shop in free zones that offer tax benefits to exporters.

The Central Valley offers a wide range of housing. Decent, affordable housing ranges from $50,000 to $100,000 in *tico* neighborhoods, while mid-range prices are $100,000 to $250,000. Low-end condos in the Escazú Santa Ana area start at $150,000. Luxury apartments in Escazú can cost between $250,000 and $750,000. To many this seems expensive but the same housing would cost several times as much or more in some places in the United States or Europe.

A recent boom in the construction industry has created a wide variety of affordable new homes from which to choose. Many gated communities have been built in Santa Ana and in the Heredia and Grecia areas. Older homes also abound and are sometimes a better deal because they often have larger parcels of land.

Deciding where to live in Costa Rica depends on your preferences. If you like the stimulation of urban living and spring-like weather all year, you will probably be happiest living in San José, Heredia or one of the adjacent smaller towns and cities in the Central Valley, such as Alajuela, Escazú or Santa Ana.

As mention later in this book, there are hundreds of activities for everyone in, around and near San José. The infrastructure is excellent, and the area offers almost all of the amenities of living in the United States.

Retirement is a big change for many people because they find themselves with more free time than before and some people get bored. This should not be a problem if you reside in San José or the nearby suburbs, since there is a large North American community and it is always easy to find something to do.

DOWNTOWN SAN JOSE

San José

San José is the capital of the country and the capitol city of the province with the same name. Living in San José proper has a couple of drawbacks. Like most cities, San José is crowded, noisy and suffers from pollution from buses and cars during rush hour with commuters driving, walking, and taking public transportation to work. There is also some crime in the downtown area. If you own a vehicle it is hard to find a place to keep it it downtown except for public parking lots.

Finding your way around San José can be confusing at first. Like most of Costa Rica's cities the streets are one-way in downtown San José. To make matters worse most buildings don't have addresses. The city is divided into *avenidas* (avenues) which run east and west, and *calles* (streets) which run north and south. This is explained later on in Chapter 10, "Getting Around."

Despite these shortcomings, there are quite a few Americans who live in the center of town because it is convenient and there is a lot to do to stay busy.

The downtown area boasts the National Theater (*Teatro Nacional*) where the National Symphony performs, outdoor cafés, eateries, pedestrian streets, bookstores, department stores, nightclubs, a whole slew of *Gringo* hangouts like the Hotel Del Rey, Internet cafes, language schools, souvenir stores, museums, supermarkets, a Costa Rican-style central market district, several large casinos, historic hotels like the Gran Hotel Costa Rica and a whole lot more.

One friend from Florida loves this area because he is right in the thick of the action in the Gringo Gulch area. Another American we know likes to spend all day in front of the Gran Hotel Costa Rica seated at one of the tables talking with other expatriates and people-watching. The latter is a favorite pastime among foreigners in the downtown area. A couple of groups of *gringos* gather for coffee and conversation most days at the McDonald's next to the *Plaza de la Cultura* and the National Theater. Newcomers can make some instant friends there.

The municipal authorities have announced plans to revamp downtown San José in an effort to draw more people back to the city. The population of the areas that make up the central San José area has dropped from about 70,000 people to 60,000 over the last 20 years, with many people moving to the suburbs. Urban planners are transforming the city by building more parks and six new pedestrian walkways, similar to the ones found on Avenidas Central and 4. The National Water and Sewage Institute will improve the city's water, sewage and drainage systems, and the Ministry of Transportation plans to improve traffic in the city by placing major transportation arteries outside of the 53 blocks that make up the heart of the city, leaving the downtown area for pedestrians. The electricity company has already placed electrical lines underground and a new network of "intelligent" traffic lights has been installed.

One of the new pet projects is the creation of a Chinatown. The area design, still on the drawing board already has several oriental supermarkets and restaurants. The new *Barrio Chino* or Chinatown will be located between *Avenidas* (avenues) 2 and 14 and will be about two acres or 8,300 square meters in size when completed. Plans call for a huge Chinese-style gate with an ornate design at each entrance to the neighborhood. If you have ever been to San Francisco's Chinatown you can visualize one of these entrances.

Another project of interest is the development of Paseo Colón. Developers now have their eyes set on turning the western entrance to San José into a street lined with sidewalk cafés, stores and high-rise condominiums like the ones that are being built around Sabana Park. The Municipality of San José backs this project and is willing to cooperate and work hand-in-hand with the developers to beautify the Paseo Colón area.

Here is an expatriate's take on San José: "I find San Jose's air to be much cleaner than 11 years ago. I go from San Antonio de Coronado to downtown San José everyday Monday through Sunday. I have walked from Sabana Park to the Central Market many days and then all over the downtown area and never had a problem. Today I went to the U.S. Embassy by taking two buses from central San José and then went back on another bus. I also did a few errands. Then I took the bus back to my house and was home by 2 pm. I know about 20 words in Spanish. For me the city is great. You could not pay me to return to the little town I came from in the U.S. I have been living here less than a month and have accomplished a lot in a little time — a Costa Rican driver's license, a bank, a post office box and a girl friend. So if a 66-year-old man with no Spanish can do it, anyone can."

Here is another foreign resident's view of the city of San José: "I can understand every expat has a different perspective about San José. After living in New York City so many years without a car, I have no intention of buying one to live in the suburbs of San José. The city suits me fine. Buses and taxis are always available if I want to travel outside the city. I have a home just a block north of Torre Mercedes, off Paseo, Colón, and easily walk to most things I need such as the weekend flea market in the *Cementerio* district, theaters and art galleries in downtown San José and Sabana Park. "

"A block or less from my house there's a supermarket, several interesting restaurants, a major bank and a few bakeries. I know the neighbors on my little street as well as the guys who knock on the door to offer the daily newspapers or a pushcart full of vegetables."

Why I live in Costa Rica

By Jo Stuart

The quality of life is not measured simply by efficiency nor by material things. For those of you who want to know why I live in Costa Rica, here are my reasons why.

(1) I was originally drawn to this country because it has no army, and as a resut has developed a peaceful mentality. Costa Ricans do not like confrontations and are not greatly into competition. Perhaps because of this, the minute I arrived, I felt comfortable here.

(2) I was charmed (and still am) because when *ticos* thank you, they don't say "*Gracias.*" They usually say"*Gracias muy amable,*" which means "Thank you, you're very kind." Being told I am kind often enough makes me see myself as kind and wanting to be more so.

My life here is enhanced each time a *tico* says, "You're welcome." Here they don't say, as they do in most other Spanish-speaking countries, "*No hay de que*" or "*De nada*" (For nothing). They say "*Con mucho gusto*" (With much pleasure or, more loosely, The pleasure is mine). My friend Jerry has said more than once that giving and receiving are the same thing, and *ticos* seem to have recognized this. I have been trying to remember to say both *Gracias, muy amable* and Con mucho gusto. Language is a powerful influence on attitude.

(3) Although I have learned that there is a downside to a peace-loving philosophy, a trait called passive-aggressiveness, I have decided that I can handle passive-aggressiveness better that I can the downside of a personal freedom-loving philosophy, which seems to be aggressive-aggressiveness.

(4) I enjoy walking in downtown San José in spite of the traffic and challenging sidewalks. When I first came here and mixed with the people on the streets, I thought there wereas many pedestrians here as there were in New York at Christmastime but without the hostility. Instead, I find myself energized and uplifted.

(5) I also noticed that Costa Ricans as a rule have fine postures. It is a pleasure to see them, and seeing them reminds me to straighten up. It is surprising how much better you feel when you walk tall.

(6) I have on a number of occasions, experienced the health care system of Costa Rica, both private and public . The cost here for medical care is far less than in the United States, and I always have felt more cared for and cared about in my experiences here. Even in the overworked and

under-supplied public hospitals, I have found attention and compassion. It outweighs the lack of Kleenex. The last time I was in the Hospital Calderón Guardia emergency section, they passed out lunches at noon and coffee and snacks in the late afternoon to the waiting patients.

(7) Although business transactions are not always speedy here, how can you not like a country where it is the law that every public building must have a public bathroom? (That doesn't mean they must supply paper.) It is true one spends considerable time waiting in lines. This is where I get a lot of my reading done. I've waited in lines in many countries, and I'll take an orderly, friendly queue of *ticos* any day.

(8) There is a custom here that many North Americans have picked up and that is the custom of brushing cheeks when seeing a friend or acquaintance. In the States, after an initial handshake following an introduction, I seldom touch that person again, certainly not my travel agent, my doctor or my landlord. Here, I do. Touching cheeks makes me feel a connectedness to others, and when you think about it, is much more sanitary than a handshake.

(9) On the comfort front, it is hard to beat the climate in the Central Valley of Costa Rica. I have lived where there were 15-foot snowdrifts and where I became accustomed to perspiration dripping down my neck all the time. Living where I need neither air conditioning nor a heater is such a pleasure, and I am sure, far healthier.

(10) Something that is changing here that I regret are the window displays in the stores. Once there was nothing that caught my attention, and I had no desire to buy. I was not lured into being a consumer. Now they are getting both more artistic and more products, and I have found myself stopping and thinking I would like something.

(11) Because the growing season is so rapid, fresh vegetables and fruits are available most of the year. If one were a vegetarian, one could live very cheaply here.

(12) And finally, what clinched my love affair with Costa Rica was discovering that their national bird is the *yigüirro*. The *yigüirro* (which I can't even pronounce) is very similar to the U.S. robin but smaller, and even less colorful. The yigüirro neither threatens no one's existence It is certainly not a bird of prey nor is it a rare or endangered bird. It is a common little dun-colored bird, an Every bird, if you will. I think people who choose the yigüirro as a national bird have something to say to the rest of the world about peaceful coexistence, humanity, self-esteem and equality.

* Jo Stuart is a regular columnist for the online daily ***Am Costa Rica***. See **www.amcostarica.com** for more details.

La Sabana and Rohrmoser

Many North Americans who do not want to live too far from San José reside around Sabana Park. Most of them live in nearby **Sabana Norte** and **Sabana Sur**. Restaurants, gyms, two *Más x Menos* supermarkets and a variety of stores and services are all found in this area.

Located at the west end of Paseo Colón, the sprawling **Sabana Park** with its forest of eucalyptus trees, is the largest of Costa Rica's urban parks and is within walking distance of San José and neighboring Rohrmoser. The park is right on the outskirts of the center of the city and has nice upscale neighborhoods on the north, south and west. La Sabana was originally the site of the country's international airport. The old control tower is the present art museum. The park is now covered with tall trees and features a museum, a lake, jogging trails, an Olympic-size pool, soccer fields, recreational facilities and many more attractions for the general public.

China donated the workers and materials to build a new world-class, state-of-the-art soccer stadium at the north-west corner of Sabana Park. It will be finished in 2010 and will take the place of the old decrepit National Stadium.

The fashionable suburb of **Rohrmoser**, on the northwest side of Sabana Park, is very popular with people who want to live in a suburban area close to San José. Living in Rohrmoser is much like having a home near New York's Central Park or San Francisco's Golden Gate Park. This is especially true now since high-rise condos are being built around the perimeter of Sabana Park and in Rohrmoser. The area around Sabana Park is undergoing something of a building boom. Some say this area will become the Manhattan of Central America. Overnight, it seems, about a half dozen developers began building towers with as many as 12 stories on all sides of the park to take advantage of the views. The condos in the mixed-use developments are pricey: $350,000 and up, for the most part, with penthouses selling for more than $1 million. The new developments are sure to attract more builders and homeowners, and of course, the new highway will place any La Sabana homeowner only about a one-hour drive from the coast.

Sabana and Rohrmoser are middle-class Costa Rican neighborhoods, which are generally pretty safe. Its residents are predominantly *tico* families, along with a few expatriates. Several embassies are located there, as is the house of President Oscar Arias. The light traffic and the area's multiple parks make it safe for children to play outside.

The main tree-lined street called Rohrmoser Boulevard runs right through the center of this neighborhood, virtually bisecting it in half. Rohrmoser is bordered on the south by the Pavas Highway. Just about any type of store you might need is found along this busy thoroughfare as well as the U.S. Embassy to the west.

The neighborhood is made up of homes, apartments, condos, a few businesses and has some lovely neighborhood parks. Rohrmoser has many upscale homes owned by wealthy Costa Ricans and is considered very safe, since a large number of well-guarded foreign embassies are found here. Home prices start at about $100,000 on the low end, from $100,000 to $250,000 for a mid-range home and $350,000 to $750,000 or more for an upper-end home. Rent begins at $700.

At one time my family and I lived in Rohrmoser and paid $600 for a three-bedroom, three-bath penthouse apartment with a panoramic view of the mountains and indoor parking. We found living there to be very convenient since it is close to everything.

Excellent supermarkets, boutiques, international restaurants, the Cemaco department store, several small strip malls, an English-language bookstore, fast-food restaurants, upper-end eateries, Más por Menos and Automercado supermarkets, pharmacies, bars, discos, doctor's and dentists, offices, health clubs, beauty parlors, cafés with pastry shops, movie theaters, the Plaza Mayor and Plaza Rohrmoser shopping centers are located in and around this upscale neighborhood.

For you nighthawks there is even a 24-hour mini-market at the Shell gas station. The only thing bad about Rohrmoser is that bus service to downtown San José is not good, but you can always take a taxi since they are so affordable.

A $400,000 + home in the upscale Rohrmoser neighborhood.

East of San José - Los Yoses, Barrio Escalante, San Pedro, Curridabat and Tres Ríos

These eastern suburbs have a surprisingly wide variety of large shopping malls, supermarkets and other stores. There are three major shopping malls, including Terramall in Tres Ríos (a few kilometers east of Curridabat); Multiplaza del Este in Curridabat/Zapote; and Mall San Pedro in San Pedro. There are also plenty of appliance stores, interior design stores and cinemas on that side of town.

About five minutes east of downtown San José sits the residential neighborhood of **Los Yoses.** Like all areas east of downtown San José, Los Yoses features a mixture of new and old homes and businesses. Many foreigners live in this area because it is only a short walk to downtown San José. The *Centro Cultural Costarricense-Norteamericano* (Costa Rican-North American Cultural Center) is located in this area (there is also a smaller branch in Sabana Norte next to the American Chamber of Commerce). Los Yoses boasts a bowling alley, a supermarket complex, a bookstore and many bars and restaurants. The gigantic San Pedro Mall is found on the eastern edge of this neighborhood. So, there are interesting activities to keep a person occupied.

Barrio Escalante, slightly to the north of Los Yoses, has many older homes and stately mansions. The area provides a glimpse of how the upper crust used to live in Costa Rica. Many foreigners prefer this area since it is so close to downtown and some reasonably priced housing is available. Prices range from about $100,000 on up. Rent starts at about $500 for a small apartment.

Just east of Los Yoses is **San Pedro** — the home of the University of Costa Rica (UCR) or "La U" as it is affectionately referred to by Costa Rica's youth. The campus and surrounding area resemble many U.S. college towns with numerous student hangouts, restaurants, pizzerias, bookstores, nightspots, boutiques and two large shopping malls.

You can spend the day sitting at a table at one of the many sidewalk cafés along the Calle de La Amargura and check out the students as they pass by. A distinctly Bohemian ambience fills the air. Some interesting event or cultural activity is always happening in or around the university. During April, the annual University Week celebration takes place. This spectacle includes floats and a carnival-like atmosphere. Low-priced student apartments are available within walking distance of the university.

Curridabat or "Curri" as it is called by the locals is just east of San Pedro. There are some gated communities and condominiums going up on the extreme eastern edge of Curridabat – entering into Tres Ríos – where some inexpensive land is still available. Most of San Pedro and Curridabat

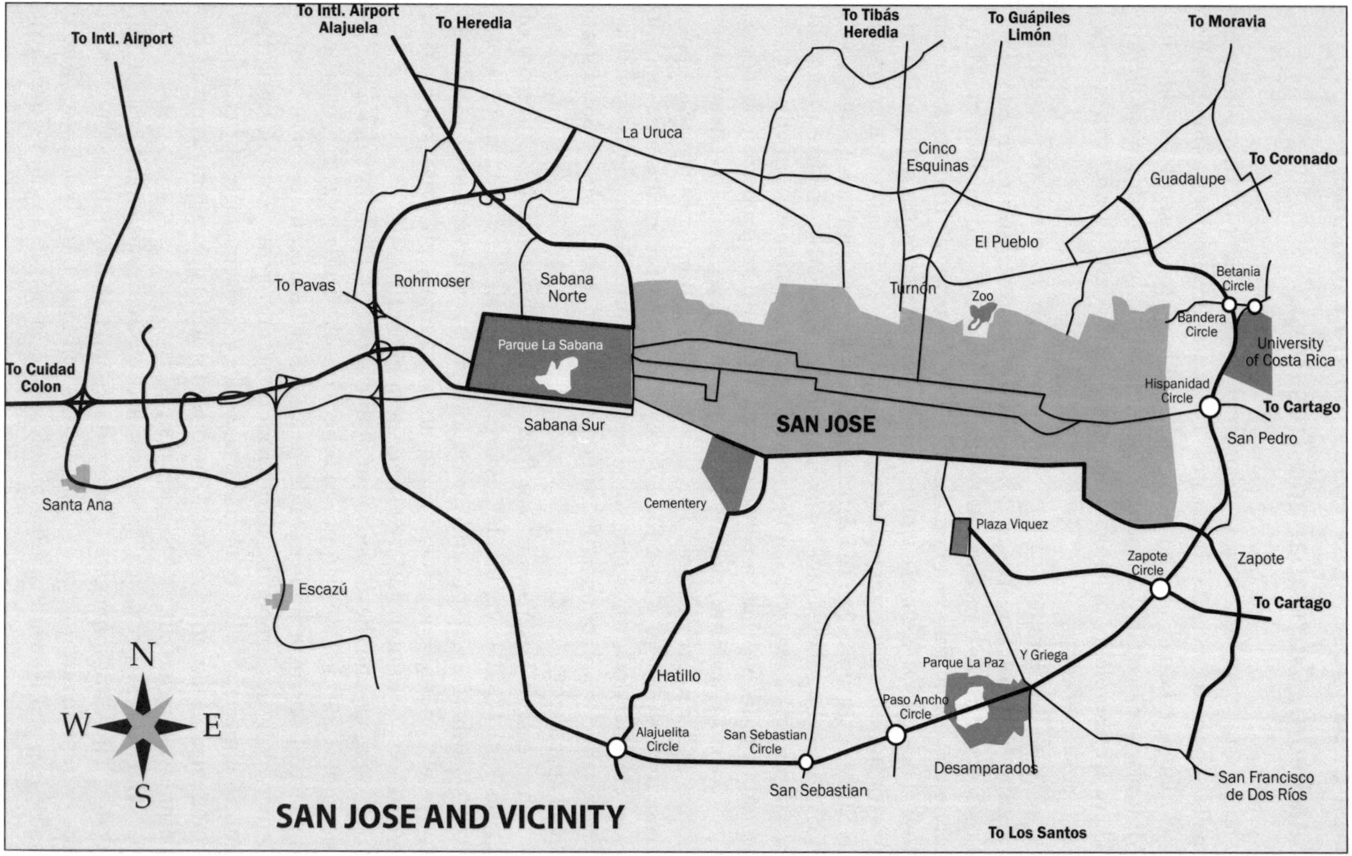
To Intl. Airport
To Intl. Airport Alajuela
To Heredia
To Tibás Heredia
To Guápiles Limón
To Moravia
La Uruca
Cinco Esquinas
To Coronado
Guadalupe
El Pueblo
To Pavas
Rohrmoser
Sabana Norte
Turnón
Zoo
Betania Circle
Bandera Circle
University of Costa Rica
Parque La Sabana
To Cuidad Colon
Hispanidad Circle
To Cartago
Sabana Sur
SAN JOSE
San Pedro
Santa Ana
Cementery
Plaza Viquez
Zapote Circle
Zapote
To Cartago
Escazú
N
W
E
S
Y Griega
Parque La Paz
Hatillo
Paso Ancho Circle
Alajuelita Circle
San Sebastian Circle
Desamparados
San Francisco de Dos Ríos
San Sebastian
SAN JOSE AND VICINITY
To Los Santos

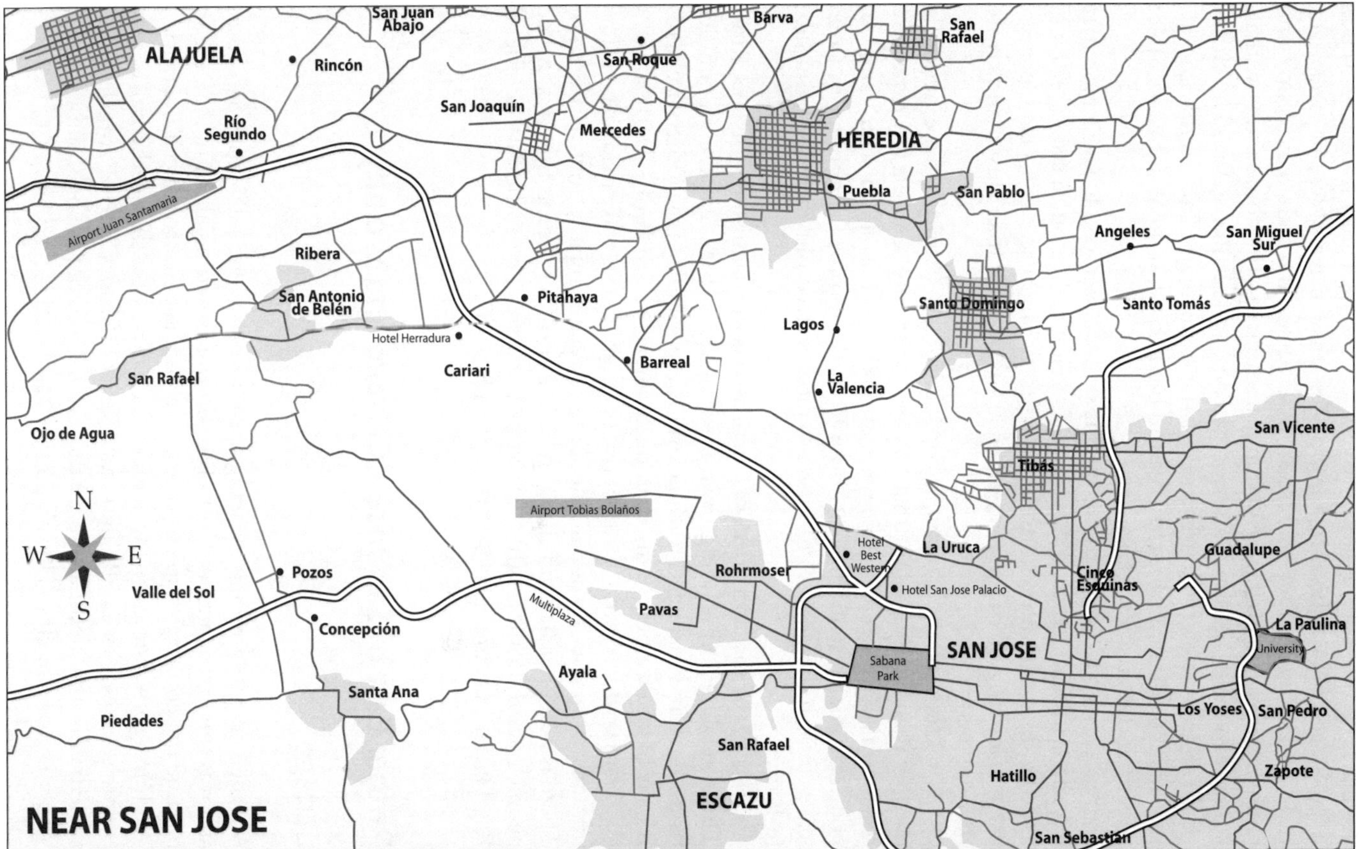
NEAR SAN JOSE
ALAJUELA
Rincón
San Juan Abajo
San Roque
Barva
San Rafael
San Joaquín
Mercedes
HEREDIA
Río Segundo
Puebla
San Pablo
Airport Juan Santamaria
Angeles
San Miguel Sur
Ribera
San Antonio de Belén
Pitahaya
Santo Domingo
Santo Tomás
Lagos
Hotel Herradura
Cariari
Barreal
San Rafael
La Valencia
Ojo de Agua
San Vicente
Tibás
N
W
E
S
Airport Tobias Bolaños
Hotel Best Western
La Uruca
Guadalupe
Pozos
Rohrmoser
Cinco Esquinas
Valle del Sol
Hotel San Jose Palacio
Multiplaza
Pavas
La Paulina
Concepción
SAN JOSE
University
Sabana Park
Ayala
Santa Ana
Los Yoses
San Pedro
Piedades
San Rafael
Hatillo
Zapote
ESCAZU
San Sebastián

are made up of medium, large, or very large single family homes, as well as a few gated communities. In a few places, lots are available, but expensive.

The main four-lane road that passes through San Pedro and Curridabat toward Cartago is certainly nothing to write home about, with its aging strip malls, plentiful fast food eateries, and terrible traffic. The charm of these areas, however, is found off the main drag. The neighborhoods that branch off the main street feature big houses, some good views, quiet streets, and even a few parks.

If you do decide to live on this side of town, you'll have a more *tico* experience than in Escazú. Not many foreigners live on this side of town, and the ones who do tend to blend in to the local scene – speak Spanish, eat at *tico* places, live in a stand-alone house – rather than cluster and create their own communities.

Property and houses in San Pedro and Curridabat are generally cheaper than in Escazú, but that has been changing. Quite a few expensive restaurants have been popping up, though there is still a wide range of good, cheaper restaurants to choose from. In terms of shopping, the area leaves little to be desired, though it's more spaced out than what you find in Escazú.

Just to the east and north of Curridabat is the community of **Tres Ríos**. This sprawling and winding town is seeing quite a few gated communities being built and marketed to the Costa Rican middle class. Otherwise, Tres Ríos is basically a bedroom community similar to San Pedro or Sabanilla.

Lomas de Ayarco is an upper-scale area east of Curridabat a few minutes from the TerraMall shopping area and on the way to Cartago. There is an Hipermás and there are other good services in this area. Some people refer to Lomas as the "Escazú of the east." The author's good friend Ray Hagist lives in this area with his family.

Farther East of San José - Cartago and Vicinity

Cartago

Another neighboring city, **Cartago**, is "just over the hill" from San José, and was the first capital of Costa Rica during the colonial period. San José became the country's capital when an earthquake destroyed old Cartago.

Cartago is home to the largest and most beautiful cathedral in the country, known as La Basilica de Nuestra Señora de los Angeles;.The cathedral is the destination of the annual pilgrimage in honor of the Virgin of los Angeles. The pilgrimage takes place every August. Literally

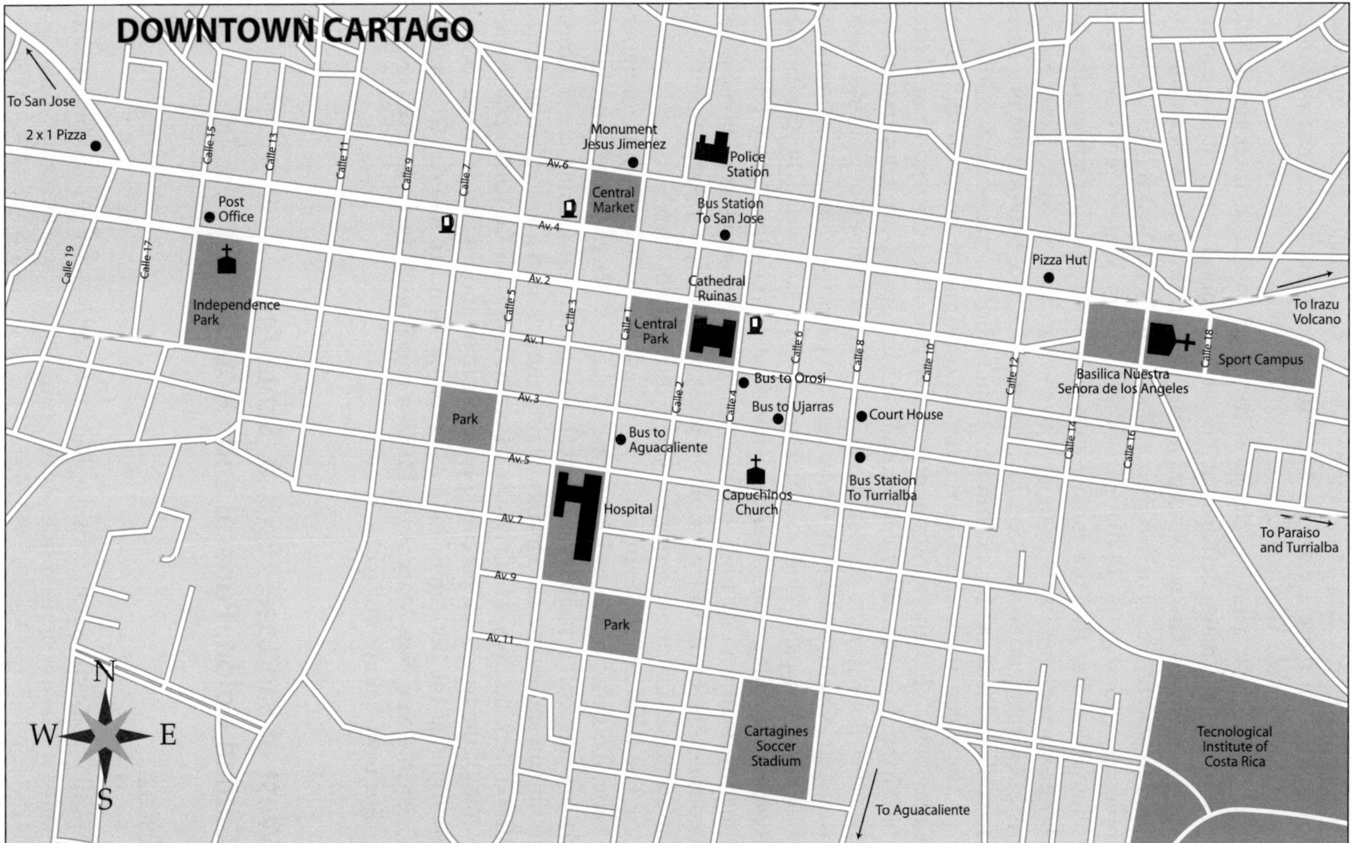
DOWNTOWN CARTAGO
To San Jose
2 x 1 Pizza
Monument
Jesus Jimenez
Police
Station
Central
Market
Post
Office
Bus Station
To San Jose
Pizza Hut
Cathedral
Ruinas
Independence
Park
Central
Park
To Irazu
Volcano
Sport Campus
Basilica Nuestra
Señora de los Angeles
Bus to Orosi
Bus to Ujarras
Court House
Park
Bus to
Aguacaliente
Bus Station
To Turrialba
Capuchinos
Church
Hospital
To Paraiso
and Turrialba
Park
Cartagines
Soccer
Stadium
To Aguacaliente
Tecnological
Institute of
Costa Rica
Av. 6
Av. 4
Av. 2
Av. 1
Av. 3
Av. 5
Av. 7
Av. 9
Av. 11
Calle 19
Calle 17
Calle 15
Calle 13
Calle 11
Calle 9
Calle 7
Calle 5
Calle 3
Calle 1
Calle 2
Calle 4
Calle 6
Calle 8
Calle 10
Calle 12
Calle 14
Calle 16
Calle 18
N
W
E
S

millions of people make the journey every year, usually starting from San José, although there are always a few devotees that walk all the way from Guanacaste or the Southern Zone.

Cartago is at a higher elevation than San José, and therefore a little more chilly and rainy. Perhaps the cooler year-round temperatures explain why fewer North Americans reside here. The air, however, is clean, and the views are spectacular. There is plenty of space to build, which is usually what foreigners choose to do in that part of the country. Quite a few services are still available, but they are further away. The style of living for expats who choose Cartago and its environs is relatively more sedate. Many Costa Ricans live in Cartago and work in San José, since bus service between the two cities is excellent. Plans call for a commuter train linking Cartago and San José.

The nicest thing about Cartago is its proximity to the beautiful **Orosi Valley**, which lies about 60 minutes east of San José. Viewed from above, this Shangrila-esque valley is breathtaking. The spring-like temperatures on the valley floor stay the same all year. At one end of the valley is a large man-made lake, **Cachí**, and a park where one can participate in many recreational activities, from picnicking to water sports. The lake is fed by the famous **Reventazón** white-water river that runs through the Orosi Valley The area's other main attractions are waterfalls, nature reserves and several hot springs. I consider the Orosí Valley one of the most beautiful spots in the country and am surprised that more foreigners don't choose to live here.

The **Route of the Saints** is an area near Cartago where some foreigners reside. This part of Costa Rica is one of the few places where you can find dairy farms, coffee plantations, log cabins, country inns, pine trees and fresh mountain air. Surrounded by mountains, the towns in this area are all named after different saints, which is how it became known as *La Ruta de los Santos.* Some of the towns are perched precariously on mountainsides while others are found at the bottom of valleys. **Tarbarca**, **San Ignacio de Acosta**, **San Cristóbal Sur**, **San Marcos de Tarrazú** and **Santa María de Dota** are the major towns along this scenic route.

West of San José - Escazú, Santa Ana, Ciudad Colón, Puriscal and Orotina

Escazú

Another place you might consider living is **Escazú** — a popular suburb where many North Americans reside. At one time Escazú was known as the town of the witches, not because there are a lot of women in a bad mood there, but because at one time there were many indigenous women who were *curanderas* or female witchdoctors.

Escazú is sometimes referred to as the Beverly Hills of Costa Rica because of its upscale cosmopolitan atmosphere. In the words of one American who lives there, "Escazú is an odd modern conglomeration of micro niches and little islands of green, stitched together by pot-holed roads and pocked with condo complexes, great mansions behind ominous gates and little tin barrios where the wash bakes in the noonday sun."

The town is about five miles west of San José, 10 to 15 minutes driving time on the old two-lane road or newly revamped *autopista* (highway). Since most of this suburb is located on hilly terrain, it is especially appealing to those people who like cooler temperatures. In fact, Escazú is one of the most popular places for English-speaking foreigners to live. Bus service is excellent to and from San José. You can catch either a mini-bus or regular bus in the park behind the church in downtown Escazú.

The old village center retains some of its quaint traditional feel, despite the condominiums and strip malls going up all around it. In some places adobe buildings still line the narrow roads, and the whitewashed church, the park, and the soccer field still dominate the center. Often farmers can be seen trotting their horses up the lanes to and from their farms, a reminder that not everything in Escazú has been quick to change.

Despite being quaint and country-like, Escazú has all the amenities of any North American suburb including the best shopping and dining in Costa Rica.

The recognized center of Escazú is called the "Golden Mile," where fast food restaurants and pricey clubs and cafés line a four-lane road jammed with traffic. In Escazú you can find just about anything including: small strip malls and commercial centers filled with clothing stores, beauty salons, pharmacies, English-speaking private schools, Hipermás (Walmart), trendy shops with name-brand clothing, doctors, dentists, two private mail services and more.

One advantage to living in Escazú is that you are near **Hospital Cima**, one of the country's best private medical facilities. I personally see two specialists in Cima's medical building, have had a surgical procedure there and am very pleased with the quality of care he received.

The largest shopping complex is **Multiplaza Escazú**, a shopping mall full of U.S.- and European-brand chain stores, several restaurants, a multiplex cinema and an Automercado supermarket. Several large furniture and interior stores, PriceSmart and Office Depot, the Real Intercontinental Hotel, and the Plaza Roble office complex can be found in the same area. More office and condo complexes start construction in that part of town every day.

Plaza Izcazu on the north side of the highway, offers trendy dining for the Costa Rican yuppie set. Gentlemen will be happy to know that there is even a **Hooters** restaurant found here.

The new **Avenida Ezcazú** project, next to Cima Hospital, is Costa Rica's version of Rodeo Drive. It features a Marriott Courtyard hotel, a block of buildings to house business on the ground floor with offices on upper floors, movie theaters, upscale restaurants and apartment-type houses with one or two bedrooms. There is a multitude of shops, including brand name designer stores.

The main road in Escazú has so many U.S. franchises, you may find it hard to believe you're not in the States. If you reside here you won't have to go to San José for basic services unless you want to. There is even a beautiful private country club and golf course.

Escazú has a variety of residential areas, from pricey Trejos Montealegre, just off the highway, to San Antonio, which is up in the hills and has cheaper land. Hillside properties in Escazú have fantastic views of the twinkling lights of the Central Valley. Housing is plentiful but expensive, as Escazú is popular with wealthy Costa Ricans and well-to-do foreigners. You can find simple *tico*-style single-family homes, condos, high-rise penthouses and even country estates scattered around this area.

Escazú is the home of many a high-rise condo.

An up-and-coming area is Guachipelín. Though growth in land value in much of Escazú has paused, Guachipelín is still experiencing appreciation in value. As far as style, you can get pretty much anything in Escazú, from low-, mid-, and high-rise condominiums to houses in gated communities to traditional *tico*-style houses up in the hills. A few lots are still available as well, though not many, and they're very pricey.

Trejos Montealegre, has many condos and apartments from which to choose. Some upper-end homes in Escazú cost a couple of hundred thousand to a million dollars. However, if you are living on a budget or small pension, you can find more affordable housing in San Antonio de Escazú. Many affordable *tico*-style homes are scattered around this area.

Escazú's upper-crust lifestyle isn't for everyone. Here is one local's critical view of present-day Escazú which appeared in the *Escazú News*. It summarizes how some expatriates feel in a nutshell: "There is no way around it: Escazú has become the Costa Rican Miami. Along the main highway to the west of Escazú, PriceSmart, Office Depot, Payless Shoes and Liz Claiborne can be seen to your left and the Marriott Courtyard Hotel, Outback Steakhouse and Comfort Suizo can be seen on your right. The new highway passes by the mall. This is the Dadeland of Costa Rica, the glamour capital where people from all walks of life converge."

"If you enter Escazú from the old road, it looks the same, with Tony Roma's and T.G.I.F. on the right and Häagen-Daz, Bagelmen's, U.S. Laundry and Big Dog's on the left. As you continue on, just like on tropical Flagler Boulevard, you will see on both sides of the street, KFC, McDonald's, Hollywood Video, TCBY and Hugo Boss."

"It seems that the only thing missing in Escazú to make it exactly like Miami is the ocean."

"Continuing on, there exists another constellation of luxury shopping centers within Escazú with such chic names as Delights Gourmet, Mommy Basics, Underwear Options and Dry Clean USA. There are sales and clearances every week as well as coffee shops where Perrier is the drink of choice."

It isn't any coincidence, though, that in Escazú you will find upper-crust North Americans, with the Ambassador's residence leading the group, and where, just like in Miami, there are Venezuelans, Colombians and even a 'Little Havana,' which is headed by well known-local Cubans.

"The schools have names such as Country Day, Blue Valley, Saint Mary and Lighthouse. There is even a Spanish School. "

"The former forest of **Guachipelín** and yellow barks has been turned into condominium complexes that offer a more secure, yet more boring, lifestyle. Nowadays, you can't even plant a garden in your backyard, much less have hens to lay fresh eggs every day."

"But what really stands out in the center of this big Floridian landscape, erect and upright, the great pioneer of this colony, is the Costa Rica Country Club."

"Most of the girls are blondes; they go to the gym and they wear tight, attention-getting clothes. They carry Louis Vuitton or Burberry purses, wear Chopard watches, styled hair and sun visors. The guys drive only the coolest cars, wear only the coolest sunglasses, aerodynamic and galactic, and talk only about business, parties and their trips outside the country."

"And to finish off, the Escazu newspaper, as the Miami Herald, has an English name: *Escazú News* see **http://newsletter.escazunews.com/index.php.** "

Santa Ana

Santa Ana, nestled in the "Valley of the Sun," is slightly more rural than Escazú. This fast-growing village is about four miles west of Escazú, and a good mix of Costa Ricans and foreigners resides here. Santa Ana's warm climate makes it an almost perfect place to live. At one time Santa Ana was a popular weekend retreat and summer destination for well-to-do Costa Ricans. Some of their large estates still exist today. Many foreigners and ordinary Costa Ricans reside in this town of 30,000 inhabitants now. Lately the town has become very popular with upper-class Costa Ricans and *gringos.* You can get to Santa Ana by taking the old scenic road from Escazú through the hills or by the new toll-highway that goes through Ciudad Colón to the Pacific Coast.

I recommend checking out this town. Downtown Santa Ana retains a small-town flavor. It is more rural and less developed than Escazú but offers good supermarkets and some shopping. You don't have to go to San José for your essential products.

Lately there has been a building boom in the area. Every day it more closely resembles the suburban sprawl found outside U.S. cities. There are new high-end strip malls in the Lindora area with restaurants, spas, supermarkets and fast-food chains like Taco Bell, Wendy's and McDonald's. However, this area is not as densely populated or developed as Escazú - yet.

Builders there are focusing on gated communities rather than towers. **The Lindora**, **Pozos** and **Río Oro** neighborhoods have really experienced a lot of growth. *Tico*-style homes in the older areas are more reasonably priced than in Escazú. Luxury homes in a secure gated community are a popular choice for middle-to-high-income budgets. An upscale four-bedroom home in a gated community will cost from $250,000 on up. **Valley de Sol** is a gated-golf course community with upper end homes. When this development was opened over ten years ago lots cost around $50,000. Today there are homes that cost over $1,000,000.

Ciudad Colón, Puriscal and Orotina

Ciudad Colón, about 20 minutes or six miles beyond Santa Ana, is the farthest western suburb or bedroom community of San José. There is a small expat community including an art colony there. The new highway from Ciudad Colón to the town of Orotina has opened and has reduced driving time to the beach from Ciudad Colón in half.

Ciudad Colón retains its small-town feel and is still very much a working service town, with small Costa Rican stores and the inevitable fried chicken – *pollo frito* – joints. Every year the city (it recently became a city from a town, and thus changed its name from Villa Colón to Ciudad Colón) hosts a horse parade, or *tope*, and everyone gathers along the streets to watch the horses prance through town, owners dressed in their best riding gear.

The city is the home of the **University for Peace** where students from many countries study in order to make the world a better place.

As Escazú and Santa Ana become more and more expensive and crowded, *tico* and expatriate builders look further west, towards the fast-growing Ciudad Colón. Property owners in this town have seen the value of their land shoot up along with the construction of gated communities and new single-family homes in what used to be cattle pasture and coffee fields. Cerro Colón which overlooks Ciudad Colón from a steep mountain side, is an example of one of the new communities that is being built there.

Puriscal

Santiago de Puriscal (called Puriscal or just *Puri* by the locals) is about 17 miles west of Ciudad Colón in the mountains. The word Puriscal comes from the word *purisco* which is the flower stage of a bean plant. The cool mountain climate with its clean air, magnificent views and relaxed rural character are the main appeal of this area.

Foreigners also choose Puriscal for both convenience and ambiance. While the beaches are beautiful, most people feel that the perpetual spring-like climate of this area is more comfortable to live in than the increased heat and humidity at the beach.

This town is perfect for people seeking affordable housing, more land for their money and rural living. A few properties offer panoramic views of the Pacific Ocean, Gulf of Nicoya and the Central Valley. There is even a back road from Puriscal to just before Quepos. The road is mostly unpaved, so be prepared for a rough trip. There is also a scenic paved country road that goes from Puriscal to Orotina.

This picturesque area is within easy reach of the most modern conveniences and services in Costa Rica. Many who live in Puriscal commute daily to San

José since bus service is good. Thirty minutes away is the Escazú/Santa Ana area where you'll find a state-of-the-art, USA- affiliated medical center, the largest mall in Costa Rica, and lots of quality restaurants. There are new homes for sale in the area but the only real development is **Orchid Point Estates** in San Antonio de Puriscal. It offers breathtaking views of the Central Valley and prices of the home sites are very attractive.

Orotina

Orotina, located over the hill and west of Atenas, is a nice-size little *tico* town. Fruit and nuts is what they do best, but there are plenty of horse farms and cattle ranches around. This area is gradually developing and there is a lot of land for sale including nice country estates or *quintas* and a couple of new projects. My Costa Rican friend Fernando, has a new project just west of Orotina. If you want a quiet Costa Rican town, Orotina could be for you. Few North Americans live here, but there is a bilingual school where some people send kids from as far away as Jacó Beach.

Things are about to change in the Orotina area. The town lies right in the path of western growth and improved infrastructure. The new highway is going to make Orotina more accessible and within 30-35 minutes by car from Santa Ana and Escazú. This will turn the whole area into a bedroom community for San José and its western suburbs.

Belén, Cariari and Alajuela

Belén

A bout five miles northwest of San José and just south of Juan Sanatamaría International Airport is the town of **San Antonio de Belén.** It is a laid-back town with a middle-class neighborhood. It is located behind the airport, just a couple of miles off the main highway west of Cariari on the way to Santa Ana. It is another good spot to live. This town has experienced a great deal of growth since Intel's mammoth plant opened and Marriott built a five-star hotel in the area. There is an upscale shopping center called **Centro Comercial La Rivera** in this small town as well as basic services.

A couple of nice gated communities can be found here like La Joya. Home prices, rent and land cost less than in Escazú, Santa Ana and Cariari. The popular *Ojo de Agua* recreational complex is also in this area.

Cariari

Ciudad Cariari, about five miles northwest of San José and five minutes before the airport, is an upscale neighborhood of mostly newer homes and condos. It was originally developed two decades ago with foreign residents in mind. The area has plenty of security and areas for children to play. Housing in this semi-gated community ranges between $170,000 for a small condo to $750,000or more for a palatial home.

This area is perfect for those interested in country-club living. Within this area are the Cariari Hotel and Costa Rica's oldest golf course, the **Cariari Country Club**, plus a small shopping center with a restaurant and 24-hour AM/PM mini-market, the Los Arcos neighborhood and the American International School — one of the best English-language schools in the country. A couple of golfer friends of mine live in this area and enjoy living next to the golf course. Right across the main General Cañas highway from Cariari sits the **Real Cariari Mall** with shops, restaurants and movie theaters.

Alajuela and La Garita

If you wish to combine an urban life and warmer weather, you can reside in San José's neighboring city Alajuela, Costa Rica's second largest city located almost next to the airport. The country's main airport is not in San José as most people believe but in Alajuela. The city is also known as the "City of the Mangos" for the mango trees which dot the main square.This quiet city is about 30 minutes by bus from downtown San José and has everything you want in a city without the city feeling. The bus service is excellent during the day, so it is easy to commute to San José if necessary.

Because of the warm climate, many Americans live in Alajuela, so you can easily make new acquaintances. The city's shady Central Park is a perfect place to sit and relax or socialize with the many locals or fellow expatriates who gather there in the afternoon. The park is impressive with a lot of tall, ancient trees that are a testament to the city's grandeur. There are other nice parks, movie theaters, restaurants, doctors, supermarkets and more in this city.

The Jalapeño Tex Mex Restaurant and Café Delicias north of the main park are hangouts where a lot of *gringos* gather. If you are new in town you can make some new friends there. Another place to find foreigners is at the nearby **Fiesta Casino** on Sunday afternoons during the NFL's football season.

Hospital San Rafael is the new public hospital located on the road going out of town toward the airport. Directly across the street is **Mall Internacional**, the city's main shopping center. On the north side of town

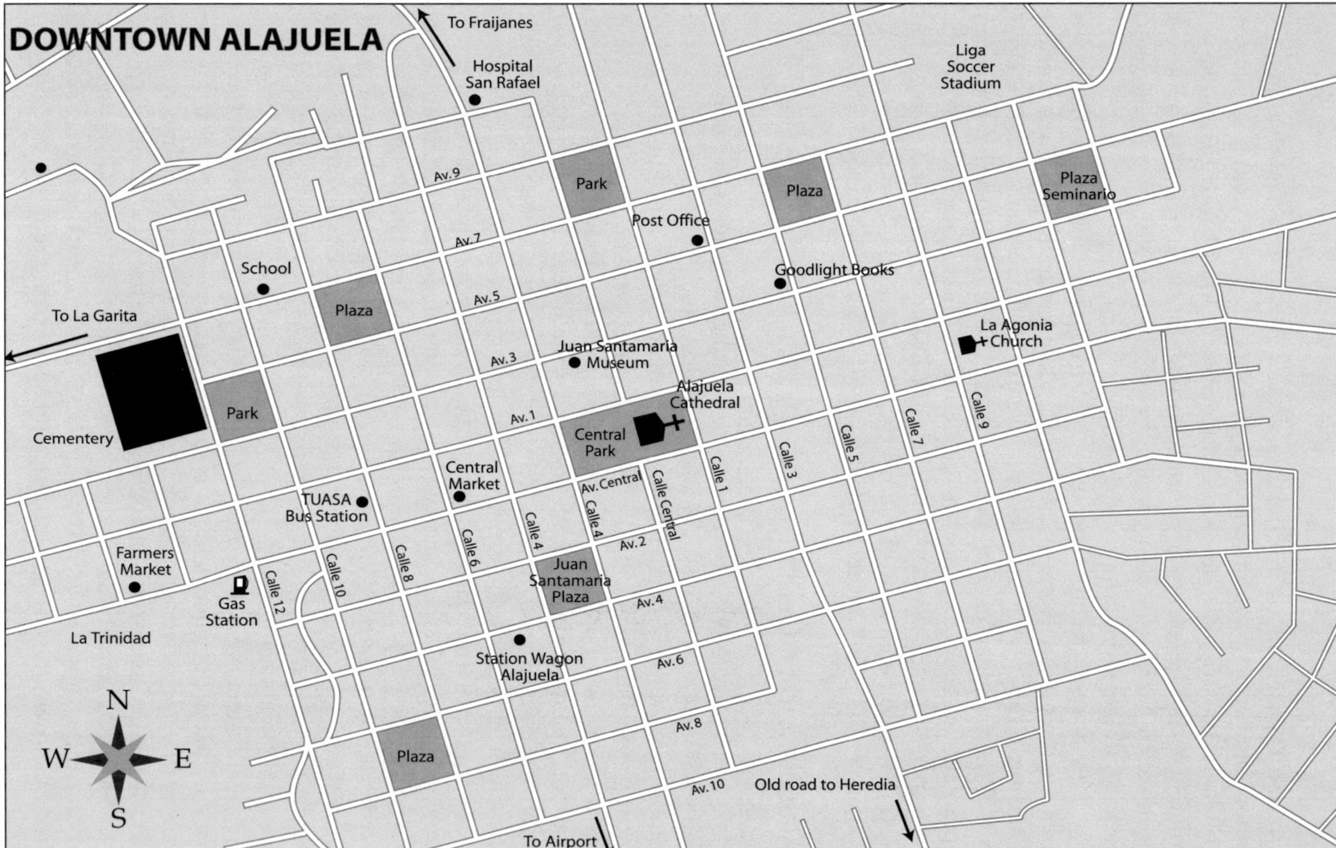
DOWNTOWN ALAJUELA
To Fraijanes
Hospital San Rafael
Liga Soccer Stadium
Park
Plaza
Plaza Seminario
Post Office
School
Goodlight Books
To La Garita
Plaza
La Agonia Church
Juan Santamaria Museum
Alajuela Cathedral
Park
Cementery
Central Park
Central Market
TUASA Bus Station
Farmers Market
Gas Station
Juan Santamaria Plaza
La Trinidad
Station Wagon Alajuela
Plaza
Old road to Heredia
To Airport
Av. 9
Av. 7
Av. 5
Av. 3
Av. 1
Av. Central
Av. 2
Av. 4
Av. 6
Av. 8
Av. 10
Calle 12
Calle 10
Calle 8
Calle 6
Calle 4
Calle Central
Calle 1
Calle 3
Calle 5
Calle 7
Calle 9
N
W
E
S

sits Alejandro Morera Soto soccer stadium. It is the home of La Liga the city's premier soccer team. Costa Ricans also refer to the city of Alajuela as *La Liga* in slang.

The town's Central Market is only a couple of blocks west of the Central Park. Fresh meats, fish, vegetables, fruits and a variety of other odds and ends can be found under one roof. On Saturdays the city holds a large outdoor farmer's market where a lot of bargains can be found. If nothing else the carnival-like atmosphere of this outdoor marketplace provides an excellent opportunity to mingle with the locals. Many Americans gather in the bar and restaurant area. Some people say Alajuela has by far the best farmers market in all of Costa Rica. Other local attractions are a bird zoo, a butterfly farm, national parks, the spectacular Poás Volcano and much more.

Pricemart recently opened one of their warehouse-style facilities on the west side of town.

Housing in the Alajuela area is plentiful and very reasonably priced compared to San José. Prices range from about $50,000 to $300,000 or more and rents begins at about $400.

La Garrita

La Garita, is a pleasant area that extends from the west end of the city of Alajuela to the area off the General Cañas Highway on the way to Atenas and the Central Pacific beach areas of Jacó, Hermosa Quepos and areas south.

The area is known for its mild climate of 72 degrees and is a popular place for *ticos* to own second homes. Many foreigners live in this town. Some of the upscale homes come with large parcels of land. I have a friend who rented a home with a pool, a couple of acres of land and a security guard for a very reasonable price. The town has very little to offer in terms of services but there is a small bird zoo and a lot of good restaurants that serve typical Costa Rican dishes. Good shopping is located about five miles away in Alajuela

The Heredias

The City of Heredia

The city of Heredia is Costa Rica's third biggest city, capital of the province with the same name, located between (and north of) San José and Alajuela and is very suitable for living . The towns around the city – including San Rafael, San Pablo, Santo Domingo, Santa Barbara, San Isidro and San

Joaquín de Flores – have become popular places among both expatriates and upwardly-mobile *ticos* looking for a safe place to raise a family.

Heredia is known as the "City of the Flowers" because of its beauty, and some say due to its gorgeous women. The surrounding countryside is beautiful, especially above the city. The hills overlooking the city offer some of the most spectacular views of the Central Valley. The climate is cooler here, especially as you go higher up into the mountains.

This lovely city is only a short distance from San José by car or by the new commuter train. Three bus lines offer service to San José every five minutes.

At one time hillsides were filled with verdant coffee fields. Now that real estate in the area has become so valuable a lot of the coffee fields have been replaced by housing developments. Nevertheless when viewed from afar the hills in around and above the city are still predominantly green from the remaining coffee farms and abundance of trees.

It is rumored that at one time the Sánchez family owned all of the coffee fields between Heredia and the airport. Costa Rica's Nobel Peace Price winner, President Oscar Arias Sánchez is a memeber of this prominent family.

Heredia is also a university town and still retains its rich colonial heritage. Many old Spanish-style buildings made of adobe with tile roofs can still be found near the center of the city. Heredia's beautiful Central Park is one of the finest in the country. It has an imposing old church and a large water fountain. Concerts, celebrations, crafts fairs, music festivals and other activities are often held in the park.

Plans call for the construction of a *Paseo de la Cultura*, a cobblestone pedestrian street. This eight-block promenade will run east-west from the National University along the north side of Central Park and end at the *Palacio de Deportes.* It will pass though the heart of the city's historical district, where many old architectural gems are found.

The new **San Vicente de Paul** public hospital will be finished in 2010. It will replace the old Heredia hospital with the same name. It is located about four blocks due south of the old hospital and about a block south of where the outdoor farmer's market is held every Saturday.

I know a lot of foreigners who live in and around the city of Heredia. A group of expatriates hangs out at a couple of restaurants in the downtown area. They can be found sitting there every morning. You will find it easy to strike up a conversation. You can meet colorful local characters such as Mr. Goldman, "Search Engine" Bill, Hamster Rudy, "Marvelous" Marvin and even the author of this book.

In recent years, the city's entertainment and nightlife scene has improved. Bars catering to college students and thrill-seeking tourists dot the area around the **National University.** Numerous Internet cafés coffee shops and bookstores contribute to the college atmosphere.

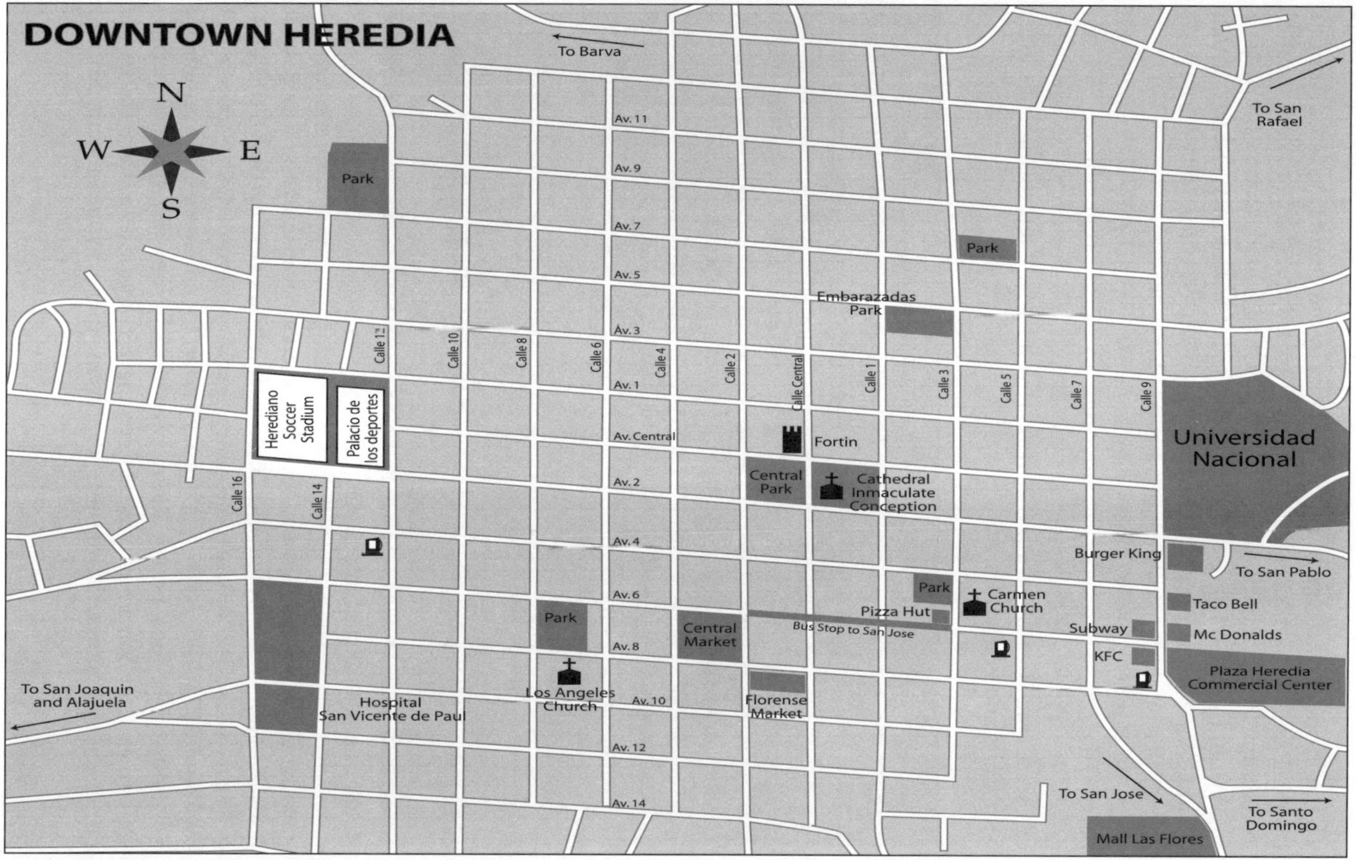
DOWNTOWN HEREDIA
N
S
E
W
To Barva
To San Rafael
Park
Av. 11
Av. 9
Av. 7
Av. 5
Av. 3
Av. 1
Av. Central
Av. 2
Av. 4
Av. 6
Av. 8
Av. 10
Av. 12
Av. 14
Calle 12
Calle 10
Calle 8
Calle 6
Calle 4
Calle 2
Calle Central
Calle 1
Calle 3
Calle 5
Calle 7
Calle 9
Calle 16
Calle 14
Embarazadas Park
Herediano Soccer Stadium
Palacio de los deportes
Universidad Nacional
Fortin
Central Park
Cathedral Inmaculate Conception
Burger King
To San Pablo
Park
Carmen Church
Pizza Hut
Bus Stop to San Jose
Taco Bell
Subway
Mc Donalds
KFC
Plaza Heredia Commercial Center
Central Market
Los Angeles Church
Florense Market
Hospital San Vicente de Paul
To San Joaquin and Alajuela
To San Jose
To Santo Domingo
Mall Las Flores

Heredia also has unique restaurants offering international fare. Pane e Vino is one of the best Italian restaurants in the country as is La Antigua Roma. **Paseo de las Flores** is a new shopping mall near the southern entrance of the city. **Pricesmart**, across the street from the mall is a warehouse style store from the U.S. There is also an **Hipermás** (owned by Walmart) which is a huge supermarket that sells hardware, appliances, automobile parts, patio and garden supplies, clothing and a whole lot more.

On Saturday there is a large open-air farmer's market (*fería*) in the south part of the city where you can buy fresh fruits and vegetables at bargain prices. It stretches for about eight blocks and is a beehive of activity. You can see Costa Ricans leaving the market with large overflowing bags filled with fruits and vegetables.

Heredia's beautiful Central Park

Many foreign retirees now live in Heredia because of the low cost of housing. Here, you may find a lot of affordable homes for less than $100,000. For example, a 1200 square foot home in gated community can be purchased for about $125,000. A few years ago my good friend Terry Ortiz purchased a 1,500-square-foot house about two blocks from the huge Hipermás supermarket in San Francisco de Heredia for about $95,000. Today the home is worth almost $150,000. At present, there is a construction boom in small gated communities on the outskirts of the Heredia area. Heredia is now one of the fastest growing areas in the country.

I know several foreigners who rent nice apartments in downtown Heredia for only a few hundred dollars per month. Carson Smith has a beautiful three-bedroom apartment near the university with all of the amenities. Five or six other Americans live in the same building. Carson loves his apartment because of its great location. He says, "I can walk around the corner to the pharmacy. I have three supermarkets within four blocks. There are several restaurants and places where my friends gather, all within walking distance. My brother lives in the States and makes more than $500,000 yearly. I would never trade my lifestyle here in Heredia for his."

If you prefer living in a cooler alpine-like setting, you can find nice homes and cabins all over the pine-covered mountains surrounding the Central Valley.

San Rafael de Heredia is in the hills above the city of Heredia. The most notable feature of this area is the climate, which is considerably cooler than that in San José. Wealthy Costa Ricans and some foreigners live there. The town's most salient feature is a huge church that can be seen from many miles away. The Sunday *feria* or outdoor market is a real plus here. Although not as big as the one in downtown Heredia, almost any fruit or vegetable can be found there.

My good friend Joe Brennan bought a nice home overlooking San Rafael and the Central Valley for less than $100,000. His view is to kill for. every year he hosts an annual Thanksgiving Dinner for his friends, which everyone looks forward to.

Los Angeles de Heredia, to the north of San Rafael, is a favorite with foreigners because of its pastoral setting. The nearby areas around **Monte de la Cruz** and **San José de la Montaña** are all similar but sparsely populated and cooler because of their higher elevation. I know several Americans who live near the mountain towns of **Barva** and **Birrí** north of downtown Heredia.

San Isidro de Heredia is an absolutely spectacular area to the east of Heredia. Gently rolling, verdant hills and meadows surround this Swiss alpine-like town. This area remains green even during the dry season due to its cool climate. Many Americans live in the San Isidro area. Bruce from San Diego just purchased a huge parcel of land with an unbelievable view of the Irazú Volcano. He paid about $80,000 for the land that includes a farmhouse. He is presently refurbishing it and plans to build his dream home on another part of the property. My friend Ana Brown built a quaint home in the Calle Chávez area of San Isidro.

Grecia, San Ramón and Atenas

Grecia

Grecia (Greece in Spanish), known as the cleanest town in Costa Rica, is also a place worth investigating. This charming town is located about 10 minutes off the Pan-American Highway making it very accessible. It is also about half an hour from the country's main airport and about an hour from San José. You can get to the new highway leading to the Pacific beaches in about 30 minutes by taking the old road to Atenas through the scenic countryside. Once in Atenas you can pick up the connection to the new highway a short distance away.

The area around the town of Grecia is absolutely beautiful. Gently rolling, green hills and sugarcane fields with a backdrop of spectacular mountains in the distance dominate the surrounding landscape. This tranquil agricultural town, has a beautiful Central Park, a famous church made of metal panels and an ideal climate. On Sunday evenings many residents stroll around the park just like in the days of old. The hills surrounding the town are full of nice spots to live. **Plaza Grecia** is the town's new mall and will eventually house more than 50 shops, a supermarket, food court, movie theaters and parking for over 300 cars.

One clear advantage Grecia has over the town of Atenas is its public hospital.

Grecia is rapidly becoming a bedroom community for people from San José. Many people choose to live here because of the laid-back lifestyle, cheaper housing prices and other factors. They make the hour-long commute to and from San José by bus or car on weekdays. My good friends Mike and Ed both live there and love it. Most expats hang out at the Café Delicias diagonal to the town's main square.

There are a lot of Gringos who live in the Cajón de Grecia area. In the last five years, more than 20 housing projects have been built and close to 1,500 construction permits have been issued in the area around Grecia. There is no indication this trend will change.

Nearby is the town of **Sarchí**, famous for its handicrafts and wood products. Other towns worth checking out for living northwest of San José are **Naranjo**, **San Ramón** and **Palmares**. I know of a few Americans and Europeans who are happily living in and around these laid-back towns . My friend Gino and his Costa Rican wife live on the outskirts of Naranjo in a beautiful 3,000-square-foot home they purchased for less than $100,000.

San Ramón

San Ramón, with a Population of 70,000, is a great place to live given its terrific climate, friendly people, wide array of services, and proximity to both the Pacific coast and to San José. Home to ex-presidents and leading literary figures, San Ramón (locals are affectionately called *monche os*) is known as the "City of Poets and Presidents." Additionally, the area's value-priced real estate makes it one of the best places to invest in Costa Rica.

San Ramón is directly off the Pan-American highway heading northwest from San José, is only a 35-minute drive from the airport to town, and an additional 35 minutes to the port town of Puntareans on the Pacific. However, because of its location it is difficult for residents of this town to take advantage of the new highway to the Central Pacific beaches. In order to reach the new highway you will have to backtrack to Atenas which can take up to an hour.

Some *gringos* live in and around San Ramón but the area has not been overrun like other more popular parts of the country.

A new improved highway to the capital is in the works and should reduce driving time to San José and the airport. The stretch between San Ramón and the airport will receive special much needed improvements to speed up the flow of traffic.

San Ramón boasts a shopping mall, modern movie theatre, cultural center/museum, and many supermarkets and restaurants. There is a major hospital, many doctors' offices, and the only branch of the University of Costa Rica outside of San José.

Surrounded by lush mountains and located at 4000 feet above sea level, temperatures usually range from 70 to 80 degrees Fahrenheit every day of the year. However, because the town's elevation it can get very cool at night. The winds are also fierce in the summer months. Air conditioning and heating are not necessary but you do have to bundle up on some of the cooler nights. During the rainy season, from June through December, one can expect sunshine in the morning and rain showers in the mid to late afternoon. The skies tend to clear toward the early evening.

Until recently, there was a limited selection of high-quality homes in the San Ramón area but this is changing as communities catering to foreign retirees are sprouting up rapidly. Because development is still relatively new, real estate remains under-priced compared to other towns in the Central Valley.

Some absolutely beautiful areas can be found above the town of San Ramón. Helene from Austria has a hotel and health resort in Piedades Sur de San Ramón. Located in the coastal mountains, it has an absolutely incredible view of the Gulf of Nicoya.

The nearby town of **Palmares** is known for its yearly carnival held in January. The town fills up with Costa Ricans and foreigners in search of a good time.

Atenas

Nestled in the foothills at the western edge of the Central Valley at 2,500 feet in altitude, the rural and picturesque town of Atenas offers panoramic views of the Central Valley and nearby volcanoes. The town is 13 miles from Alajuela — the main city that services the area— and about 45 minutes to an hour from San José. Atenas is Spanish for Athens. So you can visit Grecia (Grece) and Atenas (Athens) in Costa Rica without ever going to Europe.

The town's weather is its claim to fame. According to *National Geographic*, Atenas has one the world's best climates. You can see the slogan *Atenas, el mejor clima del Mundo* (Atenas the best climate in the world) painted on the commuter buses that go back and forth between Atenas and San José and Alajuela.

Atenas is located on the highway that currently serves as the Central Valley's main connection to the Central Pacific. About a 25 minute drive from the international airport and close to a large city with all requisite services, Atenas also boasts a cool, breezy climate is wooing beach lovers away from the relentless sun. It is a popular place for both retirees and younger generations.

The town is a friendly, small-town with a laid-back atmosphere and 5,000 residents. Another 15,000 people live in the surrounding area. The town is clean with a beautiful central park lined with palm trees. There are schools, banks, several supermarkets, a health care center, an Internet café and good restaurants in this quaint town. About 200 North Americans and Europeans have chosen to live in here. Many Costa Ricans have their country homes in the surrounding hills.

The other advantage of Atenas from an investor's point of view is that it is one of the communities easily reached by the new highway. This will help to bolster land prices in the area. The big advantage of the new highway is that it will make the amenities of Santa Ana and Escazú and even San Jose more accessible. Atenas doesn't have a hospital but with the new road, Escazú's Cima Hospital is fairly close. Driving time to the beach just takes minutes.

Atenas itself doesn't have much in the way of variety. It's a traditional farming town with all the basic necessities plus a farmer's market on Fridays. For imported goods, clothes and housewares, it's a better bet to head for Alajuela, which has a large shopping mall, or go a little further to Escazú.

The expatriates living in Atenas are generally from the U.S. or Canada, though you do come across Europeans as well. Only a handful of gated communities have been established to date, but more are on the way, and it

Why Small Is Better

By Christopher Howard

The first week of December I visited my home town of Thousand Oaks, California. I had not returned in almost seven years. The first thing I noticed was that a lot had changed dramatically. Due to a construction boom, I could barely recognize some of the areas of town. It seemed like everything had become a great deal more commercial and homogeneous on much larger scale. Everywhere I went there were people driving a whole gamut of sports utility vehicles or as they are more commonly known, SUVS. The streets were filled with gas-guzzling vehicles we rarely see in Costa Rica - the Ford Excursion, the GMC Yukon, the Ford F-250 monster truck and a couple of models of Hummers – to name a few. The latter is similar to the military vehicles that are blown to pieces by roadside bombs in Iraq. The version sold in the States is more luxurious with its leather seats, colorful paint and sporty trim. In California it appears that the bigger the vehicle, the better it is and more status a person has. You are defined by what you drive. I guess the car's size reflects the owner's ego. The interesting thing is that very few of the owners use these mammoth vehicles to go off- road. They use them to commute at a snail's pace on the overcrowded freeways, to go to the grocery store and to take the kids to soccer practice.

The freeways are also bigger than ever. They usually have four or five lanes in each direction. Rush hour is almost an all-day affair. Traffic begins to get bad at 5:30 in the morning and ends around 8:00 at night. Sprawling, massive, slow-moving traffic jams can extend from Ventura Country in the north to the Mexican border just south of San Diego. These are normal conditions. God forbid if there is an accident! The freeways are indeed bigger but not a faster means of transportation than our pothole-filled roads in Costa Rica. Costa Rica's *presas* or traffic jams are small in comparison.

Everything else is supe sized up north. There are enormous 24-hour gyms to keep those perfect bodies in shape. Almost every major shopping center and strip mall has a Starbucks, a Subway sandwich shop, a Home Depot, a Walmart, a Target, a big chain vitamin store, a Borders or Barnes & Noble bookstore, a branch of Best Buy and almost every other colossal chain store. There are supermarkets that even dwarf our Hipermás. They have a huge selection of every imaginable food. There are gigantic bags of potato chips, barrel-sized bottles of soda pop, and a variety of mouth-watering delicacies to stimulate your appetite. No wonder obesity is such a monumental problem in the U.S. Restaurants supersize everything. There is even a chain of pet stores called Petco. Most of their stores are as big or larger than a Costa Rican supermarket. I guess most pets are also overweight in the States. It would not surprise me if there is a Weight Watchers for pets.

Then there are the massive Kinko's copy centers. They basically offer every conceivable type of service from making photocopies to using the Internet. Everything is under one roof and they are conveniently open 24-hours. These stores are extremely handy for the traveling business person. I accessed my e-mail everyday by using one of their computers. I was going to use the local public library's computer services at $5 an hour but there was an hour limit The price at Kinko's proved to be astronomical. I paid $12 per hour to use a state of the art credit card device connected directly to the computer. The cost of the average net café in Costa Rica is about a dollar an hour. However, none of the Internet cafés in Costa Rica that I have seen feature new Dell computers like the ones at Kinko's.

Everything else is geared towards large-scale consumption. People seem very happy and caught up in their fast-paced lifestyles of expensive SUVS, the "shop until you drop" mentality and living in their palatial upscale housing tracts which seem like ritzy suburban ghettos where every house looks almost exactly like it had been cut from the same mold.

After a few days of experiencing everything on the large scale, I began to yearn for my simple down-sized lifestyle in petite Costa Rica. People here seem to be a lot happier with much less. The average person here is materially poorer than the average American, but their lives are far more richer. Here people seem to live with gusto (enjoyment) and *sabor* (a flavor or spice). In Costa Rica every day can be filled with adventure and exciting activities. Sure we have the malls and a dose of U.S. culture but we also have a lot more little things that truly make life immensely more worthwhile. People up north exist, we live the pure life on a much smaller scale. The phrase, "*¡Pura vida¡*," says it all.

seems to be an increasingly popular choice for security reasons. Quite a few smaller, *tico*-style homes are also on the market, and further outside town many farms are for sale that might be good for development.

Developers are building gated communities within a short distance of the town center, and there are wonderful views of the area's mountains and valleys. In general, Three-bedroom homes range from $80,000 in a ***tico*** neighborhood to $500,000 in one of the newer gated developments like Roca Verde.

The cost of living in this area is lower than in Escazú, but mainly because life is simpler and there are fewer options. Good restaurants are hard to come by, and the ones you do encounter have mainly local cuisines, as opposed to international.. While that's good for the pocketbook, the town's charm may wear thin for those looking for a more fast-paced or sophisticated lifestyle. This is rural living, and you have to be ready for it.

Downtown Atenas has good shopping

The Northern Zone

For those not interested in the ocean, or who want to avoid the heat and prices of the Pacific coast by living a rural life away from the traffic of the Central Valley, Northern Costa Rica – particularly around the visually stunning lake and volcano – is a great choice for either a vacation home or a permanent residence.

Verdant rainforest blankets the hills in a chaotic tangle of vines, canopy, and aerials. Beneath it, delicate flowers bloom at various times of year, swaying in the slightest breeze. Countless species of animals dwell in this wilderness. The majestic cloud forest of Monteverde is an important ecosystem whose inhabitants are being threatened by climate change. Other parts of the area consist of endless cattle pastures demarcated by fence lines. Further north, in the flatlands, lie the fruit plantations.

The quaint mountain town of **Zarcero** is famous for its sculptured bushes. The park in front of Zarcero's church is full of shrubs that have been sculpted into the shapes of arches, animals, people and even an oxcart complete with oxen.

San Carlos, or **Ciudad Quesada** is about two hours from San José and is considered the capital of the country's Northern Zone. Note here that San Carlos often refers to two things: The city, which also goes by the name Cuidad Quesada, and San Carlos the area around the city, including towns such as San Isidro. It's easy to get the two mixed up, as locals (*los Sancarleños*) and expatriates familiar with the area really use the two names interchangeably. So ask if you're not sure which is which. The climate is mild and there are a few North Americans who own ranches in this area.

Almost everything of importance is found within several blocks of the town's main square. **Plaza San Carlos** is a new mall with about 143 stores including a supermarket, movie theaters, food court, travel agencies and much more.

Around the San Carlos area, you might notice lots of black sheets covering large portions of steep or sloping farmland on the drive up from San José. These are ornamental plant farms, and there are quite a few of them in the region. They take advantage of the region's heavy rains by growing plants that they either export to other countries or sell in booming real estate markets in Northwest Guanacaste and the Central Pacific.

Northern Costa Rica's crown jewel is the **Arenal Volcano**, an active volcano that trickles lava and smoke almost constantly, giving the landscape a sense of mystery found nowhere else in the country.

Here, the four medieval elements are found in abundance: fire from the volcano, water from Lake Arenal, fresh air thanks to the work of the rain forest, and rich soil from the volcanic ash that has blanketed the ground since the volcano's last big eruption in 1968.

The 48-square-mile, man-made **Lake Arenal** is northwest of San Carlos. It is surrounded by rolling hills covered with pastures and patches of tropical forest. The very active Arenal Volcano can often be seen in the distance with plumes of smoke emanating from the top.

Lake Arenal is the largest lake in Costa Rica and the second-biggest in Central America, after nearby Lake Nicaragua. It receives water from

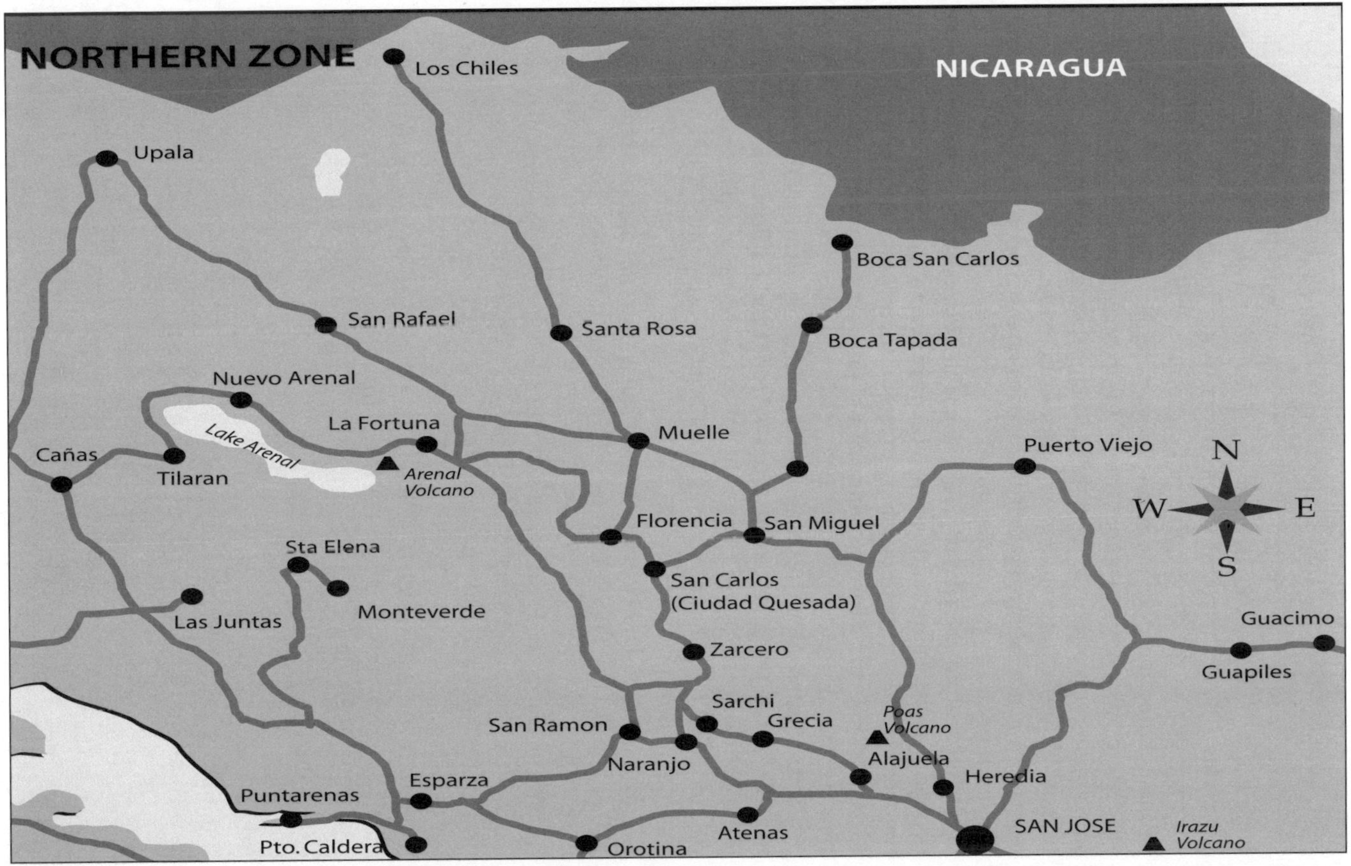
NORTHERN ZONE
NICARAGUA
Los Chiles
Upala
Boca San Carlos
San Rafael
Santa Rosa
Boca Tapada
Nuevo Arenal
La Fortuna
Muelle
Lake Arenal
Cañas
Tilaran
Arenal Volcano
Puerto Viejo
N
W
E
S
Florencia
San Miguel
Sta Elena
San Carlos (Ciudad Quesada)
Las Juntas
Monteverde
Guacimo
Zarcero
Guapiles
Sarchi
San Ramon
Grecia
Poas Volcano
Naranjo
Alajuela
Esparza
Heredia
Puntarenas
SAN JOSE
Irazu Volcano
Atenas
Pto. Caldera
Orotina

at least three rivers in the region, in addition to a 400-meter tunnel that connects it with the beautiful (and natural) Lake Cote.

Lake Arenal was created to be a reservoir when engineers flooded a large valley. The lake was an engineering feat for Costa Rica at the time and generates 70% of the country's electricity. Water from the lake is also used for irrigation in the Pacific area of Guanacaste, which is the most arid part of the country and goes months without rain

There are many enjoyable things to do around Arenal. The lake and surrounding area offer excellent fishing, sailing, hiking, windsurfing, mountain biking, bird-watching and other outdoor activities. With all the area has to offer, it is not surprising that this area is rapidly becoming popular with foreign residents.

Land around the lake is readily available. Prices vary per square meter depending on location and views. There are several large developments in the area like the one being built by my good friend John Wilson from Santa Monica, California. He owns quite a bit of prime real estate with spectacular views of the lake.

Several interesting towns are found in this area. Nearby **Tilarán** is home to a number of foreigners, as are **Nuevo Arenal** and **La Fortuna**. The latter is a tourist-oriented town east of the volcano and a good place to view the volcano. The town has numerous small hotels, restaurants, tour companies and many souvenir stores.

The Catarata La Fortuna is a spectacular waterfall that plummets some 100 feet into a deep pool surrounded by luxuriant foliage. To get there you have to hike down a steep trail.

At the **Tabacón Resort** you will find a hot spring in a lush valley at the base of the picture-perfect Arenal Volcano. This is the place to soak your tired bones after a day of participating in one of the many activities this area has to offer.

Nuevo Arenal (which will herein be referred to simply as Arenal) is a relatively pretty town on the northern tip of the lake that was built with government funding after the original town got in the way of the planned lake. The center of the town lies just up the hill from the lake and is on the main road linking Tilarán (and the main part of Guanacaste) with the Arenal Volcano. It's therefore a route much traveled by tourists. The little community has a bullring and neighborhoods of prefab houses, each with its own unique garden, porch extension, colorful facade and ironwork.

The town is a typical one-of-everything small town, with a handful of shops and restaurants near the lake that are obviously aimed at tourists. The town has a bank, a post office, a couple of grocery stores and some construction supply stores. Like many places in Costa Rica, you will need to visit San José for a good selection of furnishings, appliances, and nice clothing.

The Northern Pacific Zone

The northwest region has vast plains and is drier than the Central Valley and central and southern coastal regions. Nevertheless, some of the country's most beautiful beaches, breathtaking views, history, culture and nightlife can be found here. The city of Liberia and the Tempisque Bridge are the entry points to Guanacaste's beaches.

The capital city of **Liberia**, located 125 miles north of San José on the Pan-American Highway, is considered the heart of Guanacaste, andis a full-service city. Sometimes called the "white city" because of its architecture, Liberia is the most colonial of Costa Rica's cities. Due to the area's growing popularity, Liberia is quickly becoming one of the country's largest and most important cities, offering restaurants, hotels, several museums, good shopping, a mall with movie theaters, a public hospital and the **Daniel Oduber International Airport.** Liberia is a good place to visit while on your way to Guanacaste's many beaches. My good friend Bud from Las Vegas owns a small farm in the Liberia area.

More good news! The Holiday Inn Express announced plans to invest $10 million in the construction of a new 120-room hotel and mall in Liberia. The new mall will house approximately 40 stores with parking for 450 cars. Holiday Inn also plans to build a golf course near the hotel.

Another exciting development is the wild animal park, **Africa Mía**, a 100 -acre open-air zoo with free-roaming animals. Mario Sotela, the developer of Africa Mía, also owns Libería Mía which is the town of Liberia's soccer team.

Contributing to the development of this area are approximately 40 weekly flights from the United States to Liberia's Daniel Oduber International Airport and better infrastructure than can be found around the beaches on the southern part of Nicoya Peninsula.

A wide range of condos may be found on both isolated and popular beaches. Prices range from $100,000 to $750,000 depending on location. A number of nice gated communities and golf resorts are found in this section of the country. Undeveloped beach and ocean-view properties can still be found in some areas.

More than 50 spectacular beaches of all sizes, shapes and colors with clear blue water are found all along the Pacific coast in the Guanacaste Province. This area is sometimes referred to as Costa Rica's "Gold Coast". However, a few of the adjacent beach communities may have too much tranquility for some people or have too much of a resort atmosphere for others.

The area around the **Peninsula of Papagayo** has been the scene of recent development. The spectacular, upscale all-inclusive **Four Seasons Resort** on Playa Blanca is found in this area. It was selected as the best resort in Central and South America.

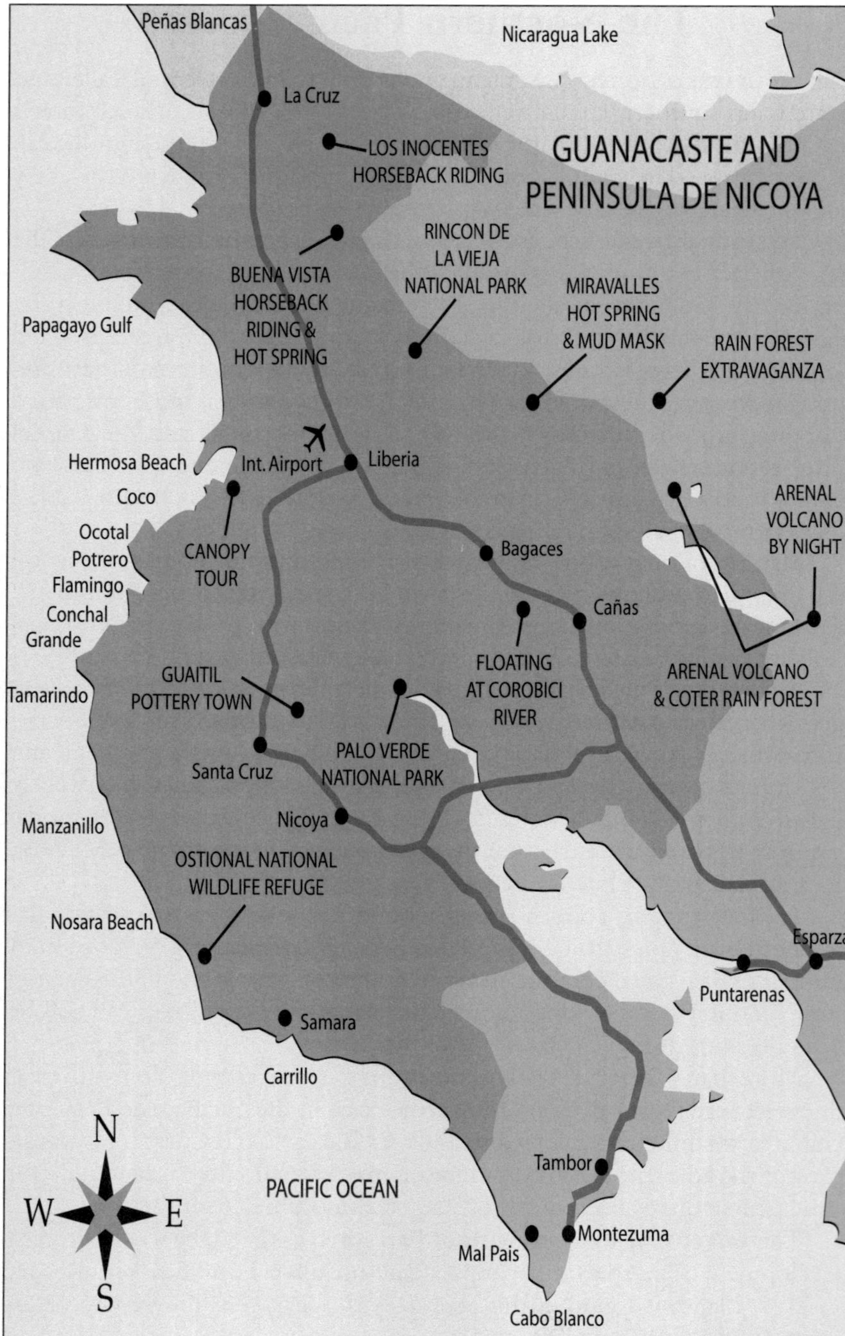
GUANACASTE AND PENINSULA DE NICOYA
Peñas Blancas
Nicaragua Lake
La Cruz
LOS INOCENTES HORSEBACK RIDING
RINCON DE LA VIEJA NATIONAL PARK
BUENA VISTA HORSEBACK RIDING & HOT SPRING
MIRAVALLES HOT SPRING & MUD MASK
RAIN FOREST EXTRAVAGANZA
Papagayo Gulf
Hermosa Beach
Int. Airport
Liberia
Coco
CANOPY TOUR
Ocotal
Potrero
Flamingo
Conchal
Grande
ARENAL VOLCANO BY NIGHT
Bagaces
Cañas
FLOATING AT COROBICI RIVER
ARENAL VOLCANO & COTER RAIN FOREST
Tamarindo
GUAITIL POTTERY TOWN
Santa Cruz
PALO VERDE NATIONAL PARK
Manzanillo
Nicoya
OSTIONAL NATIONAL WILDLIFE REFUGE
Nosara Beach
Esparza
Puntarenas
Samara
Carrillo
N
W
E
S
PACIFIC OCEAN
Tambor
Mal Pais
Montezuma
Cabo Blanco

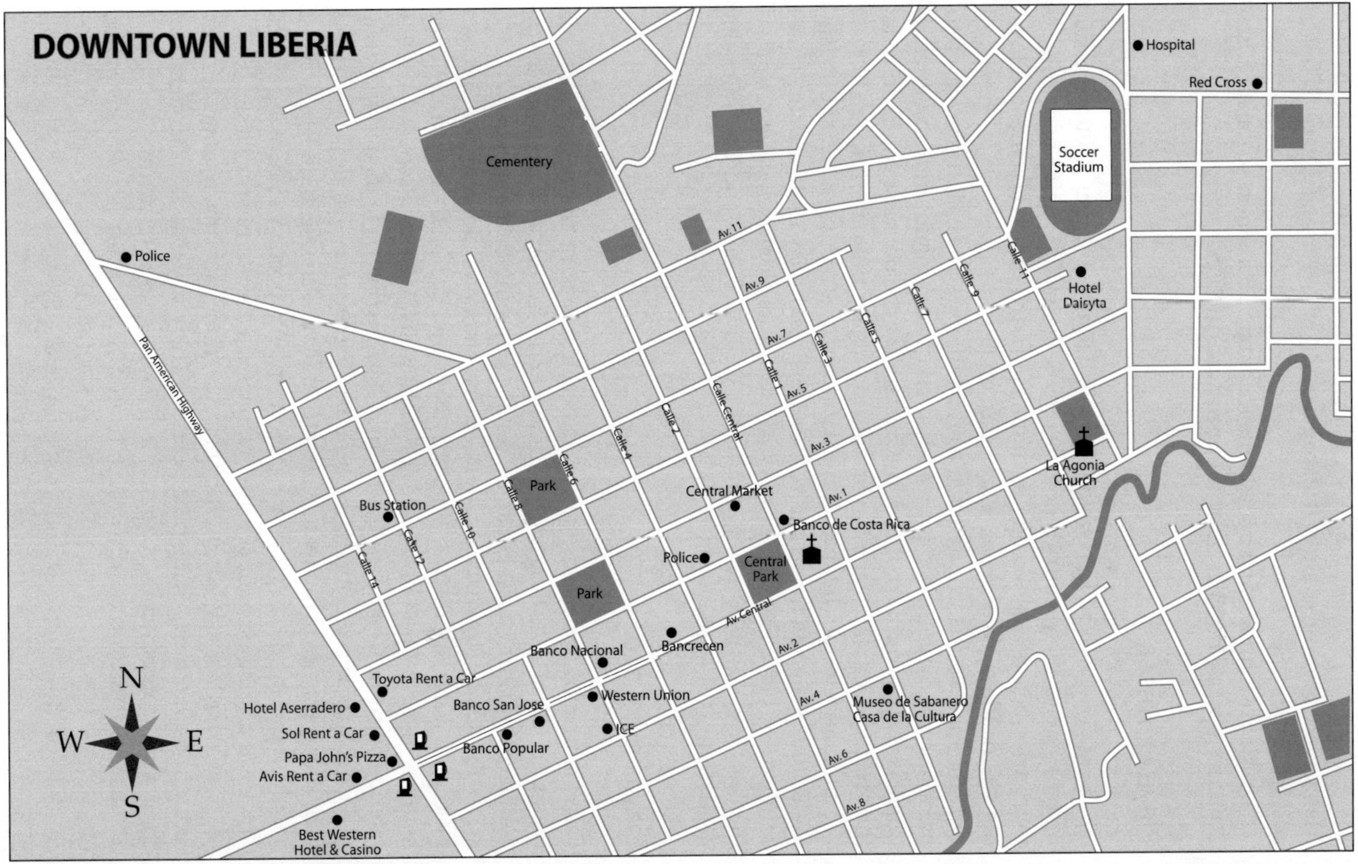
DOWNTOWN LIBERIA
Cementery
Hospital
Red Cross
Soccer Stadium
Police
Av. 11
Av. 9
Av. 7
Av. 5
Av. 3
Av. 1
Av. Central
Av. 2
Av. 4
Av. 6
Av. 8
Calle 11
Calle 9
Calle 7
Calle 5
Calle 3
Calle 1
Calle Central
Calle 2
Calle 4
Calle 6
Calle 8
Calle 10
Calle 12
Calle 14
Hotel Daisyta
Pan American Highway
La Agonia Church
Park
Central Market
Banco de Costa Rica
Bus Station
Police
Central Park
Park
Banco Nacional
Bancrecen
Toyota Rent a Car
Western Union
Hotel Aserradero
Banco San Jose
Museo de Sabanero
Casa de la Cultura
Sol Rent a Car
ICE
Banco Popular
Papa John's Pizza
Avis Rent a Car
Best Western
Hotel & Casino
N
W
E
S

The new $15 million 370-slip **La Marina Papagayo** is being built in Manzanillo Bay in the Gulf of Papagayo. It will eventually have 370 slips and will cover 100 acres.

AOL co-founder Steve Case is spending $23 million to build a new 200-acre upscale hotel at nearby **Punta Cacique**.

Playa Hermosa

The next cove north of Playas del Coco is Hermosa. It has white sand and offers some of the country's best diving. It lies in the center of a string of four major beaches, all within 30 minutes of each other: **Hermosa**, **Playas del Coco**, **Playa Ocotal** and **Playa Panamá**.

The hillside that slopes down to the little bay and its long beach offers plenty of opportunity for great views, and both condo and single family home construction. Like Coco, the beach isn't the prettiest you'll find, but the great views make real estate in this town a bit more upscale.

Ocean-view lots in the Hermosa area range between $250,000 and $500,000. My good friend and realtor Les lives there with his family. Don't confuse this Playa Hermosa with two other beaches with the same name — the one just south of Jaco Beach in the Central Pacific and the other one near Dominical in the Southern Zone.

Playas del Coco

Coco is one of the most developed beach towns in the region but still retains much of its fishing-village atmosphere. It is set in a deep cove with consistently calm waters, making it a safe swimming beach.

This seaside town is surrounded by emerald-colored hills, offers a variety of water sports and boasts a small international community. The nightlife here is good and includes restaurants, bars, a disco and casinos catering to those looking to have fun. A new marina is planned in this area.

Coco has the advantage of offering a greater availability of services than the nearby growth areas of Hermosa, Playa Panamá and Ocotal. Most people in the area go to Coco for their shopping, postal and banking needs. The town also has several dentists, medical clinics and pharmacies.

Coco has always been a popular vacation spot for *ticos* and, more recently, U.S. retirees living on a pension. These days the area has plenty of cheap studio apartments, though not always of the best quality.

Land in the Coco area ranges from $20 to $200 per square meter. Ocean view lots can be found for under $100,000. Grupo Mapache offers condos for those retirees and *tico* vacationers for between $50,000 and $75,000 depending on the size and amenities.

Playa Ocotal

Ocotal is just south of Playas del Coco. This gray-sand beach area is much smaller, secluded and laid-back than neighboring Coco. Ocotal is a base for sport fishing and scuba diving. The main feature is the Ocotal Beach resort.

Playa Potrero

This small fishing village with its gray-sand beach is located immediately north of Playa Flamingo and about a 30-minute drive from the city of Liberia. Potrero does have its charm, boasting one resort and a few small hotels. We have a friend who owns a couple of nice condos right on the beach.

Flamingo

Flamingo is a hilly peninsula of beautiful million-dollar vacation homes nestled among trees with splendid ocean views. It is situated in the province of Guanacaste only 50 minutes away by car from the Liberia International Airport. The fact that the area is a peninsula naturally restricts development, however land is still available in the hills just off the peninsula. Flamingo's picture-perfect, mile-long, white-sand beach to the south of the peninsula is one of the most beautiful in the country. (Flamingo was originally called Playa Blanca because of this long mile-ling white sand beach.)

Flamingo is considered to be one of the finest resort areas in Costa Rica. It is also Guanacaste's sport fishing capital and offers some of the best sailfish and marlin fishing in the world. Excellent skin diving and snorkeling are also offered in this area. All of this plus good nightlife and several restaurants have led some to call Flaming the "Acapulco of Costa Rica."

Good news! Now that there is finally a company approved to build the new Flamingo Beach Marina, there is a lot of excitement in this Costa Rican coastal town. Initial plans will give the marina more than 440 boat slips that will accommodate many different sizes of boats and yachts. For more info see: www.flamingomarina.com.

There is an abundance of real estate in Flamingo, including condominiums dotting the surrounding hills. Land prices range from about $150 to $350 per square meter. A 1000 meter square lot can be found for about $500,000.

Golf lovers are happy here, with three golf courses located nearby.

Flamingo attracts retired foreigners as well as people with children because of all it has to offer. **The Country Day School**, one of the country's most prestigious private primary and secondary institutions, has a branch near here.

Neighboring **Sugar** beach has calm waters, ocean views and breathtaking sunsets. Many foreigners reside around the neighboring areas.

Brasilito and Conchal

South of Flamingo, there are other beaches worth checking out. Brasilito is a quaint *tico* beach town near the Reserva Conchal luxury resort. A few other large resorts are planned for that area, but have been stalled by environmental regulations and a loss of financing. The road from Brasilito to the small towns of Surfside and Potrero isn't paved. The area has seen plenty of development recently, and prices aren't as high as Flamingo.

Conchal is famous for its powdery sand, made of small white seashells or *conchas* in Spanish. It is also the home of the all-inclusive 18-hole **Playa Conchal Golf Resort**. There are a lot of high-priced condominiums and townhouses for sale at the resort.

Tamarindo

Tamarindo, often referred to now as "*Tamargringo,*" is a beach town overlooking a long stretch of beautiful beach. It is a popular spot among surfers. Most people seem to have a love-hate relationship with this epicenter of northwest Guanacaste's real estate boom. A lack of planning and regulation and an easily corruptible former municipality have led to uncontrolled development that is now threatening the surrounding environment.

Tamarindo has the most developed tourist infrastructure in Guanacaste and it indisputably has the best services for miles around. The foreign community has given birth to plenty of restaurants, clubs, bars, hotels and a variety of stores for all tastes that line the main road. The town also has several small grocery stores, a supermarket, many real estate brokers and property management companies, plus a few strip malls with lawyers' offices and title insurance companies. An increasing number of banks are opening branches there as well. **Plaza Tamarindo** is the town's new mall. It will eventually be the largest mall built in a beach community, boasting 50 businesses and a couple of restaurants.

In general, the place is very cosmopolitan, with residents from all over the world adding a very exciting cultural diversity to the area. The Tamarindo community is a mix of North Americans, French, Italian, British and other Europeans, with a few South Americans thrown in the mix. Fewer *ticos* live in the area simply because property prices have gone too high. The community is young and active and most of its members are involved in the tourism or real estate industries.

Property and everything else has become rather expensive in the Tamarindo area because of its popularity. Condos and homes can cost from $200,000 to $700,000. Homes about five minutes from town can be purchased for $150,000 plus.

South of Tamarindo is **Hacienda Pinilla Resort,** which has a championship golf course and offers every imaginable water sport.

Playa Grande

This long white beach to the south of Tamarindo has, until now, been a low-key backpacker and surfer destination with just a few small hotels, residences, and surf schools. Although located adjacent to bustling Tamarindo, the natural barrier of an estuary means it is only accessible either by a 30-minute drive through Villa Real, Huacas and Matapalo, or by a foot ferry which runs only when there's enough traffic.

Its secluded location and the existence of Las Baulas National Marine Park – which includes a large swath of ocean, as well as the sandy beach 50 meters inland to protect the nesting grounds of the endangered leatherback turtle – has kept development to a minimum. Access to the beach at night is closed to all but tour guides with visitors to watch the turtles laying their eggs.

Playa Grande is a very beautiful piece of real estate, but its proximity to the park has caused fierce legal battles that have yet to be resolved. The government has been in the process for some time of expropriating land along the beach, and landowners have countersued. Considering the high prices that developments like Playa Grande Estates are asking, and the ever-present risk of expropriation that will not reimburse you nearly what you paid, investing in Playa Grande is much too risky at this point. Once again, it's a fantastic location, but a smart investor would either wait to see how all the legal battles pan out, or be prepared to spend a lot of money on a very good attorney.

The Nicoya Peninsula Beaches

Junquillal

Junquillal is an isolated white-sand blue-flag beach which is starting to be developed. The Ecological Blue Flag, is a distinction granted to beaches with excellent or very high sanitation and cleanliness. There is a strong ocean current here, so only experienced swimmers should venture out into the water. My good Costa Rican friend, Ricardo Lara and his two sons, are building a small real estate development there.

Nosara

Presently one has to drive along a dreadful (sometimes impassible) road for about 45 minutes to reach the town of Nosara. A person really has to love Nosara to get there. The main route is a gravel, mostly dirt road bisected by runoff ditches and dotted with mud holes. The current gravel road cannot be used during the rainy season or when there is high water in the many rivers. Only buses and large trucks can traverse the route and drivers now have to ford the rivers and streams. This road parallels the coastline.

Change is coming. Work has been started on the first stage of what will become a paved road all the way to Nosara. Workers are grading the road now, and preparing it for paving. This is only half of the story. In the planning stages for the Pacific coast community is a new $60 million highway project that will include seven bridges. The road will more or less follow the path of another seasonal gravel road that leads from Sámara to Playa Garza and Nosara. It will be about 40 kilometers or 25 miles long.

When this project is completed it will open up a section of Pacific coast property that has been a backwater. Sámara, which is further south on the Nicoya Peninsula Pacific coast is already connected to the business center and community of Nicoya with an all-weather, hard surface road.

Despite the bad road, Nosara has developed much more quickly than Sámara, though the pace of development is still much slower than in Tamarindo or Flamingo. A small group of North Americans has been living in Nosara for decades, so the town has a strong sense of community.

Nosara is an attractive area to live in if you are a nature lover. Years ago, the area's North American pioneers donated parcels of land to the government maintain as a reserve, something that has helped keep the area green with controlled development. The community is more family oriented, so it's not a party town. A flourishing expatriate community of 300-400 people gives the town a slightly California-like flavor.

The actual *tico* town of Nosara is located a few kilometers inland. Most expatriates live either in houses in town with great ocean views, or around **Playa Guiones**, away from town, where they've built a little enclave with many day-to-day services and a construction supply store. Small U.S.-style restaurants and services exist for the growing foreign community.

Playa Guiones has a medical clinic and dentist, a couple of pharmacies, and some great restaurants and cafés. The beach also has a surf shop and several surf schools that take advantage of the area's great waves.

Nosara is a famous yoga center. **The Nosara Yoga Institute** is a world-class yoga retreat located just outside of town. They specialize in training yoga teachers; numerous celebrities have been known to take courses there.

Most properties on the market there are single-family homes, many located on the steep hillside to take advantage of the gorgeous sunsets. Construction quality appears high, and the area has an impressive variety of architectural styles. Inland from Guiones, there are several farms for sale. Gated communities and low-rise condominium projects are just starting to get underway. The community doesn't want high rises and will probably do what it can to stop them. As development has picked up the pace, land values have skyrocketed in the past six years, though there is still no zoning plan in place.

Sámara and Carrillo

Sámara and Carrillo south of Nosara, are laid-back beaches really worth exploring. Both beaches are located on bays that are good for swimming. Property is still affordable since the area is not as developed as some of the beaches to the north.

Sámara has a small fishing village-like atmosphere with a few good restaurants, hotels and nightlife. Carrillo, the southern-most of the two beaches is an exceptionally beautiful, palm-lined, white-sand beach on a curved bay, yet it lacks the development of Sámara. A new asfhalt road connects Sámara to Carrillo

The area is popular as a tourist destination with both *ticos* and foreigners, so there's lots of room for tourism-related investment. Both Sámara and Carrillo are perfect spots for families with young children, and generally nice places to relax. Carrillo is more laid-back and doesn't offer many services you, so you will have to shop in Sámara which offers only the basics you would expect from a small town: a doctor, a pharmacy, a few shops and grocery stores, and (of course) real estate brokers. For your main shopping, you head to Nicoya, the nearest service town.

Although there hasn't been as much development here as in the northern part of this region, it is only a matter of time before things will change given the beauty of the area. There are homes and a development scattered in the hills overlooking Carrillo where the views are incredible. On a clear day you can see all the way to Cabo Blanco at the tip of the Nicoya Peninsula.

South of Sámara and Carrillo

In the Southern Nicoya Peninsula there is a whole string of unspoiled beaches. However, accessibility is a big obstacle because of the poor condition of the road and several rivers that cannot be crossed during the rainy season. But in the dry season you can make it all the way down to Mal País.

Sámara is a laid-back beach town

Camaronal

The word *camaronal* means a place where a lot of shrimp are found. The place originally got its name for the number of shrimp that are found around the area. Camaronal has a long beach that is good for surfing. I visited there a couple years ago to look at a large piece of land a friend of mine was going to purchase.

To the south of Camaronal is the isolated community of **Islita**. It is the location of Hotel Punta Islita which is one of Costa Rica's premier hotels. It has been recognized by *Condé Nast Travel* and *Travel and Leisure World* as one of the best hotels in the world.

Playa Coyote is another pristine beach in the area and lies between Punta Islita and Manzanillo.

Santa Teresa, Playa Manzanillo and Malpaís

These towns are located about 3 kilometers apart on the Pacific side of the Nicoya Peninsula. To the north lies **Playa Santa Teresa**. Its seemingly endless beach is one of the best places for surfing on the entire Nicoya Peninsula.

Nearby **Playa Manzanillo** is also becoming popular with surfers and expatriates. A German friend has lived there for several years and really loves this part of Costa Rica.

Malpaís, immediately northwest of Cabo Blanco near the southern tip of the Nicoya Peninsula, is a surfer's paradise. The word Malpaís means "bad country" in Spanish and is a misnomer because nothing could be further from the truth. Nobody knows why or how this beautiful place got the wrong name. There are several beaches at which to swim, dive and snorkel, though the area's main attractions are its unique conditions for surfing. Malpaís has been featured in numerous surfing documentaries and magazines and attracts surfers from all over the world.

This isolated area is becoming very popular with some foreigners because of its scenery and incredible sunsets. The community is young, close and very international, with large contingents of Israelis and Argentines. The area's residents make a living running businesses catering to tourists and real estate companies, and the pace of life is slow but active. Like many surfing towns, the schedules are set by the surf rather than the clock.

Both Santa Teresa and Malpaís more or less consist of a row of small hotels, cabins, restaurants, cafés, bars and houses lining the unpaved road that winds its way up the coast.

The area's reputation has attracted its share of celebrities. Matthew McConaughey spent a week there surfing and partying with his buddies. Even Leonardo DiCaprio went there to surf and relax before an Academy Awards ceremony a few years ago. He ended up falling in love with the place and purchased some land that he gave to his then girlfriend supermodel Gisele Bundchen. She in turn married New England Patriot's star quarterback in a ceremony at their home in there area

To date, the property market in Santa Teresa and Malpaís is dominated by the sale of raw land and houses. The area's first gated community was under construction at the time of my research, and other developers have begun building model homes, so there should be more residences for sale over the next few years. A few large *fincas* are still available in the Santa Teresa area, but most of the action now appears to have moved inland toward the town of Cóbano.

Montezuma

Montezuma, a remote little fishing village near the southern tip of the Nicoya Peninsula, has almost perfect beaches with clear-blue water just right for bodysurfing. Tucked into the foot of a steep and wooded hillside, Montezuma is a lively but quaint tourist town. Unlike almost every other beach town on Costa Rica's Pacific Coast, Montezuma faces east, which allows residents to enjoy the sunrise rather than the sunset.

There are miles of beaches with tide pools and even a tropical 50-foot waterfall nearby. Fortunately, Montezuma and its surroundings have not been destroyed by developers. The area is teeming with birds, monkeys and all sorts of exotic wildlife.

Montezuma is a funky beach town

Jimmy, a 45-year old retiree from Boston, told us he moved there 10 years ago and bought a small home because he found living in San José too expensive. He gets by on about $1000 or less monthly—beer included.

This cozy town is a magnet for hip and Bohemian types interested in alternative lifestyles. European backpackers, yoga enthusiasts and people in search of something new visit here. In this town one can either hangout at the beach or at a local restaurant. The Sano Banano is a vegetarian restaurant where many locals and tourists congregate.

Actually the town really got its start as a popular hippy hangout. During those times, the place was jokingly referred to as *Montefuma – monte* being the *tico* colloquial word for marijuana and *fumar* being the Spanish verb "to smoke." Those days, while not entirely over, have certainly passed their former glory. The hippie crowd has given way to a more sophisticated profile of tourist and resident – possibly the very same clientele as before, but grown up. They now have money and children, so they're looking for a more comfortable lifestyle that's nevertheless off the beaten track.

The change seems to have resulted in a thriving little town that's popular with families who have imagination and a sense of adventure and would be frustrated in Tamarindo or Jacó. The economy has come to rely heavily on tourism and increasingly on real estate. Some beautiful houses and villas are under construction on the cliff tops that ring the town and offer fabulous views of the coastline.

The ocean, as always, is an attraction for expatriates, and it is here that Montezuma's difference with its neighboring markets is most pronounced: Montezuma doesn't have any surfing beaches. The sea is usually calmer than in Malpaís and Santa Teresa, and therefore more attractive to families. As with many other places in Costa Rica, many more families are moving to the area to relocate permanently, a fact reflected by a new demand for schooling in the area. Montezuma is also attracting the first wave of baby boomers, a group that will probably keep demand for property in the area high during the next few years.

Montezuma's community is an interesting mix of *ticos*, North Americans, Germans, Italians, Swiss, and other Europeans. Most expatriates moving permanently to Montezuma work in real estate or construction, or run tourism businesses. Despite its size, Montezuma has some wonderful restaurants thanks to the European and hippie influences.

The town doesn't offer many services like banks or grocery stores. However, the town does have an organic vegetable market once a week, and Cóbano – with its banks, supermarkets, and high-speed Internet, is just 7 kilometers up the hill. For shopping and going to the movies, you'll need to either hop the ferry to Puntarenas or Jacó or, better yet, go to Tambor to catch a flight to San José. Construction supplies can be found in Cóbano or Paquera, though as in other coastal areas you'll probably want to ship in your furnishings from either San José or North America.

Tambor

Originally a fishing village of tiny houses wedged onto a narrow strip of land between the ocean and a small cliff, Tambor is undergoing a massive transformation that will probably spell the end of the village and usher in a number of large resorts, a marina, and a lot of real estate development.

It would be hard to find a more perfect location for an upscale resort community. The sea is gentle and the golden-sand beach that stretches for kilometers forms a perfect crescent across Ballena Bay. The deep circular bay is good for swimming and other outdoor activities. Behind the bay, level ground stretches back to a road, then rises to the farm town of Pánica.

The all-inclusive Hotel Barceló Playa Tambor is located here. The nearby Delfines Golf Club also attracts many visitors. I know a few Americans who reside in the Tambor area and there are some excellent real estate buys. Most live at the Tango Mar development three miles southwest of Tambor or in and around the newly developed Tambor Hills area.

Two of my good friends from California, have a beautiful $2,000,000 ocean-front home in the nearby **Tango Mar** development. They lived at the beach for a few years but found it too laid back for them. They now live in a beautiful condo in Escazú with a panoramic view of the Central Valley. They rent out their beach home and can pay their expenses with the money it generates.

If it's so perfect, why is Tambor still so sleepy? Two factors have prevented a mad rush of development: Difficulty in accessing the area, and the Spanish hotel group Barceló. As for the former, the road from Paquera past Tambor to Cóbano was paved only recently, and visitors from San Joseé still must endure several hours of driving time plus a ferry ride (if you catch it in time). The nearest city is either Puntarenas, or Nicoya, the road to which is still unpaved. More paved roads would certainly add to the area's popularity.

As for Barceló, in the 1970s the company managed to basically control real estate development in the area by purchasing the seven kilometer stretch of land fronting the beach (yes, it's titled) reaching three kilometers inland back in the 1970s. It built the Los Delfines Resort and Barceló Hotel, the only large resort in the whole region and simply left the remaining land unused. This resort has some villas and a 9-hole golf course.

Barcelo is starting to loosen its grip, however. A few years ago, the group began selling parcels of land to developers, and now several large resorts are under construction, with more planned.

Riverside Developers – the same ones who built Riverside Escazú and the Sonesta Jacó Resort – are building two condotel resorts in Tambor, to be known as Bayside and Ocean Whisper. Also under construction are a five-story condominium project called Tambor Hills, and Terramar, a 72-unit low-rise condo project. A mega project called Punta Piedra Amarilla is also in the works. Supposedly this project will include a marina and four boutique hotels, but as of the time of research it was still in the permitting process. The developers are also hoping to bring in a new car ferry to connect their facility with Port Caldera (which connects by the new highway to San José).

In addition to all that, investors are buying up farms with ocean views around the Pánica area. With those areas developed alongside the condominium resorts that are under construction and planned, Tambor is soon going to look like a very different place.

So what's it like now?

It consists of an upscale resort, a sleepy fishing village, and a row of upscale single family homes on a strip of titled beachfront owned by expatriates enjoying their retirement. There are very few services outside the resort, just a tiny grocery store, a couple of restaurants and one or two souvenir shops.

Just outside of the Barceló property is a strip of titled beachfront property with single family homes and a bar, all worth in the high hundred thousands and very likely to have appreciated more.

Locals and expatriates tend to mix because there are very few places to go, but the budding retirement community is close-knit and has a Friday-evening jam session at a beach bar, as well as meetings to discuss what's happening in the area and to exchange experiences. It's known as the TGIF club. As you can see, there is very little to do right now in Tambor, so until the amenities come, a quiet life would be your only option. For now, many property owners live in the area permanently.

In addition to growing interest from retirees, there should also be increasing demand from the yachting and fishing crowd once the marina is up and running. Interest from families wanting a resort area with a safe swimming beach should be on the rise as well, all of which will help keep prices growing for some time to come.

The Central Pacific

The Central Pacific is one of Costa Rica's jewels. It extends from Puntarenas in the north to the Barú River in the south. The closest and most accessible beaches to San José are found in this area. The beaches are sunny year-round, the weather is hot and the ocean is warm. Whether you want to retire or just live in a tropical paradise, the Central Pacific Coast has something for you. Some of the outdoor activities the area offers are: golfing, sport fishing, yachting, canopy tours, river rafting, parasailing, hang gliding, mountain biking, snorkeling, diving, kayaking, bird watching and a lot more. There are even places to study Spanish and practice yoga in this part of Costa Rica.

Here is one expat's take on the Central Pacific: "It was our experience that the west coast was very much like where we came from in San Diego, California. The ocean was similar to that of California (but warmer). There has been a lot of American-style investment here. Prices, as you'd expect, are higher as you get closer to the water. "

The Central Pacific, like Northwest Guanacaste, has been going through quite a building boom over the past few years, and a whole lot of resorts, condominiums, condotels, and gated communities are set to come onto the market there in the near future. The rate of development is such that it's spilled out from the beach areas up and down the highway that runs along the coast into the hills set back a few kilometers from the ocean.

Puntarenas

The Central Pacific's largest city, Puntarenas (meaning "sandy point"), sits on a long, narrow peninsula or spit in the Gulf of Nicoya, a short 62 miles from San José. The town itself is about three miles long but just a few blocks wide. It is also the capital of the province of the same name. Costa Ricans affectionately refer to Puntarenas as"*El Puerto*" or "the port." Due to its proximity, Puntarenas has been the main beach destination for Costa Ricans from the Central Valley for more than a century. *ticos* still flock here to spend a day or weekend. The seven-mile brown-sand, palm studded, Blue Flag beach runs along the narrow spit of land. The beach is cleaned and raked every day.

The Paseo de los Turistas is a seaside palm-shaded walkway with a series of souvenir kiosks, open-air bars and inexpensive restaurants that dot the waterfront and add to the city's atmosphere. This tourist promenade is also the place where dozens of huge cruise ships anchor yearly. It buzzes with activity day and night. Puntarenas also boasts year-round spectacular sunsets.

Puntarenas is also home to the country's only aquarium, and is one of the best places to savor fresh seafood, including *chuchecas* (ink-black clams). In fact, the people who live in Puntarenas are affectionately called *chuchequeros.* Some of the best *marisquerías* or seafood restaurants in the country are found all along the Paseo de los Turistas. Puntarenas is also the home of another local delight called the Churchill, a beverage similar to a snow cone over which layers of syrup and ice cream are poured.

I know a few Americans who call this port city their home. Bill, is a colorful local character who used to live in the San José area where he managed a huge penthouse right in the heart of the city. When he started to receive his monthly Social Security checks he moved to Puntarenas and seems to be very content there.

The Central Pacific Coast to the south of Puntarenas offers superb locations for living. This area has something for everyone: swimming and

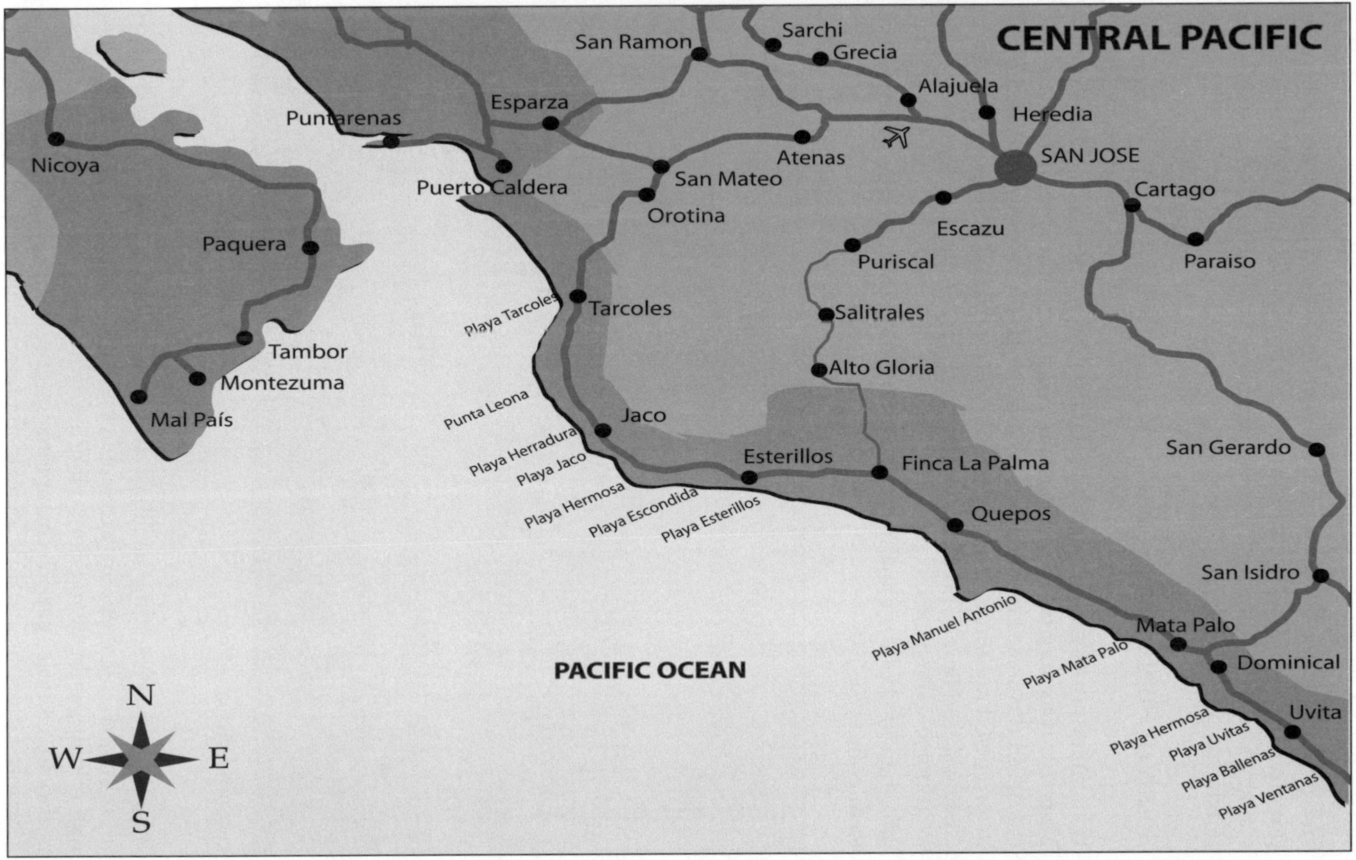
CENTRAL PACIFIC
San Ramon
Sarchi
Grecia
Alajuela
Heredia
Esparza
Puntarenas
Nicoya
Atenas
SAN JOSE
San Mateo
Puerto Caldera
Orotina
Cartago
Escazu
Paquera
Puriscal
Paraiso
Tarcoles
Playa Tarcoles
Salitrales
Tambor
Montezuma
Alto Gloria
Mal País
Punta Leona
Jaco
Playa Herradura
Playa Jaco
Esterillos
Finca La Palma
San Gerardo
Playa Hermosa
Playa Escondida
Playa Esterillos
Quepos
San Isidro
Playa Manuel Antonio
Mata Palo
Playa Mata Palo
Dominical
PACIFIC OCEAN
Uvita
Playa Hermosa
Playa Uvitas
Playa Ballenas
Playa Ventanas
N
W
E
S

surfing beaches, excellent sport fishing, developed and undeveloped beaches and natural parks. The area is a magnet for beach lovers because of its proximity to San José, especially now that the new Ciudad Colón-Orotina-Caldera Highway is finished. You can get from San José to the Central Pacific beaches in about an hour.

South of Puntarenas

Four miles north of Jacó, at Bahía Herradura, is the upscale **Los Sueños Marriott Ocean and Golf Resort**, considered the premier resort and marina in the area. Los Sueños is set on a 1,100-acre property surrounded by protected rainforest. The largest full-service marina between Mexico and Chile is found here. This 200-slip marina can accommodate vessels from 20 to 200 feet with all of the amenities international boaters expect. For more information about the marina, call 1-866-865-9759 toll-free or see **www.lsrm.com**.

Los Sueños Resort

In addition to boating facilities, the marina offers restaurants, bars, a supermarket, gift shop, marine supplies and concessions for jet skis, kayaks, water skiing, scuba diving, snorkeling and other recreational activities. There is also an 18-hole, par-72 championship golf course, a 201-room palatial Marriott Hotel, home sites, deluxe condominiums for sale and a number of nature walks. All of the condos and the hotel feature elegant Spanish colonial-style architecture. Condo prices start at about $500,000. Some affluent visitors have been known to visit Los Sueños and like it so much they never leave.

The improving infrastructure makes it idea for living with all of the amenities of home. **Plaza Herradura** is located on the main Pacific Ocean coastal highway (La Costanera) at the entrance to Playa Herradura and the Los Sueños Resort. This new shopping center has an AutoMercado supermarket that caters to the many North American residents of Los Sueños, providing American brand names and products. The Fischel pharmacy is the largest chain in Costa Rica, and carries typical medications and antibiotics. In addition to the fast food restaurants at Plaza Herradura, Pizza Hut, Subway and Spoon, the center also hosts four fine dining restaurants, Inka Grille, Long, Samurai Sushi and Asian Cuisine. The mall also has Radio Shack, furniture and appliance stores, resort wear, boating supplies, and other services.

Playa Jacó

If you like a lot of action, good waves and partying, I recommend **Jacó Beach.** Lately, it has become known as *Jacopulco* due to the many high-rise condominiums under construction and its similarity in appearance to Acapulco.

Jacó is conveniently located just 72 miles from San José. This Key-West-like town is a very popular weekend retreat with both *ticos* and foreigners since it is only one to two hours from San José. With a floating population of about 40,000, it is by far the most developed beach town in the Central Pacific region and has an excellent tourist infrastructure. An eclectic mixture of foreigners and locals gives Jacó a sort of cosmopolitan feeling.

Central Jacó changes constantly, with new shops, strip malls, condos and restaurants popping up almost monthly. A new shopping mall was completed in 2007 and the area has a couple of large supermarkets (AutoMercado in Herradura and Mas x Menos in downtown Jacó) that are stocked with both Costa Rican and high-end imported products.

There are pizza parlors, international restaurants, handicraft shops, bars, discos and late-night spots where you can party until the wee hours of the morning. Water sports, especially surfing and sport fishing, attract scores of people to the area. You can also explore the natural wonders of nearby forests on foot, horseback or a canopy ride through the treetops. The Jacó community's new **Plaza Coral Mall** features 60 stores, a food court and two formal restaurants and caters to both tourists and local residents.

Because of its fame, Jacó is usually packed on most summer weekends, holidays such as Easter Week and special occasions such as surf tournaments.

Lodging ranges from four-star hotels to small, inexpensive cabins for locals on a tight budget. Boredom will not be a factor here.

Like many beach spots popular with foreign men past their prime, Jacó is a happening place to find a prostitute. The infamous **Beatle Bar** is the hub of this activity.

Development in Jacó began earlier than in Tamarindo, though the latter has now more or less caught up. Real estate brokers estimate that the frenzy of condominium, resort, and condotel development will put about 2,000 new units on the market over the next few years. Of course, as with any real estate development, some of the proposed projects may never get built, especially considering the current woes of the global economy. It's something to look into before buying anything pre-sale in Jacó or anywhere in the country. Overall, however, the message is that Jacó and its surrounding areas will keep growing, though maybe not as quickly.

Many of the expatriate residents of the area are involved in the real estate business in some way, whether developing, selling, marketing, or building. A lot of the area's developers, however, don't live in the Jacó area. Other expatriates here work in the tourist industry, managing hotels and beachfront cabins or restaurants and clubs.

Down Jacó Beach is always bustling with activity

Of course, plenty of *ticos* are also involved in real estate and tourism, working as real estate lawyers, developers, construction workers, electricians, plumbers, waiters, and receptionists. The importance of tourism to the area means there is plenty of English spoken. *Tico* residents who work in the service industry mostly live in the small villages around Jacó such as Tarcoles, as well as along the main road just outside Jacó.

Playa Hermosa

Hermosa, about 10 minutes south of Jacó, has a completely different feel. Do not confuse this idyllic community with the beach with the same name in Guanacaste or the one near Uvita to the south. Hermosa ("beautiful"), as its name indicates, is protected as a national wil life refuge.

Unlike Jacó, Hermosa has remained a low-key village popular mainly with surfers because of good year-round waves Many international surfing tournaments are held here every year. However, there is plenty to keep non-surfers busy, especially at nearby bustling Jacó.

A number of expatriates live in the area, running hotels or just enjoying a quieter life. The village itself hasn't yet been caught up in the condo boom. Surfers apparently aren't too worried about where they sleep, as long as they have enough money for sex wax and beer. Expensive rooms there would probably be a difficult sell.

Nevertheless, more building is underway on the land behind the beach that rises steeply into areas of dense woodland. In that area, projects are appealing to buyers seeking ocean views rather than the Jacó party scene. The views from developments, especially like Hermosa Highlands, have to be seen to be believed.

Esterillos

Esterillos means small estuary in Spanish. It is easy to get confused here because the area is divided into Esterillos Oeste (West Esterillos) and Esterillos Este (East Esterillos). This area has long, uncrowded beaches with treacherous currents surrounded by African palm trees, estuaries and mangroves. Many *ticos* have vacation homes along here, and there is a smattering of hotels as well. Monterey del Mar and Xandari are two of the nicer hotels. The latter has a great open-air restaurant with a good panoramic view of the beach. We stop for lunch there on all of my Central Pacific retirement and relocation tours.

There has been a lot of building in this area. Cabo Caletas and Del Pacifico are two huge projects in the Esterillos vicinity. Both projects are supposed to eventually include golf courses.

Playa Bejuco is a nice beach with a few small developments nearby and strong ocean currents just south of Esterillos Este.

Parrita

The town of Parrita is located south of Esterillos or about half way between Jacó and Quepos. It is a center for the African palm oil ranch founded by the United Brands Fruit Company many years ago. In Parrita you can find almost any service you may need. Parrita boasts a long seven-mile beach. There are a few new housing developments being touted in the foothills a few miles in back of the town.

There is good news for the town of Parrita. A new two-lane bridge eliminates traffic congestion, which at peak hours, added an hour or more to driving time. It replaces the one lane bridge that saw its better days decades ago. The old bridge was lower and was sometimes submerged when the Parrita river flooded.

Palo Seco is a gray-sand beach on a small peninsula a few miles south of Parrita. There are a couple of new projects being built here . Tesroro promises to be a good project but is currently on hold because the local banks are not lending money due to the economic crisis in the U.S. **Los Pelícanos is** an ambitious development that will be built along the canals of the estuary. Many of the homes will come with a dock located on a canal.

Quepos and Manuel Antonio

The **Quepos** and adjoining **Manuel Antonio** area is one of the country's most popular tourist destinations, and offers some of the most beautiful beach resorts in the world. Few other places in Costa Rica offer so much in one spot. You will find endless activities to keep you busy in this quaint beach town. Some of the area's most prominent features are white sand, paradise - like beaches, beautiful hidden coves, abundant wildlife, good nightlife, fine cuisine, unforgettable sunsets from many vantage points and even a chance to mingle with the Hollywood crowd at a five-star hotel. This area offers other activities such as rafting on either the Naranjo or Savegre rivers, horseback riding, four-wheeling, hiking and canopy tours in the incredible mountains that serve as a backdrop to this part of Costa Rica.

Quepos and Manuel Antonio lie about an hour's drive south from Jacó and host a very different community altogether. Of the two, Quepos is the bigger town but still very much a working fishing town rather than a tourist destination. Its real estate market isn't as developed as that of Manuel Antonio, a 10-minute drive up the road.

Downtown Quepos is a beach community surrounded by forested hills facing the Pacific Ocean. It's not, however, the prettiest of Costa Rica's beach towns. Quepos has all the services one would expect to find in a large Costa Rican town, including bars, boutiques, eateries, a mini-bookstore, good nightlife banks, small supermarkets, tourist shops and a whole lot more to keep local foreigners entertained.

The infrastructure is good here with a public hospital, an airport for small planes and limited docking facilities. Construction of a new 200- slip $11 million ***Pez Vela*** Marina began in 2006. Expect to see the commercial real estate market heat up as the marina comes online in the near future and attracts more sport fishermen and other tourists to the town. Until then, Quepos is likely to remain a *tico* town bypassed by second-homeowners or permanent residents fro the more attracative Manuel Antonio up the road.

Known for its sport fishing scene, Quepos is the site of several yearly tournaments. Hotels, businesses and even an old airplane converted into a restaurant are scattered around the hills and line the highway between Quepos and Manuel Antonio. Many of the hotels are situated on large properties that extend into the forest.

Most foreigners live in and around the town of Quepos and along the road leading to **Manuel Antonio National Park**, just a few kilometers south and over the hill. The community living here is relatively young and run the numerous local tourist businesses. The coastal road connecting Quepos to the Manuel Antonio National Park is filled with boutique hotels, restaurants, bars, clubs and spas, all with their share of the ocean views that make the town so special (and expensive) for many.

The park is nestled on some 682-plus hectares of land. The park receives more visitors than any other park or reserve in the country. If you are a nature lover you can always explore the national park or go to one of its pristine white-sand beaches that slope down from tropical forests into the clear blue waters of the Pacific Ocean. The park teems with paradisiacal flora and fauna.

Despite its distance from an international airport and city-quality shopping and services, real estate prices in Manuel Antonio have risen to be some of the highest in the country. It comes as no surprise that the popularity of the park, the beauty of the beaches, and the quiet magnificence of the ocean views have all played a part in pushing vacation rental prices for family homes high. Renting a vacation home in Manuel Antonio can be a profitable business.

In the past, many real estate investors came to Manuel Antonio to build large individual houses and buy tracts of land for segregation. The condominium market, however, has yet to take off. There are a couple of mid-sized towers under construction, but for now the Manuel Antonio buyer is more interested in a single-family home for personal use and vacation rental.

The long-awaited *Costanera Sur* (Costal Highway)

By Christopher Howard

The idea of coastal highway linking Quepos in the Central Pacific with Dominical in the South Pacific was originally conceived during the government of José María "Don Pepe" Figueres Ferrer in the year 1970. Work was begun in 1976 under the government of Daniel Oduber Quirós, but the concession was cancelled when a Spanish company pulled out of the project. Thirty years of delays were basically due to a lack of funding and bureaucratic snags which kept the project in limbo until the Arias administration (2006-2010) made it a priority to finish this baldly needed north-south artery.

The transportation ministry (*Ministerio de Obras Públicas y Transportes* or MOPT) promised that by the end of the 2009 the entire 42 kilometers (26 miles) between Quepos and Dominical would be paved. Well his prediction was almost correct. As of April 2010 only about three kilometers just north of Dominical are unpaved and one bridge has to be completed.

The project is a boon to tourism and will open up the whole area south of Quepos. Trucks can now easily go north and south along the coast without traveling on the Pan-American Highway that passes through San José, and Cartago and thus avoid also crossing the dreaded *Cerro de la Muerte* or "Hill of Death" (appropriately named due to the sometimes treacherous driving conditions and cold temperatures) twice when going from one border to another.

The paving was done in two sections. Consorcio Meco-Santa Fe had the job between Savegre and Quepos. That stretch is about 19 kilometers (about 13 miles) and cost $16.4 million. The section from Savegre to Dominical is 22.6 kilometers (about 14 miles) and was the responsibility of Constructora Solís-Sánchez Carvajal. The contract was for $15.5 million. The Meco-Santa Fe contract had a deadline of eight months. The Solís-Sánchez Carvajal had a 10-month deadline, according to MOPT. In both sections the workers installed a 30-centimeter (12-inch) sub-base, a 20-centimeter (eight-inch) base and a 13-centimeter (5.1-inch) road surface.

The new highway has changed everything. It used to take at least two hours or more to travel from Dominical to Quepos. Now it can be done in under an hour. The highway is a as smooth as glass and a far cry from the old pothole filled-road.

Expect, to see the commercial real estate market heat up as a marina comes online in the near future and attracts sport fishermen and other tourists to the town. Until then, Quepos is likely to remain a *Tico* town bypassed by second-home owners or permanent residents for the more attractive Manuel Antonio up the road.

On the downside, the area between Quepos and Manuel Antonio National Park has been overbuilt and there is little land available near the coast. Consequently, more and more people are purchasing land in the spectacular foothills and mountains to the east.

One of the best opportunities I have seen in this area are lots offered in **Vistas de Manuel Antonio**, where a 5,000 square meter ocean-view lot costs around $150,000 with a log home on it. For additional information call toll-free **1-888-581-1786** or e-mail: **robert@costaricaretirementvacationproperties.com, http://www.costaricaretirementvacationproperties.com/index.php?op=view_property&PropertyID=1044**

Matapalo

Matapalo located about 15 miles south of Quepos and along the new coastal highway, between Quepos and Dominical, is a little town with a laid-back beach community and a virtually unspoiled beach. The long beach is perfect for walking, horseback riding or just soaking up the rays. A lot of beachfront property can still be had this area. There are also many beautiful homes and lots with ocean views in the foothills behind Matapalo. The town has a few hotels, restaurants and places to buy basic groceries.

I know quite a few foreigners who live here. My friend Robert Klenz has built a large equestrian development called the Hills of Portalón in the mountains high above this area.

All of the property between Quepos and Dominical will increase dramatically in value because the new 26-mile coastal highway or *Costanera Sur* (see sidebar). The main reason this area had escaped development for over forty years was its inaccessibility. The old road from Quepos to Dominical was described as "a road from hell." Driving along it used to be like sitting on a vibrating bed at full speed or riding a mechanical bull like in the movie "Urban Cowboy." Some locals theorized that the *políticos* (politicians) and rich businesspeople in Quepos deliberately used their influence to keep this stretch of the coastal highway from being paved because they feared they would lose a lot of business given the natural beauty of Dominical and the areas to the south. One thing is for sure the new highway will sure beat the old one from having to travel over the inland route or *Cerro de La Muerte* and through San Isidro to get to the Southern Zone.

The South Pacific

The area extending from Dominical to the Osa Peninsula all the way to the Panamanian border on the Pacific coast is called the South Pacific.The spectacular Corcovado National Park, Drake's Bay and Isla del Caño are a few of this area's salient features.

For years, the region has remained one of the country's best-kept secrets, and for good reason. A difficult four-hour drive from San José to Dominical through the country's highest mountains and sometimes dangerous highway and the horrendous road between Quepos and Dominical kept this area relatively isolated and undeveloped for decades. Hippies who moved there to live out their peaceful existence in the 1970s, their ranks swelled by a groups of surfers, are now being joined by expatriates seeking a less stressful life. The developers, of course, are right behind.

The area generating the most interest is the coastal zone from Dominical south to Ojochal, but development is spreading in every direction and is set to continue for the foreseeable future.

This part of Costa Rica possesses a striking beauty. In many places, the rain forest sweeps down the coastal hills right to the shore line. The area has some of the largest mangrove forests on the Pacific side of the Americas, and represents an ecological fantasy land. Corcovado National Park on the Osa Peninusula has been dubbed the most ecologically intense place on earth, containing, as it does, 6% of the world's biodiversity.

A new international airport intended to boost tourism in this region of Costa Rica will be constructed in the community of Sierpe at the entrance to the Osa Peninsula or in Palmar Sur, according to the *Coordinador General de Aeropuertos.* The government expects the airport, whatever its exact location, to invigorate the entire region. The government wants to promote economic, commercial and mostly tourism development. Once the airport is built, more people will come to this area, which is just like what happened when the Daniel Oduber Airport was built in Liberia, Guanacaste.

Another exciting development designed to improve the area's infrastructure is the construction of the new 28-mile stretch of the coastal highway between Quepos and Dominical which will be finished in 2010. It will have three and four lanes in some places and a bike path. Once this stretch is completed, more people will come to the area and property values will increase, so now is a good time to invest.

The new **San Buenas Golf Resort** in the San Buena Ventura Valley is sure to add to this area's appeal. The 18-hole championship golf course is dedicated to preserving the surrounding ecology and community. When completed it will provide amenities like, a sunset ocean-view restaurant, a

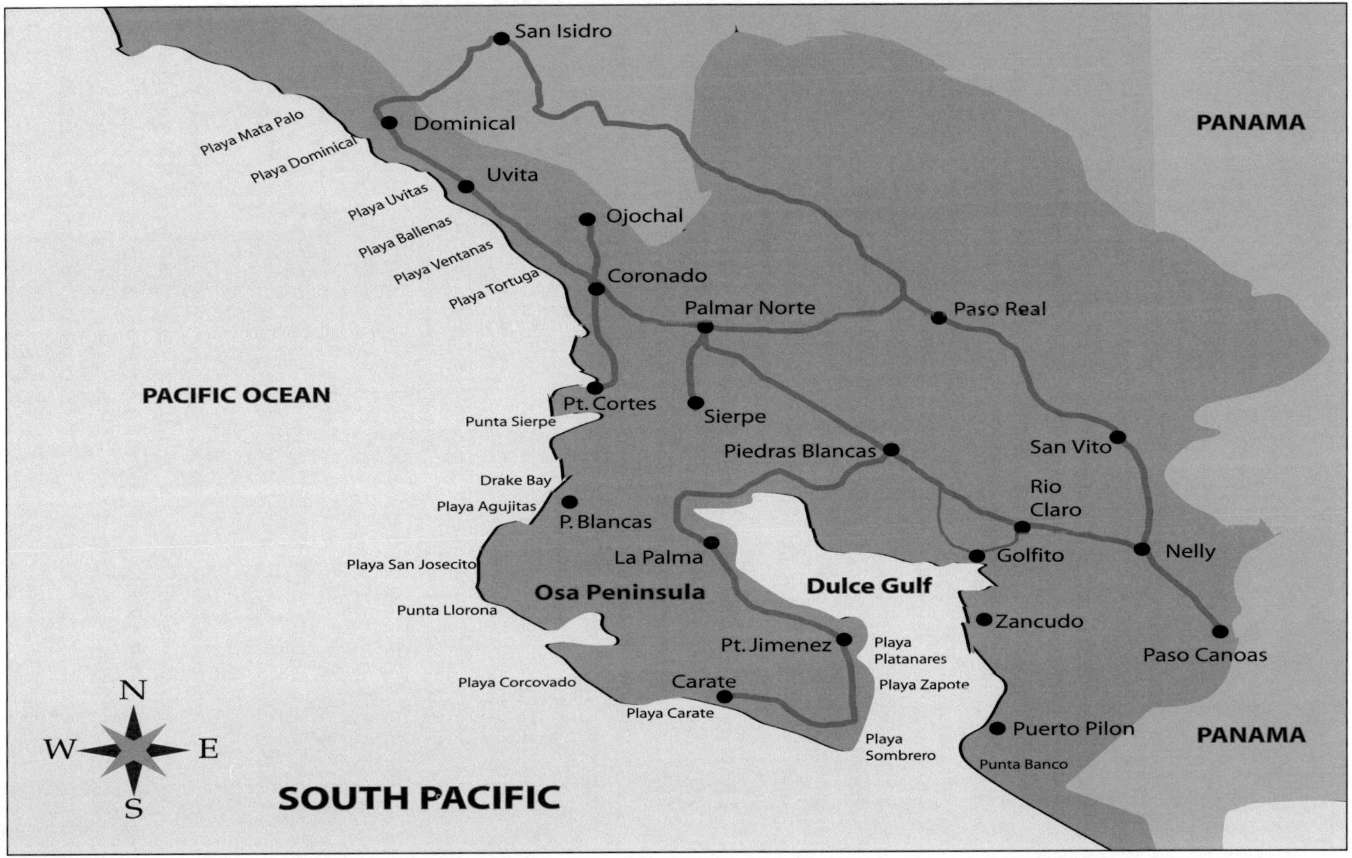
San Isidro
Dominical
PANAMA
Playa Mata Palo
Playa Dominical
Uvita
Playa Uvitas
Ojochal
Playa Ballenas
Playa Ventanas
Coronado
Playa Tortuga
Palmar Norte
Paso Real
PACIFIC OCEAN
Pt. Cortes
Punta Sierpe
Sierpe
Piedras Blancas
San Vito
Drake Bay
Rio
Claro
Playa Agujitas
P. Blancas
Nelly
La Palma
Golfito
Playa San Josecito
Osa Peninsula
Dulce Gulf
Punta Llorona
Zancudo
Pt. Jimenez
Playa
Platanares
Paso Canoas
Playa Corcovado
Carate
Playa Zapote
Playa Carate
N
W
E
S
Playa
Sombrero
Puerto Pilon
PANAMA
Punta Banco
SOUTH PACIFIC

COSTA RICA
A country that lives up to its name.

by Julie Campbell

"In my capacity as Fashion and Travel Editor of *Sports Illustrated* magazine, I've produced every one of the magazine's swimsuit issues from 1965 to 1996, thirty-two in all. My annual search for beautiful and unspoiled locations has led me to every continent except Antarctica, and I've walked literally hundreds of miles of beaches, mountain trails, deserts, and even glaciers in order to take our readers to some of the most exotic, and often overlooked, corners of our planet. Sometimes my choice was a resort so new that it could only be envisioned from an architect's blueprint; in other years I've settled on an island or a country or even an entire continent— Australia.

So what brought me to Dominical, Costa Rica? Looking at the map I was struck for the first time by how near a neighbor Central America was, and at the same time how little I knew about it. I had to know more, and when I discovered Costa Rica, the jewel of the Central American chain, and traveled its length and breadth, I knew I had found something very special—a country that truly lives up to its name.

Costa Rica means Coast of Abundance or richness of nature. Its rainforests comprise a virtual cornucopia of flowers, lush vegetation, birds and wildlife—all still unspoiled. Rising from the coastline at Dominical are the majestic green mountains with rushing clear streams leading to crystal waterfalls and swimable fresh-water pools.

Coming down from mountains that were often tucked behind mist and clouds I found myself in a beautiful and varied stretch of coast. One side of the country faces the Pacific and the other the Caribbean. For our shoot I chose the Pacific at a place called Dominical, where one beach is more lovely and dramatic than the next. The diversity was breathtaking. And on these immaculate beaches there is no one to step over you while sunning, and only the sound of tropical birds and rolling surf.

I came to Dominical to take gorgeous pictures of gorgeous models in a gorgeous setting, and indeed I was able to do that. But the real discovery was a small piece of God's Country that I'll want to revisit again and again—and on my own time!

***Courtesy of Sports Illustrated**

wellness spa, multi-tiered swimming pools, and a tennis facility. The ultimate goal is to create the premiere lifestyle-investment option in the area.

Dominical

Dominical, located 40 kilometers (30 miles) south of Quepos, is a tiny laid-back resort town surrounded by some of the most breathtaking coastal scenery Costa Rica has to offer. The town lies just off the main road where the Costanera highway coming south meets the road to San Isidro. The beautiful **Barú River** winds its way down from the surrounding mountains and empties into the sea at the north end of town.

Dominical is a charming town with friendly people who say hello and greet you with smiles. The place has a spring break vibe that's a little rough around the edges, with young surfers and backpackers riding the bus in to hang out and catch waves. It has an unpaved main street, which runs right through the center of town and down to the ocean. On either side of the street are a few restaurants and bars, such as the San Clemente Bar and Grill. You'll find limited entertainment, touristy souvenir shops, backpacker and surfer shack hostels,. It's a fun and lively place that's growing at a reasonable pace, and the many activities to choose from in the area leave little to be desired.

Some of the expatriates who have stayed have built lovely vacation homes in the forested hillsides behind this small village. More ambitious foreigners have started businesses or are buying land in the area. Plenty of people have rediscovered their inner hippie here, finding the place to be the perfect antidote to their hectic lives. Others simply want a quieter life for their families. Much like Montezuma, this town attracts those seeking an alternative lifestyle. It is not unusual to see people practicing the Oriental art of tai chi or yoga on the beach.

This area is reminiscent of California's Big Sur because of its spectacular coastline towering mountains that meet the sea, spectacular shoreline, mountain backdrop and unbelievable panoramic views. One of the area's claims to fame is that it was used as a backdrop to shoot the 1996 *Sports Illustrated* swimsuit issue.

There are unlimited options for adventure and sightseeing in this pristine area of Costa Rica. Several spectacular jungle waterfalls are found here. Pozo Azul is a 30-foot waterfall close to the village of Dominicalito. The Barú River Falls, also known as Santo Cristo or Nauyaca Falls, is located in the mountains above Dominical. This series of waterfalls is considered one of the most picturesque in Costa Rica, if not all of Central America. It cascades down into a huge natural pool that is 20 feet deep and perfect for swimming. The surrounding area is verdant rainforest with abundant wildlife. The mountains between Dominical and Ojochal are filled with dozens of smaller waterfalls.

The hills behind Dominical and south into Escaleras have an endless ocean view framed by thick rainforest that most people can only dream about. Large homes with incredible views that cost in the hundreds of thousands of dollars dot the steep hills above the beach. Some properties in this area have their own private waterfall. A few small developments are going up in the area.

In general land prices are lower than the Quepos-Manuel Antonio area and at one time were rising fast. Because of the economic meltdown in the States prices came down in 2009 as many people tried to unload their properties.

Playa **Dominicalito** (or little Dominical Beach) lies two kilometers south and has perfectly calm water for swimming. Spectacular views of the coastline may be seen from nearby rocky **Punta Dominical** which juts out into the ocean. The Parcela Restaurant is located on the outcropping of rock. There are several developments in the hills above Dominicalito.

Playa Uvita

Ten 10 miles south of Dominical is **Uvita.** A smaller and slower-paced town than Dominical with a good swimming beach. Uvita has a nice vibe and you will be quick to notice how friendly everyone is. The town's location between Dominical and Ojochal makes it ideal for development. In the last few years a number of businesses have sprouted up around Uvita because of the area's growing popularity. There are a couple of new supermarkets, furniture stores, watering holes, pharmacies, real estate offices, eateries, small hotels and banks. **La Fogata** is a rustic restaurant serving excellent pizza and chicken at very reasonable prices.

The setting with mountains in the background is very similar to Dominical. The countryside in the hills to the east affords some stunning ocean-view properties. It comes as no surprise that many foreigners now live in the hills above Punta Uvita, just as they do in Dominical. Prices are still affordable and there are plenty of mountainside homes and lots with spectacular views. A friend just purchased a beautiful mountaintop home overlooking the beach.

Some of the activities available in the Uvita area are kayaking, snorkeling, horseback riding, waterfall and jungle hikes, beachcombing and a lot more.

The **Ballena National Marine Park** is located here as is the so-called Whale's Tail sand spit, which protrudes in the shape of its namesake, providing great snorkeling and a lovely spot for a walk when the tide is out. To get a fantastic view of the Whale's Tail and surrounding area, venture up to the Hotel Ballenas and Delfines for a cocktail at sunset. It has to be one of the best views in the world.

Just north of Playa Uvita is **Playa Hermosa**. It is a long beach that is suited for swimming. My son and I go there all the time and really enjoy it. In case the tropical sun is too strong, there are trees near the beach where you can enjoy the shade. **Playa Pinuela**, to the south of Uvita is another good spot to swim and to enjoy the sun.

Tortuga/Ojochal/PlayaVentanas

The Tortuga/Ojochal/Cinco Ventanas area is also well-suited for living. **Ojochal**, about 20 miles south of Dominical, is a quaint country village with a nice mixture of *ticos*, French Canadians and other foreigners. It has grown into more of a community than Dominical and Uvita to the north, and an increasing number of people are buying residences in the area.

The village is set off the main highway and is easy to miss and quite spread out.. The town has a surprising number of excellent restaurants (reportedly over 30) owned by locals from all over the world. On my retirement tours we have dined at restaurants run by people from such faraway places as Belgium, Estonia, Holland, Indonesia, Italy and Israel. My tour clients say the food here is as good as you'll find in any first-class restaurant back home . **Exotica Restaurant**, virtually in the middle of the jungle, has some of the best cuisine I have ever tasted in all of my travels. The owners are French Canadian and really take pride in the gourmet food they prepare. **Citrus** is another great place to eat.

This area has a few shops, including a grocery store, liquor store, a few bars, hardware and a *pulpería*, but for the most part it is a residential area with a handful of tourist ventures. There are some good ocean views, though not as spectacular as those found in Uvita or around Dominical.

Although this area is somewhat off the beaten track, DirecTV and other forms of entertainment are available. The members of this community are tight-knit and share many activities. Annie Drake, a local tour expert and resident says, "There is something happening almost every night here. There is a potluck dinner, party or 'get-together' once or twice a week."

Area activities include good fishing, snorkeling, boat and river tours, bird-watching, horseback riding, kayaking and boat trips to Caño Island and nearby Drake Bay. You can even watch whales and see turtles lay their eggs on the beach.

Steep coastal mountains with tropical rainforest forests serve as a backdrop for this beautiful part of the country. The area's popularity is growing as word spreads about all the natural wonders it has to offer. The beach at **Playa Ventanas** got its name because of five spectacular 50-foot, tunnel-like blow

Village Life in Costa Rica

By Annie Drake Expert Tour Guide

About 10 years ago I moved to Costa Rica. Initially I found work as a tour guide in the San José area. Eventually my work took me to all corners of the country. On one of my tours I visited Dominical and the areas to the south. I was overwhelmed by the sheer beauty of the area. Unlike Guanacaste in the north this area stays green and tropical all year. It is set against a backdrop of towering mountains covered with a lush tropical rain forest reaches down to the sea. The surrounding area is teems with wildlife and has several spectacular waterfalls and abundant fauna.

Eventually I discovered the hamlet of Ojochal. Since the village is set off the highway you could drive by and never know it existed. At the turnoff to the town there is a small general store, real estate office and police station. As you drive along the bumpy dirt road about two kilometers the town starts to emerge. There is a small river on the left with homes and restaurants along both sides of the road. There is even an Internet café and a couple of small hotels.

I spent some time there and absolutely fell in love with the area. The town has a thriving community of Costa Ricans, French Canadians, Europeans and Americans. There are actually people from 19 countries living there. The town literally has an international flavor. Foreigners have opened a score of excellent restaurants. A gourmet would be in heaven. There is even a houseboat restaurant where you can dine at the mouth of a nearby river. The cook is from Belgium and the food is absolutely incredible. My friends and I go there to watch the sunset and to eat dinner.

Exotica Restuarant in Ojochal is another real treat. The place only seats about 25 people but it is so popular with the locals that without a reservation, you'll be turned away. I take all of my tour groups there and they leave saying it was one of the best meals they had ever tasted.

It didn't take me long to find a great house with a view and pool which I decided to buy. It also has another large building lot above it. As time goes by my love for Ojochal and the surrounding area has grown even bigger. I've been working as a tour guide and really know the area inside out. In fact, I now consider myself an expert. People come to me when they want private tours or want an orientation.

The best part of living in my village is the great people and sense of a tight-knit community. We share and do so much together from community projects to a myriad of group activities. One night we may gather at the local pizza parlor. Another time we get together at somebody's home for a game of Trivial Pursuit. On other occasions we may have a Latin Dance night. We even have a rodeo once a year. Not only do we share activities with the people in Ojochal but we get to get together with friends in the neighboring towns of Dominical and Uvita a few kilometers to the north.

We never get bored here. Outdoor activities abound. There is good swimming at nearby Pinuela and Ventanas beaches. The latter is in a secluded cove with rock formations which have five giant blow holes. At Tortuga Beach you can see turtles laying their eggs on the shore. The area is also good for whale-watching at certain times of the year. If the ocean isn't your cup of tea you can swim in one of the mountain streams and soak under a gushing waterfall. There is a lot more to do here. Hiking, fishing, kayaking, snorkeling, bird-watching, hiking and excellent surfing are just a few of the many activities from which to choose. You can even take a boat trip up the Sierpe and Terraba Rivers or to to Caño Island 17 kilometers off shore. The island has coral reefs and is good for snorkeling. The waters teem with all sorts of creatures like moray eel, tropical fish, dolphins, sperm, pilot and humpback whales.

The new highway from Dominical south links all of our communities and makes travel easy. Everyday the local infrastructure improves. New businesses like a hardware stores, small supermarkets, restaurants, a gas station and a small hotel have sprung up in the area.

For essentials we either travel forty-five minutes north through the beautiful mountains to the town of San Isidro or south to Palmar Norte or Puerto Cortez. Panama is only a couple of hours to the south and has excellent shopping.

Plans call for an international airport to be built somewhere to the south of us in the not too distant future. Also the last stretch of the coastal highway from Quepos to Dominical will be completed soon. All of these improvements should make our area more accessible, really spur development and boost property values.

holes in the rocks. At low tide, you can actually walk through the tunnels. The dark-sand beach and high rocky cliffs resemble something right out of the book *Robinson Crusoe*. This beach is truly a work of Mother Nature and has to be seen to be believed. **Playa Tortuga** and **Playa Ballena** are other spectacular beaches in the area.

A big draw to the southern zone is the **San Buenas Golf Resort** located south of the town of Ojochal. San Buenas is a private, gated eco-development encompassing a 332 acre tropical rainforest, rolling hills, and lush green flatlands. It will feature an 18-hole championship par 72 golf course, designed by golf course architect Dan Lavis, that challenges all skill levels. The resort will also have a driving range, tennis center, stunning condominiums with views and a whole lot more (Please see their full-page ad at the end of this book).

San Isidro de El General

Named for the saint of farmers, San Isidro de El General, about 120 kilometers (75 miles) south of San José and a half hour inland from Dominical along the Pan-American Highway, offers inexpensive housing and a warm climate due to the town's elevation of 2,300 feet. The area is a major producer of high-quality Costa Rican coffee, sugarcane and dairy products.

San Isidro is considered by many to be the fastest-growing city in Central America. As a municipal center, it houses all of the government offices of the province of Pérez Zeledón. **Monte General** is the city's new shopping mall. It has a Megasuper supermarket, Universal department store, three movie screens, nine restaurants in a food court, a Scotiabank branch, 60 stores and 220 parking spaces. The mall is the anchor for the large Monte General residential community adjacent to it.

The city is a full-service commercial center for the southern zone. It is the ideal place to live because of the low crime, mild climate, plentiful goods and services, hardware stores, supermarkets, banks, farmers markets, professional services schools and a public hospital. Regarding the latter, a friend of mine was in Playa Uvita and had to have an emergency appendectomy. He was rushed to the hospital in San Isidro where he had the operation and lived to tell about it.

The area does not have a good selection of restaurants. However, there is one good eatery where many *Gringos* hang out called Bazookas on the Pan-American Highway on the north side of town. The place is a "required stop" on my monthly retirement and relocation tours. The restaurant is owned by a Costa Rican couple who lived in the U.S. and who really know how to cater to the likes of foreigners. A lot of gringos also hang out at the Chirripó Restaurant across from the city's newly-refurbished central park.

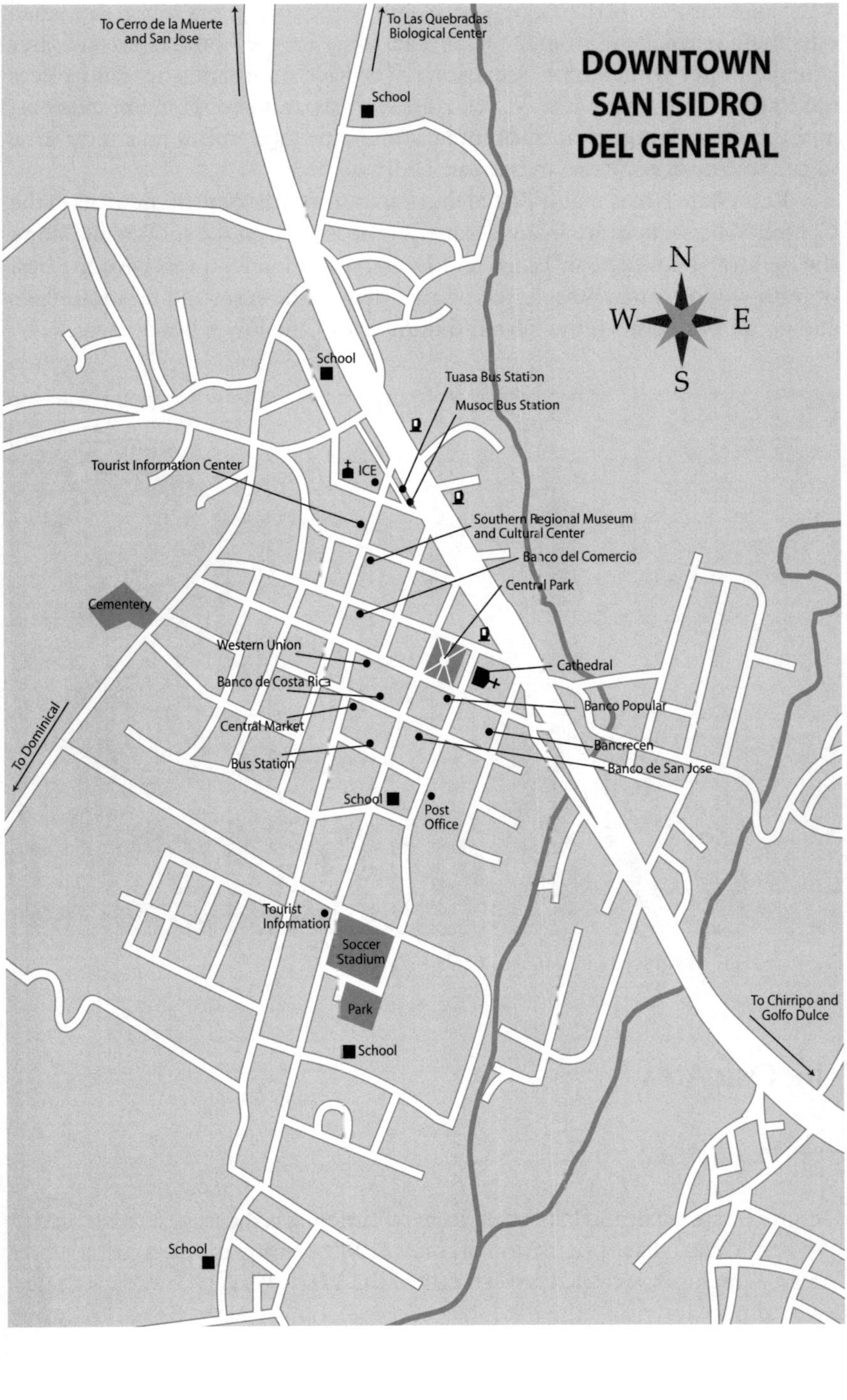
DOWNTOWN
SAN ISIDRO
DEL GENERAL
N
W
E
S
To Cerro de la Muerte and San Jose
To Las Quebradas Biological Center
School
Tuasa Bus Station
Musoc Bus Station
Tourist Information Center
ICE
Southern Regional Museum and Cultural Center
Banco del Comercio
Central Park
Cementery
Western Union
Banco de Costa Rica
Cathedral
Banco Popular
Central Market
Bancrecen
Bus Station
Banco de San Jose
To Dominical
Post Office
Tourist Information
Soccer Stadium
Park
To Chirripo and Golfo Dulce

San Isidro is off the beaten path, but some foreigners make this small city their permanent home. Of all the areas in the southern zone they actually prefer to live near San Isidro. The views are fantastic, land prices are lower, the municipality is well run, services and shopping are close by, and there is a better chance of integrating with local culture, as most *ticos* in the southern zone live in the San Isidro area.

Real estate is reasonably priced in comparison with some of the areas in the Central Valley. There are many ocean-view properties in the mountains along the highway between San Isidro and Dominical. Here you can have the best of both worlds: a magnificent panoramic view of the surrounding mountains and ocean but without the heat and humidity of the lower beach areas.

San Isidro is the largest city in southern Costa Rica

The Osa Area

Puerto Jiménez

Despite being small and laid-back, **Puerto Jiménez** is the largest town on the Osa Peninsula. It has a population of about 6,000. During the gold rush, 1980s Puerto Jiménez resembled a town out of the Wild West. Nowadays things have calmed down and the town has become popular with the backpacking set, surfers, lovers of adventure tourism and devotees of ecotourism. Its location on the Golfo Dulce makes Puerto Jiménz and its environs perfect for snorkeling, scuba diving and kayaking.

There are only a couple of ways to reach Puerto Jiménez: over a bad dirt road, by small plane or by boat.

There are a few expats living in and around Puerto Jiménez. However, it takes a special breed of foreigner who is willing to do without a lot of conveniences and services and who wants to "get away from it all." I had a couple on one of my retirement and relocation tours that ended up in Carate, an area even more remote than Puerto Jiménez.

By far the most famous park is the Corcovado National Park on the Osa Peninsula, the place that the *National Geographic* dubbed as one of two places in the world with the most biological diversity Here you will find everything from jaguars and peccaries, to many varieties of frogs, birds, and reptiles, as well as several kinds of monkeys.

The new Golfito Marina is expected to revitalize this area and cause a major land boom. The ICT (Costa Rican Tourism Institute) also considers the Puerto Jiménez area suitable for a future marina project. I have heard of a wealthy Costa Rican who bought a huge $30,000,000 million piece land in anticipation of things to come.

The Gulf Area

Golfito

Some expatriates live around the port of Golfito on **Golfo Dulce Bay**. The town is sort of drab and somewhat abandoned. However, the surrounding scenery is beautiful. There are several restaurants and *gringo* hangouts in town where you can strike up a conversation with local expats. Sport fishing and surfing attract many tourists to this area. As one local foreign resident points out, "The town has basic services like banks, a hospital, courthouse, a couple of supermarkets, butchers and doctor's offices. Transportation is decent with a small airfield and ferry transportation to Puerto Jiménez and Zancudo and plenty of taxis and buses. Panama is not far away and is a great place for good shopping."

Golfito, is synonymous with the United Fruit Company. In the late 1800s, the company established banana and pineapple plantations in the area to produce export products for its U.S. market. United Fruit was by far the largest employer, and the local economy came to rely almost entirely on this "father figure" to provide them with work, medical care, and public works infrastructure.

Despite starting out as a banana port the town was virtually abandoned when the United Fruit Company closed down its operation. Over the years, the government has made attempts to help the local economy. In 1990 it opened the *Depóstio Libre* or Free Trade Zone. Many *ticos* make the long journey to Golfito since appliances and other items may be purchased for much less than in San José. Foreign residents and tourists with a passport can also purchase an ample variety of goods at the duty-free warehouses.

Plans call for a world-class marina and condo complex that will improve infrastructure and change the face of this area. Local residents have a lot to be excited about. The Costa Rican Tourism Institute (ICT) and the Commission for Marinas approved the installation of two marinas in the southern Pacific port of Golfito. The **Banana Bay Marina** will have 16 slips and the **Bahía Escondida** or **Golfito Marina** will have 217 slips for boats up to 150 feet. This marina will have a hotel, stores, two restaurants, a health club, a yacht club, 84 condominiums with prices ranging from $300,000 to $800,000 and 280 residential units. The ICT approval was long-awaited and it will be a big boost for the economy of the struggling port town of Golfito.

The new marina planned for the town is expected to play a principle role in defining the fortunes of the area's real estate market. Because of this some people expect the Golfito area and the town **of Puerto Jiménez** to be the sites of the next land boom in Costa Rica.

Such a large infrastructure investment is extremely important for a region trying to leverage its tourist potential. Right now, tourists are more likely to be of the more adventurous kind, those coming to buy duty-free appliances, and surfers looking for waves in beaches like Pavones.

The marina will bring in higher-spending tourists, including sport fishermen, their families, and the yachting crowd. This is all speculation, however, as large infrastructure developments in Costa Rica tend to take a very long time to materialize, if they ever do. For now, Golfito remains a place of *tico* homes, colonial buildings, a few small hotels, and several large parcels of land outside town. Prices are lower than in the Dominical-Ojochal area, as getting here from San José takes at least five hours by bus or car.

Zancudo

Zancudo ("mosquito beach" in Spanish), a slow-paced beach community just south of Golfito, is home to some foreigners. Despite being nearby, you'll need to go to the Pan-American Highway and take about a two-hour drive over an unpaved road to get there. During the rainy season you will absolutely need a four-wheel-drive vehicle. Some foreigners come only for the winter months while others live in the area year-round. Several bars and open-air restaurants serve as gathering places for expats. Zancudo's uncrowded beach has gentle surf and is very good for swimming. Middle-priced housing may be found here.

Jim, my friend from Baltimore, makes this town his winter home. He has built a small house and even has DirecTV (called SkyTV here). When he leaves to go back to work in the United States, he has a caretaker oversee his home.

Playa Pavones

Pavones, 40 kilometers south of Golfito, is a surfer's mecca, renowned for having the longest left-breaking waves in the world. The surrounding scenery is downright spectacular. Surfers from all over the world are attracted to this area. Everything including the nightlife revolves around the surfing scene.

Numerous North Americans and foreigners own large *fincas* (ranches or farms) in this area while others live in the more isolated areas. My dentist, a sometimes surfer, has a vacation home in Pavones. Because of the excellent surf some say Pavones has the potential to become another Jacó.

Beware of the many land disputes in this area . You should do a complete title search on any property you are thinking of purchasing here.

The Caribbean Zone

The 150-mile Caribbean coast extends from the border with Nicaragua in the north to the border with Panama in the south.

The South Caribbean, as the area is known, is small, comprising a handful of beach towns and settlements that dot the approximately 18 kilometers between Cahuita and Manzanillo. It's about 250 kilometers and a breath-taking four-hour drive from San José, through the rain forest-draped mountains of Braulio Carrillo National Park, down onto coastal plains with their road-side *tico* restaurants, and on to one of Costa Rica's most important port cities, Limón.

Puerto Limón is one of Costa Rica's two important ports. It is the cradle of the country's Afro-Caribbean culture and its Creole language. Few Americans live in this city.

A further half-hour drive south along the palm-fringed coast takes you to the small but lively Afro-Caribbean towns of **Cahuita** and **Puerto Viejo**.

The South Caribbean is a lush part of the country, where jungle sweeps down the hillsides, sometimes right up to the beach. More often, plains about half a kilometer to 1km deep act as a buffer between the beach and the Talamanca foothills. The hills are also home to pasture land and farms with ocean views.

The Caribbean coastal area offers many places to live. It is particularly appealing to young people who like beautiful tropical settings, surfing, reggae music and the Afro-Caribbean culture. A large colony of foreigners from Europe and the United States live here.

Despite having some of the most gorgeous beaches in the country and a more interesting local culture than most other areas of Costa Rica, the area's awkward location and reputation for crime and drugs has kept it off the real estate map for the most part. In addition to the locals and the small but visible expatriate community, the towns are a haunt for backpackers and surfers, who come from all over the world to ride the waves at *Salsa Brava*.

Cahuita

Until a few years ago, the village of Cahuita, about 25 miles south of the city of Limón, was a more popular tourist town. Its reputation as a drug spot, however, provoked an exodus from the area. Since then, Puerto Viejo has taken over as the spot to stay on the Caribbean coast, though these days Cauhita has begun to make a comeback. Many Europeans own or operate hotels in and around Cahuita.

Cahuita lies next to Cahuita National Park which has one of the best beaches in the country. The park includes a strip of jungle that runs along the bay and covers the point just to the south. The park is home to sloths, white-faced capuchin monkeys, and all manner of birds and insects. The park also includes a marine park to protect the coral close to the shore and the more than 500 species of fish endemic to the reefs. Unfortunately, the reef has begun to die out in recent years and the snorkeling isn't as good as it used to be. However, the beach that is part of the park is connected to the town, very well cared for by the local park volunteers, and truly one of the most consistently nice, safe, and accessible places to swim in Costa Rica. The endangered leatherback turtle also breeds within the park, on the other side of the point from the most popular beach.

Puerto Viejo

Puerto Viejo, 12 miles south of Cahuita, is a funky town with a Jamaican-like ambience. It is a great place for lovers of the Caribbean lifestyle and ocean activities such as snorkeling and surfing. There are some lovely swimming beaches with good waves and crystal- clear water. A large number of Europeans and a few Americans live here.

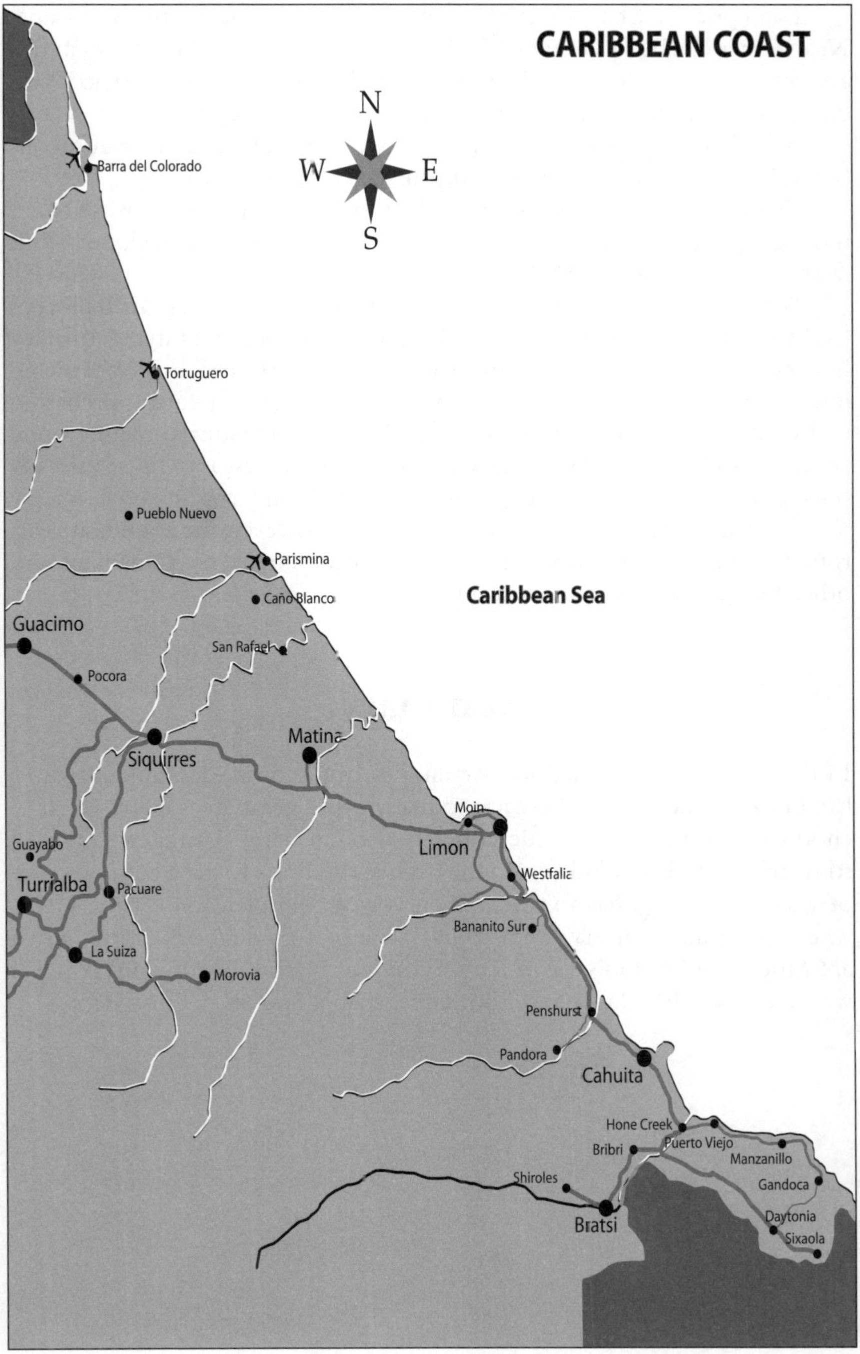
CARIBBEAN COAST
N
W
E
S
Barra del Colorado
Tortuguero
Pueblo Nuevo
Parismina
Caño Blanco
Caribbean Sea
Guacimo
San Rafael
Pocora
Matina
Siquirres
Moin
Limon
Guayabo
Westfalia
Turrialba
Pacuare
Bananito Sur
La Suiza
Morovia
Penshurst
Pandora
Cahuita
Hone Creek
Puerto Viejo
Bribri
Manzanillo
Shiroles
Gandoca
Bratsi
Daytonia
Sixaola

Land prices start at about $100 per square meter and are rising in value. Nice homes can be found for $150,000. There are no condo projects in this arearea. However, there are plans for a 400-slip marina in Puerto Viejo. Plans call for the marina to be built in a place called Playa Negra.

A few kilometers south of Puerto Viejo are **Punta Uvita**, with a gorgeous beach for swimming, and the fishing village of **Manzanillo**.

The surrounding landscape is lushly tropical, and wildlife such as howler monkeys and iguanas abound. This area is spectacular and undeveloped—but it won't be for long.

People are relocating to the South Caribbean and buying small plots of land to build their homes, cabins or businesses. Others are buying turnkey houses and more ready-built properties now, partly because of growing interest from baby boomers. However, the majority of people purchasing real estate in the area are couples, families and individuals, mainly quite young, searching for a less hectic lifestyle. Serious investors who are already buying up land in the area are doing so for the long term.

The Caribbean coast sounds very enticing; however, the abundant year-round rainfall and humidity make most North Americans, Canadians and other foreigners choose to live on the drier west coast.

Summary

In this chapter I have tried to give an idea of the more desirable places to live in Costa Rica. Since there are so many other great areas from which to choose—it is impossible to describe all of them here—I suggest you read some of the guide books listed in the back of this book to get a better picture of what Costa Rica has to offer. Then you should plan to visit the places where you think you may want to live. The best guidebooks of the bunch are Moon Publication's *Costa Rica Handbook* by the award-winning travel writer Christopher Baker and Eliot Greenspan's *Frommers Costa Rica.*

Christopher Howard's

World-Famous Relocation and Retirement Tours

Featured on:

The NBC Today Show
CNBC World News
Good Morning America

Seen in
Newsweek Magazine

One-of-a-Kind Tours for Those Who Might Want to Move to Costa Rica

"Tours that Change People's Lives"

One way to get an overview Costa Rica is to take one of the introductory tours operated by Christopher Howard's **Live in Costa Rica Tours**. The cost is no more than that of a regular guided tour. You could *not* possibly do a tour like this by yourself and gain the same knowledge, contacts and information about living or retiring in Costa Rica. **Nobody** else offers an in-depth tour like this.

Why not see the country on your own, you might wonder. Consider these disadvantages of *self*-guided retirement tours:

* When thinking of retirement in Costa Rica one of the first things that comes to mind is the best way to explore the country, learn about it and decide where to settle. A lot has been written in publications and web sites about this subject and some of the information is incorrect.
* Those who have a high level of Spanish fluency, who have traveled extensively abroad or visited Costa Rica on numerous occasions will probably have success touring the country on their own. However, those people are few and far between.
* On the other hand, almost one hundred percent of participants on these retirement and relocation tours have stated that they could never have explored the country on their own, made the contacts the tours provide, nor learn so much from Christopher Howard's own experience.
* At some point independent travelers will have to drive or take buses which can prove tiresome and time-wasters. There have also been cases where people traveling by bus have had their luggage stolen. Even if you choose to fly around the country, at some point you will take a taxi or bus since you won't have ground transportation, and that can add up to a lot of money.

On top of that most travelers speak little or no Spanish and may feel helpless when asking directions and trying to get around. Remember: Not all Costa Ricans speak English. Imagine having car troubles or some other emergency in the middle of nowhere and trying to communicate with people. One client on a private two-day consultation insisted on renting an automobile and driving as he and the guide toured the Central Valley. After the tour he remarked that he saw very little.

Wouldn't it be easier to take a guided retirement and relocation tour than to have to deal with all the situations above? One would think so.

The knowledge and contacts you get from an experienced retirement guide are invaluable. And best of all you can leave all of the headaches like finding lodging, transportation, viewing the inside of homes and looking for good restaurants to your guide. By the time you add up your valuable time and monetary and emotional costs of a self-guided tour, a guided retirement tour is a no-brainer.

NOTE: The retirement and relocation tours are lifestyle tours for people who are thinking of moving to Costa Rica. They are *not* real estate tours. At the request of former clients a few carefully selected properties are included to give you a sampling of what different living situations are like. If you have a high interest in property, the names and contact information of reliable and trustworthy real estate professionals will be provided as part of our service.

What you learn from a personalized retirement and relocation tour

When you finish one of these tours, you will have enough information to know whether Costa Rica is for you, and if so, which area you can see yourself living in. You will learn what it took Christopher Howard years to learn: the good, the bad and the ugly. Your guide tells like it is and pulls no punches.

Specifically, the tours cover the following:

* The best locations suited for your lifestyle and specific needs.
* You will see a sampling of Costa Rican homes in the path of progress with high resale vale and not in remote areas. All properties in the Central Valley are in neighborhoods with high-speed Internet access and near the best private hospitals in case of a serious medical emergency. You won't find any of these indispensable amenities in the outlying areas.
* A two-day highly informative seminar with experts in the fields of real estate, law, moving to Costa Rica, health care, banking, insurance and more.
* Expats who have moved here will relate their experiences to you.
* You will make valuable contacts to help ensure your success move here.
* How to access inexpensive health care.
* Investors will receive insider information and tips, and learn how to

make money and opportunities that are can be compared to Hawaii 60 years ago.

* What to expect when you first arrive.
* How the banking system will work to your advantage
* Time-proven shortcuts for learning Spanish by Christopher Howard, the author of the popular one-of-a-kind *Guide to Costa Rican Spanish.*
* Learn about the satisfying and exciting lifestyle you can have living in Costa Rica.

How are Christopher Howard's retirement and relocation tours different from other tours and relocation services?

1) Christopher's tours are the only retirement tours and relocation services to be legally approved and licensed by the Costa Rican government's tourism department (ICT). In order to obtain the approval of said entity of the government, all applicants have to have an unblemished criminal record, the nature of their particular business has to be investigated and studied and the tourism department's legal team has to approve the company. The whole process can take over a year in order to ensure that the applicant is reputable.
2) Christopher Howard has lived in Costa Rica for 30 years and in Latin America for over 40 years He he has written and published 15 previous editions of his perennial best=seller, "The New Golden Door to Retirement and Living in Costa Rica." Experience is everything and Christopher stands out above the crowd.
3) Christopher invented and pioneered the concept of retirement in Costa Rica and put the country on the map for baby boomers with his books and tours. Because of this success, his tours and books have been imitated but never equaled by anyone.
4) In addition to his 30 years in Costa Rica, Christopher has a Masters Degree in Spanish linguistics and therefore understands Costa Rica, the Latin culture and mindset better than any other foreigner in Costa Rica. He has written the only Spanish guide to help beginners learn Costa Rican slang. The book has already helped thousands master the basics of the local language. Knowing Spanish will save you time and money.
5) No other retirement tour guide has the the range of contacts that Christopher does. He has personally met with Costa Rica's Nobel Prize winning president, Oscar Arias, on several occasions. On Christopher's tours you will make the connections you need to be successful in Costa Rica. You meet lawyers, moving specialists, medical experts, the best

contacts in the field of real estate, and people who have actually move here successfully.

6) Christopher is the most read authority on living in Costa Rica and has appeared on the NBC Today Show, CNBC World News and other television and radio programs because of his extensive knowledge and experience living in Costa Rica. In addition, he is the only author of guides about living and retiring in Costa Rica who lives in the country full time. Thus, he stays up-to-date on everything that affects foreigners living in Costa Rica. This ensures that the information you receive on the tour is accurate and current.
7) No other tour or relocation service has been in business over six years. Some of the guides who lead other tours have only lived in the country a few years! How can you become an expert retirement guide or offer relocation services in such a short time? One tour is even led by a travel agent who is not even a relocation tour guide. Just moving to Costa Rica and spending a few years here does not qualify them to impart three decades worth of knowledge and experience.
8) Over the last two decades Christopher has personally helped thousands of people relocate to Costa Rica and live their dreams. Nobody else can make this claim. You could not be in better hands and could never learn what you do from Christopher on your own. Christopher takes great pride in helping his clients find happiness in Costa Rica.
9) Christopher has a successful investment portfolio and will share his methods of how to profit by investing in Costa Rica, if you so desire.

What others say about Christopher Howard's tours

"If you're fantasizing about living in Costa Rica, Christopher Howard is the go-to guy. His tour of the beaches is worth taking just for the food and scenery. Chris knows where to find the most delicious meals and gorgeous beaches, and is a fountain of information about what you'll encounter as an expatriate. His tours are a great way to learn if Costa Rica is for you. And they're fun!" - ***Sara Davidson, contributing editor of Oprah magazine, October 2005***

"Visit early and often. To help you choose a country for retirement, companies like www.liveincostarica.com offer pre-retirement tours. It's sort of like a vacation but you may end up staying forever." - ***Linda Stern, Newsweek, March 2005***

"This was the tour of a lifetime for us" - ***Dan and Lani Curtis, Camarillo, California"***

"I took your retirement tour in June of 2005. First, let me say it was

Some of Our Happy Tour Participants

one of the BEST INVESTMENTS I have ever made. I could not have seen the Central Valley on my own for twice the money and I had someone to explain all the wonders of Costa Rica to me. Anyone thinking of moving to Costa Rica should take the tour, have an open mind and a dream in their heart. - ***Don Autry Okemah, Oklahoma***

THE RETIREMENT AND RELOCATION TOURS

I, Christopher Howard, the author of this book and other books on Costa Rica, lead tours in Costa Rica for people who are interested in seeing first-hand what it would be like to live here. Continue reading this book about the tours I offer. If you are interested in having additional information, or if you would like to book a tour, contact Live in Costa Rica Tours toll free 877-884-2502 AFTERNOONS, 1-877-322-4690 or 800-365-2342 (24 hours) e-mail liveincostarica@cox.net or christopher@costaricabooks.com, or go to www.liveincostarica.com.

TOUR 1

Five-Day Central Valley (Inland) Tour

This is an excellent way to get to know the Central Valley where most of the population lives, meet expatriates who have made Costa Rica their home, and learn about how you can make the move. This is an excellent tour to get to know the country, especially the infrastructure.

Participants will be given a packet with maps, valuable contact information, special articles with insider information by Christopher Howard and a free copy of his perennial best-selling guidebook, *The New Golden Door to Retirement and Living in Costa Rica*.

Call Toll-free 800 365-2342 or 1-877-884-2502
for new discounted prices. Airfare is not included.
Reserve now and see why the baby-boomer generation is choosing Costa Rica as a favorite tropical place to live and retire!

Below is a sample itinerary from my one-of-a-kind five-day Central Valley Tour:

Wednesday - Day 1:

Arrival. You will be met at the airport and transported to the Hotel Torremolinos in San José.

Thursday - Day 2:

* Breakfast at the hotel
* Pre-seminar orientation by Christopher Howard
  First day of the Association of Residents of Costa Rica (ARCR) highly -informative all-day seminar featuring:
* 8:10 Welcome by the President of the ARCR
* 8:20 Real Estate - Buying, Selling and Renting by Mercedes Castro (First Realty)
* 9:00 Questions about real estate
* 9:20 Costa Rican Laws and Regulations by Lic. José Carter
* 10:05 Questions about Costa Rican laws
* 10:25 US Veterans Services
* 10:30 Coffee break
* 10:50 Moving and Customs by Charles Zeller (ABC Mudanzas)
* 11:35 Questions about moving and customs
* 11:55 Women's Club of Costa Rica
* 12:05 Lunch break (cost is included in tour)
* 1:00 Residency by ARCR Residence Advisors
* 1:35 Questions about residency
* 1:45 Banking and Investing in Costa Rica and by Ryan Piercy
* 2:30 Questions about services
* 2:45 Culture of Costa Rica, by Eric Liljenstolpe or Ryan Piercy
* 3:05 Questions about culture
* 3:15 Dentistry in Costa Rica, by Dr. Peter Aborn
* 3:35 Questions
* 3:55 The Move to Costa Rica, by Jerry Ledin (ARCR member)
* 4:15 Questions about moving to Costa Rica
* 4:25 Happy Hour

Friday - Day 3:

* Breakfast at the hotel
* Second day of the ARCR's highly informative, all-day seminar
* 8:10 Welcome by the President of the ARCR
* 8:20 CCSS Public Health System in Costa Rica by Ryan Piercy (ARCR)

* 8:50 Questions about the CCSS (Public Health System)
* 9:10 International Health Insurance, by Brad Cook of the Clínica Bíblica
* 9:30 Questions about insurance
* 9:40 Tico Times Newspaper
* 9:55 Coffee break
* 10:00 INS and Insurance in Costa Rica, by Latin American Coverage
* 10:40 Questions about insurance
* 10:50 Health Care Quality, by Ricardo Schaechter
* 11:10 Questions about health care
* 11:30 Learning Spanish, by Christopher Howard (Author of *Official Guide to Costa Rican Spanish* and Relocation and Retirement Tour Guide)
* 11:45 Questions about learning Spanish
* 11:50 US Tax, by Randy Linder
* 12:00 Lunch break (cost is included in tour)
* 1:00 Internet and Communication, by Kevin Huey
* 1:45 Questions about internet
* 2:10 About the ARCR and Charity Committee, by Earl Tomlinson (ARCR Board)
* 3:00 Questions about the ARCR
* 3:10 Living in Costa Rica, by Terry Renfer, (ARCR President)
* 3:45 Closing remarks for the two-day seminar
* **NOTE: All seminar speakers and schedules are subject to change at any time.**

Saturday - Day 4:

Tour of the city of San José including: Clínica Bíblica Hospital, markets, San Pedro Mall, University of Costa Rica, Hipermás superstore, neighborhoods where Americans live (Los Yoses, Barrio Escalante, Sabana Norte, Sabana Sur, Rohrmoser and Escazú), Hospital Cima and Multiplaza Mall. Tour continues around the Central Valley to see other choice areas where foreigners reside: Escazú, Santa Ana, San Antonio de Belén, Ciudad Cariari, Alajuela, Heredia and Moravia. Lunch at La Cocina de Doña Lela where they serve authentic Costa Rican cuisine. Free night.

Sunday - Day 5:

Breakfast at the hotel. Tour the best areas for living west of San José including the city of Atenas famous for having the "best climate in the world," according to National Geographic," the charming town of Grecia, known as the "cleanest city in Costa Rica," Alajuela, Costa Rica's second largest city with its thriving expatriate community and finally the area of Santa Bárbara and San Joaquín de Herecia. You will view the inside of several homes and developments after a mouth-watering lunch at one of Costa Rica's best restaurants. Final questions, answers and other concerns.

* 6:00 - Dinner at the home of a local resident and wrap up session of quetions and answers.

Monday - Day 6:

* Breakfast at hotel.
* Transportation to the airport.

TOUR 2

Eight -Day Central Pacific Beach Tour

This tour is for those who are certain they want to explore only the beach as their option. It includes the majority of your meals and all of your transportation while in Costa Rica. Hotel and continental breakfasts are included.

Participants will be given a packet with maps, valuable contact information, special articles with insider information by Christopher Howard and a free copy of his perennial best selling guidebook, *The New Golden Door to Retirement and Living in Costa Rica.*

Call Toll-free 800 365-2342 or 1-877-884-2502 for new discounted prices. Airfare is not included. Reserve now and see why the baby-boomer generation is choosing Costa Rica as a favorite tropical place to live and retire!

Saturday - Day 1:

* Arrive in San José.
* You will be met at the airport and transported to the Hotel. Torremolinos in San José

Sunday - Day 2:

* A buffet breakfast at the hotel. Then a 7:30 departure for Jacó Beach where you will stay at the beachfront Arenal Pacífico Lodge. On the way, you will receive a packet of materials and orientation about the tour. Prior to arriving

at the hotel we will stop at the Nativa Resort and then tour the five-star Marriott Los Sueños resort, marina and golf course. Lunch will be served at the Barco de Mariscos in downtown Jacó Beach. After lunch we will visit the new Del Pacífico Development in Esterillos Este and Faro Escondido. To end the day on a fantastic note, you will view one of the most beautiful sunsets in the world from a Greek-style amphitheater on a hilltop at the Hotel Villas Caletas. The view alone is enough to make you want to live in Costa Rica. Dinner will be at the Colonial Restaurant in Jacó.

Monday - Day 3:

* After breakfast we will depart at 7:30 for the Dominical -Tortuga beaches. On the way, we will pass through the towns of Parrita and Quepos. We will take a break in Quepos/Manuel Antonio before continuing to Dominical to meet our local contacts and have lunch. Because the mountains meet the sea in Dominical, it is called a "tropical Big Sur." Next, we will have lunch and then travel along the pristine coast with its beautiful seaside rock formations and tropical rain forest as a backdrop to the beautiful Ojochal/Tortuga area. On the way you will see the areas where whales can be observed during most of the year. This sight is spectacular. This part of Costa Rica just recently became accessible when the new coastal highway was finished. A world of possibilities now exists here to live or retire. During the rest of the day, we will explore the area and learn about the amenities, unique lifestyle and activities it has to offer: waterfalls, tropical rain forests, birdwatching, fishing, diving, horseback riding, hiking, boating, kayaking, surfing and much more.

Tuesday - Day 4:

* An early breakfast, then we will hook up with a local guide to see more of the area and its infrastructure and sample some of the properties. We will have lunch at a special restaurant. You will also have the chance to meet some of the Americans who have retired in this part of the country. In the afternoon there will be a visit to Cinco Ventanas, a beach with a rock formation featuring five tunnel-like blow holes. Finally, to end a great day we will have an unforgettable dinner at Exotica, the area's premier restaurant. Your taste buds will never recover!

Wednesday - Day 5:

* Breakfast at the hotel and a 7:30 departure for San José. We will travel along the Barú River through the beautiful coastal mountains to the city

of San Isidro, “the fastest growing city in Central America.” After a brief stop to rest, we will take the Pan-American Highway over the country’s most spectacular mountains on our way to San José, where you will stay at the Hotel Torremolinos again. Free afternoon and evening.

* **NOTE: From this point on the activities are the same as the Central Valley Tour**

Thursday - Day 6:

* Breakfast at the hotel. At 8:00 we’ll start the first day of a highly-informative relocation, living and retirement seminar sponsored by the Association of Residents of Costa Rica. See the Central Valley (Inland) Tour previously mentioned for a list of speakers and topics. Happy Hour is scheduled after the seminar. Free evening.

Friday - Day 7:

* Second day of the seminar with lunch included. You will hear more from Costa Rica’s experts, including your retirement tour guide, Christopher Howard. See the Inland Tour on a previous page for a list of speakers and topics. Surprise group dinner at a local restaurant or a resident’s home.

Saturday - Day 8:

* Transportation to the airport included.

TOUR 3

Combination Tour (Beach and Central Valley Tour):

This tour is our most popular. It allows you to see both the beach and the Inland Valley extensively, so you will know which one of the two areas you prefer. Participants will be given a packet with maps, valuable contact information, special articles with insider information by Christopher Howard and a free copy of his perennial best-selling guidebook, *The New Golden Door to Retirement and Living in Costa Rica*.

Call Toll-free 800 365-2342 or 1-877-884-2502 for new discounted prices. Airfare is not included. Reserve now and see why the baby-boomer generation is choosing Costa Rica as a favorite tropical place to live and retire!

Saturday - Day 1:

* You will be met at the airport and taken to the Hotel. Torremolinos

Sunday - Day 2:

* A buffet breakfast at the hotel. Then a 7:30 departure for Jacó Beach where you will stay at the beachfront Arenal Pacífico Lodge. On the way you will receive a packet of materials and orientation about the tour. Prior to arriving at the hotel we will stop at the Nativa Resort and then tour the five star Marriott Los Sueños resort, marina and golf course. Lunch will be served at the Barco de Mariscos in downtown Jacó Beach. After lunch we will visit the new Del Pacífico Development in Esterillos Este and Faro Escondido. To end the day on a fantastic note, you will view one of the most beautiful sunsets in the world from a Greek-style amphitheater on a hilltop at the Hotel Villas Caletas. The view alone is enough to make you want to live in Costa Rica. Dinner will be at the Colonial Restaurant in Jacó.

Monday - Day 3:

* After breakfast we will depart at 7:30 for the Dominical -Tortuga beaches. On the way, we will pass through the towns of Parrita and Quepos. We will take a break in Quepos/Manuel Antonio before continuing to Dominical to meet our local contacts and have lunch. Because the mountains meet the sea in Dominical, it is called a "tropical big sur." Next, we will have lunch and then travel along the pristine coast with its beautiful seaside rock formations and tropical rain forest as a backdrop to the beautiful Ojochal/Tortuga area. On the way, you will see the areas where whales can be observed during most of the year. This sight is spectacular. This part of Costa Rica just recently became accessible when the new coastal highway was finished. A world of possibilities now exists here to live or retire. During the rest of the day, we will explore the area and learn about the amenities, unique lifestyle and activities it has to offer: waterfalls, tropical rain forests, birdwatching, fishing, diving, horseback riding, hiking, boating, kayaking, surfing and much more.

Tuesday - Day 4:

* An early breakfast. Then we will hook up with a local guide to see more of the area and its infrastructure and sample some of the properties. We will have lunch at a special restaurant. You will also have the chance to

meet some of the Americans who have retired in this part of the country. In the afternoon there will be a visit to Cinco Ventanas a beach with a rock formation featuring five tunnel-like blow holes. Finally, to end a great day we will have an unforgettable dinner at Exotica the area's premier restaurant. Your taste buds will never recover!

Wednesday - Day 5:

* Breakfast at the hotel and a 7:30 departure for San José. We will travel along the Barú river through the beautiful costal mountains to the city of San Isidro, "the fastest growing city in Central America." After a brief stop to rest, we will take the Pan-American Highway over the country's most spectacular mountains on our way to San José, where you will stay at the Hotel Torremolinos again. Free afternoon and evening

* **NOTE: From this point on the activities are the same as the Central Valley Tour**

Thursday - Day 6:

* Breakfast at the hotel. At 8:00 the first day of a highly-informative relocation, living and retirement seminar sponsored by the Association of Residents of Costa Rica. See the Inland Tour on a previous page for a list of speakers and topics. Happy Hour is scheduled after the seminar. Free evening.

Friday - Day 7:

* Second day of the seminar with lunch included. You will hear more from Costa Rica's experts including your retirement tour guide, Christopher Howard. See the Inland Tour on a previous page for a list of speakers and topics. Surprise group dinner at a local restaurant or resident's home. Free evening.

Saturday - Day 8:

* Tour of the city of San José including: Clínica Bíblica Hospital, markets, San Perdo Mall, University of Costa Rica, Hipermás superstore, neighborhoods where Americans live (Los Yoses, Barrio Escalante, Sabana Norte, Sabana Sur, Rohrmoser and Escazú, Hospital Cima and Multiplaza Mall. Continue tour around the Central Valley to see other choice areas where foreigners reside: Escazú, Santa Ana, San Antonio de Belén, Ciudad

Cariari, Alajuela, Heredia and Moravia. Lunch at La Cocina de Doña Lela where they serve authentic Costa Rican cuisine. Free night.

Sunday - Day 9:

* Breakfast at the hotel. Tour the best areas for living west of San José, including the city of Atenas famous, for having the "best climate in the world," according to National Geographic," the charming town of Grecia, known as the "cleanest city in Costa Rica," Alajuela, Costa Rica's second largest city with its thriving expatriate community, and finally the area of Santa Bárbara and San Joaquín de Heredia. You will view the inside of several homes and developments after a mouth-watering lunch at one of Costa Rica's best restaurants. Final questions, answers and other concerns.

Monday - Day 10:

* Breakfast at hotel.
* Transportation to the airport.

Another Option

Tour 4

Private Tailor-made Tour/Consultation

This one-of-a-kind, time-tested, custom tour was created to meet the specific needs of individuals, couples or small groups. It is also designed for those who cannot come for regular fixed-date tours. This fact-filled tour was created over 13 years ago and nearly 1000 people who have taken it have successfully moved to Costa Rica. In 2007 this tour was mentioned on "Good Morning America."

Participants will be given a packet with maps, valuable contact information, special articles with insider information by Christopher Howard and a free copy of his perennial best-selling guidebook, *The New Golden Door to Retirement and Living in Costa Rica.*

Virtually everything is covered on this tour in an unbiased and informative way. You will come away with the knowledge you need to successfully relocate to Costa Rica. The country's most prominent lawyers, realtors, movers, builders, educators, insurance people, health care specialists and more will be on call to address your specific concerns if you need their services.

I look forward to helping you design your own custom tour. **Prices depend on the number of people, the number of days and your specific needs.**

Tour 5

Guanacaste Tour

Located in the North pacific region of Costa Rica, Guanacaste is famous for its string of beautiful beaches. This tour is given from time to time, depending on demand. You can arrive at Daniel Oduber International Airport, conveniently located in Guanacaste. Contact me if you are interested in exploring Guanacaste as a place to live.

Participants will be given a packet with maps, valuable contact information, special articles with insider information by Christopher Howard and a free copy of his perennial best selling guidebook, *The New Golden Door to Retirement and Living in Costa Rica.*

Call Toll-free 800 365-2342 or 1-877-884-2502 for new discounted prices. Airfare is not included. Reserve now and see why the baby-boomer generation is choosing Costa Rica as a favorite tropical place to live and retire! This tour is only given occasionally.

Saturday - Arrival

Sunday - Day 1

* Visit Coco, Ocotal Hermosa beaches. **Playa Hermosa** has some of the country's best diving. It lies in the center of a string of four major beaches, all within 30 minutes of each other: Hermosa, Playa del Coco, Playa Ocotal and Playa Panama. Playa del Coco is a colorful beach town with an active nightlife and a small international community.

Monday - Day 2

* In the morning finish Coco, Ocotal Hermosa beaches.
* In the afternoon, go to Flamingo. Flamingo is one of the finest resort areas in Costa Rica and has the country's second best full-service marina and a beautiful white-sand beach.

Tuesday Day -3

* **Visit** Tamarindo is a laid-back beach town overlooking a long stretch of beautiful beach. It is a popular spot among surfers. It has the most developed tourist infrastructure in Guanacaste.

Wednesday - Day 4

Return to San José

* **NOTE: From this point on the activities are the same as the Central Valley Tour**

Thursday - Day 5

* Breakfast at the hotel. At 8:00 we'll start the first day of a highly-informative Seminar sponsored by the Association of Residents of Costa Rica. See the Central Valley (Inland) Tour previously mentioned for a list of speakers and topics. Happy Hour is scheduled after the seminar. Free evening.

Friday - Day 6

* Second day of the seminar with lunch included. You will hear more from Costa Rica's experts, including your retirement tour guide, Christopher Howard. See the Five-Day Central Valley (Inland) Tour previously mentioned for a list of speakers and topics. Surprise group dinner at a local restaurant or a resident's home.

Saturday - Day 7

* Return home or stay for the Central Valley Tour.*
* This tour may also be combined with our Central Valley Tour by adding two days at the end.

Our Concierge Services

For more than 20 years I have helped people successfully move to Costa Rica. The monthly time-proven tours and seminars have been the first logical step to moving here. To complement the tours, my company now offers the very best concierge services to my clients.

Moving to a new country and dealing with a new culture and language can be difficult for the average person. We will provide you with all of the necessary contacts and information you will need to adjust successfully to a new culture. We strive to make this process as easy as possible. In no time you will feel at home in your new surroundings.

Our associates will show you how to do all daily tasks from A to Z. They will guide you every step of the way to significantly shorten the time it takes to get acclimated to your new country.

The organizations with which we work come highly recommended and have excellent track records. Please let us know your specific needs and we will connect you with the organizations that provide the services below. Our associates will charge you accordingly for their time.

* Airport pick up
* Assistance in dealing with various government departments in Costa Rica.
* Attorneys
* Banking procedures
* Buying furniture
* Cable TV
* Car, home and health insurance
* Computer repair
* Cosmetic surgery
* Courier service
* Culture shock awareness
* Daily errands
* Doctors, dentists and hospitals
* Expert legal advice from the best lawyers in Costa Rica
* Finding a mechanic
* Finding a maid
* Finding a rental in San José or at the beach
* Finding a school for your children
* Getting a phone
* Home finding
* Home repairs
* Home security system
* Household maintenance program
* How to use Costa Rica's taxis
* Immigration
* Importing your pets
* Insurance for automobile and homeowners
* Locating hard to find items
* Medical plans
* Moving of household items and assistance with shipping and customs
* Obtaining a Costa Rican P.O. box
* Obtaining a gun permit
* Offshore corporations to protect your assets
* Opening a bank account
* Paying utilities
* Pet transportation
* Photocopies
* Placing ads in local newspapers
* Private mail service

* Private taxi driver
* Psychiatric services
* Purchasing a car
* Real estate brokers
* Receiving your Social Security benefits in Costa Rica
* Residency
* Residency renewals
* Safe real estate investments
* Satellite TV
* Shopping
* Social activities
* Spanish schools
* Supermarkets
* Tax and accounting assistance
* Translations
* Understanding the bus system
* Vehicle and property title searches
* Veterinary service
* Work permits for foreign domestic staff.

To Contact us:
Locally 2261-8892
International toll-free 800-365-2342, 877-884-2502,
or 1-877-322-4690
E-mail: christopher@costaricabooks.com

3

Saving Money in Costa Rica

How Much Does it Cost to Live in Costa Rica?

An important factor that determines the cost of living for foreigners in Costa Rica is their lifestyle. If you are used to a wealthy lifestyle, you'll spend more than someone accustomed to living frugally. Either way, you will still find Costa Rica to be a bargain.

Despite having one of the highest standards of living in Latin America, purchasing power is greater in Costa Rica than in the United States or Canada.

San José's cost of living ranks close to last when compared to 144 cities worldwide. To see where Costa Rica ranks, see http://www.finfacts.com/costofliving3.htm. The cost of living in Guatemala City or Panama City is about 14 percent higher than in San José. Corporate Resource Consulting, a firm that compares costs of goods and services, rates San José among the least expensive cost-of -living cities in the world. It is second to Quito, Ecuador, in the Americas in terms of affordability. CNN reports that Mercer Human Resource Consulting also finds the country of Costa Rica an inexpensive place to live.

In most areas, housing costs less than in the United States and hired help is a steal. Utilities (telephone service, electricity, and water) are cheaper than in North America. You never need to heat your home or apartment since Costa Rica's climate is warm. You need not cook with gas, since most stoves are electric. These services cost about 30 per cent of what they do at home. Bills for heating in the winter and air conditioning in the summer can cost hundreds of dollars in the United States, neither of which is necessary in the Central Valley. Public transportation is also inexpensive. San José and surrounding suburbs occupy a small area. A bus ride across town to a neighboring city like Alajuela, usually costs $0.50 to $.90 depending on the distance. Bus fares to the provinces cost no more than $20 to the furthest part of the country (see Chapter 10). Taxi travel around San José is also inexpensive.

Water is relatively inexpensive in Costa Rica, and most monthly water bills amount to no more than $8 to $15. Low per-unit costs are not the only reason for cheap bills – many Costa Rican-style appliances are geared toward water conservation: Semi-automatic washing machines consume very little water, and low-flow, on-demand showers save additional water. Most dishes are washed by hand.

A gallon of regular gasoline costs about $4.20, making Costa Rica's gasoline prices among the lowest in the Americas (To figure the cost of gasoline per gallon in dollars take the actual price per liter in *colones*, divide it by the exchange rate in *colones* and then multiply by 3.8). You can find out the actual gas prices see: **http://www.recope.go.cr/info_clientes/precios_productos/.**

Only oil-exporting countries such as Mexico and Venezuela have cheaper gasoline. However, you do not really need a car because public transportation is inexpensive and accessible. If you must have a *new* car, remember that they are very expensive here due to high import duties. In Costa Rica people tend to keep their cars for a long time and take good care of them. We recommend buying used cars since they are usually in good mechanical condition and their resale value is excellent. Food, continuing education, entertainment (movies cost about $3 to $4) and, above all, health care, are surprisingly affordable. Both new and second-hand furniture is priced very low.

When you have lived in Costa Rica a while, finally get settled, learned the ins-and- outs and made some friends and contacts, you can cut your living costs more by sharing a house or apartment, house-sitting in exchange for free rent, working full-or part-time (if you can find legal work legally), starting a small business or bartering within the expatriate community. Doing without packaged and canned imported brand-name foods and buying local products, eating in small cafés or *sodas* instead of expensive restaurants and buying fresh foods in bulk at one of the weekend farmers markets (*ferías*) or

Is affordable even for people on a low budget?

Retirees range from the person squeaking by on $700 a month in U.S. Social Security to someone who can write a check for a $450,000 oceanside condo.

But those short on funds usually want to know how low can you go. Because Costa Rica is a socialist country, great attention is paid to the costs of public services. In simple terms, they are a steal. And they will continue to be. Want a cell phone? The Instituto Costarricense de Electricidad will charge you a base rate of 3,375 colons or about $8.10 a month. A land line will cost 3,220 colons or $5.88 a month.

Basic Internet hookup can be had for 8,350 colons a month or $28.25. But then there also is the charge for using the telephone to connect to a server. The alternative, a cable hookup, can cost about $18 for basic service which usually is sufficient for one household. And there is an obligatory purchase of cable television. The price also depends on which company has the service contract for the specific geographical area.

Shopping at the weekend farmer's market or ferias where vegetables and otherv agricultural products are sold far below supermarket prices.

Even in the supermarket, some products are price controlled. Milk is 1,430 colons a gallon or $2.61.

Seats in the Teatro Nacional for a major orchestra performance can be just 8,000 colones or about $14.60. The cheap seats are 3,000 colons ($5.50) and all tickets are subject to a 10 percent discount for senior citizens. Movies are only $4.00.

The ciudadano de oro card is accepted universally and can mean deep discounts. To get one, an expat has to have a *pensionado, rentista, inversionist* or *residencia cédula.*

Bus fares are a steal to begin with. The fare from San José to Tamarindo on the far Pacific coast is 3,055 *colones* or $6.23. That's nearly an all-day ride. And in the city few routes are more than 250 *colones* (about 45 cents).

Taxis also are a deal, although recent increases have Costa Ricans unhappy. The first kilometer of a taxi ride is 420 *colones* or about 77 cents. Additional kilometers in the city are still 380 *colones* (69 cents). Those are definitely not New York City prices.

There are the apartments. Even after paying the informal tax levied on those who do not speak Spanish well, a decent two-bedroom, secure unit can be had for $450 a month. An A.M. Costa Rica reporter just vacated a one-bedroom with loft where the rent was $275 a month. And this was no slum.

Electrical and water bills are designed for the low-end user. The *Compañía Nacional de Fuerza y Luz* rates favor low use. The current rate is 43 colons (8 cents) for each kilowatt for the first 200 kilowatts of use. Each of the next 100 kilowatts is 66 colons (12 cents). Larger consumers pay more per unit.

The government water company just got a 25 percent overall raise but the actual rates have not been set yet. Company officials promise to favor low users.

Then there is free. Like nearly all the country's beaches from high water to 50 meters inland. And the parks. And frequent entertainment.

Again, prices and use of utilities depend a lot on where the expat lives. Air conditioning can add a lot of an electric bill. So can alcohol or cigarettes. Remember, socialist countries like to control your bad habits.

Beer is about 800 colons a can, about $1.45. Local beer is cheaper by the two-liter bottle, but still it is no bargain. On the other hand, a glass of decent Chilean or Italian wine in a four-star hotel restaurant will cost between 3,100 and 3,500 colons (from $5.66 to $6.39). Better to buy by the bottle (4,000 to 6,000 colons or $7.30 to $10.95) except for infrequent sprees.

Bars that cater to expats will reflect that in their beer prices where 1,200 colon beer means nearly $2.20 a bottle.

The big ticket items here are automobiles because the government levies a gigantic tax. So an expat can figure paying twice for what a vehicle costs in the States. But the insurance is very reasonable, again based on coverage and type of vehicle. But $100 a year is possible.

Those who simply have to have imported U.S. goods will pay handsomely. They shop at Pricesmart or Automercado.

A lot has been said about the Costa Rican health system. And one must accept the fact that most U.S. medical benefits do not extend outside the States. An exception is the health plan for retired military and some federal employees. Patients in the government system probably do not have their own assigned physician. And the waits are legendary.

However, older patients of the *ciudadano de oro* category usually get to go to the head of the line. Expats find they can obtain very reasonable health insurance from the only provider, the Instituto Nacional de Seguros. Some group plans reduce the cost even more.

Costa Rican employees are covered because the *Caja Costarricense de Seguro Social* takes 10 percent of their gross pay as a salary deduction. Employees add to the total.

***Courtesy of AM Costa Rica**

the Central Market like Costa Ricans do can also reduce your living costs. You can also help yourself by learning Spanish so you can bargain and get lower prices when shopping.

If you take lessons from the locals and live a modest *tico* lifestyle, you can save a lot of money and still enjoy yourself. By not following a U.S.- "shop-till-you-drop" mentality, you can live reasonably. Taking all of the aforementioned and personal lifestyle into consideration, the minimum needed for a decent standard of living for a single person ranges from $1,200 to $1,500 monthly. A person can indeed live for as little as $35 a day, excluding housing. Some single people scrape by on considerably less and others spend hundreds of dollars more, again depending on what one is accustomed to. A couple can live on $2,000 per month, and live better on $2,500 to $3,000. Couples with husband and wife both receiving good pensions can live even better. Remember, two in Costa Rica can often live as cheaply as one. Any way you look at it, you will enjoy a higher standard of living in Costa Rica and get more for your money.

Considering that the minimum monthly wage is $287 and the average Costa Rican earns only $250 to $350 a month, you should be able to live well. The upper one-fifth of per capita income in Costa Rica involves families that make $387 to $577 per month.

Here is one expat's view of the cost of living here: "If you go completely native, you can even live on $600 a month, counting $75 a month to rent a room with no bath but kitchen privileges where there is no hot water to disinfect the communal dishes. But would you like it? NO!

"Most Costa Ricans eat small amounts of meat, rice and beans, and mostly fruits. Their dress is clean and neat if not stylish. They do not, at this salary, have cars. Their homes are not plumbed for hot water, nor do they seem to miss it. Their children are not given textbooks in public schools. They ride the bus, they seem happy, their clothes are often homemade, they own miniature washers and hang their clothes out to dry. They often share housing, with several earning family members occupying the same house, making for crowded conditions. The older generations leave a piece of their backyard to the newer generations. When they can scrape together the money, they build a house for the new bride and groom.

"On the other hand, wealthy Costa Ricans, live on, what seems to be, by observing their restaurant eating habits, their clothing and large 4 x 4's, in excess of $4000 per month. They buy CD's, eat at restaurants where the tab is often more than $20 per plate, send their kids to expensive private schools costing up to $700 per month, have places in the country and live in $300,000 homes."

One American retiree stated, "Most Americans I know in Costa Rica are frugal, live on a fixed income, drive older cars, and are just getting by.

Many have had to get temporary jobs or start their own small businesses. They live on $1,500 a month. You need to realize that this may exclude many perks that we as Americans are accustomed to having: good quality clothes, travel, electronic toys, eating in steak houses rather than beans-and-rice places, using imported condiments and other nice imported foods that double your food bill."

Another foreigner said, "The long and the short of it is, it can be hugely cheaper to live in Costa Rica. Like others have said, the average *tico* family lives on $4,800 a year. They're not wallowing in abject poverty, either. They haveplenty to eat, attractive clothing and a clean appearance. They also have a TV, they own their own home and they might have a computer. Nothing is stopping us from also living on $4,800 a year.

"The question is how you want to live. It is no different in Costa Rica than in the United States. There are families who live quite comfortably on $30,000 or $40,000 a year, and families that wouldn't feel comfortable spending less than $80,000 (or $100,000 or $150,000, etc.). Some things are more expensive in Costa Rica (goods), some are less (services). You can live very well here for less money than would buy you "good living" in the United States, but it may not be the same kind of 'good living' you'd enjoy in the States. Costa Rica is a different country; adjustments are always required.

"If you are prepared to shed some of the luxuries you enjoyed back home (i.e., big kitchens, nice bed linens, long luxurious baths, fast food [if you consider that a luxury], high-quality spices, etc.), then you can live very inexpensively. But you will live like a *tico*, and *ticos* live in a third-world country. Prepare for the differences, embrace your new life and enjoy every minute of the *pura vida*, and you can live the good life *a la tica* (Costa Rican style) for less money than you evercould in the United States."

Jim, a fellow expat remarked, "Costa Rica is a place where one can live whatever lifestyle one desires and can afford to live. I am a 72-year-old *pensionado* who has been living in Costa Rica for more than three years now. I am retired on Social Security and live on less, yes, I said less, than $700 per month. I do not feel that my lifestyle is much better or worse than it was in California. In the United States I lived on more than $25,000 a year. Now I own a small plot of land on which I have built a small (750 square feet) Swiss chalet-style log cabin and have a view that many of my California friends would literally die for."

Here is what another expatriate wrote to an on-line forum: "I am discovering that it is actually much easier than I would have dreamed to live in Costa Rica on Social Security benefits alone, even though mine are quite meager. I am astonished when I realize that I am living a comfortable middle-class life on less than $1,000 a month. That includes traveling around the country and paying to stay in hotels when friends come to visit occasionally.

How to Get By on a Shoestring in Costa Rica: The Story of Banana Bread Steve

By Christopher Howard

The purpose of this article is to show one person's resourcefulness and courage in the face of adversity. The author is not advocating moving to Costa Rica with little or no money.

About three years ago I met Steve who had lived in Hawaii for many years. He moved here because Hawaii had become very expensive and he wanted to make his early retirement "nest egg" go farther. Steve had always been used to living frugally and in the process amassed a few hundred thousand dollars.

Within a few months of moving here Steve invested his life savings in two high interest -yielding investments with the idea of doubling his money in a few years. This was his game plan but unfortunately both of his investments went "belly up." Steve was left with only a few thousand dollars to his name. As we mentioned Steve had mastered the art of living on very little money but had never been faced with having no resources and living in a foreign country. He knew that he would not be able to draw his pension for four more years. Steve thought of returning to the States to work and then moving back to Costa Rica when he got back on his feet. However, he became involved with a nice Costa Rican woman and had also fallen in love with the country.

His close friends provided him with a place to live for free, but he still had to find a way to generate income. Since he was born with the ability to repair almost anything, he did odd jobs in exchange for small sums of money and food.

After a while he figured that the only way he could continue to live in Costa Rica was to start a business. Steve had one big problem; no money with which to start a business. His pride kept him from asking for a loan from friends. He started to look at small local business and do research on the Internet. It did not take him long to come up with a good idea for a small business. He came across a good recipe for banana bread and his business was born.

At present he sells the bread to tourists and his many friends in the city of Heredia where he lives. He has purchased a mixing machine, an oven and his lady friend is helping him.

Steve is a born survivor. All of his friends are sure he will continue to do well and continue to enjoy living in the country he has adopted as his home.

I am actually saving money while living on Social Security and haven't had to touch my savings. I did come with the intention of simplifying my life, which I have done. I do not own a car. I enjoy taking public transportation. I do not buy every electronic gadget and gizmo that comes down the pike. And you know, I am not missing anything. I feel richer than ever."

Another American stated something similar: "I've been living here now for one year (exactly), and I have spent more than $1,000 per month in only one month so far. I didn't expect to live so cheaply. I do not deprive myself of much of anything. For amusement, I travel about the country quite a bit, staying in fairly nice hotels. I eat well. I rent a two-bedroom, *gringo*-style apartment and have all modern conveniences. I also have a serious book- and CD-buying habit that I support.

"The big money-saver for me is not owning an auto. Instead, whenever I want or need, I rent a car or truck and its driver, — for the hour or for the day. I also use public transportation — buses, of course, and taxis, — a lot! I go where I want, when I want but I don't worry about auto repairs, buying gas or insurance, or getting a vehicle inspected every year. I promise that at the end of the month, my transportation costs are way lower than the transportation costs of all my auto-addicted friends. Of course, your mileage may vary, particularly if you cannot imagine living without a car in order to drive to the corner *pulpería*.

"Besides, I've lost 20 pounds in the past year, which I attribute to walking. Remember walking? What a concept! The only problem is trying to walk in places where you can avoid the autos!

"I was bragging to some friends about living on less than $1,000 per month. Two of those friends accused me of being a 'spendthrift.' Both have lived here for more than 10 years, and neither spends more than about $600 per month."

When you take into account all these factors and others, such as good year-round weather, the friendly Costa Rican people, the lack of political strife and a more peaceful way of life—no price is too high to pay to live in a unique, tropical paradise like Costa Rica.

Before closing this section, I want to emphasize that you should not be alarmed by high real estate prices you may hear about or see advertised in English-language publications such as the *The Tico Times.* This recent rise in land prices is a result of the current land boom and increasing popularity of Costa Rica. Inflated real estate prices do not reflect the real cost of living in Costa Rica, which is still relatively low when compared to North America and Europe . Even more important, the Costa Rican government must keep the cost of basic goods, transportation and services affordable for the Costa Rican people in order to avoid the social problems found in most other Latin American countries.

Approximate Cost of Living and Prices as of June 2010 in Dollars*

Rentals - Monthly	
House (small, unfurnished)	$400
House (large, luxurious)	$1000–1500
Apartment (small, 1–2 bedrooms, unfurnished	$300+
Apartment (large, luxurious)	$700+
Property Taxes	$100 a year on a small home

Home Prices	
House (small *tico*)	$70,000+
House (large)	$175,000+
House (luxury/gated)	$300,000+

Miscellaneous	Monthly
Electric Bill (apt.)	$15–25
Electric Bill (home)	$50+
Water-Sewage (apt.)	$8
Telephone (850 impulses)	$13
Telephone (cell) 200 minutes	$24
Cable TV	$30
Satellite TV (full package)	$60
Internet (ADSL 1024/512 kb/sec) (per month)	$40
Taxi	¢510 first kilometer, and ¢510 thereafter per kilometer
Bus Fares (around city)	$.45
Gasoline (regular gas)	$3.94 per gallon
Gasoline (super)	$4.11 per gallon
Gasoline (diesel)	$3.50 per gallon
Maid/Gardener	$2.00 per hour, $200 per month full-time
Restaurant Meal (inexpensive)	$5.00+
Soda (a diner or coffee shop) Meal	$2.00
Restaurant (mid-range)	$10.00
Airmail Letter	around $.33 to the U.S.
Doctor's Visit	$25–35
National Health Insurance	$450.00 yearly for permanent residents
New Automobile	$15,000–$50,000
Light Bulbs, soft white 60W (4ct)	$1.90
Freezer Bags, Ziploc gallon (30bags	$2.02 (15ct)
Laundry Detergent, liquid (100 fl.oz)	$5.25

Man's Haircut with shampoo (styling salon)	$10-$15
Man's haircut at local barbershop	$5.00

Foods

Banana	$.05
Watermelon	$.85
Soft drink	$.50
Beer	$.70
Pineapple	$1.25
Apple	$.50
Papaya	$1.00
Grapes (per lb)	$2.70
Orange	$.08
Papaya	$.70
Orange Juice (46oz)	$1.06
Avocado (large)	$.50
Lettuce	$.50
Carrots (per lb)	$.24
Eggplant (per lb)	$.75
Red Bell Pepper	$.20
Potato (per lb)	$.60
Broccoli	$1.85
Cereal (large box of corn flakes)	$3.50
Bread (loaf)	$1.00
Tuna (small can)	$.75
Oatmeal (imported)	$2.86
Rice (1lb.)	$.45
Lasagna, (8oz box)	$.90
Refried Beans, Del Monte canned (16oz)	$1.26
Chicken Soup, Campbell's(10.5oz)	$1.27
Kraft Mac & Cheese, (7.25oz box)	$.75
Eggs, Grade A large (per dozen)	$1.75
Syrup, Aunt Jemima Imported (24oz)	$3.46
Steak (per lb)	$4.60
Beef, ground chuck (per lb)	$2.60
Chicken breast, boneless (per lb)	$2.99
Milk, whole (1/2 gallon)	$1.03
Beer	$.85
Sugar, white (5lb)	$1.45
White Flour (5lb)	$1.54
Splenda, packets 100ct.	$4.02
Salt, (26oz)	$.41

Coca Cola (20 fl.oz)	$.78
Popcorn, microwave (each)	$.43
Doritos (13oz)	$3.52
Oreos (15oz)	$1.87

Sundries	
Secret Deodorant (2.6oz)	$ 2.95
Razors, Mach3 Turbo refills	$11.69
Toothpaste, Aqua fresh (6.4 oz)	$1.76
Sunscreen (8fl.oz)	$7.07

* These prices are subject to fluctuations and where items are purchased.

How to live for as little as $1500 per month in Costa Rica Living in Costa Rica

At the request of one of the clients on my monthly Retirement and Relocation Tours, I wrote an article about how a couple can live well on $3000 to $4000 per month. In it I broke down the costs using a typical budget and proved it was possible. But what about the single person with a limited budget?

A single person can live cheaply in Costa Rica. I know a couple of single men and women in the Heredia area who have mastered the art of living on less than $1500 monthly. They don't live in luxury nor do they live like paupers. Typically, they do not own an automobile but rely exclusively on public transportation which is very affordable. They don't own a home and rent small apartments. They do part of their shopping at the local weekend farmers' markets where they can stock up on a lot of fruits and vegetables like many Costa Ricans do. Some buy their clothes at second-hand stores. When they eat out they tend to eat breakfast and lunch at one of the small cafes or *sodas* in Heredia's Central Market. They go to bargain matinees and seek other inexpensive forms of entertainment. For health care they belong to the Caja, the public health care system which costs them $50 dollars or less for complete health coverage. They use Internet cafés at less than a dollar an hour instead of owning a computer.

Most of these people are very happy with their simple lifestyle which they could never have in the States for the same price. When you take into consideration that most Costa Ricans earn far less than $1000 monthly and get by easily you can see that with $1500 monthly you will be able to live well. In the States or Canada a person would be below the poverty line with that income. I have actually met retired foreigners who live on less than $1000 per month and seem to live well.

On my monthly retirement tours I give people additional advice and methods on how they can live affordably in Costa Rica. After almost 30 years of living here, I know how live well and save money.

Here is an example of a budget for a single person who has no more than $1500.

Rent	$200 to $300
Electricity and water	$20
Cable TV	$25
Monthly Transportation	$50
Monthly public health insurance (medicines included)	$50
Food	$200
Entertainment	$100 -$150
Misc.	$200

How to live like a king or queen on $3000 or $4000

When you read the title of this article you will probably think that it is impossible to live so cheaply and so well. This is especially true if you reside in an expensive area of the U.S. like California. You could probably scrape by on a few thousand dollars a month up north but you certainly wouldn't be living in luxury.

Let's see why the title of this article is true. A couple who owns a $150,000 home (three bedrooms and three baths) free and clear and has a car will probably have the following monthly expenses in Costa Rica.

Private medical insurance	$200
Dental care	$50 per month
A part time maid	$100 to $150
Part time gardener	$30
Beauty parlor	$75
Food including inexpensive fruits and vegetables from a Farmer's market and many imported American products	$500 per month
Entertainment (movies, socializing)	$200- $300
Dining out a couple of times a week	$300
Private gym	$50 - $100 per couple
Country Club (after you pay initial fees)	$100 to $200 per month
Car insurance for a relatively new car	$100

Item	Cost
Utilities (water and electricity)	$100
Telephone (using Vonage or Skype for long distance)	$75-$100
High speed Internet	$50
Cable or satellite TV	$50
Car repairs	$50
Garbage	$40 per year
Property taxes on your $150,000 home	$20 per month
Misc. expenses	$300
Other possible expenses	
Travel to U.S. or other countries	$3000-$5000 or more per year

Really your lifestyle determines what you will spend here. You can choose to spend a lot more money if you are a high roller or yuppie type or substantially less if you wish to live modestly. I know single people who live for less than $1000 per month and others who have expensive tastes who spend what they would in the States. Nevertheless, you can live very well on the budget above. I should know because I have lived here almost 30 years and buy and do everything I want for under $4,000 monthly.

Money

The ***colón***, named for Christopher Columbus, is Costa Rica's official currency. One of the most stable currencies in Latin America, the *colón* used to be devaluated regularly, but a change in the Central Bank stopped that practice. Fortunately, the fluctuations are relatively small when compared to the mega-devaluations and runaway inflation rampant in other Latin American countries. Since your main source of income will probably be in dollars, you should not worry too much about fluctuations unless you have large amounts of money in *colones,* which is not advisable for long-term investments. Fluctuations can be good because they increase your purchasing power until prices catch up, however towards the end of 2009 the dollar dropped against the *colón.*

Coins come in denominations of 5, 10, 25, 50,100 and 500 *colones.* Bills come in 1000 (called *rojos* in slang), 2,000, 5000 (called *tucanes* in slang) and 10,000 (called *pumas* in slang) *colón* denominations. The Central Bank of Costa Rica (BCCR) will issue new bills in 2010. They will be different sizes according to their denominations and both 20,000 and 50,000 *colón* bills — about $35 and $88 respectively—will be introduced.

Also the older, silver-colored 5, 10 and 20 *colón* coins were removed from circulation.

The rate of exchange, which is set by the Central Bank, was around 550 *colones* to the dollar as of April 2010. You may view exchange rates at **http://**

indicadoreseconomicos.bccr.fi.cr/indicadoreseconomicos/Cuadros/frmVerCatCuadro.aspx?Idioma=1&CodCuadro=400. You can also see the current exchange rate or convert currency at **http://www.xe.com/.**

You can exchange money at most banks between 9 a.m. and 4 p.m., Monday through Friday. Some banks are now open even later, and some are open Saturday mornings as well. Remember to bring only U.S. currency, since other monies are difficult and expensive to exchange. When you exchange money at a bank, do so early in the morning because lines can be long later in the day and you may have to wait for what seems like an eternity. You should always carry your passport, a certified copy of your passport or *pensionado* or resident I.D. when exchanging money or for other banking transactions.

Banks, businesses and most money changers do not accept damaged or torn foreign currency. There is really no need to worry about changing money since a large number of businesses in Costa Rica will accept U.S. dollars. However, some may be reluctant to accept $50 or $100 bills.

Money can also be changed on the street, where you get the same rate of exchange as in the banks. I advise against this because many slick change artists distribute counterfeit bills or attempt to shortchange you.

Banking

Before selecting a bank it is necessary to decide what services you will need.

There are branches of Costa Rica's state-owned banks in San José and in other large cities and towns. The headquarters of Costa Rica's largest banks: **Banco Nacional**, **Banco de Costa Rica** and **Banco Crédito Agrícola** are in downtown San José near the Central Post Office. The government guarantees all monies deposited in these state banks.

Here is a list of banks:

BAC San José (private) .... Tel: 2295-9595
Banco Promérica (private)
E-mail: solucion@promerica.fi.cr .... Tel: 2296-4848
Banco Bantec (private) .... Tel: 2242-2222
Banco Cathay (private) .... Tel: 2290-2233
Banco Central de Costa Rica .... Tel: 2243-3333
E-mail: webmaster@bccr.fi.cr.
Banco Crédito Agrícola de Cartago .... Tel: 2550-0202
Banco de Costa Rica .... Tel: 2287-9088
E-mail: bancobcr@bancobcr.com

Costa Rican Coins and Bills

1,000 Costa Rican *colon* bill

2,000 Costa Rican *colon* bill

5,000 Costa Rican *colon* bill

10,000 Costa Rican *colon* bill

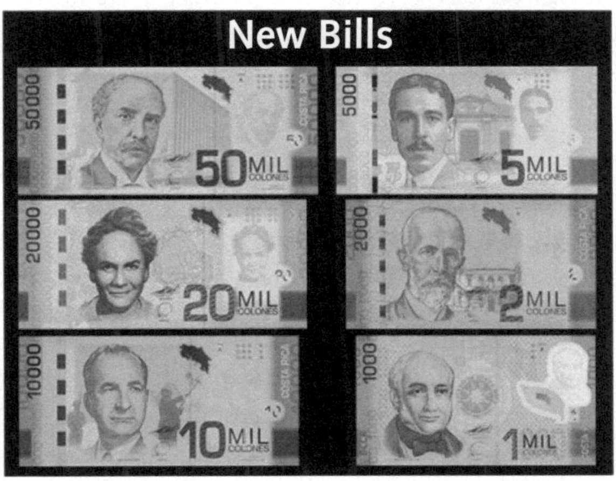

¢5 (silver) ¢5 (gold) ¢10 (silver) ¢10 (gold) ¢25 (gold) ¢50 (gold) ¢100 (gold) ¢500 (gold)

Banco Nacional	Tel: 2212-2000
Banco Popular	Tel: 2257-5797
Citibank (private)	Tel: 2201-0800
Mutual de Alajuela (private)	Tel: 2437-0865
Scotiabank (private)	Tel: 2287-8700
E-mail: scotiacr@scotiabank.com	

When making deposits in national banks, you should consider the following. Checks from outside Costa Rica, including bank cashiers checks, sometimes require 15 or more working days minimum before funds are usable after they are deposited. Checks issued by private Costa Rican banks will usually take a couple of working days before the funds will be available. Checks deposited from the same bank and branch are usually available the same day. Wire transfers are usually available in 2 to 4 days.

There are also numerous private banks affiliated with international banks. Private banks can offer many of the same services that the state banks do. When the minimum deposit is not maintained, service charges for account operations at private banks can sometimes be higher than at the national banks.

Many private banks pay higher interest than state banks but cannot guarantee your deposits as the government banks do. Remember, the higher the interest, the more the risk. In the mid-1980s private finance companies were offering up to 45 percent interest in *colones*. As recently as 2002, several other companies were paying as much as three percent monthly. Needless to say they all failed and the investors lost everything (Please see Chapter 4 for the whole story).

Some of the better private banks are **BAC**, **HSBC** and **Citibank**, . Check the yellow pages for more private banks. It is advisable to open an account at one of these banks or state banks so you can have a dollar account to protect against unexpected currencyfluctuations, cash personal checks, obtain a safety deposit box for your valuables and facilitate having money sent to you from abroad.

Regarding the latter, you should make sure that the bank you choose works with a U.S. correspondent bank to avoid untimely delays in cashing checks.

Warning: Be careful of **Scotiabank**. I have heard many foreign residents complain about unfair treatment at this bank. They complain about having to open their safety boxes for random inspections (which is illegal without a court order) and general lack of privacy at this overly intrusive bank.

Costa Rican Banks offer a full range of services.

Here is what one resident said about Scotiabank, "I was with Scotiabank for over a year. They were awful. And I mean bad. Their statements were impossible to read. But worse is they didn't know how to read them and often took two months to research the problems. The worst was telling me they would have a decision for a home loan in two weeks and then taking three months. In the end they said the property was worth $4 per square meter when all other sales in the neighborhood were $25 to $35. I moved to Promerica and they have been tons better. Not to say they are perfect. But compared to Scotiabank, they are amazing."

Another local who works in the real estate business said about Scotiabank: "Atrocious service, and they outright mislead. I have seen them pull the rug out of a sale at the last minute, when sellers and buyers both had their house packed up to go. No good reason. I have heard this tale from others, too. Overall, I regard them as the worst because they seem so up-to-date and modern with the fancy air conditioning and slick offices. I avoid them like the plague and have no clue why they behave this way."

Here is another bad experience a local resident had at Scotiabank. "I have a good excuse to report an experience at Scotiabank from several years ago (downtown branch). I withdrew some money, which the teller gave me after opening an unusual number of drawers (not all at his window) and roaming about a lot. Within 10 minutes of leaving the bank, I discovered I had been given a $100 counterfeit bill. I returned and they wouldn't do anything about it saying, of course, "You left the bank." Whenever I had occasion to be in the bank, I would look at him in passing and he would duck his head and look away. I think he was just waiting for someone to pass it to. I avoid Scotiabank every opportunity I get."

The author has a safety deposit box at Banco Nacional that is readily accessible during working hours. We also have a dollar account, certificates of deposit and an ATM card. My only complaint is that service in state run banks tends to be very slow. You can spend up to an hour in the bank waiting to make a simple transaction.

ATMs are found all over the country in banks, supermarkets and other convenient locations. These 24-hour automated tellers disperse a few hundred dollars at a time from your account, cash advance in *colones* only. When using one of these machines, be sure to exercise the following precautions:

1. Look for an ATM that is not isolated or unknown.
2. Use ATMs located in well-lit areas with good visibility.
3. Use an ATM that allows you entry and a door to lock rather than one on an open sidewalk.
4. Cancel the transaction at the first sign of suspicious activity.
5. Take all paperwork with you and do not throw away anything that has your account number printed on it.
6. Do not carry your ATM card with you unless you are going to use it.
7. Don't go alone.
8. Concerning residency receipts — ATM receipts will NOT work as proof of exchange.

Other banking services are high-yield certificates of deposit in *colones*, certificates of deposit in dollars on par with U.S. interest rates and credit card related services.

All banks have different requirements for opening accounts or obtaining credit cards, possibly entailing banking or personal references, identification and most certainly minimum deposits. Requirements will vary slightly from bank to bank, so check with the banking institution of your choice.

Permanent and non-residents may open a savings account in state and private banks. All that is needed is a minimum deposit, in some cases a letter of reference and a passport or *cédula*. To open a local checking account, you have to be a resident and may be asked to provide a Costa Rican ID card or passport as a form of identification.

You may be asked to show your water, telephone and electric bills in your name to prove you live here. If you cannot provide these documents you will need two references from banks in the United States or from two account holders in the same bank where you wish to open your account. If opening a checking account in local currency you will need an initial deposit of about $500. A local dollar checking account may require an initial deposit of $2,000.

Here is an example of what some banks require for various services:

HSBC

Personal Accounts

Initial Deposit and Minimum Balance

Checking Account:	$ Account	¢ Account
Transactional	none*	none*
Classical	$1,000	¢100,000
Savings Account:	none*	none*

*Must maintain a minimum balance to write checks

Requirements:

1. Must have resided at least 6 months in Costa Rica.
2. Passport or Resident Visa or Costa Rican ID (*cédula*).
3. Letter of recommendation by a Costa Rican or a letter from the applicant's respective embassy.

HSBC Personal Accounts have 2 Checking Accounts:
Transactional - fee $1 or ¢250 (respective of the currency of the check) per check written.

Classical - up to 25 checks per month free. The penalty for not maintaining the minimum balance in this account is $10 for the USD account or ¢2,000 for the *colón* account.

Corporate Account:

Initial Deposit and Minimum Balance
Initial Deposit: (No Minimum Balance)* .... $1,500 / ¢250,000
*To write 50 checks

Requirements:

1. Passport or Resident Visa or Costa Rican ID (*cédula*).
2. *Carta de Constitución de la empressa.*
3. *Personeria Juridica* (no more than three months since issued).
4. *Cédula Jurídica.*

Checkbooks: Book of 25 checks................................$3 (or ¢1,000)
Limit on checks written per month: none
Debit Cards: free
Online Banking
Issues Credit Cards

CitiBank

Personal Accounts

Initial Deposit and Minimum Balance

	$ Account	¢ Account
Checking Account:	$300	¢100,000
Savings Account:	$100	¢5,000

Requirements:

1. Passport or Resident Visa or Costa Rican ID (*cédula*).

Corporate Account:

Initial Deposit and Minimum Balance

Initial Deposit: (No Minimum Balance) .... $500/¢150,000

Requirements:

1. Passport or Resident Visa or Costa Rican ID (*cédula*).
2. *Carta de Constitución de la empressa.*
3. *Personeria Juridica* ((no more than three months since issued)
4. *Cédula Juridica.*

Checkbooks: Book of 25 checks .... ¢8,000
Limit on checks written per month: .... none/Per Year
Debit Cards: .... free
Savings Account: .... ¢1,200
No Web-based Online Banking Customers may purchase
PC software to view their accounts online for $30
Issues Credit Cards

BAC

Personal Accounts:

Initial Deposit and Minimum Balance

Checking Account	$ Account	¢ Account
Initial Deposit:	$250	¢50,000
Minimum Balance	$250	¢50,000

Savings Account

Initial Deposit:	$250	¢50,000
Minimum Balance:	$100	¢25,000

Requirements:

1. Passport or Resident Visa or Costa Rican ID (*cédula*).
2. Reference from another bank.

Corporate Account:

Initial Deposit and Minimum Balance

Initial Deposit & Minimum Balance:.......................... $250/¢50,000

Requirements:

1. Passport or Resident Visa or Costa Rican ID (*cédula*).
2. *Carta de Constitución de la empressa.*
3. *Personeria Juridica* (no más de tres meses de emitida.
4. *Cédula Juridica.*
5. Reference from 2 other banks.

Checkbooks: .... Book of 24 checks
Personal Account:... ¢1,250
Corporate Account: .... ¢750
Limit on checks written per month: .... Arranged with bank
Debit Cards:.. free
Online Banking
Issues Credit Cards

BANCO NACIONAL

Personal Accounts:

Initial Deposit and Minimum Balance

Checking Account	$ Account	¢ Account
Initial Deposit:	$2,000	¢300,000
Minimum Balance	$2,000	¢300,000

Savings Account

Initial Deposit:	$30	¢3,000
Minimum Balance:	$30	¢3,000

Requirements:

1. Passport or Resident Visa or Costa Rican ID (*cédula*).
2. Original telephone or utilities bill with the applicant's name.
3. Reference letters from 2 people who have accounts with BN.

Corporate Account:

Initial Deposit and Minimum Balance

Initial Deposit: (No Minimim Balance) .... $2,000/¢250,000

Requirements:

1. Passport or Resident Visa or Costa Rican ID (*cédula*).
2. *Carta de Constitución de la empressa.*
3. *Personeria Juridica* ((no more than three months since issued).
4. *Cédula Juridica.*
5. Original telephone or utilities bill with the applicant's name.

Checkbooks: Book of 40 checks $5
Limit on checks written per month: .... none
Debit Cards: .... $7.50/¢2,500
Online Banking
Credit Cards: .... No annual fees

SCOTIABANK

Personal Accounts:

Initial Deposit and Minimum Balance

Checking Account	$ Account	¢ Account
Initial Deposit:	$500	¢50,000
Minimum Balance	none	none

Savings Account

Initial Deposit:	$100	¢5,000
Minimum Balance:	none	none

Requirements:

1. Passport or Resident Visa or Costa Rican ID (*cédula*).
2. Reference from 2 other banks.

Corporate Account:

Initial Deposit and Minimum Balance
Initial Deposit: (No Minimim Balance) .... $500/¢100,000

Requirements:

1. Passport or Resident Visa or Costa Rican ID (*cédula*).
2. *Carta de Constitución de la empressa.*
3. *Personeria Juridica (no más de tres meses de emitida.*
4. *Cédula Juridica.*
5. Reference from 2 other banks.

Checkbooks: Book of 25 checks .... ¢1,000

Limit on checks written per month: 8 in conjunction with bank card use
Bank Cards: .... 8 transactions a month:
(in conjunction with checks written)* .... ¢600
Additional 20 transactions a month: .... ¢500

* To avoid additional charges, bank card transactions and number of checks written per month combined cannot exceed 8.

BANCO DE COSTA RICA

Personal Accounts:

Initial Deposit and Minimum Balance

Checking Account	$ Account	¢ Account
Initial Deposit:	$500	¢50,000
Minimum Balance	none	none

Savings Account

Initial Deposit:	$100	¢10,000
Minimum Balance:	none	none

Requirements:

1. Passport or Resident Visa or Costa Rican ID (*cédula*).
2. Reference from another bank.

Corporate Account:

Initial Deposit and Minimum Balance

Initial Deposit:	$500	¢50,000
Minimim Balance:	none	none

Requirements:

1. Passport or Resident Visa or Costa Rican ID (*cédula*).
2. *Carta de Constitución de la empressa.*
3. *Personeria Juridica (no más de tres meses de emitida.*
4. *Cédula Juridica.*

Checkbooks: Book of 25 checks $3
Limit on checks written per month: .... none
Free Debit Cards
Online Banking
Issues Credit Cards

Banking Terms

account	*la cuenta*
application	*solicitud*
ATM	*cajero automático*
bank	*el banco*
bank book	*la libreta de depósitos*
fixed	*fijo*
balance	*saldo*
bill	*billete*
bond	*bono*
cash	*dinero en efectivo*
to cash	*cobrar, cambiar*
cashier, teller	*cajero/a*
change	*cambio*
to change	*cambiar*
check	*cheque*
check book	*la chequera*
checking account	*cuenta corriente*
coin	*moneda*
compound interest	*interés compuesto*
credit card	*tarjeta de crédito*
customer	*cliente*
debit	*débito*
debit card	*tarjeta de débito*
debt	*deuda*
deposit	*depósito*
deposit slip	*hoja de depósito*
to deposit	*depositar*
dollar	*dólar*
draft	*giro bancario*
endorso	*endorse*
to endorse	*endorsar*
foreign exchange	*divisas*
income	*ingresos*

insured .... *asegurado*
interest .... *interés*
interest rate .... *tasa de interés*
invest .... *invertir*
line .... *fila*
loan .... *préstamo*
manager .... *gerente*
money .... *dinero/plata*
money order .... *giro baancario*
mortgage .... *hipoteca*
to mortage .... *hipotecar*
payment .... *pago, abono*
to pay .... *pagar*
pay off debts .... *saldar las deudas*
profit .... *ganancia*
receipt .... *recibo*
safe .... *caja fuerte*
salary .... *sueldo/salario*
savings .... *ahorros*
savings bank .... *caja de ahorros*
savings account .... *cuenta de ahorros*
to save .... *ahorrar*
securities .... *valores*
stock, share .... *acción*
tax .... *impuesto*
taxable .... *gravable, sujeto a impuesto*
to tax .... *gravar*
teller's window .... *la ventanilla*
traveler's check .... *cheque de viajero*
withdraw .... *retirar, sacar dinero*
withdrawl .... *retiro*
withdrawl .... *slip hoja de retiro*
to withdraw .... *retirar*
vault .... *bóveda*

If you have a Costa Rican corporation, you may also open a local corporate checking account, or *cuenta corriente empresarial.* You'll have to provide the following: passport or *cédula* (Costa Rican ID), the name of the corporation or *personería jurídica*, proof that it is active, a letter from the person who has general power of attorney of your corporation authorizing who can sign on the account, along with their ID numbers, and an initial deposit of about $1,000 for an account in local currency or $2,000 for a local dollar account.

International dollar checking accounts are offered through BAC. Individuals and corporations may open these accounts, but specific requirements must be met. Check with the bank of your choice.

Most banks are normally open from 8 a.m. to 5 p.m., Monday through Friday. Two branches of the Banco Nacional in downtown San José open at 7:30 a.m. Branch offices at most malls don't open until the mall opens. More and more banks are open on Saturdays and a few even on Sundays. **Mutual de Alajuela** has a service called SERVICAJA. Some of its branches are open after regular banking hours, on Saturdays, Sundays and holidays.

Warning: Never plan to do any banking on the second or last Friday of the month; this is payday for most Costa Rican workers and lines sometimes extend outside the bank.

The state banks are also very crowded after holidays and on Monday and Friday mornings. It is always best to get to the bank at least a half-hour before it opens to get a good place in line. Bring some good reading material, since the lines often move at a snail's pace.

Tipping (*propinas*)

A 15 percent sales tax, as well as a three percent tourist tax is added to all hotel bills. Cafés and restaurants include a 10 percent service charge or tip, so tipping above that amount is optional. The tip is almost always located on a bill below the food/beverage and just above or below the tax *(impuesto)* Employees such as bellhops and taxi drivers are appreciative of any additional gratuity for excellent service. It is also customary to give a small tip to the parking attendants who watch your car on the street, called *cuidacarros.* Two hundred fifty to three hundred *colones* or about $.50 is usually sufficient.

Supermarket box boys should be tipped for carrying groceries to your car, since they do not receive a salary. If you live nearby, they will even take your bags to your home. I used to live four blocks from the supermarket at Plaza Mayor in Rohrmoser and liked to walk to the market. My favorite box boy delivered our food to our front door for about 75 cents.

Paying Bills

Although your bills are sent to your home or post office box, the procedure for paying bills is different than in the United States and Canada. In Costa Rica you may pay your phone, electricity, water and cable TV bills at any supermarket, at some banks or by going directly to the company that issues the bill. Nobody sends a check by mail to pay bills in Costa Rica. Some banks allow you to pay bills online. Check with your local bank to see if it offers this service.

Affordable Hired Help

As you know, full or part-time domestic help is hard to find and prohibitively expensive for the average person, not to mention a retiree, in the United States. This is not the case in Costa Rica. A live-in maid or other full-time help usually costs about $200 per month. Often you can hire a couple for a bargain price, with the woman working as a maid and the man working as a full-time gardener and watchman. Before hiring any employee, be aware of all your requirements as an employer. Contact the ARCR for up to date information.

In Costa Rica, a maid usually does everything from washing clothes to taking care of small children. You can also use your maid to stand in line for you or run errands and bargain for you in stores, since foreigners often pay more for some items because of their naiveté and poor language skills.

After you have had an employee for a number of years, they can begin to think of you as a parental figure. As a result, it is not unusual for an employee to ask for loans, advances, help with money for family members who wish to build a home, furnish their house, provide school clothes for their children, or provide medical care and medications for family members.

General handymen and carpenters are also inexpensive. If you are infirm, one of the above people can assist you with many daily tasks. To find quality help, check with other retirees for references or look in local newspapers (*Tico Times*, *La República or La Nación*).

Gardeners, maintenance, construction and other workers should be asked if they are registered with the Caja as a *trabajador independiente* and if they have individual coverage for workers compensation. If they are, doing business with them is probably safe as long as they do business with others as well. However, if they are not legal and do not have insurance, one either needs to add them to a payroll or not work with them and look for someone else.

Unless your business is going to be a one-person operation, you will need to hire employees. Be very careful, because the labor laws are stringent and there are minimum salaries depending on the type of work. Ignoring these regulations can be very expensive for you if you get caught breaking the labor law.

Costa Rica's labor laws for domestic workers are even stricter, and difficult to interpret. All full time domestic employees have the right to Social Security benefits from the ***Caja Costarricense de Seguro Social*** (roughly the equivalent of the U.S. Social Security System). This important institution pays for sick leave, general health care, pension funds, disability pensions and maternity care.

Costa Rican labor law states all workers must be signed up with the Caja Costarricense de Seguro Social and be protected by workers compensation insurance for work related accidents. Employees and owners both have to be signed up. All workers, whether they are hourly, salaried or independent, must be covered.

Workers should be put on a payroll and the corresponding amount paid into the social security system. If the employees are temporary, they too should be signed up because the law states so even though the system seems to be unfair.

It is the *employer's* responsibility to pay monthly Social Security payments for each employee. The employer must make monthly payments of about 22 percent of the worker's monthly wage, and an additional nine percent is deducted from the employee's earnings. In return, the worker is entitled to the Social Security services mentioned above.

New employees must be registered with Social Security within a week of being hired. All new employees must register in an office in downtown San José (2223-9890). There is an automatic trial period of one month for domestic help, during which time an employee may be released without notice or termination pay.

One huge mistake is giving the employee too many "in-kind" benefits. These include anything not in the form of money. For example, meals, clothes, education, lodging and transportation. In Costa Rica, these "in-kind" perks which an employee receives can become part of their payment for work performed.

As alluded to above, it is also mandatory to insure employees against work-related accidents (*seguro contra riesgos de trabajo*). A workers' compensation policy should be purchased from the *Instituto Nacional de Seguros de Costa Rica*, the national insurance company, to cover work accidents. This coverage can be included in a homeowner's policy if only a few workers are involved. This type of worker's compensation costs 8,000 colones monthly for domestic employees and must be reapplied for annually. By not covering an employee with workers compensation you are setting yourself up for possible problems that will have to be settled in court.

Employers must also pay at least minimum wage to employees. This wage is set by the Ministry of Labor and depends on the job and skills required. Average wages for unskilled workers start at about $120 per month. Live-in help can receive an additional 50 percent more that is not actually paid to them but is used when computing certain benefits and bonuses.

Live-in domestic help cannot be required to work more than 12 hours a day, although few expect this. Live-in workers usually work-eight hours a day like other workers. Most regular employees work an eight-hour day, five days per week. Live-in employees can work more than this but have to be given some time off.

Domestic help is affordable in Costa Rica

Furthermore, employees are entitled to a paid vacation depending on their length of employment and whether they are full-or part-time. The law requires one day of vacation for every month of employment. A two-week vacation is due after 50 weeks of work. The employer can choose the time the vacation is taken and can require that half be taken at two different times, but they must be granted within 15 weeks of the time when they were due. Upon termination of the employment contract, unused vacation time should be paid using as a base the average of salary earned during the last six months.

Employers must also pay ***aguinaldo*** (end-of-year bonus) if an employee has worked from December 1 through November 30, or an amount proportionate to the time worked, if less than a year. The amount is the equivalent of one month's salary. This bonus should be paid in early December. Do not forget that live-in employees receive an additional 50 percent year-end bonus. Employees must also be paid for eight official holidays: January 1, Easter Thursday and Friday, April 11, May 1, July 25, August 15, September 15 and December 25.

A maternity leave of one month before a baby's birth is required; the employee receives 50 percent of her normal salary. Dismissal of a pregnant employee is also a bad idea, as it is frowned upon and could be very costly to the employer.

Maternity leave is a total of four months, one month before birth and three after. I believe it is at 60 percent pay, but am not sure about that. New mothers are entitled to up to a year of *lactancia*—an hour for breast-feeding. In practice, I've seen most people leave an hour early— I don't recall anyone taking it at lunchtime. I believe this is granted by the doctor for three months intervals (although I've never asked anyone how they decide if you are entitled to three more months). I don't believe there are any restrictions as to, length of time at work, etc.

In some cases, when a worker is terminated, it is the employer's responsibility to pay severance pay, all unused vacation time, the proportionate *aguinaldo*, and any wages due.

An employee must be given notice prior to being laid off. Severance pay, or *cesantía*, is usually one month's salary for each year worked. If an employee resigns voluntarily, the employer does not owe severance pay.

After three months of employment, an employee has the right to receive notice in the event of termination of employment without just cause by the employer (if notice is not given, he must be paid one month's salary, or a fraction if he has been employed for less than one year).

If the worker is fired without justification after at least three months of service, the employer has to pay a severance payment, the amount of which increases in accordance with the time worked and could be up to 22 days per year worked, with a maximum calculated on the basis of eight years, all according to a specific calculation table indicated by the Labor Code.

While countries such as the United States and Canada have standard minimum wages, Costa Rica has a separate minimum wage for nearly every type of job. Monthly minimum salaries are reviewed by the government every six months (January 1 and June 1).

Every six months, the government negotiates salary increases with various employee unions. If the negotiations fail, as they do from time to time, the president may issue a decree setting the new salaries in conjunction with the *Consejo Nacional de Salarios.*

Unskilled workers earn about $230, semi-skilled workers $260, skilled workers $285, technicians $290, technicians with higher education $450 and employees with a university degree $530. To give you a more precise idea of what salaries are like in Costa Rica, here are some samples of the approximate starting minimum monthly wages as established by the Labor Ministry or *Ministerio de Trabajo y Seguridad Social*: accountant $400, bartender $240, bus driver $250, carpenter $240, chauffeur $175, clerk $175, computer operator $300, dentist or doctor $1000, other professionals $430, farm hand $125, domestic worker (maid) $146 plus food, executive bilingual secretary $375, guard $180.00, journalist $550.00, messenger $175, nurse $375, plant supervisor $400, phone operator $170, secretary $295, tour guide $250 and unskilled laborer $120.

Only inexperienced workers receive these starting salaries. Experienced workers command higher wages. Keep in mind that these figures vary and are subject to change at any time. Such factors as bonuses and other perks also increase actual salaries. A list of minimum salaries is available at legal bookstores and some newsstands.

Many professionals work for salaries established by their *colegios* or trade organizations. For instance, a lawyer is supposed to get 10 percent of the value of any contract he or she prepares.

Companies try to pay about the legal minimum, although more enlightened ones reward good employees with higher salaries. Although the salaries appear low by North American standards, they are good for Latin America, and employees here have perks such as pensions, free medical care and other benefits in additional to their salaries.

This site provides you a list of all of the basic salaries **http://www.mtss.go.cr/Macros/Salario/Salarios%20Minimos.htm**

We have touched only briefly on the main points of Costa Rican labor law because it is **very complex**. If you have any questions, we advise you to contact the Ministry of Labor (2223-7166) or better yet your attorney. Have your lawyer help with any labor related matters to avoid unnecessary problems arising between you and your hired help. Information about Costa Rica's labor law in Spanish is at **www.leylaboral.com**.

Two new books can help you communicate better with your hired help: Crown Publishers' *Home Maid Spanish* and Barron's *Household Spanish*. Both books enable you to converse with your Spanish-speaking help without being fluent in the language. They are filled with all of the essential words and phrases you need to know.

Health Care

A Healthy Country

Costa Rica is a very healthy country. Costa Rica's health status is comparable to that of developed nations. The country's private health clinics have international fame and attract people from around the world for everything from dental care and ocular laser surgery to major cosmetic surgery and life extension treatments.

Unlike other countries in Latin America, especially Mexico, Costa Rica's water supply is good and perfectly safe to drink in San José and in the majority of small towns. In most places, you can drink the water without fear of Montezuma's Revenge (diarrhea) or other intestinal problems. However, be careful when you drink water in the countryside. We have lived in Costa Rica for years and have not heard many people complain about the quality of the country's water. If you prefer, bottled water is available. Just as in the United States, there are about 20 brands of bottled water in different-size containers sold at the supermarkets. You will be pleased to know that Costa Rica's water is soft for bathing and washing your hair.

Although the Costa Rican government takes precautions to monitor the quality of the water and the country has high sanitation standards, there are some precautions you should take. Wash and peel all fresh fruits and vegetables. Avoid drinking water-based fruit drinks sold in stands on the street. You should also watch out for raw seafood dishes, such as *ceviche*, served in some bars and restaurants. This type of seafood is soaked in lime juice and not cooked with heat. In general, restaurants are clean so you shouldn't have to worry what you eat. Low-end establishments display chicken and other food under lamps to keep it warm. If the food doesn't look fresh, use your judgment.

Costa Ricans are proud of their nation's achievements in the field of health care. Their up-to-date, affordable, state-run "cradle to grave" health care system reaches all levels of society by offering the same medical treatment to the poor as to those with greater resources. Hospitals, clinics and complete medical services are available in all major cities and some small towns. More than 90 percent of the population is covered by the Social Security System.

There is either a public clinic or hospital in almost every area of the country, making medical care accessible to everyone including foreigners. I know a U.S. couple near Dominical, on the southern Pacific coast, who either use the public hospital in San Isidro or the one in Ciudad Cortez. The wife said her husband fell when he was working on their house and sustained a compound fracture of the wrist. He was treated at the public hospital in Ciudad Cortez and was very pleased with the emergency treatment he received.

Medical Care Cost Comparison

by Martin Rice

Just got a really rude awakening that I thought I might share with you, given the fact that there's been quite a bit of discussion about medical care here lately.

Robin and I went to the States for two weeks over Christmas. While there, I had to go to the emergency room in Knoxville, TN where we were visiting family. The hospital, Baptist Hospital, West, is a brand new

(1 1/2 years) super impressive place. They took great care of me in the emergency room -- all the speedy intense care you would expect for chest pains. The reason it was a bit more scary than it might have been is that just three months ago I had an angioplasty here at CIMA.

After they saw that I was doing OK and all the signs were on the money, they said that I had to have a stress test. The kind of stress test I get is a chemical one in the Department of Nuclear Medicine. I had one at CIMA before the angioplasty. It's this that tells them whether you need to have the angioplasty done. Here comes the first cost comparison: The doctor said that based on the results of the stress test, they'd decide whether I'd need another angioplasty. I told him that if at all possible I'd prefer to go back to CR to have it done because there it would cost me about $13,000 in total and I figured in the States it'd be about $25,000. He laughed and said "more like $40,000 or $50,000!" Now THAT almost gave me a heart attack.

At any rate, the results of the stress test were great and I didn't need anything else at all. When the doctor told me that, he said that I'd be able to leave right then. At this point I had spent a night at the hospital and about a total of 24 hours.

That same stress test at CIMA cost me $750. There was also comple blood work done which was another $150. I did it on an out-patient basis, but I know that a nice room at CIMA, with a sitting room attached is about $150 per night. No emergency care, but, again from experience there, I'd estimate that what I had done at the ER in the States would have been about $1,000 to $1,500. So a total of about $2,550.00.

What was the bill at the hospital in the United States? $8,000! One night in the hospital and no operation or any other kind of invasive procedure. Is that sick or what? Talk about a broken system. So when people talk about the high cost of private medicine here and at hospitals such as CIMA, remember that everything is relative, extremely relative.

Anyway, I'm doing just great now and feel fine.

Many international medical authorities rate Costa Rica as having one of the best low-cost medical care systems in the world, when preventive and curative medicines are considered. The United Nations consistently ranks Costa Rica's public health system as the best in Latin America and one of the top 20 in the world. The world Health Organization (WHO) ranks Costa Rica 36th out of 191 countries with respect to the quality of its health care systems. The United States for example ranks 37th.

Costa Ricans are a healthy people. The infant mortality rate of less than 11 in 100,000 live births is lower than that in the United States. This figure is on par with any industrialized country in the world. Life expectancy is 76.3 years for men and 79.8 years for women. Today, an 80-year-old man has a life expectancy of at least eight (actually, 8.4) years. This puts Costa Rica in *first* place in the world for life expectancy from this age up. Iceland and Japan follow with 7.7 years. Costa Rican women at age 80 are expected to live longer than men of the same age, 9.5 years, slightly behind the women of Japan and France.

Hospitals have the latest equipment, and laboratories are excellent. You can feel safe having most operations without returning to the United States or Canada. Most surgical procedures cost only a fraction of what they do in the United States. For example, a heart bypass operation costs about a third of what it does in the United States.

It is no wonder a large number of foreigners are attracted to Costa Rica because of its affordable health care. In the United States, for example,millions of people do not have health insurance because it is prohibitively expensive. For this reason, Costa Rica attracts many retirees from North America. It doesn't matter if you are a legal resident or a traveler. Everyone is entitled to emergency care at a government hospital.

Even if you are in good health, the probability of needing medical care increases with age. The security of knowing that good health services are available presents an enormous relief.

Medical Costs

Medical Procedures	USA	Costa Rica	Average Savings
Heart Bypass	Up to $130,000	$24,000	70-80%
Heart Valve Replacement	Up to $160,000	$15,000	80-90%
Angioplasty	Up to $57,000	$9,000	70-80%
Hip Replacement	Up to $43,000	$12,000	60-70%
Hysterectomy	Up to $20,000	$4,000	70-80%
Knee Replacement	Up to $40,000	$11,000	60-70%
Spinal Fusion	Up to $62,000	$25,000	50-60%

Plastic and Reconstructive Surgery			
Facelift	$7,000-$9,000	$4,600 – $5,000	30-40%
Rhinoplasty	$8,000-$12,000	$3,500 – $3,900	50-65%
Breast Lift	$5,000-$8,000	$3,000 – $3,400	40-55%
Breast Augmentation	$5,000-$8,000	$2,700 – $2,900	50-65%
Blepharoplasty (Eyelid Surgery)	$4,000-$5,500	$2,000 – $2,200	50-60%
Brazilian Butt Surgery	Up to $10,000	$3,000 – $3,300	55-65%
Tummy Tuck	$6,000-$8,500	$3,900 – $4,200	45-50%
Facelift	$7,000-$9,000	$4,600 – $5,000	35-45%
Male Breast Reduction	Up to $6,000	$2000 – $2600	50-60%
Bariatric Surgery			
Laparoscopic Gastroplasty	Up to $30,000	$10,500	55-65%
Laparoscopic Roux-en-Y	Up to $35,000	$14,000	50-60%
General and Cosmetic Dentistry			
Bridges	$1,000+ per tooth	$250 – $400 per tooth	60-70%
Crowns	$1,000+ per tooth	$250 – $400 per tooth	60-70%
Implants	$3,500+ per tooth	$700 – $900 per tooth	70-80%
Porcelain Veneers	$1,500+ per tooth	$300 – $500 per tooth	65-80%
Root canal	Up to $800	$315	55-60%
Teeth whitening	Up to $700	$250	55-65%

Costa Rican Doctors

Most Costa Rican doctors are excellent and have been trained in Europe or North America. If you don't speak Spanish, you don't have to worry. Many local doctors speak English, but most receptionists and nurses do not. Doctor's fees for office visits vary. A good private specialist usually charges between $40 and $60 for each visit, although some doctors charge a little more and others a little less.

Unlike many other places, doctors in Costa Rica take time with patients to answer questions and listen. Doctors usually give you their office, home and cell phone numbers as well as pager number. It is not unusual for doctors to call their patients at home to follow-up on care and medications, and they will make house calls.

Doctors here are much less interested in making a profit than serving the people. Considering there are no high malpractice premiums to pay, physicians can make a good living without charging exorbitant prices.

If you join Costa Rica's national health care system, you do not have to pay for each office visit, only a small monthly membership fee. If you have any questions about medical fees or doctors, you should direct them to the *Colegio de Médicos*, which is the Costa Rican equivalent of the AMA.

To find a good English-speaking physician or specialist, talk to other expats, look in the Yellow Pages under *Médicos*, look for doctor's ads in the *The Tico Times* or see the list at the end of this section.

Hospitals and Medical Facilities

Public medical facilities are so good that you don't usually need private care. Most private specialists are required by law to work part-time in public hospitals. However, private clinics and hospitals provide quicker services with more privacy, enabling you to avoid long lines and the bureaucracy of the public system.

In Costa Rica, the term ***clínica*** is used for private institutions that generally include inpatient medical/surgical facilities, doctor's offices, laboratories, radiology, pharmacy and outpatient services. **Hospital** generally refers to public inpatient medical/surgical facilities that also provide laboratory, radiology, pharmacy and related services.

Most Costa Ricans find the cost of private clinics too expensive. However, foreigners will find private clinics very reasonable compared to similar institutions back home.

You will be happy to know you can receive first-rate care at any of San José's three largest private hospitals.

If you have to enter a private hospital, costs will be lower than in the U.S. A single room a spacious, with bathroom and cable TV including English channels. Private and semi-private rooms often have an extra bed or sofa bed so a relative may spend the night, if necessary. It is important to note that the doctor's bill will always be separate from the hospital bill.

A few years ago my son was operated on for an appendectomy at the Clínica Bíblica. The total cost including the surgeon's fee was under $3,000. My INS insurance covered all but $140.

I know an American who spent a couple of days in the private Clínica Católica hospital and said, "The attention was first-class, the food was as good as home cooking, and the same care would have cost thousands of dollars in the States." It is important to know that payment can be made at most hospitals and clinics with any major credit card. Foreign medical insurance is accepted, if they cover you abroad. In some cases, especially if arranged in advance, your foreign insurance can be used so you can just pay the deductible. Talk to your private hospital.

- The **Clinica Bíblica** (Tel:2522-1000, 800-911-0800, Fax: 2255-4947,E-mail:asoserme@racsa.co.cr, www.clinicabiblica.com) in downtown San José is now affiliated with the Blue Cross and Blue Shield network. There is a small chance that Medicare may be accepted someday, but don't hold your breath. A first-class private hospital with an excellent coronary unit, this fine facility is staffed with highly trained doctors. Complete hospital services including maternity, an ER room, MRI equipment and lab work are available. I have used the lab on many occasions and found the service to be excellent. In order to keep pace with the country's needs for first-rate private care, the hospital acquired a new multi-storied medical tower in the next block and added a large wing to the main hospital.

In addition to the main branch in downtown San José, the Clínica Bíbilica has smaller satellite branches with a doctor on duty, pharmacies and express delivery of medicine in Heredia (2260-4959), Cartago (2551-0511), San Francisco de Dos Ríos (2218-0035), and in the San Pedro Mall (2283-6058). Since I live in Heredia, I have used the local Heredia branch of the Clínica Bíblica on several occasions for minor ailments and tests. The service has been very good and fast.

- The newely refurbished **Clínica Católica** (2246-3006, E-mail: info@clinicacatolica.com, www.clinicacatolica.com) in Guadalupe, a suburb of San José, is another fine private hospital with complete hospital and emergency services 24-hours a day, 365 days a year. However, it is not as popular with foreigners as the Clínica Bíblica or Hospital CIMA. This facility takes private INS insurance, Blue Shield and Blue Cross. During an acute asthma episode, I spent three days in this hospital and found the care very good.

- **Hospital CIMA** (Tel: 2208- 1000, E-mail cimahsj@racsa.co.cr, www.hospitalsanjose.net) in Escazú, right off the highway, is the newest private hospital in the San José area and is affiliated with the Baylor University Medical Center in Dallas, Texas. It is managed by International Hospital Corporation of Dallas. It is a full-service hospital that boasts the latest health care technology, state-of-the-art medical equipment and the most sophisticated physical plant in Central America. It offers complete services including X-ray, ultrasound, emergency and intensive care, as well as an advanced coronary unit.

  The average cost of a room per day is between $130 and $140, which is very reasonable compared to the cost of a hospital in the United States. An adjacent seven-story medical office building houses the offices of more than 100 specialists.

  Hospital CIMA plans to open a full-service branch near Flamingo Beach in Guanacaste. The International Hospital Corporation (IHC) announced the construction of CIMA Guanacaste, a new hospital in Guanacaste, Costa Rica. Besides CIMA San José, IHC has other hospitals in Brazil and Mexico.

Costa Ricans and foreign tourists will no longer have to travel to San Jose for quality medical attention. Now, they will have access to general physicians, specialists, surgeons, operating rooms, and hospital services in Guanacaste," said Carole Velos, General Director of CIMA San José.

The new CIMA Guanacaste will be the entry door for Pacific Plaza, an international campus specializing in completely integrated health and retirement community services.

CIMA Guanacaste will be strategically located next to Do-It Center in Carrillo, Guanacaste, on the road to Liberia's International Airport and to the beach resorts and retreats of the region. This location will provide tourists and residents with top quality medical services, and the exact same standards as in CIMA San José.

Pre-construction works have already started, and they are expected to be completed by the end of 2010 or beginning of 2011.

The Clínica Bíblica is one of Costa Rica's best private hospitals.

Note: Lately there have been a lot of complaints about Cima's high prices from some of the contributors from the Costa Rica Living newsgroup. You can look up these articles by going to ther site listed in Chapter 14.

- The **Clínica Santa Rita** (2221-6433), near the court buildings, has an excellent maternity center and is used for cosmetic surgery procedures.

- The **Hospital Cristiano Jerusalem** (2216-9191), in Alto de Guadalupe, offers limited services. Although not a hospital, the **Clínica Americana** (2222-1010), next to Clínica Bíblica, offers private out-patient service and some U.S.-trained doctors on call 24-hours a day.

- **Hospital Clínica Santa María**, (Tel: 2523-6000, Fax: 2523-6060, E-mail: servicioalcliente@hospitalcsantamaria.com), offers a variety of high-quality services in downtown San José.

- **Hospital Universitario de La Universidad Iberoaméricana,** (Tel: 2297-2242, Fax: 2236-0426, E-mail: admisiones@unibe.ac.cr), located in San José's suburb of Tibás, is the country's newest private hospital. It is a full-service university hospital where specialists treat all patients with students as observers.

- **C.A.R.E.** 8353-7456 or 2282-2626 (beeper) or 2637-8606 (Los Sueños Resort) or 643-1690 is a private emergency medical center in the Jacó Beach area. It offers medical consultation, an advanced life support ambulance, minor surgery and special events coverage. The clinic's regular hours are from 8 a.m. to 6 p.m.

- **Emergencias Médicas** (2290-4444) is a private company offering quick ambulance service. For a small yearly fee you can take advantage of its first-rate service. **Emergencias Metro** (2263-2983, emergenciasmetro@yahoo.com) is another company offering emergency medical transportation and care. **Costa Rica Life Guard** (8824-5227) offers emergency transportation by airplane.

Public Hospitals

As you can see, public hospitals and clinics are found in most parts of the country, with the three major facilities in the San José area. Although public hospitals are generally crowded and waits can be long for appointments, there is no problem when it comes to emergency treatment.

The author can personally vouch for the care at Costa Rica's public hospitals. After many hours in labor my wife gave birth to my son by cesarean section at the public San Juan de Dios Hospital. He was taken to the Children's Hospital next door because he required some special care and was placed in an incubator while my wife recovered. About three days later both mother and baby were released without any complications. Today I have a healthy 18-year old son.

The major public medical centers in San José are:

Hospital Blanco Cervantes .... Tel: 2257-8122

Hospital de la Mujer (Carit)
(Maternity Hospital) .... Tel: 2257-9111

Hospital México .... Tel: 2242-6700

Hospital de Niños (Children's Hospital) .... Tel: 2222-0122

Hospital Psiquiátrico Manuel A. Chapul
(Psychiatric Hospital) .... Tel: 2232-2155

Hospital Rafael Angel Calderón Guardia .... Tel: 2212-1000

Heredia's new hospital is the largest **public hospital in Central America**
Tel: 2257-6282

Major public medical facilities in other areas of the country:

Heredia
San Vicente de Paul .... Tel: 2277-2400

Alajuela
Hospital San Rafael .... Tel: 2436-1001

Cartago
Hospital Max Peralta .... Tel: 2550-1999

Ciudad Neily
Hospital de Ciudad Neily... Tel: 2783-4111

Guanacaste (Liberia)
Hospital Dr. Enrique Baltodano .... Tel: 26690-9700

Limón
Hospital Dr. Tony Facio .... Tel: 2758-2222

Los Chiles
Hospital Los Chiles... Tel: 2471-2000

Nicoya
Hospital de la Anexión.. 2685-8400

Pérez Zeldón
Hospital Escalante Pradilla .... Tel: 2785-0700

Puntarenas
Hospital Monseñor Sanabria................................. Tel: 2663-0033

San Carlos
Hospital San Carlos.. Tel: 2460-1176

Health Care for Veteran's in Costa Rica

The Clínica Bíblica now accepts medical coverage through **Tri Care Latin America** and **CHAMPUS** for hospital and pharmacy services.

Here are the requirements for medical benefits for U.S. military retirees and their families:

1. A current U.S. military retiree ID card (20 years of active duty)
2. 65 years or over and have Medicare Part B.
3. Current ID cards for all dependents under 21 years of age if in college with proof of enrollment
4. Unmarried widows must have the related documents above for their husband.

Medical benefits for U.S. veterans:

The disabled veteran can only be treated for the disabilities listed on the Treatment Authorization Sheet from the VA. If the veteran is 100 percent disabled, all dependents will receive total health care, not including dental and glasses. The following documents are required:

1. Current CHAMPUS VA card.
2. Current ID card for all dependents under the age of 21 and up to 23 years of age if in college with proof of enrollment.
4. Copy of DD 214
5. Unmarried widows must have the related documents above for their husband.

To find out about benefits for military retirees and their families and for disabled veterans, call 2522-1500/221-7717 or E-mail: sguros@clinicabiblica.com.

Low-Cost Medical Insurance

Costa Rica's health care system is available to retirees and other foreign residents. Residents may join the **Caja Costarricense de Seguro Social** (Costa Rican Social Security System) and enjoy the same inexpensive medical coverage as most Costa Ricans do. Most foreigners do not enroll in this system because of the long waits for medical appointments, some medications and other delays. However, despite being overburdened, the emergency care provided is very good. There are clinics all over the country. At a low cost of around $80 monthly, the Caja is a good deal for foreigners.

The cost to affiliate directly is about 13 percent of your monthly income by law; however the ARCR (www.arcr.net) has a legal contract with the Caja to affiliate at a very reasonable price.

As just stated, according to the law you must pay 11 to 13 percent of your income to the *Caja* for voluntary medical insurance. Some foreigners who try to get around this by lying about their income and paying the minimum of about $25 monthly. If they are legal residents, the government will know they have at least an income of $600 per month and should be paying about $70 monthly. If they are caught underpaying, they can be fined and ordered to pay the difference in what was not paid in the first place. My advice to you is: Don't try to cut corners.

If you are a resident or hold a work permit, the first step is to join the *Caja*. If you need a medical consultation, go to the **EBAIS** or clinic closest to home and request an appointment (go early, as there is usually a long line for appointments). If your case merits attention by a medical specialist, you will be referred to the nearest clinic or hospital for evaluation.

Most foreigners opt for the medical insurance offered by the government's insurance company—the **National Insurance Institute** or **INS**. Everyone is eligible to apply, including permanent residents, *pensionados* and *rentistas* and even tourists. Elderly people have to submit to a physical before they can be insured. The medical policy covers expenses resulting from illness, accidents, hospitalization, office visits, lab work, medicines and medical costs in foreign countries. However, if you incur medical expenses abroad, INS will pay only the amount equivalent to the same treatment in Costa Rica and you have to pay the difference.

When you purchase a policy, INS will supply you with an identification card and a booklet that lists the names of affiliated groups such as hospitals, doctors, labs and pharmacies. Most surgical procedures are covered 100 percent. You pay a small deductible for office visits, labs, medicines and treatments. If you seek medical services not affiliated with INS, you have to pay up front. You then submit a claim to INS and will be reimbursed in a few weeks.

Depending on age and sex, the annual cost of this insurance is about $800 for a man 50 to 69 For example, rates for a man 18-39 years run about $250 per year; $1,800 for a 70-year old man ; and women of all ages pay an average annual rate of about $1,500. Women of childbearing age pay slightly more than men. There is a discount if more than one person is insured on the same policy. It is easy to enroll an entire family for a low monthly rate. If you belong to a group of 15 or more people—such as the Association of Residents (ARCR) or the American Legion— you can obtain an approximate five percent discount.

Since medical costs are so low in Costa Rica, this policy is more than enough to take care of your medical needs. Retirees and other residents need not worry about lacking adequate medical coverage in Costa Rica. For information, go to the (ARCR) or contact them at: (Tel: 2233-8068, Fax: 011-(506) 2222-7862) or see www.arcr.net or contact Franklin Martinez 2258-7041 or 8318-2255.

INS now offers a new international insurance policy that covers your needs in Costa Rica and the rest of the world. This new medical policy covers medical expenses resulting from accident or sickness. Here are some of the items covered: hospitalization and ambulance expenses, maternity, prosthesis, organ transplants, air evacuation, repatriation of remains, funeral costs and a yearly check-up and eye test. The rates are high but the coverage is complete.

Mixed Medicine

One of the services offered by *Caja* is that of mixed medicine, whereby a patient can go for treatment to a private doctor, pay those bills and receive medications and other services from the *Caja*. In this sense, the *Caja* uses mainly generic medications certified by quality control laboratories, even in some cases using the original medications. The idea of Mixed Services is that the patient can been seen by a trusted physician and avoid the long line for treatment at an EBAIS or rural clinics.

Some Costa Ricans and many foreigners use the *Caja* as a type of back up insurance for extra protection. They see a private doctor for minor ailments and the *Caja* for major problems, while others use the *Caja* for certain tests and expensive medicines and minor illnesses. Another way to do it is to use a private physician for problems that require a long wait through the *Caja*. The waits for some tests and procedures can take months, so people with cancer and other serious problems often go to a private lab to get faster test results.

Many doctors who have a private practice and also work in the public system will operate on their patients in a public hospital to reduce costs.

Be careful of a ***biombo***. A *biombo* is a medical practice that has been used from time to time by some unscrupulous individuals in the medical profession. For example, a couple of medical professionals employed by the *Caja* were just arrested for taking samples of blood at their own private laboratory and then using equipment at a public hospital to do the analysis.

Comparing Costa Rica's Public and Private Health Care Plans

What follows is a brief comparison of the *Caja* and the INS medical plans available in Costa Rica.

Caja — National socialized system.

1. Covers doctor's visits, medications, examinations and hospitalization.
2. Doctors are assigned to the patient.
3. Covers pre-existing conditions.
4. Covers all medications including dental and eyes.

Some reasons to consider this plan:

1. Have pre-existing health condition and do not qualify for INS insurance.
2. Take medication on a regular basis.
3. Have it as major medical in case of serious illness.

Monthly premiums cover all illnesses for the member and his immediate family for that month. The cost through the ARCR if younger than 55 years old is $58 per month; $37 per month if 55 years or older.

INS — The semi-autonomous government insurance company.

1. Covers 75 percent of the cost of doctor's visits, medications, examinations and hospitalization.
2. Individual chooses the doctor.
3. Does not cover any pre-existing medical condition.

4. Does not cover most dental or eye exams, treatments or glasses, preventive medical check-up, illness or disorders related to female reproductive organs during the first 12 months of coverage, or birth of a baby during the first six months of coverage.

Some reasons ARCR members have the INS plan.

1. Can choose a doctor.
2. Can make doctor's appointments with less red tape.

Rates of coverage depend on age and sex; 20 percent deductible for each doctor's visit.

Plan 16 Medical Insurance Policy

Plan 16 is the medical insurance policy INS has been selling since 1990, and a lot of people from the foreign community have obtained coverage through the Canadian Club, the American Legion and the ARCR.

Who can be insured? Anyone up to age 100, regardless of legal status in Costa Rica. Applicants over 69 must undergo an examination by an INS doctor. It takes INS about three weeks to study applications; you can't pay until your application is accepted. The policy parallels the calendar year; if someone applies and is accepted part way through the year, the yearly premium is prorated.

What does the policy pay for? It covers expenses due to sickness, accident or childbirth. Outpatient services are paid for up to 10 percent of the insured amount, per year. The rest of the policy, the other 90 percent, is for hospitalization, surgery, pre- and post-operative care, private room, food, support systems, intensive care, rehabilitation, ambulance, home care, therapy, medication, etc. In case of death, 50 percent of the insured amount is paid to the named beneficiary. Please note that there is no payment for checkups or "preventive maintenance," No changes.

What does it exclude? Pre-existing conditions. Also not covered are medical expenses as a result of cataclysmic events, fighting except in self-defense, tournament sports, martial arts and other dangerous activities. Accidents when under the influence of alcohol or drugs. Mental or nervous disorders. Checkups. Allergies. Stress. Plastic surgery. Only accident related eyeglasses, dentist's bills or reconstructive surgery are paid. Some ailments (e.g. glaucoma, cataracts, ENT, women's reproductive organs, breasts, asthma, hernias, pregnancy, prostates, stones, osteoporosis) have a 12-month moratorium during which claims are not allowed.

How much does it cost? You can choose from three levels of insurance. The insured amount refers to the maximum amount INS will pay for your health in the calendar year. Premiums depend on the level of insurance, and on the age and sex of the insured.

Group policies for companies Associations or clubs, (ARCR, American Legion, etc.) cost about 40 percent less. Cost of renewal may increase if there is a high claim/premium ratio.

How does it work? In case of ambulatory care (when hospitalization is not needed), you must pay for your care and later submit an INS claim form signed by you and your main doctor, attaching original receipts and corresponding prescriptions for medicine, treatments and lab tests. Your agent will push your claim through INS, which usually pays after three to six weeks, based on usual and reasonable charges. If you require hospitalization, a week before you go into hospital, through your agent you should obtain pre-authorization from INS, which will negotiate prices with your caregiver. When released from the hospital, you must show your insurance card and so pay the deductible only. If you didn't get the pre-authorization, you must pay the entire bill and make a claim as described above.

Deductibles? providers are classified as A, B or C. If you go to an A provider, INS will pay 80% of usual and customary prices; B providers, INS pays 75%; C providers, 70%. CIMA is classified A. Clínica Bíblica is B. For additional information contact the author of this last section, **David Garrett,** at **2233-2455** or E-mail: **info@segurosgarrett.com.**

INS Medical Regional

INS Medical Regional is an alternative to Plan 16 and provides broader coverage.

Who Can Be Insured?

Residents of Costa Rica ages 18 to 65 can apply. Sometimes people up to 70 have been accepted. Once insured, INS will renew indefinitely so long as the premium is paid. Dependents from birth up to age 24 can also be insured.

What is Covered?

Medical expenses due to accident, sickness or maternity, up to $200,000 per year. For people over 69, the coverage is reduced to $60,000 per year. The policy will also pay for an eye test and checkup, as of the second year. It covers hospital care and ambulatory care. Subject to sub-limits, also maternity, cancer, epidemic diseases, prosthesis, organ transplants, ophthalmic care, air ambulance if treatment can only be administered abroad, repatriation of remains, death benefit for burial, etc. By means of surcharges you can increase the cancer coverage, and coverage for severe medical conditions, to $400,000.

Where is coverage offered?
Worldwide coverage. But the policy is designed for and works best in Central America.

What are the main exclusions? Conditions existing when the insurance is bought. Treatments for obesity, cosmetic surgery, sterility, congenital conditions, dental care, sex change, insemination, mental disease, addictions, attempted suicide, self-inflicted lesions, pregnancy of dependents except spouse, accidents when the insured was under the influence of drugs or alcohol, correction of vision, AIDS and HIV positive, erectile dysfunction, chiropractic and podiatrist care, tranquilizers, antidepressants, vitamins, non-prescribed expenses, experimental treatments, accidents while practicing high-risk or speed sports, medical expenses as a result of cataclysmic events, terrorism, civil insurrection or war.

What about preexisting Conditions?
Chronic conditions, at the discretion of INS, can be covered if the applicant has had no symptoms in the last two years.

How are claims and deductibles handled?
In Central America there is a network of providers (doctors, hospitals, labs, clinics and pharmacies), which includes Clínica Biblica, Hospital CIMA, Clínica Católica and others, where you pay less because they are bound to a price limitation imposed by INS, and you pay a lower deductible. Also, for hospital care you use your insurance card to cover the balance. With preferred providers, for hospital care you pay for one day of hospital room, plus 10 percent of the following $5,000; for ambulatory care you pay $10 per doctors' visit, plus 10 percent of other prescribed expenses. With outside providers, for hospital care you pay for one day of hospital room with a minimum of $200, plus 20 percent of the next $20,000; for ambulatory care, you pay $20 per doctor's visit, plus 20 percent of other prescribed expenses.

How much does it cost?
You can choose from three levels of insurance. Premiums depend on the level, and on age and sex of applicants (costs shown in U.S. dollars). Some averages of yearly premiums:

Adults

Age	Men	Women
0-18	US$ 448	US$ 524
19-25	470	562
26-29	526	633

30-34	553	678
35-39	640	783
40-44	692	865
45-49	829	931
50-54	953	1,086
55-59	1,068	1,179
60-64	1,348	1,364
65-69	1,625	1,599
70-75	2,090	2,046

Children to 10 years.

Both genders

1 child .... US $ 226
2 children 291
3 + children 376

* Check for current rates

Applications

No medical examination is normally necessary. For bureaucratic reasons, policy applications are best filled out by an agent. You must pay the first premium at the time of applying. The policy goes into effect 30 days later. Some medical conditions have a 10-month moratorium.

What numbers do I phone for medical assistance when I am away from Costa Rica ?

- Within the United States: 1-866-543-6307 (toll free)
- Any other country except Costa Rica : +1 (305) 463 9635 (you may call collect)

INS Medical International

Who can be insured?

Residents of Costa Rica ages 18 to 65 can apply. Applications from people up to 70 have sometimes been accepted. INS will renew indefinitely so long as the premium is paid. Dependents from birth to age 24 can also be insured.

What is covered?

Medical expenses resulting from accident, sickness or maternity, up to $2 million per year. For people over 69, coverage is reduced to $600,000 per year. The policy will also pay for a yearly eye test and checkup, as of the second year. Covers hospital and ambulatory care. Subject to sub-limits, maternity, cancer, epidemic diseases, prosthesis, transplants, ophthalmic care, air ambulance if medically required, repatriation of remains, death benefit for burial, etc.

Where is coverage offered?
Worldwide coverage.

What are the main exclusions?
Conditions existing when the insurance is bought. Treatments for obesity, cosmetic surgery, sterility, congenital conditions, dental care, sex change, insemination, mental disease, addictions, attempted suicide, self-inflicted lesions, pregnancy of dependents except spouse, accidents when the insured was under the influence of drugs or alcohol, correction of vision, treatment for AIDS and HIV positive, erectile dysfunction, chiropractic and podiatrist care, tranquilizers, antidepressants, vitamins, non-prescribed expenses, experimental treatments, accidents while practicing high-risk or speed sports, medical expenses as a result of cataclysmic events, terrorism, civil insurrection or war.

What about preexisting conditions?
At the discretion of INS, these can be covered if the applicant has had no symptoms in the two years before an application is submitted.

How are claims and deductibles handled?
In Central and North America there is a network of providers (doctors, hospitals, labs, clinics and pharmacies) where you will pay less because they are bound to a price list imposed by INS — and you pay a lower deductible. Also, you use your insurance card to cover the balance for hospital care. (You can also get this insurance with a blanket, per-year deductible, where you accumulate your medical expenses and, if in the policy year they exceed the limit, you can claim for the excess.)

With preferred providers, for hospital care you pay for one day of hospital room, plus 10 percent of the following $5,000; for ambulatory care you pay $10 per doctor's visit, plus 10 percent of other prescribed expenses.
With outside providers, for hospital care you will pay for one day of hospital room with a minimum of $200, plus 20 percent of the next $20,000; for ambulatory care, you will pay $20 per doctor's visit, plus 20 percent of other prescribed expenses.

How much does it cost?
You can choose from three levels of insurance. Premiums depend on the level, and on age and sex of applicants (costs shown in US dollars).

Large Individual Deductibles			**Minimum Deductible**	
Standard Deductible				**US$ 5.000**
Age	Men	Women	Men	Women
26-29	1,043	1,254	539	634
35-39	1,332	1,622	674	803
45-49	1,715	1,921	863	951
55-59	2,199	2,425	1,116	1,206
65-69	3,331	3,279	1,720	1,668

Minimum Deductible			**Minimum Deductible**	
US$10.000				**US$ 15.000**
Age	Men	Women	Men	Women
26-29	402	463	323	365
35-39	495	580	392	451
45-49	630	684	493	530
55-59	819	873	647	680
65-69	1,279	1,226	1,023	972

How to apply?

No medical examination is normally necessary. For bureaucratic reasons, policy applications are best filled out by an agent. You must pay the first premium at the time of applying. The policy goes into effect 30 days later. Some medical conditions have a 10-month moratorium.

What numbers do I phone for medical assistance when I am away from Costa Rica ?

- Within the United States: 1-866-543-6307 (toll-free)
- Any other country except Costa Rica: +1 (305) 463 9635 (you may call collect)

  Courtesy of 2005 Garrett & Associates www.segurosgarrett.com

Alternative International Medical Plans

In addition to the medical plans mentioned above, companies such as **Blue Cross and Blue Shield** offer international coverage for their policyholders. The majority of private clinics in Costa Rica work with companies offering international medical coverage.

With some of these policies you may have to pay out of your own pocket and provide receipts for reimbursement at a later date. Other companies will pay "right on the spot." It is a good idea to have a policy that provides international evacuation which in some cases may be a viable option. A friend of mine went on a trip from Costa Rica to Nicaragua and became very ill while there. He developed a problem with internal bleeding. Because he had an international evacuation policy, he was flown to New Orleans. He was unconscious for several days but eventually fully recovered. Needless to say, he would have probably died without this policy that allowed him to go to the United States for specialized treatment.

I.M.C. Asociados, S.A. offers **BUPA International's** health plan in Costa Rica. They have health care plans specifically designed for residents of Central America with worldwide coverage wherever and whenever needed. They guarantee lifetime coverage without excessive increases in premiums with age. Contact them at: Tel: 2256-5848 or E-mail: imccr2002@yahoo.com.

Global Insurance offers medical plans for people living abroad. You may contact them at: Tel: (305)-2274-0284, Fax: (305)-2675-6134, toll-free 1-800-975-7363, E-mail: cperez@globalinsurancenet.com or www.globalinsurancenet.com.

Medibroker (Tel: 0-191-297-2411/44-191-297-2411, Fax: 0-191-251-6424, www.medibroaker.com, e-mail: medibroker@aol.com offers medical coverage for retirees, expats and others living abroad. They have various plans from which to choose.

The **AARP** may also offer a program for foreign coverage.

While checking out Costa Rica, to see if it is the place for you to settle, you can get temporary medical insurance as a tourist through the Costa Rican Social Security office and the **International Organization of Cultural Interchanges (O.I.C.I.)**. Contact them at 2222-7867.

Medicine and Pharmacies

Pharmacies are numerous in Costa Rica and they stock most standard medicines available in Europe, Canada and the United States. In general, the cost of most medicines is lower than in the U.S. However, it pays to shop around. There has been a continuous price war going on among most of the pharmacy chains. So, good bargains may be found.

Many drugs requiring a prescription in North America are freely available "over the counter" in any Costa Rican *farmacia* .Exceptions are strong pain relievers and narcotics that require a special prescription. In Costa Rica, pharmacists are permitted to prescribe medicines as well as administer on-the-spot injections. They are also available to answer your questions and give free medical advice about less complex conditions. In general, Costa Rican pharmacists usually give you the correct advice and appropriate medication. This can save you a trip to the doctor's office.

Foreigners who can't find their specific medication will have no problem. Pharmacists have a thick medical guide listing most medicines in the world and their generic equivalents. Some caution should be taken when figuring out the specific dose. I have a friend from Fort Lauderdale, Florida, who mistakenly purchased blood pressure medicine that was twice as strong as what he needed. He ended up feeling very ill and had to be taken to a local hospital. The problem was quickly resolved when the doctor realized the dosage was incorrect.

Some pharmacies open 24-hours a day are in downtown San José at **Clínica Bíblica**, 2223-6422; at the **Clínica Católica,** 2225-9095; and the **Farmacia del Este** in San Pedro 2253-5121.

The main branch of the **Fischel** pharmacy 2223-0909, across from the main post office in San José, has a doctor on duty to give medical advice. Fischel will deliver medicine and prescriptions in most areas. Many of their employees speak English. They also have smaller pharmacies in other locations around San José and in Heredia, Alajuela, Cartago and Puntarenas.

For home delivery call them toll-free at 800 Fischel 800-347-2435. Recently, Fischel opened the country's first online pharmacy. They offer the sale of prescriptions and over-the-counter products. In addition, their staff of pharmacists and doctors will answer your questions. Their site also provides general information on topics such as proper use and storage of medicines. You may view their site at **www.fishel.co.cr**. Fishhel doesn't give very good discounts. You can find the price of most medicines by accessing their site at:**www.fischel.co.cr/Default.asp?Usu=Anonimo.**

Farmacia Sucre and **Farmacia Catedral** are other large pharmacy chains in the Central Valley.

MEDICINA (800-633-4246). They offer 24-hour home delivery seven days a week and don't close for holidays. They have 14 locations and plan to open more. Contact them to find out about their discount programs.

A Costa Rican full-service pharmacy

Dental Care

Many tourists come to Costa Rica to have their cosmetic dental work done inexpensively. The quality of dental work in Costa Rica is equal to that found in Europe, Canada or the United States. On the average, dental work costs about 25 to 30 percent less than in the United States. Most dentists charge about $40 for an initial exam. The approximate costs of the most common cosmetic procedures are: wisdom tooth surgery $175, single root canal $150, new crown $250 to $500, implants start at around $750, fillings about $30 per tooth, and regular tooth extraction $40. If you have children, orthodontics are very affordable. Check prices with the dentist of your choice, since rates vary.

Costa Rican dentists offer the following services: implants, gum treatment, root canals, whitening, oral surgery, crowns, bridges and nitrous oxide sedation.

Orthodontics for children and adults are available and affordable in Costa Rica. The author's son had braces. The total cost for a two-year treatment is about $1,500 which can be paid in monthly installments of $50.

Here is what one expat remarked about dental costs here. " Braces for my 10-year-old ran about $1,000 .Other dental prices I've encountered to date:Teeth Cleaning - 15,000 *colones* ($27.27 USD) performed by the actual dentist not the assistant); White Cavity Fillings (composite); 13,000 *colones* ($23.60 USD) each-including painless local anesthesia where needed; Pre-orthodontics, Complete X-rays, Pictures and Full Dental Molds , 33,000 *colones* ($60.00 USD)."

One word of caution for foreigners, some Costa Rican dentists advertise in English-language publications and cater almost exclusively to foreigners. Patients will sometimes pay more for the dental services these doctors provide. It's a good idea to shop around and ask for recommendations. **The Costa Rican Surgeons and Dentists Association** (Tel/Fax: 2256-3100, E-mail: dentista@racsa.co.cr, www.colegiodentists.co.cr) will give you a list of dentists practicing in Costa Rica. Check with other residents for recommendations. Above all, be sure to find out if the dentist you are considering is practicing legally.

You may now combine a dental vacation with one of **Christopher Howard's Relocation/Retirement Tours**. Please see www.costaricabooks.com/travel for all details or call toll-free 800-365-2342.

Williams Dental **(English speaking)** Tel: (506) 2228-2914 E-mail: info@williamsdental.com www.williamsdentalcostarica.com	**Dr. Simon Mermelstein** (Pediatric dentist) Tel: (506) 2296-3546/2291-6778

Do Not Hesitate to ask Who's Who in Costa Rica

By Dr. John Williams

When trying to find a competent doctor, lawyer, dentist or other professional in Costa Rica, it's best to make sure you are in the right hands. Just because someone knows how to market their services, doesn't guarantee quality work or customer satisfaction.

When I started placing dental implants in my patients way back in 1982 my colleagues thought I was crazy! Very little information about the procedure had been published and dental schools offered no implant courses. Early ideas were exchanged only in whispers within the dental underground. By the early 1980s two pioneer implantologists, Dr. Linkow and Dr. Weiss, had made available insertable blades as a base structure to support prosthetic work. New companies emerged like Oratronics and supplied the new industry. Blades quickly became the method of choice. Dr. Babbush published his first book regarding implants in 1980. The American Academy of Implant Dentistry and The Alabama Implant Study group soon became major information sources. Dr. Branemark then published his studies on osseous integrated implants. This important system was slow to catch on due to its start-up costs.

My personal break-through came when visiting Dr. Lazzarra in Palm Beach who took time out of his practice to show this Costa Rican dentist all about his new system. The lights came on and I immediately adopted his superior methodology. Today Dr. Lazzarra heads Implant Innovation Inc.(3i), theworld's leading implant supplier organization. I subscribe to 3i due to their use of certified high grade titanium and state-of-the-art precision fittings. Their prescribed dental rehabilitation procedures are most reliable, fully functional, and esthetically beautiful.

Currently our team offers the implant patient highly qualified professional services ranging from oral surgery to an American-board certified periodontist and endodontist. I personally do the treatment planning, team coordination and the final prosthetic work. Starting very young, twenty years ago, in the implant field has given me great experience and sufficient knowledge to treat both the most complicated cases and the routine with great confidence. Our lab work is all done with certified high noble alloys and vita porcelain which are worked by an Italian artist of international repute.

To combine dental work, cosmetic surgery or a language study vacation with **Christopher Howard's Retirement Tour, go to www.liveincostarica.com/travel for all details or call toll-free 800-365-2342**.

Cosmetic Surgery

Costa Rica has long been the destination for those in search of the "Fountain of Youth." People from all over the world flock to Costa Rica for cosmetic surgery because prices are lower than in the United States for comparable procedures. Costa Rica's surgeons are among the world's best. Most of Costa Rica's plastic surgeons are trained in the United States or Europe. They keep up-to-date on new trends and methods in their field and attend professional seminars regularly. Rates for different operations vary from doctor to doctor. You can combine several procedures to reduce the price substantially. There are even package prices that combine surgery, hotel and hospitalization.

In general, prices average 25 to 60 percent less than in the United States, although the final cost is open to negotiation with the surgeon. The low cost of cosmetic surgery should not, however, be interpreted as a sacrifice of quality for affordability. The cost of a full-face lift is between $2,000 and $3,500 (add a few hundred dollars per day in the hospital to recuperate from the surgery); nose surgery about $2,000; liposuction $800 and $1,500; with a tummy tuck, $2,000 to $3,000, breast implant $2,500 to $3,500 and eyelid surgery between $800 to $1,500. Many doctors send their patients to special recovery houses for about $70 a day. Rates vary from surgeon to surgeon. I suggest you contact **Dr. Arnoldo Fournier** (please see the article in this section). He is among the best plastic surgeons in Costa Rica and will be more than happy to send a brochure and answer any of your questions. For information about travel arrangements or cosmetic surgery vacations see

Unique Costa Rica Tours at **www.costaricabooks.com/travel**. You may combine cosmetic surgery, dental work or language study vacation with Christopher Howard's Retirement Tour.

One quick word about cosmetic surgery in Costa Rica. There are a couple of doctors who advertise their services as cosmetic surgeons but have no specialized training in the field. Therefore to get the best results from your surgery, we suggest you do the following:

(1) Ask the U.S. Embassy for a list of certified plastic surgeons; (2) Check with the ***Colegio de Médicos*** (the local equivalent of the A.M.A.) to see if a particular doctor is trained as a plastic surgeon. All doctors in Costa Rica must be registered with the **Costa Rican Doctor's Association** or *Colegio de Médicos* (Tel:2 232-3433, Fax: 2 232-2406, E-mail: medicos@racsa.co.cr, www.medicos.sa.cr). Only registered plastic surgeons may advertise their services; (3) Ask a local family doctor for a recommendation for a good plastic surgeon. (4) Talk with former patients of the doctor of your

Plastic Surgery in Costa Rica

By Arnoldo Fournier M.D.

Within the American Continent, Costa Rican Cosmetic, Plastic and Reconstructive surgeons, has been recognized more and more for their natural post-surgical results.

Most of these surgeons, most likely, are fluent in more than two languages because they have earned the opportunity to study abroad for their post-medical graduate studies in cosmetic procedures.

For the last ten years, cosmetic tourism has increased significantly. One of the pioneers in this field is Arnoldo Fournier, M.D., F.A.C.S., Founder and Board Member of the Society of Plastic Surgeons in Costa Rica, Correspondent Member of the American Society of Plastic Surgeons, and the American Society for Aesthetic Plastic Surgery. "When I came back to Costa Rica (more than twenty years ago) from St. Luke Hospital in New York, I was told by a former Plastic Surgeon, that cosmetic procedures were not in demand by Costa Ricans."

As a result, this stubborn Surgeon decided that if he was not going to have Costa Rican clientele, he was going to look for a demand outside the borders of Costa Rica. He placed his first advertisement in the *Tico Times* (a national English language newspaper) offering his services for Cosmetic, Reconstructive and Plastic Surgery. As time went by, he also placed more advertisements in other well known magazines such as LACSA Magazine, Eastern Magazine, Skyword Magazine, Passages Magazine, etc. "I was the seventh Cosmetic Surgeon in the world to own a web site when the era of the internet began".

The majority of his patients come from overseas, especially from the United States. Cosmetic Surgery Vacations have become more and more attractive, due to the natural beauty of Costa Rica. Most people come to Costa Rica, and tour around for one week, and then have their procedures done. Others, simply come for their procedure, relax during their post surgical recovery, and do day tours to nearby volcanoes, National Parks, etc. Costa Rica's wonderful year round weather (75 ° F year round!), is an adequate place to recover. Its not too hot, and not too cold, and it has the humidity every skin desires.

The most attractive things about the Cosmetic Vacations, are their affordable costs, excellent quality surgery, and safety. "Within the U.S., you can find rates that vary from $10, 000 to $15,000. In Costa Rica, for the same procedures, I offer rates that are $3,000 and lower The Secretary of Health, annually supervises several public and private hospitals in Costa Rica. They all need to have the appropriate, updated equipment for the procedures performed at hospitals' operating rooms. There is a requirement for the patients receive their pre-surgical medical exam results prior any procedure, and antibiotics. The procedures are done with local anesthto esia and sedation to reduce the risk of general anesthesia. "This means, that the patients are given pills for sedation prior to and during the procedures, and intravenous medication that is given by an anesthesiologist". Therefore, the patients will not be aware or awake during the procedures.

Dr. Fournier leads a Surgery team that includes his assistant, anesthesiologist, and two certified nurses. Over time, more and more patients have called and written to him from around the world for his services. He is known for his personal care with every patient. "I do one to two procedures a day in the morning time. I perform all procedures myself". Dr. Fournier, says that he likes to work first thing in the morning because he feels fresh, clear and energetic for the procedures he performs. "It is better to do one or two procedures a day, than five to twenty supervised or half done. As a result, I can explain to the patient precisely was done in the operating room".

He personally answers all the emails and telephone calls he receives from his patients. He personally visits them in their hospital rooms, and accompanies them throughout their post-op period. Patients are asked to stay in San José for a few days at any recovery center after surgery. During this time, he sets up appointments in his office several times a week, and revises the recovery time for every patient.

Today, his best advertising is done by the "word of mouth". His former patients spread the news about the good things good things dome by Dr. Fournier who has "the hands of an surgeon, the eyes of an artist, and the heart of a Friend".

For more information you can visit his website at **www.drfournier.com**, E-mail at: **fournier@racsa.co.cr** , or call him at **011-506-2223-7314**.

To combine cosmetic surgery, dental work, or a language study vacation with **Christopher Howard's Retirement Tour** see **www.costaricabooks.com/travel** or call toll free **800 365-2342.**", says Dr. Fournier.

choice before you make a decision and find out if they are pleased with the results of their surgery (5) Just because some cosmetic surgeons advertise in English-language publications doesn't mean they offer the best quality or prices. Contact the Costa Rican Plastic Surgery Association (Tel: 2258-0396, Fax: 2257-9413, E-mail: drmacaya@msn.com) for additional information.

Health Tourism

Medical touris m has become a very lucrative field since medical tourists spend two or three times what a regular tourist does. The Costa Rican government has a multi-faceted plan to promote medical tourism here. More than 750,000 U.S. citizens traveled to Thailand, Mexico, Argentina and Costa Rica in 2008 to have medical procedures done at a lower price than at home. However, Costa Rica has the competitive advantage of geography, a stable economic and political system and an international reputation for the quality of its health care system.

In 2008 Costa Rica had almost 30,000 visitors for medical tourism. The most common procedures they had done were stomach bypass for weight reduction, plastic surgery, cosmetic dentistry like implants, joint replacement and eye surgery. In addition a few thousand tourists came from Europe and South America to have similarprocedures.

Presently, there are 45 million Americans without any type of health insurance. Furthermore, citizens in the United States, Canada, Europe, Australia and New Zealand are getting older and some 220 million will need major medical care by 2015. It is predicted that by 2010 six million North Americans will travel to other countries to receive medical attention Some of them will need joint replacements and heart operations they could never afford to pay out of their pockets. Costa Rica may be the solution for some of the people in this group because of lower medical costs.

Medical Tourism has become a very lucrative field since medical tourists spend two or three times what a regular tourist does.

Only two hospitals now, Hospital Clinica Biblica in San José and Hospital CIMA in Escazú, are certified with the international division of Joint Commission Resources. More than 220 public and private health care organizations in 33 countries have been accredited by this organization, which basically sets the standards in international health care. Other health organizations are in the process of seeking accreditation, including Hospital Clinica Católica. Officials also promised to work with insurance companies elsewhere, principally in the United States, so that their customers would be covered for health treatment here. In addition, the government said it would approach large employers in the United States to interest them in sending employees here for health treatment.

Health care in Costa Rica is about a quarter of what it would in the United States because of less administrative costs and a generally lower cost of living and salaries. The *Instituto Costarricense de Turismo* expects that by next year, the income from treating foreign patients will approach $100 million annually.

Here are some examples of people who came to Costa Rica from the United States for medical procedures. Jane Doe came to Costa Rica and had a face lift, liposuction and tummy tuck. The total bill was $10,000, less that what she would have paidback home.

John Doe, 62 years old, had a total hip replacement. The cost was $20,000. In the U.S. The same procedure is approximately $60,000. Doe said, "My operation lasted six hours and before and after they made me feel like a real person and not just a number."

A number of recovery centers have sprouted up here where people can recuperate from their different surgeries in Costa Rica. The cost can be as low as $100 per day. Even with air travel, surgery and the recovery center, the cost of these procedures is much more affordable than in the U.S. Or Europe. Most of the recovery centers offer a whole gamut of tours for their guests, so they can explore Costa Rica's many natural wonders while they recover.

Approximate Costs:

Bariatric surgery	U.S. $30,000-$60,000	Costa Rica less than $10,000
Knee replacement surgery	U.S. $12,000	Costa Rica around $4,500
Hip replacement	U.S. $50,000 to $60,000	Costa Rica $20,000 to $25,000
Breast Implant	U.S. $5,000 to $7,000	Costa Rica $2,500
Rhinoplasty (Nose Job)	U.S. $5,700	Costa Rica from $2,000
Face lift	U.S. $10,000 to $20,000	Costa Rica from $3,000
Liposculpture	U.S. $5,000	Costa Rica from $3,000
Cataract	U.S. $4,000	Costa Rica from $2,200
Crown for a tooth	U.S. $800 to $1,600	Costa Rica from $350

To find a good surgeon check out the following websites
Clínica Bíblica
Clínica Católica
Hospital Cima
Www.medicaltourismco.com
Www.18000mysurgeon.com
Www.abilitymagazine.com
Medretreat.com

Ophtalmology

Costa Rica has excellent ophthalmologists. Lasik Surgery costs $800 to $1200. Johan Fernández runs the Oftalmología Laser Center (2258-3031 or 2522-1000 ext. 2430) or see www.OftalmologiaLaserCenter.com. His email is: JFernandezJ@ClinicaBiblica.com. He has an English- speaking staff. His office is located in the Torre Médica Omega, Clínica Bíblica, 8th floor in downtown San José. See the Yellow Pages for more "*Oftamólogos.*"

Care for the Elderly

Although the Costa Rican government funds homes for the elderly, foreigners are probably better off in a private facility. Full-service custodial health care is available in Costa Rica for the elderly at a very low cost. Care for less independent senior citizens is about $1,500per month. **Retirement Centers International** offers comprehensive medical care and assistance that includes all medicines, lab work, dental care, physical therapy, rehabilitation and special diets.

Villa Alegría (Tel:2433-8590 or 2372-1244, E-mail: info@ costaricanursinghomes .com, www.costaricanursinghomes.com) is a full-service facility for the elderly. The staff has more than 15 years of experience is specializes in elderly illnesses such as Parkinson and Alzheimer's. This makes Villa Alegría a unique facility in Costa Rica. Love and dedication are the main ingredients that inspire this group of professional caregivers.

These programs are some of Central America's best and are considerably less expensive than in the United States. However, if these facilities are beyond an elderly person's means, a full-time, live-in domestic worker can be hired as a nurse for a couple of hundred dollars monthly. In addition to caring for an elderly person this worker can manage other household chores.

For private home nursing, contact **SISCA** Tel: 8394-4804 or 8341-2131. **Homewatch Caregivers** also provides personal assistance for adults, Tel:2201-5265, info@hwcentralamerica.com or www.homewatchcaregiverscr.com.

Physicians

*Once again, to find a good physician or specialist talk to other retirees, look in the Yellow Pages under ***MEDICOS*** or look for doctors' ads in *The Tico Times*. Below are the names of some English speaking physicians. There are more doctors listed in Chapter 14 of this guide.

Dr. Daniel Alfaro — Rheumatologist/Internal Medicine
Tel: 2208-1511
E-mail: dalfaro@hospitalcima.com

Dr. Mauricio Buitrago — Ears, Nose and Throat
Clínica Bíblica
Tel: 2257-2121
E-mail: mbuitrago@clinicabiblica.com

Dr. Arieh Grunhaus Z. - Urologist
(English-speaking and excellent)
Hospital Cima
Tel: 2208-1716 Fax: 2208-1736
E-mail: agrunhaus@hospitalcima.com

Dr. Harry Hidalgo — Dermatologist
San Pedro
Tel: 2280-9292
E-mail: hidalgoh@racsa.co.cr

Dr. Stephen Kogel—Physician/Psychiatrist
A U.S.-born doctor who has helped many American clients with alcohol and drug problems.
Tel: 2224-6176

Dr. John Longworth, M.D.— Family Medicine
(English-speaking, excellent doctor with a good bedside manner)
Clínica Bíblica
Tel:2 221-3922 or 2221-3064

Dr. Oscar Oeding Bermúdez - Orthopedic Surgeon
Clínica Bíblica
Tel: 2522-1000 Ext. 2306 Fax: 2223-7678
E-mail: ooeding@clinicabibilica.com

Dr. William Pérez Matínez - Gastroenterologist
Clínica Bíblica
Tel: 2248-0930
E-mail: wperez@clinicabiblica.com

Dr. Manuel Trimiño Vásquez—Physician/Psychiatrist
He has many clients from the United States and is bilingual. He has helped many foreigners adjust to living in Costa Rica.
Tel: 221-6140 or 2233-3333

For names of more doctors and dentists, see the section in the back of this book titled " More Phone Numbers." Also there is a publication called *Guía Integral de la Salud* that lists hundreds of health- related services including doctors, laboratories, hospitals and clinics.

Alternative Healing

Costa Rica has more than a hundred acupunturists, chiropractors, homeopathic doctors, therapeutic massage specialists and natural health practitioners. Check *The Tico Times*, talk to other foreigners, health-food-stores, the Yellow Pages.

Taxes

You will have many tax advantages in Costa Rica. Investors pay no capital gains tax on real estate investments. Interest-bearing bank accounts are also tax -free. The maximum Costa Rican tax rate is around 30 percent with no city or state taxes and low property taxes. There is no personal income tax on a salary of less than $750 monthly. Self-employed people can earn up to $3000 a year without paying taxes. The most a corporation has to pay in taxes is 30 percent on an income of more than $100,000 (tax percentage is applied to net income after all expenses). However, it is easy to form a Costa Rican "offshore" corporation, or ***Sociedad Anónima***, to shelter earnings and pay significantly fewer tax. There are also many write offs to lessenthe tax burden. Tax information is available in Spanish from a government website: **www.hacienda.go.cr**.

Briefly, a *Sociedad Anónima* is an anonymous corporation anyone, even tourists, can set up without their names appearing on any rthat ecords. The initials S.A. will appear after a corporation's name instead of Inc.. A Costa Rican corporation is similar to its U.S. counterpart in having a board of directors, shareholders and shares that can be bought and sold freely. You control all the stock in the corporation but your identity remains unknown. This practice is illegal in the United States but not in Costa Rica. Thus you are able to maintain some degree of secrecy in financial matters and protect yourself from minor tax problems.

Each corporation has a set of six legal books in which changes may be made. Many corporations never even use their books because they never engage in any commercial activity, they exist only to hold vehicles or real estate and other investments.

These offshore corporations are used in most business transactions in Costa Rica and abroad. Because they are foreign corporations they are not subject to U.S. taxes. Furthermore, Costa Rican corporations pay only minimal taxes in Costa Rica, or none at all.

There are additional benefits to establishing an "offshore" corporation. If you put your property in your corporation's name, it is easier to transfer title. All one has to do is exchange the company's stocks. This way your assets can be transferred or sold by simply giving your shares to the new owner or vice versa. Owning one of these corporations entitles you to start a business and open a checking account in the company's name, even though you are not a legal resident or citizen. If you have relatives on the board of directors of your company, there will be no probate taxes in the event of your death. It is almost impossible to find out whose name appears in the public records since ownership is confidential. Furthermore, if you get involved in any serious litigation, it will be difficult to sue you directly. You will be protected against most judgments and liens. This affords your assets greater protection. If you are a non-resident foreigner, you must have one of these corporations to own a business.

Contact your attorney if you are seriously thinking about forming one of these anonymous corporations. Your lawyer can explain how they work and their advantages and disadvantages. The fee for starting one of these corporations is usually between $300 and $1,000. It will usually take a few months to finish all of the paperwork, depending on how fast your lawyer works.

In order to form a corporation, your attorney will have to make sure there are no other corporations with the same name as your company. The name of your company will have to be in Spanish, not English. Your corporation must have a minimum number of shareholders. It also must have a board of directors, consisting of a president, secretary and treasurer—all of whom have the option of being shareholders. The final steps are preparing a set of books, registering your company, establishing a charter and advertising the charter in the local newspaper.

Be forewarned: Many individuals have lost large amounts of money and property by not understanding fully how the corporate structure works, and therefore have been defrauded by their lawyer or other persons (often foreigners). Please contact Ryan Piercy at 2221-2053 to obtain an appointment if you wish to better understand this structure.

Costa Rica's bank secrecy is not "foolproof." This is especially true since the September 11, 2001 terrorist incident in the United States. If you attempt to use your corporation for fraudulent purposes, you are asking for big trouble. Fortunately the IRS usually will not go after you unless you are a "big fish" who has done something obvious to attract their attention. This rarely happens, since the country's banks are not very cooperative with U.S. authorities in such matters. Furthermore, the U.S. also has to obtain the authorization of a Costa Rican judge, which is difficult.

If you desire better protection for your assets or business, form a Panamanian corporation. Many savvy investors put their Costa Rica corporation in a Panamanian corporation. This way they are guaranteed maximum protection of their assets. Since I do not know all of the nuances of setting up one of these corporations, I suggest you contact one of the companies listed at the end of the next section.

Foreign income is exempt from taxation in Costa Rica. You will have to pay taxes on income earned in Costa Rica. *La Tributación Directa,* the local equivalent of the IRS, is in charge of collecting taxes, but is far less efficient.

However, if you go into business in Costa Rica and form a tax-sheltered corporation, many of your expenses can be written off. You will pay an income tax on your company's earnings during the prior fiscal year, or *año económico* which runs from October through September 30. Corporations are taxed only on the income earned within Costa Rica. Every company needs to file form D110 in March. If your corporation owns property, there are property taxes to be paid. Corporations that are inactive pay a small tax.

You must report all income earned in Costa Rica. All net income is subject to taxation. Current taxes for salaried employees run from about zero to 15 percent on a monthly income above $900. Taxes for the self-employed range from zero to $3,000 annually to 25 percent above $15,000 annually. Small companies pay from 10 percent to 30 percent depending on their profits. Though it must be declared, bank interest is tax free to the depositor (therefore deducted as non-taxable income), as the rate offered at the bank is net interest.

Due to the need for more revenue, the government has cracked down on individuals and businesses that attempt to evade their fiscal responsibilities. With the help of the U.S. Internal Revenue Service, Costa Rica is getting better at collecting taxes. Under the new tax law, evaders are now subject to big fines, interest, penalties and possible prison terms. Don't panic! A good accountant or tax lawyer can help you minimize your taxes and avoid problems later on.

Also, unlike some other places, a foreign retiree is not required to pay Costa Rican taxes on his external income (income generated abroad), so you can see why Costa Rica is considered a tax-haven by many people.

There is a yearly municipal property tax of 0.25% on your land or home and a sales tax of 13 percent paid for goods and service. In addition to paying your property taxes at the municipality, you may also pay them at the Banco Nacional. If you have an account at the Banco Nacional and use Internet banking, you can see what you owe in property taxes by typing in the *cédula* number of the owner of the property or corporation. Then go pay in person and be sure to get a receipt and save it, in case the municipality has a dispute.

U.S. Citizen's Tax Responsibility

U.S. citizens are subject to income tax wherever theylive. You must file your U.S. income tax return yearly through the U.S. E mbassy. If you have your full time residence abroad for a full calendar year, or live abroad for 330 days out of any consecutive 12 month period, you can exclude up to $91,500 of earned income from U.S. Income Taxation for 2009 and lesser amounts in earlier years. If you are married, and both of you earn income and reside and work abroad, you can also exclude up to another $91,500 of your spouses income from taxation.

This exclusion does not apply to passive income such as interest, dividends, capital gains or overseas pensions. It only applies to a foreign earned income. You must reside outside of the United States for at least 330 days a year or be a legal resident of a foreign country to qualify for this exemption. Your primary business must also be located abroad to qualify for the foreign-earned income exemption.

Fortunately, if you live outside the United States you qualify for a two-month extension and may wait to file your taxes until June 15. However, if you mail your return from outside the United States, it is best to mail your return at least two weeks before the due date. You can speed this up by using DHL, FedEx or UPS. You need to use a U.S. tax form 2555 to apply for this extension. Even if you earn no income in Costa Rica, it is imperative to file a standard 1040 tax form to avoid problems. The biggest mistake made by individuals is assuming that since their income is under the exclusionary amount, they do not have to file a return. Payment of taxes, interest and penalties can now be done by credit card by dialing **1-888-2PAY-TAX**.

If you have any tax questions, contact the U.S. Embassy or the IRS. Call either the Consular Section of the U.S. Embassy (2220-3939) or the nearest IRS office in Mexico City at (525) 211-0042, ext. 3557. You may consult the IRS Web sites at www.irs.gov or www.irs.gov/faqs/faq13.html.

There is also a book titled *The Expats Guide to U.S. Taxes.* It may be purchased through www.amazon.com. Another good resource is found at www.filetax.com/expat.html.

If you need help with your tax forms and returns while living in Costa Rica, contact U.S. Tax and Accounting288-2201, E-mail: ustax@lawyer.com for income tax assistance or for help with IRS problems.

Don D. Nelson, Attorney at Law and CPA, specializes in expatriate tax services. You may call him toll-free (866) 712-0320 or E-mail him at: don@taxmeless.com. You may view his website at www.taxmeless.com.

If Canadians want to be exempt from income taxes in Canada they need to have severed major residency ties for at least two years. These "residency

Living in Costa Rica and U.S. Taxation

By Randall J. Linder E.A.

For U.S. citizens living in a foreign country, there is little or no relief in income tax filing requirements. Often we are faced with new requirements, new situations, and given wrong advice from fellow citizens.

As a professional U.S. Income Tax preparer specializing in U.S. citizens living in a foreign country, I have personally provided answers to some of the most frequently asked questions.

Now that I am living in Costa Rica, do I need to file a U.S. income tax? Most U.S. citizens must file an annual income tax return on their worldwide income. As a general rule, if you were living in the U.S., and thought you needed to file a return there, you should probably file one here. It is better to file than not.

My only income is from a Costa Rica company and I pay taxes in Costa Rica. Do I have to include this income on my U.S. tax return? U.S. citizens must include worldwide income on their tax returns. This income could qualify for the foreign earned income exclusion, but the exclusion in not automatic. You must include the income on your tax return and then exclude it by using the IRS form 2555. If you do not meet the requirements for the exclusion, then the tax you paid in Costa Rica could be taken as foreign tax credit.

I live in Costa Rica and work for a U.S. Company Does this income qualify for the foreign earned income tax exclusion? If you meet the other requirements for the foreign earned income exclusion, the wages you receive from your U.S. employer can also be excluded. Your employer is still required to withhold Social Security and Medicare from your wages.

I have my own business in Costa Rica and work as a self-employed person. My business is not incorporated. Does this income qualify for the foreign earned income exclusion? Yes. This income can qualify for the exclusion just as if you were working for a U.S. employer. Caution: The exclusion is for federal income tax only. You will still be required to pay self-employment tax (Social Security and Medicare taxes) on your profits.

I have dividends from a Costa Rican company. Are the dividends "foreign earned income" and do they qualify for exclusion? No The foreign earned income exclusion does not apply to income such as interest, dividends, capital gains, pensions, annuities or gambling.

The exclusion applies strictly to earned income. Note: If you own

10% or more of a foreign corporation, you are required to file with your individual income tax return IRS form 5471.

I receive interest from my Costa Rican bank account, Do I have to report this interest on my U.S. income tax return? ? Yes, U.S. citizens must include in their income monies received worldwide. This includes interest and dividend income. In addition, if the aggregate value of your foreign accounts is greater than $10,000 at any time during the year, A Report of Foreign Bank and Financial Accounts must be reported to the U.S. Treasury Department.

I transferred money from the U.S. to Costa Rica, Is there anything special that I need to do? If a U.S. citizen has a financial interest in, or signature authority over any financial accounts, including bank, securities or other types of financial accounts in a foreign country, and if the aggregate value of these accounts exceeds $10,000 at ant time during the year, the accounts must be reported the the U.S. Department of the Treasury.

Last year I got married to a Costa Rican citizen. Can I file a joint return with my spouse who is not a U.S. citizen? Yes, but in doing so, *you make* the choice of reporting your income and your spouse's income worldwide.

My Costa Rican wife has a child from a previous marriage. The child is living with us. Can I claim the child as a dependent on my tax return? To be claimed as a dependent, the dependent must be a U.S. citizen or a resident of the U.S., or in certain cases a legally adopted child of a U.S. citizen.

I have been living in Costa Rica for years and have not filed a tax return. What Should I do? It is to your advantage to seek professional help to determine whether or not you need to file.

My business is incorporated as a Costa Rican S.A. (*sociedad anónima*). Currently it is not making a profit, and I am not receiving a paycheck. Does this have to be included in my tax return? Yes. if you own 10% or more of a foreign corporation, you are required to file with your individual income tax return IRS form 5471 (Information Return of U.S. Persons With Respect to Certain Foreign Corporations). This includes inactive S.A.'s and corporations not making a profit.

* **Courtesy of Randall Linder, U.S. Tax & Accounting Service, Tel: 011-506-2288-2201, Cell: 011-506-8839-9970, Fax: 011-506-2288-0120, e-mail: ustax@lawyer.com. http://www.ustaxinternational.com**

ties" can include an unleased house, Canadian health coverage, automobile registration, spouse or child support in Canada, banking or investment ties. Canadians will have to contact **Revenue Canada** concerning their tax obligations while living abroad.

A foreign tax credit is often available for taxpayers who pay tax in another country, i.e. Costa Rica. To find out your tax status, consult form IT221R3 on the Canadian Customs and Revenue Agency Web site: www.ccraedrc.gc.ca. Canadian tax returns should be in by April 30. Self-employed people have until June 15.

A word of caution

Proposed U.S. legislation to restrict the use of so-called tax shelters would invoke the Patriot Act to punish firms that are deemed to be impeding U.S. tax enforcement.

The legislation would also would uncooperative foreign banks the authority to issue credit cards that would be valid in the United States. The use of the Patriot Act now is reserved for institutions that are active money launderers.

In addition, U.S. citizens who deposit money or receive a benefit from a private foreign corporation would be considered to have control of that firm for U.S. tax purposes. Under current law U.S. citizens who hold a foreign bank account that accumulates more than $10,000 at any time in the year have to file paperwork with the U.S. Internal Revenue Service. The legislation would expand that requirement to all foreign bank accounts located in one of 34 countries identified as a tax haven.

The legislation would have wide impact in Costa Rica because many expats here own corporations. Some are involved in businesses but others are used to hold the ownership of real estate or automobiles. Even a U.S. citizen with a minor interest in a corporation could become involved in reporting and tax requirements under the proposal because the bill presumes that the person owned and exercised control over such entity, regardless of the paper ownership.

In other words, the U.S. citizen would have to provide clear and convincing evidence to the contrary if he or she really did not operate the corporation.

Costa Rica is one of those countries.

Panamanian (Offshore) Corporations an Added Advantage

Offshore corporations enable you to act as an international citizen with complete confidentiality, privacy and safety. Offshore corporations can legally open offshore bank accounts, brokerage accounts, hold credit cards, own property, stocks etc., and in many cases completely exempt you from any tax reporting requirements and with complete confidentiality.

Why Panama?

For many years Panama has been recognized worldwide as a major international offshore banking center that offers very attractive legal and tax incentives to Panamanian corporations. For example, Panamanian law allows Panamanian corporations to issue "bearer" stock certificates. This means the owners who control the corporation do not have to be named in any public record, since ownership is through physical possession of the "bearer" shares. Panamanian corporations are not subject to Panamanian tax on income earned outside of Panama. Also, Panama allows you to name your corporation with an English name. This gives you many advantages when using your Panamanian Corporation in English speaking countries. These are just a few of the more important reasons why Panamanian corporations are so popular.

Forming a Panamanian Corporation:

First, it is best to select a name in English followed by: Corp., Corporation Inc. or Incorporated. You cannot use the words Bank, Trust, Foundation or Insurance in the name of your corporation. You may use any name as long as it is not being currently in use in Panama. If you own a U.S. corporation, you may find some advantages in using the same name for your Panamanian corporation, if it is available. This would allow you to have identically named offshore and onshore bank accounts as well as other similar advantages.

Panamanian corporations are typically formed with nominee directors, president, secretary and treasurer. These are Panamanian citizens who are modestly paid office workers. If you wish, you may select your own directors and officers. However, the original directors and officers selected are registered with the Panamanian public registry, and this public information becomes available to anyone who inquires. Therefore, if you wish confidentiality, I recommend that you select the nominee director option. Officers and directors can always be changed later.

Panamanian law allows corporate shares to be issued in "bearer" form. This means that whoever physically possesses the shares, owns the company. This allows for total confidentiality of ownership, since the person who physically possesses the shares is not identified in any public or even private record. Having a Panamanian corporation with "bearer" shares also makes transfer of ownership completely private and not a matter of public record, since transfer of ownership is a simple process of physically transferring the "bearer" shares to a new owner, which is similar to passing a $20 bill to someone versus writing them a check. This feature makes it very easy to sell or transfer properties confidentially by simply transferring the "bearer" shares and ownership of the Panamanian corporation. Thus you may avoid many forms of taxes and closing costs because title to the property remains in the name of the Panamanian corporation. Essentially you are simply selling the corporation that owns the property.

Your Panamanian Corporation comes with a notarized General Power of Attorney (in English) signed by two officers named in the articles of incorporation. This power of attorney provides a blank space for you to fill in the name of any person you want to act as the legal agent of the corporation with the authority to open and sign on corporate bank accounts, enter into contracts for the corporation, sign and transfer assets for the corporation, etc. Although you fill in your name or another person's name as having power of attorney, this is not evidence of ownership.

The person named is simply an agent, similar to an employee empowered to act for the corporation. You may order as many additional Power of Attorney forms as you wish.

As you can see there is a world market for Panamanian corporations because they are extremely popular. Older Panamanian corporations with established bank accounts sell for thousands of dollars or more. Selling your Panamanian corporation is simply a matter of physically transferring the "bearer" stock certificate together with the other corporate records to the new owner.

The one-time cost for setting up a simple Panamanian Corporation is about $1600. You will have to pay an annual Registered Agent and Director's fee of $595 yearly, due one month before the anniversary date of the corporation.

For help in forming a Panamanian corporation or foundation, we highly recommend **Roberto I. Guardia**. A number of Americans we interviewed speak very well of him. You can contact him at: Tel: (507) 263-3917, Fax: (507) 263-3924 Cel: 612-5429 **E-mail: rig@orcag.com**, **http://www.panamavirtualofficecorp.com/Panama_legal_services.htm.**

Insurance

The Instituto Nacional de Seguros, or INS, is a state-run insurance company that controls all insurance in Costa Rica. They will handle all of your insurance needs. INS has a new English section on their website at **www.ins-cr.com** or **www.ins.go.cr**.

All insurance is less expensive in Costa Rica than in the United States. Auto, fire and theft insurance will cost less than half the U.S. premiums. All vehicles in Costa Rica have Obligatory Insurance or *Seguro Obligatorio*, which comes automatically with your vehicle registration. It is renewed every December when you pay your car's road tax (*marchamo*). This insurance gives you a small amount of personal liability coverage, which is the type that protects you if you hurt, kill or maim another person when you are driving your car.

About 65 percent of cars have only the obligatory insurance which is not really complete coverage. If you want real coverage you must buy a supplementary policy. For an additional cost, supplemental insurance policies provide broader coverage than the basic compulsory policy. Your car's value determines the price of your premium. These supplemental policies are paid in full every six months. They cannot be paid in monthly premiums as in the United States. Also, as in the States, premiums are increased when you have an accident. However, these increases are not as big as in the United States. It doesn't matter if an accident was your fault or not.

When considering coverage, remember the general rule of thumb: Insure against everything you would find yourself hard-pressed to overcome financially. The essential coverages are A and C; if you don't get those, INS won't sell you any of the others. For coverage F or H, you must also have D. (By the way, coverages B and G have never existed). Rates are determined by the vehicle's and applicant's characteristics.

Here is a breakdown of the basic automobile coverages in Costa Rica:

(A) **PERSONAL LIABILITY** — Covers liability established by the courts as a result of death or injury caused by an accident for which the driver of your vehicle was guilty. The benefits are paid once the Obligatory Insurance is used up and does not cover injury or death of family members or employees of the policyholder or driver.

(C) PROPERTY DAMAGE — Covers damage to property (car, house, etc.) belonging to other people if the accident was the fault of the driver of your vehicle. Excludes items being transported by your vehicle.

(D) COLLISION — In case of collision with another vehicle, persons, or property belonging to someone else, this policy pays for damage sustained by your vehicle: (1) if the accident was not the fault of your driver, or (2) if the accident was not the fault of your driver but the other vehicle has no insurance and the owner cannot pay.

(E) **FIRE** — Covers damage to your vehicle caused by fire due to either internal factors such as short circuit, or to external factors such as lightning, or if the place where the vehicle is parked burns.

(F) **THEFT** — Covers total theft of the vehicle or loss derived from the total theft. If it is not recovered, policy pays for damage and/or missing parts. If not recovered within a month, the insured amount is paid or the vehicle is replaced.

(H) **ADDITIONAL RISKS** — Covers damage resulting from overturning, running off the road, vandalism, floods, hurricanes, quakes, explosions, collisions with birds, falling objects, accidents within parking lots or private property, riots, etc.

OTHER CONSIDERATIONS

- **Insured values** — Cars should be insured at their market value in Costa Rica, and it is up to the policy applicant to determine it. To determine values of vehicles, it is sometimes best to use the newspaper classified ads. Only you can change the value on your policy; INS will not automatically reduce the insured values on vehicles as they depreciate.
- **Renewals** — Auto insurance is normally for six months, after which you have a grace period of 10 working days to pay for renewal. After that, you have to apply for new insurance or reinstatement.
- **Coverage outside of Costa Rica** — For cars with Costa Rican registration, coverage extends to all of Central America and Panama.
- **Deductibles** — All coverages except "A" have standard deductibles. "A" has no deductible. Double deductible if the driver is under 22, in cases of vandalism, birds or accidents on private property.
- **Alcohol** — Policies will not pay for accidents to vehicles being driven by people under the influence of alcohol or drugs, even if the condition did not cause the accident. An alcohol count of 50 mg or more in 100 cc of blood will invalidate insurance coverage, except for liability coverages A and C.
- **Roadside Assistance** — This comes free for vehicles less than 15 years old that have coverage "D". Call 800-800-7000(toll-free) if you have a flat tire, dead battery, are out of gas, or need a tow truck.

- **Special Notes for Tourists**— When you bring a car into Costa Rica, you will be given a permit to drive the car into the country. The permit is usually for three months, renewable once. For issuance of the permit you must state who is going to drive the car— they allow the owner and one other person, usually one's spouse. If you don't have Costa Rican plates on your automobile, you can't cover it against collision or theft. All other coverages are available under these circumstances. However, in most cases, after 180 days you can get Costa Rican plates when you pay the corresponding taxes on your vehicle.

(I) **HOMEOWNERS INSURANCE**—A homeowners insurance policy is called *Hogar Comprensivo* in Spanish. It protects your home against fire and natural disaster. The home fire policy has four sub-coverages: "A" is for fire and lightning; "B" covers damage caused by strikes, vandalism, hurricane, cyclone, explosion, smoke, falling objects and vehicles; "C" pays for damage caused by floods and landslides; "D" covers natural disasters: earthquakes, tremors, volcanoes, etc. You can take coverage A by itself, A+B, A+CD or complete coverage A+B+CD. Rates are based on a percentage of the value of the building and include a 13 percent tax and an inflationary factor whereby there is a small yearly increase. Depreciation is also factored in at a rate of one to two percent yearly.

If you have one of these policies you have to insure your house's contents as well as the house itself. You have to submit a complete list of household effects with the value of each item, and the respective brand name, model and serial number. If you want to insure the contents of your home, you must put a value on the objects based on depreciated value. The same rate for the house applies to the contents. You should have your house appraised so you can carry enough coverage.

Some people doubt whether INS would be able to settle claims from a major earthquake or hurricane. INS is by far the largest insurance company in Central America. In fact, INS is one of the largest insurance companies in Latin America, is financially solid and most importantly, it re-insures worldwide a large percentage of the risk.

I have already mentioned the affordability of medical insurance in Costa Rica in the section titled "Medical Care." Because not everyone's insurance needs are the same and because laws and coverages work differently in Costa Rica, we suggest you consult your attorney or the English-speaking insurance agent, Dave Garrett, we have listed below.

Latin American Coverage S.A.
They work closely with the Association of Residents of Costa Rica and have many retirees and other foreigners as clients.
Franklin Martinez
Tel: 2258-7041 / Cel: 8318-2255
Email: fmartinez.1@laccr.com
Web site: www.laccr.com

Garrett y Asociados
SJO 450
Miami, FL 33102-5216
Tel: 2233-2455 / Fax: 2222-0007
E-mail: info@segurosgarrett.com www.segurosgarrett.com

4

Making Money in Costa Rica

Investing in Costa Rica

Why invest in Costa Rica?

A study by the *Miami Herald* rated Costa Rica the 27th safest country for investment of 140 countries surveyed. Another study of Latin American Security conducted by FTI Consulting on behalf of the *Latin American Business Journal*, indicates Costa Rica is the safest place in Central and South America for business executives and multi-national companies to do business. If you are not impressed by Costa Rica's ranking, consider that the United States was ranked only 22nd. Another study found Costa Rica to be the least corrupt country in Latin America.

Costa Rica has been ranked 32nd of 104 countries in the third edition of the Legatum Prosperity Index. The country ranks higher than any other Latin American country. Uruguay, the next highest, is thirty-third.

In addition, U.S. business magazine *Fortune* ranked San José Latin America's fifth best city in which to do business and placed it within the 25 best cities in the world. According to the report, *Fortune* considered the city's ability to create opportunity for its residents, its business climate and how well it can satisfy the business needs of companies that invest here. San José ranked tops in the quality of its labor force, its business environment and the lifestyle it offers resident executives and investors.

According to the magazine *Foreign Direct Investment* (FDI) Costa Rica is the second best place to invest in the region which comprises Central America and the Caribbean. Said publication focuses specifically on foreign investment. Only Puerto Rica tops Costa Rica in an area that consists of 31 nations.

In order to rank the countries in this region the magazine studied each country's economic potential, human resources, cost efficiency, quality of life, infrastructure, business climate and strategy for attracting investors.

San José ranked tops in the quality of its labor force, its business environment and the lifestyle it offers companies who provide tourism services

Studies like this one should make individuals and retirees feel comfortable about investing in Costa Rica.

Here are more reasons why you should consider investing in Costa Rica:

* Year-round spring-like weather in the Central Valley
* Untarnished international image. How often do you hear bad things in the news about Costa Rica? Only good news!
* Latin America's oldest democracy
* No army and NO terrorism. Costa Rica has NO enemies.
* Excellent health care at a fraction of the price you pay at home
* Good real estate investments. Costa Rica is considered one of the world's best emerging real estate markets. Many properties are in locations with breathtaking views
* More American residents proportionately than any country in the world
* A tightly-knit expatriate community
* Time-tested organizations in place to help you with everything you need to know to make the move from A to Z
* Excellent quality of life
* Good communications with high-speed internet in many areas
* Tax savings
* Opportunities for entrepreneurs of all ages
* Affordable utilities
* Friendly people
* Many people who speak English
* Hundreds of activities to stay busy and happy
* A nature lover's Disneyland

Costa Rica is the Most Stable Country in Latin America

A World Bank study released in May aims to provide a "set of governance indicators that can help de-politicize efforts to track the quality of institutions, support capacity building, improve governance and address corruption."

The index, which analyzed 209 countries between 1996 and 2004, focuses on six components of good governance: political, civil and human rights; political stability and violence; government effectiveness; the incidence of unfriendly market policies; rule of law; and control of corruption.

"On average the quality of governance around the world has remained stagnant, highlighting the urgent need for more determined progress in this area in order to accelerate poverty reduction," said the World Bank.

The percentile ranks below indicate the percentage of countries worldwide that rank below the selected country. For example, 83 percent of countries studied worldwide have less political stability than Costa Rica, meaning that according to this study, it is the most stable country in Latin America.

Country	Percentile
Costa Rica	83.0
Chile	76.7
Uruguay	62.1
Panama	55.3
Dominican Republic	48.1
Mexico	43.7
Brazil	43.7
Nicaragua	43.7
El Salvador	39.8
Argentina	38.3
Bolivia	28.6
Peru	27.2
Honduras	26.7
Paraguay	25.7
Ecuador	23.3
Guatemala	21.8
Venezuela	13.6
Colombia	5.8

Costa Rica Number One in Latin America in Economic Freedom

Costa Rica and Chile are tied for first in the area of Economic freedom in Latin America. Hong Kong offers the most economic freedom in the world with Costa Rica and Chile in nineteenth place. One hundred twenty-seven countries were studied in the survey.

Factors such as the flexibility of the labor force, monetary regulation and more were studied in order to determine a country's ranking.

Other Countries in the region:

Country	**Ranking**
Costa Rica	19
Chile	19
Panamá	24
El Salvador	29
Uruguay	44
Guatemala	53
Perú	38
Honduras	59
Bolivia	59
Mexico	59
Paraguay	65
Dominican Republic	68
Nicaragua	68
Ecuador	86
Brazil	86
Haití	86
Argentina	92
Colombia	101
Venezuela	120

* Affordable hired help
* The beauty of the country
* Fantastic beaches and warm water
* Latin America's #1 tourist destination according to *Travel Weekly Magazine*
* Many American products and services available
* Fruits and vegetables all year
* Good public transportation
* Any many more intangibles

Areas of investments

Let us review a few of the reasons why Costa Rica has such magnetism for qualified foreign investors. First, and perhaps most important, is the enduring political stability. As you already know, Costa Rica has had a strong, democratic government without interruption since the 1940s and an excellent centralized banking system. The trend towards an open economy and possible trade pacts with such nations as the United States and Mexico are conducive to investment in Costa Rica. Privatization of many state-run institutions will undoubtedly help economic growth in the future. There are also no government expropriations or interference, unlike in many Latin American countries.

Costa Rica is easily accessible from all parts of the world by land, sea or air. Outstanding phone and Internet systems link Costa Rica internationally to other parts of the world. Also, investors in Costa Rica have equal rights and laws to protect them. Regulations for conducting business in Costa Rica are the same for both local and foreign corporations. Both can fully own and control local corporations, as well as real estate without any access limitations or restrictions. Many opportunities await foreigners who start new businesses previously nonexistent in Costa Rica. In addition, the cost of labor is low.

Asset Protection, Tax Advantages and Incentives

Additional reasons for investing in Costa Rica are: asset protection (creditors, judgments, liens, bankruptcy and divorce), privacy from individuals and governments and fewer taxes (income tax, inheritance tax, estate taxes and probate fees).

Many attractive incentives are available to foreigners investing in Costa Rica. Investments of $50,000 or more in an approved project qualify the investor for legal residency. However, it is not necessary to become a resident to own or manage a business. Anyone who owns a business can import some

Costa Rica: Bright Outlook

Costa Rica's economic outlook is bright, thanks to an attractive environment for business, a new pro-trade government and a planned free trade agreement with the United States. (Courtesy of *Latin Business Chronicle*)

During the 1980s, when Central America was dominated by political violence and armed conflicts, Costa Rica provided an oasis of peaceful stability and was often referred to as "the Switzerland of Central America." While the area subsequently has returned to normalcy, Costa Rica remains an attractive destination not only in Central America, but also compared with the rest of Latin America.

Foreign investors emphasize the country's democratic system as one of the key benefits of Costa Rica. The Central American nation is only one of three countries in Latin America with a perfect score in terms of political and civil rights, according to Freedom House (the others are Chile and Uruguay).

"It's a long-standing democracy," was among the first things Peter Cardinal said when asked about the advantages of doing business in Costa Rica. Cardinal is the executive vice president for Latin America for Canada-based Scotiabank, which acquired Costa Rica's largest bank, Interfin, in July of 2006.

Jose Antonio Rios, international president for Global Crossing, also emphasizes the democratic credentials of Costa Rica. "It's a very democratic country that also calls for stability of institutions in the longterm," he says. "The way they have handled that has been incredible." Global Crossing last month announced plans to extend its core network to Costa Rica.

ATTRACTIVE BUSINESS CLIMATE

But Costa Rica wouldn't be garnering all that attention from investors if a strong democracy were the only thing it could offer. "They have a clear and aggressive tax benefit program for companies that invest there," says Rui da Costa, managing director for Latin America and the Caribbean for U.S. computer giant HP, which employs almost 1,800 people in the country, making it home to its largest number of employees in Latin America. "They have a very updated infrastructure in terms of telecommunications, very good level of education - in terms of tech skills and also in terms of language. And it's also a more secure area. There's not as much violence as other places."

Thanks to high penetration rates of Internet, PC and wireless and fixed telecommunications, Costa Rica ranks second in Latin America in technology level, according to the Latin Business Index published by *Latin Business Chronicle*. Costa Rica has a fixed line telephony rate of 31.6 percent, and a PC penetration rate of 23.9 percent - both the highest in Latin America, while its Internet penetration rate of 23.5 percent is the second-highest in the region, according to 2004 data from the ITU (the latest available).

Costa Rica has one of the highest education levels in Latin America and ranks fourth in the region on the latest UN Human Development Index, which measures the adult literacy rate and combined gross enrollment ratio for primary, secondary and tertiary schools as well as health conditions and purchasing power. And Costa Rican capital San Jose is among the three safest cities in Latin America, according to a ranking published in the pan-regional business magazine *America Economia* recently.

In terms of competitiveness, Costa Rica ranks third in Latin America (behind Chile and Argentina), according to the 2006 Latin America Competitiveness Review from the World Economic Forum, while it also came in third (behind Panama and the Dominican Republic) on the Latin American Globalization Index published by *Latin Business Chronicle*.

ECONOMIC FREEDOM

And Costa Rica's economy is among the freest in Latin America. It came in third on the 2006 Heritage Foundation/*Wall Street Journal* survey of economic freedom in the world. Costa Rica shared the third place with Uruguay and was only beaten by Chile and El Salvador. Finally, Costa Rica also ranked third on the FTAA Readiness Indicator developed by the Institute for International Economics in 2001. The indicator measures how prepared Latin American countries are for the Free Trade Area of the Americas (FTAA).

As a result of its high scores in business, political and economic environment, Costa Rica came in third on the Latin Business Index (behind Chile and Mexico).

Apart from investors like Scotiabank, Global Crossing and HP, Costa Rica has attracted significant investment from US-based chip giant Intel, which employs 2,200 people and has become the top exporter. Intel operates two micro chip factories and a distribution center at Heredia, 19 kilometers (12 miles) west of San Jose.

"Costa Rica was originally selected for its export-oriented infrastructure, reliable power and advanced telecommunications, as well as its talented and educated workforce, high literacy rate (95.5 percent) and supportive business environment," Intel says on its web site.

The chip giant, which has operated in Costa Rica since 1998, also chose the Central American country over other candidates such as Mexico due to lower corruption, according to Intel officials. Costa Rica is the third-most transparent country in Latin America, way ahead of countries like Mexico and Brazil, according to Transparency International.

MOTOROLA AND MICROSOFT

Other key investors in Costa Rica include Microsoft, Motorola and pharmaceuticals like Baxter International Inc. and Boston Scientific. "It's very open to investment [and] open to people," Rios says.

Costa Rica is one of the leading tourism destinations in Latin America. In 2004, the number of visitors to the country reached 1.4 million, an increase of 17.3 percent from 2003, according to the World Tourism Organization (UNWTO). While it ranked eighth in the region in terms of visitors, it came in fifth in terms of receipts: $1.3 billion.

And Costa Rica can also boast a significant expat community of both retirees and current workers, which in turn is helping drive demand for real estate. "On the plane down there, you see a lot of people not just visiting for meetings, but living there or visiting people living there," Rios says. "There are now direct flights from [and to] the West Coast of Costa Rica and not just from capital San Jose."

WAITING FOR CAFTA

There is now much anticipation surrounding the implementation of a free trade agreement with the United States. Costa Rica was one of five Central American countries that signed the Central American Free Trade Agreement (CAFTA) with the United States in May 2004, but is the only one that has yet to ratify it. (El Salvador, Honduras and Nicaragua have implemented it, while implementation is pending in Guatemala. The Dominican Republic signed the pact later and is also awaiting implementation.)

Pacheco delayed sending CAFTA to the local legislature for approval until October last year. And there has been strong opposition to the pact from local unions and other interest groups. However, Arias has made the ratification one of his top priorities.

"The president is committed to going into the CAFTA with the US," Cardinal says.

Arias, who narrowly won the presidential election in February, named Marco Vinicio Ruiz as commerce minister. Ruiz was a business leader who led Costa Rican private sector efforts to support CAFTA. In a meeting with US investors at the Council of the Americas last year Arias pledged support for open markets and private investment.

At the same time, Costa Rica will benefit from a free trade agreement between Central America and the European Union. Negotiations for such a pact were announced in Vienna in May, although talks will likely take some time and result in implementation after 2008, some experts predict.

Costa Rica's total trade grew by 13.4 percent last year to $20.1 billion, according to the United Nations Economic Commission for Latin America and the Caribbean (ECLAC). Exports increased by 13.3 percent to $9.7 billion, while imports grew by 13.4 percent to $10.4 billion.

KEY US PARTNER

Trade with the United States grew by 5.6 percent last year to $7.0 billion, according to US Census Bureau data. That was the strongest growth of any Central American country except Nicaragua. Exports to the United States grew by 2.5 percent to $3.4 billion, while imports from the United States increased by 8.8 percent to $3.6 billion. The United States is Costa Rica's top trading partner and Costa Rica is the top US trading partner in Central America.

Meanwhile, trade with the European Union grew by 0.7 percent to 3.8 billion euro (approximately $4.7 billion). Costa Rican exports to the EU fell by 1.1 percent to 3.0 billion euro, but imports from the EU grew by 8.0 percent to 809 million euro, according to Eurostat.

This year, total trade is expected to grow even stronger than last year. Exports during the first five months were up 17.4 percent compared with the same period last year, according to Costa Rican data quoted by Bear Stearns. Top export items were microchips, bananas and textiles.

This year, GDP growth is picking up. In April, the economy grew by 6.3 percent and growth of more than 5 percent during each of the first four months of the year has taken the 12-month rate of expansion through April to 5.5 percent, its highest level since July 2004.

items used to operate it and get a tax break on some of the usual duties. Contact the incentive section of the **Costa Rican Tourism Institute (ICT)** for more information about incentive programs.

Tourism and Related Ventures

Costa Rica's strategic location, political stability and adventure tourism, have all contributed to increase tourism development. Tourism is now the leading industry in Costa Rica. Numerous opportunities exist in this field. However, sometimes there can be a lot of red tape and competition. Small hotels and bed-and-breakfasts were good investments a few years ago, but there may be a surplus of them now. I have a good friend who refurbished an old building and turned it into a small hotel in the 1990s. He has done very well only because he has been in the country for a while, knows all the ropes, and was a pioneer in the field.

Bank Investments

Foreigners can invest with Costa Rica's nationalized banking system or private banks. Interest rates are higher than in the United States and there are many attractive savings accounts and time deposit programs from which to choose. Presently there is no tax on interest from bank accounts. However, when investing in *colón* accounts, you have to figure in yearly inflation to see if you are really getting a good deal. There are some degrees of bank secrecy, liberal money transfer regulations, and favorable tax laws for foreigners (see the section in Chapter 3 entitled "Taxes").

Costa Rica's Stock Market

Foreigners can also invest in the local stock exchange (**Bolsa Nacional de Valores**) to get better returns than from traditional financial systems. The stock market presents a safe investment alternative with great opportunities for the investment to grow through stock appreciation, dividends, stock splits, mergers and acquisitions.

Costa Rica has the largest stock exchange in Central America. Approximately 29 firms or *puestos de bolsa* are registered with the National Stock Exchange. Costa Rican stockbrokers can study economic trends and give you advice on investing in government bonds, real estate, time deposits and other investments.

The Costa Rican Stock Exchange is regulated by the National Securities Commission or *Superintendencia Nacional de Valores de Costa Rica*

(SUGEVAL), which is the counterpart of the U.S. Securities and Exchange Commission. They can give you information about the reliability of firms and brokers. There exists a strong possibility that the local exchange will be linked with other Latin American trade blocks in the very near future.

Here is one local investor's take on the Costa Rican stock market. "This market was virtually non-existent in Costa Rica just a few years ago. At this time there are only five publicly traded companies in Costa Rica, the most liquid of which is FIFCO, the beverage company that makes Imperial beer and the Tropical drinks. Other companies include Atlas Electric and Durman Esquivel. The local stock indexes have done quite well over the past year with almost a 100 percent return.

You may be thinking "OK, it isn't perfect, but higher risk means higher reward!" Not always. As a guy that likes to speculate now and then, I can tell you that a vital component of a good market is liquidity. There are few instruments here with good liquidity, so *caveat emptor*!

Right now there are few products which offer a good return for the risk level. On top of that, commissions can be quite high, and sometimes the broker will try to ask for a cut of your earnings when you sell. For example if you made a 10 percent return (which is way above average for Costa Rica) your broker may say "Hey, nice return. How about 8 percent for you and 2 percent for me". I have never heard of such a thing elsewhere! If your broker tries this, find another broker.

More and more local investors are looking to international markets outside of Costa Rica to avoid the problems locally, but all is not lost with Costa Rican markets. I know that the exchange and the regulators are working hard on new ideas and new projects to improve regulation, liquidity, and diversity."

For more information about the Costa Rican stock market, contact **Grupo Busátil Aldesa** at 1-888-5-ALDESA (United States only) or 2223-1022, or E-mail: grupo@aldesa.com. Investors can find additional information about the local stock market at www.capitales.com.

You may also invest profitably in blue-chip, offshore mutual funds. Most people do this to protect their assets from creditors, judgments, liens, bankruptcy, malpractice claims, divorce and separation claims, liability claims not covered by insurance and seizure by the U.S. government.

AmCham's Guide to Investing and Doing Business in Costa Rica is another source of information for the potential investor. It is available through the **Costa Rican-American Chamber of Commerce**, or **AMCHAM**. The Chamber of Commerce also publishes a monthly magazine entitled *Business in Costa Rica* that has advice on how to invest in Costa Rica.

Before investing or starting a business, you should take the time to do your homework. Under no circumstances should you invest right off the plane, that is to say, on your first trip to Costa Rica. Unscrupulous individuals and scamsters prey on buyers throughout the world. Be wary of any salespeople who try to pressure you into investing. Remember, it is hard to start a business in your own home country; don't imagine it will be any easier in Costa Rica, where both language and customs are different. The **Better Business Bureau of Costa Rica** will help you find reliable businesses and services.

I also suggest you ask a lot of questions and get information and assistance from any of the organizations listed below in order to thoroughly understand the business climate of the country. However, don't depend on the help of these organizations. You'll have to garner a lot of information and learn on your own by some trial and error. This way you can find out what works best for your particular situation.

Costa Rican-American Chamber of Commerce of Costa Rica: (AMCHAM)

Address in Costa Rica:
P.O. Box 4946-1000
San José, Costa Rica
Address in United States:
Amcham SJO 1576
P.O. Box 025216
Miami, FL 33102-5216
Tel: 2220-2200
Fax: 2220-233-0969
E-mail: chamber@amcham.co.cr

Coalition for Investment Initiatives-(CINDE)
P.O. Box 7170
San José, Costa Rica
Tel: 2220-0036
Fax: 2220-4750
E-mail: aheilbron@cinde.or.cr

Export Promotion Center (CENPRO)
P.O. Box 5418
San José, Costa Rica
Tel: 0i1-(506) 2220-0066
Fax: 011-(506) 2223-5722

The Costa Rican Stock Exchange (Bolsa de Valores)
Bolsa Nacional de Valores
P.O. Box 1756
San José, Costa Rica

Tel: 2222-8011
Fax: 2255-0531

National Securities Commission
P.O. Box 10058
San José, Costa Rica
Tel: 2233-2840;
Fax: 2233-0969

Canada Costa Rica Chamber of Commerce
Tel: 2257-4466

Investment opportunities according to risk

(1) **Certificates of Deposit** in dollars through a state-run bank pay about 2 percent annually. That amount dropped from over 4 percent because of the financial crisis in the U.S. **Advantage:** Your money is insured by the Costa Rican government and earns tax-free interest.

(2) **Real Estate Advantage:** If purchased at the right place and in the right location, you are assured your property will double or triple over the next 10 years. Some beach areas such as the Central and Southern Pacific are good investments if you look for value and don't pay overinflated prices. Real Estate In vestment Trusts are also a good bet. **Disadvantages:** Overpaying or purchasing in a bad location can hurt your investment. See the section in Chapter 3 and this chapter about investing in Costa Rican real estate.

(3) **Certificates of Deposit** in *colones* (local currency) from a government bank. **Advantage:** Pay annually and are insured. **Disadvantage:** If there is a huge fluctuation, your principal and interest will be worth less than when you invested.

(4) **Personal Loans on Secured Property** in dollars or colones. **Advantage:** Can earn up to 3 percent monthly in *colones* and hold a note on the property. **Disadvantage:** If the borrower defaults, you might have to go to court to recover your property.

(5) **Certificate of Deposit** from a private bank in an offshore account. **Advantage:** You can earn a little more interest than through the state-run banks and investment is tax-free. **Disadvantage:** Your money will

not be insured. Several private banks offer these types of investments. It is best to visit different banks and shop around for the best interest rate.

(6) **Starting a Foreign-Based Internet Business**. **Advantages:** You don't have to depend on the small local economy. Dependence is on a larger market. You have a low U.S. tax liability if you use a Costa Rican or Panamanian corporation. An example of this would be an export or Internet-based business. **Disadvantage:** Not doing your homework and choosing the wrong business.

(7) **Starting a Local-Based Business. Advantages:** There are a lot of opportunities for entrepreneurs here. It is highly advisable to have prior experience in the venture you undertake. You should do a thorough feasibility study. **Disadvantages:** Not understanding the local economy, not doing your homework and thinking that what works abroad will work here. On average, only three out of 10 foreigners succeed here for a variety of reasons including a lack of disposable income by the locals. There is a section in this chapter with details and advice about going into business in Costa Rica, including success stories and failures.

(8) **Offshore Mutual Funds. Advantages:** All the wonderful benefits of investing offshore with the peace of mind of knowing your assets are held safe and secure with a major New York Stock Exchange firm. By moving liquid assets offshore, you achieve substantial protection from illegitimate creditors and financial predators and limit your tax liability. **Disadvantages:** Although mutual funds have more built-in safeguards than regular stocks, they are still subject to fluctuations in the market.

Finding work

Foreigners can only work when they are legal residents, and depending on the type of residency they have. They don't need a work permit. The only exception to this rule is when you can do a job a Costa Rican is unqualified to do. In this case, you can obtain a work permit (see Chapter 6). However, jobs that will qualify you for a work permit are very scarce. If you do obtain a work permit, it must be renewed annually. *Pensionados*, *rentistas* and foreigners without permanent residency may only own a company, invest or start a business. If you have questions about work permits, contact a lawyer or Costa Rican Immigration.

I have some discouraging news for those living on small pensions and hoping to supplement their income with a part- or full-time job or for others who need to work just to keep busy. Finding work can be difficult, but it

A Sample of Jobs for English Speakers

Rawlings
RAWLINGS DE COSTA RICA S.A.

A Baseball and Apparel Company in Turrialba
Is looking for:

1. **Manufacturing and production supervisor for the baseball area**
- Four years university degree in Industrial Engineering
- Bilingual (100% Spanish-English)
- Have full command of MS Office applications
- Be proactive, fast learner, team player, and quality oriented
- Be willing to live in Turrialba

2. **Supervisor de Planta de producción para el área textil**
- Mínimo cinco años de experiencia en puestos similares en el área textil
- Facilidad para trabajar en equipo
- Conocimientos en el uso de diferentes máquinas industriales de coser.
- Experiencia en la elaboración y construcción de muestras de prendas.
- Conocimiento en telas, hilos y materiales necesarios en la confección de prendas.
- Disponibilidad de vivir en Turrialba.

The company offers a competitive salary, excellent working environment and the necessary training will be given.

Los interesados enviar su oferta de servicios a sgomez@rawlings.com especificando el puesto al que aplican.

BROKERS
First Year Income
$90 To $100 K
For the Right Individual

IF YOU HAVE A BURNING DESIRE TO SUCCEED, AND ARE A SELF-STARTER, WITH FULL UNDERSTANDING AND PERFECT PRONUNCIATION OF THE ENGLISH LANGUAGE. WE WANT TO TALK TO YOU TODAY!

Company Offers:
-Paid Training
-No Cold Calls
-Top Industry Pay
-Fresh Leads

E-mail resume in English to: Kathia@wellingtoncr.com or fax your resume in English to (506) 291-7074
On your response, please specify BROKERS

WESTERN UNION

Exciting opportunity to join a multinational industry leader appointed to provide a fast and reliable money transfer service all over the world. We have a challenging job for a:

GENERAL DIRECTOR OF CONTACT CENTER OPERATIONS

This position has the responsibility of leading a Contact Center team of 600+ employees in areas related to Customer Service. The candidate will be actively involved in defining strategies for the business by providing decision, support and analysis to the ... performance improvement to ensure ... lationships with internal and external ...

... nagerial role in a Call Center environ- ... ills to manage talent in a proper way, ... der to adapt to business needs, and ... ship skills. MBA with an International ... nguage is highly desirable.

... s package and the opportunity to work ...

... icating your salary expectations, to the ... ternunion.com

WE ARE SEEKING CANDIDATES FOR OUR
Global Procurement Organization

Project Leader

- Professional in Industrial Engineering, Business Administration or any other administrative-related career. MBA is a plus.
- Experience required 4-6 years in financial analysis, process controls, quality ...

aplicor

a U.S.-based commercial software company is now hiring full-time professionals!

Senior Software Developers

- 5+ years professional software development experience
- 2+ years full-time experience programming using .NET
- Technologies: ASP .NET, Dynamic HTML, JavaScript, Ajax, Multi-Tiered Architectures, Patterns, SQL, OLAP, Reporting
- Good spoken and written English is required

We are seeking self-directed professionals with deep technical expertise interested in creating enterprise-grade commercial software solutions.

We offer an **excellent work environment, stability, regular schedule, and extremely competitive salaries, paid in US Dollars.**

Please visit our web site at http://www.aplicor.com and submit a letter of interest and your current resume (in English, please) to: hr@aplicor.com

We Are Hiring Now Experienced Sales Executives
We are an established International company with offices worldwide

- **Excellent base monthly salary $1.500/$2.000 plus daily bonuses, weekly team bonuses daily prizes and monthly commissions.**

Requirements:
- Experience in Call Center Sales Environment (Sportsbook, Sykes, ITS)
- Exceeding monthly sales team quotas
- Excellent verbal and written English skills (100% Fluent)
- Strong computer, customer data entry & Internet skills

To apply, please send us your resume in ENGLISH Attn: HR/Director of Human Resources

Villas Sol
Hotel & Beach Resort

IS LOOKING FOR STAFF TO FILL SEVERAL POSITIONS

Would you like to work at the Beach in Guanacaste?
This is a once in a lifetime opportunity

Requirements
- Over 19 years old
- Full English
- Excellent personal grooming
- Great communication skills

We offer
- Excellent compensation
- Opportunity to grow
- Training
- Great working environment

IF YOU ARE INTERESTED
Please APPLY IN PERSON from 8 a.m. to 5 p.m., Monday 28 and Tuesday 29, at the office of Villas Sol, 400 m north the Centro Colón.

Grow with us!
FUJITSU

TECHNICAL SUPPORT REPRESENTATIVES (SCHEDULE FLEXIBILITY REQUIRED)
Provide professional technical assistance to customers.

CUSTOMER SERVICE REPRESENTATIVES (SCHEDULE FLEXIBILITY REQUIRED)
Provide accurate information and assistance to customers.

CALL CENTER MOD (Manager on Duty) (SCHEDULE FLEXIBILITY REQUIRED)
Previous experience as Call Center MOD - Real Time monitoring is a must.

We offer:
- Paid training
- Competitive compensation in US dollars
- Bonus opportunity
- Transportation
- Employee-focused work environment
- Professional development
- Advancement opportunity
- Asociación Solidarista

Qualified candidates, PLEASE EMAIL TO: CAREERSCR@US.FUJITSU.COM PLEASE INDICATE POSITION YOU A... IN THE SUBJECT. One page resume.

Fujitsu Consulting, a $45 billion global technology leader, is expanding its services in Costa Rica. We seek talented, enthusiastic, candidates for several key positions.

All positions require:
- Full bilingual skills with 100% English fluency.
- Proficient in Internet and Microsoft Office tools.
- Customer service and call center experience a plus.
- Ability to work in a fast-paced, high growth environment.

Fujitsu - The possibili...

International Sales Professionals

U.S. PEACE CORPS IS LOOKING FOR A

SAFETY AND SECURITY COORDINATOR

Responsible for supporting the Country Director and Senior Staff to insure the safety and security of Peace Corps Volunteers and Trainees in Costa Rica in compliance with the guidelines.

Qualifications
- B.S., B.A. or equivalent college or professional training
- Fully bilingual in Spanish/English.
- Strong computer skills, especially using Windows, Excel, Word, and database software.
- Experience in conducting training sessions.
- Strong written and verbal communication, office organization and information processing skills.
- Ability to analyze situations of potential risk and develop contingency plans.
- Highly developed interpersonal skills, willingness to travel country wide when required, team player, professional attitude and individual commitment to excellence.
- Valid driver's license.

Also Desirable: Knowledge or experience in emergency response and/or safety and security issues. Bicultural experience.

Interested applicants may obtain a full position description and instructions for applying by sending an e-mail inquiry to:

PCTrabajo@cr.peacecorps.gov
Deadline for application: **4:30 p.m. - Monday, February 27, 2006**

doris peters

Our client, a global company in the automotive leather industry with facilities throughout the Americas, Europe, Asia and South Africa is currently looking for :

GLOBAL LOGISTICS MANAGER

- The successful candidate will have a minimum of a Bachelor's Degree and 5 years experience in overall logistics management, working for a global organization in a truly global capacity.
- The individual should have experience in dealing with **Purchasing, Product Planning, Customer Service and Sales Departments in a Demand-Based, Just-In-Time** Manufacturing environment, and should be **experienced in freight negotiations with freight forwarders, airlines and steamship companies.**
- The individual must be a hands-on, detail-oriented, self-starter with the ability to communicate verbally and in writing with all levels of management.
- English proficiency and excellent computer skills a must.

For immediate consideration please send resume to:

DORIS PETERS & ASOCIADOS, S.A.
Oficentro Centauro, 3er piso, oficina 7, Guadalupe
E-mail: doris.rodriguez@dorispeters.com

American Company is seeking for:
ACCOUNTANT
- 3 years experience minimum
- Full experience in the whole Accounting Cycle
- Knowledge in Quickbooks Software or similar Accounting Systems

If you fulfill 100% of these requi...

QUALFON

Multinational company located in Costa Rica is looking for

Bilingual Customer Service Representatives

Requirements:
- 100% English conversational skills: comprehensive, oral, written and reading areas.
- Computer literate.
- Customer service experience preferable.
- Availability to work 6 days a week, weekends and holidays.
- Updated ID documents.

We offer:
- Positive working atmosphere.
- Job stability.
- Growth opportunities within the company.
- Social guarantees.
- Cafeteria / Transportation.

Language Institute
needs:
English Teachers
For Greater Metropolitan Area
We Offer:
Competitive salaries
Training opportunities
Pleasant working conditions
We requires:
Full command of English
Costa Rican or resident
Telephone: 281-1818

is not impossible. In the first place, it is not easy for a Costa Rican, not to mention foreigners who do not speak fluent Spanish, to find permanent work.

If you are one of the few foreigners who have mastered Spanish, you will probably have a fair chance of finding work in tourism or some other related field. However, your best bet may be to find employment with a North American firm doing business in Costa Rica. The best-paying jobs are with multinational corporations. It is best to contact one of these companies before moving to Costa Rica. Depending on your qualifications, you may be able to find a job as a salesperson, an executive or a representative.

When local companies hire foreigners, they are generally looking for a solid educational background and an entrepreneurial spirit that some companies find lacking in Costa Ricans. It helps to have a degree, preferably an MBA, from a well-known U.S. university.

Even if you speak little or no Spanish, you have a chance of finding work as an English teacher at a language institute in San José. Do not expect to earn more than a survival salary from one of these jobs because the minimum wage in Costa Rica is low. Working as a full-time language instructor will not bring you more than a few hundred dollars monthly.

As supplemental income or busywork, this is fine, but you won't make a living on a par with the kind of lifestyle to which you are probably accustomed. If you can find work at a private bilingual school, you can earn more than $1000 a month. The competition for these jobs is very stiff; preference is given to bilingual Costa Ricans and most foreigners hang on to these coveted positions.

There is some work available for English speakers in the sportsbook industry. However, some sportsbooks may be forced to move to other countries because of a change in regulation here.

Try putting one of your skills to use by providing some service to the large expatriate community in Costa Rica. Most people have a talent or specialty they can offer. For example, if you are a writer, journalist or have experience in advertising, you might look for work at one of Costa Rica's two English-language newspapers. Unfortunately, if you are a retired professional such as a doctor, dentist or lawyer, you cannot practice in Costa Rica because of certain restrictions, but you can offer your services as a consultant to other foreigners and retirees.

As if finding work were not hard enough in Costa Rica, a work permit or residency is required before foreigners can work legally. Labor laws are very strict and the government does not want foreigners taking jobs away from Costa Ricans. In theory, companies are not allowed to have more than 10 percent foreign labor. It is actually much lower in practice. You are only allowed to work if you can perform specialized work that a Costa Rican cannot do. However, many foreigners work for under-the-table pay without a work permit.

What brings younger people to Costa Rica?

By Jacqueline Passey

Costa Rica is not just for retirees! Younger folk move to Costa Rica too. Younger folk move to Costa Rica for many of the same reasons older people do – the climate, the natural beauty, the lower cost of living, the culture and lifestyle, or to start a new life somewhere new. However, they usually move here without as many assets as older people possess and thus are not ready to retire or invest a substantial amount in a local business. So most come here as students, volunteers, teachers, employees of multinational companies, freelancers or self-employed businesspeople, with their parents, or as spouses of *Ticos.*

Many younger people who visit Costa Rica as tourists, students, or volunteers like the country so much that they want to stay. One of the easiest legal ways to do this is to teach English or teach in an international school. Although it doesn't pay very well (frequently not enough to pay off debts or save for a house or retirement in their home countries) many people find it to be enough to live on here, and teachers with more qualifications (degrees, teaching certificates, experience) make a lot more and have more job opportunities than less qualified teachers.

Globalization and the internet are bringing more and more multinational businesses to Costa Rica. Many companies have set up customer support offices in Costa Rica employing a mix of English-speaking *Ticos* and foreign consultants. In particular, the internet gambling industry (online sports books, casinos, and poker rooms) employs many foreigners as consultants, managers, specialists, etc.

The internet is also making it possible for many freelancers and self-employed people to move here as well. Writers, artists, graphic designers, webmasters, computer programmers, internet marketers, professional gamblers and other knowledge workers can now work and sell their services online from anywhere in the world and many of them choose to do it here. They find that self-employment or freelancing via the internet is a great way to make money at North American rates while only spending it at Costa Rican rates, often allowing them to save money or support themselves with only part time work. Family and romance also brings younger people to Costa Rica. Many children, teens, and young adults tag along when their parents move to Costa Rica for retirement or business. Also, with so many travelers to and from Costa Rica there are many opportunities for international romance.

As you can see, there are many opportunities to live in Costa Rica even if you're not ready to retire yet!

Some of the fortunate who have found work here complain about contract discrepancies like getting paid the full amount offered during the interview, getting paid in *colones* and not dollars, payment delays, unannounced, gradual salary cutbacks, not recognizing college degrees from the States (English teachers who have master's degrees or Ph.D.s do not get better salaries or positions in language schools unless they have mastered Spanish as well), crazy work ethics, no political correctness or professionalism and other issues that can rub foreign employees the wrong way.

If you do not seek remuneration, you can always find volunteer work to keep yourself busy. Volunteer work is legal, so you will not need a work permit or run the risk of being deported for working illegally.

Check out **www.supereconomicos.com** and the Sunday classified job ads in *La Nación* for possible jobs. You will see some firms are seeking English speakers for sales, call centers and sportsbooks.

Starting a business

Of 115 countries, Costa Rica came in first in Latin America and ninth in the world with respect to nations offering the greatest commercial freedom and protection for private business, according to Freedom and Development, a Chilean research institute.

As a foreigner, you can invest in Costa Rica and even start your own business with only a few restrictions.

If you plan to go into business here, it is very important to be aware of the local consumer market in order to succeed. Most of the country's purchasing power is located in the Central Valley. A total of 75 percent of the country's population resides in the central provinces of San José, Alajuela, Heredia and Cartago. About 60 percent of the population is under 30 years old. Intelligent businesspeople will try to meet the needs of this group.

You may also think about targeting tourists and upper-class Costa Ricans. A wealth of opportunities is available in tourist-related businesses. Upper-class *ticos* have a lot of disposable income and the greatest purchasing power. They do not mind spending a little more on good quality products.Just look at their expensive designer clothing, their expensive imported automobiles and many palatial homes.

The majority of the country's middle-class consumer values are now more akin to their U.S. counterparts. You can see this starting to take hold with a number of shopping malls being built around the Central Valley and the popularity of stores such as Radio Shack and mega-warehouses like PriceSmart and the Latin American Walmart, Hipermás. Middle and upper lower class Costa Ricans seem to want all of the goodies so much that sales of cellular telephones soemthimes exceed the availability of cellular phone lines.

Success Stories in Costa Rica

By Christopher Howard

A Coffee Baron

Cafe Britt was founded by American Steve Aronson. Today the company has gone international with their many products. They grow, roast and sell some of the best "Mountain Grown" coffee in the world. They even make a coffee liqueur. Their coffee farm tour is one of the most entertaining half-days you will spend in Costa Rica. It takes place on a beautiful farm nestled in the verdant hills of Heredia. You will learn about the history of coffee, see how it is grown and purchase many interesting products in their gift shop at the conclusion of the tour.

A Service for Expats

About 15 years ago, Jim Fendell realized the need for a fast reliable mail service as an alternative to the regular Costa Rican mail system. Thus Aerocasillas was born. Today they offer similar services in Panama and several other countries in the region. See Chapter 9 for more details about the history of this company and the services they offer.

A Company that Protects Nature

In 1978 Michael Kaye founded the first whitewater tour company, Costa Rica Expeditions, when tourism was in its infancy. The company was started to help the sophisticated traveler explore Costa Rica - its flora and fauna, its people and culture, its wildlife and beautiful places. Their goal is to create unique travel experiences.

An American-Style School

Country Day School was started by American Woodson Brown around twenty years ago. The present campus is located in the hills of Escazú overlooking San José. You cannot beat the school's beautiful setting. The actual campus evolved from a few buildings into a huge complex which rivals any private U.S. school. The owner is a visionary who recognized the need for a first-rate U.S. type English-speaking school to cater to both the local and foreign population.

A Newspaper for Foreigners

Many years ago the late American journalist Richard Dyer founded *The Tico Times* newspaper. It has become Central America's leading independent weekly covering news, business, tourism, culture and developments in Costa Rica and Central America. The classified ad section is comprehensive, and there is now an on-line version of the paper. Fifteen thousand copies are printed weekly with some being shipped overseas.

Satellite TV

Reiny and Kathy have lived in Costa Rica for 14 years. After having visited 43 countries on a two-year trip around the world, they decided Costa Rica was the place to live. For years they ran a small restaurant in Jacó Beach. However, four years ago they started Sun Sat TV Services, a satellite dish company, which offers American TV programs to people living in Costa Rica. Now viewers can watch their favorite TV shows on NBC, CBS, ABC, FOX, ESPN, HBO and many more networks.

A Hotel Fit for a King

Three people run one of San Jose's most successful hotels. They spent a couple of years and a lot of money refurbishing the old building. Their hard work paid off. Today this downtown hotel boasts one of the highest occupancy rates in the country. It is a haven for fishermen, tourists, expatriates and many local characters. The bar on the first floor is the most successful operation in Central America. At night the place really heats up. The ladies of the night are the main draw and are solely responsible for the hotel's success.

A Place to Learn Languages

American David Kaufman is the founder of Conversa, Costa Rica's oldest and most successful language school. David earned a Masters Degree in linguistics and served in the Peace Corps in the Dominican Republic. At his school's two campuses, Spanish is taught to foreigners and English to Costa Ricans. Please see more about Conversa in Chapter 11.

A Real Estate Genius

Canadian Robert Shannon came to Costa Rica as a retiree about 20 years ago. He was very successful and was able to retire at an early age. After years of playing golf in and investing he became bored and decided to start a real estate and development business in Costa Rica. That is how **Costa Rica Retirement Vacation Properties** was born. The result is an highly innovative web-based company. Mr. Shannon has used his marketing skills to make his business one of the best in Costa Rica. He has also developed two projects between Jacó and Manuel Antonio on the Pacific Coast. Vistas de Manual Antonio is 200 acres and the other one is 900 acres. Both offer lots with stunning mountain and ocean views at affordable prices.

One group to target is the lucrative foreign-resident market. There are approximately 50,000 full-time foreigners living in Costa Rica. All you have to do is look for a product to fill their needs. Most yearn for hard -to-find-products from home and would rather buy them in Costa Rica than go to the United States to shop.

Costa Rica is ripe for innovative foreigners willing to take a risk and start businesses that have not previously existed. Start up costs for small businesses are less than in the United States or Canada. Many of the same types of businesses that have been successful in North America will work if researched correctly. There is definitely a need for these types of businesses. You just have to do your homework and explore the market. Be aware that not everything that works in the United States will work here. Also you may have to adapt your idea due to the vagaries of the local market and different purchasing power. Don't get any grandiose ideas since the country only has about 4.5 million people. You cannot expect to market products on a large scale as in North America.

Costa Rica's local artisans make scores of beautiful handcrafted products such as furniture, pottery and cloth. With so many choices, a smart person can find something to sell back home.

Real estate speculation can be lucrative if you have the know-how and capital. You could buy or sell small homes for middle-class Costa Ricans or foreigners. Here are other potential business opportunities worth exploring: an import-export business, desktop publishing, computer services and support, U.S. franchises, importing new foods, specialty bookstores, restaurants and bars, an auto body and paint shop, consulting or specialty shops catering to North Americans and upper-class Costa Ricans.

Costa Ricans love anything novel from North America. Many stores sell both new and used trendy U.S.-style clothing. Costa Rican teenagers dress like their counterparts in the United States and even watch MTV and VH1. U.S. fast-food restaurants such as Taco Bell, Burger King, Pizza Hut and McDonald's are extremely popular here.

Common business sense in Costa Rica

It is important to keep in mind that running a business in Costa Rica is not like managing a business in the United States because of unusual labor laws, the Costa Rican work ethic and the Costa Rican way of doing business.

In order for a foreigner to own a business, a Costa Rican corporation or *sociedad anónima* must be formed (see the section entitled "Taxes" in the last chapter).

If you do choose to establish your own business, keep in mind that you can be limited to managerial or supervisory duties and will have to hire Costa

Ricans to do the bulk of everyday work. Do a feasibility study. Spend at least a few months thoroughly analyzing its potential. Do not assume that what works in the United States will work in Costa Rica.

Check out restrictions and the tax situation. And, most importantly, choose a business in which you have prior experience. It's much more difficult to familiarize yourself with a new type of business in a foreign country.

Remember, a trustworthy partner or manager can mean the difference between success and failure. Make sure you choose a partner with local experience. Do not trust anyone until you know him or her and have seen them perform in the workplace.

You will be doomed to failure if you intend to be an absentee owner. I know of someone who founded an English-language book distribution business that initially did very well. However, the owner moved back to the United States and put a couple of employees in charge, everything eventually fell apart: sales began to lag, money went uncollected, checks began to bounce, expenses were unaccounted for and incompetent salespeople were hired. The potentially successful business just could not be run from abroad.

You have to stay on top of your business affairs. At times it is hard to find reliable labor, and the bureaucracy can be stifling. If you have a business with employees, be aware of your duties and responsibilities as an employer. To avoid problems, know what benefits you need to pay in addition to salary to avoid problems. Remember that the more employees you have, the more headaches.

In case things get rough, be sure you have enough money in reserve, in case of an emergency. You should have an ample reserve of capital to fall back on during the initial stage of your business.

Newcomers should not count on obtaining financing in Costa Rica for a new business. If you become a resident, you may be able to obtain some type of financing. Neophytes should learn not only the language but also the rules of the game.

One option is to buy an existing business from someone else. Intheory, this can save you lots of time and trouble, which means you can bypass most of the cumbersome start-up procedures and usually save a lot of time and energy.

While this is a definite advantage over starting a business from scratch, there is a downside. You can be taken advantage of by an unscrupulous seller trying to dump his problems on you. These problems may include unpaid back wages to employees, loss of a license or lease, or other legal problems that may not be apparent at first.

The best thing to do is to have a good lawyer check into the legal status of the proposed purchase and investigate potential problem areas. He can then tell you whether he thinks the business is feasible and if there is any

How I Came to Open a Language School

By David Hansen

The year was 1978 and I had just returned to the U.S. from an incredible junior year abroad in Madrid, Spain. I was looking for someone who spoke Spanish and wore high-heeled shoes. One particular morning in late September my roommate and I drove to American University and when we arrived for our 11am classes we looked at our watches and saw it was only 10am. We had no idea why we were there one hour early. We just couldn't figure it out. You never arrive an hour early for anything much less a morning class at the university. Since we had some time to kill we decided to go to the cafeteria for a cup of coffee. As soon as we walked in my roommate spotted, Zaida, his Costa Rican roommate from the previous year. We got talking and as they say, the rest is history. (She did wear high-heeled shoes back then.)

After coming to Costa Rica a couple of times on extended vacations in the early 80's I wanted to move down here. Zaida, my wife by then, didn't really want to go back home, been there done that. Also, living in DC was very exciting back then for a couple of 23-year-olds. However, the president of Costa Rica at that time threw out the IMF and the World Bank and the international credits dried up very quickly and the local economy went into a tail spin. Zaida's dad, who was one of the most exceptional people I have ever met, was a pilot and had a small, two plane air-taxi service that went down along with everything else in the economy. So at that point she was ready to come down and help out her parents for a couple of years in 1983 Well, we are still here.

I love it. We run the IPED language school in Heredia where we teach English to the Costa Ricans and Spanish to people from all over the world. It is the best of both worlds. I live in a great town where I know many of the locals and spend my days with really interesting people from Asia, Africa, Europe, North America and the Caribbean. They live with lovely Costa Rican families, study Spanish, go to some amazing nearby attractions like the Coffee Tour, the Waterfall Gardens, InBio Park, ZooAve or the Poas or Irazú Volcanoes during the week. In the afternoons their senses are delighted by the great dance classes and delicious cooking classes. At night they have dinner with their family and talk and practice Spanish with them and then study a little. If they still feel like it we go out to the great places around Heredia to meet the locals and go dancing or listen to music. On the weekends they go to all of the wonderful, beaches, volcanoes and rain forests around the country.

It is *Pura Vida* (Pure Life) in Costa Rica.

unwanted baggage. You will also need to have a good accountant do a complete inspection of the books and records, and perhaps even conduct a complete audit to make sure all taxes, wages and Social Security payments are up-to-date.

Any one of these items could cause untold headaches if not detected before you buy the business. Taking care of these matters is the best investment you could possibly make.

Talk to people, especially the "old-timers," who have been successful in business, and learn from them. Profit from their mistakes, experiences and wisdom. Do not rush into anything that seems too good to be true. Trust your intuition and gut feeling at all times. However, the best strategy and rule of thumb is, "Test before you invest."

Long-time Costa Rican resident, Mark, runs a successful travel bookstore in downtown San José.

Newcomers find themselves seduced by the country's beauty and friendly people and are often lured into business and investment opportunities that seem too good to be true, and often are.

When it comes to making money in Costa Rica, it has been said: "The best way to leave Costa Rica with a million dollars is to bring two." In the case of some foreigners, this statement is true. During the time we have lived in Costa Rica, we have seen many foreigners succeed and fail in business ventures. Only about three in 10 foreigners succeed in business in Costa Rica. There are few success stories and a lot of failures, in areas as diverse as bars, restaurants, car-painting shops, language schools, real estate, tourism, and bed-and- breakfasts to name a few. People have impossible dreams about what business will be like in Costa Rica. It is a gigantic mistake to assume that success comes easily here. Initially, starting any business usually takes more time and more money than originally thought. Also, many unforeseen problems are sure to arise.

If you decide to purchase an existing business, make sure it is not over-priced. Try to find out the owner's real motives for selling it. Make sure you are not buying a "white elephant." Ask to see the books and talk to clients if you can. To ferret out a good deal, look for someone who is desperate to sell his business. Check the newspapers and ask everyone you know if they know of someone selling a business. Finally, make sure there are no lawsuits, debts, unpaid creditors or liens against the business.

There are some benefits to investing in certain businesses in Costa Rica. As mention in Chapter 7, you can obtain Costa Rican residency by investing in tourism or a reforestation project. Also, part of your profits can be sheltered in your corporation.

Business tip: Dealing with people is always the best way to develop a business relationship here. All business in Costa Rica is based on friendship and mutually respectful behavior. In fact, when dealing with all government officials it is a good idea to treat them to a snack, a drink and chat. You will be amazed at the difference in their attitudes.

After reading the above information, if you still have questions or are confused, I advise you to consult a knowledgeable Costa Rican attorney for further information. If you plan to invest or do business in a Spanish-speaking country, you should definitely purchase Wiley's *English-Spanish Dictionary*, Barron's *Talking Business in Spanish*, or Passport Books *Just Enough Business Spanish*. All of these guides contain hundreds of useful business terms and phrases.

Beware of the so-called experts and overnight gurus

Costa Rica's popularity and good business climate has brought with it a whole slew of enterprising foreigners. Unfortunately, some of these people lack qualifications in their fields of endeavor.

In Costa Rica, the word "expert" is sometimes used very loosely in the expatriate community, on numerous web sites in English publications and on business cards.

Do not get me wrong; there are some highly qualified native English speakers here. Nevertheless, one should be extremely cautious when dealing with foreigners who consider themselves experts in Costa Rica. Just because a person was a professional in his home country or has gone through the

Opening a Real Estate Company in Costa Rica

By Lester Núñez

I originally came to Costa Rica from Victoria, British Columbia where I was licensed as a broker and worked in both residential and commercial real estate sales for over fifteen years. My interest grew in Costa Rica because of the country's weather and culture. Basically, I guess I just wanted to seek my Hispanic roots.

My plan was to open a real estate office in Costa Rica. Shortly after arriving I met my present partner, Mercedes Castro, who had been working as an independent real estate agent here. My goal was to provide excellent service combined with professionalism and integrity, just like North Americans are accustomed to back home. However, much to my surprise I soon discovered that the local real estate scene was very disorganized. There was no licensing of agents, no formal training and little regulation. Anyone was permitted to sell anything. Now all of this has changed.

I quickly aligned our real estate franchise with the Costa Rican Chamber of Real Estate (CCBR). My partner and I have worked very closely with them over the last five years to formalize real estate training and licensing as in the States and Canada. This has mainly been achieved by educational courses, creation of an Internet-based multiple listing system and licensing requirements.

The Costa Rican Chamber of Real Estate in conjunction with UNED University have created a twenty-two unit course which takes six months to complete and trains future agents.

Multiple listings were also created to further modernize the local real estate profession. The local multiple listing system is now affiliated with MLS Today which has its base in the U.S. and Canada. Now both the agent and client are now better off. Also, there is legislation pending to regulate the real estate business. All the government has to do is give its approval.

It initially took us a couple of years to get our business off the ground. Our international listings and advertising have been our "bread and butter." It is well-nigh impossible to make a living off the local market alone.

I love Costa Rica because of the climate, inexpensive health care, tax benefits for foreign residents, Spanish culture and much more. You really couldn't get me to return to Canada for anything in this world.

process of moving here does **NOT** qualify him to be an expert here. Some foreigners consider themselves experts just because they have lived here for a short time. Remember, anyone can build a web site and say anything about themselves.

I know people who move here, and go into business and miraculously become experts overnight. Costa Rica is indeed a magical country!

Many naive newcomers have been taken advantage of by other foreigners who call themselves "experts," but are really incompetent imposters. So, be careful!

If you happen to come into contact with any foreigner who calls himself an "expert," no matter how convincing he may be, do all of the following:

1. Ask for references from other foreign residents who have used the expert's services. Don't rely on the testimonials that appear on a person's web site. They may be slanted. If your expert will not give you any references, you will know immediately you are being duped or sold shoddy second-rate services. Also, try to contact the person's last employer before they moved to Costa Rica. Again, if they will not give you the contact information, you can bet the person is hiding something. If a person who is younger than retirement age claims to have been highly successful in his or her former country, they may be trying to cover up something about their background.
2. Check with the Association of Residents of Costa Rica (ARCR) to see if they are familiar with the person's services.
3. Enter the person's name in a search engine such as Google to see what comes up. There are even companies you can pay to do a background check if you suspect something.
4. Ask how long the person has lived in Costa Rica. If they have been here for less than 10 years, be careful. It takes more than a year or two to know all the ropes; it takes years to understand this country. For example, many of the relocation and entrepreneurs mean well but just don't have enough experience under their belts to tell you the entire story.
5. Find out what the person's educational background was when they lived in their home country and if they have any formal training in the Latin American culture, studies or foreign investments. If someone was a plumber, janitor, welder or doctor prior to moving here, this does not qualify them to give professional advice about Costa Rica.
6. Be ware of colorful, well-designed web sites built by so-called experts to express their admiration for the country to attract naive foreigners.
7. Be cautious about publications that appear to be helpful on the surface but incessantly hype the services of the person(s) or organization behind them.

8. Over the years I have run into so-called foreign experts who live comfortably in upscale in "Ivory Towers" and gated communities in *gingo* enclaves such as Escazú. The majority of their friends are other English speakers, so they have never really immersed themselves in the local culture. They are virtually still foreigners living among other foreigners. These people live in virtual isolation of the real Costa Rica. Few of them have any contact with Costa Ricans except for their maids and servants and rich Costa Rican friends from the country-club set. They rarely venture out of their safe environment to gather the necessary experience to confront real life situations here. Most live as if they were still in their home country, and give advice about a country and culture they really don't know.
9. Beware of the information and advice on the so-called "hobby web sites." These include the growing number sites put up by expatriates in Costa Rica to share their experiences. On the surface these sites seem helpful but the majority of the people behind them are neophytes who have not lived here long enough to really be qualified to give good advice. Most of these individuals don't even speak enough Spanish to really get an objective view of the country and culture.

   There are even a few video-type blogs portraying people's experiences who have moved here. While they are entertaining they shouldn't be considered a true source of information. Unfortunately, the internet has now given every "Tom, Dick and Harry" a chance to be the star of their own reality show.
10. Most importantly, find out if the person is truly fluent in Spanish. There is no way a person can have expertise unless he or she can communicate with the locals and understand the nuances of the local humor, culture and language. **Beware:** there are many foreigners who say they speak fluent Spanish with a vocabulary of only a couple of hundred words. I have run into many of them in my 30 years here.

What was one of the best ways to make money in Costa Rica

As the old saying goes, "If it sounds too good to be true, it usually is." Until 2003, a large number of North Americans living in Costa Rica earned "high returns" on their money by investing in private finance companies. In general, these returns in dollars ranged between 13 to 42 percent, depending on the duration and amount of the investment.

Those who got in at the beginning made out like bandits. While those who let their money ride or got in at the end usually lost everything. The author personally knows some people who did very well in these investments and others who lost their shirts.

The most famous of these companies was the **Villalobos Brothers** or "the brothers" as almost everyone called them. They ran what turned out to be a Ponzi-like scheme for about twenty years.. They paid faithfully for years. Unfortunately, most people chose to let their money compound so that they would eventually become millionaires. Compound interest grows very quickly.

The way the Villalobos brothers could get away with this scam for so many years was the ingenious method of loaning money to "friends." They claimed that their investors were their friends who gave them personal loans. In return investors received a check with the amount of the investment. However, it could not be cashed unless they informed the Brothers first who then covered it. Really, all people were getting was a worthless piece of paper. Over the years people did ask for their investment back, sometimes with interest, and were returned all of their money.

Originally only a few expats invested but as word spread of the incredible returns more and more people jumped on the bandwagon and the list of investors swelled to nearly 6,000 people.

According to estimates the "Brothers," took in almost $800 million dollars over the years.

In July 2002 everything went to hell. The government froze the Brother's bank accounts while they were investigated for money laundering.

Enrique Villalobos fled and his younger Brother Osvaldo was left holding the bag. Osvaldo was eventually convicted and "sent up the river."

There were many theories about what the Brothers did with their investor's money. Some say that they were a clandestine bank to fund CIA operations. Others say Enrique was a genius and was involved in selling arms to foreign countries. One theory had him working in the one-time highly-profitable business of exchanging Colombian *pesos*. Whatever they did to pay the high interest we may never know. During Osvaldo's trial the defense could not demonstrate how the brothers made money. This led most people to believe that the money came in the front door and went out the back door which is how a typical Ponzi scheme operates. Since most people let their money ride and didn't withdraw their monthly interest, this business could have theoretically gone on forever as long as new money kept coming in.

It must be pointed out that the Villalobos Brothers have their supporters who to this day believe blindly in their innocence and think they will recover their investment. Many believe that the Brothers were shut down because they had a corner on the investment market and bankers conspired with the government to put them out of business. Other think that if 9/11 had never occurred the government would have continued to turn a blind eye to the Brother's operation. In case you don't remember the U.S. pressured foreign countries into stricter banking policies to supposedly stop terrorists from moving funds. The draconian Patriot Act was the result of this.

A few years prior to the brother's demise a couple of similar copycat operations were born. What they did was prey on people's gullibility and the brother's reputation to attract investors. Many expats and others said, "If the Brothers can do it, Why can't these guys?" **Savings Unlimted** (aka "the Cubans") and "the Vault were other companies that offered high returns.

Savings Unlimted was called the Cubans because the owner was a portly Cuban by the name of Luis Milanes. To attract investors, he started out offering a higher monthly rate of interest than the Villalobos Brothers. Investors could earn a whopping four percent per month. Furthermore, if you got other people to invest you could make five percent monthly. The Cubans claimed they generated income from the chain of casinos they operated in Costa Rica. To make a long story short, they skipped town with approximately a quarter of a billion dollars on the books a few months after the Brothers were raided. The fugitive owner was arrested about five years later in El Salvador and still hasn't gone to trial to face criminal charges. He is out on bail and roams freely around San José with his body guards. None of his assets like the casinos have been seized.

The **Vault** was a small-time Villalobos-like business that operated from a storefront on Avenida Central. Soon after the Brothers went down the owner, Roy Taylor, committed suicide under strange circumstances.

The Yanquis are Coming!

By Coley

Prior to the passage of the Central American Free -Trade Agreement (CAFTA), the anti-globalization doomsayers were out in force with bold predictions about the "final blow" the deal would mean to the economies of Central American countries. Pro free-traders argued just as vehemently that CAFTA was a major step in building the foundations for a democratic community of nations in our hemisphere.

What's largely been overlooked from both sides, however, may have little to do with CAFTA at all. Instead, one of the biggest economic forces reshaping Central America in the coming years may be a demographic shift occurring right here in the Unites States, spurred by the massive retirement of the baby boomer generation.

According to a recent *New York Times* story, starting in January of next year baby boomers — defined as those born between 1946 and 1964 — will start turning 60 at a rate of more than 4 million a year. The leading edge of the baby boomers is beginning to turn 59 now — the age when Americans can start collecting certain retirement benefits without penalty. The number of Americans 55 and older is expected to skyrocket from 67 million this year to 97 million by 2020.

In many ways, boomers are a different breed altogether than the generations that preceded them. They are healthier, live longer and are more active, mobile and adventurous than prior generations. Trends suggest many will continue working beyond the traditional retirement age of 65, launching second careers, becoming entrepreneurs or focusing more on charitable and volunteer projects.

But in one fundamental way, baby boomers may not be so different from their parents and grandparents. Consider what I call the "Del Boca Vista" migration.

Del Boca Vista is the mythical Florida retirement community Jerry Seinfeld's parents, Helen and Morty called home. Like Helen and Morty, the enduring cliché about older Americans is that, once retired, they pack up their belongings, bid adieu to colder climes, and move to Florida to enjoy rounds of golf and blue-plate specials in Del Boca Vista-like retirement communities.

Like many stereotypes, this one contains a kernel of truth. According to a 2001 *American Demographics* study based on 2000 census data, Florida registered the highest share of seniors of any state in the country in the1990s, but other sun-belt centers such as Phoenix, Sacramento, Raleigh-Durham and Las Vegas were also highly attractive "elderly magnets."

William Serow, professor of economics at Florida State University in Tallahassee has been studying migration patterns of the elderly for years, and believes that since the end of World War II younger, more well-off "roving retirees" in their 60s still instinctively seek out warmer climates in "fun" places such as Arizona, North and South Carolina, and Florida.

According to Serow, the other key goal of this more affluent group of retirees is reducing living expenses by moving to sun-belt communities with cheap housing and lower taxes. And therein lies the big conundrum for today's boomer retirees: just as millions of retiring baby boomers are getting ready to migrate to warmer sun-belt states, these attractive retiree destinations are experiencing skyrocketing real estate prices and property tax assessments that may put these locations out of reach for all but the most wealthy boomers.

So, what's the significance of all of this for Central America? Tomorrow's Del Boca Vista migration won't necessarily be to the sun-belt states in the United States. It's just as likely that a large subset of boomer retirees — call them "boomer gringos" — will bypass southern sun-belt states altogether for more affordable Central American alternatives headed by Costa Rica, Nicaragua and Panama. Most Central American countries are still only a two or three hour flight back to the United States and have adequate infrastructures allowing retirees to stay in touch with friends and loved ones back home—good cell phone coverage, broadband Internet connections, even satellite television.

Having recently returned from vacation in Nicaragua and Costa Rica, the anecdotal evidence suggests it's already happening. Costa Rica is experiencing a housing boom that rivals anything here in the United States. and is driven in part by new boomer retirees. Two-or three-bedroom homes that were selling for $270,000 in December of last year are now selling for $350,000 and $400,000 in some parts of the country. While coastal areas may be experiencing their own version of a housing bubble, there are still very reasonable prices for many boomer retirees.

The story to the north in Nicaragua—the second poorest country in the Western Hemisphere, and a country that still conjures up images of right-wing dictators and left-wing revolutionaries—is even more interesting. Small coastal communities such as San Juan del Sur and cities such as Granada are swarming with retired expat boomers who are buying land and building dream retirement beach-front homes for a fraction of what it would cost in the United States.

Costa Rica: Imposes no tax on income earned outside the country, and allows retirees to buy into the national health care system offering care at public hospitals by participating doctors, many of whom are U.S.-educated.

Nicaragua: The government recently passed Law 306 that includes provisions exempting qualified investors from paying income or property taxes for up to 10 years, and providing generous exemptions from import duties for "pensioners" and investors that qualify.

Panama: Positioning itself as the world's greatest retirement destination.

RE/MAX and Century 21 have opened offices in the country, and affordable housing developments on some of the most coveted and pristine coastlines in the Americas are now dotting Central America's's Pacific coast. New developments have launched sophisticated marketing campaigns to attract boomer retirees, and publications geared toward retirees are hosting retirement summits and conferences to sell Nicaragua as a retirement destination.

While exact figures are difficult to obtain, the U.S. State Department estimates that about 380,000 Social Security checks are delivered to beneficiaries outside the United States each month. Almost 4 million Americans not including embassy officials and military personnel—are now living overseas, although how many of those expats are retirees is unknown.

What is known is that governments in Central America are luring gringos with new laws that include impressive incentive packages for retirees. And despite the inherent volatility and political risks that remain in many of these countries, boomer gringos (and Central American governments themselves) are betting that the economic benefits of a retiree migration to Central America will be a two-way street. Retirees get a lower cost of living, warm weather and cheap housing and create a virtual cycle; in return,—more retirees equals more local jobs, resulting in more economic stability and less political instability, resulting in more retirees.

But will this new economic model pay dividends? Serow figures that each retiree household in the United States is responsible for a little more than one job being attracted to the community. While he cautions that such jobs tend to fall into the low-paying, service category here in the United States, for developing economies that are starting at close to zero, service jobs are the best way to get a first foot on the economic ladder.

And it appears that many are already climbing the ladder. The national newspaper in Nicaragua *La Prensa*, published a story earlier this year about how the boom in tourism and the influx of retirees has benefited the economy. The story described workers who no longer had to look for seasonal work six months out of the year as "illegals" in more developed Costa Rica because they were now employed as full-time laborers close to home, building housing developments for a new wave of foreign investors.

And while the debate rages here at home about the impact of illegal immigration on our own economy and government services, there's no question that "low-paying" service jobs here in the United States filled largely by illegal immigrants benefits local communities back home. (Remittances from foreign countries such as the United States to families in Mexico, are one of the largest sources of foreign currency in the country.)

Wouldn't it be more beneficial to Central American countries if in the future these service jobs were created locally by an influx of American retirees? It's possible that the emigration of wealthy boomer gringos to Central America in the years ahead could slow illegal immigration here as workers become part of a home-grown service economy driven by retirees.

Are American retirees a panacea for Central American economies? Not by a long shot. There are still fundamental economic and political issues that will need to be addressed by the governments themselves that neither an influx of retirees nor CAFTA will completely mitigate. Stamping out corruption, increasing government transparency and bolstering education and the rule of law all need to be top priorities at home before the hemisphere can develop strong and sustained economic growth.

But the facts seem to indicate that barring some unexpected political upheaval or economic calamity, the Yanquis are going to keep on coming in larger and larger numbers. Central American governments have already placed their bets. They see our retirees not as a drag on the economy as we here in the Unites States often do, but as a potentially huge source of much-needed capital, investment and job creation. The smart money should be betting that they're right.

Coley Hudgins is a Washington D.C.-based government affairs consultant. He has lived and worked in West Africa, and has traveled extensively throughout Central America and Asia.

Common business Lingo

A pagos.......Payments, buy on time
Abogado, licenciado.......Lawyer
Acciones.......Stocks
Accionista.......Stockholder, shareholder
Activo.......Asset
Agrimensor.......Surveyor
Al contado.......For cash
Anualidad.......Annuity
Año fiscal.......Fiscal year
Anticipo, prima, depósito.......Down payment
Arrendamiento.......Lease
Autenticar.......Notarize
Avalúo.......Appraisal
Certificado de depósito.......CD.
Cheque.......Check
Cláusula.......Clause
Comprador.......Buyer
Contrato.......Contract
Corredor.......Stockbroker, real estate broker
Costo.......Cost
Cuenta.......Bank account
Cuenta corriente.......Checking account
Déficit.......In the red, deficit
Depreciación.......Depreciation
Deuda.......Debt
Divisas.......Foreign exchange (hard currency)
El Justo Valor del Mercado.......Fair market value
Embargar, enganchar.......Attach assets
En efectivo.......Pay in cash
Escritura.......Deed
Estado de cuenta.......Bank statement, statement
Facilidades de pago.......Payment plan
Fideicomiso.......Trust
Fidecomisario.......Trustee
Financiamiento.......Financing

Gastos .... Costs, expenses
Giro .... Money order
Hipoteca .... Mortgage
Impuestos .... Taxes
Intereses .... Interest
Impuestos prediales .... Property taxes
Inversiones .... Investments
Justo valor del mercado .... Fair market value
Lote .... Lot
Montar, poner un negocio .... Start a business
Negocios .... Business
Notario .... Notary
Pagaré .... Promissory note
Parcela .... Parcel of land
Plazo .... Term, period of time
Precio .... Price
Préstamo .... Loan
Principal .... Principal
Propiedad .... Property
Registro .... Record of ownership
Renta .... Income
RentabilidadAA .... Profitability
Saldo .... Balance of an account
Seguros .... Insurance
Socio .... Partner
Sociedad .... Corporation
Subcontratar .... To subcontract, farm out
Superávit .... In the black, surplus of capital
Tasa de interés .... Interest rate
Testaferro .... .Person who lends a name to a business
Terreno .... .Land
Traspaso .... Transfer
Timbres fiscales .... Tax stamps
Valor .... Value
Vendedor .... Seller

5

An Introduction to Real Estate in Costa Rica

Note: Any book of this type would be incomplete without a discussion of real estate. The section that follows is a detailed introduction to the subject and has been used for reference by many publications. Nevertheless in order to cover this topic thoroughly this guide would have had to be about 400 to 500 pages longer. But at 1000 pages it would have been too bulky and impractical for a travel guidebook of this genre.

So what I did was publish a separate 550- page real estate guide that amply covers the subject. The result is Christopher Howard's ***Guide to Real Estate in Costa Rica: a primer for investing profitably and safely in real estate in Costa Rica***. People need to understand all aspects of life before moving here or making a real estate purchase. Too many people have not done their homework or have bought strictly on emotion. People need to have the facts before they buy and know how to find value.

Please see **www.officialguidetocostaricanrealestate.com** for a free preview of this comprehensive book.

Events in the United States and the rest of the world have affected the Costa Rican economy and real estate market. However, there have never been sub-prime loans here nor did the government or banks invest in the U.S. stock market. The economy here has slowed down, but when compared to the larger economies like the U.S., the effect has been minimal. Costa Rica continues to be one of the most popular travel destinations in the world, the premier country in Latin America and the #1 retirement haven south of the border. All of this will combine to fuel the real estate market now and in the future. Costa Rica is a brand name and that will never change.

Why Costa Rica real estate?

In 2006 the first Baby Boomers turned 60 and every 90 seconds another Baby Boomer reaches retirement age Behind this first wave is a virtual tsunami of graying, affluent soon-to-be-retirees desperately seeking some affordable sunshine. And they're not only Americans. Swedes, Germans, Japanese, Brits, Canadians, and others are all looking to escape cold weather, dark skies and their dreary, over-regulated, under-performing high-priced economies. Costa Rica boasts an international market of people seeking their piece of the" Latin American Dream." Even the Chinese want in on the action. Not only are they interested in trade but tourism and investment as well.

So where are you (and your global counterparts) going to land? Do you want to risk building your dream home on the Gulf Coast only to have it flattened by Hurricane Katrina's uglier, meaner sister? How long will it take to restore the equity which has been lost, if that's even possible?

Look around the rest of the investment landscape and you can be just as depressed. Even Wall Street's deep thinkers will tell you that we're most likely in for decades of tepid, single-digit returns in stocks. Don't even think about living off your fixed-income investments either.

A savvy, soon to retire investor with a few bucks tucked away might look at it this way:

The dollar is weak and will continue to fall; the current world financial mess, wars, record deficits and more will keep the pressure on.

Can you rely on a money market account? With certain continued deflation of the value of the dollar, high rates of taxation, soon to be high inflation; the value of your savings will continue to erode at a record pace.

The U.S. government will be staring at a colossal tax increase in just a few years to fund social security, universal health coverage and Medicaid benefits for the flood of retirees. Some say that under Obama's plan, federal

No Real Estate Fire Sale on Horizon Despite economic woes in U.S., Tico property values not plunging

By Devon Magee

"The sky is not falling. There's just a healthy correction going on," says Bob Davey, owner of Century 21's Marina Trading Post in Flamingo Beach. His agency represents properties from Potrero to Tamarindo on the Pacific Coast.

"There were more realtors during the boom than ever," he says. "Many were unqualified, and they overpriced their properties. Now, that correction is setting in. People who are waiting for the markets to "recover" need to face that reality, whether they be brokers or sellers. It will be a while before the buyers will be back in the numbers they were before.

A recent Reuters article reported that prices of vacation houses and condos in Costa Rica have dropped as much as 40 percent. An overpriced listing will sit, reduce and then sell. This doesn't mean that the property values are down," explains Brian Freedman, an agent for Century 21 in the central Pacific town of Jacó. "It just means that sellers are getting more realistic."

Les Nuñez, owner of First Realty Pacific Beach Properties in Playa Hermosa in the northwestern province of Guanacaste, says that region has experienced a "supercharged" market over the last four years. "It was a very speculative market. I saw people flipping properties in four months for $100,000 in profit. Now, they're going to have to get real."

But Nuñez estimates there are fewer than 100 units on the market on the northwestern coasts, whereas in Miami, for example, "there are (about) 3,000 units on the market."

On the whole, he says, single-family homes in Costa Rica have not been affected by the U.S. mortgage crisis, although he cited two families from the U.S. who were forced to sell here because of mortgage finance problems back home.

The Costa Rican real estate market might be most susceptible to local, seasonal factors. September and October are the rainiest months on the Pacific Coast. This is typically the tourist down season and the annual lull in real estate sales. This year, Delta Air Lines has cut back flights to Liberia, the capital of the northwestern province of Guanacaste. European carriers have not offered direct flights into Liberia since the British charter First Choice recently suspended its weekly direct flight from London to Liberia. The European market never really evolved as had been anticipated.

Baby boomer retirees, for instance, who are living on a fixed income, are less affected by the vagaries of the real estate market. They are more interested in finding an affordable place to settle down where they'll get more bang out of their pension buck.

However, Costa Rica still represents a travel value when compared to alternatives such as Europe.

Costa Rica still offers a very friendly price-per-square-foot to build."

Unfinished developments that depended on pre-sales and U.S. dollar lending to finance their projects might feel the biggest crunch as their production costs rise and the price of building a home for prospective clients becomes more expensive. A realistically priced market could obligate them to be more than realistic in order to pay back loans. Due to the current economic problems that the world is facing, as well as the speed at which the real estate market in Costa Rica was moving before the present downturn, it is inevitable that there would be casualties.

Lucke, the economist, predicts the Costa Rican real estate market will ramp up again, not once the U.S. mortgage mess is cleaned up, but when the cost of raw materials – concrete, iron, gas – "starts falling or stops going up."

" Costa Rica is not in danger of a fire sale," says Davey. "We're really just back to where we were. We're back to normal."

The long-term property value determinant – on both a monetary and lifestyle level – may be the natural beauty that continues to attract travelers here, he says.

income taxes will increase dramatically possibly give the United States one of the highest tax rates among developed countries.

Where is the end of the huge financial burden the government is placing on every taxpayer?

Diversifying out of a falling currency and into hard assets outside the U.S. just might be the only way to protect your hard-earned wealth—while enjoying and preserving your lifestyle.

Many people who have had their new worth and retirement drastically reduced can now salvage what they have left and their lifestyles by moving and investing abroad.

The super rich have been doing this for years to protect their wealth and reduce liability. They safeguard their money and diversify their investment portfolio by investing in international assets. Now the average Joe can protect what he has left from the world economic fallout by using the same strategy.

Is there a way to profit from this mess?

Consider your options, run the numbers, and think about everything you'll need: an ideal climate, accessibility, advanced infrastructure, excellent health care, and so on. Over and over again—Costa Rica is the brightest blip on the radar.

Getting in before the crowd has always been the secret to making a lot of money with real estate investments. People who took a chance and invested in real estate in beach property in California, Hawaii and some parts of Florida were ahead of their time. They saw opportunity where others saw nothing. They took well-planned risks and were paid handsomely for their investments and created better lives for themselves and their families. What really gets people excited about Costa Rica is that it offers some of the most undervalued prime beach and Central Valley real estate in the world. As the rest of the world finds out about Costa Rica, prices will only go up.

Let us look at why this real estate boom is happening. The simple fact that almost every bit of coastline worldwide is becoming overcrowded, overpriced and scarcer contributes to a high level of interest Costa Rica's beach areas. The U.S. National Association of Realtors says Americans are buying second homes in record numbers, thus driving up the cost of vacation homes everywhere in the country. A recent newspaper article stated one in every seven people in the Unted States now lives in areas bordering the coast. This trend is driving the great baby-boomer migration. As a result, land in prime sunbelt areas of the United States has, become prohibitively expensive and hard to find. This is not the case in Costa Rica.

Costa Rica has one of the most appealing investment environments in the world. One of the reasons is that its tax system is much less complicated than those in the United States, Canada and Europe, offering great tax incentives for foreign investors, including tax free transactions. Such conditions, definitely contribute to Costa Rica's real estate market boom.

Where else can you get in on the ground floor of the new Latin America Riviera? Where else can one successfully shelter investments and profits?

Where else can one keep a fair amount of profits? Where else are property taxes on valuable properties paid in hundreds, not tens of thousands of dollars per year?

Where else in the world can you purchase a fully titled luxury beach front condominium for under $350,000 or luxury ocean view home for under $500,000?

A local real estate expert shares his perspective on the future of Costa Rican Real estate: " One has only to look here in Costa Rica, and see what has happened in the last five years. Now the baby boomers are coming and the market should continue to improve."

Easy to live and work in paradise

Another reason people consider Costa Rica today is how easy it is to live and work here. The next wave is for retiring boomers and younger entrepreneurs to move "South" for at least part of the year. Telecom is much more prevalent than people realize. With a laptop, cell phone, VPN (virtual private network) and the latest VOIP (voice-over Internet protocol) phone services, you can stay in touch more cheaply than ever. Costa Rica is easily reachable from major U.S. airports. Health care is superior. The people are friendly and welcoming. English is widely spoken. The Costa Rican government has made a major commitment to protecting and enhancing its spectacular natural environment.

Can this be done in other countries?

Forget Europe it is too expensive. Asia is too far and there are terrorism issues. Even traditional retirement havens as Thailand and the Philippines have their problems.

In this part of the world Nicaragua is just too poor, underdeveloped and plagued by political instability with no end in sight. Several countries have cancelled much-needed aid because the lack of true democracy institutions in the country.

Panama is too warm. Air conditioning bills in Panama City can run into the hundreds of dollars per month. There is talk of some benefits being cut for retirees and crime is growing. The latter is underreported so as not to scare away tourists.

Mexico used to be the number one retirement spot south of the border but people are starting to get turned off to the place. The country is currently being torn apart by a war between the government and the powerful drug cartels. Kidnappings have increased manifold. It is only a matter of time before foreign investors and retirees will become targets for this growing trade.

South America is just too far away and not ready yet. International retirement publications hype Medellín and Cali Colombia, Ecuador and Uruguay. Someone in Ecuador has even copied Costa Rica's national motto, *Pura Vida*, in an effort to promote the county. Ecuador's slogan is "Life in its pure state."

Most of these publications or web sites are selling real estate in those places knowing that the quality of life can't come close to Costa Rica's. None of the countries mentioned has an Association of Residents as Costa does to look out for the interests of expatriates. Nor do they have as much experience providing the quality of health care that foreigners demand.

The Central and South Pacific Coasts are perfectly situated in the path of growth

As explain in great detail in Chapter 2, Costa Rica's Central and South Pacific Coasts are pristine and unspoiled. Along Costa Rica's Central and South Pacific Coasts, you will find the most spectacular scenery, endless empty wide white-and dark-sand beaches, rocky outcrops and clear water set against a tropical backdrop of primary rain forest, as much privacy as you want and the best surfing and superb sport fishing. The beaches are reminiscent of those in California and Hawaii, but you can buy here for a fraction of the cost. For a very reasonable price, you may purchase a couple of acres of land with an ocean view. You can have a spectacular home perched on a hill, complete with custom tiles and finished in mahogany, teak and precious woods you never knew existed. The geography looks like California or Hawaii years ago.

According to an article in the country's financial daily, *La República*, property in the Central and South Pacific regions has risen 250 percent in value over the last six years. Although there has been some correction in prices due to the world downturn, long-term investment is still a good bet.

Even better, it's getting easier and easier to reach this slice of heaven. Two new highways are reducing the driving time by half between the country's capital, San José and the nearest beach resorts. The first stage of the new highway will link Ciudad Colón in the Central Valley to the town of Orotina near the Central Pacific Coast. The other section of new highway will link the towns of Quepos and Dominical to the south. Furthermore, there is a new marina in Quepos, a water park with artificial waves between Quepos and Dominical and a new international airport near the town of Palmar Norte. All of this will combine to make real estate values increase. Without question, over the next five years the Central and Southern Pacific Coasts of Costa Rica will be the sweet spot for investors.

As an example of this boom, the Marriott Corporation built its crown jewel of Central America, "Los Sueños Resort" and pre-sold 50 condominium units of 2,000 square feet each for $250,000. The next year they sold another 50 at $350,000 and this year's upper-end units sold between $600,000 to over $1,000,000 million.. And there is a waiting list! Seven years ago Los Suenos was selling its condos at a price of $150/ sq. ft. The price today is $750/sq.ft. Next door, the new St. Regis project is asking $1,200/sq.ft.! Why? Because the market is changing, to a more mature, demanding and affluent "resort type" buyer. These people want luxury and are willing to pay for it. They want—make that demand—first class amenities, not a funky and fun "experience." An investor friend saw lots for $50,000 when Los Sueños first opened over ten years ago and thought they were over priced. Now he kicks himself in the butt because the same lots are worth more than $1,000,000 million. (Part of this section is Courtesy of Martin Strudwich)

Add to this the fact that, "They aren't making more of this real estate." Costa Rica is a small nation and the amount of prime property here will eventually become limited. Given the fact that Costa Rica is a warm-weather destination like Hawaii it will always be popular and its land in high demand. Baby Boomers, tourists, those disenchanted with politics and other factors in their homeland and savvy investors and developers will continue to flock here to buy property. Thus your investment here can only appreciate in the future.

Central Valley is a good bet

Although there has been an real estate boom in Guanacaste and the Central and South Pacific are coming into their own, the Central Valley is still a good bet.

As I mention in detail in Chapter 2, the Central Valley is the heart of the country's activities. It has the best infrastructure, ideal spring-like climate, good Internet connections (very important) the best hospitals, incredible shopping, unending activities to stay busy and happy and unparalleled growth.

The Central Valley has had the greatest amount of construction and number of building permits issued in recent years. High-rise construction has already begun around the Sabana Park and Rohrmoser and is now extending along Paseo Colón. The Heredia area leads the pack with many new housing projects and gated communities. Santa Ana, Atenas, Alajuela, Ciudad Colón and even outlying areas like Grecia, Atenas, Naranjo, San Ramón and Puriscal are all following suit by experiencing growth.. With the new highway to the beach the Orotina area is going to experience a boom. The new road will bring everything closer.

There is more product in all price ranges in the Central Valley. Buyers have their choice of different microclimates, city or rural locations, a full range of prices from affordable to high end and virtually something for every lifestyle and taste. This area really can't be beat when you consider all of the options.

Guanacaste an initial explosion

Until the economic crisis of 2009, Guanacaste experienced a boom in tourism in the real estate market due to several important factors. Rumor has it the politicians and wealthy chose to develop this area rather than the Southern Zone because of their vested interests. Therefore they pushed for the construction of the Liberia International Airport. The result was a huge influx of tourists from all over the world and a subsequent real estate boom as more and more people visited the formerly undeveloped and inaccessible area of Costa Rica.

Condos under construction in Guanacaste

An initial building boom ensued and the land rush was on. Huge projects like the five-star Four Seasons Resort in the Gulf of Papagayo mushroomed as the developers moved in.

Realtors were popping out of the woodwork. Some of them were tourists and working illegally. Fortunately immigration cracked down on many of these carpetbaggers with fly-by-night operations.

The word spread and the rich and famous and Hollywood crowd arrived to bask in the sun on the province's string of beautiful beaches.

Unfortunately development happened so fast that infrastructure lagged behind. There are still many unpaved roads in the area. Because the region is very dry there have been problems with the water supply. Couple this with the economic downturn of 2009 and construction in many places has ground to a halt.

Things should get back on track as the world gets its economic house in order and consumer confidence increases. Also don't forget Costa Rica is such a unique place with such magnetic appeal and has so much to offer, investors will not stay away for long. The baby boomers are still pouring in.

The big developer's projects like Marrriott, Hyatt Regency, Ritz Carlton continue full steam ahead. The mammoth Solarium Project, directly in front of the Daniel Oduber Quirós International Airport, will spread out over 104 hectares (257 acres), and will include warehouses, a hospital, a gas station, 800 condominiums, and Guanacaste's very own *zona franca*, or free-trade zone. The project is being developed to help bring business and health services to a region whose tourism industry will soon demand these amenities.

The Solarium Project will be developed over seven or eight years, in six different phases, each catering to a different niche. In addition, Solarium's director believes that the project will bring about 15,000 permanent, stable jobs to the market, stimulating a micro-economy that currently waxes and wanes with the demand of the area's tourists.

In addition, Solarium is working to preserve nature and help maintain Costa Rica's image of green living: 50% of the project's 104 hectares will be devoted to landscaping, keeping the lands fertile and beautiful.

Housing and Real Estate Investments in Costa Rica

Finding a Temporary Place to Stay

While exploring Costa Rica or looking for an apartment, house or other type of residence in the San José area, you may choose to stay at one of the many accommodations listed below.

If staying in downtown San José, I recommend the **Dunn Inn** (2222-3232). It is run by North Americans and is a very popular *gringo* hangout. The service is excellent and you can make some good contacts. At night the new bar is a happening place.

In the beautiful city of Heredia I recommend the **Hotel America** (260-9292) E-mail: info@hotelamericacr.com, www.hotelamerica.com. The owners also operate three other quaint and affordable places in the same area: **Hotel Ceos** (262-2628), **Hotel Heredia** (2238-0880) and **Hotel D'Cristina** (2237-3036).

There are other accommodations for all tastes and budgets in the metropolitan area. The price range is from a few hundred dollars at the top end to less than $20 at the lower end of the scale. I don't have the space to list every hotel, motel, *pensión*, aparthotel and bed-and- breakfast in the section below. If you want a more extensive list I suggest you purchase Christopher Baker's *Cost Rica Handbook* or any of the guides listed in the last chapter of this book.

Vacation Rental Homes

Vacation Rental Homes are another possibility for your stay. They are fully furnished, and have cable TV, Internet, a fully-equipped kitchen, laundry room, phone and other amenities. To find out more, look on the Internet in places like www.craigslist,com Costa Rica, the *Tico Times* and *AmCostaRica.com.*

Aparthotels

Apartotels function something like a cross between an apartment and a hotel, but rent for longer periods of time. They include a kitchenette, cooking facilities. and are fully furnished, down to the hand towels. Aparthotels, are a good first option because they are completely equipped and have phone access as well as bilingual management. From there you can comfortably survey the market. If you are living in Costa Rica only on a seasonal basis, an aparthotel is probably your best bet. Usually they are less expensive than hotels with similar amenities, but more expensive than apartments. **The Don Carlos** and **Los Yoses** are centrally located and have nice accommodations. **Aparthotel Castilla** (2222-2113), **Aparthotel La Sabana** (2220-2422) and **Aparthotel El Sesteo** (2296-1805 round out the list.

Bed-and-Breakfasts

Bed-and-Breakfasts, or B&Bs as they are sometimes called, have sprouted up all over Costa Rica in recent years. Most of these establishments are smaller and in many cases less expensive than hotels. What sets them apart from other lodging is their home-like, quaint ambience. Many have a live-in host or owner on the premises and some are located downtown. Most B&Bs advertise in the local English -language newspapers, but there is now a service to help you find the "right" b-and-b for you. Call or fax the **Bed-and-Breakfast Association** at 2228-9200. To make a reservation, call, 2223-4168.

Homestays

Homestays can be a good option if you would like to check out *Tico* home life. They provide a great introduction to the Costa Rican way of life and the opportunity for you to improve your Spanish. Best of all, you have the experience of living with a Costa Rican family. Meals may be included depending on how you negotiate it. You must ask around with your local contacts in order to find one, although they're fairly common pretty much anywhere in the country.

I highly recommend **Bell's Home Hospitality**, 2225-4752, Fax: 2224-5884, E-mail: home-stay@racsa.co.cr.

Apartments

Here are three apartments that cater to foreigners. All are furnished and located in or near downtown San José and offer kitchens, a telephone, cable TV. **Apartments Scotland** (Tel: 2223-0833, Fax: 2257-5317) and **Apartments Sudamer** (2221-0247, Fax: 2222-2195).

Rentals

Some people are buyers while others are renters. People from the second group will be happy to know that housing is affordable and plentiful in Costa

Rica. Renting is the least risky and most flexible. It can, however, be costly in the long term, and depending on where you want to live, there may not be much rental product available on the market. Neither do renters have the chance to see a return on their investment. On the other hand, if you have limited resources and are not planning on staying in Costa Rica for the long term, renting is by far the best option.

If you do plan to live in Costa Rica for a long time, in some cases it's highly recommended that you rent before you buy depending on your financial situation. Neighborhoods and cultures reveal their secrets reluctantly, and six months of renting will teach you things about your new home that a simple visit would never expose. This is especially true considering that your move will include a measure of culture shock. If you discover something you don't like, you can pull up stakes and try out another region of Costa Rica. In the event that you decide to move here permanently, you will still have to consider whether to continue renting, or to buy or build something.

No matter what kind of rental you get, it will either be furnished or unfurnished. These are loaded terms, and don't mean the same thing as they do in the United States or Canada. For one thing, unfurnished apartments are completely unfurnished. That means they don't even include basic appliances like stoves and refrigerators. Furnished apartments, meanwhile, are generally decorated very poorly, with knick-knacks, cheap picture frames, and tacky curtains. The furnishings themselves are usually hand-me-downs – castoffs from the landlord's residence. Shockingly, this is often the case even in pricey properties in the $500 to $1,000 range. Landlords in Costa Rica typically put the bare minimum of upkeep into their properties as well, so before you settle on a place, you will probably view a parade of gloomy concrete boxes with cracked tiles, peeling paint, ancient kitchen and bathroom fixtures, and faded wooden cabinetry, all being rented at absurdly high rates. Newer properties, by the way, won't necessarily have these same problems, and in all likelihood they rent for the same rate.

If you're looking for a house rental, your two basic options are stand-alone houses and houses (or townhouses) in gated communities. The former might be cheaper because your landlord does not have to pay condo fees. The latter will be safer, since the condo fees usually include 24-hour security, and your landlord may not ask you to pay them. Be careful since some apartment buildings lack safe, strong gates or security systems to protect tenants.

There are quite a few gated communities in the Central Valley and the surrounding areas, and more are being built every year. That kind of housing is more difficult to find in rural areas, and in beach areas it's usually targeted toward tourists, and therefore quite expensive.

Apartment rentals are most common in city areas, although you can find them more or less anywhere if you look long enough. Like house rentals, you can get one with or without 24-hour security. Newer apartments come with their own parking spaces in a guarded area, which is something to check on if that's important to you. Also, when renting ground-floor apartments, you usually also get any garden space that comes with the building.

Rental prices vary just as in your hometown. With the exception of downtown San José, rent for houses or apartments is reasonable (half or less than the cost in the United States). Depending on location and personal taste, a small house or large apartment usually rents for a few hundred dollars per month. A luxurious house or apartment will go for $800 to $1,500 per month or more. Most of these upper-end houses and apartments have all the amenities of home: large bedrooms, a spectacular view, pools, gardens with fruit trees, bathrooms with hot water, kitchens, dining rooms, a laundry room and even maid's quarters, since help is so inexpensive in Costa Rica.

In the lower range—from $300 to $700—you can expect to find a two-to three-bedroom house or apartment in a middle-class neighborhood. Since most Costa Ricans pay less than $150 monthly for rent, $400 or more should get you a nice place to live. Most affordable houses and apartments are unfurnished. However, you can usually buy a complete household of furniture from someone who is leaving the country. This way you can save money. Most of the cheaper places will not have hot water. In the shower there will probably be an electric device that heats the water. If the shower doesn't have one of these devices, you can buy one for about $30 and have it installed for a few dollars.

When looking for a place, remember to check the phone, the shower, closet space, kitchen cabinets, electrical outlets, light fixtures, the toilet, faucets and water pressure, locks, general security of the building, windows and the condition of the stove, refrigerator and furniture, if furnished. Look at the ceilings for telltale signs of leaks and stains.

Also, check for traffic noise, signs of insects and rodents and what the neighbors are like. Ask about the proximity of buses and availability of taxis.

Have your lawyer inspect the apartment before moving in and document its condition to help avoid any potential problems.

As a final note on rental options, there is a rather distinct difference between rentals for *ticos* and rentals for foreigners. *Tico* houses and apartments have a rather dreary style that includes block construction, small or no windows, tin roofs, and shabby furnishings. That being the case, *tico* rentals also come with a lower price, so if you can handle "going local" for a bit, you'll get to both experience some of the culture and save money. Also, if you have pets, make sure to ask your landlord about them ahead of time.

Here is an example of a rental from an ad in the newspaper. "New "fully furnished" two bedroom*/one bathroom apartment for rent at $500.00 per month. The apartment is located near the Real Cariari Mall. It is minutes away from Heredia's Ultra Park/Global Park, ten minutes to the airport and twenty minutes to downtown San Jose or Escazú.

"Apartment features private telephone line, Amnet cable TV / RACSA Internet cable modem, leather sofas, hot water tank, dishwasher, clothes washer/dryer, 28" TV with DVD player in living room, 14" TV mounted on wall in bedroom, bedroom closets, vacuum cleaner, pantry closet, all necessary kitchen utensils, a gym quality "Life Fitness" Elliptical Cross Trainer** and secure parking for one car. 24 hour neighborhood guard service is included in rental price. Utilities (telephone / electricity / water / basic Amnet cable TV / basic 256kbps RACSA cable modem internet) average $100.00 per month. No pets. Long term, i.e. one year, rental agreement only. $600.00 security deposit required."

Below are some more tips a local real estate expert recently wrote about renting here:

1. Be clear on what you are looking for and what you can pay. Better rental equals more money.
2. Ask your agent to negotiate the rent down for you. Some landlords will.
3. Try prepaying the rent a few months to get a better rent. Some landlords like this.
4. Remember that the majority of landlords in Costa Rica never read the rental law (No. 7527). So, they have no idea about their rights or duties as property owners or about legal procedures that protect both tenants and owners. Also they will sometimes violate the rental law, and most of the time they will get away with it. Many landlords will break the rental law, if it means saving money.
5. Widen your choices by furnishing it yourself. We have a real shortage right now of furnished places.
6. Be a good tenant. Costa Rican landlords have become accustomed to bad renters, slow payers, fussy people who say, 'please come over and change my light bulb.' Make yourself a model renter, the one you would want to rent to, if you were a landlord. This gives you moral and economic leverage. It just makes sense."

Be sure to have anything you sign translated into English before you sign it. **Don't sign anything you don't understand based on the landlord's word of honor.** You should be aware that by law landlords can raise rents where the contract is in *colones* a maximum of 15 percent annually. On the other hand, contracts in dollars may be raised only once every three years.

You can read about the rental law in detail in my book, *Christopher Howard's Guide to Real Estate in Costa Rica*, available at www.amazon.com. Also, you can read about *La Ley General de Arrendamientos Urbanos y Suburbanos Ley* 7527 in Spanish at **www.asamblea.go.cr**.

Principal points of the rental law:

1. A rental contract can be either verbal or written.
2. No matter what a contract says, a renter who duly fulfills the terms of a rental agreement, can stay for three years minimum, no matter what. If the period of the contract is more than three years, the longer term takes priority.
3. At the end of the term, if the landlord wants the rental property back, he or she needs to notify the tenant at least three months before the term expires. Otherwise the term is automatically renewed for another three years or whatever the original term of the contract states.
4. When property is rented to an individual as a home and in *colones*, Costa Rica's currency, the rent amount increases automatically 15 percent every year. When the rental price is agreed to in any other currency, the automatic increase does not apply. Usually rent is stated in *colones* or U.S. dollars in Costa Rica, but it can be negotiated using any worldwide currency. Businesses can negotiate any payment method and/or yearly adjustments agreeable to both parties.
5. Public services and utilities are to be paid by the tenant except for property taxes, which are the responsibility of the landlord.
6. If a property is sold or otherwise transferred, it should not affect the tenant's rights and the new landlord must respect any existing contract.
7. Any improvements made by a tenant automatically become the property of the landlord.
8. A tenant cannot change the original, agreed-upon use of a property. For example, a home cannot be turned into a pet store or a pet store into a bar.
9. Landlords have the right to inspect their property once a month.
10. Tenants have the legal right to pay rent up to seven days after it is due.
11. In negotiating a rental contract, a landlord can request any guarantee deposit they deem necessary to protect their interests.
12. Tenants can not sublet/lease a property.

Rooms in homes usually rent for about $100 monthly. We know of several foreigners who live this way to save money.

As I mention later on, before deciding to live in Costa Rica permanently, it is a good idea to rent a place first or find a real estate agent who can show you around and guide you through the buying process. As you have just seen, a variety of rental options and price ranges is available to match almost any taste or budget. However, for *gringos*, the prices are generally much higher.

The main advantages to buying and not renting are the appreciation you gain on your investment and the rent money you save,

You will need a map of the area where you want to live. *The Tico Times* is a good place to start looking. *La Nación* is the most prestigious Spanish-language daily with ads. It has an excellent real estate section on Saturdays. However, relying solely on classified ads in newspapers is a mistake and can prove to be misleading. Some places are outright disappointing when compared to the way they are described in ads.

Other sources for finding an apartment are supermarket bulletin boards and word of mouth. Tell everyone you know you're hunting, and ask them to tell everyone they know, and so on. The Blue Marlin Bar, in the Hotel Del Rey, McDonald's in San José, around the Central Park in Heredia and other *gringo* hangouts are other places to inquire about rentals.

When hunting for an apartment or house to rent, contact the **Association of Residents of Costa Rica (ARCR)**, Tel: (506) 2233-8068 or 2221-2053, Fax: (506) 2255-0061, www.arcr.net. They will help you look in those areas that suit your personal needs and help take the headaches out of finding a place to live.

When reading the ads in the Spanish-language newspapers you should be familiar with the following words:

Air conditioning	*aire acondicionado*
Apartment	*Apartamento*
Backyard	*Patio*
Balcony	*Balcón*
Bars (window)	*Verjas*
Bathroom	*Baño*
Beach	*Playa*
Bedroom	*Dormitorio*
Building	*Edificio*
Carpeted	*Alfombrado*
Cable TV	*Televisión por cable*
Condominium	*Condominio*
Contract...	*Contrato*
Deposit.	*Depósito*
Dining room	*Comedor*
Dryer	*Secadora*
Elevator	*Elevador, ascensor*
Farm	*finca*
Floor	*El piso, La planta*
Furnished	*Amueblado*
For rent	*Se alquila, en alquiler*
For sale	*Se vende*

Garage	*Cochera, garaje*
Garden	*Jardín*
Grassy area	*Zona verde*
Ground floor	*Planta baja*
Guard	*Guarda*
High speed internet	*Internet de alta velocidad*
Hot water	*Agua caliente*
House	*Casa*
Kitchen	*Cocina*
Laundry room	*Cuarto de pilas*
Living room	*Sala*
Lower floor	*Planta baja*
Maid's quarters	*Cuarto de servicio*
Parking lot	*Parqueo*
Patio	*Patio*
Peaceful, quiet	*Tranquilo*
Refrigerator	*Refrrigeradora refri*
Rent	*Alquiler*
Rooms	*Habitaciónes, cuartos*
Safe	*Seguro*
Shower	*Ducha*
Stove	*Cocina*
Swimming pool	*Piscina*
Telephone	*Teléfono*
Tub	*Bañera*
Unfurnished	*Sin muebles*
View	*La vista*

Buying Real Estate

If you can't afford to buy a house in the United States or Canada, you might be able to here. Prices for homes in many neighborhoods in Costa Rica begin at about $60,000 with financing available for new homes if you become a resident. In 2003 I purchased a new $85,000 home in Heredia with financing. Our payments are about $560 monthly on a 15-year, 7.0 percent loan—$150 less than I used to pay for rent in Rohrmoser. The monthly payment includes a life insurance policy that pays off the loan in full in the event of death of the owner.

Just like in the U.S., Property ownership is fee simple title. You do not have to be a resident of Costa Rica to own property and you are entitled to the same ownership rights as citizens of Costa Rica. Ownership of real estate in Costa Rica is fully guaranteed by the constitution to all foreigners. This means your purchase here can be fully secured and safe. Title can be held several ways in Costa Rica: by a single person, jointly by several persons, by a corporation, a limited liability company or a trust.

Though the buying process isn't as neatly predictable as one might want it to be, here are the basic steps in more or less chronological order:

- Find a property
- Check it out by doing some preliminary due diligence
- Meet the owner and start the negotiation
- Offer and counter-offer
- Sign the sales agreement and put down a deposit or purchase an option
- Line up financing
- Complete the due diligence process
- Make any contract adjustments according to what you turned up
- Have notary draw up the document that will be the deed
- Sign (along with the seller) the deed at closing, along with the seller
- Send the notary to the National Registry to register the deed
- Pay transfer taxes, notary fees, broker fees, and administrative fees
- Within two weeks of submitting the deed to the National Registry, the property should be registered under your name or corporation.

Some of these steps can take place simultaneously, especially on the financing end, which is something to keep in mind even before you find the property you want to buy, as lining up the actual payment can take some fancy logistics.

How to locate a property

Though Costa Rica has drawn the developed world's attention as a great place to buy real estate, it's still very much a developing market, which is something to keep in mind as you begin your search for a house, a condo, or a piece of property. The market is still not very efficient at finding buyers what they want. And the lack of a multiple listing service makes it hard for buyers to quickly find fair prices. That's not to say that there aren't lots of nice properties out there at good prices – just that they're harder to find in Costa Rica than in developed markets like Canada and the U.S., and finding the good deals requires more than picking the low-hanging fruit in newspapers and on the Internet.

Fortunately, though there's work to be done, the Costa Rican market is indeed becoming more sophisticated, and there are a lot more places to shop for real estate and compare prices than there used to be.

Classified ads in local newspapers will probably give you a closer idea of fair prices. You may also want to check out the listings in the back of the *The Tico Times.* If you want to save money, look in the daily Spanish-language newspapers *La Nación* or *La República,* because prices are more realistic. Also, look around; go door-to-door in areas you like, and talk to other expats. If you drive around an area you like, you are bound to see a number of for-sale signs for properties not listed in the newspaper.

Like most other things in today's information marketplace, the best place to start looking for a Costa Rican property is the Internet. A few hours on -line will give you at least a basic idea of what's out there. The sites addressing Costa Rican real estate split into three rough categories: Those offering services (brokers, lawyers, fixers, property tours), those selling their own properties (developers), and those offering third-party listings (newspapers, Internet classified ads). The first two kinds of sites can have good information, but should be taken with the proverbial grain of salt. For one thing, anyone with a few hundred dollars can set up a decent Web site these days, and it's not proof of competence. For another thing, most of them directly profit from high real estate prices, so there is quite a bit of hype and their price quotes (if they offer them) will be a bit high. Still, those kinds of sites can give you an idea where price negotiations will start, especially if you're in the market for a condo or a house in a gated community.

These sites are also a good place to start researching the service people you will need to hire to complete your transaction. The best way to find them is through Internet search engines like Google.com and Yahoo.com, preferably searching with the name of the region you're interested in (Jacó, Escazú) and the product you're looking for (condominium, broker, etc.).

Keep in mind that housing costs are much higher in *gringo* enclaves such as Escazú , Rohrmoser and touristy beach areas. Be sure to remember that the farther away you live from San José and the upper-end areas the more you get for your money.

To find a house or land to purchase, look for a well-recommended realtor who can identify true market value. If you're on a tight schedule and you know where you want to buy, you can hook up with a broker, fly in, and pound the pavement hard for a few weeks.

If you don't know the country or you want to check out places you haven't been (but are still on a tight schedule) you could take a retirement/ lifestyle tour like the kind offered by Christopher Howard (**Live in Costa Rica Tours,** www.liveincostarica.com), which will show you the best areas to live and their amenities, infrastructure like malls, hospitals, supermarkets, appliance stores, etc. You will also see a sample of different living situations including actual properties in order to gain a broad perspective of the local market. You will also be introduce to trustworthy brokers, developers, and real estate lawyers.

Another alternative is the lifestyle real estate tours offered by **Costa Rica Retirement Vacation Properties** (www.costaricaretirementvacation-properties.com). They interview you to determine your needs, then create a streamlined process to find properties that you will like.

In the best case scenario, however, if you have a few months to poke around, you may want to rent an apartment or house somewhere central, rent a car, and take short trips to the different markets. Talk with brokers, drop by different developments – it's sometimes even a good idea to hire a *tico* fixer who can go with you as a translator so you can stop at all the little farms with the *se vende* signs out front, if it's raw property you're after.

Tico homes in *Tico* neighborhoods

Some *gringos* want to live in predominantly Costa Rican neighborhoods. However, most Americans don't want to downgrade but rather upgrade or preserve their present lifestyle. Unless you have the money to live in a gated community or high-end area like Escazú, Santa Ana most *tico* housing and neighborhoods are substandard for a lot of foreigners. Older areas like Guadalupe, Desamparados or isolated neighborhoods, for example, have a scarcity of adecuate housing. The *tico*-style homes in these types of places usually have poor plumbing with no hot water, are noisy, can have boisterous neighbors and small dark bedrooms without closets. Although living among the locals is a good way to meet people, Costa Ricans tend to keep to themselves. If you don't speak Spanish you may often feel isolated in a *tico* neighborhood. Also crime may be a factor. Criminals often prey on foreigners in these types of living situations. You may find cheaper property in one of these neighborhoods but most likely won't be happy with it.

Value of land

Pricing of land in Costa Rica can be relative. One way to find out is to hang out with the locals and see what land is really going for in an area. By cross-referencing one can usually arrive at the real value of property in a specific area. Another method of pricing is to put a value on it according to what person needs. A property may be worth only $10,000, but the owner needs $15,000. So he puts an arbitrary asking price of $15,000 on the property. The best way to find the true value is to compare the price of similar properties in the area, look for a motivated seller and work with a competent broker who knows the area. Many established brokers have sold properties in the area and keep a list of their previous sales. Some foreigners, including North

Americans, charge outrageous prices to make a quick buck. So, be careful with whom you deal.

To find a good buy, you should study the market. Remember it takes time to understand the market so you learn what a good value is. It is also a good idea to negotiate in *colones* since you will come out ahead in the long run as the *colón* continues to devaluate. This will make your home appreciate over time. Don't depend too much on the newspaper. Talk to as many people as you can. Nothing works better than word of mouth for finding good deals. Practice your negotiating skills. *Ticos* love to haggle. You may be better off having a trustworthy, bilingual Costa Rican search for you and do your negotiating. Your realtor or lawyer should also be able to assist you.

How value is assigned to a property depends, of course, on the property. Generally, however, turnkey properties like condominiums are priced according to their constructed square meters (i.e. - any space that's under a roof) plus any additional property (outdoor parking, garden, etc). A square meter equals 10.76 square feet. The price you pay per square meter of the building will vary according to concrete factors like the quality of the furnishings and the building materials, as well as intangibles like location and market conditions.

Land Measurement Chart

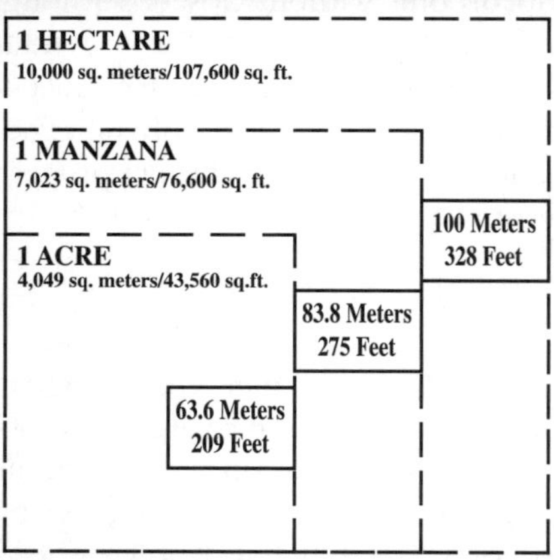

CONVERSION CHART
1 mile=1.61 kilometers
1 kilometer=.6214 miles
1 meter=3.28 feet
1 foot=.304 meters
1 yard=.914 yards
1 square meter=10.76 square ft.
1 square foot=.093 square meters
1 manzana=.698896 hectares
1 acre=.43,560 square feet
1 acre=.405 hectares
1 hectare=10,000 square meters
1 hectare=2.47 acres
1 hectare=107,600 square feet
1 inch=2.54 centimeters

Generally speaking, anything costing over $1,000 per square meter – especially large houses – should have top-of-the-line furnishings and be in excellent condition. That per-meter price tends to be higher the smaller the house or apartment, and will vary wildly according to location. A small condo in a prime Guanacaste beach location can cost upwards of $2,000/m2, while large country homes around Cartago or on the Caribbean slope can be down in the hundreds of dollars per square meter – once again, depending a lot on the furnishings.

Pricing large tracts of raw property is traditionally done differently. Pasture and farmland is sold by the hectare, a unit equivalent to 10,000 square meters, or 2.47 acres (occasionally in rural areas you may also run into *manzanas*, a unit of area measurement equivalent to 1.72 acres). In rural areas, these prices can often break down into a few dollars per square meter, which is certainly a deal. You can tell an area is becoming more valuable (or anyway, more residential) once the tracts of land get smaller and the prices are posted by the square meter, as is the case now in beach towns and has always been the case in urban areas. In really hot markets the price for raw land can go above $1,000 per square meter, though this isn't common, and expensive land should certainly come with added value, like sewer and electric hook-ups and road infrastructure.

Price comparisons

As mentioned elsewhere in this book, finding a nice property is one thing, and finding a property at a realistic price is an entirely different matter. Property is regularly overpriced to see if the *gringo* will bite, although that overpricing isn't entirely the fault of the owners: Lots of property bought in rural areas is farmland, with no residential pricing precedents in living memory. A few other market factors make it difficult to put a clear price on many properties and homes. The biggest issue is the market's lack of a multiple listing service, especially one that keeps a record of past sales. This makes it difficult to find out how much other properties are selling for ("comparables," in real estate jargon).

One solution is to hook up with a well-established broker with lots of listings and years of experience. Name-brand brokers like Century 21 and ReMAX have offices all over the country whose databases are connected, but beware: Some of those brands are just carpetbagging operations. In many areas of the country, the best brokers don't have a branded franchise. An experienced broker with many years in the market will be able to give you price comparisons, as well as an idea of the market's past performance. If you're looking for a somewhat liquid product (residential condominium) in an active market (Jacó or Tamarindo) there should be plenty of product on the move that will allow you to take an educated guess as to the value. Be careful, however, to get some sort of documentation or proof of sales values, as rumors run fast and wide.

What is a *perito*?

Another option – actually, a recommendation – is to get a quote from a professional property appraiser, the famous so-called *perito*, or expert. A *perito* will visit a property, measure it, note the materials used, examine the construction, and take the local market into account to place a value on the property. Keep in mind that the final quote is just an estimate, and should be taken only as a starting point for negotiations. But the *perito* is there to serve you, the buyer, not the seller or the broker, so the evaluation plus a short sit-down interview should give you a clear picture of what's going on. *Peritos* usually have a university degree in architecture or some sort of engineering. There are a handful of reputable companies that offer this service, for whom contact information is available in the resources section of this book. You can also use local companies or individuals that are based in the area where you're looking to buy.

A word about beach property

As we alluded to in a previous section of this chapter, the value of beach property has skyrocketed over the last decade due to the country's increased popularity. Many people want to realize their dream of owning a beachfront lot in a tropical paradise.

For most foreigners, the main beach development areas worth considering for retirement or vacation homes can be found in Guanacaste areas of Hermosa, Junquillal and Tamarindo. The Central Pacific beach areas around the towns of Jacó Beach, Quepos and Manuel Antonio are also attractive. The Central Pacific area has great potential, as it is much closer to the Central Valley and San José. The new Ciudad Colón-Orotina and Quepos-Dominical highways will have a huge effect on real estate values in this part of the country, as it will reduce driving time to the Central and South Pacific areas.

As in nearly every country in the world, Costa Rica's beaches are public property. So, if you would like to build or buy a beachfront home or business, you should familiarize yourself with the special rules regarding beach property in Costa Rica. Unlike in Mexico, some beachfront property may be purchased. The 1977 Maritime Zoning Law for beach property (*Ley sobre la Zona Marítimo-Terrestre - Ley Número* 6043) regulates the ownership and usage of beachfront property in Costa Rica.

Beach property here has its own set of rules so you have to be careful. The 200-meter strip of land along the seacoasts is owned by the government and is for public use. It is prohibited to build anything within the first 50 meters (*Zone Pública)* of the high-tide line. This zone is for the public and cannot be turned into a private beach.

Also, you can no longer build within the next 50 to 200 meters of the high tide line—this is called the Maritime Zone, or *Zona Marítima,* —unless there is existing housing or a new tourism project involved. If this is the case, you can lease the land from the municipality, which is overseen by the Costa Rican Tourism Institute (ICT).

The Maritime Zone runs for more than 1,500 kilometers (932 miles) along both coasts. More than one third of this (590 kilometers (367 miles) is open to legal development. The rest is invested in mangrove swamps, National Parks, mouths of rivers and other protected areas.

Most of this land is already developed, much of it illegally. Only a small fraction is still open to development.

There are two types of beach properties — titled and untitled. Titled properties are those acquired before 1977 before the law changed. The Maritime Zoning Law is not applied retroactively. Any shoreline property previously titled can be freely transferred After that date costal properties can only be obtained by means of a concession. A concession is a type of lease which is good for five to twenty years and is usually renewable but there is no guarantee.

Life is a beach

Obtaining a concession is a bureaucratic nightmare. The Instituto Costarricense de Turismo (ICT) authorizes leases in the Restricted Zone, but the local municipal governments grant and administer the government concession for possession of land in the maritime zone. The Registry of Concessions in the Public Registry in San José records all concessions. Before a concession can be granted, the particular beach where the property is located must have an approved Zoning Plan (*Plan Regulador*) in place. You will also need an *uso de suelo* (ground use) permit, and approval from the *Instituto Costarricense de Vivienda y Urbanismo* or IVU and whatever else they think up to make you jump through the hoops.

Only the actual Concession will clearly define the rights and terms of ownership that the occupant has to the property. In theory, foreigners cannot lease this land, but there are loopholes in this law. One of the ways to circumvent this regulation is by obtaining a lease through a corporation owned mainly by a Costa Rican. However, this is illegal and you can get into trouble and end up losing the lease. Check with a lawyer to find out how this works.

* Concessions for maritime zone beach property cannot be granted to:
* Foreigners who have not been residents for five years
* Companies with bearer shares
* Foreign companies based abroad
* A company set up in Costa Rica exclusively for foreigners.
* A company with more than fifty percent foreign capital (ZM Art. 47)

Concessions on maritime zone beach property can be forfeited for the following reasons:

* Failure to apply for an extension of a concession in a timely manner
* The forfeiture of rights by the interested parties
* The death or legal absence of the concession holder with no heir
* Not abiding by the established obligations of Article 51
* Cancellation of the concession (ZM Art. 52)

The ICT can cancel a concession on maritime zone beach property for:

* Non payment of the yearly canon or royalty
* Breach of contract (e.g. use of the land for purposes other than those expressly stated by ICT)
* Violation of the ordinances of the law that grants the concession
* Impediment of the use of the public right of way
* Other causes that this law establishes (ZM Art. 53)

Beachfront property is being bought-up fast, and the price of this and other prime real estate is soaring. However, before you move to the beach, you should know that for some people the novelty of living at the beach wears off fast. Visiting the beach for a few days or weeks is very different from living there full-time. The humidity, boredom, bugs, lack of emergency medical facilities in a few areas and the occasional inconveniences of living in an often out-of-the-way area are factors that might deter some from moving to any beach area. However, in general the positives of beach living far outweigh any negatives. Due to Costa Rica's increasing popularity and improving infrastructure, beach property can be an excellent investment.

Finding a Broker

You are advised to use the services of a real estate broker to buy or sell property in Costa Rica. Real estate agents normally collect a five or six percent commission on the sale of a home and up to 10 percent commission on the sale of raw land. In general, this commission is paid by the seller of the property to the realtor.

After you decide where you want to live and what you want to buy, then select a broker. This can pose a problem because no one needs a license to sell real real estate in Costa Rica. One of the most infamous and inconvenient characteristics of the Costa Rican real estate market is that the law does not regulate real estate brokers. Anyone can sell you a property, and everyone will probably try to. Deals have been found through taxi drivers, but so have scams and endless runarounds. Even if you're looking to purchase something from a development with its own sales office, it's a good idea to ask a broker to help you choose the development. Though picking a good one from the mass of mediocre ones seems like a daunting task, it's doable.

Since selling real estate is in vogue and there are a lot of *gringo* opportunists looking to make a quick buck it may be hard to find an agent who looks out for your interests more than just making a sale.

On top of that many foreigners who sell property here aren't even legal residents of Costa Rica and don't have permission to work. Would you buy real estate from a tourist in the U.S. or Canada? Some of these characters just come down for the high season to sell properties and then disappear into the wood work. If you need to find them for anything, you can't. Also many of these people have never had any experience working in real estate in their home country.

It seems that everyone is selling property in Costa Rica: cab drivers, waiters in restaurants, your friendly gringo neighbor, hotel employees and a lot of people without papers as I just mentioned. Even fugitives have gotten into act. The AM Costa Rica on-line newspaper reported on September 3, 2008 than a U.S. citizen on the lam was arrested while working as real estate broker in an office on the Pacific Coast. In December 2005 and in December 2007 two other *gringos* wanted in the U.S. were arrested here. Both had been working as real estate salesmen. Many U.S. citizens are hired illegally in the real estate business because of their English-language abilities.

Bad brokers come in three flavors: the incompetent, the dishonest, and, most commonly, those who are both incompetent and dishonest. To make matters worse, some brokers are working here illegally, either because they haven't established legal residency and therefore aren't allowed to work or because their company has not been legally incorporated. Incompetent, dishonest realtors are all attracted by the lure of making a quick buck. And, if they are here illegally and have no investment in the country or family ties here, then there is nothing to prevent them from skipping town after having committed a malfeasance.

The most common trick of the trade—unethical but not illegal—is to sell property at a higher price than the asking price and to pocket the difference. Another common misdeed is to claim something about the property that isn't true (e.g., that it has access to water) or to conceal some problem with the property (e.g., problems with title). Perhaps the most common fraud is committed when someone poses as a property owner (or as an agent of the owner) and sells land that doesn't belong to the putative "owner." Again, you can avoid all these problems by relying on common sense, acting prudently, and relying on the services of a lawyer who specializes in property law.

Since the real estate industry is virtually unregulated—business and contract laws do apply to real estate deals as well—you might find that realtors are especially zealous and wary when it comes to ensuring that they receive their commissions. After all, if the seller refuses to pay the commission, the broker doesn't have a regulatory body to back him up and his only recourse would be to file a lawsuit. So, you'll need to understand the broker's position, and work with all parties involved to allay any concerns the broker might have about not getting paid.

A good broker, indeed any professional salesperson, must have good listening skills. If you meet with a broker and describe exactly what kind of property you are looking for, then find that the broker proceeds to show you five properties that don't match your description at all, it's time to move on.

This is why it is important to work with a good broker:

1. A good broker can help you find a fairly-priced property.
2. Only a small percentage of properties for sale are advertised in the newspaper. A lot of brokers have their own listings, which they don't share with other brokers.
3. A broker can save you time and aggravation by showing you just what you want. He will do this by pre-qualifying you.
4. Good brokers have excellent contacts and will help you with every-step of the process.

5. A good broker will know all of the good areas and will not waste your time showing you undesirable neighborhoods. A broker who knows you are working faithfully with him will go all out to help you find what you want. Be sure to tell your broker from the beginning if you are working with other agents.
6. A good broker can form a relationship with you and truly understand your specific needs.
7. Working with a broker in Costa Rica is similar to working with a broker back home. If you are patient, loyal and have confidence in your broker, you will find what you want.
8. Brokers offer a wide range of properties. They sell a little bit of everything.: houses, lots, commercial property, condos, and even *fincas* (farms). Therefore, it is best to find a broker who specializes in exactly what you are looking for. A person who sells at the beach cannot possibly be an expert in properties in the Central Valley.

In order to find a competent, honest broker, it is wise to talk to other expatriates or contact the local Chamber of Real Estate Brokers or *Cámara Costarricense de Bienes Raíces.*

Here are more tips on finding a good broker:

(1) Shop around: You wouldn't buy the first car you test drive, and you shouldn't go with the first broker you lay eyes on. Talk to at least two or three. They can be found on the Internet, in local offices, in real estate guides, through recommendations and in the resource section of this book. Personality is very important, and if you don't get along with your broker, the buying experience will be a miserable one.

(2) Communication: Just as in a marriage, communication is a key component of the relationship between a homeowner and an agent. If the communication isn't there, the relationship won't work. So if your agent doesn't return your phone calls in a timely fashion or disappears without warning for weeks at a time, you should probably find someone else.

(3) Stay local: Pick a broker who specializes in the area where you want to buy. Since there is no MLS in Costa Rica, local connections are very important, especially if you're looking for raw land.

(4) Even homeowners who have been through several real estate transactions can benefit from a little advice from their agent. But if an agent doesn't offer any advice, it could be an indication that he or she is not fully engaged in the process.

(5) Go bicultural: Most brokers can spit out a few words of Spanish, and some speak fairly well. The ideal broker, however, understands both

the language and the culture, or has teamed up with another broker who does.

(6) Demand residency: Ask that agent to show you their Costa Rican *cédula* (ID) or work permit. Ask how long the agent has lived in Costa Rica (5-7 years minimum). Costa Rica has a history of so-called "tail-gate realtors," or foreigners that parachute in, sell a few properties while here on a tourist visa, and leave whenever they want.

(7) Today, the market is mature enough that most regions have at least one broker who's been here for years and has Costa Rican residency. This is a sign of commitment to reputation and to the country, and it should figure importantly in your final decision. If your real estate agent is actually a waiter, waitress, or another profession, then you are probably not going to be happy with where their priorities.

(8) Ask for references: Satisfied customers are a good sign that a broker is doing his or her job. Request contacts for a few and ring them up. Be sure to ask what the customer didn't like about the broker as well. Do an Internet search on the agent's name and see what comes up.

(9) Brand isn't everything: All the big U.S. real estate brands are in Costa Rica: Century21, RE/MAX, ERA, Coldwell Banker. Remember, though, what they're doing. On the upside, branded brokerages often communicate with their other franchises in the country and offer you a bigger pool of product. On the downside, many of them may be newbies in the country who simply bought a franchise. Some branded brokers are good and some are bad, just like everyone else in theindustry. Experience in the market and good referrals should be more important to you than brand.

(10) Ask how long the agent has lived in Costa Rica (5-7 years minimum) (11) Ask for a few happy customers to contact.

(12) Just as in a marriage, communication is a key component of the relationship between a homeowner and an agent. If the communication isn't there, the relationship won't work. So if your agent doesn't return your phone calls in a timely fashion or disappears without warning for weeks at a time, you should probably find someone else.

(13) Let's face it, even homeowners who have been through several realestate transactions can benefit from a little advice from their agent. But if an agent doesn't offer any advice, it could be an indication that he or she is not fully engaged in the process.

(14) Real estate agents who insist on clients' using a particular lender or affiliated company for the transaction may trigger alarm bells. That's a huge red flag because odds are they are probably getting a cut on a referral fee.

(15) If your real estate agent is actually a waiter, waitress, or (another profession), then you are probably not going to be happy with where their priorities are.

Would You Buy Real Estate from a Tourist?

By Christopher Howard

Again and again I hear stories about people making mistakes when purchasing property in Costa Rica. I really feel it is my responsibility to share the following with my readers.

As you probably know, by now Costa Rica has become very popular over the last couple of years. From all indications, interest in the country is not going to wane for some time to come. Recently, one economist told me the local boom could last for up to 10 years more.

Therefore, it is not surprising that investors are pouring into the country to purchase all kinds of homes and land. Unfortunately, in many cases they are not using their common sense.

Scores of would-be entrepreneurs have set up shop here. Most have eye-catching web sites proclaiming their expertise and real estate offices. The problem is that some of these people are little more than modern day carpetbaggers with no credibility trying to cash in on the real estate gold rush. They are here to get what they can take and ride happily off into the sunset.

A large number of these JCLs or "Johnny Come Latelys," are not even legal Costa Rican residents but tourists.Would you buy real estate in your hometown from a tourist? Of course not! Only a fool would do it. A realtor friend of ours had the immigration department run a check to see what the status was of foreigners selling real estate in a certain beach area of Costa Rica. The results were frightening. Many of the realtors in the area turned out to be tourists living here illegally. Furthermore, the Costa Rican government prohibits anyone from working here who is not a resident.

Fortunately the world economic mess and resultant slowdown in property sales has eliminated the majority of these illegal real estate agents and fly-by-night operations.

So, when looking for real estate in Costa Rica you should only deal with time-tested real estate agencies and people who are legal residents of the country. Do your homework, ask a lot of questions and don't "leave your brain on the plane."

(16) A real estate agent who shows buyers only properties that are listed with his or her brokerage could be subordinating the client's best interests. Since selling agents earn a separate commission off a real estate transaction, agents who make listings available just from their company may be trying to steer that commission to the brokerage as well.

As I mention repeatedly above, the real estate industry is not regulated here as it is in the United States. So, it is sometimes hard to find a good broker in Costa Rica. Fortunately, one of the companies I recommend contacting is **Costa Rica Retirement Vacation Property**. They have more than 35 years of combined experience in the real estate market and have helped thousands of people make safe and profitable investments and find success here.**Costa Rica Retirement Vacation Properties toll-free 1-888-581-1786,** E-mail: **robert@costaricaretirementvacationproperties.com**, or see **www.costaricaretiementvacationproperties.com.**

Due Diligence — Tips Before you Actually Make the Purchase

Due diligence is the process of researching the physical and legal status of the property you are about to buy before you buy it. If you do a good job in this process you will save yourself a lot of headaches, heartache and money down the road. Do not rely solely on information that the broker or owner provides you. Do your homework during this important phase of purchasing a property. Once again, take nothing for granted.

During this process, you are confirming that the property is what the seller says it is; that it brings with it no legal complications that will make your life difficult; and that you can do with it what you have planned. Depending on the identity of the owner, the size of the property transaction, and your plans for the property, your lawyer could carry out due diligence or you could hire a due diligence professional. Likely your lawyer would handle the hiring of this person and receive all the data that person collects. Once again, be sure to ask for references. Along with the due diligence professional, you will likely want to hire a site surveyor as part of the due diligence process.

Once you have found the property or home you like, there are a few precautions you need to take as part of the due diligence process.

1. Make sure you know the real value of the property.
2. Do not assume the seller or broker is trustworthy just because they speak English. This is a common pitfall.

3. Make sure the property you are about to purchase is not part of a national park or subject to restricted use. There are areas near Dominical, for example, that abut a rainforest where it is forbidden to cut any trees.
4. If you purchase raw land, be sure to get a soil sample and hire an engineer, especially if your lot has been cut out of a hillside. I know of one man who built a million-dollar home on a bluff overlooking the beach. About a year later he had to spend $100,000 to build a retaining wall because the rain started to undermine his lot.
5. If you buy in a remote region make sure you can bring electricity to the land. This can be expensive.Also check to see if the water supply is good in the area.
6. Do not rely on a verbal contract if you decide to make an offer. Get everything in writing.
7. Check out your neighbors. There is nothing worse than buying property and finding out later that you have bad neighbors.
8. If buying in the city or near a major street, check the noise level. Make sure there are no dancehalls, bars, rowdy neighbors or noisy buses.
9. If you purchase a home, have an engineer make sure it is structurally sound. Also, check the plumbing, wiring, roof for leaks, water pressure and septic or sewage system.
10. If buying in the city it is extremely important to be familiar with the neighborhood where you decide to buy. Make sure you are not buying in a crime-ridden area. There are a few areas around San José where you would not like to live. A good broker and doing your homework can help you avoid this disaster.

This is advice from an experienced local realtor.

1. It is always important to ask the person selling the property for his *cédula* or I.D.
2. Are you certain that all of the amenities you want and need are available? Don't assume anything in Costa Rica. People over -promise and under-deliver here. Internet and the satellite TVs and even good medical care or a good mechanic are not things that exist here with any assurance. Make a checklist for yourself. Make sure the clubhouse, pool golf course etc., will really be built in an upper end development.
3. Are you positive that your lot can, in fact, come with water, electric and telephone? There are more than a handful of communities in Costa Rica where water shortages are preventing building permits from being issued. Talk to the municipality and a good attorney and insist upon proof of these simple questions. Don't take utilities and roads in Costa

Rica for granted. A salesperson's assurance of a new highway or road to the property is definitely not a guarantee.

4. If you are buying a predevelopment or preconstruction property, what guarantee do you have that the infrastructure will be completed?
5. If your salesperson tells you that you can subdivide the property and resell it for a quick profit, don't take his word for it. Tell him you want proof. Many municipalities have minimum size lots and sometimes the promise of quick profits can cloud sound judgment. How are you going to arrange for utilities to your new subdivided lots?
6. Don't let yourself be fooled by a salesperson's promise of quick profits, a new marina or a hospital or highway "right around the corner." Things move slowly in Costa Rica, and installing the infrastructure you are counting on could realistically (and probably will) drag on for years.
7. If you have responded to a TV ad, an E-mail, or Google ad, you will get a telephone call extolling the virtues and profitability of the property in question. Ask the salesperson where he is calling from. The odds are that he is calling from Florida and that he has not even seen the property. Ask yourself what kind of credibility this person could possibly have if he has not even seen the property or doesn't even live in Costa Rica.
8. If you are one of the many potential buyers who is thinking about buying a property sight unseen, you should think twice. You wouldn't do it in your own hometown. Why would you do it in a foreign country?

Negotiating

The seller's lawyer will present the asking price and your broker responds with a counteroffer that will contain all the conditions you might have for the purchase – for example, any work you want done on the property or house, the time frame for payment or financing, the deposit and length of time necessary to allow your lawyer to carry out due diligence, etc. Here are a few important features of the property to keep in mind when negotiating:

- Grade: How steep is the property? Will it be hard to build on it?
- Bodies of water: While a river running through a property is a nice feature, bodies of water can be either a plus or a minus. Its presence will limit the use of the property, as there are building restrictions within 15 meters of bodies of water.
- Water source: If you need to drill a well, remember that getting water rights where there are none is a separate process. If those rights are already locked in, it will save you a potentially major headache.

New Rules to Protect Buyers

Projects in development must now comply with strict rules for the protection of consumers.

Those offering real estate for sale with delivery at a future date to register with the *Ministerio de Economía, Industria y Comercio* and show they have the financial capability to carry out the project.

Costa Rica's recent real estate history is filled with cases where developers promised certain amenities or improvements and never followed through even though some purchasers paid substantial sums. In some cases, all the developer did was erect a gateway or a welcome center or bulldoze a few roadways.

The new rules also require that purchasers pay for the real estate or services in a proportional way rather than with all the money up front. There also are restrictions on what may be in a sales contract. For example a purchaser cannot surrender his or her rights. Some current contracts required arbitration or require the buyer to hold the seller harmless in case of problems.

Purchasers also have eight working days to back out of the deal. Previously the rule was eight calendar days to rescind.

In the past some developers set up shop, obtained an option on land and began selling lots, houses, apartments or other real estate that they did not really own and which had not yet been built. Some tried to zero finance their projects by accepting substantial sums from purchasers and using the money for development instead of putting the money into escrow.

The decree also requires a seller to provide his or her exact home address and to assume the obligation to notify purchasers of any changes allowing them to exercise an escape clause.

The rules specify mathematical calculations of the solvency of sellers and what appears to be a complex application process. If ministry employees do not think that the seller has the funds to met the obligations, they are empowered to require additional financial guarantees, according to the decree. The decree also said that the ministry will review contracts.

The ministry also has the right to file complaints against vendors who are not registered.

Developers of projects already in the works have six months to comply with the new regulations, the decree said. The new rules are updates and additions to existing laws and rules which mostly covered just time shares, said the ministry.

* Courtesy of AM Costa Rica

- Utilities: Water and power connections to the property (or, more to the point, lack thereof) could have an important affect on the price, as they can be fairly difficult to arrange.
- Access: Is there a way to get to your property? What's the road like? As a helpful exercise, try to imagine it with five inches of rain falling in the space of a few hours.
- Encumbrances: Does a neighbor have a right-of-way that passes through the property? Are there power lines or pipes that will restrict how you can use the land?
- View: Is it up or down? Does it look out over the Pacific Ocean or a sea of tin roofs?
- Landscape: Cow pasture and other farm land is relatively easy to build on; forest is not, as you have to get special permits from the Ministry of the Environment to cut down trees.
- Security: Does the development include the infrastructure for 24-hour security, such as a guard shack?
- Financing: Is the seller financing the deal? Is he or she willing to accept balloon payments or some other kind of option that will better meet your needs? Does the seller need quick cash? Will you be forced to wait for any legal issues to be resolved before you close on the deal?

As far as the human side of the negotiations, negotiating with a *tico* landowner versus negotiating with a professional developer are two distinctly different experiences. Business negotiations in Costa Rica are quite circuitous, and if you decide to take part, you will be expected to drink a lot of coffee and begin meetings with long, winding discussions on the weather, family, and other such niceties. It can be pleasant once you get used to it, which you might as well do, because though language barriers may cut down the chitchat somewhat, American-style aggressiveness and brusqueness will get you nowhere.

This is perhaps the most important thing to keep in mind when going into a business negotiation with a *tico*, especially in rural areas. If you are an impatient or pushy person and have a difficult time containing yourself, it might be a good idea to find a bicultural broker who can handle the negotiations on your behalf.

Negotiations will, of course, have a different quality if the seller is a developer – local or foreign – with product to move. Developers have a set range in which they will negotiate, and it's a range that varies depending on the newness of the development. Make an offer and see what happens. Newer developments will be anxious to get some sales on the board and their sales staff is probably more likely to come down in price. One advantage of buying a place still under construction is that you can negotiate the interior, including the fixtures, cabinetry, floor, lighting, and even appliances. If the developer doesn't want to do things the way you like them, you can negotiate the furnishings right out of the contract and do them yourself once you take possession.

One final caveat to negotiating with *tico* landowners is that though you can usually talk the "*gringo* price" down, it depends on the landowner's motivation. Some property owners simply slap a *se vende* sign on the front gate after seeing their neighbor rake in a million bucks. They're not motivated to sell the property, but they will if the price is right. Oftentimes, however, their expectations are unrealistic and you won't be able to negotiate that seller's price down much at all. In that case, it's best to move on.

Purchasing property

Purchasing property in Costa Rica is very different from making a similar purchase in your home country. The laws of Costa Rica and the property registration process can be somewhat confusing to a foreigner. Your best bet is to work with a broker (brokers are not licensed in Costa Rica) or real estate consultant when looking for property, such as the people I recommend in the section, "Finding a Broker." When you find a property, your broker can help you negotiate the price and explain your financing options.

If you decide to buy real estate, an attorney is absolutely necessary to do the legal work. We strongly recommend that a competent, English-speaking lawyer do a thorough search of all records before you make your purchase to make sure there are no encumbrances (*gravámenes*) on it.

Your Lawyer and Notary

Your lawyer will play an important role in this transaction, and a larger one than is traditional in the United States or Canada. Your lawyer could do any number of the following tasks:

- Title search
- Due diligence
- Permitting
- Sales contract drafting/revision
- Negotiation
- Act as escrow agent
- Certify the deed
- Register the deed

Because the role of the lawyer is so large during a property transaction, it is crucial that you find a trustworthy one. For more detailed advice on how to find one, see Chapter 6 on finding a lawyer.

Most likely your lawyer will also be a notary. All notaries are lawyers, but not all lawyers are notaries. A notary is basically a lawyer with extra training and, as a public official, authority to draw up deeds and submit them to the National Registry for inscription. Every property transaction in Costa Rica is done through a notary.

One of the biggest errors made by foreigners buying real estate is not properly researching the title for liens. You can obtain information about property at the ***Registro de la Propiedad*** (like your land title office) in the suburb of Zapote, about five minutes from downtown San José by car or taxi. Because Costa Rica is so small, all land records are kept at this office.

Costa Rican law requires that all documents relating to an interest and/or title to real property be registered in the property section of the Public Registry (Article 460 of the Civil Code).

You can also find the status and ownership of a piece of property and get any title documents and surveys you may need at the *Registro*. If the property is registered in the name of a corporation, the legal representatives must be verified, since they have power of attorney to make the sale. Information may also be obtained from the registry's website at **www.registronacional.go.cr.**

Your specific property can be researched by using the owner's name, *cédula* (national ID card) or registration number, called a *folio real.* The more information you obtain the better.

The first information that appears should be the owner and registration number. If the registration number ends in 000, chances are you are dealing with an individual owner. If there is another number within the 000, there are probably co-owners. For example, a husband will have the number 001. If a 002 appears, this indicates the property has two different, non-married owners.

The printout you receive will give you the following information in Spanish. You may need someone to translate.

(a) The description of the property and the name of the province where it is located.
(b) The boundaries of the property
(c) The area in square meters (make sure the property you are buying really is the same size).
(d) The survey number of record.
(e) Origin of land or history (perhaps it was a farm before, etc.)
(f) Government assessment for transfer purposes
(g) Data concerning the owners— whether an individual, individuals or a corporation.

(h) *Cédula* (ID) of the owner(s) or corporation
(i) Estimated price (this can vary in Costa Rica; there is sometimes a difference between what is paid and what is actually recorded).
(j) Statement of full ownership
(k) The number that was recorded in the registry when the owner took over the property.
(l) Date registered.
(m) *Anotaciones*—this is very important point since there may be pending activity concerning the property.
(n) *Gravámenes*— has to do with liens, mortgages and encumbrances.

Deposits and Escrows

Let us hear what one local expert has to say about this subject: "In Costa Rica a real estate transaction is different. I have read various Internet articles about "crooked" real estate transactions in Costa Rica. The first step in protecting yourself here in a real estate transaction is to realize you are in a different country governed by a different legal system and you fall under the umbrella of the way things are done here and not the way they are done in the United States. For instance, real estate deposits and escrows here are very different. Escrow accounts are virtually nonexistent unless you are dealing with a company like Stewart Title or have a legal arrangement with your lawyer. I will focus on deposits, since you definitely need to be aware of how they work in Costa Rica.

"The majority of the time the deposit is going to be held by the seller. Instead of 'held,' I should have said 'given' to the seller. I do not think many sellers in Costa Rica hold deposits very long. Therefore, you should place as little money as possible in the hands of the seller. Five percent is a start, with a maximum of 10 percent. When asked how much I would like to deposit, I usually say, 'the least amount of money possible.' Then, when the seller names a figure I always say it is too much. What is the least amount possible? It is amazing how much sellers will come down to initiate a sale.

"If you back out as a buyer, the seller who already has your deposit will most likely keep it. I would venture to say that in Costa Rica, in many cases the seller has already spent the deposit money. You can put a protective clause in your contract, but the bottom line is, that deposits, once lost, are hard to recover here. The one clause I advise clients to put in the contract is that if the seller does not honor the contract or other unforeseen circumstances occur, the buyer will be returned double the original deposit. I do not think this clause scares away anyone, but it might help you in another situation. It is not uncommon for the seller to sell the property to someone else if they offer a higher price.

"You may think that if you lose your deposit you can take the seller to court to recover it. The legal process can sometimes take years.

"Concerning monies, I advise clients never to use cash because there is no paper trail and cash can do funny things to people. Certified or regular checks from the United States can take a long time to clear. It is better to open an account here, wire your money and get a certified check from your bank in Costa Rica."

Transferring Title

If a property appears free and clear of encumbrances, the lawyer can then proceed. Your lawyer should then draft a transfer deed or *escritura de traspaso* to move the ownership from seller to buyer. The transfer deed should include details about financing of the property. In Costa Rica the buyer and the seller usually share the closing costs, which normally runabout four to five percent of the total purchase. A small real estate transfer tax, or 1.5 percent of the actual value, is included, as well as a registration fee, stamps and notary fees, which vary depending on the price of the sale. Title insurance is optional but advisable. It is common practice with many lawyers in Costa Rica to lower the actual amount paid on a sale to a much lower sum on paper to reduce land transfer tax. This can be risky and problems may arise later on. Make sure you understand what you are expected to pay.

In Costa Rica, the seller transfers land to the buyer by executing a transfer deed (*escritura*) before a notary public. Unlike common law countries, such as the United States and Canada, in Costa Rica the notary public has extensive powers. The notary public must be an attorney and may draft and interpret legal documents, as well as authenticate or certify the authenticity of documents. In order to close on the property, the buyer must select a notary/attorney who will draft the transfer deed and register the sale in the Public Registry (*Registro Nacional*).

If the purchase price is financed, there are 3 options for selecting the notary/attorney:

1. If the seller is financing a large percentage of the purchase price and a mortgage needs to be drafted to guarantee payment, then the seller may request that her or his notary/attorney draft the transfer deed.
2. If a property is purchased with 50 percent cash and 50 percent financing, it is common for the buyer's attorney and seller's attorney to jointly draft the transfer deed and mortgage in a single document.
3. Finally, the buyer may insist that his or her notary/attorney draft the transfer deed and let the seller's notary/attorney draft a separate mortgage

instrument. In this case, because the mortgage is being drafted separately, it carries a higher registration fee.

Property may be purchased individually, between several people or in the name of a corporation (*sociedad anónima*). Buying and registering a property in a corporation has many advantages, mainly, asset protection in the event of a divorce or a lawsuit. When a corporation owns the property, the sale or purchase of the company can be negotiated so you don't have to pay property taxes or stamp fees. All you have to do is change the board of directors, the legal representatives of the corporation, and transfer the shares.

Do not hire the same lawyer used by the seller of the property. In Costa Rica an attorney can legally represent both parties. Also, do not forget to check that you are buying the land from its rightful owner. Some owners have sold their land to several buyers. You can protect your real estate investment further if you talk with neighbors about water shortages, safety and burglaries in the area.

Remember, always see the property in person and never buy sight unseen. Don't forget to check if you need special permits to build. Be sure to check the comparative land values in your area to see if you are getting a good deal. If you are thinking of living in a remote area, check to be sure that roads, electricity and telephone service are available.

Closing costs for a sale include a transfer land tax, a stamp tax, and legal fees. Closing costs typically run 3 – 6% of the sales price and are usually paid buy the buyer. The transfer taxes (if not owned by a corporation) and land taxes are assessed based on the declared value, while legal fees are charged based on sales price of the property. If the property is held by a Costa Rican corporation (often the case) a large portion of these costs can be avoided

Stewart Title (Tel: 2258-5600, Fax:2 222-7936, see www.stewarttitle.com) can assist you with title searches and full title guarantee. **American Title** also has a representative in Costa Rica.

Recently the **Costa Rica Realtors' Chamber** opened the country's first out-of-court conflict resolution center specializing in property disputes. It specializes in solving property disputes for both sellers and buyers within six months. The same process in the courts can often take up to 10 years or more to get to trial. Anyone in need of such services may contact them at Tel:2 283-2891, Fax: 2283-0347, or E-mail: caccbr@racsa.co.cr.

Property Taxes

You will be pleased to know that no capital gains taxes on real estate exist in Costa Rica, so real estate is an excellent investment. You do have to pay yearly taxes, but they are low by U.S. standards. Yearly property taxes are on a sliding scale up to .25 percent of the stated value of a particular property. So on a house valued at $100,000 you pay about $250 yearly. This is a bargain compared to what most people pay in the United States.

Property taxes are collected by the local municipal government, which also collects a separate tax for garbage. The latter has to be paid when you pay your property tax. Every year the author goes through this painless procedure at the *Palacio Municipal de Heredia*. The taxes on my home run about $280 including garbage. I have found the clerks at the city offices to be very courteous and helpful.

New tax on luxury homes

The new luxury tax law went into effect October 1, 2009 and affects owners of homes worth more than 100 million *colones* or $172,000. For example, a homeowner with a house worth just 100 million colons could expect to pay a tax of just one-fourth of a percent. That is 250,000 colons or about $430. The law, No. 8683, is designed to provide funds to give housing to the extreme poor. The income from the tax is earmarked for the *Banco Hipotecario de la Vivienda*, which would use the funds to build housing for the poor now living in slums, according to law. For help see: www.amcostarica.com/chart101209.jpg

The Complete Guide to Property Taxes and the Luxury Home Tax in Costa Rica is a new book ebook which will help you learn how the local government calculates, collects and spends the property taxes in Costa Rica. The answer to your questions are all contained in this book. It has direct links to government land valuation maps for Costa Rica, construction valuation manuals, directory of municipal governments of Costa Rica, property tax and luxury home tax filing forms and much more. To order a copy go to www.costaricalaw.com/bookstore/costaricalawbooks_orderpage.html

Squatters

Squatters, or *precaristas*, as they are known in Costa Rica, can be a real problem.

In Costa Rica squatters have certain rights. The laws that protect them were originally passed to prevent wealthy people from acquiring too much land, as in some Latin American countries. Land ownership here is an active process — stop taking care of it and it will go to someone who will. It is the law and the intent of the law. Costa Rica did not establish its law so that foreigners could buy large chunks of land and leave it idle as a future investment. They established their law originally so that they wouldn't have a large class of people denied land because a few very rich owned it.

Undeveloped land is a prime target for squatter invasions. Once they establish themselves on your land, it is difficult to get rid of them. If they occupy the land for less than a year, it is fairly easy to have them removed, especially during the first three months. The sooner you get them off the land, the fewer problems you will have. Be careful! After a certain period of time they can claim the land as their own.

The best way to avoid squatters is to prevent them from settling on your land. Visit the land periodically to help prevent people from settling on it. If you cannot live on your property year-round, then you will have to hire a guard, caretaker or a reliable house sitter to watch it for you. If you have a caretaker make sure to obtain a receipt each time you pay him. Have your lawyer or some other person keep an eye on your caretaker. There have been cases in which caretakers have tried to squat on land.

Also, make sure boundary fences and limit signs are well maintained and visible. If you have to be an absentee owner, you can have a friend or attorney stop by to check your property periodically.

There is a trustworthy professional house-sitting agency in San José that will watch your home while you are away. It is bonded and will provide references upon request. You may contact the agency at 2256-7890.

Building a Home

In Costa Rica you can build your retirement dream house since land, labor and materials are inexpensive. However, think twice about undertaking such a project because you could be flirting with disaster. Many foreigners who have built homes complain that it sounds easier than it really is. They would not do it again because of costly delays, unreliable labor, fussy building inspectors, different laws and building codes and many other unforeseen problems. Be sure to talk with foreigners who have built homes to see what obstacles they encountered. Costs depend on location, materials and the size of the home you want to build. You generally pay $500 to $1,000 a square meter or $45 to $90 a square foot.

One common mistake some newcomers make is to hurry to build their dream home while they are still on their "honeymoon" with the country. Many have been shocked by substantial cost overruns. Months or years later, they realize too much of their capital has been spent on their new home.

If you do decide to build a home on your land, there are several steps required. First, conduct a preliminary study, which should be completed before you buy the land. Also, be sure to see if your lot has access to water, drainage, electricity and telephone services.

The law says you have to hire an architect or civil engineer to file all of your construction permits.

A building permit must be obtained from the municipality where you plan to build. An architect can usually handle building permits and work jointly with the contractor to supervise the construction. It may take a couple of months or longer to get all of the permits in order.A reliable contractor will also have to be hired. You should get several bids and ask for references. Expect to visit the construction site almost daily to ensure things are getting done. If you cannot be there, have a reliable person inspect the construction site for you on a daily basis.

According to one local realtor, this is how you can lose money while building a home:

1. Give money to a real nice and friendly contractor and then leave the country and tell him you will be back in a couple of months.
2. Take the first bid you get because it seems so incredibly cheap, far cheaper than anyone else's. Halfway through, when the real price emerges, it is nearly impossible to get a second contractor to come in and finish what the first one started. So, you are stuck with him and have to pay the real price to build, but now you are working with someone you do not trust.
3. Pay no attention to the amount of cinder-blocks delivered to your construction site.
4. Live in the city while building in the country and only drive out on weekends.
5. Give the power of attorney to almost anyone. There is a special trick here for people getting your deed number (*escritura*), and suddenly you don't own the property anymore.
6. Ignore the advice of experienced people because the taxi driver and the guy on the bar stool are "locals" and must give good advice.

In short, I buy my materials directly through local hardware stores (*ferreterías*), get receipts, place orders by phone and live on the land while building on it. Some people do it by contract. I pay the workers once a week, pay my building supplier once a month and use a hardware store I know and trust. The contractor supervising the project gets a bonus of about 10 percent of the total building cost."

One local resident's experience building a home in Costa Rica

"Lots of folks seem interested in building a house in Costa Rica. My wife and I have done this twice and thought that maybe knowing about some of our experiences might prove useful to others.

"Because we're focusing on building here, I won't talk about buying land. I'll assume that you've already acquired the land you want to use.

"We arrived here with plans we had purchased in the States. We found them in one of a myriad of home plan books that you can buy at bookstores. When we made our decision, we sent off with the plans.

"Although we loved the plans, we had to make a lot of necessary changes to make the construction suitable for Costa Rica. For example, we didn't want the house built with wooden studs and sheet rock. We decided to use concrete block and stucco.

"Clearly we needed an architect to help us with all this. So we asked the realtors from whom we had bought the land if they could recommend one. They had someone they had worked with in the past and recommended highly. After twice meeting with the architect, we asked him for a quote, found it reasonable, and contracted him to make the modifications.

"Of course we weren't contracting him to design the house from scratch by any means. Had we been doing that, the process would have been different. In any case, if you're going to build a house, you must have some relationship with an architect so that the plans you submit for approval are properly stamped by a professional architect in good standing in Costa Rica. You also use the architect to obtain the building permits for you.

"Make no mistake about it: you must get your building permits. I can't tell you how many times I have heard of people who had their building projects stopped dead in the water because they had no permits. The interesting thing is that after you've submitted your plans and received your permits, there's not a lot of checking that goes on to make sure that what you're building agrees with the plans. Personally, however, I would not take the chance of submitting plans that are not what you're going to build.

"Also in our agreement we contracted him to be the supervising architect, that is, he would submit the plans, as mentioned above, would do all the paper work, keep the on-site log required by law, work closely with the builder, etc. We paid him $10,000 for all of that. The funds were paid over the course of the project, according to an agreed-upon schedule.

"We had already found a builder. He lived right in our little town. In fact, our property was part of a huge farm his father had once owned. He had built a lot of the houses for our neighbors, and we examined those very closely. We also looked very closely at houses in the neighborhood built by others. Our guy's work was really superior, plus he had an excellent reputation with our friends and neighbors, almost all North Americans. We never regretted our decision to go with him.

"When the architect had the plans ready, we gave them to the builder and two weeks later he came back with a price for all labor and materials. The price was more than we had expected. We now know that the reason for this was that he was concerned because the house was more complex than anything he had ever built before, and he was padding considerably to help ensure that he didn't lose money. The fellow did everything on scraps of paper and didn't have any kind of estimating system of any sophistication at all; he didn't even have a computer. Some houses he made money on, on others he lost money.

"Although the price was higher than we wanted, it was not unreasonable by any means. We both made some adjustments and soon agreed on a price. One thing should be stressed here; the price was for all labor and materials, that is, it was a fixed price. I'll talk about alternatives later. It was agreed, of course, that any changes we wanted to make would cost extra. As it turned out, we did, indeed, make a handful of changes, one of which was significant and the others rather minor. But for each one we agreed beforehand on the cost so that we knew all along what the project was costing us.

"Three things we talked about quite a bit before signing our agreement had to do with allowances, infrastructure improvements, and payment structure.

"The question of allowances is extremely important in a deal such as this, that is, where there's a fixed price. Clearly you, the owner are going to select things such as finishes (tiles, floors, counter tops, for example), paint, light fixtures, plumbing fixtures, doors, windows, cabinets, shelving and many other things.

"The builder has already estimated what these are going to cost him, otherwise he couldn't give you a fixed price. So you have to know what he estimated so that when you pick things out you'll know whether you're right on the money or whether you're going over budget, in which case you'll owe the builder if you decide to purchase these things anyway, or whether you're under budget, in which case he will owe you money.

"The question of infrastructure is important, too. One must make sure, for example, that the price includes bringing water to the property. In the rural areas where we built both times, there's no such thing as 'city water.' What about telephone lines to the property? What about electricity? All of this has to be planned beforehand, and there are costs the builder isn't responsible for.

"For example, both times we built, although there was electricity available, there was no transformer on the road from which to supply our houses. So we had to pay the electric company for buying and installing a transformer. We had no phones where we first built, so there was no problem about installation. At our second house, telephone service was available, but the nearest pole was a kilometer away. We were responsible for paying for poles and cable and having the work done to bring the lines from that last pole to our house.

"These things about electricity and phone might strike you as being strange or unusual. But if you live out in the country in Costa Rica, that's the way it's done.

"Finally there was the question of payment. We worked out a schedule of how much we needed to give the builder and at what intervals. That made it easy for both of us to watch our cash flow.

"Another important consideration while building is where you will be while the building is going on. The first time we built a large house, we were living in a small guest house right on the property and were always right there. Indeed, every day the foreman (who, by the way, was fantastic) would consult with us numerous times as did the subcontractors. Living on site is absolutely the best arrangement. It's even better when, as in this case, the builder lives right in the neighborhood.

"When we built the second house, we were living in a rental house that was exactly a 20-minute drive from the building site. In addition, the architect/builder lived in San José. What a difference that made. We were obviously not always available to the foreman and subcontractors. We had to schedule regular meetings at exact times on certain days with the builder who had to travel about an hour and a half to get to the site. Although it was doable, it was far from ideal.

"We have friends who continued to live in the States while their houses were being built. In most cases this resulted in large problems and great frustration.

"All in all, the building of our first house went extremely well. The house itself was magnificent, we had all the input anyone could ask for and at the end of the day we still had a fine relationship with the builder.

"I wish I could say that after the first experience, the second was even better because of all we had learned the first time. But the second time we did it differently and I must say that even though in the end, we were extremely pleased with the house, getting to that point was much more difficult than our first venture.

"In this case, we didn't start with pre-drawn plans, but we did have a highly detailed plan that my wife worked out with just a little bit of help from me. Then she built a model that would have done her proud in any school of architecture.

"We met the builder by calling him after seeing his full-page ad in an upscale Costa Rican home and building publication. He was an extremely bright young man who built only log homes, which is what we wanted. There are other log home builders in Costa Rica and we investigated them all. But the type of homes they built were not what we were looking for.

"What we did was to have a series of meetings with the architect at which we would present our ideas, he would make sketches, we'd come back, look at what he did, discuss it and then go to the next round. The purpose of this was to end up with a plan, on paper, with drawings (but not final blueprints) of what we would go ahead with. He charged us a set price for the series of meetings that was quite reasonable, less than $1,000.

"Eventually we agreed on a plan about which we were quite excited. At that point, we contracted, but on an entirely different basis than we did during the first project. This time there was a fixed cost for plans, labor and labor supervision. The idea here is that if they don't meet the deadline for completion, we don't pay anything extra regardless of how long they take.

"The architect's company was also the builder. Materials, however, were only estimated and we would pay for the materials as we went. In most cases they would buy the materials and I would pay the invoices directly to the vendors, unless the architect had already paid for them and gave me a cancelled invoice, in which case I would reimburse him.

"All the things that are normally considered allowances, that is, the things the client picks, we ourselves would just pick and buy, since there was no set price for materials.

"There are two potential dangers in doing this. The first is that the estimate made by the architect/builder is way off, in which case you could go way over budget on materials. The second is that the architect/builder could be in cahoots with the suppliers and we could be overcharged, with them getting a 'commission.'

"The latter was not the case. I was convinced at the time that these were honest people and even after all the difficulties we later had, I still believe them to be honest men. But ... that's the only thing that went well.

"We had the estimate for materials and a completion date five months out. They spent a great deal of time explaining to us why we could be sure that the estimated materials cost was right on the money and the job was going to be on time. Unlike our first builder, these folks were highly computerized—which just goes to show that the old saw about garbage in, garbage out, as far as computers are concerned is absolutely right.

"They were to start working on January 3 or 4 and were to finish on May 30. I fired all of them about early April because it was clear that at this point they had no real idea of when the house was going to be done -- I estimated that it was about 90 percent done.

"At that point we were a good 20 percent over budget and I was having a hard time getting a fix on what was to come. As you can imagine, there was a lot of other stuff going on that contributed to my reaching the point of firing them. One significant problem was, as I mentioned, that they were from San José and weren't here nearly as often as they needed to be, and the foreman here was as bad as our first foreman was great. Additionally, they were always late on their estimates about when we, the clients, had to make certain material choices. This, in turn, resulted in either falling further and further behind schedule or our settling for something that wasn't our first choice.

"Eventually, after I fired them, the job was finished by a terrific local guy. Before we started the house, he had been the architect and supervisor for a large stable, a nice little house for our workers, a large gate, water system, etc. He had done a great job and he's extremely competent and, in general, an exceedingly nice and honorable young man. We didn't consider him for the main house because we wanted someone with experience in building log homes. That was a mistake.

"He did a fantastic job in getting the house and remaining infrastructure work done and had an extremely efficient crew of local workers. Man, what a difference between using local workers and workers who have no tie to the community.

"Clearly, the first arrangement with a fixed price was far superior to this open-ended material purchasing arrangement. We'd certainly never go into an arrangement such as the second one again.

"Concerning prices per square-meter for building, there is a great, great range of prices, so it is difficult to speak generally. The variables involved are many. For example, a huge part of the cost of materials is based on transportation charges. Thus, if you're far away from the suppliers your materials cost can easily increase by as much as 30 percent. At times, I've had delivery charges that were 50 percent of the value of the materials delivered.

"Labor costs, especially unskilled labor, vary from builder to builder, regardless of what the law says. This, too, tends to be influenced by location. If you're building in a generally economically depressed area, the builder will pay the workers less than in an urban area where there might be more work available.

"The type of house you're building will make a great difference in cost per square meter as well. For example, the log and stone house of the second project required much more handcrafting than a block, concrete and stucco house, such as the first one we built. But then comes design. The first one had many curved walls, niches, a curved stairway to the second floor, etc. All of this takes a lot more time to do and thus results in great labor charges.

"In the second project, in addition to the house, we built a large stable, a small house for animal rehabilitation, a large flight cage for un-releasable bats we've rehabilitated, a small house for our workers and a large storage facility. All the prices per square-meter varied greatly, not only because of the usual variables but also because we used several different builders for the several projects.

"But, just to give a general idea, a very good price for a simple home would be between \$270 and \$323 per square meter (\$25 to \$30 per square foot). A simple house would be basically a one-story, rectangular structure with straight walls and a simple roof line built with block, concrete, and stucco. Some people refer to this type of design as a "*tico* house."

"On the other hand, you should be able to build just about anything you want, regardless of how complex and complete, for between \$540 and \$645 per square meter (\$50 to \$60 per square foot).

"If you're building a simple block and concrete house and you're paying between $40 and $45 per square foot, you're probably paying quite a bit too much.

"And if you're building anything for $65 per square foot and above, you're probably building a mini Taj Mahal."

Long-time Costa Rican resident Martin Rice is the author of *At Home in Costa Rica* ISBN 1413460283.

Commercial Real Estate

There is commercial real estate for anyone thinking of starting a retail business or looking for office space. Office space in and around San José can be leased for anywhere from $7 to $20 per square meter, depending on the location.

Downtown San José has outgrown itself. The majority of office space is now found west of the city. More and more tenants are moving into new buildings on the outskirts of town. The new Torre Mercedes and Centro Colón are huge office buildings west of downtown. Oficentro is a huge complex of five office buildings, to the south of Sabana Park. About five minutes to the west is Plaza Roble, located next to Multiplaza Mall. In Santa Ana, the newly constructed Plaza Forum Center has abundant office space.

Many large homes in the Rohrmoser area have been turned into businesses because of the lack of adequate space and office facilities in San José. All of the growth toward the west has happened because many Costa Rican landlords have not refurbished buildings in the downtown area.

Financing

Until about 15 years ago it was difficult for anyone to obtain financing here. The only thing available was owner financing. Up to three years ago, non-residents were not allowed to take out home mortgages at Costa Rica banks. That did not deter home sales. Instead, potential property owners would come with ready cash or take out a second mortgage in their respective countries.

Now all of that has changed. Costa Ricans and foreigners may now apply for loans from public and private banks (There has been a tightening up of credit because of the financial crisis in the U.S. in 2009, but this should change as countries emerge from the recession). However, foreigners need to have a residency permit and/or a job to get a mortgage. Interest on the loan and requirements may vary from bank to bank.

A well-kept secret is that foreigners may use pre-tax IRAs from the United States to purchase property here (see the next section). This procedure is perfectly legal. They can also take out a line of credit on the equity of their home in the United States. I also know of some people who have obtained financing in Costa Rica without being residents as long as their credit rating was good in their home country.

Interest rates for mortgages (*hipoteca*) depend on the market and the institution making the loan. In this section I include samples of what banks require to qualify and interest rates. Most lending institutions require a life insurance policy to cover a loan.

Lehman Brothers Bank has agreed to finance mortgages for foreigners hoping to call Costa Rica their new home.

Lehman is the first foreign bank to provide home financing to non-residents. The Delaware-based institution struck a deal with Stewart Title, which has an office in San José, to facilitate the process on local soil. The company is looking to expand its mortgage lending opportunities outside of the United States, Stewart Title is a natural fit. However, the bank does not mean for the deal to be exclusive.

Stewart Title alone works with seven local banks – ranging from private institutions such as HSBC and Scotiabank to the state-controlled Banco Nacional and Banco de Costa Rica – to help non-residents obtain mortgages.

In general, future clients can pick from six different amortization periods, ranging from one- to 30-year, fixed-rate mortgages with 20 percent down on the home purchase price. The mortgages will be secured with the property through a lien filed with the National Registry of property.

Lehman will deal solely with U.S. citizens first, planning to expand its operations with time.

When you look at the demographics of the baby boomer population, I believe that there will be a lot of baby boomers looking for vacation (and living) opportunities outside of the United States. Costa Rica has built a very nice brand, and people are heading there.

Buying real estate in Costa Rica with IRA funds

If you are looking at real estate in Costa Rica, or for a way to get better returns in your IRA, here is a little secret your stockbroker will never tell you about: The IRS lets you purchase real estate with income that is tax- deferred. This means many savvy investors are investing their IRA funds in real estate. This is a great way to beat the ups and downs of the stock market, diversify your portfolio or provide a stable income as you transition from riskier investments.

How can you do this? The rules governing ownership of real estate in Costa Rica in this regard are simple. First, you may purchase practically any real estate you can imagine: raw land, condos, office buildings, single or multifamily homes, apartment buildings or improved land. You can also own a fraction of real estate, with other entities or investors owning other fractions. You can purchase an option on the real estate or you can buy it outright using a land trust, limited liability company or similar entity. Also, you can roll over your IRA, so you are buying the real estate with retirement assets.

The one exception is that you can't use the Costa Rican real estate in your IRA as your residence or vacation home if you are under 59 and a half years of age. This is logical, since your retirement funds are tax-deferred and are meant to be used for your retirement. In other words, it can be any kind of property, but you can't use it personally, unless you are already retired and take the amount as a distribution. Your business can't lease space in your IRA held property, nor can you place real estate that you already own into your IRA. Also, your spouse, parents or children can't have been the previous owners of the real estate. Property owned by siblings may be allowed, since the Internal Revenue Code (section 4975) specifies that only "lineal descendants" are qualified.

Your IRA custodian must actually buy the real estate you are investing in. So, the title will really be in their name, not yours. You may put up the deposit with your personal funds, in order to reserve the property until the legal structure is in place; in this case, you have to be sure to include that amount in the total due, so you get your money back from your IRA at closing.

You will need to work with an independent IRA custodian that allows real estate investments to set up an IRA account. Most banks and brokerage companies limit your choices to products they sell. However, section 408 of the Internal Revenue Code permits individuals to purchase real estate with funds held in many common forms of IRAs, including a traditional IRA, a Roth IRA and a Simplified Employee Pension plan (SEP IRA).

To find a custodian that specializes in real estate, search under terms such as "real estate IRA" or "self directed IRA." In Costa Rica, your realtor or the developer may be able to help you find a reputable tax attorney or organization to assist you with this. You can't serve as the custodian of your own account. It is important to select a custodian knowledgeable about the types of investment you're interested in, because the custodian holds title to the real estate. It is vital you find a custodian who will permit foreign property or leveraged property.

If the property is financed, you must structure the purchase correctly to avoid adverse tax consequences down the road. Also keep in mind that if the property is leveraged, the debt must be a non-recourse promissory note. But it is possible for your IRA to take on a debt.

Another way is to purchase an interest in the property along with others, such as a spouse, business associate or friend. Because all property expenses, including taxes, insurance and repairs, must be paid from funds in your IRA, you'll need liquid funds available in your account.

A Sample of Requirements for Obtaining a Loan

Note: All of the data below is subject to change

Private Banks

HSBC

www.banex.co.cr
INTEREST RATES IN DOLLARS \$8.5% revised
INTEREST RATES IN COLONES ¢25%
TERM 20 years
MINIMUM LOAN AMOUNT \$30,000
MAXIMUM LOAN AMOUNT (% OF APPRAISAL VALUE) 80%
COMMISSION FEES Approximately 6% including legal fees, bank commission and first month's insurance.
WHO QUALIFIES Residents and non-residents who have lived in the country for at least a year

BAC

www.bancosanjose.com
INTEREST RATES IN DOLLARS Prime rate or 8% minimum, revised quarterly
INTEREST RATE IN COLONES Not available
TERM 15 years
MINIMUM LOAN AMOUNT \$30,000
MAXIMUM LOAN AMOUNT (% OF APPRAISAL VALUE) 70%
\$400,000 maximum
COMMISSION FEES Approximately 10%
WHO QUALIFIES Residents only

Scotiabank

www.scotiabank.com
INTEREST RATES IN DOLLARS From 7.25% for residents. From 8.25% for non-residents.
INTEREST RATES IN COLONES 19.95% 1st year, options start at 22.5%
TERM Up to 30 years
MINIMUM LOAN AMOUNT None
MAXIMUM LOAN AMOUNT (% OF APPRAISAL VALUE) 75% for living purposes
65% recreational or rental purposes
COMMISSION FEES From 5 to 10%

WHO QUALIFIES Residents and foreigners/non-residents who must have two types of ID (including passport), SSN, income tax statements from last three quarters, last bank and credit card statements certification of ownership of house, car, etc. Legalized by the Costarican Consulate or Embassy in US (or Homeland)

Public Bank

Banco Nacional
www.bncr.fi.cr
INTEREST RATES IN DOLLARS $7,5% fixed first year, variable from 9% minimum subsequent years (currently 9.25%)
INTEREST RATES IN COLONES ¢20% fixed first years, periodically adjustable subsequent years (currently 24,5%)
TERM $Up to 20 years ¢Up to 30 years
MINIMUM LOAN AMOUNT $1MAXIMUM LOAN AMOUNT (% OF APPRAISAL VALUE) $80 % / ¢ 90%
$200,000 maximum
COMMISSION FEES 2% Comission: appraisal fees (vary with amount); various other fees
WHO QUALIFIES Residents Only

Banco de Costa Rica
www.bancobcr.com
INTEREST RATES $9,5% ¢23.5%
TERM 15 years
MINIMUM LOAN AMOUNT $40,000
MAXIMUM LOAN AMOUNT (% OF APPRAISAL VALUE) $70% / $80%
COMMISSION FEES Approximately 10%
WHO QUALIFIES Residents Only

Banco de Crédito Agrícola
www.bancocreditocr.com
INTEREST RATES In DOLLARS $9,5%
TERM 20 years
MINIMUM LOAN AMOUNT $30,000
MAXIMUM LOAN AMOUNT(% OF APPRAISAL VALUE) $75% / ¢80%
COMMISSION FEES Aproximmately 9%
WHO QUALIFIES Residents Only

Of course, all income generated from the property will be deposited into your IRA account, so you could use that money to cover your costs. Or you can make annual contributions within federal guidelines: $6,000 annually to a traditional or Roth IRA ($3,500 if you're 50 or older), and as much as 25% of your annual compensation – up to $40,000 – if you're a self employed individual with a SEP IRA.

If your account doesn't have funds to cover property expenses, you will have to withdraw the property from your IRA and pay taxes on the value of the property, as well as possible penalties for early withdrawal. If you decide to sell, the buyer cannot be a family member. Once a deal closes, your IRA account now holds the cash ready for you to make your next move.

A great way to build up your retirement fund is to sell property with seller financing so all payments made by the buyers are paid to the IRA. You can withdraw real estate in Costa Rica from your IRA and use it as a residence or second home when you reach retirement age (59 and a half or older for a penalty free withdrawal).

Either the IRA can sell the property, or you can take an in kind distribution of the property. In this case, your IRA custodian transfers the property title to you. If you expect the property to appreciate and you want to eventually take it as a distribution, the Roth IRA is your best vehicle.

Know Your IRA Options:

A traditional IRA lets you deduct annual contributions (currently set at $6,000) from your income. However, once you begin withdrawing money, those funds will be taxed as regular income.

A Roth IRA gives you no deduction on your current contributions (again $3,000) but does allow you to withdraw funds tax free. If you expect to buy a real estate investment in an IRA and hold it for a long period, this is probably your best option, particularly if the property increases in value over that period. If the property was held in a traditional IRA, you have to pay income taxes on the current value of the property when you sell it or take it as a distribution. With a Roth IRA, you won't owe taxes at distribution; this is the best way if you anticipate your real estate investments will appreciate over time.

A SEP IRA is designed for self employed individuals and small companies. You can contribute up to 25% of your compensation, or $49,000, whichever is less. However, keep in mind that if you have employees, you must make contributions for them as well. This option is a great alternative for real estate practitioners who can make higher contributions, because they can build up funds more rapidly to purchase properties. Withdrawals from a SEP IRA are treated like those of a traditional IRA for tax purposes.

* Courtest of the *Tico Times*

Speculating

If you are interested in purchasing real estate for investment purposes, you will be pleased to know that the government welcomes your investment. If you choose to speculate in real estate, there are some prime areas to choose from in the Central Valley. This area offers a lot more potential because of its proximity to San José, the large number of services available and excellent infrastructure. The towns of Escazú, San Rafael de Heredia, Santa Ana, Ciudad Colón, Alajuela (Costa Rica's second biggest city) and San José's suburbs of Rohrmoser, Los Yoses and San Pedro are all hot spots.

Homes range from about $50,000 in some *tico* neighborhoods to $250,000 on up in high-scale areas such as Rohrmoser and Escazú. It is best to speculate in middle and lower-end properties since they are more affordable for the average Costa Rican and financing is available. A standard rule of thumb is the farther from town you go, the lower the price.

The current housing shortage, the popularity of Costa Rica and the Central Valley's weather assure excellent investment opportunities. Whether you are buying a home or an investment property, you are bound to make money if you hang on to your property. Real estate values are expected to double over the next decade or two. During the last 10 years some property values have risen 10 times. There is limited land in some urban areas, so the resale value goes up as population grows. Beach property is also a good investment because of the demand.

Presently there is a building and investment boom in Costa Rica's Central Pacific and Guanacaste beach areas. Infrastructure continues to improve in these once inaccessible areas. The Central Pacific area is like Hawaii or California, but only a fraction of the price. If you cannot afford to live in a prime coastal area in the United States, you may be able to find the property of your dreams in Costa Rica in a much more spectacular setting.

Remember this when thinking of investing in Costa Rican property. Real estate will not become more plentiful in Costa Rica and the demand will increase based on the number of retirees world-wide. Furthermore, the exodus from the United States due to government policies will increase the worldwide demand created by North Americans looking for a simpler lifestyle.

Another excellent investment is Costa Rica's nascent Real Estate Investment Trust Market. Briefly, a Real Estate Investment Trust (*fondo inmobiliario*) or REIT is a type of public investment fund that buys and rents out real estate and distributes the profits among investors. Depending on the fund, dividends are paid on a monthly, quarterly or yearly basis. Revenues for these types of funds depend mainly on the price at which the property was bought and the price at which it rents. For more information,

Scenes from life in Costa Rica

A perfect ending to a day in paradise

Natures wonders await you in Costa Rica

A view from a high-rise condo in the Central Valley

A beautiful home in the Central Valley

In Costa Rica you can have a kitchen with all of the amenities of home.

Many condos and apartments have swimming pools in a tropical setting

Participants on Christopher Howard's tour check out a beautiful home in the Central

Modern supermarkets stock all of the goodies from home and more.

An older middle-class home in Heredia

Modern strip malls and shopping centers abound in the Central Valley

One of Costa Rica's many pristine beaches

In Costa Rica you can have a beach all to yourself.

Outdoor farmers markets are the place to buy inexpensive fruits and vegetables

It is easy for foreigners to go into business in Costa Rica.

One of Costa Rica's laid-back city parks

A quaint neighborhood watering hole

Costa Rica is one of the world's best surf ng spots

An upscale home at the beach

Mother Nature at work again

A couple of Christopher's tour participants checking out the shopping at Jaco Beach

Your can be comfortable in a condo like this at the beach

Homes in the hills at beach community

Costa Rica is a tropical paradise

Anyone want a fresh coconut at the beach?

contact **Costa Rica Retirement Vacation Properties** at **E-mail: robert@costaricaretirementvacationproperties.com, christas@racsa.co.cr** or call toll free 1-888-581-1786.

Banks offer properties that were collateral for a mortgage loan and were legally repossessed by the bank after the client defaulted on the loan. Properties are awarded to the highest bidder. Most banks require a five percent security deposit when making a bid. Some good deals may be found by checking with a local bank.

Property management companies are available to take the hassle out of home ownership. Most property management companies charge a monthly fee to cover general maintenance, security and upkeep costs. The fee ranges from $50 to $150 monthly. If you have a rental in the Central Pacific or Guanacaste beach areas, one of these companies is essential. A list of property management companies can be found in the local Yellow Pages under "*Administración de Condominios.*" In addition, many real estate companies have partnerships with property management companies. I have friends who own a rental property in an exclusive gated community in the Central Pacific area who use a local realtor to manage their condo. They are very pleased with this service.

Helpful Real Estate Publications

Before buying a home or making any other real estate investment, I suggest you educate yourself by studying the Costa Rican real estate market. Fortunately, there are excellent guidebooks available to assist you and answer most of your questions.

Once again, *Christopher Howard's Guide to Real Estate in Costa Rica,* is the definitive work on the subject. Costa Rica's top real estate minds collaborated to write this one-of-a-kind guidebook. It leaves no stone unturned. To order contact **Costa Rica Books** toll-free at **1-800-365-2342, liveincostarica@cox.net,** visit **Amazon.com** or obtain it through your local bookstore. The eBook version may be ordered through www.escapeartist.com.

Another good source of information is the *The Tico Times* biannual *Real Estate and Investment Supplement*. It is packed with useful articles and advice. Reading this guide will keep you up on the local real estate scene. It is also filled with ads from local real estate brokers.

Costa Rica Real Estate Magazine is an informative publication that lists numerous properties for sale as well as brokers. To subscribe, see www.thecostaricaguide.com.

Real Estate Terms

amortization .... *amortización*
appraisal........ *el avalúo*
appreciation........ a*preciación*
back yard .... *el patio*
bathroom .... *el baño*
bedroom .... *el dormitorio*
borrower .... *el prestatario*
to borrow .... *pedir prestado*
buyer .... *el comprador*
cash price........ *precio al contado*
closing costs........ *el cierre*
collateral .... *la garantía*
clear title........ *título libre de gravámenes*
closing costs .... *costo de los gastos de cierre*
compound interest........ *interés compuesto*
condo .... *condominio*
contract .... el contrato
counter offer........ *contraoferta*
credit rating .... *el historial crediticio*
debt........ *deuda*
declared value .... *el valor declarado*
deed .... *el título de propiedad*
depreciation........ *depreciación, desvalorización*
down payment .... *la prima, pago inicial, enganche*
easement........ *el servidumbre*
encumbrance, lien .... *el gravamen*
equity .... *el activo neto*
extensión of time .... *la prórroga*
extensión of credit .... *concesión de crédito*
farm........ *a finca*
first mortgage .... *hipoteca en primer grado*
fixed-rate mortgage........ *hipoteca con tasa de interés fija*
fixed term .... *plazo fijo*
for sale........ *e..n venta, se vende*
gated community .... *residencial amurallado*

Hall of Records for property .... *El Registro de Propiedad*
hectare (2.5 acres .... *la hectárea*
house .... *la casa*
interest rate .... l*a tasa de interés*
investment .... *la inversión*
joint tenancy .... *tenencia conjunta*
kitchen .... *la cocina*
landlord .... *el casero*
lease .... *el contrato de arrendamiento*
lender .... *el prestamista*
letter of credit .... *carta de crédito*
line of credit .... *la línea de crédito*
list price .... *precio de lista*
loan .... *el préstamo*
market value .... *el valor de mercado*
mortgage .... *la hipoteca*
to mortgage .... *hipotecar*
offer .... *a oferta*
permit .... *el permiso*
pool .... *la piscina*
prime interest rate .... l*a tasa de interés preferencial*
property .... *la propiedad, bienes inmuebles*
property tax .... *impuesto territorial*
real estate .... *bienes raíces*
real estate broker .... *corredor de bienes y raíces*
real price .... *precio real*
rent .... *el alquiler*
to rent .... *alquilar*
second mortgage .... *hipoteca en segundo grado*
sold .... *vendido*
tenant .... *el inquilino*
tax .... *el impuesto*
title .... *el título*

6

Red Tape

Dealing With Bureaucracy

Just as in the rest of Latin America, Costa Rica is plagued by a more inefficient bureaucratic system than the United States is. This situation is exaggerated by the Latin American temperament, the seemingly lackadaisical attitude of most bureaucrats, and the slower pace of life. The concept of time is much different from that in North America. When someone says they'll do something *"ahorita"* (which literally means "right now"), it will take from a few minutes to a week, or maybe forever. It is not unusual to wait in lines for hours in banks and government offices and experience unnecessary delays.

This situation is very frustrating for foreigners who are used to fast, efficient service. It can be especially irritating if you don't speak Spanish well. Since very few people working in offices speak English, and most North Americans speak little else, it is advisable to study basic Spanish. However, if language is an insurmountable obstacle at first, use a competent bilingual lawyer or ask the **Association of Residents of Costa Rica** (ARCR) to help you deal with Costa Rica's bureaucracy or "red tape jungle," as it is known. Above all, learn to be patient and remember that you can get the best results if you do not push or pressure people. Try having a good sense of humor and using a smile. You will be surprised at the results.

You shouldn't despair if Costa Rica's "bureaucrazy" gets you down. For a small fee, you can get a person (*gavilán*) to wait in line for you while you run errands or make better use of your time.

A few words of caution: there are some individuals, (*choriceros* in popular jargon), who pass themselves off as lawyers or who befriend you and offer to help you with red tape, claiming they can shortcut the bureaucratic system because of their contacts. As a general rule, avoid such individuals or you will lose valuable time, run the risk of acquiring forged documents, most certainly lose money, and experience indescribable grief.

Since bribery and payoffs are common in most Latin American countries and government employees are underpaid, some people advise paying them extra money to speed up paperwork or circumvent normal channels. This bribery is illegal and not recommended for foreigners, who can be deported for breaking the law. However, in some instances it may be necessary to pay extra money to get things done. Use your own discretion in such matters. A tip here and there for a small favor can accelerate bureaucratic delays. I have a friend who was in the process of getting all of the required paper work to marry a Costa Rican. He was in a hurry and did not have time to waste. He went to the National Registry to get his future wife's birth certificate and was told he would have to wait a week. So, he passed out a little extra money and had it the next morning.

United States Embassy Services

Everyone planning to live, retire or do business in Costa Rica should know that the U.S. Embassy (in the San José suburb of Pavas) can help with Social Security and veterans benefits, notarizing documents, obtaining new U.S. passports, reporting lost or stolen passports, obtaining a marriage license, registering births of your children, registering to vote, complying with Selective Service registration requirements, private mail service, reporting deaths of U.S. citizens abroad, and getting a U.S. visa for your spouse (if you choose to marry a Costa Rican). They also assist in obtaining absentee ballots for U.S. elections and getting U.S. income tax forms and information. However, if you get into any legal trouble in Costa Rica, do not expect help from the U.S. Embassy.

Social Security — In the past there were two ways of receiving your Social Security check if you lived abroad. First, you could have it sent directly to your P.O. box in Costa Rica through the U.S. Embassy. The only problem with this method was that the checks did not arrive until almost the third week of the

A Trip Through Costa Rica's Bureaucratic Maze

by Loyd Newton

It's always an adventure in paradise when you have to deal with the bureaucracy in any of its many forms. Fortunately, it's not something I have to do very often. I've been in Costa Rica for a little over two years now and things are starting to expire and renewal times coming near. My driver's license was due to expire at the end of this week so Monday I went down to the offices in San Jose on Calle 7 to renew it.

I parked my car in one of the public parking lots and they conveniently had a sign posted with the requirements for new and renewed licenses. Besides money, I needed to get a doctor's exam for my renewal. I didn't even make it halfway from the parking lot to the drivers license office when I was waved into a doctors office. The exam took about 5 minutes which consisted of answering a few questions and reading the eye-chart above the green line. The doctor also mentioned he had a private practice near my home town and handed me a few business cards to take with me.

At the office I discovered a line that went out the door. Luckily for me, the line that stretched out the door was for new licenses. The one for renewals was doubled around the inside of the offices. I noticed a lot of people armed with newspapers for the long wait. My helper (interpreter, guide, etc.) went to get us a newspaper while I started my hour long wait in line. The people in line near me were very friendly and immediately started up conversations. The man ahead of me spoke English pretty well and was a fountain of information about the process. So instead of reading a newspaper, I spent my hour in line conversing with the *ticos* and the time went by quickly.

Once I got to the head of the line, I showed my doctors certificate and old license to the man at the first stop. He was very concerned about the fact that my residency card was expiring in June but said I could renew my license. Just use my passport he said and don't show them the residency card. Well, to be honest, I figured out what he was saying at the time but didn't understand what he meant until I hit the last stop.

I took my papers, got back in another line for the bank. There I paid 10,000 *colones* for my 5 year license. I told them the sign said it was only 4000 *colones* but they explained that was for the 2 year license. Sounded good to me, so I took my receipt and got into another line for the cameras. After about 15 minutes, I made it to the head of the line and went up to have my photo taken for the new license. When I got there, I handed over my papers and receipts and the man asked for my *cédula*. My big mistake was in giving it to him. He took one look at it and said he would not take my photo. He took me back to the start, "do not pass go, do not collect license". There the man asked me why I showed the man my *cédula* and I explained because he asked me for it. He told me, that the man would not take my photo or give me the license because my *cédula* was expiring in two months. This didn't make any sense to me, since I don't even need residency to get a license here.

When people get a little excited here, they talk very fast so I was having a hard time understanding what they were telling me. My helper had gotten separated from me between the last stop and the return to go. Fortunately, a *tica* came over and translated for me. There are some wonderfully helpful people here! While they were explaining the man's reason for not taking my photo, another photographer stepped up and said he would do it. So they took me around to another camera station, and within 5 minutes I had my new driver's license.

A low level bureaucrat that likes to have little power or just doesn't like gringos decided that a *cédula* that expires in 2 months was a big problem. Fortunately for me, kinder hearted people stepped in and took care of things. "I have always depended upon the kindness of strangers." So I left the place with mixed feelings....distaste for the petty bureaucrat and the hitch after over an hour of waiting and happiness that the good *ticos* and *ticas* won out and I could finish business that day.

I felt so good about not having anything else to do this week, that I went out and played 18 holes of golf today at Valle del Sol. First time I've played golf in a year so I gave up keeping score on the first hole. A great day to be outside and enjoy the weather though so I thoroughly enjoyed it though my golf game needs a lot of work. Guess I'll just have to get out once a week and practice on it.

Pura vida,
Loyd Newton

month. The other way was to have your check directly deposited into your U.S. bank account. Now, things are much simpler. Your Social Security payments may be deposited electronically to your account in a Costa Rican bank by the third of each month. Banco Nacional, Banco de Costa Rica, Banco Interfin and Citibank offer direct deposit of Social Security checks. All you have to do is complete a form and make sure it gets sent to the Federal Benefits Unit of the US Embassy. Call the embassy at 2220-3050 if you have any questions. Your bank will charge $6 for this service. Here is a bank link with information about direct deposit. **http://www.bancobcr.com/bcr_in.php?id=331**

The Social Security Administration's guide tells you how to receive your Social Security checks while living abroad. See **www.ssa.gov/pubs/10137.html**

Passports — Since 2002, U.S. citizens residing or traveling abroad who need a U.S. passport are issued the latest, state-of-the-art passport incorporating a digitalized photo image and other innovative security features. U.S. embassies and consulates will send the applications to domestic U.S. passport facilities. This increases processing time at some embassies and consulates, but it ensures that U.S. citizens receive secure documents in a timely manner. Therefore, U.S. citizens are encouraged to apply early for renewal of expiring passports.

U.S. embassies and consulates issue passports in emergency situations. Such passports have limited validity and cannot be extended. Bearers are required to exchange their limited validity passports for full-validity digitalized photo passports upon completion of their emergency travel, either through passport facilities in the United States or U.S. embassies abroad.

First-time Passport Applicants — To apply for a U.S. passport, a native-born, U.S. citizen must present a certified copy of his or her birth certificate, two passport photos measuring two inches by two inches (color or black and white with a light background), photo ID and the applicable fee. You will need to present the certificate of naturalization together with the photos, a photo ID, and the fees.

Passport Renewal — You need your current passport as evidence of citizenship and two passport photos measuring two inches by two inches (color or black and white with a light background). To be eligible, you must have been issued a U.S. passport in your name within the past 12 years. There are different fees for adults and for those under 16.

Lost or Stolen Passport — You will need to report the loss of your passport to the police and obtain a copy of the police report. In addition to the two passport photos, you will need to present proof of identity and proof of a U.S. citizenship. The proof of identity could be any photo ID such as U.S. driver's license. Proof of citizenship could be a certified, sealed copy of your U.S. birth certificate and/or an old cancelled U.S. passport.

Report of a Birth Abroad — Children being registered as U.S. citizens must be brought to the embassy or consulate by the U.S. -citizen parent along with the following documents:

1. Child's Costa Rican birth certificate, which may be obtained from the Civil Registry, or *Registro Civil.*
2. Evidence of parent's U.S. citizenship. This may be in the form of an original U.S. birth certificates, U.S. passports, Certificates of Citizenship or Naturalization Certificates. Military IDs are not proof of U.S. citizenship.
3. Parents' marriage certificate.
4. Evidence of dissolutions of previous marriages. If either parent has been previously married, submit original divorce decrees or death certificates.
5. If only one parent is a U.S. citizen, there are additional requirements. Please check with the embassy.

The U.S. State Department provides links and information for U.S. citizens living abroad. See **www.travel.state.gov/travel/living/living_1243.html.**

Here are other matters the embassy can assist you with.

How can I teach school or volunteer in Costa Rica? There are several U.S.-curriculum and English-medium schools in Costa Rica, and some of them recruit teachers in the United States. If you are interested in teaching school in Costa Rica or another foreign country, see the U.S. Department of State's Overseas Schools page for a list of recruiting organizations and for information on schools that are supported by the U.S. government overseas.

The Peace Corps has a small number of volunteers in Costa Rica. Other U.S. non-profit programs such as WorldTeach have placed volunteers in Costa Rica in past years. The Embassy has no specific information on volunteer opportunities at this time. The Embassy of Costa Rica in Washington, DC (202-234-2945) may have additional information about volunteer programs.

Can I receive my Social Security checks at the U.S. Embassy? Only military personnel can receive their Social Security checks at the U.S. Embassy. The recipient should have at least 20 years of service. In order to receive checks at the embassy, you must fill out a registration form to be submitted to and approved by the Office of the Defense Representative in the embassy.

At one time, all other beneficiaries could receive checks in Costa Rica by registering with the Federal Benefits Unit. You needed to provide the embassy with your home and mailing addresses, phone number, identification document and Social Security number. The checks were received through Diplomatic Pouch and were mailed via "registered mail" to the address indicated in your registration document. The problem was the checks did not reach the post office boxes until the middle of the month.

The good news is that a couple of Costa Rican banks now offer direct deposit to your account by the third of each month. Please check with the embassy to see which banks provide this service and what forms have to be filled out.

For information about all of Social Security's programs, see their website at **www.socialsecurity.gov**.

What inoculations do I need for Costa Rica? How is medical care in Costa Rica? There are no required inoculations for Costa Rica, but it is a good idea to check with your physician for recommendations of optional inoculations and health precautions. Costa Rica is suffering an outbreak of dengue fever, although the incidence remains lower than in other Central American countries. Dengue is transmitted by mosquito bite and there is no vaccine. Anyone planning to travel in affected areas should take steps to avoid mosquito bites. These include wearing long sleeves and pants, using insect repellent on exposed skin, and sleeping under mosquito netting.

Medical care around the capital city of San José is very good. However, in areas outside of San José medical care is more limited. Doctors and hospitals often expect immediate cash payment for health services. U.S. medical insurance is not always valid outside the United States. Supplemental medical insurance with specific overseas coverage, including provision for medical evacuation, has proven useful in many emergencies.

How can I register with the U.S. Embassy? All travelers should register with the embassy in case an emergency occurs in Costa Rica or at home. Go to the Embassy Consular Section, Window C, Mondays 8 a.m. and 11:30 a.m. and 1:00 p.m. and 3:00 p.m. or Tuesday to Friday between 8:00 a.m. and 11:30 a.m.

You can also send the embassy your information on-line: include name, passport number, travel plans, local contact in Costa Rica, and next-of-kin contact information in the United States. Registration on-line will not serve to prove citizenship in case of passport loss, but will provide a basis for which an emergency passport may be issued.

In person registration is necessary to be entered in embassy records as an American citizen.

Those American citizens who are living in Costa Rica, whether or not they are official residents, should also register.

Do I have access to APO privileges in the U.S. Embassy? If you are a holder of a U.S. military identification card, you may use the embassy's Army Post Office privileges.

What if I Work Outside the United States? If you work or own a business outside the U.S. and are younger than full retirement age, notify the nearest U.S. Embassy or consulate or Social Security office right away. If you do not, it could result in a penalty that could cause the loss of benefits. This loss of benefits is in addition to benefits that may be withheld under one of the work tests explained on the following pages.

For people born in 1937 or earlier, full retirement age is 65. Beginning with people born in 1938, full retirement age increases gradually until it reaches age 67 for those born in 1960 or later.

Report your work even if the job is part-time or you are self-employed. Some examples of the types of work which should be reported are work as an apprentice, farmer, sales representative, tutor, writer, etc. If you own a business, notify them even if you do not work in the business or receive any income from it.

If a child beneficiary (regardless of age) begins an apprenticeship, notify the nearest U.S. Embassy or consulate or the Social Security Administration. An apprenticeship may be considered work under the Social Security program.

The following work tests may affect the amount of your monthly benefit payment. Work after full retirement age does not affect the payment of benefits.

The Foreign Work Test Benefits are withheld for each month a beneficiary younger than full retirement age works more than 45 hours outside the U.S. in employment or self-employment not subject to U.S. Social Security taxes. It does not matter how much was earned or how many hours were worked each day.

A person is considered to be working on any day he or she:

* Works as an employee or self-employed person;
* Has an agreement to work even if he or she does not actually work because of sickness, vacation, etc.; or
* Is the owner or part owner of a trade or business even if he or she does not actually work in the trade or business or receive any income from it.

Generally, if a retired worker's benefits are withheld because of his or her work, no benefits can be paid to anyone else receiving benefits on his or her record for those months. However, the work of others receiving benefits on the worker's record affects only their own benefits.

* **Courtesy of the U.S. Embassy**
American Citizen Services Section
Embassy Hours:
Monday 8-11:30am 1-3pm
Tue-Fri 8-11:30am
Phone 519-2000 ext 2452

Purchasing an Automobile

High taxes make the purchase of a new vehicle in Costa Rica more expensive than in many other countries. In the past, people chose to buy new cars in the United States, where prices are much lower. Now, prices of new cars in Costa Rica are more affordable than before, and more people are choosing to purchase locally rather than deal with the paperwork of importing a vehicle and high taxes.

One more reason to buy locally is to ensure your vehicle will be under warranty in case anything goes wrong. Most local dealers offer two to three-year warranties on new cars.

Due to the high price of new cars, used cars are plentiful in Costa Rica. Most of these second-hand cars are priced higher than they would be in the United States or Canada, so Costa Ricans tend to keep them longer and take better care of them. This makes resale value high.

The majority of automobiles in Costa Rica are made in Japan, so most replacement parts are for Japanese automobiles. Mechanics know these brands and have equipment to diagnose them. Parts are available nationwide for Japanese automobiles.

Spare parts for U.S. cars must be imported, are expensive and sometimes hard to come by. Brands such as Ford, Chevrolet, Saturn and Jeep only have parts available from the dealer or by special order. With some cars, an owner has to be careful about which country version he or she has. Therefore, you should think twice about bringing an U.S. car to Costa Rica.

Other brands such as Honda, Mitsubishi, Mercedes, BMW and Land Rover have good quality parts that are available but they are much more expensive here. These vehicles hold their resale value very well (Other brands such as Kia and Daihatsu have very low values on the secondary market)

If you do decide to bring a car from the United States or Canada, it is best to bring a Toyota, Nissan, Honda or other Japanese import for the reasons just mentioned.

If you plan to drive mostly in the country's larger cities, smaller, new or used cars will help reduce fuel consumption and are easier to maneuver on crowded streets. Prices for new small cars are extremely affordable and range between $12,000 and $16,000,while new mid-sized vehicles cost between $17,000 and $23,000. Those of you who plan to drive outside the city and off-road should consider a sport utility vehicle (SUV), pick-up or jeep. Many of the country's roads are unpaved and filled with potholes, and a solidly built vehicle is absolutely necessary especially during the rainy season. Prices of new SUVs run $20,000 to $75,000, depending on the model and size of the vehicle. Used cars are priced substantially lower.

Here are sample prices of some used cars found in the *The Tico Times'* classified ads. Also check out **www.crautos.com** for prices.

All prices are in U.S. dollars

95 Chevy Lumina	$4,900
91 Isuzu Amigo	$2,900
02 Chrysler Caravan	$21,500
00 Mercedes S-500	$30,000
04 Mercedes E240	$48,000
91 Isuzu Rodeo	$5,500
4X4s	
99 4-Runner	$14,000
03 Pathfinder	$27,000
91 Land Cruiser	$13,900
00 GMC Jimmy	$18,500
01 Jeep Wrangler	$22,500
80 Land Cruiser Diesel	$13,900
87 4-Runner	$8,900
03 Dodge Dakota	$25,000
95 Mitsubishi Montero	$11,000

On the road between the Pan-American Highway and the town of Grecia there are sixty-five used car dealerships. Check this area for a wide selection of used cars.

Since new cars are so expensive in Costa Rica, buyers have the option to lease or finance. The dealer can usually arrange financing. If not, many Costa Rican banks offer financing for cars. Interest rates are generally in dollars instead of *colones* and vary according to market rates.

Bringing a car to Costa Rica

If you decide to bring a car to Costa Rica, there are two ways to do it: by sea or by land. If you ship your car to Costa Rica by boat, contact a shipping company near where you keep your car in the United States or one of the companies mentioned in this chapter. This method of transportation is relatively safe since your car can be insured against all possible types of damage.

If you have all of your paperwork in order, your vehicle should not take more than a month at most to reach Costa Rica, depending on your port of departure. If you send your car from Miami, it takes only one week to reach Puerto Limón on the east coast of Costa Rica and costs about $800 plus taxes. From the west coast or New York, you can expect to pay more than $1,300 plus taxes and some other fees to process your paperwork.

To import a new or used vehicle, you will have to make sure your shipping company sends the following documents: a driver's license for all potential drivers, the original clear title or pink slip (*título de propiedad*), original registration, copy of passport, original bill of lading (*conocimiento de embarque*) if the vehicle has been shipped, and the name of the shipping company. Also make sure your car has Canadian or U.S. plates, or the whole process may be delayed.

Note: **ALL VEHICLES**, since June 7, 2001, require an Emissions Control Certificate certified by the Department of Motor Vehicles from your country of origin or by the vehicle's manufacturer if new, dated no later than 30 days prior to the shipping date. The certificate must be translated into Spanish by an official translator and authenticated by the Consulate of Costa Rica nearest to the Emissions Inspection Station that issued your certificate. This applies even to used vehicles, and any car without it will not be able to be registered in the country. This change, in fact, caused many vehicles to be stuck in Customs for a time, as the law passed in December 1999, but was never enforced until the middle of 2001.

To be safe, call the nearest consulate to check what documents are actually required. In many cases, they will ask for a notary public to authenticate the gas emission test and then have the State Department certify that the notary is registered.

If your name does not appear on the original title of the vehicle, you must provide a document from an attorney certifying that the owners allow you to drive their car. Said document must be notarized and approved by the nearest Costa Rican Consulate in your country of origin. Cars that are being financed in the United States and are not fully paid off fall into this category.

If you do not provide all of the documents above, including the gas emission certificate, you cannot import the vehicle to Costa Rica.

Make sure that the VIN (vehicle identification number) and all details of the car are correctly typed on all documents. Any errors will void the documents and prevent you from importing the car.

Calculating Taxes on a Vehicle

Long-term imported vehicle duties are calculated by multiplying the Vehicle's Appraised Value (VCAV) at the *Ministerio de Hacienda* by following the percentages according to model year. The VCAV is the sum of the vehicle's market value, freight and freight insurance. Freight is the cost of transporting your vehicle to Costa Rica.

If an expat does ship in a vehicle, he or she will pay the following rates on cars, SUVs and pickups.

Duties are determined by the age of your vehicle. If your vehicle is a 2009, 2008 or 2007, you pay 52.9percent of the retail value plus shipping. If your car is a 2006 or 2005, you pay 63.91 percent of its value plus shipping. For any vehicle older than 2004, a tax of 79.03 percent plus shipping will be charged.

Brand new cars purchased at dealerships here have about 30 percent worth of duties applied to the price. These rates are applied not only to the black book value of the car (regardless of the purchase price), but also to the shipping and insurance costs. If an expat would like to find out how much a particular vehicle will be taxed, he or she can check with the *Ministerio de Hacienda*.

If there is no bill of lading or if you drove your vehicle, freight will equal seven percent of the market value of your vehicle, which could equal thousands of dollars more than actual freight charges. Freight insurance is the amount of money you pay to insure your vehicle. If you did not pay insurance, Customs will multiply the sum of the market value and freight first by 110 percent, then by 1.5 percent.

As you can see, taxes are now higher for used cars. In order to establish the value of a used vehicle, you present the commercial invoice with the purchase value of the vehicle. If you do not have an invoice, you have to declare the value.

Do not think you can fool the Customs inspectors by putting an arbitrary value on your vehicle. They have a list showing the manufacturer's suggested retail price of every vehicle manufactured when it was new, including extra equipment.

In the past, Customs agents would refer to the market value based on the "Black Book," a manual published in the U.S. with a listing of new and used car wholesale auction prices for United States car dealers and loan officers, but Customs agents no longer depend on this book. However, if you want to get an idea of the value of your vehicle, contact **National Auto Research** at 2620 Barrett Road, PO Box 758, Gainesville, GA, 30503, Tel: (800) 554-1026, Fax: (770) 532-4792, www.blackbookguides.com.Another good resource is **www.crautos.com**.

Duties may be checked at the *Ministerio de Hacienda.* **(www.hacienda.go.co/autovalor** www.hacienda.go.cr/autohacienda/autovalor.aspx). However, to obtain a better estimate of the duties to be paid, send a fax or E-mail to the Association of Residents or Charles Zeller at E-mail: **shiptocostarica@racsa.co.cr**, toll- free 1-866-280-9036, Fax: 258-7123. Be sure to include the make of the car, model, serial number (VIN), automatic or stick shift, extras such as air conditioning, power windows or other non-standard equipment. Be sure to specify the country from where you plan to ship the car.

After reading the above, if you still decide to import a used vehicle, I recommend using a Customs broker to run around, obtain all the necessary documents and massive paperwork, and help with the taxes. After going through this process, a friend of mine told me, "A good customs agent can save you money." A bilingual attorney is also important and will save you days of running around from one office to another. He can take you step-by-step through the whole ordeal."

However, if you do decide to do this yourself, you will need to follow the procedure below. First, you have to go to either the east or west coast of Costa Rica to pick up your vehicle at the port of entry. This can be a real pain in the neck, requiring a lot of paperwork and patience. It is best to have a Customs agent do all of this for you or go with you in person to pick up the vehicle. A good Customs agent will have all the paper work done and your car out of the *aduana* when you arrive at the port of entry.

When I picked up my 1990 Montero in Limón, we arranged everything beforehand. I took an early-morning bus from San José and arrived in Limón with my agent three hours later. My car was waiting for me in a private parking lot. We just signed one paper, got in the car and returned to San José. The process would not have gone as smoothly had we not planned carefully and coordinated everything with my Customs agent.

Next, you need to register your car, which usually takes a few working days. First, get your paperwork from customs. Then have your vehicle checked at the nearest **Riteve SyC Inspection Center** (www.rtv.co.cr). At present there are 11 inspection centers scattered around the country. Call 800-788-0000 to make an appointment and to locate the nearest station to your home. Cars also have to be taken to these stations yearly for general inspections to assure they are roadworthy. Then take the papers they give you to the *Registro Público* or Public Registry vehicle section (*Registro de Vehículos*) in the suburb of Zapote. Call 224-0628 if you need information. The cost of your registration depends on the value of your car. Finally, take the documents from the registry to the Ministry of Public Works (*Ministerio de Obras Públicas y Transportes*) at Plaza Víquez, south of downtown San José. Your temporary paper license plates will be issued a few months later at the *Registro* in Zapote.

You will have to wait for your permanent metal plates. In the meantime, you will be issued a temporary paper plate that you have to affix to the windshield of your vehicle. There is an expiration date on the temporary paper plate. If your metal plates still aren't ready you may renew the paper plate. If you let it expire, there is a fine.

When your permanent metal plates are ready, you'll need to take the following documents to the National Registry (*Registro Nacional*) in Zapote: the temporary paper plate (*placa provisional*), title of ownership (*título de propiedad*), yellow registration card (tarjeta de circulación) and resident ID card (*cédula*) or passport.

You can find information about vehicles and property by viewing the National Registry's website at **www.registronacional.com.**

Every year you have to pay your *marchamo* or sticker indicating you have paid your obligatory liability insurance. It has to be renewed between November 1 and December 31. This is a certificate that shows your vehicles emissions are within the legal limit. It is like a smog certificate in the United States. A car without a *marchamo* decal on the windshield after the first of January may be impounded.

You may pay the *marchamo* in person at many banks and even on- line with The Banco Nacional.

Here are the locations of the Registro's Regional Offices with hours of operations and phone numbers:

- **San José** (Oeste - West San Jose) 8:00 a.m. a 3:30 p.m., Centro Comercial Plaza Mayor, Rohrmoser, Tel: 2290-2363,/2290-4914, Fax: 2290-2696,
- **Alajuela** 7:30 a.m. a 3:30 p.m., 50 metros al sur de tienda Llobet (50 meters south of Llobet department store), Tel: 2430-1697, Fax: 2430-1697
- **Liberia** 9:00 a.m. a 4:00 p.m., Segunda planta Banco de Costa Rica (2nd floor of BCR), Tel: 2666-8096, Fax: 2666-8096
- **Puntarenas** 9:00 a.m. a 4:00 p.m., Primera planta Banco de Costa Rica (1st floor of BCR), Tel: 2661-1503, Fax: 2661-1503
- **Ciudad Quesada** 7:30 a.m. a 3:30 p.m. Frente a los Tribunales de Justicia (Across from the Court House), Tel: 2460-6300, Fax: 2460-6300
- **Limón** 9:00 a.m. a 4:00 p.m., Primera planta Banco de Costa Rica (1st floor of BCR), Tel: 2798-1257, Fax: 2798-1257
- **Pérez Zeledón** 8:00 a.m. a 3:30 p.m., Segunda planta Banco de Costa Rica (2nd floor of BCR), Tel: 2770-6584, Fax: 2770-6584

Driving an Automobile to Costa Rica

If you have sufficient time and enjoy adventure, drive your automobile to Costa Rica. The journey from the United States to Costa Rica (depending on where you cross the Mexican border), takes about three weeks if driving at a moderate speed. The shortest land distance from the United States to Costa Rica is 2,250 miles through Brownsville, Texas.

Take your time to stop and see some of the sights. I recommend driving only during the day since most roads are poorly lit, if at all. At night, large animals—cows, donkeys and horses— can stray onto the road and cause serious accidents.

Your car must be in good mechanical condition before your trip. Carry spare tires and necessary parts. Take a can of gas and try to keep your gas tank as full as possible, because service stations are few and far between.

Have your required visas, passports and other necessary papers in order to avoid problems at border crossings. Remember, passports are required for all U.S. citizens driving through Central America. You also need complete car insurance, a valid driver's license and vehicle registration.

You can purchase insurance from AAA in the United States., or contact **Sanborn's Insurance** in the United States Tel: 800-222-0158, Fax: (956)-686-0732 or **www.sambornsinsurance.com**. They offer both Mexican and Central American policies.

Instant Auto Insurance offers a 24-hour 800 number and fax service so you can have your policy ready. In the United States and Canada, call 1-800-345-47-01 or Fax: (619)-690-6533.

The web site **www.drivemeloco.com** has information about border crossings and people's experiences making the trip.

You can also buy insurance at the border before entering Mexico. Having an accident in Mexico is a felony, not a misdemeanor. So do not forget to be fully insured.

If you are missing a driver's license, a vehicle registration or insurance, border guards can make your life miserable. Also, remember that some border crossings close at night, so plan to arrive at all borders between 8 a.m. and 5 p.m., just to be safe.

When you finally arrive at the Costa Rica-Nicaragua border, expect to be delayed clearing Customs. If you bring many personal possessions to live in Costa Rica permanently, some or all of them may be inventoried and taken to the Custom's warehouse in San José. You may pick them up at a later date after you have paid the necessary taxes. However, if you come in as a tourist you usually will not be hassled by Customs at the border.

As a foreigner in Costa Rica (a non-resident) you are allowed to drive a car with a tourist permit for three months without paying taxes. Your initial three-month permit to drive your car in Costa Rica may be obtained at the Customs office at the port of entry. The documents required are the title, registration of the car and proof of having paid the local minimum insurance (it is important to understand that this insurance does not cover any vehicle damage. You cannot obtain additional insurance locally while driving with this permit.) Mandatory liability insurance from the **Instituto Nacional de Seguros** is $10 for three months.

Another three-month extension is usually granted, but after six months the vehicle must leave the country or the duties must be paid. To get the one-time three-month extension, you will have to leave the country prior to the three-month limit for 48 hours. Upon re-entry, your passport will be restamped, allowing you to drive the vehicle for three more months. **Warning:** Do not drive the car if the permit has expired—it will be considered an abandoned vehicle and can be confiscated.

When your second three-month extension expires, you have to either leave the country or store the vehicle in a Customs storage facility until you pay the Customs duties and purchase your Costa Rican license plates.

Any person who brings a car to Costa Rica and pays all of the taxes, may keep the car in the country indefinitely once all paperwork is completed. One advantage to bringing your vehicle yourself by land is that you don't have to pay taxes immediately, as you do when you have your vehicle shipped by sea. **Warning**: If you have permanent residency status and bring a car by sea, you will have to pay all of the taxes almost immediately before you can get your car out of Customs.

If you keep your vehicle in Costa Rica, you will have to apply the corresponding tax formula listed above.

For additional information about driving from the United States to Costa Rica, you can see http://drivemeloco.com orpurchase a useful guidebook, ***Driving the Pan-American Highway to Mexico and Central America***, by Raymond and Audrey Pritchard, with help from Christopher Howard. You can order this one-of-a-kind book through **Amazon.com**, **www.drivetocentralamerica.com** or **www.costaricabooks.com**.

Be aware of the following rules if you want to take an automobile out of the country. As one resident who did it pointed out, "Once you have your car in Costa Rica and you want to drive a car across the border from Costa Rica and back, you need to get a *permiso para salida del país* from the Registro Nacional in Costa Rica (there is an office in Liberia, I am told), which will require:

1. A certified, written permission from the owner of the vehicle (you will need to see your lawyer for this)
2. A copy of the title

3. The paid and current *marchamo* certificate
4. The current Riteve inspection document. They will do a search of the Registro files to ensure that there are no unsatisfied liens on the vehicle. They will also make sure that the corporation that owns it, if there is one, is on the up and up regarding liabilities and unpaid taxes.
5. If the vehicle is owned by a corporation, you will also have to supply a certified copy of the corporate constitution.
6. And a recent *personería jurídica*, for the corporation showing that the person seeking authorization to drive the car out is the officer of the corporation and is legally authorized to make such a decision.

Personerías are normally good for only three months, so make sure it is new enough that it will still be valid when you try to come back. The *permiso* document you receive from the *Registro* is good for one journey of no more than 30 days. The car must leave the country within 30 days of the time the *permiso* is issued for it to be valid. At the border, you will have to have some or all of the above documents will be examined by Customs on both sides of the border, going each direction.

Be prepared with at least two certified copies of each; you may be asked for them, and if you are and don't have them, you're sunk — there's no copy center at Peñas Blancas. You will be asked for copies of the *personería jurídica* as well as the *marchamo* by the Costa Rican *aduana* (Customs) going out. Getting across takes about three hours.

Here is what one resident said about his experience at the border. "Going into Panama last year at Paso Canoas, all the officials on both sides were happy with my paperwork, yet I still had to wait in line behind a long line of truck drivers in the Customs office on the Panama side. And when my turn finally came, I had to wait while the Panamanian *aduana* typed out a six-page form, in four copies, hunting and pecking through it on her 40-year old Smith Corona that didn't advance the ribbon anymore. The document she produced was a *Derecho de Circulación* of which every cop I encountered in Panama wanted to see my copy, as did the *aduanas* on both sides coming back into Costa Rica. I was asked to surrender it to the *aduanas* on the Costa Rican side coming back."

Bringing Your Boat or Plane to Costa Rica

Those of you who own yachts and sailboats will be pleased to know that there are two marinas where you may dock your boats in Costa Rica, and plans call for a couple more to be built in the future. The country's marinas are the **Flamingo Marina** in the northwest and the **Los Sueños Resort** in the Central Pacific. The latter has 200 slips and is the only marina where you can keep your boat in the country legally for more than 6 months. Slips rent for about $13 to $15 per month, per foot. The marina offers membership in the Los Sueños Yacht Club, a full range of sport-fishing charters, day cruises as well as other water sports activities.

In the past the longest you could keep a boat in the country without having to pay taxes on it was six months. Duties can be as high as 57 percent of the boat's real value for brand name boats. This is still the case at the Flamingo Marina in Guanacaste. Most people get around this by taking the boat out every six months and then returning. However, you cannot keep doing this. The Los Sueños Marina is the only licensed marina in the country and has a special agreement whereby a boat may be kept in the country under the cover of the marina for up to two years without taking it out of Costa Rica. I understand that you can then renew your permit for another two years. This exemption is only for non-commercial boats and does not apply to those who use their boats for sport fishing. For additional information we urge you to call the Los Sueños Marina at 2643-3941/2.

I understand that a new law will be passed soon that will enable owners of small aircraft to keep their planes in the country like boat owners do at present. The government figures that anyone who owns a boat or plane will possibly make sizeable investments in the country.

Shipping your household goods to Costa Rica

As previously stated, the old *pensionado* program allowed retirees to import household items including an automobile virtually duty-free. Since most of these privileges were rescinded more than a decade ago, you may well have second thoughts about importing anything.

Keep in mind that most imported used items are also taxed. Taxes range from 40 to 90 percent or more of the value of the article plus your shipping costs. Taxes can be raised at the whim of the Costa Rican government. You can, however, save money by purchasing many imported items at the duty-free zone or *depósito libre* in the southern city of Golfito.

The duty-free zone was designed in 1990 for Costa Ricans and residents. Most popular goods sold there are domestic electrical appliances ranging from refrigerators, freezers and stoves to sound systems and television sets. Many brand names are available in a variety of models. Although you may find many of them cheaper in the United States, they are good buys compared to San José's prices—up to 50 percent off on some large appliances. When you add shipping costs from the United States, taxes and possible headaches, it is more practical to buy your appliances at the free port or look for sales at **Importadora Monge**, **Casa Blanca** or **El Gallo** appliance stores.

Some restrictions and paper-work may irk you, but this will be easier for you than importing things from the United States. You can purchase only $500 worth of items every six months. The first period of the year ends on June 30 and the second begins on July 1. You are limited to $500.00 during the first six months. You cannot carry it over to the second period of the year and buy $1,000 worth of merchandise. You can, however, combine your card with a family member's and buy $1,000 per period. You must furnish proof that the person you do this with is really a family member.

You may pick up your Purchase Authorization Card or "TAC" (*Tarjeta de Autorización de Compra*), as it more commonly called, at the booth in the duty-free zone in Golfito. You must be over 18 years old and have a Costa Rican ID or passport to do so.

To find out information about shopping, contact **ACODELCO** in San José at Tel:2 232-1198, Fax: 232-2692 and in Golfito at 2775-0717, Fax: 775-1940. Golfito is open everyday except Monday. Stores open promptly at 8 a.m.

Here is what one resident says about his experience in Golfito: "There are two routes to Golfito: one is through San Isidro de El General through Dominical and Palmar Norte. The other way is along the coastal highway through Jacó. The stretch between Quepos and Dominical used to be unpaved and in terrible shape. It is now paved and flat so you can avoid taking the sometimes treacherous route over the mountain. "

Travel time is about three hours from San José to San Isidro and three and a half hours from San Isidro to Golfito. If you go through Jacó, Quepos and Dominical, you cut about an hour off the trip."

"The duty-free shopping is at the far end of the main street going through Golfito,, The main street circles around the duty-free-area, one way. You can't miss it."

"Rules say that you have to stay overnight in Golfito. So, you need to arrive in Golfito one day before you shop because you need to buy a purchase form. You must take your passport if you are a foreigner or your *cédula* if you are Costa Rican. Each person has the right to buy $500 each semester (January through June and July through December). The trip will take approximately seven hours from San José. "

"There are many hotels available in Golfito but I recommend one that is very close to the duty-free shops. It is good quality and costs only $50 per room with everything included. Each person can buy a maximum of $500

Shopping in Golfito

By Martha Bennett

Appliances are very expensive in Costa Rica because of the import tax. Large appliances are more affordable in Golfito, comparable to U.S. costs. After pricing an American washer in San José at $600, I went to Golfito and bought a washer and dryer for $600. Golfito is near Panamá and used to thrive with the United Fruit Company. When this outfit left, the Costa Rican government allowed the residents to set up a free-zone to maintain their economy.

The procedure for buying appliances is not too difficult but there are steps to follow.

1. There are many excursions which take you there and set up your hotel arrangements. The cost is about $15 round trip plus hotel. You can drive there in about 8 hours. You may also fly, but this uses up your savings. You must stay overnight. This is one of the economy boosting rules. It is hot, but the area away from the freeport complex is quite beautiful.
2. At the shopping complex, get your *boleto.* This form is your permit to buy about $500 on each passport every six months. If you want to buy more, residents of Golfito will sell you their *boleto* for around $25.
3. Proceed in an orderly fashion while shopping. The stores are numbered but they all look alike and you won't want to hit the same one twice. Each shop will give you a paper with their price and store number. Discounts do happen but only for cash. It's worth trying to bargain. Prices vary for the same brand of appliance so throw away papers with higher prices immediately. This saves confusion. If you can decide what you want on the first day, pay for it at once. You can pay the next morning, but lines are long and there are other things to do.
4. Go to your hotel and relax.
5. Return to the stores early, 7:30 a.m., to retrieve your stuff and pay if you haven't. They inspect everything. For big items, there are boys with trolleys to gather everything in a waiting area. Then these boys will take your purchases through the gate where you need to show your passport, *boleto* and sales slip one more time. Do not lose any papers. Your life will be a nightmare. Tips are expected for trolleying your stuff around.
6. Outside, are trucking firms that will deliver your purchases the next day to a warehouse or directly to your house for less than $20. Everything is guaranteed and inspected again. Smaller items can go with you on the bus. If this sounds exhausting, it is. But remember, you can sell these appliances for more than you paid five years down the line. I don't want to do it again, but I'm glad I did it once.

for one or more products. If you go with a relative (wife, husband, sibling, etc.) you can pay for two cards and buy up to $1,000 worth of articles. There is a wide variety of products, but appliances are really worth buying. They cost about half of what they do in San José. You can also buy articles by using another person's name. There is always someone hanging around the facility waiting to sell you extra tickets."

"One word of caution: Make sure you know the retail prices of what you want to buy, and try not to buy on impulse. Stores are numbered 1 through 50, and if you want something special just ask any of the store clerks; they are happy to direct you to the right place.

"Ask for discounts!! Banco de Costa Rica, Banco National, and Banco Popular are all represented and have *cajas* to get cash. The Duty Free Stores will not give you a discount if you pay for it with a Credit or Debit card.. On some larger purchases it is possible to get up to 5 percent or more discounts with cash.. We used both debit card and cash depending on what we were buying. Also, if you buy a lot of items from one store, ask for a discount on the total purchase versus each individual item."

"If you only have a few small items (like me) then find one of the many helpers that have the big hand trucks and pick up all of your purchases going from store to store. I found these guys to be really helpful and honest, they do this everyday, watch it , they will try to take advantage of a *gringo*.the free zone." You will need two hand truck guys, one to pick up your purchased and take it to the check out station and another to take it from the check out station to your car. We paid ¢1500 (a little less than $3.00)each which is a bargain. The second day the it took about 3 hours to complete the shopping,, checking out and packing up and we were on our way home, after paying the parking attendant a little over a dollar per hour."

"If you need delivery service to San José for stoves, washers, dryers or refrigerators, contract someone directly from a cargo company. Just ask the people where you bought the merchandise. They will be happy to recommend someone. You can find these people close to the stores and if you cannot find them, ask anyone and they can help you out. The cost of delivery is two to three percent of the price of the products. It isn't worth it to take any products back with you that were not bought under your name. There are many police stops and check points along the way and they ask for documentation of the purchase, so make sure to keep all paperwork and receipts. You will need your papers at check out time. For small items, many foreign residents go to the town of David, Panama, near the Panamanian border. Prices on everything including household goods are nearly as low as in the United States. However, because of taxes you will have to pay on large electronic goods and appliances, it is better to shop at the duty-free *depósito* across the border in Golfito. Nevertheless, foreign residents living in Costa Rica on a 90- day tourist visa can go to David for 72 hours to renew their papers for another three months. (Be aware that many frown upon this status of "perpetual tourist," and the government is looking at changing this possibility.)

After taking high shipping costs into consideration, you may be reluctant to ship any household items from the United States. This is a matter of personal choice. Most foreign residents and even Costa Ricans prefer U.S. products because of their higher quality. However, many retirees live comfortably and happily without luxuries and expensive appliances.

You can rent a furnished apartment. If you choose, you can furnish an apartment, excluding stove and refrigerator, for a few hundred dollars. Wooden furniture is inexpensive in Costa Rica. You can also purchase good used furniture and appliances from expatriates and others moving out of the country. Check the local English-language newspapers. What you need to import depends on your personal preference and budget.

Make an effort to get rid of "clutter" and bulky items, and do not ship what can be easily or cheaply replaced in Costa Rica. Try to leave large appliances and furniture at home. You pay more for these items in Costa Rica, but in the long run they turn out to be less expensive when you take shipping costs and taxes into consideration. Talk to other foreign residents and retirees to see what they think is absolutely necessary to bring to Costa Rica. One person who moved here recently recommends, "Only bring what you absolutely cannot live without."

If you still want to import your U.S. belongings and household goods and want to save time and money, purchase and ship them from Los Angeles, Houston, New Orleans or, preferably, Miami. The latter is the U.S. port nearest to Costa Rica, and shipping costs are lower. Look in the Yellow Pages of the Miami phone book for a shipping company or call the company listed at the end of this section.

Ways to Bring Your Belongings to Costa Rica

Here are some money-saving tips for bringing items to Costa Rica.First, when entering the country as a tourist by plane, you can bring in a lot of personal effects and small appliances. A tourist is sometimes waved through Customs without ever having to open any luggage. Costa Rica has become a popular tourist destination.

Flying into Costa Rica

The government understands that tourists come here to enjoy the country and have many different hobbies and reasons for visiting. They know that tourists need sports equipment, such as surfboards, bicycles, kayaks or fishing equipment, photographic equipment, small stereos, clothing, toys, a personal computer, radios, tapes and musical instruments. Personal items are not limited to this list. Almost any article that will be used by the resident or traveler while in the country, whether to work or play, may be considered a "personal item."

The government permits items for personal use not intended for resale. The number of these personal items has to be reasonable in relation to the length of the stay or needed for the exercise of one's profession during his or her trip. All items have to be portable and considered luggage.

The amount of luggage allowed on the plane by airlines is limited in most cases to two pieces that must not exceed 50 pounds each. Sometimes they allow excess luggage for an additional fee. If they do allow you to take more, do so, because it is the cheapest way to bring items into Costa Rica.

While on the plane, you have to fill out a Customs declaration form. If you are bringing anything that is not considered luggage under the law, declare it at a very low price. Once you have picked up your luggage from the carousel you will have to go through Customs. If they red-light you, you must go through an inspection; otherwise you'll walk through unstopped.

Tourists and residents have the right to bring in $500 in merchandise purchased abroad every six months tax-free, in addition to personal items considered part of a traveler's luggage. Any merchandise that exceeds the $500 limit and cannot be considered a personal article will be retained in Customs until the import duties are paid. The back of your passport will be stamped *"bonificado,"* which means you will be restricted from bringing more imported items into the country for a period of six months. If you bring in more items within six months, you will have to pay the corresponding taxes. Be forewarned that Customs officials will usually stamp the passports of people who bring in obviously new merchandise.

Used clothing and books are not subject to taxes. Do not pack them with taxable articles or you may have to pay taxes on them anyway.

Ask friends bring a few things when they come to visit you in Costa Rica. Always try to take as much as possible with you on the plane rather than shipping items by boat, because most used personal things are not taxed at the airport. Even used appliances have a good chance of clearing airport Customs if you can fit them on the plane.

Air cargo

If you have a small amount of items (fewer than 500 pounds) that you cannot take with you as luggage, you should consider sending them as air cargo. One slightly crazy friend of mine, who has moved back and forth between Costa Rica and the United States six times, highly recommends American Airlines Cargo. He always uses them to ship his belongings to Costa Rica.

If you choose to ship your belongings by air, find an air cargo freight forwarder in the yellow pages. There should be a couple near any major airport. Ask them if they will take cargo shipment of personal effects to be shipped to San Jose, Costa Rica. You will then have to give them the number of boxes you are planning to ship, and the respective weight and dimensions of each box.

The operator will then figure out the approximate cost. All items will officially be weighed at the airport cargo facility. The cost is based on either the total weight or the combined dimensions of all your boxes, whichever is greater.

You will then be given the choice of sending your things by express or standard freight. The latter is your best bet if you are not in a hurry. It takes only two to five days to reach Costa Rica from the United States. The only drawback to shipping standard rate is that it will be on a space-available basis, and your merchandise may be slightly delayed. The cost works out to be about a dollar per pound.

It is highly advisable to make your travel plans so as to arrive in Costa Rica before your shipment. This way you can go directly to the Customs house and remove your things after paying the corresponding taxes.

Be sure to pack everything in boxes or unlocked plastic bins. Use duct tape to seal the bins. If you are shipping computers, stereos or other electronic equipment, I recommend packing your belongings in unmarked plain boxes. Number each box and put the name and address of the person who will be receiving them in Costa Rica. Make a list of the contents of each box for yourself, the airlines and customs. This will help ensure that your boxes get there intact. Cardboard boxes should be thick and have plenty of packing material to protect any fragile items. Airline employees often heap heavy boxes on top of other cargo. Be sure to write "not for resale"on any paperwork and air bills. This will save you a lot of money when the Customs people figure out how much you will pay in taxes.

We advise you to take a chance and not insure what you ship. This way you will avoid paying tax on the declared value of your goods.

Always consign the shipment to your name as it appears on your passport. If you consign it to a corporation the shipment will be considered a commercial shipment by Costa Rican Customs and you will pay high import duties in addition to having to provide permits and invoices.

You can use a shipping expert to clear customs or do it yourself. If you decide to get your things out of Customs yourself, the process goes like this. First, you will have to go to the airlines cargo facility, pay a small fee and take the paperwork to the Customs house. When you arrive there, you go to a couple of windows. Next, you will sit and wait until they call your name. While you wait you can peek inside a large glass window and watch the workers load and unload boxes of all sizes and shapes from the 20-foot high storage shelves. When your name is finally called you go inside and the inspector opens all of your sealed boxes and determines what the contents are worth. Due to a lack of knowledge or because the Customs inspector will want to, they sometimes apply the same rules as luggage and you will pay nothing or very little. Most of the time you do not need a Customs broker to help you with a small shipment.

Finally, you go to a window, which also serves as a branch of one of the national banks, and pay the taxes on the items you have imported.

There are small trucks or *taxis de carga* available outside the Customs building that you can hire to take your belongings to your house or apartment. Prices are quite reasonable. I took a full load to San José and the driver only charged me about $50. He even helped me load and unload.

Cargo container

If you have more than 500 pounds and large items like refrigerators, it is too expensive to ship by air. Your best option is to send your things by boat in a cargo container. It is more cost-effective to use a large container, and the transit time will be shorter. As a rule of thumb, a small 20-foot container will cost $1500 plus tax and a large 40-foot container will cost around $2000 plus tax. So it is best to use a whole container. Your Customs agent can get all of your household items and belongings out of Customs. Surprisingly, it is cheaper to ship your items to Costa Rica by container than to ship your household goods across the United States.

If you don't have enough to fill even a half container, then you should use a freight consolidator like Charles Zeller. A consolidator has a warehouse and receives small shipments going to Costa Rica. Once he has enough small shipments to fill a container he lumps them together and sends a container to Costa Rica with many small shipments inside.

Here is what one expat said about the experience of shipping his things by container: "I moved down with everything that would fit in a 40-foot container, from the Indianapolis area, and if I remember correctly I paid about $5,500 to $5,800. However, if your location is close to a major seaport, the cost should be a lot lower. My container had to go by truck to Chicago, then by rail to the eastern seaboard (possibly New York or Virginia Beach) before it got onto the ship, and the cost for the land portion was probably greater than the cost of the sea voyage.

"The best part is that they left the container parked in my driveway for several days at no extra charge. It was up on wheels of course, so I had to build a ramp to load it. I loaded it myself with some friends and hired a crew for the real heavy stuff.

"Having that kind of time was key to getting everything to fit right, which was important to me because not a cubic foot was wasted — and there were 2,261 of them. Instead of selling or giving away a ton of stuff in the States, we brought it all down and gave it away here, and brought a lot of additional supplies we needed for our mission work here, in addition to all our household stuff, a couple thousand books and my 17-foot canoe."

Driving

Driving through Mexico and Central America is another way to bring your household goods and personal belongings to Costa Rica. However, because of the length of the journey, delays at border crossings, risk of theft and other hassles, this method is not recommended. Some trucking companies will ship your belongings overland.

Customs (*aduana*)

Whether you choose to send some of your possessions by ship or plane as unaccompanied luggage, you will learn to exercise extreme patience. Be prepared to face some unnecessary delays and frustrations when dealing with the Costa Rican Customs house, or ***aduana***. Since the new modern Customs warehouse opened near the airport, this process has been somewhat streamlined.

However, it is more usual than not to make several trips to the Customs warehouse to get your belongings. At worst you may spend all day dealing with mountains of paperwork, only to hear at the end of the day that you must come back tomorrow. Furthermore, fickle Customs officials sometimes decide the value of the shipped goods, and two identical shipments can be taxed differently depending on who examines them at the *aduana*.

The documents you need to clear your shipment through customs:

- A copy of the main page of your passport and a page with the last entry stamp when you last entered Costa Rica. In order for the shipment to qualify as personal effects, it has to clear customs within 90 days of your arrival.

- Original Airway Bill which the freight forwarder usually sends this with the shipment and the airline agent will have it in Costa Rica for you to pick up after paying the Terminal Handling Fee.
- Packing inventory with the declared value of the goods.

Because of this lengthy process and hassles, most people pay a local Customs broker, ***Agencia Aduanera***, or hire some other person or their lawyer to do this unpleasant task for them. It may cost a little more this way, but it will save valuable time and hassles.

I recommend the following company (please see their ad in the classified ads section of this guide):

Ship to Costa Rica
Tel: 258-8747
Fax: 2258-7123
Toll-Free from the United States or Canada: 1-866-245-6923
E-mail: shiptocostarica@racsa.co.cr

Here is what Susan said about Ship to Costa Rica's services: "Well, finally, we have our stuff! The container arrived a week ago, but we had to store our things because we considered moving to another spot. Then after a hectic week of looking around, we decided we liked our spot just fine and we had a great deal, talked to the neighbors about the reasons we considered leaving and decided to stay here."

"So today was the BIG day. We got a call at 8:30 this morning to say the truck was ready at the warehouse and did we want them to come NOW. That was three hours early—imagine that! And I groaned and said, 'But we're not even dressed.' So we did the Keystone Cops thing and ran around throwing on clothes, throwing cats in the maid's room, throwing the dog in the laundry room, throwing the sheets in with the dog and getting ready for the big day."

"And the truck came and unloaded and the other truck came and unloaded and unloaded, and unloaded. The only space they didn't unload into was the hall bathroom. So that's where we hung out for a moment of peace from the boxes and piles of stuff. Even though we de-stuffed multiple times back in the States we still had so much stuff that I have no idea where it will go."

"Our maid stood wide-eyed through the entire day wondering when the stuff would stop arriving and dreading having to unpack it. She deserves a medal."

"Today I truly felt like an American with many of the undercurrents of what that word means to people who are not and have not got what we have. It was almost embarrassing. But I was assured that we were perfectly normal for Americans moving to Costa Rica."

"After it was all delivered, the guys unwrapped all the furniture and took away the garbage. They helped us bully several dozen boxes into a handy storage area we have under the stairs and smiled the entire time, except for when they delivered my 500-pound fire-proof filing cabinet up a long flight of stairs—we affectionately call this the 'pig'."

"Many thanks to and hats off to Charlie Zeller of **Ship to Costa Rica** and his son Charlie, Jr., the head of the moving crew. From start to finish, these are the most professional movers I have ever worked with. They are honest, gave me a quote up front and stuck to it right down to when I paid them, delivered on time to my door, arranged all the paperwork and Customs stuff. They stored my stuff in their warehouse for a week after it arrived in Costa Rica for free and overall did a fantastic job for us. Not one piece of furniture was damaged. I do give myself a little credit because I know how to pack. There have been so far a few little items, mostly dishes, chipped or broken. Nothing that can't be replaced."

"Five stars to Charlie and his crew. If you are looking to move to Costa Rica, I definitely recommend them and you can find them through the ARCR, another wonderful organization that has been immensely helpful.

"So now we are starting the unpack and my animals are sniffing around wondering what the heck went on here all day; they are checking out every box and all the new nooks and crannies and we are all thinking, gee, this looks like home and it don't echo no more in my place."

Be sure to ask the following when choosing a customs agency: Does the agency have English-speaking employees? Talk to them to see if they are customer-service oriented. Find out if they have the resources to access computerized Customs information. Talk to long-time residents who have dealt with reputable agencies and get referrals.

You may also choose to consult the Yellow Pages for a listing of *Agencias Aduaneras* (Custom's brokers). The **Association of Residents of Costa Rica** (ARCR) can give you the names of several Customs agencies.

How to Find a Lawyer

If you plan to go into business, work, buy or sell property or seek long-term residency status in Costa Rica, you will definitely need the services of a trustworthy and professional attorney.

Your attorney can help you understand the complexities of the Costa Rican legal system, which is based on Napoleonic law. You are guilty until proven innocent, just the opposite of the system in the United States. Also, one of the most frustrating experiences in Costa Rica is the amount of time and money it takes to accomplish anything judicially. It is well known that the judicial process in Costa Rica is complicated and requires time, patience and money to traverse. So, a good lawyer is one of the best investments you can make because he can assist you with bureaucratic procedures and handle other legal matters that arise.

If you are not fully bilingual, be sure to choose a lawyer who is bilingual. The secretary should be bilingual too (Spanish/English). This helps avoid communication problems and misunderstandings and enables you to stay on top of your legal affairs.

It is very important to watch your lawyer closely, since most Costa Rican lawyers tend to drag their feet as bureaucrats do.

Never take anything for granted. Refuse to believe that things are getting done, even if you are assured they are. Check with your lawyer on a regular basis and ask to see your file to make sure he has taken care of business. As you might imagine, paperwork moves slowly in Costa Rica, so you do not want a procrastinating lawyer to prolong the process.

When you first contact a lawyer, make sure he is accessible at all hours. Make sure you have your lawyer's office and home telephone number in case you need him in an emergency. If you are told your lawyer is always "in meetings" or "out of the office," this is a clear sign your work is being neglected and you have chosen the wrong lawyer.

Know your lawyer's specialty. Although most attorneys are required to have a general knowledge of Costa Rican law, you may need a specialist to deal with your specific case. Some people find it is a good idea to have several lawyers for precisely this reason.

Take your time and look around when you are trying to find a lawyer. This should be fairly easy since there are more than 7,000 lawyers from whom to choose. You should ask friends, other people, retirees and other knowledgeable people for the names of their lawyers. Above all, make sure your attorney is recommended by a reliable source. Then try to inquire about your potential lawyer's reputation, his work methods and integrity.

Here are some tips for finding a lawyer in Costa Rica:

1. Ask your fellow ex-pats for recommendations. They have been there and done that. be careful here because almost every *Gringo* brags that he or she has the best lawyer with the best connections.
2. Do not let advertising influence your decision. It is only a paid ad. Anyone can do that.
3. If you do have a problem, you CAN file a complaint against an attorney, but it is extremely difficult, if not impossible to get another attorney to represent you so be prepared to represent yourself which requires fluent Spanish.

4. Do not automatically trust someone who appears in forums as an "expert". There is way more involved in Costa Rica legal transactions than "knowledge".
5. Never, ever pay the entire amount required up front. Pay no more than one-half initially and one-half upon completion.
6. Remember that sometimes the "giving your word" concept is not understood here as in other countries.
7. A good clue is if the attorney makes the appointment for 2 or 3 in the afternoon, it is possible that is when he begins the work day. Most government offices close from 3 to 4:30 for the day, leaving little time for attorney "work".
8. Ask for at least 2 recommendations for a particular attorney.
9. And if you are personally involved with an attorney, go elsewhere for your legal work.
10. Do not trust an attorney (or anyone else) just because they speak English.

If you find yourself in a jam before finding a lawyer, contact the Association of Residents of Costa Rica (ARCR) for assistance, ask a friend for a recommendation or contact one of the lawyers mentioned in this section.

All over the world, there are always a few incompetent, unscrupulous attorneys, so be careful with whom you are dealing before you make your final choice. Remember, one of the most important people in your life in Costa Rica is your lawyer, so it is imperative that you develop a good working relationship.

Most attorneys charge from $25 to $50 or more an hour depending on your problem and their expertise. It is inadvisable to select your lawyer solely on the basis of legal fees. Lawyer's fees, or *honorarios*, vary. The fee table used by attorneys and notaries in Costa Rica is more of a guideline than a strict pricing rule. However, when it is convenient for the professional to use it, they adhere to it rigidly. This is normally the case when something is easy to do and takes virtually no time at all and should cost much less than the fee schedule states. On the other hand, with truly complex matters that go far beyond the scope of the pricing of the fee table, the same professional will discard it and ask for more money. Understand the fee table they use is a guideline and realize that all fees can be negotiated.

Just because a lawyer is expensive does not mean he is good. Likewise, you should not select an attorney because his fees are low. When hiring a lawyer to do a job it is advisable to pay a third to a half up front, with the balance to be paid when the job is completed. If the attorney insists on more than 50 percent up front, you should get another attorney.

Check with the Costa Rican version of the Bar Association (*El Colegio de Abogados*) **www.abogados.or.cr** if you have any questions about legal fees. They responsible entity for setting all fees for attorneys and notaries, however some fees are determined by the amount of the transaction.

A notary is needed to transfer a vehicle because they need to put the transaction in their protocol book, make a testimony of the act, and submit it to the *Registro Nacional.* The same is true for the transfer of a property in this country.

In addition to forms for transferring assets, most states in the United States have approved, standardized forms that people can use for a variety of other legal matters, even divorce. There are very few forms one can use here for certain legal activities. The most common is for renting of an apartment or a house. Forms are available but very hard to find for a rental agreement. The rule of thumb in this country is a person needs an attorney for court and a notary for anything official that needs registration in the Registro Nacional.

The notary fee, as much as 1.5 percent of the deal for property transfers, is a drag on the economy.

In theory, all this mumbo jumbo and added official paperwork is to curb fraudulent transactions when, in fact, what it has done is contributed to an increase in property crime and the illegal transfer of other assets as well.

Here are two facts most people do not know regarding legal professionals. Attorneys and notaries have a kind of insurance to cover errors and omission and outright negligence. However, the amount of insurance is so minuscule that it is virtually worthless in a legal dispute. In addition, the statute of limitations for the bar association to discipline, as in suspend or expel a legal professional, is only two years from the date of the act. Not the date one finds out about it, but from the actually date of the mistake.

In Costa Rica it is not uncommon to hire a lawyer on a full-time basis by paying what amounts to a small retainer. If you find a lawyer who will handle your *pensionado* or residency paperwork for under $500, you have found a bargain.

However, if you speak fluent Spanish and have a lot of patience, you can do your residency or *pensionado* paperwork yourself. Just pick up a list of the requirements from the Immigration office.

If you choose this route you can save yourself hundreds of dollars in attorneys' fees. All a lawyer does is just sign a couple of papers, turn them in at the Immigration office and take your money.

There is a small amount of paperwork involved in giving your lawyer power of attorney *(poder)* so he can take care of your personal business and legal affairs.

This is not a bad idea when you may have to leave the country for a period of time or in the event of an emergency. However, first make sure your lawyer is completely trustworthy and competent. You may either choose to give your attorney *poder general* (general power of attorney) or *poder especial* (special power of attorney). You may revoke both types of power of attorney at any time.

If a foreigner lives or has assets in Costa Rica he or she should have a will. Your lawyer can help you with this.

A successful Costa Rican attorney,

By the way, lawsuits can last longer than in the states.

One thing that you should know is that prenuptial agreements work differently here. Unlike many countries, in Costa Rica one can sign this type of agreement before or during marriage, and even after it has been signed and during the marriage itself, it can be changed or terminated if both parties, so wish.

Costa Rica does have common law marriage, in which two people living together, without being officially married, acquire rights similar to married couples if certain requirements are met. However, the law here does not permit prenupcial agreements to govern or wave rights acquired through common-law marriage.

If you want answers to most of your questions about the complex Costa Rican legal system, purchase *The Legal Guide To Costa Rica* by Roger Petersen. Although this book is no substitute for a good lawyer, it is still very useful for the layman. This guide may be purchased from www.amazon.com. If you have any questions, contact Mr. Peterson at: Tel: 2233-5219, Fax: 2233-2507 or E-mail: crlaws@racsa.co.cr.

This comprehensive guide contains sample forms and documents. It covers the most common situations you will encounter in Costa Rica: real estate transactions, corporations, commercial transactions, Immigration, labor laws, taxation, wills, marriage and much more.

We suggest you also purchase the forthcoming ***Christopher Howard's Simplified Guide to the Costa Rican Legal System***. The latter will simplify Costa Rica's often confusing legal system, clear up many of your questions and be very user friendly. This guide is written by Adolfo García who is one of the best legal minds in the country.

We also recommend purchasing a copy of *Diccionario de Términos Jurídicos* by Enrique Alcaraz. It is a complete English-Spanish dictionary of legal terms. McGraw-Hill's *Spanish and English Legal Dictionary* by Henry Saint Dahl is another good legal dictionary.

Here is a partial list of bilingual attorneys who have many North American clients:

Lic. Ruhal Barrientos Saborio
Tel: 011-(506) 2291-5884
Cel: 8996-2379

Lic. Adolfo García
Tel: 2201-0300
E-mail: agarcia@lexcounsel.com

Lic. José Fernando Carter Vargas
Tel: 2257-6646
Fax: 2258-4101,
E-mail: jfcarter@racsa.co.cr

Lic. Henry Lang
Tel: 2204-7871
Fax: 2204-7872
www.langcr.com

Costa Rica Business and Legal Summary

With the proper guidance and preparation, Costa Rica can be a profitable place to establish a business enterprise while enjoying the tranquility and diversity of the countryside. The business practices, customs and organization that you may be accustomed to in your country of origin may not be applicable to those in Costa Rica.

Be patient; learn the procedures and the local way of doing things before you embark. If you arrive trying to change the country, attitudes and practices you will be in for a surprise. The summary that follows will hopefully assist you in understanding the basic structure of Costa Rican business.

The Costa Rican political system

Costa Rica is recognized worldwide for its stable and democratic political system. All changes of government have occurred by way of free elections which are held every four years. The core of Costa Rica's democratic political system is its Constitution. Originally adopted on November 7, 1949, it remains in effect today, establishing a clear system of checks and balances between the three branches of government: the Executive, Judicial and Legislative.

The legal system

The Costa Rican legal system is based upon the French civil law system as opposed to English common law that is used in England and the United States. The common law system relies more on case law which is generated by the judicial system and binding on lower courts. In the civil law system, the laws passed by the legislature are codified into codes which are then applied by the courts. Only the decisions of the Supreme Court of Costa Rica are binding on the lower courts. The court system is made up of: Lower Courts, Trial Level Courts, Appellate Courts and the Supreme Court.

At the present time, delays in processing claims through the legal system are a serious problem. There is a backlog of cases and the government does not have the financial resources to adequately staff and modernize the judicial system to handle those cases.

The country has recently passed legislation which allows for private mediation and arbitration services in the hope that more cases will be resolved by way of alternative dispute.

Foreign investors may also participate or invest in Costa Rica using any of the legal entities recognized by Costa Rican law.

Costa Rican corporate law

The most common corporate entity used in Costa Rica is the Sociedad Anónima (S.A.), mainly because the liability of the shareholders is limited to their capital contributions, and the shares of the corporation may be freely transferred. The corporation must maintain the following three books: (1) Shareholders' minutes book, (2) Board of Directors' minutes books, and (3) a Shareholders' log book.

Taxes in Costa Rica

Yes, we have them also. The Costa Rican tax laws were completely overhauled in 1995 with the passage of the new Tax Code. Taxation is based upon source income; in other words, Costa Rica only taxes revenue that is generated within Costa Rica and not worldwide as other countries do.

Personal income taxes range from 10% to 25% depending on the amount earned. Corporate taxation ranges from 10% to 30% depending on the amount. Costa Rica applies a sales tax of 13% and a special consumption tax on selected items which ranges from 8% to 10%.

The government also collects a property transfer tax of 1.5% which is triggered whenever a property deed is presented at the Costa Rican National Public Registry to record the transfer of ownership of property from one person to another. The same applies to the transfer of ownership of a motor vehicle which triggers a 2.5% transfer tax.

Property taxes are levied and collected by the municipal government where the property is located. The property values on the books of municipalities is far below the actual market value of the property and each municipality is implementing its own property tax program to update its property tax data base.

*Courtesy of Roger Petersen

How the Justice System Works in Costa Rica

Let's start with the *tico* system of justice. If you find it strange that *las cortes* (courts) in Costa Rica don't have room for the *jurado* (jury) then you probably haven't heard that Costa Rica practices a justice system based on the Roman and French codes that came to us by way of Spain.

The system has several interesting features that make it different from the common law system practiced in the United States, Canada and England.

The most outstanding of them all from the *gringo* perspective, is the lack of a jury. Another is that judges don't have much room for interpretations and must apply the law as a *receta* (recipe); if the crime doesn't fit, they must acquit.

The precept of *inocente hasta que se pruebe lo contrario* (innocent until proven guilty) is also a principle in the Costa Rican system, but whereas in the common law system judges usually are content to set bail for most types of crimes, in Costa Rica judges seem more inclined to deny it.

In fact, there is a good number of other measures at the disposal of a *tico* judge, collectively known as *medidas cautelares* (precautionary measures) that can make the whole process a nightmare for the *imputado* (suspect).

The four most famous *medidas* are: *arresto domiciliario* or *casa por cárcel* (house arrest), *fianza* (bail), *impedimento de salida* (prohibition to leave the country) and last but not least *prisión preventiva* (preventive prison), a measure intended to keep the suspect from obstructing justice.

You can say that *tico* justice guards evidence jealously. If you ever find yourself in hot legal water, by all means try to breathe very carefully and keep a low profile. A certain ex-president of ours did not answer his phone or tell his assistant where he was going for four days, and that cost him an *orden de arresto internacional* (international arrest warrant). He should have known better.

There is some confusion also as to who presses charges, but there should not be as practically anybody with a stake in the matter can do it. For instance, Alcatel pressed charges against two of its former managers, who are in addition to those already charged by the government. By the way, in this case there is a difference between *el estado* (the state) and *el gobierno* (the government). The former is represented by the *Ministerio Público* (Attorney's Office) and belongs to the Judiciary, the latter is represented by the *Procuraduría General* (the Government's Lawyer, known as *Procurador)* and belongs to the Executive branch. Together they have most of the powers of what many of you know as a Justice Department, though none have powers as far reaching when it comes to interpreting the law.

The process itself is composed of four phases, and the name of the defendant changes accordingly. When the *Ministerio Público* thinks it has a possible reason to start an investigation, it opens a process called *de instrucción* (instruction) and it is presided over by one or several judges, each making decisions apart from the other judges. During this phase the defendant is called *imputado* (suspect), and it is the job of the judge to say if there is *falta de mérito* (lack of merit), if there isn't, the judge elevates the issue to a higher office known as a *Tribunal*; from here on the defendant is called *indiciado* (indicted), but you can also call him *acusado* (defendant) as well.

A *Tribunal* is made up of three judges, one of whom is the president of the panel. This system is called *colegiado*. This is by all means a process similar to that of common law except for the missing jury. After hearing all the arguments, examining all the *evidencia* (evidence) and listening to all the *testigos* (witnesses), the judges retire to their offices and make their decision alone, then meet up to vote; this is why a verdict by a *Tribunal* in Costa Rica is called a *voto* (vote).

Regardless of the outcome there is a statutory period during which any of the parties can file an *apelación* (appeal); this is the third phase and it is called *casación*. This job belongs to the Sala III of the Supreme Court, which confirms the verdict, orders a retrial or even modifies the punishment. From here on, the *acusado* turns into *culpable* (guilty) or *inocente* (innocent) and the big *Cosa Juzgada* seal is put on the whole matter. Reopening it constitutes double jeopardy. If found guilty, there is yet one more phase to go through called *ejecución de la pena* (execution of the verdict), also headed by a full-blown judge who though limited by the penal code, can still change the sentence and even trade it for something else, such as *casa por cárcel* (house arrest).

In the Costa Rican system, unlike the common law system, subtle differences in vocabulary and actions may lead to completely different crimes and equally different lengths of sentences. The operative word in our system is *la tipificación* (the configuration) of the crime.

It all comes down to how Congress worded the law. *Tico* judges must closely observe the letter of that law first, and only then consider whatever *jurisprudencia* (jurisprudence) may already exist.

With that in mind, let's begin our journey into the types of crimes that Mr. District Attorney has at his disposal for doing his job, but just to keep it manageable let's limit that journey to *crímenes económicos* (money related crimes) committed against the state.

Got an easy way to squeeze money out of the government? Did your pal learn about this tip of yours and join in? You want to explore the loophole as far as it takes you? Well then, you are part of a *corruptela*, a type of *actividad* (activity) that may or may not be considered a *crimen* (crime). It all depends.

Let me explain that one again. The squeezing easy money from the government part is definitely a crime, so don't get too excited; what is not a crime is the casual nature of the affair.

In the *tico* system the *dolo* (intent) makes the difference between *cárcel* (doing time) or walking free, in almost all instances. That is why legislators came up with *asociación ilícita* (conspiracy to commit a crime), which to me is sort of like "mail fraud" in the United States. If the DA can't get you for the big crime, he will get you for mail fraud, at least.

The difference between a *corruptela* and *asociación ilícita* is then *dolo* and all it takes is to prove that there was some kind of understanding between the parties. Illicit association carries a six-year sentence.

The situation of the three *tico* ex-presidents had a lot to do with these type of *tenue* (subtle) differences, with two of them in jail and the other without as much as a formal accusation. At the time this article was written, both presidents have since released.

Ex-president #1 used to have a rather well-known lawyer's office that was equally well-connected. He was hired by a certain corporation, *supuestamente* (allegedly) for *asesoramiento político* (lobbying). However, he understood differently; to him he was hired to carry out legal work in agreement with his profession. The problem was that the person who paid him says he did it as part of a payment requested by the head of a certain *agencia gubernamental* (government agency) who was part of a large scheme to defraud the state of a $40 million dollar loan given by a certain Scandinavian country. Willingly or unwillingly, he became part of the scheme and therefore is in deep trouble.

What is left to be determined, then, is his *grado* (degree) of participation. That is, how much did he actually know? Let's start by giving him *el beneficio de la duda* (benefit of the doubt), as we should, and let's say he was completely unaware of what was going on, thus ruling out intent. This is the lowest degree of participation, in which case he could be charged with *favorecimiento real* (obtaining an actual benefit) from the whole transaction. Being the good lawyer that he is, however, he proceeded to put all of the money he got from the transaction into a *depósito judicial* (escrow account in the hands of the court). He now can go to the court and say he got no benefit since he returned the money. That works, too.

If the *fiscal* (DA) can find so much as a thread ofevidence to prove intent, however, he can then be charged with illicit association and *corrupción*, a crime usually reserved for *servidores públicos* (government employees), but that applies to him by way of the head of the government agency. Just to clarify, contrary to popular belief, an ex-president is not a public servant.

Nevertheless, he has an uphill battle because the head of the government agency involved in the scheme says (allegedly) it was he who organized everything and they were simply following his lead; that could turn him into the *corruptor* (the corrupting party), which is the highest degree of participation and the individual who gets the biggest prize in real jail time.

Ex-president #2 has sort of a different story, as he was not as close to the action. He considers himself, and he may be right about that, a big shot when it comes to *tecnologías de la comunicación* (communication technologies) and as such he was hired by a friend of his to do some *asesoramiento* (professional consulting). Nothing wrong there, so far.

In another rather friendly transaction, his friend hired another friend, who happened to be a prominent member of a prominent party. Her expertise: *filología* (philology) or correcting papers, essays and the like in the proper usage of the Spanish language. She seems to be an expert on the subject, as she got paid allegedly $900,000 for the job. This is strange because Mr. Big Shot ex-president also got paid exactly the same amount.

In addition, the friend who hired them also kept another $900,000 for himself as payment for his networking abilities that provided Alcatel with so much *talento* (talent) at so high a price. At this point, I should add that the *gerente* (manager) of Alcatel Costa Rica, who hired the friend in the first place is the brother of the *filóloga*.

Remember the definition of *corruptela* above? Well, the *Fiscal General* (DA) is working hard to find out if this situation was a *corruptela*, and, if so if a crime was committed. Nobody is calling anything a crime yet, except Alcatel which seems to believe that its manager for Latin America and its manager for Costa Rica conspired to commit *fraude* (fraud).

This brings us to ex-president #3. His problem is that he apparently is into asking for *préstamos* (loans) from anybody. According to his own declarations he borrowed from a certain former ICE director a total of $140,000; Mr. Director says, instead, the money was allegedly part of the *comisión* (commission) for helping Alcatel get a government contract. In total, that company circulated about $13 million dollars in *pagos* (payments) and the like. So generous they were that even a certain head of a certain government agency, if you catch my drift, who had NOTHING to do with this deal, got money as well. Charges for this case include *corrupción agravada* (aggravated corruption).

That is not all, however. He also allegedly borrowed money from the Taiwanese government and got a contract for *asesoramiento* (consulting) to the Spanish company that is working on the under-ground electrification project of the city of San José. He did drop the consulting gig and his relationship with the Taiwanese government is not really that clear, either.

Some of these events allegedly took place while he was still in office, which qualifies him for a whole set of crimes that may or may not apply to the other ex-presidents, among them: *enrequicimiento ilícito* (illegal enrichment) and *negociaciones incompatibles* (conflict of interest).

Last but not least is the oldest *crimen económico* on the books: *peculado* (embezzlement), which is nothing but the use of state assets to procure a personal or patrimonial benefit. Which one do you think can be charged with that?

*Courtesy of Guillermo Jiménez

Wills and *testamentos* in Costa Rica

The name for a will in Spanish is *testamento* and Costa Rican laws give several options for the person writing one: Open Testaments, Privileged Open Testaments, and Closed Testaments, each of which will be explained briefly.

El Testamento

Here is how one is written and its benefits. To preface the definitions are the things you may not do.

You may not make a Will giving your power of attorney to someone else to write the will in your name or by the arbitration of a third party

You may not include secret instructions or recommendations given to a third party

False motive invocations do not invalidate the Testament, unless the motives are announced as conditions to the applicability of the Testament, or that the testator him/herself intended that the legacy or inheritance depend on the existence of the invoked clause. The expression of a motive against the law will always nullify the disposition.

Substitutions are prohibited. The disposition in which a Third is called to recollect the benefits of the said disposition if, for some reason, the first named beneficiary will not or can not accept the legacy, does not constitute substitution, and, in this case, the disposition is valid.

The Open Testament

An open testament is one that you make without secrecy: everyone may know what your final decision is about your assets. The Open Testament is written and signed by you in front of a Notary Public in the presence of at least three witnesses: only two witnesses are required if the Testator writes the Testament in his own hand (a holographic will). If no Notary Public is present, four witnesses are necessary. Normally, you go to the Notary Public and he makes a deed with your final dispositions for your death and the distribution of assets you desire. If you want to make your will in a language different from Spanish, then in addition to the Notary Public, you will need the services of at least two translators chosen by yourself, who will translate your final dispositions into Spanish and who will dictate it for the Notary Public.

These are the basic requirements of an Open Testament

It has to be dated, indicating the place, hour, day, and month and year it was written.

It has to be read aloud to the witnesses by the Testator or by the person he designates or by the Notary Public. If the Testator is deaf. but can read, the Testament is read for him; if he is unable to read, he has to designate the person who will read it in his place.

The completed Open Testament has to be signed by the testator, the Notary Public, and all the witnesses. If the Testator does not know how to write his signature or is physically unable to sign, this information will be stated in the Open Testament. You may also distribute future assets and leave instructions for what to do with money, goods, and services that you do not yet have.

The Privileged Open Testament

The privileged open testament is created for specific situations: all the formalities are omitted because of the special circumstances and only certain people can issue these Testaments. Those who may do so are: a soldier in the Army and on campaign, or as a prisoner of war in the hands of the enemy, may write a Privileged Open Testament before two witnesses and an officer; a sailor in the Navy may do the same before two witnesses and the Captain of the ship. The Privileged Open Testament is only valid if the subject dies in the special circumstance that originated the dispensation of the normal requirements.

The Closed Testament

The closed testament stays secret until your death: nobody will know what is in it and it is kept secure until you die. You complete it personally: it comes from your own hand, or is at least signed by you.

You place it in an envelope and take it to a Notary Public. In the presence of at least three witnesses the Notary Public writes a notation in his *protocolo.* (The bound book given by the Costa Rican government to each Notary Public in which are described all deeds and actions that they perform) making reference to the envelope presented to him: how many pages it includes, if it was written and signed by you, if the Testament includes overwriting, alteration or notes, and noting for the *Protocolo* the hour and date the Testament was received, including the names of the witnesses present at that moment. The envelope is in turn; marked with the information from the *Protocolo* of the Notary Public and it is kept safe until the time of death of the Testator. The Closed Testament cannot be opened until the death of the Testator.

There are certain people who cannot issue a valid Testament i.e. children under 15 years of age and the mentally ill.

There is 'Relative Prohibition' of receipt for the following persons named in a Testament:

From a minor child to his tutor.

From a minor child to his teachers or caretakers.

From the ill person to his caretakers at the moment of his death
From the adulterous spouse to his lover if the adultery is judicially proven.
From the Testator to the Notary Public making the Testament.

The Testator can freely decide how to distribute his assets as long as he provides financially for each of his minor children until they reach the age of 18, and for their natural life if physically or mentally handicapped or disabled. If, at the moment of the Testators death, the children under age 18 and those children who are disabled already have enough assets, this is not applicable.

* Courtesy of the ARCR and top 10 Costa Rica.

Death of a friend or loved one overseas

Facing the death of a friend or loved one is difficult under any circumstances, let alone when it occurs in a foreign country. Since the majority of Americans living in Costa Rica are middle-aged or seniors, it is advisable that they know what procedures to follow if their spouse or a friend passes away.

First, you should contact the U.S. Embassy to report the death of an American citizen. The American Citizen Services section of the U.S. Embassy may be reached at 519-2000, extension 2452. If necessary, they will contact family members, hold valuables for the family, act as a liaison to help the family make funeral and/or cremation arrangements, and help with repatriation of the body (this cost is covered by the government if the deceased was an active member of the military, if so desired). They will also issue a Certificate of Death Abroad, an official copy of which is sent to the State Department in Washington, D.C. This document may be important for both insurance, tax and probate purposes. Note: If your spouse or a friend passes away anywhere else except in a hospital, the body has to undergo an autopsy. A police report will also have to be made. You will have to get a death certificate from a doctor before the body can be sent to a funeral home. Without a death certificate the body will be taken to the judicial morgue, no matter the circumstances under which the person died. Then you'll have to go though a bureaucratic process to get it released. If your relative dies in the hospital, you do not have to worry about this.

You can find out additional information by calling the U.S. Embassy at 2220-3050.

Cremation is not that common in Costa Rica. Jardines de Recuerdo pioneered cremation in Costa Rica with its sponsored regulation *Reglamento de Cremación de Cadáveres y Restos Humanos* on Nov. 25, 1986. The funeral firm brought the first cremation oven to the country in 1985. Over the years,

Legal Terms

By Christopher Howard

LEGAL TERMS / TERMINOS LEGALES

A person who lends his name - *Testaferro*
Absolve - *Absolver*
Accusation - *Denuncia*
Accused person – *Acusado*
Accuser – *Denunciante*
Alibi - *Coartada*
Alimony - *Pensión alimenticia*
Appeal - *Apelación*
Appearance in court – *Comparecencia*
Acquit – *Sobreseer*
Arrest warrant. - *Orden de captura, orden de aprensión, orden de arresto*
Attach assets - *Embargar/enganchar*
Bar – *Colegio de Abogados* (Costa Rican equivalent)
Bail – *Fianza*
Beyond a reasonable doubt – *Más allá de una duda razonable*
Case – *Caso*
Civil code – *Código civil*
Civil law - *Derecho civil*
Common property (in a divorce – *Bienes comunes*
Contract - *Contrato*
Copyright - *derecho de autor*
Court - *Tribunal/corte*
Court of appeals .- *Corte de apelaciónes*
Court appointed attorney - *Abogado de oficio*
Courtroom - *Sala de justicia*
Crime - *Crimen*
Criminal law - *Derecho penal*
Criminal lawyer - *Abogado penalista*
Custody - *Patria potestad*
Custody while awaiting trial – *Prisión preventiva*
DA - *Fiscal*
Defend - *Defender*

Defense attorney - *Abogado defensor*
Defraud - *Defraudar*
Demandado – *Person being sued*
Disbar – *Echar del Colegio de Abogados*
District Attorney – *Fiscal*
Divorce - *Divorcio*
Due dillgance – *Diligencia debida*
Easement - *Servidumbre*
Executor - *Albacea*
Execution of the verdict - *Ejecución de la pena*
Embezzlement – *Desfalco*
Encumberance - *Gravamen*
Evidence – *Evidencia* or *pruebas*
Eye witness - *Testigo ocular*
False witness - *Testigo falso*
Fees - *Honorarios*
Felony - *Delito mayor*
Fight case -.*Pelear el caso*
Find guilty - *Encontrar culpable*
Find innocent - *Encontrar inocente*
Fine - *Multa*
Fraud - *Fraude*
Guilt - *Culpa*
Guilty - *Culpable*
Hearing - *Audiencia*
Higher court - *Corte superior*
House arrest - *Arresto domiciliario or casa poir cárcel*
Illegal- *Ilegal/prohibido*
Illegal enrichment - *Enriquecimiento ilícito*
Impediment to leave country - *Impedimento de salida*
Innocent - *Inocente*
Judge - *Juez* (masc.)/*Jueza* (fem.)
Jury – *Jurado* (none in Costa Rica)
Key witness – *Testigo clave*
Law suit - *Demanda*
Lawyer - *Abogado*
Lawyer's bar - *Colegio de Abogados*
Legal - *Legal*

Legal form - *Papel sellado*
Lose a case– *Perder un caso*
Lower court - *Corte inferior*
Manslaughter – *Homocido simple or homicidio sin premeditación*
Misappropriate funds - *Malversar*
Misdemeanor - *Delito menor*
Not guilty - *No culpable/absuelto*
Notary – *Notario*
Notary's records - *protocolo*
Notarize – *Autenticar*
Out of court settlement – *Llegar a un acuerdo extrajudicialment*
Party (people) - *La parte*
Person who plans a crime – *Autor intelectual*
Protective measures - *Medidas cautelares*
Plaintiff. - .*Demandante or Querellante*
Plea – *Alegato or Alegación*
Possession is 9/10 of the law - *La ley de posesción*
Press charges – *Presentar cargos*
Power of attorney - *Poder*
Probate - *Sucesorio*
Property - *Propiedad*
Prosecutor - *Fiscal/procurador*
Restraining order - *Orden de alejamiento*
Retainer - *Pago anticipado de honorarios*
Ruling- *Fallo*
Sentence - *Condena/sentencia/pena*
Stockholder/shareholder - *Accionista*
Signature – *Firma*
Squatter - *Precarist*
Suit - *Demanda/ Querella*
Summons - *Citación*
Suspect - *Imputado*
Take the case (lawyer) - *Llevar el caso*
Take to trial - *Llevar a juicio*
Tax evasion- *Evasión fiscal*
Testify - *Declarar*
Testify against - *Testificar/declarar contra*
Testify for - *Tesitificar/declarar a favor de…*

The right to enjoy a thing owned by another person – *Usofructo* (Like living in their home)
To appear in court – *Comparecer*
To dismiss a case - *Desestimar*
To record in the nation al registry - *Protocolizar*
To rule against – *Fallar en contra de*
To rule in a case – *Fallar*
To rule in favor of - *Fallar a favor de*
Trial - *Juicio*
Tribunal - made up of three judges
Trust – *Fidecomiso*
Trustee - *Fidecomisario*
Try - *Juzgar/enjuiciar*
Verdict - *Fallo*
Will – *Testamento*
Win a case – *Ganar un caso*
Witness - *Testigo*

* From ***Christopher Howard's Guide to Costa Rican Spanish*** and the forthcoming ***Guide to the Costa Rican Legal System.***

most of the cremations done by Jardines de Recuerdo have been performed for foreigners. However, slowly the trend has been catching on among Costa Ricans. Currently, cremations are estimated to be about 15 percent of deaths in Costa Rica, compared to the United States, 25.5 percent, and Canada's 42.7 percent.

Article 5 of the regulation states that all bodies to be cremated need to undergo an autopsy and that a permit must be issued by health officials. Both procedures are now easily accomplished and done at the crematorium in most cases.

Jardines de Recuerdo is currently the only funeral company in Costa Rica offering cremation. The funeral charge of cremation is around $2,100 today in Costa Rica.(about US$1,600 for cremation and $500. for autopsy). Transporting a body from anywhere in Costa Rica to San José for cremation costs about 500 *colones* per kilometer. There are no choices of urns at the funeral parlor, they only have one model, but some interesting alternatives exist in the market. There are no services currently offering the spreading of ashes in Costa Rica. The urn provided by Jardines de Recuerdo is hermetically sealed and the company can provide a special authorization to transport remains out of the country.

Here is the contact information for Jardines de Recuerdo. **Jardines de Recuerdo (www.jardinesdelrecuerdo.co.cr/cremacion_y_cenizarios.htm). Montesacro** (2233-1129) also does cremations and burials.

By the way, you can prepay either cremation or burial at today's rates for these services.

Here is a person's recent experience with the cremation of a member of the family: "A relative passed away late on a Monday night, the autopsy was completed around noon on Tuesday, and the funeral home refrigerated the remains until they could schedule the cremation at their facility on Saturday morning. "I was present and viewed my relative's remains immediately prior to the cremation, which took place next to the chapel. I also viewed the crematory unit and it was void of any previous remains. I needed to do this for my peace of mind."

"The funeral home obtained all permits, including the Consular Mortuary Certificate from the U.S. Embassy. If you are returning the ashes to the United States for burial, you need to allow time for this to meet airline regulations."

Here is an another person's experiences. "My mother in law passed away in San Ramon last Sept. La Jardín in Alajuela came and picked her up, did the cremation, we picked her up a few days later. She was in a nice box with her name and birth and death dates and it cost about $1600. We took their paperwork to the US Embassy, got a report of death of a citizen in a foreign country, and a permit to take her remains back to the states. This costs nothing. We were not charged nor did they do an autopsy, she died in a private home, and her doctor filled out the death certificate. It was a relatively easy process."

Costa Rican Consulates and Embassies Abroad

Costa Rican consulates provide information about visas, work permits, marriage and residency. They can issue tourist visas, authenticate documents and assist Costa Rican citizens living abroad.

Anyone seeking permanent residency in Costa Rica needs to have certain documents notarized by a Costa Rican consulate or embassy in their country of origin. Documents that must be notarized are a birth certificate, police certificate (stating you have no criminal record) and proof of income statement. All this paperwork should be taken care of before coming to Costa Rica.

If you apply for permanent residency in Costa Rica, it may take months to get notarized documents from your home country, if it's possible at all. If worse comes to worst, you may have to make a trip home to take care of these matters. While you are waiting for papers from abroad, other documents may expire and you will have to start all over again. Bureaucracy is slow enough as it is in Costa Rica, and it is foolish to delay this process any more than necessary.

Each Costa Rican consulate has its own business hours and its area of coverage (jurisdiction) based on the origin of the document. Please locate your nearest consulate for personal attention. If there is no consulate in your state, locate the state or city nearest your residence in the list below.

Consulates in the United States:

Atlanta: 1870 The Exchange Southeast N.W., Suite 100, Atlanta, GA, 30339. Tel: (770) 951-7025 Fax: (770)-951-7073 E-mail: consulate_ga@costarica-embassy.org.

Boston: 175 McClennan Highway, East Boston, MA 02128. Tel: (617) 561-2444, Fax: (617) 561-2461. E-mail: consulate_bos@costarica-embassy.org.

Chicago: (includes Illinois, Indiana, Michigan, Ohio, Iowa, Minnesota, Missouri, North Dakota, South Dakota, Indiana and Wisconsin): 203 North Wabash Avenue, Suite 1312, Chicago, IL 60601. Tel: (312) 263-2772 Fax: (312) 263-5807 E-mail: crcchi@aol.com.

Dallas (Area of coverage: Dallas): 7777 Forrest Ln., Suite C-204, Dallas, TX 75231. Tel: (972) 566-7020 or (972) 566-2871, Fax: (972) 566-7943.

Denver: 3356 South Xenia Street, Denver, CO 80231-4542. Tel: (303) 696-8211, Fax: (303) 696-1110, E-mail: crconsul@hypermall.net

Houston: (includes Colorado, Kansas, Nebraska, New Mexico, Oklahoma and Texas): 3000 Wilcrest, Suite 112, Houston, TX 77042. Tel: (713) 266-0484, Fax: (713) 266-1527 E-mail: consulatecr@juno.com or consulatecr@sbcglobal.net.

Los Angeles: (includes Southern California, Arizona, Nevada, Utah and Hawaii): 1605 West Olympic., Suite 400, Los Angeles, CA 90015, Tel: (213) 380-6031 Fax: (213) 380-5639. E-mail: costaricaconsulatela@hotmail.com.

Miami (area of coverage: Florida): Consulate General, 1101 Brickell Ave., Suite 704-S, Miami, FL 33131, Tel: (305) 871-7487, 871-7485, Fax: (305) 871-0860. After hours emergency phone line: (305) 331-0636 E-mail: consulate_fla@costarica-embassy.org or consulate_mia@costarica-embassy.org.

New Orleans: (Includes Alabama, Arkansas, Kentucky, Louisiana, Mississippi and Tennessee): World Trade Center Bldg., 2 Canal St., Suite 2334, New Orleans, LA 70130. Tel: (504) 581-6800 Fax: (504) 581-6850. After hours emergency phone line: (504) 256-2027 E-mail: consulno@aol.com.

New York (includes Connecticut, Maine, Massachusetts, New England, New Hampshire, New Jersey, New York, Pennsylvania, Rhode Island and Vermont): 80 Wall Street, Suite 718, New York, NY 10005. Tel: (212) 623-6310 or (212) 509-3066, Fax: 212 509-3068. After hours emergency phone line: (908) 623-6310. E-mail: consulnewyork@hotmail.com or costaricaconsul@yahoo.com.

Phoenix (area of coverage Arizona): 7373 E. Doubletree Ranch Rd.,Suite 200, Scottsdale, Arizona, 85258. Tel: (480) 951-2264 Fax: (480) 991-6606, E-mail: burkeap@aol.com.

Puerto Rico Avenida Ponce de Leon, Edificio 1510, Oficina P1, Esquina Calle Pelaval, San Juan, Puerto Rico 00909. Tel: (787) 723-6227 Fax: (787) 723-6226. After hours emergency phone line: (787) 627-3220 E-mail: consuladopr@yunque.net.

San Antonio: Continental Building , 6836 San Pedro, Suite 116, San Antonio, TX 78216 Tel: (210) 824-8474 Fax: (210) 824-8489 After Hours
Puerto Rico Avenida Ponce de Leon, Edificio 1510, Oficina P1, Esquina Calle Pelaval, San Juan, Puerto Rico 00909. Tel: (787) 723-6227 Fax: (787) 723-6226. After hours emergency phone line: (787) 627-3220 E-mail: consuladopr@yunque.net.

San Antonio Continental Building, 6836 San Pedro, Suite 116, San Antonio, TX 78216. Tel: (210) 824-8474, Fax: (210) 824-8489. After hours emergency phone Line: (210) 386-6839 E-mail: mrojasconssulsa@msn.com.

San Francisco (includes, Alaska, Idaho, Montana, Northern California, Oregon, Washington and Wyoming)**:** P.O. Box 7643, Freemont, Ca 94536. Tel: (510) 790-0785, Fax: (510) 792-5249. After hours emergency phone line: (800) 790-8561 E-mail: consulsfo@hotmail.com.

St. Paul (area of coverage Minnesota): 2424 Territorial Road, St. Paul, MN 55114. Tel: (651) 645-4103 or (651) 293-1816,Fax: (651) 645-4684, E-mail: cr-consulate@2424group.com.

Tampa 2204 Barker Road, Tampa, FL 33605. Tel: (813) 248-6741, Fax: 813) 248-6857 E-mail: crica@integracom.net.

Washington (includes all U.S. states, District of Columbia, Dela ware, Maryland, Virginia and West Virginia, North Carolina and South Carolina): 2114 "S" Street, NW, Washington, D.C. 20008. Tel: (202) 328-6626 Fax: (202) 265-4795. After Hours emergency phone line: (202) 215-4178, E-mail: consulate@costarica-embassy.org. Web: www.costarica-embassy.org.

Costa Rican Consulates Abroad:

England
14 Lancaster Gate
London, England
K2P 1B7
Tel: 071-723-1772

Canada
135 York St., Suite 208
Ottawa, Ontario K1N 5T4
Tel: (613) 562-0842
Fax: (613) 562-22855
E-mail: rolomadrigal@hotmail.com

Canada
614 Centre A. Street N.W.
Calgary, Alberta

Canada
164 Avenue Road
Toronto, Ontario M5R 2H9
Tel: (416) 961-6773

Canada
145 Chadwik Court
Suite 320
North Vancouver, BC
V6C 1H2
Tel: (604) 983-2152
Fax: (604) 983-2178
E-mail: consulado@sprint.ca

Canada
1425 René Levexque-West
Suite 602
Montreal, H3G 1T7
Tel: (514) 393-1057
Fax: (514) 393-1624

* **To obtain a complete list of embassies and consulates visit the Costa Rican Foreign Ministry website at www.rree.go.cr or see www.embassiesabroad.com**

Embassies and Consulates in Costa Rica

If you are planning to travel and explore Latin America and other parts of the world, when you are settled in Costa Rica, you will need the addresses of the embassies and consulates listed below in order to get visas and other necessary travel documents.

Most embassies and consulates are located in downtown San José. The rest are found in upscale neighborhoods such as Rohrmoser, Los Yoses and San Pedro, about 10 minutes from the center of the city. Before visiting any of the consulates or embassies below, I suggest you find out their hours.

Argentina — Curridabat	2234-6520
Austria — San José	2255-0767
Barbados — Trejos Montealegre	2289-9918
Belgium — Los Yoses	2225-6255
Belize — Guadalupe	2253-9626
Bolivia — Sabana Sur	2290-8844
Brazil — Paseo Colón	8383-1904
Canada — Sabana Sur	2242-4400
Chile — Los Yoses	2224-1547

China — San Pedro	2224-8180
Colombia — Barro Dent	2283-6871
Cuba — Sabana Norte	2291-1604
Czech — Rohrmoser	2232-1471
Denmark — Rohrmoser	2220-0242
Dutch — Sabana Oeste	2296-1490
Ecuador— Rohrmoser	2232-1503
El Salvador — San José	2257-7855
Finland — Barrio Amón	2222-6555
France — Curridabat	2234-4167
Germany — Sabana Norte	2290-9091
Great Britain — Paseo Colón	2258-2025
Guatemala —Sabana Sur	2220-1297
Honduras — Boulevard Rohrmoser	2231-1642
India	2220-3810
Italy — Los Yoses	2234-2326
Israel — Centro Colón	2221-6011
Jamaica - Curridabat	2253-5604
Japan — Sabana Norte	2232-1255
Malta — Rohrmoser	2290-3738
Mexico — San José	2257-0633
Nicaragua — Barrio California	2257-9006
Panama — San Pedro	2280-1570
Peru – Curridabat	2225-9145
Philippine — Curridabat	2225-4122
Poland — San José	2234-6024
Portugal — Barrio Mexico	2221-4202
Puerto Rico — Ave. 2, Calle 11-13	2257-1769
Russian — Lomas de Ayarco	2256-9181
Spain — Barrio Escalante	2222-1933
Sweden — La Uruca	2232-8549
Switzerland — Centro Colón	2221-4829
Taiwan — Barrio Escalante, Guadalupe	2224-8180
United States of America, Pavas	2220-3050, 519-2000
Uruguay	2234-9909
Venezuela — Los Yoses	2225-8810

* Check the phone book or information for more consulate and telephone numbers or see **www.rree.go.cr**

7

Residency and Related Matters

How to Become a Legal Resident of Costa Rica

People find Costa Rica attractive and want to live in the country for a myriad of reasons: good year-round weather, tired of the rat race and hustle-bustle, a new start in life, inexpensive living and retirement, tax benefits, the country's low-cost health care system, to start a business or invest, to learn Spanish, separation or divorce, to enjoy the country's large expatriate community and even to find companionship. Whatever your motives may be for wanting to move to Costa Rica, there are a number of ways to remain in the country on a long-term basis.

Tourists from North America and many countries in Europe may remain legally in the country for three months without having to apply for legal residency. You may own property, start a business or make investments with no more than a tourist visa.

I know many Americans, Canadians and other foreigners who started businesses as tourists (be aware that a tourist cannot legally work in any company, as they can in most other countries). If you plan to reside in Costa Rica full-time, however, one of Costa Rica's residency programs will appeal to you.

Several residency categories permit you to retain your current citizenship and obtain long-term legal status in Costa Rica. They are ***pensionado***, ***rentista*** and ***inversionista*** (resident investor). Which program you choose depends on your needs and financial position. Becoming a legal resident will by no means affect your U.S. or Canadian citizenship. Be very aware that residency procedures and requirements can change frequently, so always check for current requirements with the ARCR at www.arcr.net.

In March 1992, a change in the *pensionado* law eliminated many tax privileges that retirees had enjoyed since the program started in 1964. Under the old system, foreigners with official *pensionado* or *rentista* (permanent retiree) status were required to live in the country four months a year. They were entitled to the following perks: residency without immigration hassles, all the privileges of Costa Rican citizens except the rights to vote and work for hire, and the right to import one of each of the major appliances such as refrigerator, stove, microwave, television, washer and drier, as well as many personal household goods free of taxes.

Pensionados could import a new car every five years duty-free, provided it was worth less than $16,000. In 1992, low taxes on imported cars and duty-free household goods were eliminated. Since then, all *pensionados* have to pay taxes on their automobiles and household goods the same as Costa Rican citizens do.

Despite the changes in this law, Costa Rica continues to be Latin America's prime relocation and retirement haven. People continue to flock to the country because of its high quality of life, peaceful atmosphere, political stability, fantastic climate, friendly people who like foreigners, excellent business environment and natural beauty. In fact, Costa Rica has more American residents per capita than any other country in the world outside of the United States. They can't all be wrong!

The good news is that there is a good chance that a new version of the *pensionado* law will be passed by the government. The Costa Rican government realized that 10,000 more *pensionados* would create 5,000 new jobs indirectly and add about $135 million to the economy. Retirees would also contribute to the health care industry. If the law becomes reality it will offer a $5,000 exoneration on automobiles and up to $10,000 on house hold goods.

The practical benefits of obtaining residency in Costa Rica as a foreigner are very tangible, unlike in some other countries:

1. Access to Social Security continued care.
2. Access to checking accounts and credit service from some banks

3. Permission to engage in labor relationships
4. Freedom from worries about immigration checkpoints and possible deportation
5. Ability to purchase personal and business property and real estate
6. Qualify for citizenship and Costa Rican passport once requirements are met
7. Have the right to purchase telephone lines

The New Immigration Law

A new immigration law or *Ley de Migración* was approved in 2009, and with it came important changes in many residency categories, as well as in the treatment of illegal residents in the country. The law went into effect on March 1, 2010.

Both the increase in the number of immigrants, as well as alleged shortcomings of the old immigration law, led government officials to look at a series of changes they hope will improve security in Costa Rica and better facilitate immigration for foreigners looking to live here.

Costa Rica is a small country with limited resources. As but one example; Costa Rica's national health care system cannot continue to expand as needed when foreigners are allowed to flow across its borders unchecked and without having to contribute financially to the system. This is similar to uninsured or uninsured costs plaguing the United States and other worldwide health care systems.

To better address these concerns Costa Rica recently re-wrote its immigration laws, towards:

* setting-up official positions and commissions to pass rules, regulations and procedures under the directives of the new immigration laws.
* centralizing and modernizing the immigration process towards better efficiency and enforcement.
* allowing 'flexibility' in making administrative approvals fon those seeking immigration statuses that may fall outside of written guidelines.
* criminalizing human trafficking and establishing human rights for immigrants.
' Professionalizing' the Costa Rica Immigration Police force (*la Policía Profesional de Migración y Extranjería*).
* setting higher qualifications for residency - mainly to ensure that foreigners come with adequate income to support themselves.
* attempting to close the "Marriage of Convenience" loophole that is a long standing business institution where attorneys document false

marriages between Costa Rica citizens and foreigners for the sole purpose of obtaining Costa Rica residency and citizenship.

* requiring all temporary and permanent residents to contribute to the *Caja (Caja Costarricense de Seguro Socia*l –or- CCSS), The new law requires *pensionados*, *rentistas* and *inversionistas* here to join Costa Rica's national social security and health care system regardless of whether they have medical insurance elsewhere.

According to the Immigration Administration, there were nearly 284,000 permanent residents living in Costa Rica in 2007. Nicaragua, Colombia and the United States topped the list of countries with the greatest number of legal residents here, with 220,000, 11,652 and 9,000, respectively. The actual figures may be higher.

Among the changes in the law are tougher residency-through-marriage rules, a possibility for extending tourist visas and the opportunity to apply for residency from within Costa Rica.

The new law lumps *pensionados* under the permanent residency category. They are now considered temporary residents but have the right after *three* years to request permanent residency. Permanent residents **do not** have to show a specific monthly income.

Rentistas and *inversionistas* still are considered temporary residents (*residentes temporales*). But they, too, seem to have the right to seek permanent residency after *three* years here.

Tourists are considered non-residents, and they may not work in the country. However, tourists have the right to renew their stay for 90 days with the payment of $100. Tourists are allowed an additional 90 days in which to apply for other immigration categories.

The law does not address the perpetual tourists who leave the country for 72 hours every 90 days to renew their tourist visa. However, the new law beefs up the immigration police and promotes them to a status equal to other police agencies, so those abusing the tourist category might face judicial action.

The law also authorizes the nation's president and the immigration director to issue decrees to legalize foreigners who may be in the country illegally. This clause opens the door to a general amnesty for illegal aliens, however the final decision is left up to the president. Costa Rica had an amnesty in the 1990s that allowed a number of foreigners, mostly Nicaraguans, to obtain residency. Some expats took advantage of that policy, too.

Summary of Important Points from the New Immigration Law

* Foreign visitors on tourist visas may stay in the country for up to 90 days, provided they prove they have adequate means of subsistence.

* Foreigners who stay in the country beyond the time period granted by immigration authorities will be fined the equivalent of $100 for *each month* overstayed in the country.
* Foreigners will have to pay an additional $25 in order to renew residency in the country.
* *Pensionados* (retirees) looking to gain permanent residency in Costa Rica must show they receive a monthly pension of no less than $1,000. The old amount was $600 per month. Close family members may get in under this amount.
* *Rentistas* (self-employed businesspeople or foreign investors) must prove a monthly income of no less than $2,500 to gain residency. The previous minimum income was $1,000. Likewise, close family members may get in under this amount.
* Hotels and other hospitality sites must create a registry of people who stay at their establishments, which can be made available to immigration officials at any time.
* Individuals who provide work to undocumented foreigners risk being fined from two to 12 times the employee's base salary.
* To obtain residency through marriage, a couple must be able to prove cohabitation. This must also be demonstrated on an annual basis for a period of three years, if the foreigner wants to renew his or her residency.
* Foreigners may apply for residency from within Costa Rica. This will now incur an additional fee of a few hundred dollars.
* Police may not detain immigrants with questionable residency status for more than 24 hours.
* **Note: If you have any questions about the new law, please contact the Association of Residents of Costa Rica (ARCR).**

Specific Residency Requirements

Now let's look at the specific requirements and documents you will need to present to the Costa Rican government if you choose to apply for the ***pensionado*** or ***rentista*** categories

NOTE: These are the requirements under the old law. Details for the new Immigration law passed in 2009 are still forthcoming as of the publication of this book.

A ***pensionado*** is someone who lives on a pension (a U.S. Social Security check or permanent retirement program). A husband and wife cannot combine their pensions, but the wife can live under the husband's *pensionado* status or vice versa. The individual applying can combine pensions to achieve the total required. If the recipient of the pension dies, the spouse can retain *pensionado* status if the pension is inherited. Some paper work, naturally, is involved.

Here are the requirements for this category:

1. A lifetime income of at least $1000 a month generated outside of Costa Rica. Social Security recipients need a certification that can be made at the U.S. Embassy in Costa Rica.
2. A signed letter confirming that you will receive this money in Costa Rica. This is not needed if issued by the U.S. Embassy.
3. A letter from a CPA stating that you will receive at least $1000 for life if the pension comes from a company's pension plan.
4. If the money comes from a private company, two letters from bank officials showing that your company is financially sound and that the pension plan has been in existence for at least 20 years.
5. A detailed account of your company's pension plan or a yearly corporate report.
6. Join the *Caja Costarricense de Seguro Social (CCSS)*.
   As a *pensionado* you are obligated to exchange $12,000a year ($1000 per month) for *colones* at a local bank. You need proof of this to update your file. If you cannot prove that you converted enough money during the year, you can lose your status. You also have to renew your *pensionado* I.D. card every two years ($100) and reside in the country for at least four months yearly (not necessarily consecutively). As a *pensionado* you can own and operate your own business but not work. Also, as a *pensionado* you do not have to pay taxes on your income from outside Costa Rica. After three years you may change to permanent residency status. For the same $1,000 per year you can bring your spouse and/or dependent children.

Rentista is a category designed for those who are not retired or receive no government pension. To qualify for *rentista* status, you must have an income of $30,000 a year ($2,500 per month) coming from an investment or annuity from any financial institution. A good way to do this is to buy a certificate of deposit from a Costa Rican bank that yields a monthly income of at least $2,500 (from the capital). **NOTE:** Close family members are included in the requirement.

As a *rentista*, you must prove that this investment will be stable for at least five years. At the end of five years, you have to prove your source of income again or change to permanent residency if possible. Furthermore, every year as a *rentista* you have to prove that you changed $30,000 into *colones* and show your passport to prove you were in the country at least four months (not necessarily consecutively).

Why Belong to ARCR Administration and Association of Residents of Costa Rica?

By Ryan Piercy

- Assistance within Costa Rica before you arrive—advice,contacts and information.
- Recommendation of professional people you can trust, including lawyers, accountants and other specialists.
- Assistance with language.
- Service to establish residency, starting before you arrive.
- Assistance in getting acquainted with the country when you arrive.
- Recommendation of trustworthy real estate firms.
- Assistance with importation of cars, furniture and personal effects through our office.
- Assistance in locating various firms you may require who speak your language.
- Assistance with government agencies and departments, and an explanation of local rules and regulations.
- Assistance in establishing banking contacts.
- Advice about how various investments work in Costa Rica.
- Processing of resident government file updates and I.D. card renewals.
- Full insurance service through our office, including group plans for health, home and vehicles.
- Discount rates for Costa Rica social service medical insurance.
- Safe, inexpensive international mail and courier service.
- ARCR computers are on line with the computers at the Central Registry for property and vehicle title search and company name searches.
- Personal or company credit studies. ARCR computers are on line with the largest checking agencies.
- ARCR is on the Internet; We have a small net cafe for members.
- In the ARCR office, photocopy, fax, postal and document translation services are available to members.
- Hundreds of merchants and professional services provide discounts to members simply by showing the ARCR membership card.
- ARCR can arrange work permits for domestic help in Costa Rica.
- ARCR can assist in rentals and purchases for property and accomodations.

- Membership includes subscription to the bimonthly ARCR magazine, *"El Residente"*.
- Participation in the Residents Association's social and cultural events and the opportunity to meet other foreign residents.
- Travel and tourism assistance.
- Access to Costa Rica Assitance or CR Asistencia. ACCR (Automobile Club of Costa Rica)—"AAA-USA".
- Publications about Costa Rica are available from the ARCR office.
- Importing of pets.
- Funeral services.
- Newcomers Seminar. Our informative seminar is held every month,providing vital updates on banking,residency,moving, insurance, medical care and other topics important in making your decision to move here...and it's all FREE!

Who are we?
The ARCR Administration is an organization serving all types of foreign residents in Costa Rica, as well as people living abroad wishing to become residents of Costa Rica.

What do we do?
- Advocate for members before the Costa Rican government in matters of legal and human rights.
- Inform interested persons about procedures for becoming legal residents and to assist and advise them during the process.
- Organize social activities for members.
- Promote member participation in Costa Rican society and culture.

In Costa Rica:
ARCR Administration
Address: Apdo. 1191-1007
Centro Colón, San José, Costa Rica
Tel: (506) 2233-8068
Fax: (506) 2255-0061
WebSite: www.arcr.net
e-mail: arcr@casacanada.net
Street address: Casa Canada, corner of Calle 40 and Avenida 4, San José.
Tico style address: 200 meters sur del Banco de Costa Rica, Paseo Colón.

The safest banks are the public banks, which are the Banco Nacional de Costa Rica or the Banco de Costa Rica. You must keep the deposit of your money for five years in a CD and you may withdraw the interest obtained from it. If you decide to withdraw the principal, then you will be charged a penalty and will also be subject to loss of your residency, because the bank is required to notify Immigration if the deposit is withdrawn.

As a *rentista,* you can own and operate a business but **not** work for hire. The disadvantage to being a *rentista* is tying up your funds at relatively low interest. As with *pensionados,* dependents are allowed for an additional amount of income.

I just heard of a new method for obtaining *rentista* status from one of my readers. He said: "If anyone has to get residency under the *rentista* category, they can do it by setting up a business in the States if they already do not have one. The business has to hold $150,000 which is to be dispersed over five years." I urge you to check with a lawyer to see if this method will work before trying it.

In brief, to qualify for rentista status, you need:

1. An income of $2,500 per month for the next three years in Costa Rica.
2. Documentation from a bank attesting to income, if the income is from a foreign source.
3. Join the *Caja Costarricense de Seguro Social (CCSS*), with the intent that foreigners become integrated in Costa Rican life.

Inversionista is another resident status for people who are not retired and want to invest in Costa Rica. If you have a lot of money to invest, this might be the best route to go. The government will grant residency under this category if you invest at least $50,000 in high- priority projects such as tourism, $100,000 in pre-approved reforestation projects or $200,000in any other business (retail, farming, manufacturing, etc.). No dependents can be included under this category.

Most importantly, under the new law it appears that it may be possible to obtain this status with an investment of $200,000 in property or shares. Structure would be very important, so talk to the ARCR before starting this option.

The paperwork and requirements are similar to those in the other residency programs, with a few basic differences. Under this program you must reside in Costa Rica at least six months of every year (they do not have to be consecutive) and live as a temporary resident for two years. Eventually you may become a permanent resident.

If you plan to start a project, additional paperwork such as a feasibility study and bank references may be needed. If you are going to get involved in tourism, you will need permission from the Costa Rican Tourism Institute (ICT). When investing in an established company, you will have to show the company's books.

Since every circumstance is different and requirements change often, contact the Association of Residents of Costa Rica for a good lawyer to answer your questions.

The following documents are also required for *pensionado, rentista, inversionista* (resident investor), and all other types of residency in Costa Rica:

Note: All documents usually must be authenticated by the Costa Rican consulate or embassy located closest to the origin of the document (see the list for at the end of the last chapter for the nearest one). The charge is $40 per document. The people at the consulate must affix stamps worth the amount to collect the money. If the documents do not have the required stamps, you can buy them in Costa Rica. Talk to the ARCR before processing documents.

1. **Police Certificate** — From your local area stating that you have no criminal record. (This document is good for only six months, so make sure it is current.) Required for applicant, spouse, and any children ages 18 to 25. The local police in the applicant's usual residence, if different from the applicant's home state, may issue this report, but the police report usually coincides with the applicant's U.S. driver's license number. This document must also be authenticated by the nearest Costa Rican consulate. Many U.S. state and local law enforcement agencies have websites and special phone numbers to issue such reports, upon request by the applicant.
2. **Birth Certificate** — Required for applicant, spouse and all dependent children (up to 18 years old or up to 25 if a university student; proof of enrollment is required). This document has to be authenticated by the Costa Rican consulate nearest to the issuing authority of the birth certificate.
3. **Marriage Certificate** — If applicable and if spouse wishes residency. Proof of divorce is not needed. This document must also be authenticated by the nearest Costa Rican consulate.
4. **Income Certificate** — For *pensionados* and *rentistas* (required only for the applicant). Please see the previous sections for specific details. Talk to the ARCR before processing documents. This document must also be authenticated by the nearest Costa Rican consulate.
5. **Certified photocopies** of all pages of the applicant's entire passport (Not stamped by consulate),
6. **Photos** — Twelve *cédula*-size photos—six front views and six profiles. Do not bring photos, since a specific size is required and passport size will not work. Photos must be matte finish, not glossy.

Translation of Documents: Don't forget that all of these required documents must be translated from English into Spanish by an official translator. Translations from other languages to Spanish have to be done either by the Costa Rican consulate (no one else) in the country where the document was issued or in Costa Rica by an official translator for the specific language to Spanish. The Costa Rican government does not accept translation of the original language to English. The formal application should have the following information: your mother's maiden name, full name, nationality, passport number, dependents' names, date of entry into Costa Rica, origin and amount of income, address in country of origin or Costa Rica, authentication by a notary public and corresponding stamps.

All the above residency documents (other than those obtained in Costa Rica) must be:

a) Notarized by a local notary public if they do not have an official government seal. If in doubt about the need to have it notarized, check with the local Costa Rican consulate.
b) Authenticated by the Secretary of State (or other body) where they were issued (if in the United States, and possibly some other countries).
c) Authenticated by the Costa Rican consulate in the country where the document was issued.
Notarization: Your signature must NOT appear in the notarization of the document.

Authentication: A Costa Rican consulate will charge US$40 for authentication of each document. They must affix stamps worth that amount to collect the money. If they do not have the stamps, the ARCR can buy them in Costa Rica on your behalf. There is also a $100 application fee.

Translations from other languages to Spanish have to be done either by the Costa Rican consulate (no one else) in the country where the document was issued or here in Costa Rica by an *official* translator for the specific language to Spanish. ARCR can arrange for the services of a translator at the cost of the member. Translation from the original language to English is not accepted by the Costa Rica government.

If you meet the prerequisites for any of the residency categories and have gathered all the required documents, you are ready to apply for your chosen status.

Next, have the ARCR Administration or an attorney present your papers to the proper agency, which will process them in four months or so.

If you want to avoid the many inconveniences of Costa Rica's giant "bureaucrazy" and save time and money in the long run, I suggest you join the **ARCR.** The 5,000-member association has been reorganized and revitalized. It now offers services to all legal residents in Costa Rica, not just *pensionados.*

The ARCR's monthly seminar is a must

A provisional membership in The ARCR, which entitles you to all information and services, costs $100 yearly. Members with legal Costa Rican residency pay dues of $50 per year. Spouses and dependents of members may join for $10 per year as associate members. The ARCR offices are located in San José at Casa Canada, two blocks south of Centro Colón on the corner of Avenida 4 and Calle 40. They will assist you when you need help applying for *pensionado* or *rentista* status for $950 for the primary applicant, $950 for spouse or dependent and $500per child. This includes everything except the deposit to the government of $300 to $400 per person and the consular stamps you must obtain on foreign documents ($40 per document, and usually you need three such documents for an individual, or seven for a couple).

The cost for *inversionista* or *representante* status is $1,200 for the primary applicant. These prices are a good deal since many lawyers charge up to $2,000 and take much longer.

The ARCR'S other services

The ARCR can also help with buying and selling cars, obtaining a Costa Rican driver's license (see chapter 10 for details), assisting with English-to-Spanish translations of any required documents or papers, and making sure your annual papers are up-to-date. The association can notarize all your important documents, help with the renewal of your ID card or ***cédula***, and help you obtain medical coverage with the Costa Rican Social Security System and the new supplemental coverage they now offer (see the section on medical care for details). Should you desire additional information, contact:

ARCR Administration
Apartado 1191-1007, Centro Colón
San José, Costa Rica
Tel: 2233-8068 or 221-2053
Fax: 2255-0061
E-mail: arcr@casacanada.net
Website: www.arcr.net or www.casacanada.net

Residency in Costa Rica is another company that specializes in the preparation and filing of applications for prospective Costa Rican residents. Their website says that they have one goal: the approval of your residency application. To find out more about their services see: www.residencyincostarica.com or email: costarica@residencyincostarica.com, Tel: (323) 255-6116, Fax: (323) 344-1620.

To give readers an idea of what the process of obtaining residency is like, here is an account of one person's experience: "I handled all my own paperwork in the States. That amounted to following very peculiar procedures in New York State (New York City) for my birth certificate, and only slightly less complicated ones in Pennsylvania for my police report, with all of the certifications, etc. Then I took them all to the Costa Rican consulate and had them certified by the Consul in less than an hour.

"I suppose one could go to different consulates for each different document, but it would be a really trying process, as I am sure you are finding out if that's the way you do it. According to the rules, you have to take everything to the consulate assigned to your place of residence in the United States. I lived in south Philly, so New York was the place. In fact, the embassy in Washington said I could bring them all down there if I wanted, when I expressed concern on the phone that I initially had trouble reaching the New York Consul by phone or e-mail.

"I had already gone to the U.S. Embassy in Costa Rica for the paperwork to establish an account for my pension in Costa Rica.

Costa Rica Residency Types

as of March 1, 2010 (new law)

LEY GENERAL DE MIGRACIÓN EXTRANJERÍA

Pensionado	Rentista	Inversionista	Representante	Permanent
Proof of $1.000 USD Per month income From permanent Pension or retirement fund. Previously $600/mo.	Proof of $2,500 USD per month income guaranteed by a bank Previously $1,000/mo.	$200,000 investment in any Costa Rica business OR a specified amount of investment in certain Costa Rica government approved sectors.	Director, executives, representatives managers and technical employees of companies meeting certain requirements.	First degree relative with Costa Rica Citizen (thru marriage or having a child) OR may apply after 3 years in another residency.
Can claim spouse and dependents under 25 years of age or older with disabilities.	Can claim spouse and dependents under 25 years of page or older with disabilities.	Can claim spouse and dependents under 25 years of age or older with disabilities.		Can claim spouse and dependents under 25 years of age or older with disabilities.
Cannot work as an employee.	Cannot work as an employee.	Income allowed from the project.	Income must exceed Costa Rica minimum wage for specified position by at least 25%.	Can work as an employee
Must exchange $12,000 per year within a bank in Costa Rica	Must exchange $30,000 per year within a bank in Costa Rica	No exchange requirement.	No exchange requirement.	No exchange requirement.
Can own a company and receive income.	Can own a company and receive income.	Can own a company and receive income.	Can own a company and receive income.	Can own a company and receive income.
Cannot be absent From Costa Rica more than 2 consecutive yrs.	Cannot be absent from Costa Rica more than 2 consecutive years.	Cannot be absent from Costa Rica more than 2 consecutive years.	Cannot be absent from Costa Rica more than 2 consecutive years.	Cannot be absent from Costa Rica more than 4 consecutive years.

All residency types must participate in the Caja Costarricense de Seguro Social (CCSS) national social security and healthcare insurance system -or- "Caja". Proof of participations and payments for the entire term of residency are required for renewals.

US$300 guarante deposit for all types of residency

"When I was done with all this, my Costa Rican attorney took me by the hand and led me through the police fingerprinting and *Migración*. Each step took less than two hours counting lunch.

"It is really not a big deal. It is more a learning experience in patience than anything else. All told, it took me about three months start to finish, mostly waiting."

For more information on the new immigration law, see: http://central-america-forum.com/member-blogs/costa-ricas-new-immigration-law-quick-english-overview-guide

Methods of Obtaining Costa Rican Residency

As we mentioned in the last section, most of the *pensionado* program's privileges were revoked in 1992 (although some may be restored as we mention in the last section), so the only real advantage for becoming a *pensionado* is to be able to stay in the country legally. Now more and more people are looking at other ways of obtaining Costa Rican residency.

The residency program is for people who wish to reside in Costa Rica full-time but who cannot qualify for *pensionado* or *rentista* status.

(1) **Residente Inversionista** — As we mentioned in the last section, you can become *inversionistas* (resident investors) by investing $50,000 in an approved organization such as a tourism or export business, $100,000 in a reforestation project or $200,000 in another type of business. With this type of residency you have to live in the country six months a year.

2) **First Degree Relative** — Foreigners can also claim permanent residency if they have an immediate or **first-degree relative** in Costa Rica, i.e. a child, spouse or parent (mother or father), brother or sister (in this particular case, the applicant must be single) who is a citizen. Applicants must prove a relationship in the first degree, either by marriage or blood, to a Costa Rican citizen, and the Costa Rican citizen must be willing to sponsor the applicant's residency.

They must also prove they have financial means to support themselves while living in Costa Rica. Relatives of foreigners who have become Costa Rican citizens are also eligible for residency. In all cases you will be asked to prove your relationship. You can usually work under this category. All the documents required for other residency applications must be provided.

(3) **Marriage** — Marrying a Costa Rican also entitles you to residency. This is the fastest way to become a resident. I personally know of many expatriates who have married Costa Ricans for this very reason. Anyone under this category is not required to prove a minimum foreign income.

In addition, anyone who has lived for several years under another residency category, such as *pensionado* or *rentista*, may apply for Costa Rican residency. Many *ex-pensionados* do this because they can generally qualify for this status easily. With this type of residency you have to visit the country once a year. As in the other residency categories, you need an application, birth certificate, marital status certificate, police report, several passport photos and in some cases documents proving your relationship to your Costa Rican relatives.

(4) **Working for a Costa Rican Corporation** — There is a newly added residency status for those who have a working company or *sociedad anónima*. You must have a minimum number of local employees and provide financial statements. Just having a Costa Rican corporation will not qualify a person for this status.

(5) **Residency Under Special Circumstances** — Residency is sometimes granted to some people who do not fall into any of the previous categories. Not all people who apply under this category will obtain residency. If there are two people with the exact circumstances, one may be granted residency and the other may be denied. Since each case is different I suggest you talk to an attorney.

(6) **Temporary Residency** — *Residencia temporal* is for students enrolled in a university or language school, Peace Corps volunteers and members of affiliated church service groups, employees of foreign firms, employees of many national companies and other categories. Language teachers at any language institute in San José may obtain temporary residency. Others doing jobs that Costa Ricans cannot do are also eligible for this status.

Temporary residency permits are valid for three months to a year and can be renewed. Temporary residents may enter and leave the country as often as they wish, paying the exit tax. Once all documents are correctly presented, temporary permits are approved as quickly as possible.

Because each person's situation is different, the procedure is complicated. All residency programs require mounds of paperwork, so I advise you to consult a lawyer to facilitate this process. To find a competent, trustworthy attorney, go to the ARCR office or see the section in the Chapter 6 titled, "How to Find a Lawyer."

* **NOTE:** There are certain crimes which automatically disqualify you for Costa Rican residency. The list of criminal convictions for crimes that preclude a person from applying for Costa Rican residency are the following major crimes (felonies): Murder; trafficking in illegal drugs/narcotics; trafficking in human beings; trafficking in weapons or explosives; sexual crimes against minors, the elderly or the disabled; domestic violence; membership in certain designated gangs or in organized crime; etc.

Residency *Cédula* Renewal

Renewing *Cédulas*/Residency — Under the new residency law in order to renew, you must exchange a total of $12,000 per year as a *pensionado* or $30,000as a *rentista*. Even if you spend only part of the year here, you must still exchange this total amount. You can exchange it in as many increments as you like, be it once or 60 times a year. I also recommend you show your exchange each year, since it means less paperwork. This keeps you correctly up to date at immigration.

You must keep all exchange receipts for the total required. The *only* receipts accepted are those you get at a bank every time you change dollars to *colones*. You can use any Costa Rican state or private bank to change your money. The receipt *must* show your name, amount of dollars exchanged, rate of exchange, and amount of *colones* received. You can then change it all back into dollars if you wish.

You can renew up to one month your *cédula* expires (*vencimiento*). Try to plan ahead like four or five months before the expiration date to avoid long lines. You must renew at the latest within three months after the *vencimiento*.

Here are some things to remember when renewing your *cédula* at immigration:

* *Migración* (Immigration) has made a few changes to the process of renewing the *cédula de residencia*.
* ***Timbres*** (stamps) — Deposit the money in the *Ministro de Haciendas* general account at Banco de Costa Rica.
* **Copies of *cédula*** — You are required to provide a copy of the inside front cover (your picture, *cédula* number), inside back cover (*expediente* or file number) and copy of page with latest expiry date.
* **Renewal without appointment** — Thursday and Friday only. Get to Migración early, like 6 a.m. (the gates open at 8 a.m.), as it is better to wait a couple of hours early than four hours later. One resident I know renewed his *cédula* in a few hours. He arrived at 7 a.m. and left at noon.

* **Passport** — You need to carry it with you because some are asked people for their passport. For more information, see **www.migracion.go.cr/residencias/index.html.**

Here is what one couple experienced when they renewed their *cédulas*: "My wife and I arrived at 5:34 a.m. We got into line and began the wait. A man came by and offered a place closer to the front of the line for 4,000 *colones*. This practice is not legal, but is not policed either.

"The man making the offer was selling music CD's, mostly as a cover for the other offer. Having more time than money and sharing the pirate's feelings about all things not legal, I declined the offer. They also offered to rent me a plastic-chair-height stool for 200 *colones*. Later I was sorry I did not take them up on that offer.

Every Costa Rican resident is issued a *cédula* or ID card

"We stood there until a bit before 8:00 am, when the line started moving. At the gate they checked to see that we had the necessary papers:

1. My *cédula* (residency document that has to be renewed).
2. A copy of the pages with my picture, the prior validation stamp and the last page.
3. A receipt for the 1,250 *colones* deposited to the *Migración* account at BCR (Banco de Costa Rica).
4. "An application, which was passed out in the line about 7:30 . If you had these items they wrote a number on the copy of your *cédula* and

let you inside the gate to proceed to another line, actually the same line in a different place. I was number 80 in the line.

"By around 9 a.m. all of the people in line were inside and I could not tell if they were letting anyone else in. I have heard that they only accept 300 per day without appointments, and only on Thursday and Friday. I also heard that appointments were being made only in person, with a two to three hour window and were for three or four months in the future. Apparently someone else can make the appointment for you. But you have to go to get the renewal."

"It took the better part of two hours to get to the window where a person took all my papers and put my copy in their printer and printed my information from their computer on the back of the copy of my *cédula*.

"Next, they instructed me to go to Window 3.

"At window 3 they took four above-mentioned items, put them in some order and stapled them together. They told me it would be about an hour and 15 minutes. It was now 9:45am.

"We went to the coffee shop and had coffee, talked, read, and at 11:00 returned to Window three. After about five minutes, a person came out with a folder full of papers and began calling names. If you looked remotely like the picture on the *cédula*, they removed the *cédula* from the packet of papers and gave it to you. At 11:17am I had my renewed *cédula* in my hand and we were on our way to the parking lot. We got to the car before the sixth hour was up. So I paid for six hours of parking (3,000 *colones*).

Renewal at the Bank of Costa Rica

Legal residents can now renew or replace their identity *cédulas* at 32 Banco de Costa Rica offices all over the country. I mentioned the traditional method above because some people have run into snags at the bank and had to renew the previous way by going to Immigration. **NOTE:** First time applicants have to apply at immigration and not at the bank.

The Dirección General de Migración or immigration department has adopted a single format for all types of residencies, so this means that *rentistas*, *pensionados*, permanent residents and others holding a different type of residency can renew at the bank. They will get an identical *cédula*.

Those applying for their first *cédula* still will have to make their appointments directly with the immigration department.

The renewal service begins with a call to **800-BCR-CITA (800-227-2482) or see http://www.bancobcr.com/bcr_in.php?id=617.** This is the same number Costa Ricans call to make an appointment for passport or driver's license renewal, and other services offered by the bank.

During and after the telephone call, the appointments clerk checks the residency status of the caller with the immigration department. So when the foreigner shows up at the designated bank branch for the appointment, much of the paperwork already is done. At the appointment, the bank clerk collects the $48 fee and a $5 fee for delivery of the *cédula* via *Correos de Costa Rica*. The foreigner submits prints of both index fingers and poses for a photo.

The *cédula* is made at the immigration department based on the data collected at the bank. The finished *cédula* should be delivered in 22 days.

The new procedure reduces lines at the immigration department in La Uruca and saves foreigners money because they do not have to travel to the Central Valley.

The bank program also is designed to reduce the infamous immigration backlog. At one point 300,000 foreigners were awaiting immigration appointments but the department could handle just 300 a day. Some appointments were put off for more than a year, forcing foreigners to conduct their lives and businesses with expired *cédulas*.

The bank has experience in issuing documents. Clerks have handled 137,167 appointments for passports and 228,385 driver's license renewals,

Here is one person's experience renewing his *cédula* at the bank.

"I went this morning for my 9:40 appointment at BCR in Paseo Colon for my renewal and everything went smoothly. I was helped around 10:00,

Long-term residents will have to make many trips to Costa Rica's Immigrations building in La Uruca.

and was led into an office. The lady processed my payment 55USD in colones (for 2 year renewal in my case) plus the 2600 colones for shipping. They asked me for my exact address, fingerprint scan of both index fingers and signature like usual. She then scanned my old *cédula* and the receipts to keep on file I guess."

"I was then told that I needed to pick up my new *cédula* at a post office and was asked which one was most convenient for me. After I replied a form was printed out and I was told to pick it up at the post office after June 15. Once I was seen the whole process took less than 10 minutes."

"In my case I have permanent residency and didn't need to show receipts. For those who have to show receipts my guess is that they will scan them and check them later? ".

"Overall it was really great, I didn't have to wait a year for an appointment nor spend hours at *migración* on my appointment date. *Viva el Gobierno Digital*!"

"In addition the 800 number was a free call (800 BCR CITA/ 800 227 2482) and the BCR had free customer parking in the back. I little antecdote about the parking though: I pulled into the parking lot and went into the shaded/covered parking area. The guard asked me to park outside the shaded area as the covered area is for employees only. Oops, silly me, I forgot that at government banks the employees come first and customers second. ¡*Pura Vida*!"

Immigration and Other Matters

Work Permits

Applicants for work permits must submit the following documents:

1. Letter on certified paper to the Immigration's Temporary Permits Department outlining the reason for the request, with all necessary stamps affixed.
2. Temporary work permit application, available along with the list of requirements at the Immigration information desk in La Uruca district.
3. Four recent passport photographs.
4. A full set of fingerprints, taken at *Puerta* (door) 4 of the Immigration office in La Uruca.
5. Proof of guaranteed income while in the country. This could be provided via a letter from the applicant's employer here.
6. Applicants who will be working for a government or international institution in Costa Rica must provide a confirmation letter from the institution.

7. Photocopy of the photo page and last entry stamp of the applicant's passport.
8. Guarantee deposit of $100 at Immigration's temporary permit department once the permit is approved. If the applicant is also applying for a permit under a residency category, this deposit may be waived. The deposit is refunded when the applicant returns home.

Immigration will approve work permits only for Costa Rican companies authorized by Immigration's Executive Council. Businesses that have a long history of operating in the country are generally considered eligible to receive foreign workers.

Good news! There is a new government decree that would speed up residency applications for skilled professionals at multinational companies, export firms, airlines, large hotels and banks.

The decree pledges that the government will process applications within 30 days of receipt. It also allows foreigners to present their documents in Costa Rica, rather than in their home countries.

On paper, the decree markedly improves a process that lawyers, foreigners, company executives and even the Immigration Director describe as so bureaucratic and cumbersome that it reduces Costa Rica's competitiveness. Foreign investment requires speed and efficiency, and if one country doesn't make the cut, companies go elsewhere.

A main worry was competition from Panama, where foreign workers at multinational companies can get a temporary residency card in just three days. When the World Bank measured ease of doing business last year, Panama ranked 11th of 31 countries in Latin America. Costa Rica ranked 24th.

The Costa Rican Investment Promotion Agency (CINDE), a private non-profit that represents manufacturing, service and medical device companies, lobbied the government to take action in this area.

The decree will help about 500 companies. Firms can apply for the new benefits at a new, exclusive window at immigration headquarters in La Uruca, a northwestern district of San José.

Student permits

For a student permit, an applicant must submit the following:

1. A letter, on certified paper affixed with all necessary stamps, to Immigration's temporary permit department explaining the reason for the permit request as well as the name of the local "sponsor" — a legal resident of Costa Rica, *tico* or foreign, who will accept responsibility for

the applicant's actions while he/she is in the country. Letter must be certified by a local attorney or Costa Rican Consul.

2. Application form available at the La Uruca Immigration office's information desk.
3. Four recent passport photographs.
4. A guarantee of $100, which must be deposited with the temporary permit department after the permit is approved. Deposit is refunded when applicant returns home.
5. Proof of the sponsor's income here — a certified letter from the sponsor's employer, financial statements, etc.
6. Photocopy of sponsor's identification card (*cédula*) or residency card (*carnet*).
7. A full set of the applicant's fingerprints, taken at the Immigration office in La Uruca, Puerta (door) 4.
8. Photocopies of the photo page and final entry of the applicant's passport.
9. Registration letter or card from the school where the applicant will study.
10. Minors must present a certified authorization from their parents.

Perpetual tourist

In the past if you didn't want to invest the time and money to become a *pensionado* or resident, you could live indefinitely as a perpetual tourist in Costa Rica. No paper work or lawyers needed to be involved. People just had to leave for at least 72 hours every three months to renew their tourist visa. However under the new immigration law you have to pay $100 for every month you overstay. Bear in mind that the locals frowned upon this, much as we do in our own countries, as this was done frequently and avoided the "intent of the law." The ARCR recommends you consider some form of residency once you are certain you intend to stay in the country.

Under the new immigration law you can no longer repeat this process over-and-over again to stay in the country indefinitely. You also run the risk of being banned from the country for ten years if you try to do this. Also keep in mind that it is virtually impossible for a tourist to work legally in Costa Rica unless he or she marries a Costa Rican or has immediate Costa Rican relatives. The Costa Rican Government is also beginning to change their policies in relation to this, and some individuals may not be allowed to return.

If you don't want to bother leaving the country every few months to renew your papers, you can stay in the country illegally. You no longer have to pay the $0.90 fine for each overstayed month. The fine is now $100 for each month overstayed.

If you re a snow bird who comes to Costa Rica for a few months a year as a tourist on vacation and stays away for three to six months or only come for a few weeks at a time, you will have no problem with immigration.

For those who spend a long periods of time here , it is always better to have residency and your papers up-to-date because or you may be deported at the whim of an Immigration official or if you get into any kind of trouble and are in the country illegally. Costa Rica's Immigration Law gives airport or border officers the right to deport any illegal tourist.

Sometimes airlines give you a hard time if you are not a resident of Costa Rica and try to travel with a one-way ticket.

One reader found the solution: "The last time I traveled I was unable to board the flight bound for Costa Rica without an onward ticket. It was the airline that made the fuss, probably because if they bring me to Costa Rica without the onward ticket they can be forced to take me back to where I came from by Immigration (and without pay). Since I was at the counter to collect my boarding pass and ready to "come home," to Costa Rica, I bought a fully refundable ticket to Panama and got a refund in Costa Rica by showing the airline a bus ticket to Panama that I bought for $7."

Extending your stay

Effective March 2010, for a fee of $100.00 U.S. dollars, you can apply for an extension of a temporary stay in Costa Rica in the Department of Temporary Permits and Extension if:

* you were lawfully admitted into Costa Rica as a nonimmigrant in a tourist visa or a one-entry visa category that is not ineligible for an extension,
* you have not committed any crimes that make you ineligible for an extension, and
* you submit the application for an extension of stay before (at least 20 days) your current authorized stay expires.

Extension of Stay Required Documents

1. A passport valid for at least six months
2. Original Birth certificate *
3. Police record *
4. Personal letter with a 10 *colones* stamp attached to it addressed to the Director of the Department of Temporary Permits and Extension of Stays at the Immigration Department stating your name, last names, nationality, passport number, address and phone number where you will reside while in Costa Rica and your reasons for extending your stay. This letter must be signed in front of the Immigration clerk who receives

your application or it must be authenticated by an attorney. If the letter is authenticated by an attorney, you must attach to it an additional 50 colones stamp.

5. Extension of Stay Application is available at the Department of Temporary Permits and Extension of Stays at the Immigration Department
6. Four recent frontal passport sized photographs
7. A certified copy of all pages of your passport authenticated by an attorney in Costa Rica. Each copy must bear the stamp and signature of the attorney who authenticated it.
8. An original return airplane ticket to your home country. The ticket must have an expiration date and its departure date must be consistent with the date when your requested extension of stay expires.
9. Proof of financial funds: You must bring $200.00US in cash, travel checks, or a certified bank letter stating the current balance of your bank account. The minimum balance of your account must be $200.00 U.S.
10. Stamp Fees: You must pay 175 colones for each month that you are requesting the extension of stay. For example, if you are requesting two additional months you will be required to pay 350 *colones.*

* Document is not required. However, in some cases the Immigration Department of Costa Rica will require you to submit it. Document must be authenticated by a Consulate of Costa Rica prior to coming to Costa Rica, translated into Spanish (either in your home country by a Registered translator, by a Costa Rican translator certified by the Ministry of Foreign Affairs in Costa Rica, or by a Costa Rican Notary Public who speaks the language and certifies the translation), issued thirty days prior to your arrival in Costa Rica, and be no more than six months old after its issuance date.

Leaving the Country

Any tourist who has stayed in Costa Rica more than 30 days with just a tourist card will need an exit visa or *visa de salida* to leave the country. Likewise, foreigners who entered Costa Rica using just a passport and overstayed the maximum permitted time of 90 days, will also have to get an exit visa.

Costa Rican citizens, retirees and permanent residents are required to get an exit visa and *pensión alimenticia* stamps to prove to prove they have not left dependent children behind.

Everyone has to pay an exit tax of $26 at the airport. You can avoid a lot of hassles and lines at the airport if you pay before leaving. You may do so at the Bancrédito. Take your documents with you, passport or *cédula*, and the cashier will tell you the amount.

Children's Exit Visas

Children under 18, including infants, who remain in Costa Rica for more than 30 days are subject to the country's child welfare laws and will not be permitted to leave the country unless both parents request permission from the National Child Welfare Agency or *Patronato Nacional de Infancia* (PANI) (Calle 19 and Avenida 6). This can pose a real problem for a single parent traveling with children who overstay the permitted 90 days. One parent or guardian cannot get exit papers without written permission from the non-accompanying other parent. A Costa Rican Consul in the child's home country must notarize this document.

If you don't adhere to this procedure, your child <u>cannot leave</u> the country. When you go to the airport you have to take your child to a special window where an official form PANI checks to see if the child can be taken out of the country. A travel agent or lawyer <u>may</u> be able to get permission from the PANI if given the child's passport and two extra Costa Rican-sized passport photos.

If your child was born in Costa Rica, the child is automatically a Costa Rican citizen. To exit the country, the child will need an exit permit from the Costa Rican Immigration department if he or she is a minor. The child must have the permission of both parents to leave the country. This can be annoying if the child has to travel a lot with one parent. However, the parents can fill out a special permanent permission form whereby the child can leave the country with either parent as many times as necessary until the child is no longer a minor (18). My wife and I did this to make it easier for our son to travel.

Costa Rica's child protection laws can be a real pain in the neck. However, in some cases they can work to your advantage and enable you to stay in the country. All you have to do is have the cooperation of your child's mother or father.

If you support minor children, you cannot be deported from the country under most circumstances. If a mother wishes, she can ask for an *impedimento de salida*, preventing the father from leaving the country. If the *impedimento* is served, then the only way to leave the country is to pay the equivalent of 13 months' *pensión* (child support) in advance. Although I don't recommend using this method, some foreigners remain in the country indefinitely this way whether they really support their child or not. Your attorney can explain how to use this law to protract your stay in the country.

Here is one resident's experience on leaving the country with minor children: "I am not sure about a non-citizen resident, but for citizens it's just a matter of going down to Immigration with both parents and child and signing a form. Probably better to do this, just in case. The child will need a photograph too, which can be taken there. There are two types of permissions, temporary and permanent. The temporary is only good for certain period of time, say one or three months. It may even only be good for one departure. A permanent one is just that, permanent. The whole idea behind it is to prevent abductions, so if you go with a permanent, it might be a good idea to keep the permission papers separate from the child's passport. When we went, the person working there said that about 75 percent go with a permanent as opposed to the temporary."

By the way, paternity laws are very strict in Costa Rica. If a mother asks for a DNA test and it is positive, the father pays for the test; if it is negative, the mother pays for it. The tests are not cheap, but there is a long waiting list of about three months for these tests.

The *Patronato Nacional de Infancia* handles adoptions in Costa Rica. This process can take a couple of years even for a newborn or child if you satisfy all of the requirements. It is easier and faster if you adopt a child rather than a newborn.

If you are an American and your father children in Costa Rica, they will be eligible for your Social Security benefits. The U.S. Social Security Administration (SSA) seems to define "natural children" as distinguished from adoptive children. Whether they are born out of wedlock is not an issue.

According to the SSA at: **http://www.socialsecurity.gov/pubs/10085.html,** "Within a family, a child may receive up to one-half of the parent's full retirement or disability benefit, or 75 percent of the deceased parent's basic Social Security benefit. However, there is a limit to the amount of money that can be paid to a family. The family maximum payment is determined as part of every Social Security benefit computation and can be from 150 to 180 percent of the parent's full benefit amount. If the total amount payable to all family members exceeds this limit, each person's benefit is reduced proportionately (except the parent's) until the total equals the maximum allowable amount."

Costa Rican Citizenship

After living in Costa Rica for a number of years many foreigners decide that they want to acquire Costa Rican citizenship (dual citizenship is permitted for U.S. citizens through marriage). If you qualify, this is another way to stay in the country legally. As a naturalized citizen, you will have the same rights as a Costa Rican, including the privilege to vote and a Costa Rican passport.

There are some U.S. citizens who give up their citizenship voluntarily to take care of tax benefits for those living abroad. This is an extreme measure and I recommend thinking about the advantages and disadvantages. I heard of one case where the founder of Tupperware moved to Costa Rica about 30 years ago and became a Costa Rican citizen for tax reasons. In this case, millions of dollars were involved. The average person would not benefit from such a move.

There are other benefits of becoming a citizen of Costa Rica for many foreign residents: you can become a member of Costa Rica's Social Security System; it is almost impossible to extradite Costa Rican citizens; and there are mutual visa exemption agreements between Costa Rica and all the European Union countries, Scandinavia, Canada, Japan and Russia.

Naturalization (citizenship) applications are processed and granted by the *Tribunal Supremo de Elecciones y del Registro Civil,* the Costa Rican electoral and civil registry. Some consider this institution the fourth most powerful government entity.

You may apply for citizenship if:

1. You are married to a Costa Rican for at least 2 years. Article 14, section 5 of the *Constitución Política* and Law 1155 of April 29, 1950, and its reforms, states that a foreigner married to a Costa Rican can apply for citizenship after being married and physically present in Costa Rica for at least two years. The section allows foreigners to reside in Costa Rica **without** the requirement to become residents under Immigration rules.

   Foreign men and women married to Costa Ricans for a minimum of two years, and who have lived in the country for at least two years may also become citizens. The Costa Rican spouse can either be through birth or naturalization. You may also be able to become a naturalized citizen if you have been divorced from a Costa Rica citizen. However, you must comply with both the minimum time requirement for marriage and residence in the country.
2. After five years of residency (accumulated in the country), if Spanish is your first language. More specifically, nationals of other countries of Central America, Spaniards and Ibero-Americans by birth who have resided officially in the country for five years and who fulfill the other requirements that the law requires. Those born in the United States who speak Spanish as a first language do not qualify.
3. After seven years of residency (accumulated in the country) if Spanish is not your first language. U.S. citizens fall into this category.
4. Items 2 and 3 require an extensive exam (very difficult and in Spanish) in order to obtain citizenship. Note: Applicants will need to take a written test through the Department of Public Education in geography, social studies and the Spanish language. This test is similar to the one Costa Rican sixth graders take to move onto the next level. The Spanish test includes two parts: writing and reading comprehension. The writing test is a short essay, not fewer than 200 words, about one of four themes

given at the time of the exam. A competent speaker of Spanish as a second language should be able to manage the literacy test.

The history section covers with pre-Columbian societies, the Spanish conquest, the process of colonization, independence, the events of the latter half of the 19th century including the annexation of Guanacaste and events of part of the 20th Century .

These exams are usually given four times a year. Applicants can register at any time. Requirements to register are a copy of one's identification, a *timbre de archivo* for 20 colons (one of those postage stamp things), 4,500 *colones* deposited in the Banco Nacional for each test, and a passport photo. This exam is not easy for most English speakers unless their Spanish is fluent. You can find out more about the exam and what it covers at **http://www.dcc.mep.go.cr/temarios%20natura.html.** The office where you register or get information (*Gestión y Evaluación* is at Avenida 10, Calle Central y Primera. Tel: 2255-2272, Fax; 2221-0376.

Applicants will need to prove they have the financial means to live in Costa Rica. They'll also need a certificate from the computer section of the Department of Immigration showing their exits and entries into Costa Rica from the time they entered Costa Rica to the day they apply for citizenship. Permanent residents and resident investors will need a certificate from the National Immigration Council showing the names of their parents, date of birth and current immigration status.

Residency under the Immigration rules is not required by a foreigner who marries a Costa Rican national and wishes to remain permanently in Costa Rica.

Here is how the process goes:

First, go to the *Tribunal Supremo de Elecciones y Registro Civil*, to the section of *Opciones y Naturalizaciones* in San José.

Ask for an application with all of the instructions, a sample solicitation letter (to be copied verbatim) in Spanish and advice as to where to go for what.

The application must be submitted with:

1. A copy of your *cédula de residencia* (I believe they will make the copy for you at this section).
2. From the Computer "Mechanized" Department at immigration a certification of the number of passport and list of times you have entered and returned to Costa Rica up to the day you file for Costa Rican citizenship, since your first time from your passport. This can be received from near the bank at Puerta 7 at *Migración*. It usually takes one week and the cost in stamps is minimal.

3. Certified copy of your birth certificate which is available at *Puerta* 2 the same day. Request by 10 a.m. and receive by 2 p.m. This was submitted for your residency initially. (You may use the same one you obtained for Costa Rican residency). In lieu of this last requirement, you may obtain either a certificate from the Immigration Department or from the Tourism Institute showing your date and place of birth, parents' names and a sworn statement of your birth. You will need to have your birth certificate notarized by a Costa Rican Consul.
4. Current copy of marriage documents (*certificado iteral de matrimonio*), if using marriage or prior marriage to a *tico(a)*. A birth certificate issued by the Civil Registry for your Costa Rican spouse is also required.
5) A few *timbres fiscales* (stamps) (19 *colones) Archivo Nacional* stamps for 5 *colones.*

Workers at the *Registro Civil* will look up the applicant's police record and don't seem to care about any to pre-Costa Rica activities.

As far as I know, the United States does not favor dual nationality for its citizens but does recognize its existence. I just checked with the embassy here, and U. S. citizens may obtain Costa Rican citizenship without renouncing U.S. citizenship.

The naturalization process is slow and can take over a year, but is much less tedious and painful than getting Costa Rican residency (no long lines, don't have to join the public health care system and other inconveniences). Once approved, you'll be sworn in at a special ceremony where you have to stand up with everyone else and sing the national anthem. Be sure to learn the words and not use lip syncing.

Check with the U.S. Embassy in San José for the latest regulations. I know of a number of North Americans who have both U.S. and Costa Rican citizenship. One expatriate friend uses his Costa Rican passport for travel because he claims there are fewer problems than with his U.S. passport.

I suggest consulting a Costa Rican attorney for all the details and specific requirements if you are really interested in this subject. Attorneys charge $700 to $1,000 for this service. However, if you speak fluent Spanish you can do it yourself. There are several people who work outside of the Immigration office who will assist you for a nominal fee.

Once you become a Costa Rican citizen you are entitled to a Costa Rican passport. To obtain a Costa Rican passport you

1. Pay $26 at either *Banco de Costa Rica* or *Banco Nacional* before you go to Immigration.
2. Present your national ID card or *cédula* and a photocopy of both sides of it.

3. For children you will need a photocopy of their birth certificates and photocopies of both parent's *cédulas*. You will also have to pay $26 for each child at either of the two banks mentioned above.
4. For children born to foreign parents in Costa Rica, you will need photocopies of their birth certificate, a photocopy of the parents' residency *cédula* or passport and to pay the $26 for each child as above.

Getting Married and Fiancée Visas

Getting married in Costa Rica is really quite simple. All you have to do is complete the required paperwork and have the appropriate documents such as a valid passport, divorce papers (if you were previously married), affidavit of single status (if applicable) birth certificate for each party and any other pertinent information. All of the above need to be authenticated by the Costa Rican Consulate to validate the signatures of officials from other countries as is needed with residency paperwork, i.e. notarized, certified by Secretary of State, then sent to the consulate.

The Costa Rica woman will need a copy of her *cédula* and proof or her of civil status. The only church wedding that is officially recognized is that of the Catholic church. Other than a Catholic church wedding one must get married by a Notary. Most often Catholics get married by the Notary because it might be easier. Non-Catholics who want to have a church wedding for friends, family, etc. first get married in a civil ceremony then have an "unofficial weddingin the non-Catholic church.

I suggest consulting your lawyer if you are marrying in Costa Rica to find out exactly what documents are needed and what procedures to follow. Lawyers can marry people in Costa Rica much like a justice of the peace in the United States. This type of marriage is called ***por civil*** and is usually quicker than a traditional church wedding or ***por la iglesia***. In Costa Rica, people get married either way.

If you choose to have a lawyer to get married, you will need to have two witnesses who are not a third-degree relatives for the ceremony. Your lawyer will be able to round up a couple of people if you can't find anyone.

It takes at least three months or so before the marriage is recorded in the *registro* to be official. You can check your marriage status at **http://registronacional.com/costarica/personas.htm**

Fiancé Visa

If you are interested in obtaining a fiancé visa, you should be aware of the following process. Marrying a foreign national is a completely different experience than marrying a resident of the United States. In this country, you go down to the license bureau, apply for a marriage license and then tie the knot. When joining your life with an alien spouse, marriage alone does not necessarily allow the married couple to be together in the country. The U. S. government must be petitioned to permit your spouse to live with you in the United States.

When a foreign marriage occurs, the American spouse must file a Petition for Alien Relative and endure many months or even years of separation from his or her new spouse while the petition is approved and finally processed at the foreign consulate abroad.

A citizen of the United States has an additional option available : the fiancée visa. A U.S. citizen can petition for a visa for his or her alien fiancé(e) to allow him or her admission to the United States for a period of 90 days, to allow them to prepare for their marriage and life together. The fiancé process can be completed in a much shorter time period than a spousal petition.

Upon entry into the United States, the fiancé(e) is only permitted to remain for a period of 90 days. There are no extensions allowed. During the admission to the United States, the fiancé(e) will receive employment authorization from INS.

The petitioner and beneficiary must marry within the 90-day window or the beneficiary must leave the United States. If marriage to the petitioner occurs, the married couple will then apply for adjustment of status to lawful permanent resident at the INS district office in their area. If the marriage does not occur and the fiance(é) returns to his or her home country within the 90-day period, then the U.S. citizen retains his or her eligibility to pursue options with other potential spouses in the future.

This is intended to provide general information on the visa process. There are many other factors in this complex and ever-changing area of the law. I divorced here several years ago, but as far as I know nothing has changed.

Getting Divorced

1. You may get divorced by mutual consent. This, of course, requires that both parties agree on child support, child custody, dissolution of assets, etc. I believe this can actually be done without a lawyer but I wouldn´t try it. It may take a year or more for the courts to recognize this, PANI to approve it, etc.
2. The judge can declare divorce by separation if the parties have been approved by the court as separated for one year, which means counting from the date of court approval of the separation. I think you have to attend counseling or reconciliation meetings or something to do this.
3. Separation for at least three years. We are not sure how you prove this.
4. Of course there is divorce for cause, too, but it does not sound like this applies, and is lengthy and usually difficult to prove.

8

Staying Busy and Happy in Costa Rica

Some Sound Advice

Retirement or just living in another country often presents new challenges for people. For the first time, they are confronted with having a plethora of leisure time and the problem of what to do with it. As you will see throughout this chapter, Costa Rica is a wonderful place to live. In addition to being relatively inexpensive, there are many interesting activities from which to choose. As one of my American friends stated when referring to his busy life in Costa Rica, "My days are so fulfilling that each day in Costa Rica seems like a whole lifetime."

In Costa Rica you have no excuse for being bored or inactive, unless you are just plain lazy. There is a hobby or pastime for everyone regardless of age or interests. Even if you cannot pursue your favorite hobbies, you can get involved in something new and exciting. Best of all, by participating in some of the activities in this chapter, you will meet other people with common interests and cultivate new friendships in the process. You can even spend your time continuing your education or studying Spanish. Most people you meet will also be expatriates, so you probably will not need that much Spanish to enjoy yourself. However, the happiest expats seem to be those who speak Spanish. They are able to enjoy the culture more fully, mix with the locals and make new friends in the process. If you don't learn the language, you will always be somewhat isolated from the real world here.

Whatever you do, don't make the mistake of being idle. The worst thing you can do is spend all your time drinking in one of the many *gringo* hangouts in downtown San José. Over the years, we have seen many fellow Americans fail to use their time constructively, and destroy their lives by becoming alcoholics while living in Costa Rica— many have died prematurely. So, use the information provided in this chapter and take advantage of the many activities Costa Rica offers.

English Books, Magazines and Newspapers

Books, newspapers, magazines and other printed materials in English are available at most leading bookstores, in souvenir shops of larger hotels, and at some newsstands.

Many bookstores carry a large selection of books in English. **7th Street Books**, in downtown San José, is one of the city's best -bookstores (Calle 7, between Ave. 1 and Central, Tel: 2256-8251, e-mail: marroca@sol.racsa.co.cr). The North American owners, John and Mark, stock a wide range of new and used books in English with an excellent selection of travel, Spanish, nature books and U.S. magazines. They will even special order books for you.

Librería Internacional is a European-style bookstore. This bookstore is not global in name only since it sells books in English, Spanish and German. Locations: Barrio Dent, San Pedro, 300 meters west of Taco Bell, 2253-9553; Centro Comercial Multiplaza, second floor, 2201-8320; Rohrmoser 200 meters east of El Fogoncito restaurant. 2290-3331; Mall Internacional, Alajuela, 2442-3800; Plaza Cemaco, second floor, 100 meters north of Garantías Sociales traffic circle, 2257-8065; Central Ave., 75 meters west of la Plaza de la Cultura 2257-2563; Paseo de las Flores Mall, Heredia.

You can also find a good selection of English books in the book section of any of the **Librería Universal** department stores all over the country (Ave. Central, 2222-2222) and **Librería Lehmann** (Ave. Central, Calles 1 and 3, 2223-1212). **Papyrus** (next to Más x Menos supermarket in Sabana Este, 2221-4664) has an excellent selection of magazines, newspapers and paperbacks in English and Spanish. They have another branch in downtown San José.

Why Did You Come Here? What Do You Do?

By Martha Bennett

There are several species of *estranjeros* living in Costa Rica for a variety of reasons and doing different things. They come to retire, for adventure, to invest or open a business, or to study with one thing in common: changing their life style.

There are tourists. Some come to appreciate the flora and the fauna, volcanoes, beaches and mountains, and observe the Costa Rica culture. Others flock for sports: deep sea fishing, diving, surfing, white water rafting, hiking and hanging out. Everything is available except snow sports. Cultural events may be added on to either group's activities. A third group comes entirely for the bars, casinos and massage parlors. No one comes for the great food which has not inspired restaurants in other parts of the world. No matter, the ingredients are available to create your own cuisine.

The people who park here for six months to life do these things and more. Missionaries come for Latin language and culture. Old men come looking for young *ticas.* They get them too. This unlikely alliance builds the men's egos and the girls like the upgraded standard of living. Others of all ages earn or supplement their income teaching languages, writing, renting rooms or acting as tour guides. There is a group, usually college educated, that can't find, satisfactory jobs in North America. These people are found in the tourist industry or working for international companies. A foreigner can work here if the task is something a *tico* can not do. There are regulations, but in Latin countries, these are worked around. A slower pace of life and close family ties appeal to people in high stress jobs who have children. They come for a change of atmosphere. There is crime and substance abuse here, but the tightly knit community provides a healthier climate for raising children.

Retirees participate in many things. Some renovate a dream house. Some pursue the World Wide Web. There is a Theater Group, a Canadian Club, Women's club, Scrabble, bridge and T'ai Chi clubs and even a society for refrigeration engineers. The country club set plays golf, graces swimming pools, and dines elegantly. One can study yoga, painting, writing, language, pottery, gardening, holistic medicine and dance.

Remember, living takes longer here. Time is spent finding things, fixing things, cutting red tape and avoiding long lines. But this pace allows more time for reading, observing, listening to music and just being. In Costa Rica, we are more human beings than human doings. *Pura vida*! Pure life!

A local bookstore

Mora Books (2255-4136, 383-8385) is located in downtown San José behind the Holiday Inn Aurora. Theyhave more than 25,000 volumes on display and specialize in used books. **Goodlight Books** (2430-4083) in downtown Alajuela offers used books in English.

Some ex-pats order books on line though **www.amazon.com** and have one of the local private mail services, such as Aerocasillas bring them to Costa Rica. Here is what one expatriate said about importing books this way: "I buy from Amazon, and Aerocasillas takes care of getting it through Customs. If there are any duties to be paid, they ask you to deposit them into their bank account or bring it by their offices prior to them getting it released from Customs. They also will deliver the merchandise to your door. Of course they charge a fee, but it is worth it because once it gets to the address in Miami, it's couriered here to Costa Rica."

Major libraries in the San José area have large collections of English language books and magazines. A good place to go for the best selection of books is the **Mark Twain Library** at the Costa Rican North American Culture Center, commonly known as the **Centro Cultural**. You can browse all day or check out books. They also have nearly 100 English magazines from which to choose. Call 2253-5783 for more information. The **Lexicon Library** in La Sabana Oeste has a good selection of novels and other English-language books. Open Wednesdays and Fridays from 9:00am to 4:00pm Tel: 2291-4383.

The **National Library**, in downtown San José, is not a browsing library but has a large selection of novels and magazines in English. You have to

Opening an English Language Bookstore in Costa Rica

By Mike Jones

My business partner and I are often asked how we decided to start a bookstore in Costa Rica. We began by listing all the businesses we thought might be interesting to operate and/or be potentially profitable. The list we came up with included a pool hall, music store, bar, pharmacy, bagel shop, bookstore and laundromat. As we were mulling over the possibilities, we heard about a bar that was for sale. After talking to the owners of the bar and consulting with our lawyer, we decided to make an offer, contingent upon our being able to discuss with the building's landlord the changes we wanted to make to the bar. When the owners of the bar told us that it wouldn't be possible to talk to their landlord prior to purchase, we balked at the deal, sensing bad faith. A few weeks later, some friends contacted us about an excellent retail location that was becoming available in downtown San José. Because the location is near the *Plaza de la Cultura*, a point visited by nearly every tourist, we decided that an English language bookstore, whose main market would be tourists, might work. And so, within the space of two weeks we went from being bar owners to bookstore owners.

Our bookstore has now been opened nearly four years, and each year sales have nudged upward. There have been moments of despair, frustration and crisis, but the business appears to have finally have left the crawling stage behind and is walking. I never owned a business before in the U.S. and do not think that only four years of business ownership prepares me to give general business advice. What I could instead offer is a handful of tips that relate specifically to expatriate business ownership.

The first relates to your decision about opening a business in Costa Rica. You must decide if you like the country! This is an obvious point, but I have seen many tourists arrive and decide to move here mainly on the basis of having enjoyed their vacation. The rhythm of day-to-day existence versus that of tourist life is entirely distinct. If you can pull it off financially, I would recommend first arriving for a six month visit to really test the idea that this is where you would like to live. Even then, you must keep in mind that there is a big difference between living here while not working and living here while running a business; all the things you enjoyed doing when you were free of work obligations, you will find little time for when you are starting up a business.

When you do decide to start a business, be prepared for a dual challenge, you will be facing all the standard problems of business ownership (managing cash, monitoring competition, attempting to increase sales, etc.) at the same time that you are learning a new culture and language.

As you go through the process of trying to decide what kind of business to open, it is common to make a list of kinds of businesses that exist in the home country but do not exist in Costa Rica. For several years we expatriates were clamoring for a bagelry and a micro brewery, and when they did finally arrive they met with considerable success. Nevertheless, it is important to keep in mind the significant cultural differences that exist between the home country and here, and that what works there won't always work here. The expatriate community is not so large that you can succeed simply by targeting that group. You need *tico* customers too, and disposable income is not too high here. Also, whatever business you choose, it is obviously important as an expatriate to respect the customs and moral standards of this country. One gentleman from Canada entered the store and told me he was planning on opening a topless car wash. I said, "I would suggest doing that in another country."

Expatriate business people need to resist the occasional pull toward paranoia, toward the notion that "they", the locals are all trying to take advantage of me. A more reasonable stance, I think, is to assume that in business everyone is trying to take advantage of everyone, regardless of national origin. So far, our only slightly significant encounters with less than honorable people have been two unfortunate business deals with other expatriate business people, who , because they had no strong family or financial ties to this country, were able to flee the country.

Despite a strong tendency on the part of the U.S. media to represent Latin American governments as bureaucratic, inefficient mazes, we have found the opposite to be true in Costa Rica. Nearly all the legal and regulatory issues that we have been required to comply with have generally been handled swiftly and fairly inexpensively by our lawyer. Get a good lawyer whose practice focuses on expatriate clients. A related stereotype about Latin America is that it is rife with corruption. While there are great differences between countries, we have never had anyone approach us and insist that we pay a bribe as a condition for conducting business. True, we have had people offer us the option of a bribe in order to receive faster or better service. I've seen similar things happen in New York. A last word of advice...don't expect to get rich.

use the card catalog to select your book and then request it at the front desk. Also, the **University of Costa Rica Library** has some materials in English.

There are 55 public libraries around the country. The vast majority of their publications are Spanish language books. Library hours are from 10 a.m. to 6 p.m. In the San José area public libraries can be found in the cities of Desamparados (2250-0426), Hatillo (2254-1028), Montes de Oca (2272-0809), Ciudad Colón (2249-3516), Santa Ana (2282-9106), Puriscal (2416-8300) and Tibás (2236-3087).

There is no problem obtaining copies of *New York Times*, *Time* or *Newsweek* in Costa Rica. The *Miami Herald* international satellite edition is now also available in Costa Rica. You can pick up most of these English-language publications at local newsstands, hotels and some bookstores. Other publications available are *Barron's*, *International Herald Tribune*, *Sporting News*, *Sports Illustrated*, *USA Today*, *Wall Street Journal* and *Washington Post*. Obviously you can find almost any publication on line.

Europrensa, S.A. (232-6682), is now offering 320 digitally produced print-on-demand newspapers from 57 countries.

The Tico Times, the largest English-language newspaper published in Central America, is available almost everywhere in Costa Rica. Reading it is an excellent way to keep up with local Costa Rican and Central American news in general. Car sales, cultural activities and other useful information can also be found in this newspaper. The newspaper costs $1 and comes out every Friday.

To subscribe to the *Tico Times* (if you live in the United States), write Dept. 717, P.O. Box 025216, Miami, FL 33102, or e-mail info@ticotimes.net. If you live in Costa Rica: Apdo. 4362, San José, Costa Rica, Tel: 2258-1558. You can read this newspaper on line at: www.ticotimes.net.

Inside Costa Rica is another good online publication. It is published daily and has both local and international news articles. *Inside Costa Rica* may be accessed at: www.insidecostarica.com.

A.M. Costa Rica is an online newspaper published Monday through Friday. In additional to the usual daily news events and features, there is an excellent classified ads section. You may access this online newspaper at www.amcostarica.com. For additional information contact A.M. Costa Rica, Apdo. 6318-1000, San José, Costa Rica, Tel/Fax: 2231-7528, E-mail: editor@amcostarica.com.

La Nación, Costa Rica's best Spanish-language daily, has a new online version in English at: www.nacion.com/In_ee/english.

Here is a list of all of the online Costa Rican newspapers:

* Al Dia (Spanish)
  www.aldia.co.cr
* A.M. Costa Rica (English)
  www.amcostarica.com

* Central America Panorama (Spanish)
  www.elpanorama.net
* Cyberprensa (Spanish)
  www.cyberprensa.com
* Diario Extra (Spanish)
  www.diarioextra.com
* El Financiero (Spanish)
  http://costarica.capitalfinanciero.com/edactual/
* El Heraldo (Spanish)
  www.elheraldo.net
* Informa-Tico (Spanish)
  www.informa-tico.com/php/informa-tico.php
* Inside Costa Rica (English)
  www.insidecostarica.com
* La República (Spanish)
  www.larepublica.net
* Nación (Spanish)
  www.nacion.com
* Prensa Libre (Spanish)
  www.prensalibre.co.cr
* Semanario Universidad (Spanish)
  www.semanario.ucr.ac.cr
* The Tico Times (English)
  www.ticotimes.net

Television and Radio

Cable TV

As in the United States, Costa Rica has satellite cable television that is available in most places in the Central Valley, Liberia, Tilarán, San Carlos, Pérez Zeledón, Orotina and in some beach areas such as Jacó and Quepos. A variety of American television channels provides viewing and entertainment at a low cost from **Amnet** (2231-38380, 2231-2811 or 2231-3939, www.amnetcable.co.cr) or **Cable Tica, www.cabletica.com** (, 2254-8858) . You will not miss much TV while living in Costa Rica since these companies offer local channels in Spanish as well as 38 channels in English including CBS, NBC, ABC, FOX, HBO, CNN, ESPN, TNT, the Discovery Channel and more. There is an initial sign up fee of about $25 and a monthly charge of $23. If you want to hook up additional TV in your house or apartment, you will pay only $2.50 extra per month.

Satellite TV

Direct TV in Costa Rica was bought out by a Mexican company. called **SKY** (www.sky.com.mx/nosusc/int/centroamerica/ Tel: 2205-5151) which is now the local provider of satellite TV. Their system works in nearly any location in Costa Rica. We have friends who live in isolated areas of Costa Rica and say the system works without a hitch.

Programming is out of Mexico, so there are both channels in English and Spanish. In all there are around 200 channels from which to choose. Satellite TV is more expensive than cable service and is occasionally interrupted during heavy rainstorms. The monthly cost for the full package including the movie channels is around $50. They also offer special seasonal packages for the NFL and other sporting events. Some English-speakers complain that SKy has too many channels in Spanish.

SKY does not offer Internet service. Direct TV equipment purchased in the United States will not work with the satellite systems in Costa Rica or the rest of Latin America.

An alternative to SKY is **Dish TV**. For a one-time installation fee and a reasonable monthly rate, you get hooked up to digital TV viewing, a "slice of home" so to speak. Some of the many channels offered include Fox, Fox Sports, HBO (10 channels), Showtime (10 channels), NBC, CBS, ABC, CNN, TNT, Movie City, Sirius Music and more than a hundred more channels. The programming is from the Dish Network in the United States. You can view what they have to offer at **www.dishnetwork.com**.

I have who have this system and rave about the wide variety of programs. Feel free to contact **Sun Sat TV** (2249-0506 or 2282-9097, E-mail: cathy@sunsattv.com, see **www.sunsattv.com**) about any interest or questions you may have concerning satellite TV and the latest technology available in Costa Rica. Good news! Sun Sat is now offering **Direct TV** from the States at the same cost as Dish TV. What they offer is better than SKY, since there are more programs in English than SKY has.

The *Instituto Costarricense de Electricidad*, known as ICE, said that it expected to be offering digital television over the Internet by June of 2010. Instead of connecting to an antenna or a cable modem, this technology utilizes a router to receive the signal from broadband which also feeds your computer.

Local Spanish-language TV stations are **Teletica** Channel 7 (2232-2222), **Repretel** (2280-6665) Channels 4, 6 and 11 and **EXTRA TV 42** (905-398-7288)

Teletica, Channel 7, has a pay-per-view system and places videos online on its own Web page. However, the new service is expected to be television on demand, hence the need for a new system.

Radio

Most radio stations play Latin music. However, there are four English language radio stations that play pop, oldies and modern rock. Both foreigners and younger locals listen to these stations since they play a lot of past and present hits. Many of the bus drivers play rock music that the English stations play. **Radio Dos 99.5 FM** plays top -40 music from the 1960s, '70s, '80s and '90s, **Radio 102.3 FM** offers soft rock, classics and oldies and **103.5** plays soft rock and classics, 60's through the 80's. **Radio 107.5 FM**, the country's only all-English radio stations, offers 100 percent rock from all decades. **Radio 95.5** plays a great selection of tasty jazz and fusion.

Video and DVD Rentals

Movie buffs will be happy that many video rental shops do business all over the country. For a small initial fee, you can acquire a membership at one of these stores and enjoy many privileges. Most movies you rent are in English with Spanish subtitles. Almost every neighborhood has a *Video* store or place where a wide selection of DVDs can be rented. The cost is usually around a dollar or two-dollars per day. Most offer specials where you can rent three videos and get the fourth for free. The good news is that a large number of DVDs are available at most of these establishments. See the local phone book for a full listing of videos in your area.

Shopping

One way to keep active is to go shopping. Although Costa Rica is not as good for shopping as the United States., you can still spend your free time doing some serious shopping, browsing or just window-shopping.

Due to the large number of U.S. and Canadian citizens living in Costa Rica, and a growing number of Costa Ricans exposed to U.S. culture by cable TV and visiting the States, there has been an influx of American products. The only problem is that many of these goods are more expensive in Costa Rica because of import duties.

Everyday, more and more imported goods from the United States are available in Costa Rica. Imported brand name cosmetics, stylish clothing, appliances and some foods can now be found in many stores in San José and other areas catering to foreigners. A number of new stores and shopping centers in or near San José now sell imported items.

In downtown San José, a few specialty shops and a couple of department stores sell American-style clothing and other imported goods. San José's Central Avenue or *Avenida Central* has virtually been turned into a pedestrian outdoor mall and walking street. This section begins a block beyond the Central Market and ends at the east end of Plaza de la Cultura. Lehman bookstore and the Universal department store are all found along this promenade.

A variety of shops around the Central Market offer products at low prices. Prices in this section of town tend to be much more reasonable than in the local mega-malls. Boutiques, a multitude of shoe stores, a record shop, a pharmacy, an outdoor sidewalk café and fast food restaurants such as McDonald's, Burger King and Taco Bell dot both sides of the street.

For you mall-rats or mall-crawlers, there are also a number of local shopping centers that closely resemble U.S.-style malls. **Plaza del Sol**, Costa Rica's first U.S.-style mall, is about five minutes east of San José in Curridabat. A mall is also found at the **Plaza Mayor Shopping Center** in Rohrmoser. It has 21 businesses, including a movie theater, supermarket, bank, pet store, pharmacy and food court. In the suburb of Escazú, home of many foreigners and well-to-do Costa Ricans, a number of U.S.-style mini-malls have sprung up. Most of these newer stores have products that foreigners seek. The **Multiplaza** mega-mall west of Escazú houses a large mall and shopping center. There are the usual chain stores here plus a host of specialty shops. A new section with over 50 stores and restaurants has been added. It is now one of the largest malls in Central America. **Multiplaza del Este,** in the eastern San José suburb of Curridabat, belongs to the same company. **Terramall**, east of San José on the way to the city of Cartago, is one of the country's newest mall complexes.

In Heredia **Paseo de las Flores** has stores, food courts, multiple- screen movie theaters, ample parking and more. A new second section of the mall was added in November of 2006 and the mall continues to grow with the addition of new businesses.

The **San Pedro** Mall is one of Central America's largest shopping centers. This mega-mall has more than 260 stores, 35 restaurants, a hotel, a couple of discos, video arcades and parking for 1,200 cars.

A few blocks east of San Pedro Mall is the **American Outlet Mall**. There is **Plaza Real Cariari**, near the Cariari Country Club with about 125 stores, a food court, theaters and recently underwent expansion.

The **Mall Internacional**, on the main road just before the city of Alajuela, is smaller than the other giant shopping complexes but offers shoppers an ample variety of shops.

Other smaller mini-malls include **Plaza Colonial** in San Rafael de Escazú, **Santa Ana 2000** in Santa Ana, **San José 2000** near the Hotel Irazú, **Plaza**

Heredia, in the neighboring city of Heredia, **Centro Colón** on Paseo Colón **Centro Comercial Guadalupe** in Guadalupe, the new **Nova Centro** in Moravia, **Plaza América** near Hatillo, **Metrocentro** in the city of Cartago, **Gran Centro Comercial del Sur** and **Multi Centro** in Desamparados south of San José. **Plaza Lincoln** will be a new mall with over 150 stores for people in the Moravia/Tibas area.

There are also music stores, supermarkets and natural food stores located in the San José area. There are even arts and crafts stores and gift shops. Check out **La Casona**, the **National Artisan Street Market** or the new **International Market of Arts and Crafts** in the suburb of Curridabat to the east of San José.

The newest shopping craze is U.S. warehouse-style mega-stores such as Walmart. They promise to change local shopping habits and pricing. The **Hipermás** stores have groceries, furniture, toys, a deli, clothing, appliances and more all under one roof. Best of all, the stores stock a huge amount of U.S. products. Costa Rica's first wholesale shopping club, **PriceSmart**, opened its first store in San José's Zapote district in mid-1999. The chain's stores are similar to the Costco chain in the United States. The company is pioneering the "club" concept in Costa Rica. The store purchases large amounts of imported products, and in turn passes its volume-buying savings on to its club members. They also have stores in Heredia, Escazú and Tibás. **GNC** (2288-1049) opened several vitamin stores in the San José area. Now all types of vitamins and nutritional products are available.

A mammoth U.S.-style mall.

The **Cemaco** department store chain operates stores in Pavas, Multiplaza, Alajuela and Zapote. The newest store in Zapote's Plaza Cemaco has 37 departments and more than 60,000 items.

In general, despite the availability of many new imported products and the growing number of malls, supermarkets, mini-malls and specialty shops, shopping in Costa Rica still leaves a lot to be desired if you are used to shopping in North America. Do not expect to find every product you may need in Costa Rica. However, you can now order almost anything you want through one of the private mail services listed in Chapter 9 of this guidebook.

Once you live in Costa Rica for awhile, you learn to substitute many local products for items you ordinarily use and do without some things. This is easy due to the variety of similar items available in Costa Rica.

If you absolutely must have products from the States, you can go there every few months—as many foreigners and wealthy Costa Ricans do— to stock up on canned goods and other non-perishable foods, clothing, sundries and cosmetics. We know of one American retiree who goes to Miami every three or four months to buy all the goodies he cannot find in Costa Rica. These frequent trips to the States are unnecessary if you learn to make do with local products.

One thing you may need some time to get accustomed to is the way purchases are handled in some stores. One clerk will wait on you, another will ring up the purchase, and finally you will pick up your merchandise at another window. You find this system in most department stores, pharmacies and older businesses. This system seems to create a lot of extra work for employees and delays for customers. The good news is that every day more and more stores adopt the American-style one-step self-service system.

Costa Rican Pastimes

Costa Rica has a wealth of indoor and outdoor activities designed for everyone, regardless of sex, age, personal taste or budget. All of us, Costa Ricans, tourists and foreign residents, can participate in river rafting (some of the world's best), camping, walking groups, dancing, racquetball, weight lifting, tennis, baseball, soccer, swimming and surfing, jogging, bicycling, horseback riding and sailing. There are also plays, ceramic classes, movies, bridge clubs, art galleries, social clubs, museums, parks, zoos and more. Dedicated couch potatoes can even stretch out and admire the lovely landscape or work on improving their suntans.

There is something for everyone, so enjoy. Check the activities section of the *The Tico Times*. If you read Spanish, there is a listing in the weekend section of *La Nación* called *Viva.* You can find activities, cultural events and all sorts of entertainment listed there.

Gyms and health clubs are a good place to socialize and make new friends while working out. Some gyms even have spas, tennis courts and swimming pools. There are more than 32 gyms in the metropolitan area.

World Gym in Escazú and the new **Pro Fitness Gym** at the Paseo de las Flores Mall in Heredia are state-of-the-art facilities. They boast an assortment of equipment, including treadmill, weight machines, stationary bikes and free weights. There are also full service workout and fitness centers that provide personal trainers, classes or scheduled aerobics with modern facilities just like in the U.S. Costa Rica has it all, including women- only programs, such as Curves.

If you wish to join a private athletic club, country club or gym, I suggest:

Arena Trek	2228-7667
Costa Rican Tennis Club	2232-1266
Curves	2288-2480
Club Olímpico Gym	2224-3560
Fitness Centre (Mall San Pedro)	2524-1025
Fitzsimons Gym	2296-0264
Gold's Gym	2256-6689
Hi-Line Gym	2232-1464
Indoor Club Curridabat	2225-9344
Ironman Gym	2233-3025
MultiSpa (San José)	2258-2220
MultiSpa (Escazú)	2289-5051
MultiSpa (Cipreses)	2271-0359
MultiSpa (Sabana Park)	2231-5542
MultiSpa (Santa Ana)	22820224
MultiSpa (Grecia)	2495-6030
Pilates Center (San Rafael, Escazú)	2289-7411
Profitness (Heredia)	2263-1111
Spa Cariari Hotel Gym	2239-0022
Spa Corobicí Gym	2232-5533
Sports Connection	2234-9668
World Gym (Escazú)	2288-4787

* Check the phone book for more listings of gyms and private athletic clubs.

Soccer is King in Costa Rica

By Chris Howard

If you move to Costa Rica, you will have to learn about soccer or *fútbol* as it is called here. The game is almost a religion. Whenever there is a major soccer game, virtually everything comes to a stop and the party begins.

Children of all ages can be seen playing soccer on the weekends. Adults even play informal games during their lunch breaks called *mejengas.*

Basically, here is how soccer is played:

Using a round ball, a soccer match is played by two teams wearing different colored shirts. Each team consists of not more than 11 players, one of whom is the goalkeeper. An official match may not start if either team consists of fewer than seven players.

Up to a maximum of three substitutes may be used in any match played in an official competition organized under the auspices of the world governing body FIFA, the confederations or the national associations.

In other competition, the rules must state how many substitutes may be nominated, from three up to a maximum of seven. The duration of an official match is 90 minutes played in two halves — each half lasting 45 minutes.

The aim of the game is for one team to score more goals than the opposing team. The winning team is the team that has scored the most goals at the end of the game. Players score a goal when they succeed in moving the whole ball over the opposing team's goal line, between the goalposts and under the crossbar. Players may use any part of their body except their arms and hands.

The ball is out of play when it has wholly crossed the goal line, or touch line - whether on the ground or in the air, and when play has been stopped by the referee.

The game is controlled by one referee on the playing field and two assistant referees placed on opposite sidelines.

The field (or pitch) of play must be rectangular. The length of the touch line must be greater than the length of the goal line.

- Length: minimum 90 meters (100 yards), maximum 120 meters (130 yards)
- Width: minimum 45 meters (50 yards), maximum 90 meters (100 yards)
- International Matches
- Length: minimum 100 meters (110 yards) maximum 110 meters (120 yards)
- Width: minimum 64 meters (70 yards) maximum 75 meters (80 yards)

The field of play is marked with lines. These lines belong to the areas of which they are boundaries. The two longer boundary lines are called touch-lines. The two shorter lines are called goal lines. The field of play is divided into two halves by a halfway line. The center mark is indicated at the midpoint of the halfway line. A circle with a radius of 9.15 meters (10 yards) is marked around it. A goal area is defined at each end of the field. A penalty area is defined at each end of the field. Goals must be placed on the center of each goal line.

Soccer vocabulary:
árbitro — referee
banda — sideline
cabezazo — header
cancha — field
defensores — defenders
delantero — forward
empate — tie
entrenador — coach
equipo — team
falta — foul
fuera de lugar — offside
fútbol — soccer
jugador — player
"Gooooooooooool! — Goal! — Said when some scores.
guardameta, portero, arquero — goalkeeper
marcar — to score
mediocampista — mid-fielder
mejenga — an informal pick-up game
mejengear — to play an informal pick-up game
partido, juego — game
pelota — ball
penal — penalty kick
penales— shoot out
primer tiempo — first half
saque — kick off
saque de banda — side throw-in
segundo tiempo— second half
tarjeta amarilla — yellow card (warning)
tarjeta roja — red card (expulsion)
tiro de esquina — corner kick
tiro libre — free kick
travesaño — cross-bar

Golf

Costa Rica's beautiful scenery and spring-like weather provide a perfect setting for playing golf. It is no surprise the sport has really taken-off over the last couple of years and is on the verge of a boom.

The country promises to become a premier golf travel destination in the future with the opening of public courses. **Golf La Ribera**, the country's first public driving range, recently opened (8381-4433) in La Ribera de Belén near a famous water park called Ojo de Agua, about 15-20 minutes from downtown. It is a good place to begin your golf experience in Costa Rica. The **Marriott Hotel** has its own range which for now is reserved for the guests. **Parque Valle del Sol** (2282-9222) is a nine-hole public course near San José. It is very popular with local expatriates.

Most of Costa Rica's golf courses have rental clubs and provide caddies. There is sometimes a staggering difference in greens fees if you are with a member as opposed to showing up at the course as a walk-in. Below is a description of some of the country's courses.

In the Central Valley, the **Cariari Country Club** is one of Costa Rica's two 18-hole course. The Cariari, long considered to be the best course in Central America, has hosted such world-famous golfers as Tom Weiskoff, Ray Floyd and many more. The Cariari is significantly more expensive than Valle del Sol or Los Reyes.

The **Costa Rica Country Club** is a nine-hole course and boasts Central America's most lush clubhouse. You have to be with a member to play but a personal chat with the pro might get you through the gate and on the course. Incidentally, almost all the Costa Rican pros speak English, so a hint at perhaps taking some lessons could help open some doors.

Los Reyes Country Club is just nine-holes for now but is designed to be a full 18 eventually. It is about 45 minutes from downtown San José.

Currently there are several places to play golf on Costa Rica's west coast. Over the next few years, more will open. A word of advice: schedule your tee-off for early in the morning or wait for a leisurely, twilight round, because the sun and humidity can be brutal during the day.

Los Sueños Marriott Ocean and Golf Resort is the jewel of the Central Pacific. This beautiful resort is bordered by the Pacific Ocean on one side and rain forest on the other.

Tango Mar Resort and Country Club is a 10-hole course at Playa Tambor on the bottom of the Nicoya Peninsula. You do not have to be accompanied by a member and chances are you will have the course all to yourself.

Garra de León Golf Course at Playa Conchal is one of the best golf courses in Central America. No expense was spared to create a course on a par with the spectacular resort that surrounds it.

A Golfer's Dream

By Landy Blank

My wife Susan and I have lived in Costa Rica for two years. We vacationed here many times before deciding to make our big move. It often feels as though we arrived here just yesterday, at other times I don't remember living anywhere else. However, I will always remember the reaction of family and friends upon being told that we were packing our bags, three large dogs and heading to Costa Rica. I thought everybody would be excited and offer lots of encouragement, but read on to get an idea.

"What will you do on that island?" "We'll bring people to Costa Rica on golf vacations, and actually it's not an island. Oh, I didn't know it was a golf destination, they must have some great courses." "Well, not exactly... They do have one great course, the Cariari, and more are being built." "Landy, they only have one course and you're going to sell golf vacations?" "We're looking ahead and new courses are being built!" "When will they be finished?" "That's a tough question, and nobody seems to know, but it will happen! The only way I can find out is to move there, get ourselves settled, and be ready when they do open."

Inevitably at this point in the conversation there was a rolling of the eyes and a small smile would pass across the face of my friend, family member, or golfing buddy.

"Why in the world would you want to leave Charleston? You get to play golf as part of your job at the country club, and then go downtown and eat and drink for free at your restaurant. You must be crazy, I just don't understand."

How do you explain that Costa Rica has gotten into your blood, the people, the beauty, the climate, and despite the bureaucratic hassles, you're determined to live there. It didn't take long for these conversations to become tiresome, and as quickly as possible we made our move to our new home. With dogs, computers, golf clubs, and anything that would fit into a suitcase, we were off to Costa Rica in search of our destiny.

Many of the people we met in Costa Rica expressed the same incredulity when we told them we were planning to bring groups of golfers here on vacation. The look we got was, "Well, you're not the first crazy *gringo* to hit Costa Rica, and I wish you all the best luck in the world. Let me buy you a drink!"

(Author's note: In the past two years, two world class championship golf courses have been completed. Costa Rica is quickly becoming known around the world as a golf destination and we are very happy that we made the move!)

Rancho Las Colinas Golf and Country Club, near Flamingo, overlooking Playa Grande in mid-Guanacaste, is one of the newest courses in Costa Rica. This course is the jewel of a quickly developing community.

The **Four Seasons Hotel** at the Papagayo Peninsula opened an 18-hole golf course in February of 2004. This course is only opened to guests. Friends who have played rave about it.

Developers of the **Guanacaste Country Club** said that construction would begin in 2010 for a Jack Nicklaus Signature Golf Course. The Guanacaste Country Club is a 2,500-acre development which is west of Liberia and the international airport and inland from the Gulf of Papagayo

The **San Buenas Golf Resort** is a new 644- acre golf community currently being built south of Dominical and Uvita in the Southern Pacific area. It will have a championship golf course, driving range, tennis center, condominiums and a whole lot more (Please see their full-page ad at the end of this book).

Golfers may now keep up-to-date on Costa Rica's growing golf scene by subscribing to *Central America's Golf Magazine*, Tel: 2231-6931, Fax: 232-1930, E-mail: golftennis@hotmail.com, www.golfmagazine.com.

For golf tours see: **Costa Rica Golf Adventures** at www.golfcr.com.

Museums and Art Galleries

There are more than 30 museums scattered around Costa Rica displaying everything from pre-Columbian artifacts to the history of railways. Many are conveniently located in downtown San José. Most guidebooks have maps showing their locations.

Although not as impressive as museums in the United States or Europe, there is still a lot to see. In general, Costa Rica's museums provide a good perspective on the history and culture of the country. Here is a list of some of the best museums:

Museums:

Museum	Phone
Calderón Guardia Museum, Barrio Escalante	2255-1218
Costa Rican Scientific and Cultural Center, (for children)	2223-7003
Costa Rican Art Museum, Sabana Park	2222-7155
Entomological Museum	2225-5555
Museum of Criminology	2221-1340
Museum of Contemporary Art	2257-7202
Gold Museum	2223-0528
Jade Museum	2223-5800
National Museum	2257-1433

Maritime Museum	2661-3666
Juan Santamaría Museum, Alajuela	2441-4775
Galleries:	
Alterna, Pavas	2232-8500
Arte 99, Rohrmoser	2232-4035
Andrómeda, Barrio Amón	2223-3529
Café de Artistas, Escazú	2228-6045
Contemporary National Art Gallery	2257-5524
Jacob Karpio, San José	2257-7963
José Joaquín García Monge	2221-1329
Kadinsky, San Pedro	2234-0478
National Gallery, Children's Museum	2258-4929

For more listings, see the yellow pages under *Galerías.*

Excellent Fishing

Costa Rica has some of the world's best sport fishing. The country's Pacific and Caribbean coasts offer anglers some of the world's best deep sea sportfishing.

The fishing is outstanding almost all of the time and almost everywhere in Costa Rica. Even when it rains, your chances of catching some excellent sport fish are very good. Catch marlin, sail, dorado, wahoo, tuna, roosterfish, tarpon and snook year round More importantly, most fishing areas are only a few hours' driving time from anywhere in Costa Rica. Fish either the Caribbean or the Pacific. Either coast is a short driving distance from the capital city of San Jose you can fly in and be on the beach, fishing on the same day. You can be in Guanacaste fishing one day and on the Caribbean fishing the next morning.

Offshore or inshore fishing, there are fishing boats, charters and or camps available for your stay in nearby areas. All of the sportsman's lodges have great accommodations and experienced English-speaking fishing guides.

Do not forget those gentle miles of meandering rivers or the fresh water lakes. Lake Arenal is famous for its *guapote* bass. The country is considered one of the best year-round fishing areas in the world.

If you need a fishing license go to the INCOPESCA office in San José, Tel: 2248-1196; sport fishing tour operators provide them for you.

If you are really hooked on fishing and want to keep up with the local fishing scene, pick up a copy of the *The Tico Times.* It has an excellent weekly fishing column. Please see www.ticotimes.net/fishing.

For a listing of other fishing camps and tours, contact **Tico Travel** at www.ticotravel.com or call 1-800-493-8426

A Fisherman Finds a Home in Costa Rica

By Todd Staley

A writing assignment first brought me to Costa Rica in 1987. Being an outdoor journalist, I was very excited to test some of the country's "world famous sport fishing". This trip brought me in contact with the late Archie Fields and we became immediate friends. While sitting on the veranda of his famous Rio Colorado Lodge, I asked Archie if he ever needed someone to run his lodge I would like to be considered. He chuckled and said I was about number 1000 on the list.

I returned to the States and told all that would listen that I didn't know how, but one day I would be living in Costa Rica. In the meantime I sought out other Costa Rican writing assignments and began bringing groups of fishermen down to Costa Rica.

In June of 1991 Archie called my house in the US and asked me to "think" about coming down and managing his fishing lodge. I took less than three seconds to think it over. In the next three months I condensed my life belongings to 7 suitcases and 35 fishing poles and headed for Costa Rica.

In Barra del Colorado where I lived there are no cars. The river, creeks and canals are the streets and avenues. I worked long hours often going as many as three months without a day off and loved every second of it. I used Norman Paperman, the character in Herman Wouk's "Don't Stop the Carnival" as my relief when problems arose concerning employees or guests.

I was awestruck by the culture of the Caribbean side of Costa Rica, especially the stories told to me by the older generations. I met people with zero education but with more wisdom than anyone I had met in my life. The people are a mix of Spanish, African, several types of Indian and Chinese. For the first time in my life, through this experience, I came to believe in "magic" both black and white.

For nearly five years I lived in the jungle. Today I'm in the concrete jungle, but you would have to drag me back kicking and screaming the whole way for me to give up the lifestyle I have grown accustomed to in Costa Rica.

What worked for me is that the first thing I did was throw any American attitude I may have had down the river that flowed in front of the lodge and immersed myself in the culture, language and people. *Tuanis*!

Pristine Beaches

Unlike many resort areas in Mexico and Latin America, Costa Rica's beautiful tropical beaches and 767 miles of coastline stretching along two oceans are virtually unspoiled. Water temperatures are very warm so you can stay in the water all day.

There are many white-and dark-sand beaches and numerous resorts along the west coast. In the northern Guanacaste area, the best beaches include: Playa Naranjo, Playa Panama, Playa Hermosa, Playas del Coco (a favorite *gringo* hangout), Ocotal, Bahía Pez Vela, Playa Potrero, Playa Flamingo, Playa Brasilito, Conchal, Playa Grande, Playa Tamarindo, Playa Avellanas and Playa Junquillal.

As we move south, the following beaches are scattered along the coast of the Nicoya Peninsula: Playa Azul, Playa Nosara, Playa Sámara, Playa Carrillo, Playa Coyote. Playa Montezuma, on the southeastern tip of Nicoya, is also a nice beach.

Moving even farther south, along the central and southern Pacific coast are Puntarenas (Costa Rica's main port), Boca Barranca (good surfing beach), Mata Limón, Playa Tivives, Playa Tárcoles, Playa Escondida, Playa Herradura, Playa Jacó, Playa Hermosa, Esterillos, Quepos, Manuel Antonio (considered by many to be the most beautiful beach in Costa Rica), Playa Dominical and the beaches around the towns of Uvita and Ojochal.

On the Atlantic side, some beautiful beaches are: Playa Bonita (Portete), Punta Cahuita (beautiful beach), Puerto Viejo, Punta Uva and Playa Manzanillo.

Beach safety is very important in Costa Rica. Inexperienced swimmers should only wade in the water. You should also be careful around surfers. Never swim alone. Be aware of rip-tides. If caught in a rip tide, don't panic! Swim parallel to the shore until you are clear of the current. If you cannot break free, let the current take you beyond the breakers. Then swim diagonally toward the shore. Never try to swim against the current.

Do not leave your belongings unattended. If you need to leave your things, ask someone you know to watch them until you return.

Surfing and Diving

Surfing

Surfers of all ages will be pleased to know that Costa Rica is quickly gaining popularity on the worldwide surf circuit due to its warm weather and great waves. The water is so warm a wetsuit is never needed. Surfing attracts about

250,000 tourists yearly. So, about one out of five tourists come to surf. The sport also generates about $275 million a year in income.

The country boasts close to 40 prime areas for surfing on both the east and west coasts. In Guanacaste, many prime surfing locations line the peninsula from tip to tip. **Roca Bruja** (Witch's Rock) inside Santa Rosa National Park is famous for its tubular waves. Other recommended places to surf in Guanacaste are **Playa Grande**, **Tamarindo, Nosara**, **Playa Coyote**, **Malpaís** and **Manzanillo**.

In the Central Pacific region, **Playa Jacó** and the surrounding area is also worth checking out. Nearby **Playa Hermosa** has been host to many surfing tournaments and is steadily gaining popularity. **Esterillos Oeste**, **Esterillos Este, Bejuco, Boca Damas, Playa El Rey** and **Playa Matapalo** are other options in the Central Pacific area. Farther south is **Dominical**, which is considered a top spot for surfers.

Pavones in the southern Pacific area is a legendary surf spot famous for its endless waves and touted as having the world's longest rideable left break. Try **Matapalo**, located near the Panamanian border. **"Salsa Brava"** at Puerto Viejo and **Manzanillo** on the east coast have good surfing. There are numerous surfing schools in Costa Rica, and **Tico Travel** offers surfing tours to the country.

To find out about surfing lessons, see **www.wavescr.com,** and for information about surfing, see **www.crsurf.com.** Also check out *H20 Surf TravelGuide:* Costa Rica, by Jonathan Yonkers.

Diving

Schools of fish, turtles, grouper, whales, rays and other species make Costa Rica a great place for divers. Most of the best diving areas are found in Guanacaste around Playas del Coco, Tamarindo, Flamingo and nearby beaches. In the southern Pacific area the diving is good at Isla del Caño just off the Osa Peninsula. The waters teem with many interesting species. I have friends in the area who dive there frequently. The Caribbean coast has famous diving off Cahuita and at Long Shoal off Manzanillo.

During the rainy season, from May to November, visibility may often be obscured in some areas. To find out about the country's diving, see **www.costaricadiving.net**, **www.richcoastdiving.com** or **www.aquacenterdiving.com**.

Boating

With miles of beautiful coastline along the country's Pacific coast, Costa Rica is a boaters paradise. Currently, there are a couple of ports and docking facilities along the coast. **Los Sueños** is the only international marina at this time. It boasts modern docking facilities for 200 boats, including potable water, electricity, 24-hour security, mini-self- storage units, a state-of-the-art fuel station, a marine supply store, bar, restaurants and more. For more information, call 2637-8886 or 1-866-865-9759toll-free, or visit www.lsrm.com. Informatio2n is also available at **http://portfocus.com/costa_rica**.

Costa Rica could have many new marinas in several years time. The ICT is currently studying applications for 15 other marinas with a total capacity of 5,000 boats. However, Costa Rica doesn't want Miami-style marinas which will affect the aesthetics of their beautiful coastline.

The Costa Rican Tourism Institute (ICT) approved new marinas in Quepos and the southern Pacific port of Golfito. The former is under construction and will house 200 boats; the latter will have more than 200 slips. The **Marina Papagayo** is a 400-slip marina being constructed in northwest Guanacaste. A new marina is also under construction in the Flamingo area. When finished it will have 420 slips. Plans have also been approved for the new $24 million 200-slip marina **"El Coco"** at Playas del Coco in northwest Guanacaste. Waiting for approval is the **Marina Carara**, at Punta Leona, just up the road from the Los Sueños Marina. It will have a capacity of 260 boats when finished.

There is also a180-boat capacity marina planned for Playa Carrillo and another one with 400 slips on the drawing board for Puerto Viejo on the Caribbean coast.

Parks for Nature Lovers

Costa Ricans take pride in their extensive national park system. The country is rich not only in natural beauty but in all varieties of wildlife. Costa Ricans have set aside 25 percent of its territory and established 36 national parks and preserves to protect the flora and fauna in the country. This is reportedly the largest percentage of any country in the world. In fact, Costa Rica is in first place in ecological tourism in the world.

Five percent of the world's biodiversity can be found in Costa Rica. The variety of birds, butterflies, amphibians, mammals, trees and flowers has to be seen to be believed. The country has 850 species of mammals, 218 species of reptiles, 160 species of amphibians, 845 varieties of birds, 360,000 species of insects and 1000 varieties of orchids as well as 10,353 species of other plants.

Costa Rica's parks are in every region of the country, with some parks more accessible than others. Additional information and a list of parks may be obtained by calling 2233-5673, 2233-5284 or 2233-4160. Most hotels and tourist information centers can be helpful to nature lovers. Foreigners pay about $6 admission and Costa Ricans and residents $1 to enter Costa Rica's parks. After an international uproar over hikes in park fees, the "Green Pass" was instituted to offer the most affordable way to visit Costa Rica's world-famous parks. For $29, you receive a coupon booklet with four tickets to any national park and one ticket to one of 10 parks.

Costa Ricans take the same pride in their urban parks. Every neighborhood in Costa Rica, from the biggest cities to the tiniest villages, always has a park usually adjacent to the Catholic Church. San José's **La Sabana Park** is the country's largest city park. The park is crisscrossed by miles of jogging, biking and walking trails. *Ticos* flock by the hundreds to this park to indulge their love of family, children, sports and the outdoors. Go to the park any Sunday and you will see people walking, jogging, picnicking, cycling or playing soccer on one of the many playing fields.

There are also free tennis and basketball courts. The park is located at the site of the old national airport and the terminal building now houses the Costa Rican Art Museum. La Sabana is also the home of the new state-of-the-art National Stadium and National Gymnasium, where events of all types are held. There is an Olympic-size swimming pool just west of the gymnasium. In the center of the park, a large lake and fountain attract many people. It is a favorite gathering spot for families.

Your whole family can have fun at Waterland aquatic park.

Another popular weekend destination in San José is **Parque de la Paz**. It does not have the peaceful seclusion of La Sabana, but it still has all the activity. The park is set around three artificial lakes. **Waterland** is the country's first U.S.-style water park. There are several pools, water slides, miniature golf and a pool with artificial waves. An even more spectacular water park is being built a few miles off the coastal highway between Quepos and Dominical. When completed, it will have artificial waves and a whole lot more.

Where to Make New Friends

You should have no problem making new friends of either sex in Costa Rica, but you might have some difficulty meeting Costa Ricans if you speak little or no Spanish. You will be surprised how many *ticos* speak some English and are dying for the chance to perfect their English-language skills while you work on your Spanish. Perhaps you can find someone with whom to exchange language lessons. This is a good way to make new acquaintances and learn how Spanish is really spoken.

You most certainly will find it easier to meet fellow Americans in Costa Rica than in the United States, because Americans living abroad tend to gravitate toward one another. Newcomers have to only find an enclave of fellow countrymen to make new friends.

A group of expats having coffee at a local hangout.

Working as a Volunteer in Costa Rica

By Daniel Spitzer, Ph.D.

Everyone has some type of talent or skill they can share to help others improve their lives. One way to spend your time in Costa Rica is doing volunteer work. This way, you will be able to give something back to the country for the privilege of living here. There is a variety of options for people who want to help others, especially in the field of teaching English to the locals.

When United States citizens Jerri and Daniel Spitzer go out for dinner on a Friday night, their conversation is always dominated by one topic: the progress of their students in the Community Conversation Program.

The growth of the government's initiative, designed to assist Costa Ricans in learning English, has been such that new people are being sought to join volunteers like the Spitzers, who dedicate a couple of hours a week to speaking English with Costa Ricans. With more than 30 groups in four provinces, 250 registered volunteers and even its own page on the social networking site Facebook, the initiative is fast helping the government achieve its goal of providing English training to 35,000 Costa Ricans by the end of this year.

"We are absolutely begging for more volunteers right now," said Jerri, formerly a piano teacher from the U.S. state of Virginia. "All they have to do is speak English. It's not really teaching, but rather conversation.

"The Costa Ricans who come along are just so grateful to have someone to practice their English with that it makes you so happy to help. I have made so many new friends and learned so much about different people from doing this.

"When Daniel and I go out for dinner after class, all we find ourselves talking about is the how the class went".

The program is just one of many that fall under the Arias government's Costa Rica Multilingual initiative, designed to assist Costa Ricans learn a new foreign language.

The success of the program has depended not only on the generosity of its volunteers, but also on the willingness of local organizations such as schools, community centers, libraries and churches to provide space where the conversation classes can take place.

Katherine Stanley, co-coordinator for Costa Rica Multilingual, said, "As word-of mouth spreads, we are finding that people, even before arriving in Costa Rica, are signing up as volunteers for the program because they realize it is a great way to meet Costa Ricans and get to know their community better.

"In return for volunteering just an hour a week, they themselves learn those important little things from their Costa Rican conversation partner, like the best place to buy bread or the best places to eat out. My hope is that it will eventually become part of the expat experience."

Volunteers are not required to have teaching experience, but simply a high level of spoken English.

The program itself was originally designed for Costa Rican teachers of English to improve their oral skills. Such has been the interest from the general public that the program has been opened to everyone, providing they first have a basic grasp of the English language.

As well as conversation classes, innovative volunteers have arranged for karaoke evenings in English and theater workshops given by the Little Theatre Group, all with the aim of helping Costa Ricans learn English in a relaxed atmosphere.

"We started off with set topics of conversation but, as volunteers and their partners got to know each other, they started choosing their own topics and it really took off. It really is up to the volunteer and partner to decide how they want to structure the hour," Stanley said.

While Costa Rica Multilingual's short term goal is aimed at 35,000 Costa Ricans, officials hope that it will have a long-standing impact on the country. By 2017, the plan guarantees that 100 per cent of high school students will graduate with an intermediate to advanced level of English.

***Part of this article is courtesy of the *Tico Times*.**

You cannot help bumping-into other Americans since Costa Rica is such a small country (more than 50,000 *gringos* live here permanently). This is especially true if you live in one of the areas where many North Americans reside, such as Escazú, Heredia, Rohrmoser or along the Pacific beaches. Another good way of contacting other foreign residents is by participating in some of the activities listed in the Weekend section of the *The Tico Times.* This newspaper serves as a vital link within the foreign community, or "*Gringo* Grapevine"and helps to put you in touch with a whole network of expatriates and the services they offer.

At any of the local *gringo* watering holes in downtown San José, such as the New York Bar, the Casino Colonial, Mac's American Bar near the La Sabana Park or the Time Out Tavern in Escazú, you can watch live sporting events from the United States on cable TV or simply shoot the breeze with your compatriots. Many Americans also congregate at the Plaza de la Cultura and at McDonald's across the street, where they linger over coffee every morning and watch the beautiful women pass by.

You have no reason to be lonely unless you want to be. Just be yourself and you will find that Costa Rica is just the place for you. Oh yes, I might add that there are poetry readings, art and sculpture exhibitions as well as other activities where people can easily socialize. The Costa Rican-North American Cultural Center has many events where you can also make new acquaintances.

Here is a sample of the many organizations.

CLUBS AND ORGANIZATIONS

Club	Phone
Aikido Club	2289-7479
American Legion Post 11	2233-7233
American Legion Post 12	2775-0567
Bridge Club	2294-7856
Canadian Club	2282-5858
Chess Club	8384-0936
Computer Club	2228-0190
Democrats Abroad	2215-4254
Disabled American Veterans	2443-2508
English-Spanish Conversation Club	2260-4869
Gay and Lesbian Association	2280-3548
Internet Club	2220-0714
Investment Club of Costa Rica	2256-5075
Language Exchange Group	2257-0441

Club	Phone
Lions Club	2670-0447
Mac User Group	2257-2160
Mountain Bike Club	2290-7870
National Bridge Association	2253-2762
Newcomers' Club	2416-1111
PC Club	2224-9926
Photography Club	2272-5329
Readers Club	2228-9167
Republicans Abroad	2239-2262
Rotary Club	2255-1001
Spanish/English Conversation Club	8390-9759
Singles Club	8360-5987
V.F.W Post 11	2750-0453
Women's Club of Costa Rica	2282-6801

* For a complete listing of clubs and related activities, look under the weekly "What's Doing" section in the *Tico Times.* You may also check out the Association of Residents of Costa Rica's community calendar. Call 2221-2053 for more information.

Love and Permanent Companionship

If you are looking for romance, Costa Rica might just be the right place for you.

Ladies will find gentleman admirers if they so desire. Due to *machismo,* Costa Rican men are more flirtatious and aggressive than North American counterparts. Some Costa Rican men think foreign women have looser morals and are easier conquests than *ticas* (Costa Rican women). Age seems to matter here, with younger men showing interest in older women. If you are interested in meeting *tico* men, consider learning the Latin dances at a dance school such as Merecumbé or Son Latinos. Be careful to take time to develop a long-term, meaningful relationship and do not rush things.

As one local expat pointed out, "*Tico* men have the best *labia* in the world. *Labia* when used in slang, means 'rap.' Costa Rican men are charming, witty, and know how to treat a woman. They can seduce almost any woman, regardless of nationality. I have a few *tico* friends that could get a woman into their car and to a *mirador* overlooking the city within five minutes of meeting them.

"Usually, however, these relationships, if you can call them that, don't last too long. The conquest is a big part of the *tico* male's psyche, and then

Advice about *Gringas* in Paradise

By Margie Davis

"You've got guts," my friends told me when I moved to Costa Rica by myself, not knowing anyone, at age 55. That's what it takes to venture forth to a new country – courage and a sense of adventure. And plenty of single women have made the move.

I live in the Central Valley, the cultural center of the country. There are numerous ways to have fun and enjoy life here, but experiences are best shared with a friend or a group. It's relatively easy to find other expatriates, but be prepared to spend time alone until you make friends.

Dating is the #1 challenge of most single women here. I have dozens of single gal pals in their 40s to 70s, and none of us can find suitable men to date. Most *gringo* men who come to Costa Rica are looking for young *ticas*. While there are exceptions, I have found that most gringo males don't even realize that there is a population of women here from back home. They just don't consider that *gringa* women could have the same kind of courage and wanderlust that prompted their own move.

Personally, I would love to date a latino man, whether he's Costa Rican or from another Spanish-speaking country. Learning language and cultural differences from each other can be fun, but the same question remains: Where are the eligible *latinos*?

I've tried bars, endured karaoke, gone on nature walks, sat at cafes looking desirable and approachable. I learned to dance merengue and salsa and I go to dance halls frequently. I really put myself out there to meet men, but the ones I meet are either married or not in my league. As one girlfriend says, "Costa Rica has a definite class system. It's easy to have an affair with an uneducated man. It is much harder to find one who will be an equal, both financially and educationally."

If you do find someone appealing, the first question to ask is, "Are you married?" Some will actually answer honestly: "Yes, but I don't have a girlfriend," or "Yes, but I only have one girlfriend." This is good news if you don't mind sharing your man, but if you want a trusting, monogamous relationship, you most likely won't find one here. Also, my friends and I have found that many *tico* men drink a lot, so be careful about getting involved with a drunk.

It's relatively easy to find a hot guy in his 20s or 30s who finds older *gringas* attractive. They are either looking for a sugar mama or women their own age won't have anything to do with them, for whatever reasons. You can get lured into paying his way if he is good-looking and treats you well, but over time you could be paying his child support and supporting his mother and sisters, too.

If you do indulge in an adventure with a man, protect yourself from STDs. The macho men of Costa Rica do not like to wear condoms. They may say they will, but in the heat of passion they will resist. Stand your ground and insist if you want to protect yourself.

Respectable singles here socialize in groups. If a group goes out at night, all the members stay in that group, making it almost impossible to meet someone new without a proper introduction. I have been told by *ticos* that a woman alone at a bar might as well wear a sign that says *Puta* or whore. So find yourself some friends and go out with them.

My lesbian friends face the same challenges. Where to find a quality girlfriend? There are several gay male bars and dance halls, but there is no lesbian gathering place, except for two nights a month when *La Avispa*, a gay bar in San Jose, opens its doors to women only.

If you go to a bar, especially in the beach communities, don't leave your drink unattended. I've been told that date rape drugs are on the rise.

I'm glad I took a personal self-defense course in the U.S. many years ago, and I recommend that everyone, especially women living alone, take one too before moving to Costa Rica. The course will raise your awareness of your surroundings and just may save you from a dangerous situation.

One last note about foreign women living alone in Costa Rica: We can get hit by a double whammy when we bring our cars to a mechanic. Just like in the U.S., women who don't know about cars can get overcharged, and if you are a foreigner who doesn't speak the language, you can get charged even more. However, a benefit to being a female in this country, regardless of your native language, is that most men will stop to change your flat tire or to lift your car out of a pothole. All you have to do is smile and say, "*Por favor.*"

* **Margie Davis is a freelance marketing consultant and writer living in Costa Rica, and teaches business English to professionals.**

it's off to the next one. Don't be fooled by these modern-day Casanovas, that is of course, unless you want to."

Many single middle-aged women have a tough time finding a mate because they cannot compete with the young curvaceous *ticas.* As one expat woman put it, "We just happen to live in a country of traffic-stopping gorgeous women, — all of whom seem to have been raised in the Geisha School of Relating to Men. If you are planning to move here based on some dream of meeting a Ricky Martin or other Latin stud, think again."

Furthermore, if you do meet a Latin man, he may have a hard time handling an independent American woman. Latin men also like to have a lot of girlfriends on the side. As I mention in Chapter 1 many Latin men measure their virility by the number of women they can seduce.

Men of any age will have no problem meeting Costa Rican women. The women in Costa Rica seem to like older, more experienced men. It is not unusual to see a wife who is 10 to 20 years younger than her spouse. This practice may be frowned upon in some countries but is accepted in Costa Rica. Many retirees I know claim to feel rejuvenated and to have a new lease on life after becoming involved with younger women. Costa Rican women have an unparalleled reputation as being the most beautiful, flirtatious and accessible women in Latin America, including Brazil. The ladies of Costa Rica can be more warm-hearted and devoted than their North American counterparts. They consider you a joy. One retiree I know boasts, "The women here really know how to treat you like a king!"

One of Costa Rica's beautiful women.

A man doesn't even have to be rich to meet women; a $1,500 to $2,000 Social Security check translates into a millionaire's pay in Costa Rica.

Here is what one expat's Costa Rican wife said about her relationship in a recent edition of *The Tico Times.* "Most of the time when a young woman marries an older man, people think she's doing it for the money. I like older men. They are experienced; they've had a lot of fun in the past, so they start to think, 'I want to stay now with someone for the rest of my life.' Plus they have their life set up, so they have time to spend with their woman."

With Costa Rican men close to her age, she says, their behavior changes after marriage. With Costa Rican men, you are a princess, but when you get married the whole thing changes: "You are going to have my children. I'm working, so you should make my dinner, wash my clothes." The women get submissive and the men get possessive.

"Costa Rican men don't see their women in the home being the porn star they watch on TV. *Ticos* think the woman at home is pretty, sweet and the mother of their children."

No wonder Costa Rican women are highly sought by foreign men. However, before becoming involved with a Costa Rican woman, you should realize many cultural differences can lead to all kinds of problems, especially if you do not speak Spanish fluently. I have seen so many disasters with people who try to create a relationship without a common language. If a Costa Rican woman is in your future, you are going to have to be able to communicate with her. Even if she speaks some English, the nitty-gritty type of communication that a real relationship requires will definitely require some effort on your part. Men need to seriously consider studying Spanish if they want to have a successful relationship with a native Spanish speaker.

Generally, Latin women are more jealous and possessive than American women, and tend not to understand our ways unless they have lived in North America. Also, be aware that because of their comparative wealth, most Americans, especially the elderly, are considered prime targets for some unscrupulous Latin females.

As alluded to at the end of the first chapter, in some cases there is another bad side to marrying a Costa Rican woman. You can end up supporting her whole family, either directly or indirectly, as many foreigners complain. There is an out-of-print book, *Happy Aging With Costa Rican Women — The Other Costa Rica,* by James Y. Kennedy. It tells all about the trials and tribulations and experiences many *gringos* have with Costa Rican women. You may be able to find a used copy in a second-hand bookstore in San José or borrow it from a local expatriate.

I advise you to give any relationship time and make sure a woman is sincerely interested in you and not just in your money. You will save yourself a lot of grief and heartache in the long run. Since prostitution is legal and

How I Found Love in Costa Rica

By Brian

My name is Brian and right now I am about to take a beautiful lady on a tour of Southern California. And, at the end of our drive, she will come home with me. She is my lovely *Tica* wife, *Yanory* and this is her first day in her new home. I met *Yanory* a year ago in San Jose at an agency called Spanish Eyes.

I first heard of Spanish Eyes through a fellow surfer during one of my trips to Playa Hermosa to surf. He said it was a great way to meet ladies from Costa Rica. Having been a widower for 6 years, I was feeling lonely and wanted to find a woman who was kind, sweet, gentle and loving but I was not sure how to approach the ladies of Costa Rica.

Once I contacted Spanish Eyes and met Tom and *Purita*, I felt comfortable and sure that together we would find that perfect lady for me. I met some beautiful women and made some lifetime friends. About a year ago, *Purita* introduced me to *Yanory*, a quiet, soft spoken wonderful young woman who captured my mind and heart. We dated and I found myself coming back to

Costa Rica as often as I could to see her. We spent Christmas together and I knew that we were meant for each other so I asked her to marry me. We married in April and began the process for her spousal visa. The process took only 3 months which is unusually fast.

In less than a year, I met my future wife, married her and she is now with me in our home in California. It all seems so easy. But, every step of the way, *Purita* and Tom were there to answer questions for me, to take my phone calls and to help in any way they could.

Spanish Eyes Introductions is about service. I still do not understand how they find the time to give every client the personalized service that they do. And, how they can recommend the perfect ladies for you to meet. *Yanory* was not one of my first choices, but a recommendation made by *Purita*. To this day I do not know how she knew that *Yanory* would be so perfect for me.

available to men of all ages, be careful of the ladies of ill repute. Many foreigners, after inviting one of these females to spend the night, wake up the next day without the woman and minus wallets and other valuables. Above all, think with your brain and not with your penis.

One scam I heard of involves a well-dressed woman with a brief case who approaches strangers. She claims to be from another Latin American country and wants to celebrate her birthday. She says she is alone and has nobody to celebrate it with. She then invites the unsuspecting victim to accompany her to a bar for a drink. Once in the bar, she slips a drug into the glass of the foreigner. Within minutes he is unconscious. The woman then relieves him of his cash and credit cards. She then takes the credit cards to an accomplice who quickly charges large amounts of money to the cards. So, never drink from a glass or bottle that has been out of your sight.

Here are some tips from *AM Costa* on how to avoid be victimized:

(1) Don't bring strange women home. Get to know them first. There are plenty of love motels in Costa Rica, they are inexpensive and the girl doesn't see where you live and what you have.

(2) Ask the girl where she is from. Most will tell you they are from Colombia, Nicaragua or the Dominican Republic. Be especially careful with these foreign women. If you are planning to pick one up, don't carry a lot of money and leave your credit cards at home.

(3) There are fun places to visit, but be careful if you are planning to pick up women at the well-known hook-up bars and other bars where the women are anonymous. If you do, however, don't be afraid to ask to see her ID, write down her name and ID number. Prostitution is legal here, if she is age 18 or over, and there is no reason why she wouldn't give you her ID to look at. It is a business. They have to show their IDs when they go to hotels with a guy. This is how the hotels protect their clients.

(4) If she says she doesn't have an ID, it is not a good idea to pick her up. She obviously wants to remain anonymous for some dark reason, or she is illegal, another reason not to mess with them.

(5) There are plenty of places where the girls and the rooms are in the same building. You don't have to take the girls somewhere else. The rooms are right there. The managers of these places know the women and have copies of their IDs. The women work on a regular basis, and if any funny business is reported by the customers, the managers won't let the woman work there any more. Also, coincidently, most of the women in these places are Costa Rican women who don't have to worry about being threatened by the tough foreign girls at other bars which seem to be dominated by foreign women, many of whom are illegal here.

How to increase your chances of meeting a quality woman

Most single men can avoid getting involved with gold diggers, prostitutes and other troublesome women if they know where to look for good women. The personals section of the *The Tico Times* is an excellent place to advertise for companionship. It is relatively inexpensive and many Costa Rican and other women read this section each week. Check out the current or past issues of the *The Tico Times* for ideas on how to write one of these ads.

One American I know ran an ad in the *The Tico Times* and the local Spanish newspapers and ended up screening hundreds of women before finding his ideal mate. As far as I know he is still happily married. Taking classes at the university is another way to meet quality women. The University of Costa Rica in San Pedro is full of beautiful, well-educated females. Cafés, restaurants, bars and other places around the university are good places to meet women. If you have Costa Rican friends, they will usually be able introduce you to someone worthwhile.

The best places to meet nice women who are sincere and honest tend to be where you would met them back home. Go to church or get involved in a community service project. Most people meet their friends and mates at work. So work at something, even if as a volunteer. If you have Costa Rican friends, they will usually be able introduce you to someone worthwhile.

Meeting people in bars, nightclubs, at the beach, etc., is generally a lousy way to meet someone you really want to have a relationship with anywhere in the world.

Probably the most effective and least painless way to meet quality Costa Rica women is through an introduction service. **Spanish Eyes Introductions** provides such a service and screens their women very carefully to protect their clients. In addition to their standard services, they offer parties for their members to meet women. I have several friends who are members and rave about this service. You may contact them at: Tel: 2289-5271 or 2228-7389, E-mail: **info@spanisheyesccostarica.com** or see **www.spanisheyescostarica.com**.

The key is to find a nice, traditional Costa Rican woman and avoid getting involved with "bad" Costa Rican women. Costa Rica has plenty of working girls and hustlers. They hang out at the popular bars and discos specifically to pick up guys. They also go shopping in the malls, ride buses and go to grocery stores. So just because you have met a nice girl in a typical working-girl hangout does not mean you have met a quality person. If you know what to look for, they are easy to spot.

Many men have knowingly and unknowingly married bad women. Some girls are honest and will directly ask you for money. The hustlers are more dangerous because their agenda is to really take you to the cleaners, and they do not rule out marrying you to achieve this objective. Some men say they have lost everything from airline tickets that are cashed instead of used, to large sums of money the girls claim they need to get visas, houses and more. These are the women who contribute to the bad stories you may hear about some Costa Rican women. Unfortunately, the hustlers are the easiest girls to meet in many instances and a good number of men fall into this trap.

A very small number of these women will become good wives, find religion, etc. They are often women who have been sexually or otherwise abused at a very young age, so the problem is very deeply rooted. Your realistic chances of converting them are very slim. No matter how gorgeous the girl is, it is just not worth it.

The best way to spot a bad girl is her profile. They never have a job, never live with their parents, never have phone numbers and never invite you to their home or introduce you to their friends or family. They do not want to leave any trail for you to track them down later. They typically come from very poor backgrounds and have very little education, rarely completing high school.

They are quite aggressive and target older Americans. Often they speak a little English and will start up a conversation with you or smile at you until you make the first move. They will appear friendly and sincerely interested in you. They are always attractive or very young. They will always ask for your phone number.

Perhaps the best way to politely get rid of one of these women is to ask them to loan you a little money. You will immediately see their interest disappear. Actually, a nice woman in Costa Rica might just loan you the money.

Women you see working in stores are usually poorly educated and from poor families. Some may show an interest in an older American who is friendly toward them, but the relationship is likely to be overly influenced by a poor woman looking for a rich American husband.

Foreign men should beware of the so-called "Costa Rican set-up." I have heard countless stories where Costa Rican women get pregnant as a ploy to get a foreigner to marry them. Beware this underhanded and self-centered method of ensnaring you into an unwanted relationship.

Furthermore, there are differences in practices at hospitals when a Costa Rican woman has a baby. In the United States both parents are required to give information as to paternity. If there is any question concerning paternity a pre-birth DNA exam can be done without much difficulty. In Costa Rica this is **not** standard procedure.

While in the hospital the mother is asked for the father's name ,and she can give any name she wants. It makes no difference who she says, that is the name that will appear on the birth certificate. The man in question is never

Reasons to Date *Ticas*

by Tom

1. Accessibility: By and large, the most amazing thing about Costa Rican women is how easy they are to approach. Girls in the U.S. seem programmed to say NO, while a *Tica* three times as pretty will be happy to accept a drink, join you for a dance or offer her telephone number. It makes going out on the town an adventure, rather than a self-fulfilling prophecy of failure!
2. Sexy: There's just something about the pure sensuality that *Latinas* seem to exude effortlessly. *Ticas* are no exception. They are not embarrassed or ashamed by utilizing sex appeal and seemed to have learned from birth what turns a man on. My lord, I'm sweating just thinking about it.
3. Not Overly Demanding: What does a *gringa* NOT want from a man these days? A man who's wealthy yet not in love with work. A man who is tough and wild, yet honest and sensitive. Honestly, the ideal man that's been portrayed for women in movies and TV just doesn't exist. In my experience, *Ticas* have much more realistic expectations from men.
4. Not Body Conscious: *Latina* women are so much more confident in their own skin. We have demanded such Playboy Centerfold-like perfection up North that even drop dead gorgeous American girls are anorexic. Not the case of *Ticas*, where even a size 10 is not afraid to wear a bikini.
5. Sanity: I really believe that women in the U.S. have been given so many options and conflicting messages of what it is to be a strong woman, that many are driven to near insanity. At least I can state this is absolutely the case of my last few ex's. Ticas seem so much more grounded and comfortable with themselves. It's refreshing.
6. Compassion: Ticas really know how to take care of a man. They are just so darn sweet and considerate.
7. Fashion Sense: Costa Rican women just know what to wear. Have you ever seen so many girls who know what looks good on them? Wow!
8. Directness: Even though raised in a strict Catholic environment, from my experience *Ticas* are much more direct about expressing desires for sex. Quite refreshing, after the fiery hoops I jumped through in the U.S.
9. Femininity: I don't know when it became so unhip for American women to act, well...like women. Costa Rican females are totally unashamed to be sexy, feminine and beautiful. What's wrong with that?
10. No Nonsense: *Ticas* don't mess around or play complicated mind games, they're pretty simple human beings. That's not to say simple = unintelligent. They just know what they want.

contacted or asked if he fathered the child. The law in Costa Rica requires support for that child and will not permit the father whose name appears on the birth certificate to leave the country without first posting the equivalent of 13 months of support. It can take up to two years to unravel this problem and the chances of recovering the 'support' is somewhere between "nil and nonexistent. "

In general, a nice Costa Rica woman typically lives with her parents until she gets married. Single daughters are not encouraged to get jobs unless the parents are very poor. Instead, they are expected to study or help with taking care of the house.

Quality Costa Rican women from traditional family backgrounds are raised to take care of their man. They can be quite possessive and jealous at times, but this is only because they are very emotional and deeply in love with their man. They tend to seek out long-term relationships, starting at a very young age. It is quite rare for Costa Rican women to have any interest in casually dating many different men.

When approached by strangers, they are friendly and helpful by nature; this is their culture. All Costa Ricans value making new friends. Americans often misread this friendliness and think the woman has a romantic interest in them. In order for the woman to develop any romantic interest in you at all, she has to first know from a trusted third party that you are looking for a long-term relationship. After a brief encounter, a decent woman will never ask for your phone number. If you ask for her number, she will always give you the wrong number in order to avoid appearing rude. Nice women live with their parents and would never want to have strange men calling their house. From a romantic interest point of view, quality Latin women are very difficult to meet.

As alluded to earlier, some Costa Rican women prefer older men. Most Costa Rican women meet a boy in high school and are only interested in men their own age. However, about 40 percent do seriously prefer older men. I have met many Costa Rican friends who are happily married to women 10 to 25 years younger than them.

If the woman is convinced you are seriously looking for a long-term relationship, she will then start to show an interest in getting to know you better. Her initial physical attraction to you will usually be of very minor importance to her. Her main interest will be focused on your personality: Are you are a kind person? Can you offer minimum security to raise a family? Do you sincerely care about her family? Would you make a good father?

Over the years I have encountered a lot of foreigners who end up not using common sense and get involved with people with whom they would probably never associate back home. This brings me to the story of "Dumb and Dumber."

Dumb came to Costa Rica about 12 years ago from the United States, where he was a successful businessman. Almost upon arriving here, he became romantically involved with a woman of ill- repute. He was basically too lazy and busy getting drunk to find a quality mate. Over the course of his relationship, he lost about $300,000 because he entrusted his business dealings to his girlfriend. After splitting up with her and having to give her half of everything he owned because of their common-law situation, he went and got involved with another woman who will probably "take him to the cleaners" someday.

Dumber is even more stupid than Dumb. He came to the country as a millionaire. The first thing he did was get romantically involved with a woman of the night. Dumber also spent most of his time in bars, like Dumb. Consequently, when he broke up with his lady friend, after a few years together, he had to pay her about $50,000. He is now with another woman and most likely supporting her whole family. He will probably end up broke like Dumb. Neither Dumb nor Dumber speaks Spanish nor has made any effort to understand the locals and constantly refers to them in derogatory terms.

The majority of foreign men who come to Costa Rica don't share Dumb and Dumber's fate. Nevertheless, they should learn a lesson from this story.

A Walk on the Wild Side

The author of this guidebook feels it is his responsibility to paint a realistic picture of all of the aspects of living in Costa Rica. I would not be doing a service to my readers if I did not cover the subject of prostitution. However, let it be known that in no way do I condone the sexual exploitation of minors. In this section I only provide information about sexual relationships between consenting adults.

For some people, Costa Rica is a sexual paradise. Like Thailand, the Philippines and many other countries outside of the United States, prostitution is permitted and looked upon with general acceptance in Costa Rica. As in the rest of Latin America, many males have their first sexual experience with prostitutes. In order to control the propagation of venereal disease and AIDS, prostitutes are required by the government to undergo regular health checkups by the Ministry of Health or *Ministerio de Salud* in order to practice their trade legally. Most upscale brothels make sure their employees have their health papers and tests up to date.

It is therefore not surprising that many foreigners are attracted to Costa Rica because of the availability of women. In San José there is a myriad of bordellos, cabarets, escort services, massage parlors and bars where you can find female company. One Costa Rican remarked jokingly when questioned about the number of whorehouses in San José, " In order to put a roof over all of the houses of ill repute, you would have to cover the whole city."

I have interviewed a few tight-fisted residents and retirees who think just because they live here they should pay less for sex than tourists. Consequently, many of them go to the "houses of ill repute" that dot *Calle* 6, just north of the Central Market. Prices are "rock bottom" and you probably get what you end up paying for. I don't recommend venturing into this area at night. However, none of the people interviewed have ever had problems during the day.

In the "Gringo Gulch" area near Morazán Park two places come to mind. **Key Largo** is an institution that has been around for more than 25 years. Located in a beautiful colonial mansion directly across from Parque Morazán, the place looks like a scene taken right out of a Humphrey Bogart movie. It has recently been remodeled and offers live music and dancing nightly.

The Blue Marlin Bar at the Hotel Del Rey is under the same ownership as the Key Largo and is the place to meet women of the night. Most evenings are standing room only in the bar. During the day the bar is a gathering place where local expats and tourists "shoot the bull." The Hotel Del Rey also offers a casino and fine dining

There are a number of cabarets and nightclubs where men can also find female companionship. Most of these establishments try to get you to buy expensive drinks and run up a large tab. It is not unusual to be stuck with a large bill in a short period of time. To avoid surprises, I suggest you do not buy any women more than one or two drinks. The management can be very nasty if you complain about your bill.

Here are the most popular cabarets and night clubs: **Club Hollywood** (2232-8932), across from the south side of La Sabana Park; **Pure Platinum** (2256-9989), Avenida 3 between Calle 10 and 12 and **Night Club Olympus** (2233-4058), Central Street, one block north of Hotel Europa. Most of these establishments offer floorshows, Jacuzzis, massage rooms, VIP rooms, exotic dancing and a stable of women from which to choose. **Tango India** (2290-1235, www.tangoindia.net), and **KRISIS** (2222-7640) are other hot spots worth checking out.

About a dozen escort services operate in the San José area. Most of these services advertise in local newspapers. You may find many of the local escort services by going to search engines like **Yahoo**, **Google** or **Altavista** and typing in the keywords "Costa Rica escorts."

If you are looking for a relaxing massage and steam bath, there are a number of massage parlors to cater to your needs. Prices range from about

$15 for a straight hour-long therapeutic massage to $35 for a massage with "the works,"or *masaje completo*. As a rule these places are very clean and provide a secure, discrete atmosphere. **New Fantasy** (221-4916), located two blocks north of Morazán Park in San José, is very popular among foreign residents. It is located in Barrio Amón, on Avenida 9 and Calle 7, from the Parque Morazán (in front of the Holiday Inn), 200 meters or two blocks to the north, a right turn and you are there. It is frequented by foreign residents, Costa Rican men of means and tourists. The nearby **Sportsmen's Lodge** (2221-2533) is another place to find female company. Check out its website at www.sportsmenscr.com. The **747**, located on Calle 6, one block south of Avenida 7, is also a favorite. **Idem**, Avenidas 8-10 and Calle 11, has beautiful women and is considered one of the best massage parlors in the San José area. In western San José you will find **Oasis Masajes** (2255-1182) and **Veronica's** (2256-7354).

A map of San José's hottest spots can be found at **www.dongordo.com/dongordoSJmap.php**. There is a better map at **www.costaricaticas.com**. However, you have to be a member to access it.

There is a good ebook that can be used as a guide to all of San José's erotic places, called *Passion in Paradise*. See **www.passioninparadise.com** to find out how to order this publication. Also check out **www.costaricasex.com**.

Also check out **www.costaricamongering.com** to get a copy of *Living the Vida Loca in Costa Rica*.

An interesting phenomenon is Central America's famous "love motels." Several dozen are found around San José and the suburbs and do very good business. Most foreigners do not know the difference between a "hotel" and "motel." In Costa Rica and the rest of Central America motels are for making love and serve no other purpose.

These establishments exist for discreet liaisons between adults. Bosses and their secretaries, men with prostitutes, young lovers who still live at home and others enjoy these convenient establishments. Patrons can hide their cars as well as their lovers in one of these places. Rooms may be rented for several hours. Fresh towels, sheets, food, drink and even a condom are provided. Each room also has a small waist-level little window for you to pay and for staff to hand you alcoholic beverages, soft drinks, food, towels, and more. Clients and staff of the motel never see each other's faces.

Most rooms also have a TV, some with pornographic movies, and music. There is a big curtain or door that is closed immediately to hide the identity of the couple and their vehicle. On weekend nights and during lunch, the country's love motels fill up quickly. It is very easy to find one of these motels once you have lived in Costa Rica for a while. Just ask a taxi driver or one of your friends.

Nightlife and Entertainment

There are countless open-air restaurants, bars, dance halls and discotheques all over San José and in most other parts of the country. Costa Ricans love to party and dance. Most of these nightspots will appeal to anyone from 16 to 50, give or take a little for the young at heart.

After you have lived in the country for a while, the dance bug will bite you. There are numerous dance academies in the San José area that offer classes for all levels of experience in various styles of Latin American dance. If you want to learn how to dance like a Costa Rican, call **El Malecón Escuela de Bailes Populares** (2255-0378) or **Merecumbé** (2220-8511 in Rohrmoser, 2289-4774 in Escazú, 2240-8511 in Tibás, 2237-0851 in Heredia, 2442-3536 in Alajuela and 2219-8787 in Desamparados). The latter has schools all over the San José area in Alajuela, Heredia, Pavas, Escazú, Santa Ana, Tibás and San Pedro. Other dance schools are: **Academia de Bailes Latinos** (233-8938), **Kinesis Academia de Baile** (440-0852), **Inovación Latina** (255-1460) and **Academia Salsabor Estudio** (224-1943).

The **Fiesta Casino** in Alajuela near the airport, is a happening place. There is live music by some of Costa Rica's best bands and dancing almost every night of the week at the Pirate's Bar inside of the casino. It is also a good place to view sporting events. During the American football season the place is filled on Sunday afternoons. They have eight games going on simultaneously on different big-screen televisions. They also have an annual SuperBowl Party. The event has become so popular, that you need to make your reservations a couple of months in advance.

Once you have mastered the basic dance steps and can dance to the rhythms of *salsa*, *merengue*, *cumbia* and other Latin dances, put on your best pair of dancing shoes and go to **El Azteca** dance hall in the suburb of Desamparados. It has large dance floors and really fills up on the weekends. **Rancho Garabaldi** and **El Buen Día** are other dancehalls in the southern part of the city. Here are some more clubs where you can go to dance to Latin music: **El Tobogán,** 200 meters north and 100 meters east of La República (2223 -8920), **Castro's Bar**, Calle 22, Barrio México, San José, (2256-8789), **El Palenque** at **Balneario Ojo de Agua** in San Antonio de Belén (2441-1309), **Manolo's** Bernardo Soto Highway, Alajuela (2433-9001), **Típico Latino,** downtown Heredia, (2237-1121), **Nuevo Rancho Garibaldi,** 600 meters west of the Marcial Fallas Clinic in Desamparados, San José (2218-1149) and **Picachos,** Paraíso de Cartago, (2574-6072). For additional information about Latin dancing, see: **www.salsapower.com/cities/costarica.htm**

San José´s many discotheques and dance halls play music for all tastes until the wee hours of the morning; admission is inexpensive or free. International liquors and cocktails as well as all local beers and beverages are served. Also, keep in mind that many of these clubs serve food and the traditional heaping plates of delicious local appetizers or hôrs d'oeuvres, called *bocas.*

Most of these establishments are quiet by day and artistically decorated. Many have adjoining restaurants, live music or a disc- jockey and well-lighted dance floors. **El Centro Comercial El Pueblo** has a couple of discotheques. **La** They have huge dance floors and play a mix of American pop, salsa and reggae.

The city of Heredia boasts several excellent watering holes. **El Bulevar**, **Rancho Fofos** and **La Choza** in the vicinity of the National University of Heredia, are *the* places to party. There are also a few new bars in the commercial center where **Hooligan's Bar** used to be on the road to Heredia, in front of the Atlas Factory. The new Hooligan's in located at the Paseo de Las Flores Mall up the road.

Bohemian types should check out **El Cuartel de La Boca del Monte**. Old hippies and Costa Rican yuppies mingle there. It is one of San José's oldest and most popular bar and restaurant combinations. They have a good mix of Latin and American music. The place really fills up on Mondays and Wednesdays when they feature live music. The bar is known for its truly authentic cuisine.

For lovers of jazz, there are several good clubs in the San José area. **The Jazz Café** in San Pedro and Escazú are the best spots to hear the rhythms of soul, blues and jazz. The décor will make you feel like you are in a jazz club back home.

The **Navacafé** in the town of San Ramón is a good place to listen to jazz

The area around the University of Costa Rica in San Pedro is packed with college-type hangouts. La Calle de La Amargura , just, south of the university is filled with bars.Most of these places are full any night of the week. There is some entertainment here for everyone.

For those of you who do not like loud music, sports bars, large crowds or a boisterous atmosphere, some more sedate establishments let you relax with friends and enjoy conversation. Most hotel bars have a laid-back ambience. **The Hotel Grano de Oro** has a lovely patio where you may sit and nurse your favorite beverage. Also check out the bar on the second floor of the **Holiday Inn**. It has a great view of Morazán Park.

The Gringo Bar Scene

There are many establishments where many expatriates hang out in downtown San José or nearby. Although I do not recommend hanging out at these places 24-hours a day, there is no better way to hear stories about life in the tropics, keep up on local gossip, meet some colorful local characters and gather tips about living in Costa Rica while you sip your favorite beverage.

The Hotel Presidente's bar, the **News Café,** is a happening place in San José. The food and drinks are great and it is a fantastic spot to "people watch."

The Patio open-air restaurant/bar next to Hotel Balmoral, is another good place to hang out and observe people. Thousands of people walk by this spot each day. The food is also very good.

There is always plenty of action in the "Gringo Gulch" area.

Bar Joe B y Karen, 50 meters south of the Hotel Balmoral, and **The New York Bar** are favorite watering holes among local expats. The congenial female bartenders will make you feel right at home.

The **Time Out Tavern** in Escazú, is Costa Rica's number one Sports Bar. They offer more sports options than any other spot in the country, carry all of the NFL games on Sundays and are also your best option for NHL and NBA. They have thirteen flat screens TVs with seven DirecTV feeds from the States, two Dish Network feeds from the States, and two Sky TV feeds. The bar is located in Central Escazú, 300 meters south of the Costa Rica Country Club (up the hill) on the left side of the road, diagonally across from *Magia Verde*. Their phone number is 2289-3217.

Another *gringo* hangout is the new **Tropix Bar** at the **Dunn Inn Hotel** in historic Barrio Amón. They offer a variety of drinks and mouth-watering snacks. The atmosphere is quaint.

As previously mentioned a great gringo spot is the **Blue Marlin Bar** Sport enthusiasts frequent this bar. You'll hear a bit of friendly boasting and some tall fish tales at this unique-bar. If you want to make some acquaintances, this bar is worth visiting.

The **White House** is a hotel, bar restaurant and casino in San Antonio de Escazú where some Americans hang out..

The Sportsmens Lodge is a popular hangout in downtown San José. They offer satellite TV, pool tables, real Mexican food and rooms. For information, see: www.sportsmenscr.com.

Mac's American Bar and **Restaurant**, south of La Sabana Park, is another famous *gringo* hangout. You can savor the U.S.-style cooking and watch major sporting events such as NFL games on DirectTV and the Dish Network. They have a huge Saint Patrick's Day party every year. We highly recommend this place.

Rock & Roll Pollo Bar and Restaurant located in Santa Ana, offers satellite TV for viewing all major U.S. sports. The food is also good.

Brad's Grille at the Momentum Mall on the La Lindora road in Santana has good food, entertainment and 14 TVs with an occasional tailgate party during football season.

More good bars

Most bars open at 11 a.m. and close at 2 a.m., seven days a week. Some have happy hours.

Antojitos	Good Mexican food
Castro's	Good dancing in Barrio México
Chango	Bar-restaurant in Escazú
Gran Hotel	Nice outdoor patio in the heart of San José
Fiesta Casino	Good for sporting events and dancing
Hotel Corobicí	Good bar
Holiday Inn	Across from Morazán Park
Hooters (Escazú	Part of the U.S. chain
Infinito	Has two dance floors, all types of music
K & S Brewery	A micro-brewery in Curridabat
La Cantina	Located at the Hotel Irazú
La Soda Tapia	Nice place across from Sabana Park
Mirador Ram Luna	Family style, jukebox, dancing
Tapachula	Gringo bar near soccer stadium in Alajuela

* See the *The Tico Times* or *La Nación* for more entertainment options.

Gambling

Gambling is a pastime enjoyed by both tourists and residents. Costa Rica has about 20 casinos, most in the San José area with a few at beach resorts. Rules differ slightly from those in the United States. or Europe, but gambling is fun to learn the Costa Rican way. There are four legal casino games. Rummy, a variation of black-jack or 21, is the most popular. The remaining games are craps, roulette (played lottery style rather than with a wheel) and *tute,* a type of poker played against the house. Slot machines are legal. Most casinos are open from 6 p.m. to 3 or 4 a.m. Many casinos offer 24-hour gambling.

Most casinos offer perks for gamblers such as free *bocas* (snacks), drinks and an occasional buffet. Some foreigners gather at casinos on Sundays to watch football games.

The **Fiesta Casino** and **Club Colonial** are casinos located in the heart of San José and are by far the best places to gamble. The former has other locations in Heredia near the airport in Alajuela.

The casino on the top floor of the **Holiday Inn** offers a spectacular panoramic view of the city of San José. If for no other reason, you should go to this casino to take in the view and snap a few photos. You may also gamble on the Internet through a local company called **Grand Central Casino** and **Sports Book**.

The most popular form of gambling in Costa Rica is the national lottery or *lotería*. This game of chance is played a couple of times each week. You can purchase a whole sheet of tickets or a fraction of a sheet from any street vendor.

A substantial amount of money may be won. If you are lucky enough to win the huge annual Christmas Lottery, or *Gordo Navideño*, you will become very rich and will probably be set up for life. To find the results of the lottery, look in the local newspaper. There is also an instant-winner lottery, similar to that played in the United States, called *raspa*. In this game you scrape off an area on the ticket with a coin to see if you have matching symbols or numbers.

Chances is the people's lottery and has three large prizes. Scratch cards are another type of lottery and give winners an instant reward. ***Tiempos*** is a simplified lottery designed to compete with the country's illegal lotteries.

There are also a couple of illegal underground lotteries played the same days as the legal lottery on Tuesday, Friday and Sunday. The games are attractive to some locals because you can win from five to 70 times the amount of your ticket. Also, it is easier to claim the prize in the regular lottery. **The Changa** is played among Nicaraguans; **La Pulga** is played around the Borbón Market in San José; **La Panameña** works in conjunction with the Panamanian lottery; and **Cuatro Cantos** is played in the port town

A Bookmaker in Paradise

By Redstone Brimely

The life I led in the States wasn't working for me. My last business venture ended in failure and I was being evicted from my home. The county health inspector, alerted by my nosey neighbor, posted the notice on my front door citing me with excessive refuse from fast food establishments. If that wasn't enough, I was down to my last pair of pants, I had outgrown Big and Tall. I needed a change.

Watching infomercials at four in the morning, I heard testimony from a West Virginian illiterate expounding about teaching English overseas. I sent for the deluxe package. The exotic destinations offered were many, but I decided Costa Rica was going to be my new home. There's something about change that gives a young man a bounce to his step. I sensed good things ahead and I was right.

I went to work as an English teacher for a language institute in San José, tutoring local executives. My first week there I instructed a group of Costa Ricans who spoke excellent English but needed to brush up on their grammar. Interesting work but my biweekly stipend would barely keep me in rice and beans. An offshore Las Vegas-style sportsbook operating in San José, had sent their employees to the class. The top student in the class happened to be a supervisor in the wagering department. At the end of the term he offered me a job.

I had never before worked in the gambling business, however I knew something about gambling— my father was a gambler.

When I completed my training I was placed in the betting department along with fifty other clerks where the phones were literally "ringing off the hook." Native beauties with cocoa butter skin and pearly white teeth in halter-tops and sarongs answered the phones speaking perfect English. I was in shock!

My main concern when I took this job was whether or not I was breaking any laws. I did some investigating and found out offshore bookmaking is legal and beyond the juristiction of the United States government. The company's growth during the past football season has been phenomenal. In fact, we've both grown. I was made a betting supervisor and was given a couple of weeks off before the start of the basketball season. Until then I'll be at the beach where I've traded in my Oshkosh for Bermuda shorts and a Panama hat.

of Puntarenas. I don't recommend playing illegal lotteries; I mention them only to let our readers know they exist.

Betting on horses is legal in Costa Rica, but the local track closed in 1995 because of financial problems. At the Casino Club Colonial and Hotel Del Rey there is betting on most major sporting events. In November 2001, betting on Costa Rican soccer games was legalized.

Movies and Theaters in San José and Other Areas

There are movie theaters all over the San José area and in other large cities. Most of these theaters show first-run movies usually within a month after they are first released in the United States. *Ticos* are moviegoers. Last year more than 3.5 million tickets were sold in Costa Rica.

In the 1980s there were about 125 independent movie theaters in the country. Today there are 80 theaters with 73 belonging to three major chains and found exclusively in large shopping malls.

The first of Costa Rica's megatheaters was built in the **San Pedro Mall**. It has five-screens and is located on the second floor of the mall. The opening of this theater complex started a new trend of multiple movie screens located in shopping malls. The idea was to use the movie theaters to draw large numbers of people to the malls.

The **Sala Garbo** shows first-rate independent films with Spanish subtitles. About 40 percent of all current hit movies shown in the United States make their way to Costa Rica sooner or later. You should not worry about understanding these movies since they are all in English with Spanish, subtitles except movies for children, which are usually dubbed. You can read the local newspapers to see what movies are currently playing. At present, admission costs about $4 depending on the theater. Several theaters have more than one screen. To find out what is playing look in *The Tico Times* or any of the Spanish-language newspapers such as *La Nación*. Information about movies may also be accessed at **www.whereincostarica.com/cinema** or **www.entretenimiento.co.cr (in Spanish).**

In the Central Valley, you can experience everything from old-time Paramount-style theater palaces to ultra-modern movie complexes in suburban malls. The Cine **Variedades**, up the street from the Plaza de la Cultura, is one of the oldest. The **Cine Magaly** in Barrio La California, is a great theater for that old-time big-movie experience. It has more than 1,000 seats and second-story balconies.

The parent company of the Magaly runs other movie theaters in the country. **Cadena de Cines Magaly,** or **CCM**, is the country's largest chain with 42 screening rooms located all over the country. They receive about 50 percent of the country's movie viewers.

These theaters show nontraditional foreign films and have state-of-the-art DTS Digital and Dolby sound systems. You can purchase and reserve tickets by telephone with a credit card.The Magaly movie chain also recently opened several movie theaters at **Mall Internacional** in Alajuela, the **Paseo de las Flores** and **Real Cariari** shopping centers in Heredia, in **Plaza San Carlos** and **Plaza Liberia** in Guanacaste.

The **Real Cariari** shopping center boasts a six-screen movie theater. **Cinemark** is a U.S.-style movie theater with eight screens at the **Multiplaza** mall, in Escazú. This theater boasts a -top-quality digital sound system and tiered seating . It is one of the best places to see a movie in the country, and serves snacks and candies from the United States and even hot buttered popcorn with real butter and free refills if you purchase the large size. **Cinépolis** at the new **Terramall,** on the highway to Cartago also has a state- of-the-art theater. It has 15 movie screens, three of which have VIP rooms with luxurious seats and George Lucas' THX technology.

The First IMAX 3-D viewing theater recently opens in Escazú, Costa Rica. It is the sixth IMAX in Latin America but the first in Costa Rica. México has two, Guatemala has one and Colombia has two.

Movies (Cines)

Cinépolis 2278-3506
Terramall

Cine Cariari (six screens) 2293-3300
Plaza Real Cariari, across from the Hotel Herradura

Cine Colonial 1 and 2 (two screens) 2289-9000
Centro Comercial Plaza Colonial, Escazú

Cine Magaly 2223-0085
Calle 23, Ave. Central/1 Barrio La California

CineEl Semáforo (alternative movies) 2253-9126
San Pedro

Cinematec 2207-5732
Auditorium of the School of General Studies, UCR

Cine Universitario 2207-4271
At the U.C.R.. Law School Auditorium

Cine en el Campus, Teatro Centro de Arte del CIDEA, Universidad Nacional, 200 meters north of McDonald's, Heredia

Cinemark (eight screens).. 2288-1111
Multiplaza, Escazú

Cinemark (eight screens).. 2224-8383
Multiplaza del Este, Zapote

Cine Variedades.. 2222-6104
Ave. Central/1, Calle 5

El Cine Alternativo.. 2205-4130
Centro ComercialLa Lindora

El Observatorio 2223-0725
Calle 23, Ave. Central

IMAX(Escazú).. 2299-7666
Avenida Escazú

Internacional (four screens) 2442-6100
Mall Internacional, Alajuela

One of Costa Rica's modern movie theaters

La Fábrica 905-246-3722
Grecia

Laurence Olivier 2222-1034
Ave. 2, Calle 28

Liberia.. 2223-0085
Guanacaste

Multicines 2234-8868
San Pedro across from la Plaza Roosevelt and Kennedy Park

Multicines 2592-3133
Cartago at Mall Paraíso

Multiplex 2460-6733
San Carlos

Pérez Zeledón 2772-8780
San Isidro

Plaza Mayor 1-2 (two screens)................................ 2232-3271
Rohrmoser Blvd, Rohrmoser

Plaza Occidente 2447-7120
San Ramón

Sala Garbo 2222-1034
Ave. 2, Calle 28, 100 meters south of Pizza Hut Paseo Colón

San Carlos.. 2480-9202

San Pedro Mall (five screens) 2221-6272
Mall San Pedro

Theaters (*Teatros*) in and Around San José

San José is purported to have more theaters and theater companies per capita than any other city in the world. Most live plays are in Spanish but there are occasional plays in English at the Costa Rican-North American Cultural Center. The Little Theatre Group is Costa Rica's oldest English-language acting troupe and frequently presents plays in English. However, by going to plays in Spanish, you can improve your language skills. Current plays are listed in the activities section of local newspapers.

Teatro del Angel....................2222-8258
Ave. Central & Plaza de la Democracia

Teatro Chaplin....................2223-2919
Paseo de los Estudiantes

Teatro Eugene O'Neill....................2253-5527
In the Costa Rican-North American Cultural Center, Barrio Dent

Teatro Giratablas....................2253-6001
Diagonal to Kentucky Fried Chicken on the road to San Pedro

Teatro de La Aduana....................2223-4563
Calle 25, Ave. 3/ 5

Teatro Laurence Olivier....................2222-1034
Ave. 2, Calle 28

Teatro Lucho Barahona....................2223-5972
Behind Cinema 2000

Teatro Melico Salazar....................2221-4952
Ave. 2, Calle Central

Teatro Nacional....................2221-5341
Ave. 2, Calles 3/5

Teatro Sala 15....................2236-8940
Soth side of the Plaza de la Democracia

Teatro Sancheto....................8398-9409
100 meters west and 50 meters north of the Santa Rita Clinic

Teatro Torres....................2256-4295
175 meters from Santa Rita Clinic

* For more theaters see the yellow pages.

9

Communications

Telephone Service

Costa Rica has the most number of telephones in Latin American country and boasts one of the world's best telephone systems, with direct dialing to more than 60 countries. The country has 1.5 million regular telephones, 930,000 cellular phones and 20,000 public phones.

The country code for all of Costa Rica is 506. To call any number in the country from North America dial 011 + 506 + the eight-digit number. Calls within the country are a bargain; you can call any place in the country for only a few cents; they are all local calls. If your house or apartment does not have a phone, don't worry. Public telephones are just about everywhere in Costa Rica and use 5, 10, and 20 silver *colón* coins. Phones accepting prepaid phone cards are slowly replacing coin-operated phones.

NOTE: All telephone numbers have increased from seven digits to eight. The old telephone numbers remained intact but with one change. Now all land line numbers have to be preceded by a"2" and all cell phone numbers (which previously started with either a "3" or an "8") now must be preceded by an "8."

If you do not have your own phone and want to make a direct international call, go to the ***Radiográfica* (2287-0087)** telephone office, (open 7 a.m. to 10 p.m.) in downtown San José at Calle 1, Avenida 7. Long-distance calls may be made from any phone booth by dialing 114. You can also make long distance calls from most hotels. From private phones in homes or offices, the procedure is just like in the United States: by direct dialing or first talking to the operator *(operadora)*. As was just mentioned, the access numbers for calling Costa Rica from North America are 011 + 506 + the number. To call or fax the U.S. from Costa Rica dial 001+area code+number. You may purchase prepaid phone cards for local or international direct-dial calls. Three types of cards may be purchased from Costa Rican Electricity Institute (ICE) offices, *Correos de Costa Rica* or businesses displaying a gold and blue sign that says "*Tarjetas Telefónicas.*" **CHIP cards** sold in denominations of 300 to 2,000 *colones* may be used for local calls. **Servicio 197** cards come in denominations of 300, 500 and 1000 *colones* and allow domestic calls. **Servicio 199** cards are in $10, $20 or 3,000 and 10,000 *colón* denominations and may be used for international calls and have instructions in English.

Getting a telephone line

NOTE: To purchase a land line you need to be a legal Costa Rican Resident, citizen or do it under a corporation.

Purchasing a telephone can be a real pain in the neck depending on where you live and the number of available lines. You can expect to wait from one to three months for phone installation after paying about $50 for this service.

You can request a number and service from anywhere in Costa Rica by calling 115 to see if there are lines available. Place your request with one of the operators or ask where the nearest ICE office is to order the service. If you need assistance in English, several English-speaking operators are available to help you. If there are telephone lines available, give the electric meter number of the place where you want your new telephone line installed

You'll also need the telephone number of the nearest building to the place where you want your phone line installed so the phone company can verify if a phone can be installed and how long it will take. Your passport, identification or cellular phone number may be used to identify you for your account information. You also need to supply a copy of the electricity bill for your new location. Finally, a postal address or directions where phone bills and other information about phone service may be sent. When you have given this information to ICE, they will give you a personal identification number to be used for paying the installation fee and for making any change in your service.

The next step is to pay the one-time fee to get on the waiting list for phone service. The fee ranges from $50 for a home phone line to $70 for a business line. This payment can be made at any ICE office, or the phone company will send a messenger at no cost to pick up the payment.

They give you an ICE order number sheet that you have to hang in a visible place on the front of the new house. Make sure you hang it high enough so kids don't tear it down and so that it doesn't get rained on.

If you are having problems with the line or need to make changes in your service, call 119. Few English-speaking operators work at this extension and a lot of transactions are done by computer, so it might be better to go directly to an ICE office for this kind of assistance. Or, you may call the international phone service number at 124, where operators speak English and are often willing to help foreigners having problems with their telephone service. All of this information is clearly explained in Spanish at the beginning of the local phone book.

To have a phone installed, go to one of the following ICE offices: north side of the Sabana Park 2220-7720; Pavas Centro, 2296-0303, La Florida, Tibás, 2240-6466; San Pedro, 2225-0123; San José, 2221-0123. You may also go to one of their smaller agencies located all over the country.

Phone bills may be paid at the ICE office in downtown San José or at any other ICE office or agency in Costa Rica. You can also pay your phone and electric bills (*recibos*) at many supermarkets or online through banks such as, Banco Nacional.

The phone company offers these services with your phone: call waiting, caller ID, rerouting of calls, wake-up calls, restriction of international calls and teleconferencing.

Transferring a telephone line

To transfer your telephone line or number to a different location, first you have to find out a telephone number of an office or house that is next to or close by the place where you want your telephone line transferred. After you have this information, call 115 and give them the telephone number. They will let you know if there are telephone pairs available, or in some cases they might be in the same telephone exchange.

If everything turns out well and the transfer can be done, you need an electric meter number and a photocopy of the owner's ID document.

If it is under a company name, you will need the *personería jurídica* (legal power of attorney) with the corresponding *cédula jurídica* (corporate ID number) and the power of attorney and ID document number of the representative.

The cost of transferring the line is $37 per line plus sales tax; this amount will be charged to your telephone bill. Fill in the form sent to you by fax; afterwards you can take this form to the ICE office or send it back by fax. It's very simple.

When I moved from my old home in Lagunilla de Heredia to San Francisco de Heredia, I had to transfer two telephone lines. The people at the phone company said it would not take too long. With a lot of pushing and shoving, the whole process took six weeks.

Cell phones

Cellular phone service is available in Costa Rica. The country also offers the lowest cell phone rates per minute in Latin America.Cellular phones have become a status symbol here. It seems that any Costa Rican who can afford a cell phone has one.

The basic monthly fee is about $6, and that includes 60 free minutes of call time. Any additional minutes are 30 *colones* each from 7 am to 7 pm and 23 *colones* each from 7PM to 7AM and holidays. Text messages are 1.5 *colones* each. The basic rate for calls and text messages may go up slightly soon. See **www.grupoice.com** for additional information.

Phones are more expensive than in the United States, and there are no super deals where you get a free phone by just signing up for a year's service. Nevertheless, business is booming for the companies that sell cell phones here. Stores selling cell phones are found all over the country and in most of the large shopping malls. You can often get hooked up by the store that sells you your phone, provided there are lines available. You can save money by purchasing your phone in the United States and then getting connected to the service here. However, only certain types of phones from the United States work here.

If you want to get a cell phone line, you must go to ICE and present the following documents:

1. The original and copy of your *cédula* (ID card) and your cell phone.
2. Two copies of the invoice of the phone you purchased
3. A guarantee deposit of 12,000 *colones*
4. Original or copies of a water, telephone or electric bill with your name on it.

Cell phone rentals are available in Costa Rica. I recommend the following company: **Cellular Telephone Rentals** Tel: 2290-7534, 800-769-7137, ww.cellulartelephonerentals.com

Faxes

Sending a fax is very easy in Costa Rica. You can go to **Radiográfica** (Tel: 2287-0513, 2287-0511) . At the Radiográfica office you can send a fax or have one sent to you. You can call their office to see if they have received a fax for you. They will even call when a fax comes in if they have your phone number. Many private businesses offer fax services to individuals. You can usually find their number in the classified section of *The Tico Times* (the local English-language newspapers).

Internet Service

Computer buffs will be pleased to know that Internet services are available throughout Costa Rica. Costa Rica has Central America's highest Internet connection rate, with 20 of 1,000 citizens regularly going online. The country is second in Internet use in Latin America, surpassed only by Chile. At the beginning 2004, Costa Rica had more than 100,000 Internet accounts. It is predicted that soon one-quarter of the country's population will be frequent users of the Internet.

In Costa Rica, Internet users have several ways of connecting to the national network; by cable modem provided by local cable companies in connection with RACSA (Radiográfica Costarricense); ADSL and RDSI provided by the *Instituto Costarricense de Electricidad* (ICE) , the telephone company and parent of RACSA; or by dial-up provided by RACSA. Unfortunately, many Internet users are limited to the slow dial-up system. Most people complain that it is very slow, difficult to get connected at times and they often get disconnected while online.

To get connected to the Internet, just go to the **Radiográfica** offices and open a **RACSAPAC** account. Recently, using the Internet became less expensive and the hours more flexible.

Monthly rates for home Internet vary. For further information about these services, call 800-6283427, 2287-0321 or 2287-0087; Fax: (506) 2223-1609, or e-mail: serviciocliente@racsa.co.cr.

ICE now offers **ADSL** broadband Internet. Broadband Internet will e enable homes, schools and businesses to connect to the Internet at high speeds at a fraction of the current cost without using regular telephone lines. The monthly cost of this service varies depending on connection and download speed and whether ICE, Racsa, Amnet or Cable Tica is the provider.

Internet service cable TV hookup is also available in Costa Rica through a couple of cable TV companies. **Cable Tica** (2210-1450) and **Amnet**

(800-222-5388, 2210-2929) now offer two-way high-speed cable modem Internet service in some areas, mainly the Central Valley. The monthly cost depends on the speed of the connection you choose. At present, this service is available in San José, Heredia, Santa Ana , some of the surrounding suburbs and certain pockets of the country. The author lives in Heredia and isvery happy with the service Amnet provides.

Here is a chart with the rates as of 2009

Speed	Racsa	ICE	Amnet	Cable Tica
256/64 Kbps	$6.97	$13	$16.95	$13.95
1 Mbps/256 Kbps	$12.97	$25	$34.95	$25.95
1.5 Mbps/256 Kbps	$17.48	-----	-------	$34.95
3 Mbps/256 Kbps	$24.98	------	$69.95	$49.95
2 Mbps/512 Kbps	$34.98	$30	$69.95	$69.95
4 Mbps/768 Kbps	$49.98	------	------	$99.95
4 Mbps/ 1Mb	$64.97	$97	$168.95	$129.95

You can also get high-speed satellite Internet service from several companies. The installation cost is about $2,600 and the monthly charge is about $125. In rural areas where there is no broadband Internet, DSL or cable, this may be the way to go. Call 2290-0689 for more information.

Wifi is now available in and around San José. The rates range from $29 for 512/256 Kbps to $244 for 2/1Mbps. There are plans to expand this service to other areas.

VOIP services

Internet users can now make long distance telephone calls using Voice over Internet Protocol (VOIP). I use **Vonage** and it works well. They offer an all-inclusive phone service that can bypass the Costa Rican phone system. You can use your existing high-speed Internet connection (broadband) instead of standard phone lines. You will also need a U.S. address to use this system. I know many people who use Vonage from here and are very satisfied. To find out more about their services see **www.vonage.com**.

Skype and **magicJack** are other VOIP systems that work very well from here. ICE says they plan to offer an international Internet phone services soon.

Internet Cafés and Other Places to Connect

For an hourly fee, you may send and receive email and surf the Web and make long-distance calls from any of the many local Internet cafés. Internet café prices can range anywhere from 200 *colones* ($0.40) to 470 *colones* ($0.90) per hour in the San José area to as much as 2.000 *colones* (US $3.90) at the beach.

Here is my friend Charles Mill's experience at a local Internet café: "On my first two trips I used the Internet café. They are available almost everywhere. In Heredia you trip over them all the time. They are fast and very reasonable. The main issue that bothered me was that in some cafés the keyboards were dirty. You can find Internet café's for 150 to 500 *colones* ($0.30 to $1) or more per hour. Last year I was in Branson, Missouri and an Internet café was charging $6 per hour. In New York it can cost $12 per hour."

Many hotels, restaurants and fast food places like McDonald's now offer free Internet service to their clients, and some of them even have WiFi if you are traveling with your laptop.

Paying bills online

You can pay bills online here. There is no need to have the paper bill present; you only need to know the due date and the appropriate account number and name for your bill so you can pay them on time online. Banco Nacional has the easiest, most complete and best online bill pay system here in Costa Rica. You can have an electronic *colón* and U.S. dollar account on the same page and move funds from one to the other as needed. To pay private parties (such as your landlord) or companies not listed, you need to have their account number and account name, but you can transfer money to them online also within the same bank. They have promised that interbank payments are coming soon.

As for the U.S. side of online banking, you can use **NetBank** (www.netbank.com) and pay virtually anyone in the United States either through e-bills, if they are offered, or send them an electronically generated bank check directly. With a **PayPal** account, you can pay anyone that has an e-mail address anywhere in the world, with some political exceptions.

Mail Service

Costa Rica's postal system, or *Correos de Costa Rica,* offers postal services comparable to those in many countries abroad. The country's first mail service was officially established in December 1839.

San Jose's old post office

Curbside boxes for mail pickup are almost nonexistent in Costa Rica. You will have to mail your letters from the post office or from a hotel if you are a guest. Just as in the United States, mail may be received and sent from the post office ***(correo** or **casa de correos.)*** The main post office is in the heart of downtown San José at Calle 2, between Avenidas 1 and 3 (2223-9766). Other small cities and towns in rural areas have their own centrally located post offices. Airmail between the United States or Europe and Costa Rica usually takes about five to 10 days. At present, an airmail letter to the United States or Canada costs $0.30 or 160 *colones.* A postcard to North America is about $0.20 or 125 *colones.* An airmail stamp to Europe is about $0.35 or 200 *colones.* A registered letter cost about $.25 extra. To save money, the post office has replaced stamps with adhesive labels that show the amount of postage.

The post office also provides other services, including telegrams, fax service, courier service and delivery of documents.

As stated above, mail boxes are few and far between as are house numbers, so I recommend using your nearest post office for all postal- related matters. The country's charming but exasperating "100 meters east of the church" style addresses makes getting a post office box for local mail delivery a necessity. Obtaining a post office box *(apartado)* from your local post office in Costa Rica ensures prompt and efficient mail service.

Getting a post office box is a straightforward process, but available boxes can sometimes be hard to come by. P.O. boxes are in great demand, but you can usually get one in January, when most people give up leases on their boxes

An Expat's Adventure at the Post Office

By John Vickery

I received 4 M-bags at my *apartado* in Alejuela the last week of August. There was one bag that was missing. I'm hoping that this note might help a new person to Costa Rica understand what happens when they are required to report to the main post office in Zapote. I wondered what happened to that last M-bag but figured it would be along shortly.

Sometime in the first week of September I received the normal *adviso* in my apartado telling me to report to the second floor of the *correo* to retrieve that final M-bag. Upon reporting there the clerk told me I must report to the main post office in Zapote to retrieve my package. When asked why, the clerk responded that he did not know why but suspected there might be a problem.

I hired my trusted pirate taxi driver to take me there. We arrived at 9:30 on Friday morning and the parking lot was almost empty. I still was unsure why I had to report to Zapote but if you follow my adventure, you might find this trip less intimidating than it might appear.

As you drive into the post office compound you will see the huge post office directly in front of you. This is not the place you need to go. As you enter (through the gate) look off to the right and you'll see a small booth with a guy sitting inside. After you park, go over to that little booth and present the *adviso* you received from your local post office. The clerk inside the booth will check out your paper, and if all is in order, he will point to the guy sitting next door guarding the pedestrian entrance to the customs area. Here you will need to show your *adviso* again, then sign into the compound (name, date, passport, *cédula* number and signature. After this, the guard will ask for your passport, *cédula* and verify the info. If you have others with you, they will go through the same process.

Once you clear this gate, you will walk about 150 meters towards the back of the building. You will then turn left and enter the building and proceed past a few stations to get to station #1. If there is no one in front of you (I got lucky with only one person in front of me) you will approach this window and pass your *adviso* to the person on the other side of the glass. This person will check your paperwork on the computer and if you are there (I was), they will print out the paperwork and then grab their handy rubber stamp and stamp like crazy. Then they will hand you one of those papers for you to print your name, date, passport, *cédula* number and sign it. Then they ask for your passport/*cédula* to verify the info and if all is OK, they give you one of the papers and they tell you to go across the isle to station number 2. Station 2 is a 20 foot counter and there you'll see a sign in both Spanish and English telling you to wait until your name is called. I waited there about 20 minutes and saw a large cardboard box (too big to fit in an M-bag) delivered to the serious looking guy behind the counter. That can't be mine thought I. Wrong! The guy called my name and put that large box on the counter. I looked at the box and noticed that it had rubber stamps all over it stating that the original package had been damaged in shipment and had been directed to the re-wrapping department at the USPS post office in Jersey City, New Jersey. The serious looking guy (Customs I later found out) put the package on the counter and found a large knife (not a machete) and proceeded to cut the box open.

A quick aside here: Originally the M-bag I sent contained two of what's called bankers totes. These boxes fold up nicely and have a nice cover which is easy to write on. The USPS office where I mailed them advised that I address the top of each box (in the M-bag) just like a letter. Upper right corner of the box (where a stamp would go) was noted M-bag US postage paid. Upper left hand corner of the box had a return address in the states. Center of the box had the mailing address here in Costa Rica. Well, I looked at that box which was too big to fit in any M-bag and noticed that these re-wrapping folks in New Jersey (I assume) had cut the top of one of my boxes and taped the info to the top of the re-packaged box. Good for them and I'm certainly glad I followed the instructions of my local USPS office!

Back to the serious looking customs agent. He cut the box open and did a quick inspection of the contents. I admit that I cheated just a bit and included a few VHS tapes in amongst the books in the bag. All the guy did was look through the box and say "books". Then he picked up a few of the VHS tapes, shook his head and said "OK". He then signed a paper and asked me for the same info from the previous window (no stamp) and directed me to station number 3. I proceeded to station number 3 which was another window and handed the paper to him. This process took about 15 minutes (signing papers, rubber stamps, etc) and cost me 470 colones. I still do not know why I was charged, but for less than a dollar I wasn't about to ask. The guy at station number 3 then gave me another piece of paper and directed me to station number 4. This was another 20 foot counter and about 10 minutes later I was presented my box and had to sign another number of papers and was allowed to leave carrying my box.

All in all, I think this was a positive Costa Rican experience. I've heard many horror stories dealing with Costa Rican customs. I do not consider this one of those stories!

when annual renewal fees are due. If a box's annual renewal fee isn't paid by mid-February, it is sold to those on the waiting list at that time. Popular branches such as San José's central post office or Escazú post office have long waiting lists; it is much easier to find a box in suburban or rural areas.

Many people deal with the shortage of boxes by sharing with friends, neighbors, extended family or business associates. In theory, this practice isn't permitted, but many people do it and nobody seems to check closely.

To apply for a post office box, go to the post office nearest your office or home to fill out an application *(solicitud de apartado)*. The annual rental fee costs about $10, $30 or $40 dollars in the San José metropolitan area and provincial capitals, depending on the size of the post office box. There are three sizes: small, medium and large. In rural post offices, the costs are about half these prices.

Once you fill out the paperwork and pay your annual fee, you are given an address that reads something like this: José López, Apdo. 7289-1000, San José, Costa Rica. The number before the hyphen is the *apartado* (P.O. Box) and the number after the hyphen is the post office's code.

You may also receive mail in the general delivery section *(lista de correos)* of your local post office. This is especially useful in isolated regions of the country. Register at the nearest post office and they will put your name on the local *lista de correos.* When you pick up your mail, you pay a few cents per letter for this service. All letters must have your name, the phrase *lista de correos* and the name of the nearest post office.

The worst time to receive any correspondence through regular Costa Rican mail is between November 20 and January 1. Letters can be delayed up to a month by the enormous volume of Christmas mail and the vacations of postal workers during the month of December.

You should avoid having anything larger than a letter or a magazine sent to you in Costa Rica. Any item bigger than that will be sent to the customs warehouse *(aduana)* and you will make several trips to get it out. On the first trip to customs your package or parcel is unwrapped so you can fill out a declaration of its contents. On the second trip, you usually have to pay an exorbitant duty equivalent to the value of the item plus the mailing cost. If you refuse to pay, your package will be confiscated— not sent back, just confiscated.

So, as you can see, due to the costs involved and wasted time, it is better to have friends bring you large items, pick them up when you're visiting the United States, or use one of the private mail companies mentioned in this section.

In an effort to win back some of its customers, the government recently privatized the **Costa Rican Postal Service (CORTEL)**. The service has officially shed its public status and was reborn as *Correos de Costa Rica S.A.*

The overhaul aims to transform the notoriously slow service into an efficient operation. The country's archaic street address system will be changed to a systematic numbering of streets, avenues and buildings.

For information about the *Correos de Costa Rica's* services, contact them at: Tel: 800-900-2000 or 2253-3375, extensions 343 and 345, or go to **www.correos.go.cr**.

Receiving Money from Abroad

Do you plan on having money from abroad sent to you in Costa Rica? Perhaps the cheapest and easiest way to get money is at an ATM machines available at almost all banks and supermarkets.

Western Union in Costa Rica boasts that they offer the fastest money transfers in the country. Call Western Union at 1-800-777-7777 or 2283-6336, or e-mail: bvib@western-union.co.cr for additional information, or go to one of their local agencies in San José, Liberia, San Isidro de El General, Puntarenas or other parts of the country. You'll have to show some form of valid identification to pick up your money. **Moneygram** 1-800-328-5678, 2295-9595, www.moneygram.com, offers similar services.

One of the safest ways to receive money while visiting or residing in Costa Rica is to have an international money order or any other type of important merchandise or document shipped to you by one of the worldwide courier services, such as DHL or UPS. Letters and small packages usually take about two working days (Monday to Friday) to reach Costa Rica from the United States or Canada.

Many worldwide air couriers have offices in San José, such as **DHL** (2290-3010), **FedEx** (2255-4567), **UPS** (257-7447), **TNT** (2233-5678) and **Jetex** (2293-5838). The latter is probably the cheapest option. Until recently, Costa Rica's postal service, **Correos de Costa Rica**, was the slowest and least safe option. Its "non-priority" mail was too slow to even consider as a valid option. The Costa Rican postal service does offer priority mail service; call 2253-3375 or 800-900-2000 or e-mail: pacc_prioritymail@correos.go.cr

"Priority" mail *(certificado)* supposedly takes 12 days to reach any destination in the United States and three weeks for Europe and the rest of the world. Rates are very affordable at about $5.35 per kilo and $4.75 for each additional kilo.

However, Correos de Costa Rica offers **EMS Courier**, a national and international courier service with 127 offices throughout the country. It hopes to compete with private courier companies. You may contact them at 2221-2136, fax: 2221-1737 or e-mail: ems@correos.go.cr.

The Costa Rican postal service is planning to start a money order service allowing money orders to be sent from the U.S. to Costa Rica. This service promises to be much faster and much more economical than getting money wired to your bank in Costa Rica.

You can always have a trustworthy friend or relative bring you up to $10,000 when they come to Costa Rica.

Automatic Teller Machines (ATMs) are found all over the country.

U.S. banks can wire money to banks in Costa Rica. This method is safe, but can be slow at times, as many bureaucratic delays can develop while waiting for checks to clear. You are also charged a fee for the transfer. I had a money order sent from England to my account at the *Banco Nacional de Costa Rica* and didn't experience much delay or any problems. Once I followed the correct procedure the money arrived promptly.

To wire money you will have to use eight-letter codes for your local bank's eight-letter SWIFT account. Some of these codes may have changed, so be sure and check with your bank.

Banco BAC San Jose..BSNJCRSJ 363642
Banco de Costa Rica San Jose .... BCRICRSJ 019339
Banco Internacional de Costa Rica San Jose....... COSRCRSJ 393955
Banco Nacional de Costa Rica San Jose..............BNCRCRSJ 019462
Scotia Bank de Costa Rica San Jose..................NOSCCRSJ 394833

The Costa Rican postal service is planning to start a money order service allowing money orders to be sent from the United States to Costa Rica. This service promises to be much faster and more economical than getting money wired to your bank in Costa Rica.

You can always have a trustworthy friend or relative bring you up to $10,000 when they come to Costa Rica.

Automatic teller machines (ATMs) are found all over the country. You can't transfer money directly but can get cash advances from one of your local or international credit or debit cards. Use of ATMs, along with cashing a personal check are perhaps the fastest ways to get money.

Another safe way to have checks sent to you is through one of the private mail services listed in the next section.

The worst way to send money is through the regular mail. People report that many checks have been lost or stolen. Postal thieves are very sophisticated in Costa Rica and may work with some unscrupulous black market money changers. The postal system has received numerous complaints and has promised to do something about them. If you need to file a complaint about lost or stolen mail, go to *Correo de Costa Rica's* complaint department *(Departamento de Reclamaciones)* in downtown San José on Avenida 6, between Calles 17 and 19. If you live outside San José, you can file a complaint at any local post office and it will be forwarded to San José.

If you still choose to use the regular mail system after reading the above, be sure to have your checks or money orders sent to you in secure, non-transparent manila envelopes—ones that can't be seen through when held up to a light.

A rash of postal thefts has prompted more and more people to use the private-mail companies, which offer a variety of postal related services.

If you still choose to use the regular mail system after reading the above, be sure to have your checks or money orders sent to you in secure, non-transparent manila envelopes—ones that can't be seen through when held up to a light.

A rash of postal thefts has prompted more and more people to use the private-mail companies, which offer a variety of postal-related services.

Private Mail Services

A few mail companies provide clients with a mail drop and P.O. box in Miami and a physical address where they can send or receive packages. This enables customers living in Costa Rica to have their mail sent to the Miami address from where the companies forward the mail to Costa Rica.

Aerocasillas (P.O. Box 4567-1000, San José, Costa Rica, Tel: 208-4868, Fax: 257-1187, E-mail: servicesjo@aerocasillas.com, www.aerocasillas.com) is the oldest of these companies. Besides their main office, they have branches in the suburbs and in other areas of the country: Escazú, 2208-4848; La Uruca, San José 2232-6892; Desamparados, 2208-4848, Heredia, Plaza Bratsi 2208-4848; Curridabat, San José, 2224-6381; Novacentro, Guadalupe, 224-9843; Cartago, 2592-0000; Limón, 2798-0606, ext. 6; Ciudad Quesada (San Carlos), 2460-7454; Grecia, 2444-2230; San Ramón 2440-8793; Quepos 2777-1925; and Herradura (Jacó), 2637-7134. See the web site for more details.

Trans-Express "Interlink" (P.O. Box 02-5635, Miami, FL 33102, Tel: 2296-3973/2296-3974, Fax: 2232-3979); **AAA Express Mail** (Tel: 2233-4993, Fax: 2221-5056); **Star Box** (P.O. Box 405–1000, San José, Tel: 2257-3443, Fax: 2233-5624); **Jet Box** (Tel: 2231-5592 in Pavas, 2253-5400, in Curridabat and 2665-0017 in Liberia, see www.jetbox.com); **Daily Mail** (Tel: 2233-4993, Fax:2 221-5046); and **Air Mail CR** (2239-5775) are other companies offering similar services.

Mail Boxes Etc. (2291-0282), has a store in Rohrmoser at Plaza Amistad, Local 8, 400 meters east of Plaza Mayor. They also have branches at Parque Empresarial Forum in Santa Ana (2204-7441) and in Curridabat, across from Pops Ice Cream (Tel: 8357-9429).

They provide the same services as the companies above plus packing and shipping, office supplies and a photocopy center. They also sell Hallmark greeting cards and stationery and offer notary and legal services and more.

These companies provide much faster service than the Costa Rican mail system to access mail order products from the United States, to enable clients to subscribe to magazines and newspapers at U.S. domestic rates, to help obtain replacement parts from abroad and to order directly from mail order catalogs such as Lands' End, J.C. Penney and L.L. Bean. Large automobile parts may also be ordered from the United States. You can pick up your correspondence directly from their offices or have your letters and packages picked up and delivered to your home or office at any time you choose. They will also get packages out of Customs for you and save you a lot of headaches.

I have used one of these services for more than four years and in general their service has been good. Because of the nature of my book business, I have an unusually high volume of incoming and outgoing mail. My letters, books, packages, monies and other mail reach their U.S. destinations almost as fast as if they were mailed from another city in the United States. This reliable service makes doing business from Costa Rica very easy.

Most of the private mail companies offer Certified Mail, Registered Mail, Express Mail and FedEx, UPS, DHL or other courier services.

Rates at any of these private mail services run from about $15 to $60 or more per month, depending on the amount of mail you receive and whether you have a business or personal account.

Members of ARCR also have access to these companies, paying no monthly fee, but only for the weight of the mail received. This is very useful for receiving small amounts of mail.

Note: Taxes, Customs charges and restrictions can make shipping goods into Costa Rica a complicated business, but numerous private mail companies offer services that can help residents navigate the sometimes confusing rules for bringing in goods.

There are a few restrictions on what can be brought into Costa Rica. Restricted items such as food and medicine require approval from the Health Ministry. The ministry gives special permission for medicines that treat terminal diseases. Permits can be obtained in person at the Health Ministry. However, some private mail companies will get the documents for you for a fee.

International goods brought into Costa Rica are subject to taxes and Customs handling charges, which also make international shipping more complicated than sending packages domestically. Taxes vary widely based on the product brought into the country.

Compact disks, for example, are subject to a one percent tax, while car parts are taxed at 30 percent and electronic parts at 50 percent.

Necessity Begets an International Mail Service

By Chuck Swett

Back in the good old days, the early sixties Jim Fendell had been here 10 plus years (arrived with parents in 1951), and I was just getting over the caravan like, Pan-American Airways milk-run through Central America, things were a lot different here. The nearest beach, Puntarenas, was four hours away, via Cambronero, with fog so thick you had to ride on the hood of the car and guide the driver. You could go to the movies for a few *colones*, fill up a VW for almost nothing, and a popular priced liter of milk cost a little over one *colón*. The train ride to Puntarenas was one big long party. And you could walk down any street in San José at any hour without ever considering yourself to be in danger.

But the one thing you wouldn't even consider doing , unless you really felt generous toward the customs officer population, was subscribe to National Geographic, T*he Saturday Evening Post* or *Life Magazine*. Playboy would probably not even make it off the plane, much less through the postal system. The custom was to find out who was traveling and ask them to bring that car part or special shampoo or the latest Beatles album, when they came back.

As the country and the expatriate colony grew, communications media began to introduce new goodies and remind the foreigners of things they were accustomed to at home but couldn't easily get in the local market.

Our innovative friend Jim began to recognize the need for an alternative means of establishing and regaining that "link to home" that was missing. A reliable way to get people's important mail safely to its destination, and to allow them to enjoy a "taste of home" in their adopted country. That need finally took shape in Aerocasillas, twelve years ago.

This company was envisioned as becoming "The best personalized network for receiving and sending documents and merchandise between the rest of the world and our country," This way both national and international markets were opened to our clients.

Pioneering the field of private international mail service in this country, Aerocasillas has built a growing user base of 25,000 satisfied customers, with over 3,000 active accounts. This is the result of over twelve years of constant dedication to fulfilling the needs of our clients and seeking ways to improve on the service we provide.

Aerocasillas is one of Costa Rica's private mail services

Customs handling rates begin at $2 for books and items worth up to $25, and rise up to $50 for items worth $1,000 or more, according to the Aerocasillas website **www.aeropost.com**.

Costa Rican residents can bring up to $500 worth of goods into the country tax-free once every six months, though the limit includes the item's cost, the shipping charges according to Customs, and any insurance on the item. Documentsfor the tax exemption are available from the Customs office at Juan Santamaría International Airport in Alajuela.

Mail companies, such as Aerocasillas, guide their customers through this process, which requires: an exemption alert form with information about the package and the supplier, to be submitted at least 24 hours before the package arrives; an original identification card or passport and three signed copies; a power of attorney form; and a commercial invoice.

Aerocasillas provides these forms on its website and charges $20 plus sales tax for the service.

Mailing from Costa Rica

For those of you who choose to send something to an address outside Costa Rica, there are certain regulations and options.

You should be aware that many countries restrict what types of items can be sent across their borders. The United States, for example, has special regulations for shipping goods such as coffee, liquor, fruit and other foods, medications and drugs. For shipping these items to the United States, see the website for the U.S. Food and Drug Adminstration. **www.fda.gov.**

International couriers such as DHL, UPS and FedEx, mentioned earlier in this chapter, can help with shipping items abroad. These companies handle a wide variety of shipping orders, large or small, and have extensive services to meet individual shipping and tracking needs. Although they offer high-speed, door-to-door shipping of documents and packages, their services can be on the expensive side.

DHL, for example, can ship from Costa Rica to Miami in 24 hours, and anywhere else in the Unites States in 48 hours. To Europe, DHL can get your package or letter there in three or four days.

Shipping through DHL can be done by first calling the company's Costa Rica call center open 8 a.m. to 6 p.m. at 209-6000. Their operators will answer questions and quote prices.

For next-day delivery to Seattle, a four-kilogram box would cost $123.30 and a letter would cost $40.66. To send a box to Miami would cost $83.93 and a letter $19.12. To ship the same size box to London, England would run $198.66 and the letter would cost $68.68.

DHL also provides an array of other services, such as online tracking and shipping and printable Customs forms, the details of which can be found on its Costa Rica-specific website, **www.dhl.co.cr/publish/cr/es.high.html.**

Jet Box (2253-5400) www.jetbox.com), a smaller, Costa Rican-based company that still has a global reach, also offers courier service, with personalized pricing. Senders can set up contracts for $3 to $8 per kilogram to the United States, for example, which is their most common destination. The pricing depends on volume, location and how regularly they ship. In addition, if a person regularly ships small items and wants to ship a large item, the company will offer a special price.

Another shipping company with membership-based rates is **Star Box** (2289-9393), which offers memberships as low as $2.50 a month. With that membership, clients have the right to send a certain weight of goods per month. The per-kilo cost depends on the membership.

Aerocasillas (2208-4848, **www.aerocasillas.com**), focuses mainly on shipping items into Costa Rica; however, it does ship mail and documents to the United States through Miami.

For larger items, a freight company such as **Ship to Costa Rica** (2258-8747 or from the United States or Canada 1-866-245-6923 toll-free) will have to be used. Shipping from Costa Rica to the east or west coast of the United States takes approximately 12 days, and only six days to Miami. To Europe, for example, the shipping time is from 15 to 20 days.

* **Part of this section is reprinted with permission of *The Tico Times.* See: www.ticotimes.net.**

10

GETTING AROUND

Air Travel to-in-and Around Costa Rica

As you know one of the advantages to living in Costa Rica is that it is conveniently located only a couple hours from the Unites States. There are flights from your home city to Costa Rica by way of Toronto, Los Angeles, Denver, Phoenix, Dallas, Houston, Atlanta, Miami, New York New Orleans and other cities.

Most flights arrive at **Juan Santamaría International Airport** (Tel: 2443-2622) the country's main airport, located about a half-hour northwest of San José. The airport now boasts a new terminal with restaurants and many shops. It was named the second best airport in the under-15 million passenger a year category by International Aerial Transport Association (IATA).

Many travelers choose to fly into **Daniel Oduber International Airport**, the country's other major airport, located near the city of Liberia. The main attraction here is the airport's proximity to the excellent Pacific beaches in the northern province of Guanacaste. Many carriers like Delta, Air Canada and American West now fly daily to Guanacaste. About 200,000 passengers enter yearly through this new airport.

However, the vast majority of flights continue to land at Juan Santamaría Airport. About 3 million passengers entered through this airport in 2007. The main airlines currently offering service from the United States to San José, Costa Rica, are **Continental** (800-231-0856), **Mexicana** (2531-7921), **Grupo Taca** (800-535-8780), **American** (800-433-7300), **Delta** (800-241-4141) **United** (800-538-2929) and **Frontier** (1-800-432-1FLY (359).

Some airline tickets are good for a year, but you need permission from Costa Rican Immigration to stay in the country longer than 90 days unless you are a resident or *pensionado*. Most airlines offer excursion rates and three-or-four week packages. Others, especially Canadian airlines, offer special group and charter rates. Fares are subject to availability, change and restrictions including advance purchase requirements, minimum stops or cancellation penalties. Remember, the main tourist season in Costa Rica runs from about Thanksgiving to Easter. This period coincides approximately with local vacations, so it is hard to find available space at this time of year. If you are planning to travel to or from Costa Rica during December, you may have to buy a ticket months in advance because of the Christmas holidays. However, if you get into a jam you can sometimes find space on a flight via Panama.

If you plan to travel or explore South America from Costa Rica, you can usually save money by flying to Miami and then buying a round-trip ticket to your destination. For instance, a one-way ticket from San José to Buenos Aires, Argentina can cost more than a round trip ticket from Miami to Buenos Aires.

Tico Travel (800-493-8426) and **The Travel Store** (www.allcostaricatravel.com e-mail: travel@costaricatravelstore.com) specialize in trips to Costa Rica. **Retirement/Relocation Tours** may be booked through **Live in Costa Rica Tours** (800-365-2342).

UPDATE: There are plans to build a new international airport in the southern zone. However, this project is still on the drawing board.

International Airlines Located in San José Costa Rica

Airline	Phone
Air Canada	2243-1860
Air France	2220-4119
Airport Information	2443-1737/2443-2622
Alitalia (via Cpoa or Taca)	2295-6820
American Airlines, La Sabana	2257-1266
American West	2430-6690
Avianca	2233-3066
British Airways (via United Airlines	1-800-Airways
Continental	2442-1904

A Travel Business is Born

By Robert Hodel

So there I was, preparing for the culmination of three years of law when I realized that sinking feeling just was not going to go away.

That feeling I was referring to was the fact that I did not want to spend the rest of my life, nor even one minute for that matter, as a lawyer.

As soon as I accepted that fact I was in a quandary. What was I to do?

It was then I remembered from somewhere that the key to any successful business venture one may choose is to: 1) do what you like and 2) do what you know or do well.

With that in mind I pondered my future both day and night. Finally, I realized the thing I liked most to do was travel and the place I knew best, other than my home town, was Costa Rica.

I knew the best place to go and when. I also knew how to get the best prices on airfare, rental cars and hotels So after a long phone call with my brother, who was even more knowledgeable than I, I had a plan.

We would start a travel company dedicated primarily to Costa Rica and we would call it Tico Travel. I would move back to Costa Rica and introduce myself to the hotels, car rental companies and tour operators that we wanted to work with plus stay on top of any new developments that would be of interest to our clients. My brother moved to Florida and opened our office and was able to give our clients expert information on Costa Rica with a "*gringo*" point of view.

Within a short amount of time we became the agency of choice for people who travel frequently to Costa Rica and also for the first time visitor.

Along the way we learned many things. For instance, just because it makes sense does not mean it works that way.

We also found no matter how much we advertised, that over 80% of our clients were either clients' referrals or repeat customers, as a testimony to how important one's reputation is in this part of the world.

I have been told many times that one could make many times more money with the same effort if we were in the United States.

That may be so but I have been told something else by a longtime resident here,"We are not here for the money, we are here for the lifestyle."

See Tico Travel on the Internet at **www.ticotravel.com**.

Airline	Phone
Copa	2223-2672
Cubana	2221-6918
Delta	2440-4805/2257-4141
Grupo Taca	2296-9533
Iberia	2257-8266
KLM	2220-4111
Luthansa	2221-7444
Martin Air	2232-3246
Mexicana	2295-6969/2257-6334
Spirit	800-756-7117
United	0-800-521-243
USAirways	2520-0593
West Caribbean	2291-0580

Domestic airlines

Smaller domestic airlines such as **Sansa**, **Nature Air** or chartered planes called air taxis, are used for flights within the country. Domestic airlines use four-to-15-passenger planes. Both of these airlines, are reasonably priced, depending on your destination. Sansa flies to the beach cities of Golfito, Quepos, Barra del Colorado, Sámara, Nosara, and Tamarindo. We recommend purchasing your tickets in advance, especially during the heavy tourist season (December to May.) These flights get you to your designation quickly and economically, save you time, and give you the thrill of viewing Costa Rica's spectacular landscape from above.

Sansa's office is in the Grupo Taca office. Call 2221-9414, or e-mail; info@flysansa.com or sansa@lacsa.atlas-com or see www.flysansa.com for flight times and reservations. Some travel agencies in San José also make reservations.

Nature Air offers domestic flights. Call 2299-6070 or see www.natureair.com. Charters are available at 2257-0766 or www.costaricacharters.com. Also look in the yellow pages under "Taxis Aereos."

Traveling by City Bus

Bus fares from San José to the surrounding suburbs are very cheap. On urban and inter-urban buses, you pay the driver as you board.

Here is a list of where to catch a bus from the center of San José to surrounding neighborhoods.

Destination	Location
Alajuela	Ave. 2 across from Parque La Merced
Alajuelita	Ave. 6/8, Calle 8
Aserrí	Ave. 4/6, Calle 7
Barrio México	Ave. 3, Calle 3
Barrio Luján	Ave 2, Calles 5 /7
Calle Blancos	Ave. 5, Calles 1/3
Coronado	Ave. 7, Calle 0
Curridabat	Ave. 6, Calles 3/5
Desamparados	Ave. 4, Calles 5/7
Escazú	Ave. 0/1, Calle 16
Guadalupe	Ave.3, Calle 0
Hatillos	Ave. 2/6 Calle 6, Ave. 4 Calle 2
Heredia	Ave. 2 next to La Merced Church
Moravia	Ave. 3 Calles 3/5
Paso Ancho	Ave.4 and 6, Calle 2
Pavas	Ave. 1, Calles 16/20
Sabana Cementerio	Ave. 2, Calles 8 /10
Sabana Estadio	Ave.2, Calles 2/4
Sabanilla	Ave. 0-2, Calle 9
San Pedro	Ave. 0, Calles 9/11
Santana	Ave. 1/3, Calle16
Santo Domingo	Ave. 7/9, Calles 2
Tibás	Ave. 5/7, Calle 13
Tres Ríos	Avenida Central/ 2, Calle 13
Zapote	Ave. 2/4, Calle 5

Buses provide inexpensive transportation to any destination in the country

Traveling by bus around San José or to the surrounding suburbs may seem quite difficult to a newcomer. However, once you get the hang of it, you will find it a surprisingly easy and affordable way to travel. Most expatriates who do not have cars use the city's excellent bus system. A few who own cars prefer taking buses to avoid traffic and paying for parking.

If you do not know where to catch a specific city bus to your destination, then you will have to ask someone. If you cannot find an English speaker who knows or your Spanish is not adequate, then go to the tourism office below the *Plaza de la Cultura* in the heart of San José. They will provide you with a free map of San José's bus stops. Also, you might want to ask a policeman who can usually help.

When you finally find your bus stop, you should not assume that every bus that stops there goes to your destination. It is not unusual to have several buses with different routes using the same bus stop. When in doubt, try to ask someone who is waiting, "*¿A dónde va este autobús?*" (Where does this bus go?). Another thing you can do is look at the sign displayed horizontally above the windshield or on the lower left-hand-corner of the front window. These signs will list the final destination of the bus.

Once you figure out which bus to take, have your change in hand and be ready to pay the bus fare. You can usually find out how much the fare is by asking one of the people waiting or by looking at the sign in the bus's window. Do not be in a hurry to board, since some passengers may exit through the front door.

When you get inside the bus, hand the driver your fare. If you do not have the exact amount the driver will make change. Try to avoid giving the driver anything larger than a 2,000 *colón* bill. Be careful not to stand between the electronic counter or the driver will get mad. They were installed to replace the turnstiles most buses used to have. These devices have an electric eye and count the number of people who use the bus. Once, a friend of mine boarded a bus, and his young son accidentally stood in front of the electric counter. The driver made my friend pay an extra fare or he would have had to pay the amount out of his own pocket.

Next, you will need to find a seat. It is advisable not to sit on the sunny side of the bus. A large number of buses have large windows with no curtains. If you sit on the side the sun hits, you may feel like you are under a magnifying glass. However, many of the newer buses have curtains you can draw to keep out the sun.

During rush hour, buses tend to be very crowded and you often have to stand if you cannot find a seat. In this case, take hold of one of the horizontal bars. Most buses start and stop with a jerky motion and it is easy to fall if you are standing and not holding on to something.

Be sure to let the driver know about a block before you want to get off. You can do this by pulling the horizontal cord next to the window or by pressing an overhead button. Buses usually have one of these devices. If you cannot locate the cord or button, or if either one of them does not work, then yell, *"Parada!"* (Stop!), so the driver will know to let you off at the next stop. If you do not know at which bus stop to get off, ask the driver or someone else on the bus. Usually the name of a street, neighborhood or landmark will suffice. If you let the driver know where you want to be let off upon boarding, he will usually remember to tell you when you reach your stop.

Here is how to find your busstop: **http://www.thebusschedule.com**

Bus Travel Around Costa Rica

For a very low cost ($2 to $8, or about $1 per hour of driving time) you can take a bus to almost anywhere in the country. Most Costa Ricans do not own cars, so they depend on buses for traveling to other parts of the country. Riding a bus provides the perfect opportunity to get to know people on a personal basis, see the lovely countryside and learn something about the country and the culture. Most buses used for these longer trips are modern and very comfortable. Unlike in some parts of Latin America, Costa Rica's buses are not filled with chickens and other small animals and standing is not allowed. Buses are crowded on weekends and holidays, so buy your tickets in advance or get to the station early. Be sure to check for schedule changes.

The following are bus schedules to popular destinations in Costa Rica. All buses depart from the San Jose area. Note that bus schedules may change and fares are approximate. Contact the bus terminal for the most recent schedule and fees.

- ALAJUELA (Airport): $0.75; every 10 minutes 4:20 a.m.-11:00 p.m.; after 11:00 p.m. buses depart every 30 minutes for the airport; 30 minutes. Departs from the intersection of Avenida 2 and Calles 12/14. 2222-5325.

- ARENAL VOLCANO/LA FORTUNA: $4; 6:15 a.m., 8:40 a.m. and 11:30 a.m.; 4 hours. Departs from the intersection of Calle 12 and Avenida 7. 2255-0567.

- BRAULIO CARRILLO PARK/GUAPILES: $1.85; every hour 5:30 a.m.-10:00 p.m.; weekends last departure at 9:00 p.m.; 45 minutes; get off at the Quebrada Gonzalez Station or the Zurqui Station; wait on highway for return bus. Departs from the intersection of Calle 12 and Avenidas 7/9. 2222-0610.

- CAHUITA NATIONAL PARK: $6.75; 6:00 a.m., 10:00 a.m., 12:00 p.m., 2:00 p.m. and 4:00 p.m.; 4 hours. Departs from the Terminal del Caribe, located on Avenida 13 and Calle Central. 2257-8129.

- COCO BEACH: $5; 8:00 a.m., 2:00 p.m., and 4:00 p.m.; 5 hours. Departs from Avenida 5 and Calles 10/12. Buses also depart from and return to Liberia daily en route to Coco. 2222-1650.

- DOMINICAL: 5:30 a.m. and 3:00 p.m.; 7 hours. Departs from Avenidas 1/3 and Calle 16 (Coca Cola Station). 2223-5567. Also from San Isidro: $2; 7:00, 9:00 a.m., 11:30 a.m., 3:30 p.m. and 4:00 p.m.; 1 hour. Departs from two blocks south of the church. 2771-2550.

- FLAMINGO BEACH: $8.25; 8:00 a.m., 10:30 a.m. and 3:00 p.m.; 6 hours. Departs from the intersection of Calle 20 and Avenidas 1/3. 2221-7202.

- GOLFITO: $12; 7:00 a.m. and 3:30 p.m. (direct, no stops); 8 hours. Departs from the intersection of Avenida 5 and Calles 14/16. 2222-2666

- HEREDIA: $0.60; every 10 minutes 5:00 a.m.-midnight; 25 minutes. Buses depart from the intersection of Calle 1 and Avenidas 7/9 and Calle 4 and Avenidas 5/7. 2233-8392 or 2261-7171.

- IRAZU VOLCANO: $2; 8:00 a.m.; 1.5 hours. Buses depart from the intersection of Avenida 2 and Calles 1/3. 2272-0651.

- JACO BEACH: $2.60; 5:00 a.m., 7:30 a.m., 11:00 a.m., 1:00 p.m., 3:00 p.m., 5:00 p.m. and 7:00 p.m.; 3 hours. Departs from Avenidas 1/3 and Calle 16 (Coca Cola Station). 2223-1109.

- LANKESTER GARDENS/PARAISO: $0.75; every 5 minutes 4:30 a.m.-10:00 p.m.; 20 minutes; ask to be dropped off at Lankester Garden Turnoff, then walk seven blocks to entrance. Departs in Cartago from Avenida 1 and Calle 4. 2574-6609.

- LIBERIA: $5.75; every hour 6:00 a.m.-8:00 p.m. (19:00 departure on Fridays only); 4 hours. Departs from the intersection of Calle 14 and Avenidas 1/3 (Liberia Terminal. 2222-1650.

- LIMON: $4.50; every hour 6:00 a.m.-6:00 p.m. (direct/nonstop buses depart every :30); 2.5 hours. Buses depart from the intersection of Avenida Central and Calle 3 (Terminal del Caribe). 2222-0610.

- MANZANILLO: $8.75; 12:00 p.m.; 4.5 hours. Departs from the intersection of Avenida 13 and Calle Central (Terminal del Caribe). 2257-8129.

- MONTEVEDE/SANTA ELENA: $5; 6:30 a.m. and 2:30 p.m.; 5 hours. Departs from the intersection of Calle 12 and Avenidas 7/9 (Terminal Atlantico Norte). 2645-5159.

- MANUEL ANTONIO/QUEPOS (Direct/Nonstop): $6.50; 6:00 a.m., 9:00 a.m., 12:00 p.m., 12:30 p.m., 6:00 p.m. and 7:30 p.m.; 4 hours; Departs from Avenidas 1/3 and Calle 16 (Coca Cola Station). 2223-5567.

- MANUEL ANTONIO/QUEPOS (Indirect): $6.50; 7:00 a.m., 10:00 a.m., and 4:00 p.m.; 5 hours. Departs from Avenidas 1/3 and Calle 16 (Coca Cola Station) 2223-5567.

- NICOYA: $5.50; 6:00 a.m., 10:00 a.m., 1:30 p.m., 3:00 p.m., and 5:00 p.m.; 6 hours. Departs from the intersection of Avenida 5 and Calles 14/16 (Alfaro Terminal). Buses also depart from and return to Liberia daily en route to Nicoya. 2222-2666.

- NOSARA BEACH: $7; 5:30 a.m.; 6 hours. Departs from the intersection of Avenida 5 and Calles 14/16 (Alfaro Terminal). Buses also depart from Nicoya at 4:45 a.m., 10:00 a.m., 12:00 p.m., 3:00 p.m., and 5:30 p.m. ($2; 2 hours). 2222-2666.

- PANAMA/HERMOSA BEACHES: $7.50; 3:30 p.m.; 6 hours. Departs from the intersection of Calle 20 and Avenidas 1/3. Buses also depart from Liberia several times daily. 2221-7202.

- POAS VOLCANO: $6.75 (roundtrip); 8:30 a.m.; 2.5 hours. Departs from the intersection of Avenida Segunda and Calles 12/14. 2222-5325.

- PUERTO JIMENEZ DE OSA: $12; 5:00 a.m. and 12:00 p.m.; 8 hours. Bus departs from the intersection of Calle 14 and Avenidas 9/11 (Blanco Lobo Station). 2257-4121.

- PUERTO VIEJO DE TALAMANCA (Caribbean): $7.75; 6:00 a.m., 10:00 a.m., 12:00 p.m., 2:00 p.m. and 4:00 p.m.; 4.5 hours. Departs from the intersection of Avenica 13 and Calle Central (Terminal del Caribe). Buses also depart daily from Limon. 2257-8129.

- PUNTARENAS DIRECT: $3.75; every hour 6:00 a.m.-7:00 p.m.; 2.5 hours. Departs from the intersection of Avenida 12 and Calle 16. 2222-8231.

- SAMARA BEACH: $6.50; 12:00 p.m.; 5.5 hours. Departs from the intersection of Avenida 5 and Calles 14/16 (Alfaro Terminal). Buses also depart from and return to Samara daily en route to Nicoya. 2222-2666.

- SAN ISIDRO DEL GENERAL: $3.50; every hour 5:00 a.m.-6:00 p.m.; 3 hours. Departs from the intersection of Avenida 5 and Calles 14/17. 2222-2666.

- SARCHI HANDICRAFT: $1.50; 12:15 p.m., 5:30 p.m. and 6:10 p.m.; 1.5 hours. Departs from the intersection of Calle 18 and Avenidas 5/7. 2258-2004.

- TAMARINDO BEACH: $8; 11:30 a.m. and 3:30 p.m.; 6 hours. Departs from the intersection of Avenida 3 and Calles 14/16 (Alfaro Terminal). 2222-2666.

If your destination is not listed, check with a local travel agency or some knowledgeable person who is familiar with bus schedules and knows the different bus stops.

Bus tickets may be purchased online at **www.CostaRicaBusTicket.com.** This company covers most areas north and west of San José. You may contact them at **365-9678.**

Interbus (Tel. 2283-5573, fax 283-7655, e-mail vsftrip@racsa.co.cr, www.interbusonline.com) and **Fantasy Tour/Gray Line** (Tel. 2220-2126, fax 220-2393, e-mail fantasy@racsa.co.cr, www.graylinecostarica.com) offer direct tours between many of the country's major tourist attractions. Both companies offer transportation to more than 40 destinations and have offices around the country. *Costa Rica by Bus* is a great book that covers bus routes, fares and more. To purchase a copy, see **www.costaricabybus.com**.

Bus Travel to and from Costa Rica

If you want to travel to Guatemala, Panama or other Central American countries, you can use the bus services listed. If you want to live in Costa Rica permanently without being a legal residents (we DON'T recommend this), you can take a bus to Panama or Nicaragua, return to Costa Rica after 72 hours, and thus renew your papers so you can remain legally in the country for another 90 days. Many foreigners living as perpetual tourists in Costa Rica go through this procedure every few months in order to avoid Immigration hassles.

From time to time, the Immigration asks to see a return ticket before extending tourist cards. So it is a good idea to buy an inexpensive bus ticket to a neighboring country to prove you can leave the country.

- **Tica Bus** (tel: 222-18954), *Avenidas* 2 and 4 between *Calles* 9 and 11, offers bus service to the rest of Central America.
- **San José to Panama City** leaves daily at 10 p.m. from the Tica Bus Terminal. The 542-mile journey takes 18 hours.
- **San José to David (Panama)** leaves daily at 7:30 a.m. from *Avenida* 5, *Calle* 14. It makes the 240 mile-trip in nine hours.
- **San José to Managua** leaves the **Sirca Bus Company** at 6 a.m. The 270-mile trip takes about 10 hours.
- **San José to Guatemala** leaves daily at 6 a.m. from *Avenida* 4, between *Calles* 9 and 11. This trip takes two and a half days.
- San José to Honduras leaves at 6 a.m. daily.

* Check **www.horariodebuses.com** for more information.

Traveling by Train

Costa Rica's rail system was originally built in the late 1800s to serve the coffee and banana industry. One line ran from San José to Puntarenas on the Pacific coast and another from San José to Puerto Limón on the Caribbean. In 1995 regular passenger train service on Costa Rica's two main rail lines was shut down due to economic losses. The famous "Jungle Train" that ran from San José to the Caribbean port of Limón was discontinued because of earthquake-caused landslides. Starting in 2002, the Railroad Institute (INCOFER) offered twice weekly passenger service to Puntarenas. With any luck, full train service to both coasts will resume someday.

Tico Train Tour

By John Vickery

About a month ago I was walking down the train tracks over in Sabana Sur when I thought I heard a train whistle). Must have been the previous evenings *cerveza* confusing my hearing as I'd only seen one train in 6 months. I checked behind me and here was a 6 car train bearing down on me at the incredible speed of maybe 35 kilometers per hour. I stepped off the tracks with plenty of time to spare and watched it pass. There were people (old and young) hanging out the windows waving and smiling. Hmmmmm... I thought it would be fun to ride a train sometime. Where would this train be going, and how could I get a ride? I thought I'd done my homework after moving here. Obviously I missed something. Finding new experiences in a new land is exciting.

The next weeks Tico Times had a small article about the train I saw. I visited their web page **http://www.ticotraintour.com/** and liked what I saw and fired off an Email. I received an almost instant reply in English and they sent 5 or 6 pictures of the train ride that are not on the website. There were two small problems with the web page. The page said the train goes to the East coast but it goes to Caldera (west coast) and two of the Email addresses (both RACSA) did not work . The working address is: **americatravel@ice.co.cr** Anyway, we along with 4 friends took that train ride yesterday (8th of May) and had a good time. This was a spur of the moment decision. I received a phone call around noon on Saturday (7th of May) from a *Tico* friend asking if we'd be interested in taking the train the next day if he could get tickets? "Of course", I said. Less than an hour later I received another call saying everything was set and a taxi would be picking us up at 7:15 am at our front door. It was on time and we were off! I had no idea where the train station was in Alajuela but the taxi driver did and when we were dropped off, another group was waiting on the platform at the (seemingly) deserted train station. It's difficult to describe but everyone on that platform appeared quite exited about the upcoming train ride. I know I was and my expectations were rewarded nicely.

The company has an office in Alajuela in addition to the one at the Pacific train station in San Jose and they claim that tickets must be purchased in advance. One of our party joined us at the last minute and purchased her ticket on the train. Since we all reside in Alajuela we really did not wish to go into San Jose to catch that train at 7:00, so we asked for another pick up location. The train stopped and picked us (along with 6 others) up at the station in *Ciruelas* (spelling) here in Alajuela at 7:45.

It is a very pleasant ride through countryside and towns that are not seen from the highways. Most times you can hang out the widows taking pictures or just observing the passing countryside. Beware that this is not a routine train and there are places the trees and scrub are not trimmed back. I had a few tree branches hit my head (no bigee) and there were a few gorges (through the rock walls) where the clearance between the train and the wall is measured in inches. Just watch where you are going when you dangle out the window. There is a huge bridge just before Atenas that anyone afraid of heights should not view from the widow as you cross. Fantastic site! If you are not afraid of heights, get your camera out and take pictures.

There is a quick one minute stop just before Atenas for people to observe and take pictures of an old turn of the centuryelectric locomotive. You'll never feel any uphill grade during this ride, but think about it. How do you get out of the central valley without going over the mountains? Carefully keep sticking your head out the window and watch where you're going.

Quick aside here: I would advise not choosing a passenger car directly behind the locomotive as the engineer is constantly blasting the horn and it is very loud.

Attention: If you pick the absolute last car from San Jose, (kind of quiet) You'll then be in the absolute first car (right behind the locomotive) on the return trip. That's a hint for you. Think about it. I'm betting only about 50% of those horn blasts are required for intersections and the other 50% is to alert everyone that we are coming through so they can come out and wave to us. All ages come out but the smiles on the kid's faces are contagious. You can't help but wave and smile back! It's unbelievable as to the number of folks who come out to wave and smile.

No alcohol is allowed on the train and smoking is only permitted on the little walkway between the cars. (be careful)

This is one example of the personal responsibility that I love CR for. If you wish to stand on that platform and smoke. It is your responsibility to hold onto the hand rail. If not, you could fall off the train very easily and you might not be missed for miles or hours. There is NO big brother government watching you here. Adjust!

After passing through Atenas (no stop) you get some nice views of three of the bridges that someday may be part of that long talked about new road. One bridge appears be having quite a bit of excavation work being done at one end. I have seen very nice views up in the Atenas area from the highway (?) but those views pale compared to the scenes from the train.

Next stop (maybe 5 minutes) is in the middle of some street in downtown Orotina.

The train ride continues and everyone is watching out the windows when it appears that the train somehow has left the tracks and is driving down the road. There is pavement on both sides of the train and *pulperías* and shops on both sides. WOW!

There is nothing happening at this stop until the return trip when the train is swamped by people selling many different food stuffs. After this stop we continue on with more horn blasts and more people coming out to wave at us. (Smile!)

Lovers take note: Just before arriving in Caldera you will spend about a minute in absolute darkness (you literally cannot see your hand in front of your face) traveling through a tunnel. It's fun! Arriving in Caldera around 11:00 you have two options. You can hang around Caldera without much to do except for anyone who likes to fish. There is a bridge here that quite a few people fish from. I don't know what you might catch and have no idea of bait/lures, but that br idge appears to be quite popular). Or you can buy a round trip ticket on one of the buses already there at the train stop for 1,000 colones for the round trip ride into Puntarenas. . I was not thrilled with Puntarenas. I have since learned that if I had read up on Puntarenas I would have many activities to occupy me while the women went shopping.

We males found other things to do for the 4 1/2 hours (bars etc) Perhaps I'm a little spoiled bt Manuel Antonio, but I wasn't impressed by the beach in Puntarenas. It is swimmable but I'd not go out of my way to swim there.

Got back on the bus at 3:45 and back to the train. I wonder how they turned that train around. The passenger cars were in the same position as when we arrived but the locomotive and caboose had switched ends. My simple mind wonders about these little things. The ride back was fun too except for about an hour in the rain. We had to shut the windows and it got hot and stuffy during this period.

Odds and ends:

Round trip fare is $12.50 for residents and $30 for tourists. Obviously this is a tourist operation but I'm guessing 90% of the riders were *ticos*. Each car has a host with a small megaphone to inform you of points of interest etc. Free coffee, juice and snacks are providedon the morning ride and other soft drinks/water and food may be purchased. The ride eachway is approximately 4 hours. For females: I would not even consider sitting on the toilet seat.

Once darkness descended there were only two (very weak) lights in our car. Enough to see around you but don't consider trying to read anything! Just about the time all the exhausted travelers decide to take a quick nap, you wonder what that loud annoying noise from the next car back is. It keeps getting louder and louder and seems to be coming closer. What is it?! Now it is in your car and you can't get away from it! Can you say mini-carnival? A bunch of fools (I say that lovingly) in costumes and masks comes up the aisle in your car singing and playing music and attempting to get you out in the aisle to dance. There is no arguing with them.... either you loudly applaud them or you dance with them. Does anyone have a camera? I do! It is a fun wake up call!

Heredia's new commuter train

Due to an effort to reduce traffic in the metropolitan San José area two interurban commuter lines were started recently. One train runs from east to west from Pavas to the Universidad Latina in San Pedro.

Another line runs for about eight miles from behind the Central Market in the city of Heredia to the former Atlantic Train Station just east of downtown San José. It was announced in September of 2009 that INCOFER plans to expand train service to Alajuela and Cartago. Plans call for repairing the existing train lines for this service. At one time trains used these routes before they were put out of service, so the tracks are there but have to be refurbished.

The government also announced that they have $100 million available from the Interamerican Development Bank that is to be used for an electric train from San José to Heredia. The (TREM) or Metropolitan Electric Train is expected to beginning by 2013. Initially the only service will be between San José and Heredia, but the line will eventually be expanded to other areas.

Here is a site to find the train schedules: **http://horariodetren.com/cr/index.php?lang=en**

Costa Rica's Taxis

As mentioned in Chapter 3, it is not necessary to own an automobile if you live in San José or in any major city or town because taxis are plentiful and inexpensive. The country´s buses are cheaper, but taxis are the best way to get from point A to point B.

Taxis registered with the Ministry of Public Works and Transportation (MOPT) are red with a yellow triangle on both front doors. The triangle contains the taxi's license number, which begins with the letter(s) of the province where the cab is licensed and registered, followed by a "P" for province. For example, a taxi registered in San José province has a license plate number beginning with "SJP."

Taxis charge 510 *colones* ($.85) for the first kilometer and 510 *colones* ($0.85) per kilometer thereafter. You can rent cabs by the hour or by the day. There is a "delay" fare of 5,100 *colones* ($8.50) an hour when a taxi is going less than 10 kilometers an hour (in case of traffic jams or bad roads) for more than six minutes. Drivers cannot legally charge more to pick up or drop off a passenger at a hotel or mall, if the service is at night or if the passenger is a foreigner.

If you want the driver to wait while you do an errand or some other business, there is an hourly rate of about 2,800 *colones* ($3). There is an official rate/fare sheet published and the taxi drivers usually have a copy. You may be able to get him to show it to you or even make you a copy.

If you have to go more than 12 kilometers outside the metropolitan area, there is another rate schedule. A trip of about five kilometers will cost 2,500 *colones* ($2.50), 10 kilometers will cost 5,000 *colones* ($10.00) and 20 kilometers will cost 10,000 *colones* ($20.00). In this case the driver and the passenger should negotiate the fare (do this in advance).

Rural taxis charge taxis charge 510 *colones* ($0.85) for the first kilometer and 610 *colones* ($1.20) per kilometer thereafter. There is a "delay" fare of $6,700 ($11.20) an hour .

If you are planning to use a driver/taxi for say, half a day, you may be able to agree upon a flat rate for the time. Once decided you could ask the driver to write down the amount on a piece of paper 'so you can be sure you understand correctly' how much it is. A rate based on a certain number of hours agreed upon in advance is more likely to be honored without the driver trying to gouge a little more at the end.

If you have had your *taxista* help with loading a bunch of things or several heavy things or he has been extra helpful, you may want to include a modest tip at the end. Just remember, taxis generally don't get tips (except maybe the orange taxis from the airport), so don't overdo the tipping.

Nearly all taxis have computerized meters called ***marías***. Always insist that your taxi driver use his meter, and be sure to ask about rates before traveling anywhere. Even if you negotiate a flat rate, drivers are required to put on the meter. The meter should display the starting fare on its face. Drivers are required by law to use their meters, even if they tell you they are not. The meter must be in working order. If the *maría* is missing or broken, you might be overcharged for the trip. Always tell the driver, *"Ponga la maría por favor* or *"Con la maría, por favor."* (Please turn on the meter). If the driver won't, get out and take another cab. Don't worry; there will almost always be another nearby.

Many city cab drivers get upset if you try to pay with large bills. If you intend to pay with a big bill, ask the driver if he has change before boarding the cab to avoid last minute misunderstandings. If you tell a driver beforehand you are going to pay with a large bill, he'll usually stop along the way to get change at a gas station.

Be aware that some unscrupulous taxi drivers will take a circuitous route to your destination, which will rack up extra fare.

Here are some tips you may want to follow under certain circumstances when traveling alone by taxi:

1. Check license plates.
2. Don't get into taxis with polarized windows.
3. Don' t get into taxis without license plates.
4. Check that the identification coincides with the driver and is up-to date.
5. Don' t wait for a taxi in the street at night.
6. Once inside the car, call home by phone (cellular), giving the license plates and a description of the vehicle, and how long it will take you to arrive. If there is nobody at home, fake the conversation.
7. Never get into a taxi when there is more than one person inside.

Most taxi drivers are polite, but if you are overcharged or dissatisfied with service, you can take the driver's permit number, usually on the visor of his taxi or his license number and complain to the MOPT office. You can do this in person, by letter or over the telephone (2257-7798, ext. 2512).

Taxies can be found around every public square and park, outside discotheques, on most busy streets, and in front of government buildings and most hotels.

Be careful, since many taxis parked in front of hotels may overcharge. Some of the drivers claim they work exclusively for the hotel and will overcharge you. Taxi drivers at hotels justify their high rates because they sometimes have to wait for customers.

WARNING: Many of the taxi drivers who work in front of hotels will try to sell you property, offer you seemingly good contacts or other services. Your best bet is to deal only with professionals in your area of interest and not depend on taxi drivers for these services.

They will try to double the fare to account for driving back to the hotel, their home base, empty. Many times the explanation is fair and the driver is honest. Also, if you have a complaint and the driver works for the hotel you have immediate recourse: the hotel's management.

It is difficult to find a taxi during the rainy season, especially in the afternoon, which is when it usually rains. You may also have trouble getting a cab on weekdays or during rush hour between 7 and 9 a.m. and from 4:30 to 6:30 p.m., as in most cities.

To hail a taxi just yell, "Taxi!" If a taxi is parked just ask the driver, "*¿Libre?*" (free) to see if he is available. If the taxi is available, he will usually nod or say, "*Sí*" (yes). If you want to stay on a taxi driver's good side, NEVER slam the taxi's doors; taxis are expensive in Costa Rica and drivers try to keep them in good shape.

Some people work as informal taxi drivers using their own unmarked cars. Many look like regular cabs but without the yellow triangles on the front doors. They are called ***piratas*** (pirates) by the locals, and will often approach if they see you looking for a taxi. Since they do not have meters, we advise you not to hire any of these vehicles for transportation. Most do not have insurance to cover their passengers in the event of an accident. If you do have to take one, remember there is no meter, so negotiate the fare before you get in or you may run the risk of being overcharged.

A lot of working-class locals depend on informal taxis called *colectivos.* What they do is take an unmarked mini-van instead of a bus. They pay less and get to their destinations more quickly. These collective pirate taxis operate only during rush hour and in the areas of Desamparados, Hatillo, Escazú, Vázquez de Coronado, Tres Ríos and Pavas.

Taxis are a bargain in Costa Rica

If you call a taxi, be able to give your exact location in Spanish so the taxi driver knows where to pick you up. If your command of Spanish is limited, have a Spanish speaker write down directions to your destination. I know one old grouchy *gringo* who has never made an effort to learn a word of Spanish. He has all the directions of the places he has to go written in Spanish for taxi drivers. If you phone for a taxi, the driver can turn on the meter when he gets the call and charge for the driving time to your location.

Airport pick-ups can be arranged in advance by calling one of the taxi companies. We recommend doing this, especially during the rainy season, when it is difficult to get a taxi when you need one.

Telephone numbers of the local taxi companies are in the yellow pages of the telephone book under the heading "Taxi." **Alfaro** (2221-8466), **Coopeguaria** (2226-1366), **Coopeirazú** (2254-3211) and **Coopetico** (2224-7979) have taxis available 24-hours a day. (See the directory in the back of this book for a list of taxi companies.)

Many of these companies also rent big trucks, or ***taxis de carga***, at a low hourly rate. These vehicles can be very helpful if you ever have to move furniture.

Automobile Rentals

Major international car rental agencies and private car rentals are conveniently located all over San José. Most rental agencies operate like those in the United States. The cost of renting a vehicle depends on the year, model and make of car. You must be at least 21 years old and have a valid driver's license, an American Express, Visa or Master Card or be able to leave a large deposit. Remember, insurance is extra, mandatory by law and quite expensive.

Always phone or make arrangements for car rentals well in advance. For a list of car rental agencies, see the phone directory provided in the back of this book, the yellow pages or *The Tico Times* for ads. I recommend **Prego Rent-A-Car**, which offers all kinds of vehicles to meet your every need. Unlike many car rental companies, they give generous discounts.

The Tico Times has ads for private drivers or chauffeurs. This is a good alternative to taxis but can be expensive. I know quite a few people who do not like to drive and prefer to hire private drivers instead of taking taxis whenever they have to do errands or other business.

Driving in Costa Rica

If you intend to remain in Costa Rica, it is an excellent idea to get your Costa Rican drivers license. This is because, at present foreigners can obtain

Round Trip Back to Paradise

By the late Jay Trettien

"I never had more money or had more fun than when I lived in Costa Rica," was my response when a fellow bartender friend from southern California suggested we open a bar in Baja California.

"If you're heading South of the Border, you may as well go to Costa Rica, where the weather is nicer and the people more friendly," I said.

I was first invited to Costa Rica in 1973 by a college friend who worked for the Bank of America. Through the bank he had met an American who needed help with a bar he had just bought. My friend suggested that maybe I would come to Costa Rica to help out. A late-night phone call, and two weeks later I arrived from New York. After a few weeks of working together, the bar owner and I had developed trust and a friendship and, on the strength of a handshake, I became a partner in what was to become Central America's most popular "*Gringo*" rock and roll bar, Ye Pub. *Gringos* and *ticos* loved the place. After living in Costa Rica for a while , I was granted a *cédula*, or Costa Rican "green card."

But the time came to sell. Costa Rica had been enjoying a spectacular boom but with small countries as fast as it goes up, it can go down. After three years we sold.

With a girlfriend that was driving me nuts it was easy to leave Costa Rica. I visited every country in South America. I had already seen almost all of Europe, most of the United States and Canada. So, I ended up in Australia and New Zealand for about four years, finally washing up on the shores of southern California.

I began thinking about Costa Rica again and made a brief visit about 12 years ago to be pleasantly surprised that I still had friends in the country. I returned to California, loaded up the old Pontiac and ended up back in Costa Rica.

A lucky coincidence got me my *cédula* back when the Costa Rican government declared an amnesty for all foreigners, trying to get a grip on all the illegal Nicaraguans in the country.

Now I'm working at a popular San José hotel bar. I think I have about $150 under my mattress, but I have a good time and a lot of fun.

When guests ask me how long I've been in Costa Rica, I say, " I don't remember...10-12 years." And that's the truth, I don't really remember.

Guest, "Do you like Costa Rica?" "NO! I'm here on the United States Witness Protection Program, but they could only find this low-profile job for me!"

a Costa Rican license if they possess a valid foreign license, "valid" meaning during the 90 days after entry.

You may use your current driver's license for up to 90 days if you are a tourist. After 90 days you must have a Costa Rican driver's license, but obtain it before your 90 days are up. If you are not driving on a valid license, you have no insurance coverage even if you paid for it .If you renew your tourist visa by leaving the country and returning, your non-Costa Rica driver's license will be good for another period of time equal to your visa.

All permanent residents and *pensionados* must have a Costa Rican license to drive in Costa Rica.

It is relatively easy to obtain a license if you meet the requirements. If you're a foreigner then the first time you get your Costa Rica license you have to travel to San José to visit the main COSEVI office (Lke our DMV). It is located on the main road through La Uruca about 100 meters from the Banco Nacional on the main road through Uruca and about 200 meters from the Shell gas station. You can also obtain a license from the regional offices in Liberia, Limón, Perez Zeledón, San Carlos and San Ramón. Renewals can also be done at these COSEVI offices.

Good news! The days of long lines to renew a Costa Rican driver's license are over, thanks to new digital equipment that now processes licenses in a few minutes.

If you have a license from your own country, it is only a matter of taking an eye exam, transferring information, paying a small processing fee and, having a little—or a lot of— patience and you will have your license.

Here are the requirements:

1. Your *Dictamen Médico*, which is just a single form that is filled out by a doctor and notes any health issues. It takes about 5 minutes and there is no physical exam. Any doctor can do this and give you the proper form with tax stamps affixed The cost is 10,000 *colones*.
2. A document stating your blood type. This is easy to obtain at any medical laboratory on a walk-in basis, takes 15 minutes. There is a 5,000 *colones* charge if you don't have valid proof of your blood type.
3. Your passport and a photocopy of the photo page and the page showing your most recent Costa Rica entry stamp.
4. Your driver's license with a photocopy of same.
5. Something showing you reside (though not necessarily a resident) in Costa Rica.
6. Your physical address and phone number, if any.

Next, you take the items above and the results of your physical to the licensing area about 300 meters behind the CONSEVI building where you present your receipt, your current drivers license, your passport with a current entry stamp (or your *cédula*), and the doctor's examination certificate.

You have to wait in several lines before you receive your Costa Rican license "hot off the press." It is literally hot from the laminating machine. To renew, the procedure is similar to the steps described above. Your first Costa Rica license will be good for two years, but when you renew it, it will be good for five years.

If you do not have a current license or if your license has expired, you have to take a driver's test and written exam as in the United States. The first step involves learning the basic traffic laws, road signs and driver's etiquette which are slightly different here. There are several courses through MOPT designed to help you learn about driving in Costa Rica and pass the written test.

Courses cost about $5.00 and the required test costs a little over $3.00. After passing the written exam, you have to take the driving test. Once you pass both tests you may get your license. To find out about courses and test sites nearest you call the ministry at 2226-4201, 2226-4213, 2226-7944, 2227-5158 or 2228-9297. This is all worthwhile if you plan to live and drive in Costa Rica.

One thing I would like to point out is that in most cases a driver's license is not a valid form of identification as in the United States. In order to cash checks or identify yourself, you need a passport or a *cédula*. The latter is issued only when you have legal residency in Costa Rica.

Here is what one resident experienced when he went to get his driver's license: " Mary and I got our docs together and made the trip up to the La Uruca office this week. I was prepped by a friend of ours down here to be ready for confusion and long waits in line, maybe getting kicked back to the penalty box if I was missing a document or something. In reality, it was a relative breeze and we were both out of there with our shiny new licenses in under an hour and a half. We couldn't have done it so quickly without the expert help of the gun-carrying guard at the front door who spoke fluent English. He kept us on track as we entered the system and in fact, he was really the super-organizer of the whole place. The rest of the staff was equally pleasant and helpful."

"When we got near the COSEVI office the cab driver started asking us if we wanted to be dropped off in front or inside. I had no idea what the difference was and explained to him a couple of times what we were there for until he finally decided that 'inside' was for us. In reality, it really doesn't make much difference. The advantage of going inside is that it's a shorter walk to the *licencias* office and you don't have to traverse the line of *tramitadores* (more on them later) that are in the front entrance."

On Driving in Costa Rica

By Carlos Morton

After nearly two years of living (and Driving) on Costa Rica's scenic highways, I feel inspired to submit the following wisdom to my fellow *gringos.* I speak with the voice of experience, having been a taxi driver in Chicago and New York City. I've also lived in Mexico, driven there and in other parts of Central America.

So, without any hyperbole whatsoever, I give the following advice.

1. **DON'T WORRY ABOUT THE POTHOLES:** Three are too many of them! Trying to avoid the potholes will only cause you to crash into other cars and/or pedestrians. Best thing to do is buy yourself a monster Sports Utility Vehicle (or Hum-vee, tank, dump truck, etc.) and drive over all obstacles, including beaches, ditches and animals.
2. **IGNORE ALL STOP SIGNS, TRAFFIC LIGHTS AND SIGNS:** Everyone else does! Besides, the traffic lights are usually positioned in awkward places too hard to see. Stop signs are bent, broken, faded or hidden behind shrubbery. Translations: "*Alto*" "means speed," *"Ceda el paso"* means "get the hell out of my way!" If you find yourself in a rotunda, pretend you are in the bumper-car rides at the Parque de Diversiones (local amusement park).
3. **PARK WHERE YOU WANT:** That's right! In the middle of the street, on the sidewalk, anywhere your little heart desires. No one will give you a ticket; no one will tow your car away. Continue talking with your car in idle to Don Profundo while other frustrated motorists honk their horns and curse.
4. **DRIVE AS FAST AS POSSIBLE:** When in Rome, do as the Romans do. You may pass on the right, drive on the sidewalk, pass on the left going up hills against oncoming traffic, it's all fair game. Furthermore, this is a free country, and you don't have to wear a seatbelt if you don't want!
5. **DO NOT TRY TO BRIBE A TRAFFIC COP:** It will cost you more! Yes, he'll think your just another rich *gringo* who overstayed your tourist visa. Wait until he offers to let you give him the *propina* (tip). Then barter, always barter. Show him the certified Tico driver's license you procured from a cereal box.
6. **DISCARD YOUR MAPS:** Maps are useless without street signs or addresses. If you want directions, stop and ask three or four different people, who will probably tell you three or four different ways to get there.
7. **DON'T LET THE PEDESTRIAN HAVE THE RIGHT OF WAY:** People think they own the roads! Run them over! That also includes kamikazes on motorbikes, people on bicycles, horseback riders and oxen pulling colorful oxcarts.

"Once inside we immediately saw a line probably 50 feet long snaking out the front door of the licenses office, most people with documents and bank receipts in hand. If you've learned anything about standing in long lines, the first thing is to go to the front and make sure you really are in the right line. This I did and met up with the snappy looking security guard at the front whose first question to me was to show him our documents, which I quickly retrieved from a woman who was saving our place in line. Once he approved of them he sent us directly upstairs with no further instructions."

"Glad to have dodged one line we scurried upstairs to find a cluster of mostly closed offices and one desk in the waiting room with a clerk helping someone. There were only a couple of people waiting, but no signs or other clues to tell us who to talk to next, so I just chose an office with an open door when a customer exited. This worked fine, the lady inside asking again for all our documents. She gave them the same scan that the guard had but now added an official stamp and her signature to the stack and sent us back downstairs."

"Downstairs the guard now gave us paper number tickets and escorted us over to one of two large waiting areas telling us to keep an eye on the wall counter to know when our numbers came up and telling us which row of cubicles to head to when the number did arrive. By this time he had switched to fluent English and he could not have been more polite about the whole thing. I'd glanced at the counter the first time I'd entered the lobby and noted that by this time they'd already processed 10 numbers and we only had about 30 to go, so that we should be up in about 30-40 minutes. It actually went much faster as twice a lady came from upstairs and yelled out that the next ten numbers could come up with her. Boom, we all jumped up 10 places."

"The second time a lady came down to grab another batch of 10, our numbers were the final two in the batch. As we headed to the stairs, however, the guard intervened. He told us not to go upstairs and told the lady on the stairs that we were there for foreign licenses and so had to be processed downstairs. At this point I really appreciated how this "security guard" kept things running smoothly. As the lady on the stairs took two more folks with higher numbers, the guard had us stand next to the short row of cubicles on the right so that we could just jump in when a clerk became free, since we were now out of sync with the counter board."

"In another five minutes Mary was with one clerk and I with another. Hers was with a guy and she reported nothing but the usual dull bureaucratic routine. However, the lady I got apparently took customer service more seriously. After I greeted her with, *'Buenos Días'* she looked at me and in a soft, voluptuous voice said very slowly '*Con Mucho Gusto*'. I shook off the fleeting notion that she was coming on to me, and we proceeded with the data entry and some side conversation about the beaches near Dominical and her little toy lions around her monitor. She handed me a special ticket with the charge for the license (4,000 *colones*) written on it and gave me detailed directions for finding the bank teller where I had to pay. I'd noticed that most people in line had had Banco Nacional receipts in hand, but she explicitly told me with wagging finger '*No Banco*', meaning I was to go where she'd just told me without diversion and without leaving the grounds. So, off Mary and I went across the compound to another big administrative office, which had a BCR teller off in the corner who took our money and handed back the cancelled receipts."

"So, at this point you'd think we'd have to go back in line, but our clerks had told us that once we had the canceled receipts to come back directly to them, which we dutifully did. They entered something else in their computers, which cleared us to place ourselves at the tail end of the final line of the day, the camera line. This line worked differently than the others, just two long lines of chairs from which the 5 camera cubicles peeled off folks from the head of the line. So, we were constantly all getting up and shifting over one or two, sometimes three chairs at a time, first to the left, then to the right when we entered the front chair row. Once at the head of the line you knew which cubicle to go to either by paying close attention to which clerk just freed up or if you were a little slow then the clerk hit a button that flashed an incandescent light over their cube."

"Inside a camera cubicle they check your passport again, take the blood type certificate you've been carrying around all this time, write some stuff in a big paper ledger, then take your picture, your electronic signature, and finally a digital print of your right index finger. You sign the line in the ledger and then if you're lucky, like I was, they hand your finished license to you across the desk. If you're not quite that lucky you only need loiter about the cubicles for another few minutes and they will call your name when the machine spits out your new license. Voila'! You are now a legally licensed Costa Rican driver."

"And one last benefit that may not apply to everyone: Mary and I both agreed that the license photos were the best we'd ever had! We were back at the bus station by 10:40 and exchanged our previously purchased tickets with no questions for the 11:30 bus (despite there being a sign that said no exchanges) and were home much earlier than we'd thought when we left.

"Now, back to that note I promised above about *tramitadores. Tramitadores* (poorly translated as "transactioners") are non-government people who hang around any government office to help folks who are either intimidated by bureaucratic processes or by their own lack of Spanish, or both. For a fee (typically around 10 bucks) they will take your papers and possibly you in hand and take you through the whole deal, whatever it might be. I have enough Spanish to get through most anything (I naively think) and besides I do have something of a masochistic inquisitiveness at times to learn how things actually work in these offices. This sometimes causes me grief when I don't understand some finer points and end up going in circles for a while, but it's usually compensated for by the general courtesy and professionalism of the clerks and managers inside the system I'm dealing with (here in Costa Rica that is, not always so in the States. Oh the stories we all could tell!). Often the systems here in Costa Rica are antiquated and Machiavellian, but the employees do the best they can with what they've got and never get frustrated with me for my lack of process knowledge or the gaping holes in my Spanish. So, I have never used a *tramitador* (yet) but your mileage and inclinations may vary, so you decide what's best for you, obviously."

Advice when driving in Costa Rica

Whether you are renting a car or using your own automobile, always keep the proper documents in your car. Check with your lawyer to see what documents are required. The police will occasionally stop you to see if your paperwork is in order. If a policeman should stop you, above all be polite, stay calm, and do not be verbally abusive. Most traffic police are courteous and helpful. However, if you commit a traffic violation, some policemen will try to have you pay for your ticket on the spot. Be advised this is not the standard procedure. If this happens to you, there are two offices where you can complain. You can file your complaints with the Judicial Police (OIJ) or with the Legal Department of the Transit Police (227-2188). Finally, if you are involved in a traffic accident, **do not move your car!**

If you have an accident, be sure and follow this procedure:

1. Find out where you are *tico*-style. You are going to have to summon maybe the Red Cross, but definitely the traffic cops and the National Insurance Institute (INS) inspector — so get the location right.
2. For severe injuries. Call Cruz Roja (Red Cross) ambulance at 128 or 911. Find out where the ambulance is going to take the injured persons.
3. Call the police. Call the traffic police (2222 -9245, 2222 -9330 or 911 in the Central Valley), who will go to the scene of the accident. Be patient and don't move your car until the cops tell you. Note: it is not enough to wave to a cop on a nearby corner— the police are not the ones who report on accidents — you have to call the special traffic accident squad.

4. Call INS at 800-800-8000 (toll-free, 24 hours) and ask them to send an inspector. The INS inspector usually gets there more quickly than the cops. He will fill out an accident report and give you instructions on how to proceed with the claim. (If the INS operator tells you that an inspector can't go, take the name and number of the operator; — these calls are taped, so this gives you recourse if need arises. Later, contact your insurance agent to find out how to do the paperwork.)
5. Witnesses. Take down their names, addresses and phone numbers — also of the driver of the other car. Take note of particulars of his vehicle, and the license number.
6. Drinking. If you think the other driver has been drinking, ask the cop to give the driver a Breathalyzer test (*alcolemia*). Also point this out to the INS inspector.
7. Tow truck. If your car needs towing, ask the INS man to call one. Most INS auto policies include free towing as part of the "INS *Asistencia*" roadside assistance program. If you don't have the right to free towing, ask the cop to radio for a tow truck. Remember to bargain with the tow truck operator, get a receipt, and make sure you know where he's taking your car. Left to his own devices, he will take your car to a shop that offers him a commission — often an expensive one. Give him your input. Body shops "authorized by INS" will do most of the tedious paperwork relating to the claim, and they usually finance the repair, — but they often overcharge; other body shops tend to charge less, but you may have to finance the repair and do the claim paperwork yourself.
8. Do not assume any obligations or responsibility, — or make a deal with other parties involved in the accident. Body shops do excellent work, but they are expensive — and sometimes the "decent chap" you had your accident with and made a deal with, will become less "decent" when he finds the cost of repairing his car is more than he thought; then he may conjure up all sorts of fairy tales and false witnesses saying you hit and ran and are therefore to blame for the accident. If you stand your ground and summon the cops and the INS inspector, this is unlikely to happen.
9. Summons. At the scene of the accident, the cop will give each driver an illegible blue/green ticket, which is a summons to appear at the corresponding traffic court (*Tribunal de Tránsito*) or municipal office (*Alcaldía*) to make a deposition concerning the accident. IMPORTANT! Ask the cop which traffic court, and when to go. He will usually tell you to go eight-10 days after the accident; don't go sooner — as the paperwork will not be ready. Do not fail to react to the summons lest you be found guilty by default. The deposition is fairly straightforward, and no great command of Spanish is required. People don't usually take attorneys to the traffic court unless there was serious injury or death

resulting from the accident. Don't be alarmed if you find that the other driver's deposition is not accurate; — the ungodly often tell plausible lies to try to get themselves off the hook — here is where the value of the traffic cop's report of the accident becomes important, so the judge can separate truth from fiction. Ask for a copy of your deposition, and also ask when the *sumaria* (sentence) will be ready. You will need these in the claim process.

* **Courtesy of David Garret, insurance agent, e-mail: info@ segurosgarrett.com.**

Be very careful when driving in San José or any other city. Most streets in San José are narrow, one-way and very crowded due to heavy traffic. Names of streets are not on signposts on the street corners as in the United States. Many streets' names are on small blue signs on the sides of buildings. Some streets do not even have signs.

One thing that gets on foreigners nerves is "honking." It seems that most Costa Rican drivers are born with a horn in their hand. If traffic slows just a little, they are quick to honk. This can be extremely nerve- racking and annoying but is a well-ingrained custom here. So get used to it, and do not get upset when honked at. There is no reason to go into road-rage mode when honked at. Furthermore, male Costa Ricans have the habit of honking when they see a beautiful woman on the street.

There is some car theft in Costa Rica. To discourage thieves, you should always park your car in your garage or in public parking lots. If you park on the street, make sure there is someone like a guard who can watch your car. Always lock your car and set the alarm system.

When driving in the countryside, drive only during the day, watch out for livestock and be sure to use some kind of map. Do not get off the main paved road unless absolutely necessary during the rainy season if your car does not have four-wheel drive. You may end up getting stuck in the mud. Unfortunately, the only way to get to many of Costa Rica's best beaches and mountain resorts is by unpaved roads. So be careful!

While on this subject, let me say a word about potholes, or *huecos,* as they are called here. The Costa Rican government tries to keep its paved roads in good shape but cannot keep up with the workload. So watch out for potholes and ruts in the pavement. Your car's shocks and suspension system will be grateful.

This is one resident's experience of driving in Costa Rica: "Driving in Costa Rica can be dangerous and you had better believe it. The *ticos* pass on curves, drive the wrong way on one way streets, tailgate, weave in traffic, run red lights, make illegal turns and you name it. The buses and trucks will run one off the road. The trick here is to know what to expect. Give the guy room to pass, expect the bus to change into your lane, slow down and let the guy tailgating and flashing his headlights pass. When you have a green light, make sure a car is not running a red light in front of you.

"The roads can be bad, very bad and terrible. One night I hit a hole and bent a wheel. The tire went flat and it was raining hard. I stopped a taxi and he put my spare on for me. I gave him a few dollars and we were both happy. When I took the damaged wheel to a shop, the man knew what to do. He took a sledge hammer and beat it back into shape. I suspect he has done that many times. As others have pointed out, it is very difficult to see holes in the road when it is raining."

Things could be better if the traffic cops would patrol more. As a rule they just stand by the side of the road."

A brief summary of Costa Rica's traffic laws and some advice

1. Avoid accidents by driving carefully and defensively.
2. Unless otherwise indicated, the minimum speed on highways is 40 kilometers per hour. The speed limit varies and is posted on the side of the road.
3. On highways and secondary roads, the speed limit is 60 kilometers per hour, unless otherwise indicated.
4. In urban areas, the speed limit is 40 kilometers per hour, unless otherwise indicated.
5. Around school zones and in front of hospitals and clinics the speed limit is 25 kilometers per hour.
6. Driving on beaches is strictly prohibited everywhere, except when there is no other path connecting two towns.
7. Driving under the influence of alcohol and/or drugs is strictly prohibited. The law permits police officers to perform alcohol tests on drivers.
8. The law requires all car passengers to wear a seat belt, even when riding in a taxi.
9. Pull over if any police officer signals you to do so. Police officers may ask you to stop if there is an accident ahead, a checkpoint or if you are violating the law by not having a license plate or exceeding the speed limit.
10. Your personal documents and the vehicle's registration papers are private property and may not be retained by a police officer for any reason.
11. If you are involved in an accident, always wait until a police officer arrives. Do not move your vehicle. The officer will prepare a report. You may also report the accident by calling 911 or 800-0123456.
12. Under no circumstances give money to traffic police or other police officers.

Sometimes traffic can be heavy around San José Traffic Jam

13. If a police officer insists on stopping you and retaining your documents for no apparent reason, ask him to escort you to the nearest police station to resolve the problem.
14. If you believe a traffic policeman or any other police officer acted inappropriately or you have questions regarding their behavior, call 2257-7798, ext. 2506, and ask to be referred to the nearest police station.
15. Drive confidently and stay alert. Do not stop for people signaling you and never stop for hitchhikers.
16. Do not drive through or park your car in poorly lit areas. Do not leave any belongings in the car where they might be spotted by a passerby.
17. Check your car and make sure you are carrying the proper documents before you begin to drive. If you are given a ticket, pay it at the nearest state bank. If you are renting a car, present a copy of the receipt for the ticket you paid to the car rental agency when you return the car.

For information about traffic laws and other related matters call **800-TRANSITO** or see **www.transito.go.cr** or **www.cav.go.cr (traffic tickets)**. To check out road conditons see : **http://www.transito.go.cr/estadorutas/index.html**

New traffic laws

On March 1, 2010, there will come into effect a sweeping legislation intended to transform Costa Rica's roadways from the hazardous - free for -all that has developed in recent decades, into a network occupied by safe, conscientious and prepared drivers.

A new law will dramatically increase fines for traffic violations, while punishing drunken driving and speeding with jail time.The law raises the maximum fine for traffic violations to $410 from $36, while sending drunken and reckless drivers to jail for up to three years.

On paper, the law sends drivers to prison for one to three years for going faster than 150 kph or racing other cars. While impaired drivers now need pay only a $36 fine, the new law will send people to jail for up to three years for driving with a blood-alcohol content of 0.75 grams per liter.

The new fines, pegged to inflation, range from $40 for throwing cigarettes in the street to $410 for driving faster than 120 kilometers per hour or with a blood-alcohol content of 0.5 grams per liter. Not wearing a seatbelt, driving while on a cell phone or ignoring a stop sign carry a $310 fine.

With this in mind I suggest you purchase, *Shorty's Guide To The 2000 Ley de Tránsito* (www.newleydetransito.com). This is a complete guide for the English speaking driver to know the rules and be prepared for the changes, that include:

* Computerization of Licenses, where points are deducted for infractions
* Dramatic increase in the amount of fines
* Safety seats for all minors under 12 years of age
* Harsh penalties and jail time for driving under the influence
* Immediate loss of license for multiple offences
* New devices requirements, like hands free cell phone adaptor, fire extinguisher, first aid kit, GPS transponder, etc.
* Sanctions for left lane slow pokes and no passing on right, even on multiple lane highways
* Foreigners and their drivers license
* The new *Ley de Tránsito* also affects non-drivers. Pedestrians will have to also obey many of the new rules of the road, like crossing the street at a corner or pedestrian crosswalk.
* The accumulation of 50 points means an automatic two-year suspension. Subsequent suspensions can be for life.

Portions of this law including the reduction of fines have been changed several times. Therefore check to see what are the current laws

Driving Times in and around Costa Rica

Driving times from San José are based on 43 kph which is about 27 mph.

LOCATION	DISTANCE (KM)	TIME
Alajuela	18	25 minutes
Atenas	45	1 hour 10 minutes
Cahuita	195	3 hours 15 minutes
Cartago	20	25 minutes
Cañas	182	2 hours 50 minutes
Cd Quesada	100	2 hours 40 minutes
Golfito	330	8 hours 30 minutes
Grecia	43	1 hour
Heredia	12	25 minutes
Jacó	102	2 hours
Liberia	228	3 hours 30 minutes
Limón	153	2 hours 15 minutes
Monteverde	162	4 hours
Nicoya via Liberia	318	4 hours
Parrita via Jacó	243	3 hours 15 minutes
Paso Canoas	349	8 hours
Peñas Blancas	292	4 hours
Playas del Coco	262	4 hours
Puntarenas	105	1 hour 15 minutes
Quepos via Jacó	268	3 hours 15 minutes
San Isidro de El General	131	3 hours
Tamarindo	301	4 hours 15 minutes
Tilarán	209	3 hours 15 minutes
Volcán Irazú	53	1 hour 40 minutes
Volcán Poás	55	1 hour 30 minutes

Keeping Your Bearings Straight

You can get confused in Costa Rica trying to find your way around especially in San José. Except for the center of San José, most streets have no names or numbers, or they are not in a visible place. People use known landmarks to get around, to locate addresses and give directions. If you are unfamiliar with this system. it is almost impossible to find your way around, and easy to get lost. Don't worry. After you have lived in Costa Rica awhile, you will get used to this system. In the event you get lost, you can always ask Costa Ricans for directions—provided you understand a little Spanish or they speak some English.

Finding Your Way

By Christopher Howard

Memorize the Spanish survival phrases below and you should be able to find your way around, located addresses and hopefully not get lost.

¿A qué distancia queda...? - How far is...?
¿Dónde está...? - Where is...?
Tome la primera calle... - Take the first street
a la derecha - to the right
a la izquierda - to the left
directo/derecho - straight ahead
diagonal - diagonal to
a la par de - next to in Costa Rica
al lado de, contiguo - also next to
¿Hay un...por aquí? - Is there a ...around here?
Doble a la derecha - turn right
Doble a la izquierda - turn left
a la vuelta - around the corner
una cuadra - a block
cien metros - a block in Costa Rica
cien varas - also a block in Costa Rica
una teja - also one block in Costa Rica
entrada - driveway
la esquina - corner
cerca de - near
lejos de - far
largo - far in Costa Rica (incorrect Spanish)
enfrente de - opposite
en el cruce - at the intersection
estoy perdido - I'm lost
¿Puede indicarme el camino? - Can you show me the how to get to...?
norte - north
sur - south
este - east
oeste - west

* From *Christopher Howard's Guide to Costa Rican Spanish*

As you know, Costa Ricans are generally very friendly and are usually happy to help you find the address you are seeking. However, it is always a good idea to ask a second person, because most *ticos* are embarrassed to admit they don't know an address and will sometimes give you directions whether they know where you want to go or not.

Here are some basic tips on how to get around Costa Rica and understand how the street numbering works. It is somewhat easier to find your way in downtown San José because of the layout of the city. Avenues, or *Avenidas*, run east west. All the odd-numbered avenues are north of Central Avenue (*Avenida Central*). The even-numbered avenues are south. Streets, or *Calles*, run north south, with odd-numbered streets east of *Calle Central* and even-numbered streets to the west.

If you get lost, then looking for a street sign on the side of a building and counting by two's will usually help you get your bearings. Keep in mind that the word avenue is often abbreviated as *A* and streets as *C* when you get written directions. To find your way around Costa Rica, you also need to know that 100 meters (*cien metros*) is another way of saying one block. Likewise, 50 meters (*cincuenta metros*) is a half-block and 150 meters (*ciento cincuenta metros*) a block and a half. The word *varas* (an old Spanish unit of measurement, almost a yard) is slang and often used instead of the word *metros* (meters) when giving directions.

Landmarks, such as corner grocery stores (*pulperías*), churches, schools and other buildings, are usually used with this metric block system to locate addresses. For example, in finding a house someone might say, "From Saint Paul's Church, 200 meters west and 300 meters south." In interpreting written directions you should also know that M stands for meters.

An old trick Costa Ricans often use for finding the four compass points may make it easier for you to get your bearings straight. The front doors of all churches in Costa Rica face west. So, if there is a church nearby, imagine yourself with your back to the entrance of the church—you are facing west.

If you live in San José, there is another method for finding the compass points. Poás Volcano is north, the Cruz de Alajuela mountain approximately south, the direction of Cartago is east and the general direction of the La Sabana or Rohrmoser is west. This system of using landmarks should make it easier for you to find your way around the city.

The time wasted searching for a house or building in Costa Rica may be a thing of the past. The Costa Rican postal system plans to initiate a plan that will introduce a uniform system of street and house numbers.

Signs will be posted on street corners following a coordinated system of colors, sign sizes and symbols. Blue signs will mark international thoroughfares, yellow will be used to indicate inter-provincial highways and white will denote interurban roads. Homeowners will be told where to place their number signs. This system will be tested in several areas with the hope of extending it to all parts of the country within three years. Let us hope this system becomes a reality to make everyone's life easier.

Computer and satellite global positioning system technology (GPS) is now availble for Costa Rica through **Smart Ways**. Also check out **http://www.maptak.com/**

11

Education

How to Learn Spanish

Although many of Costa Rica's well-educated people speak English, (and more than 30,000 English-speaking foreigners live permanently in Costa Rica), Spanish is the official language. Anyone who seriously plans to live or retire in Costa Rica should know Spanish — and the more the better. Frankly, you will be disadvantaged, handicapped and be considered a foreigner to some degree without Spanish. Part of the fun of living in another country is communicating with the local people, making new friends and enjoying the culture. Speaking Spanish will enable you to achieve these ends, have a more rewarding life, and open the door for many new, interesting experiences. Knowing some Spanish also saves you money when you're shopping and, in some cases, keeps people from taking advantage of you.

If you take my advice and choose to study Spanish, you can enroll at one of Costa Rica's intensive conversational language schools for a modest fee. Costa Rica has long been a destination of choice for those wishing to learn Spanish. The majority of the schools are located in the cities of San José, Heredia and Alajuela. A few schools are located in beach areas. Most schools offer programs to fit your specific needs. They have classes for beginners as well as intermediate and advanced students. Classes are also offered for business people, teenagers, children, teachers and other professionals. Many of the schools are affiliated with U.S. universities, so college students can receive credit.

In addition to language instruction, most of these schools offer exciting field trips, interesting activities and room and board with local families, all of which are optional. Living with a family that speaks little—or preferably no—English is a wonderful way to improve your language skills, make new friends and learn about Costa Rican culture at the same time. Please check with the school of your choice for current prices.

Spanish is not a difficult language to learn. With a little self-discipline and motivation, anyone can acquire a basic Spanish survival vocabulary of between 200 and 3,000 words in a relatively short time. Many Spanish words are similar enough to English, so you can guess their meanings by just looking at them. The Spanish alphabet is almost like the English one, with a few minor exceptions. Pronunciation is easier than in English because you say words as they look like they should be said. Spanish grammar is somewhat complicated but can be made easier if you are familiar with English grammar and find a good Spanish teacher. Practicing with native speakers improves your Spanish because you can hear how Spanish is spoken in everyday conversation. You will learn many new words and expressions not ordinarily found in your standard dictionary.

Watching Spanish television and listening to the radio and language cassettes can also improve your Spanish. We suggest that if you have little or no knowledge of spoken Spanish, you purchase the one-of-a-kind best seller Christopher Howard's ***Guide to Costa Rican Spanish***. The book is designed especially for people planning to retire or live in Costa Rica. It makes learning easy without the complications of grammar. If you are interested in a deeper study of Spanish, see the list of language schools at the end of this section.

Also check out **www.costaricaspanish.net.** This site is #1 at Google for Costa Rican Spanish and has hundreds of interesting articles, useful tips and Costa Rican expressions that can help you improve your Spanish skills. It's all FREE!

One highly-innovative way to learn Spanish whether you plan to live in Costa Rica or not, is the one-of-a-kind interactive on-line program offered at **ConversaConmigo.com**. All you need is a computer with a high-speed connection and a headset. They'll show you how to download the software. In no time you'll be learning Spanish at your home or office, one-on-one with a live teacher in Costa Rica. The technology will amaze you as you discover the many ways that ConversaConmigo.com will enable you to move forward quickly with Spanish. Just go to the website and register,

Super Tips For Learning Spanish

by Christopher Howard M.A.

1) Build your vocabulary. Try to learn a minimum of five new words daily.
2) Watch Spanish TV programs. Keep a notepad by your side and jot down new words and expressions. Later use the dictionary to look up any words and expressions you don't understand.
(3) Pay attention to the way the locals speak the language.
(4) Listen to Spanish music.
(5) Talk with as many different Spanish speakers as you can. You will learn something from every one. Carry a small notebook and write down new words when you hear them.
(6) Read aloud in Spanish for five minutes a day to improve your accent.
(7) Try to imitate native speakers when you talk.
(8) Don't be afraid of making mistakes.
(9) Practice using your new vocabulary words in complete sentences.
10) When you learn something new, form a mental picture to go along with it—visualize the action.
11) Try to talk in simple sentences. Remember, your Spanish is not at the same level as your English, so simplify what you are trying to say.
12) If you get stuck or tongue-tied, try using nouns instead of complete sentences.
13) Remember that Spanish and English are more similar than different. There are many cognates (words that are the same or almost the same in both languages).
14) Learn all of the basic verb tenses and memorize the important regular and irregular verbs in each tense.
15) Study Spanish grammar, but don't get bogged down in it.
16) Read the newspaper. The comic strips are great because they have a lot of dialog.
17) It takes time to learn another language. Don't be impatient. Most English speakers are in a hurry to learn foreign languages and get frustrated easily because the process is slow. Study a little bit everyday, be dedicated, persist and most of all enjoy the learning process.

¡Buena suerte! Good luck!*
From *Christopher Howard's Guide to Costa Rican Spanish*.

Getting a Head Start

by Christopher Howard M.A.

If you are seriously considering moving to a Latin American country, you should begin to study Spanish as soon as possible.

Here are a few suggestions that will give you a head start in learning the language. Look for some type of Spanish course that emphasizes conversation as well as grammar and enroll as soon as possible. University extension programs, junior colleges and night schools usually offer a wide range of Spanish classes.

You should also consider studying at a private language school like Berlitz if there is one near you. Many of these schools allow the students to work at their own pace.

Another excellent way to learn Spanish, if you can afford it, is to hire a private language tutor. Like private schools this type of instruction can be expensive, but is very worthwhile. The student has the opportunity of working one-on-one with a teacher and usually progresses much faster than in a large group situation.

If you happen to reside in an area where there are no schools that offer Spanish classes, you should go to your local bookstore and purchase some type of language cassette. This way, at least you will have a chance to learn correct pronunciation and train your ear by listening to how the language is spoken.

Listening to radio programs in Spanish and watching Spanish television are other ways to learn the language, if you are fortunate enough to live in an area where these stations are broadcast.

You can also spend your summer or work vacations studying Spanish in Mexico or Costa Rica. This way you will experience language in real life situations. These language vacations can be enjoyable and rewarding experiences.

Finally, try befriending as many native Spainsh-speakers as you can who live in the area where you reside. Besides making new friends, you will have someone to practice with and ask questions about the language.

By following the advice above and making an effort to learn the language, you should be able to acquire enough basic language skills to prepare you for living in a Spanish speaking country. Best of all, you will acquire the life-long hobby of learning a new language in the process.

* From *Christopher Howard's Guide to Costa Rican Spanish.*

or give them a call at 1888-669-1664. They'll be happy to give you a free trial lesson."

Need a little motivation to get started learning Spanish as your second language? The following is from a June 2004 news report: "Bilingualism may help keep certain brain functions working better during normal aging, Canadian psychologists say."

"The researchers compared 'executive functions,' such as the ability to ignore distracting information, in 104 monolingual and bilingual adults aged 30 to 59, and 50 adults aged 60 to 88.

"Bilingual adults performed better and the bilingual advantage increased substantially in those over 60, the researchers found. The study appears in the June 2004 issue of the Journal Psychology and Aging.

" 'It shows that a specific experience, bilingualism, has the ability to modify a central aspect of cognitive functioning and keep the brain functioning at a higher level as normal aging inevitably slows us down," said psychology Professor Ellen Bialystok of York University"

Costa Rican style-Spanish

The Spanish spoken in Costa Rica is more or less the same as standard Castilian Spanish except for one big difference which confuses beginning students. Spanish has two forms for addressing a person: *usted* and *tú*. However, in Costa Rica, there is third form: *vos*. The verb form used with vos is formed by changing the r at the end of a verb infinitive to s and adding an accent to the last syllable. This form is seldom taught because it is considered a colloquial form, used only in some parts of Central America and South America (Argentina and Uruguay, for example). It is not found in most Spanish textbooks. The chart in this chapter provides an explanation of the use of *vos.*

Don't worry! Once you live in Costa Rica for a while and get used to the Costa Rican way of speaking, you will learn to use the *vos* form almost automatically. Costa Ricans appreciate any effort you make to speak their language.

You will notice that Costa Ricans frequently use local expressions called *tiquismos* that are not used in other Latin American countries. Some of these common expressions are *pura vida* (fantastic, super, great), *tuanis* (very good), *buena nota* (good, OK), *salado* (tough luck, too bad), and many others. If Costa Rica were to have a national motto, the choice would most certainly be, *¡Pura Vida!* This expression has become so popular you will see it on T-shirts, in Spanish dictionaries to show appreciation and

The use of *vos* — the other you

The Spanish spoken in Costa Rica is more or less the same as standard Castilian Spanish except for one big difference that confuses many people. Spanish has two forms for addressing a person: *usted* and tú. However, in Costa Rica there is a third form,*vos.* This form is seldom taught because it is considered colloquial. In fact, it is not found in most Spanish textbooks or taught to most English-speaking students in their Spanish classes.

Although the use of *vos* varies from region to region and its consideration as standard Spanish varies widely from country to country, you can hear *vos* used in many countries of Central America, in the countries of the southern South America (Chile, Argentina, Uruguay) and in parts of Colombia, Peru and Ecuador. In areas of America where there was a strong influence of the Spanish Court, places such as Mexico and Peru, the eventual change from *vos* to tú and *vuestra merced* - usted mirrored the evolution of the Spanish language in Spain. However, in regions farther away from the centers of power this evolution did not necessarily follow the same pattern. Instead, in some regions tú was displaced by *vos* in the friendly address and usted was used in the polite address.

Vos is used in Latin America in varying ways. It simply replaces tú and has its own conjugation. Though it looks similar to the *tú* verbs, there are slight differences in spelling and also in stress/pronunciation. *Vos* is used only with the present indicative tense, present subjunctive and command forms. The verb form used with vos is formed by changing the "r" at the end of a verb infinitive to "s" and adding an accent to the last syllable in the present tense. For example: *vos comprás* (*comprar*), *vos comés* (*comer*), *vos vivís.* In the present subjunctive the forms are exactly the same. For example: *vos comprés* (*comprar*), *vos comás* (*comer*), *vos vivás.* When *vos* is used in commands, just drop the final "r" off the infinitive ending of the verb. For example: *comprá* (*comprar*), *comé (comer*), *escribí* (*escribir*).

Most common set of verb forms with *vos*

Since *vos* came from a different form of the verb than tú it is not surprising to see that the vos form of the verb often (although not always) uses a different form of the verb than the *tú*.

If you remember your vosotros endings of the present tense, you will assume that the endings evolve to *áis*, *éis*, and *ís*, however the most common system of vos endings in the present tense is the following.

Type of verb	ending
ar	*-ás*
es	*-és*
ir	*-ís*

Stem changes such as o to ue, e to ie, e to i, do not occur. For certain one syllable verbs and estar, there is no difference between the tú form and the vos form (since one syllable words do not usually take accents).

For example, compare the following forms:

verb	*tú* form	*vos* form
dar	*das*	*dás*
ver	*ves*	*vés*
estar	*estás*	*estás*
ir	*vas*	*vas*

However, for most verbs there is a difference:

verb	*tú* form	*vos* form
vivir	*vives*	*vivís*
hablar	*hablas*	*hablás*

ser	*eres*	*sos*
tener	*tienes*	*tenés*
pedir	*pides*	*pedís*
construir	*construyes*	*construís*
traer	*traes*	*traés*
dormir	*duermes*	*dormís*

In most other tenses, the verb forms are the same, except for the affirmative *vos* command. That form is simply the infinitive without the r and with the vowel of the infinitive ending stressed with a written accent if it's more than one syllable or would otherwise need an accent.

verb	+ *tú* command	+ *vos* command
tener	*ten*	*tené*
ser	*sé*	*sé*
venir	*ven*	*vení*
tomar	*toma*	*tomá*
hablar	*habla*	*hablá*
vivir	*vive*	*viví*
beber	*bebe*	*bebé*
dar	*da*	*da*

*From ***Christopher Howard's Guide to Costa Rican Spanish***.

Here are some links to online Spanish courses

Some of them are free:

http:// www.pimsleurapproach.com

http://www.rosettastone.com

http://www.bbc.co.uk/languages/spanish/

http://www.donquijote.org/online/

http://www.docnmail.com/learnmore/language/spanish.htm

http://www.ihspain.com/madrid/online_spanish.html

http://www.studyspanish.com/

http://www.learn-spanish-online.de/

http://www.spanish-online.com/

http://www.speakteacher.com/

http://www.spanishprograms.com/

http://www.learnspanishtoday.com/

* From Christopher Howard's Guide to Costa Rican Spanish.

Go on line and write "Learn Spanish" in any search engine like Google and you will come up with 1000's of sites to learn Spanish. Many of these sites offer free courses.

mostly for greetings. When used as a greeting it can mean "hello" or "How are you doing?" It can also be used to say "good-bye." When you say, "*pura vida*" a person will usually smile. It can also be used to express joy. The expression is infectious.

Another Costa Rican trait is the common use of *don* (for a man) and *doña* (for a woman) when addressing a middle-aged or older person formally. These forms are used with the first name, as in the case of the famous "*don Juan*." However, you will usually hear the more traditional *señor* or *señora* used instead of *don* or *doña*. Teachers in Costa Rica are addressed as profesor or *maestro*, an engineer as *ingeniero* and an attorney as *licenciado*. Using these titles is a sign of respect, and not to do so is considered rude. Anyone with a bachelor's degree is also entitled to be addressed as *licenciado*.

In Costa Rica, as in the rest of Latin America, the father's and mother's surnames comes after a person's given name. For example, if Carlos is born to José García López and Marta Lara Pérez, his complete name would be followed by his father's first surname and then by his mother's: Carlos García Lara. All official documents must have both surnames.

For some basic Spanish phrases and more tiquismos, see the section titled "Important Phrases and Vocabulary" in Chapter 14.

Language Schools

To find a language school, start with the list below. Also, check with foreigners who have studied here, visit the school and observe its classes. Perhaps this reader's experience can help you narrow down your choice. "I have found a great school that I am planning to this fall. It is located right in downtown Heredia.

"What originally attracted me to this school are the great reviews it received from its former students that I found in various places. The prices are reasonable compared to other similar schools, and they provide home-stays with *tico* families.

"Apparently, they will even have someone pick you up at the airport and take you to your *tico* family's house. I plan to get an apartment in Heredia instead of doing a home stay for various reasons including lower costs but, I can see how home-stays can have some great advantages.

"What really cemented my decision is when I E-mailed some questions to the school. They responded to my message within a couple of hours and really took the time to explain things to me. I guess the big advantage to this school is that they have smaller class sizes and give you more personalized

Conversa is Costa Rica's oldest and best Spanish school

attention. They e-mailed me pictures of the school as well — any school with a hammock out back is right up my alley."

This list should start you on your way. Private, individualized language classes are also available. For listings, look in the classified section of The Tico Times.

- **Academia Tica's** various courses and home-stays cost between $120 and $180 for 20 hours of instruction. Apdo. 1294-2100, Guadalupe, San José, Costa Rica. Tel: 229-0013, E-mail: artica@racsa.co.cr, www.academiatica.com.
- **Berlitz** offers different language programs to meet all of your needs. Tel:(506)-2204-7555. (506)-2253-9191 Fax2: 204-7444, 2253-1115, Web: http:www.berlitz.com.
- **Centro Lingüístico Conversa** was founded in 1975 and has an excellent track record. Unlike many of the language schools here the owner has a degree in Spanish and a graduate degree in Applied Linguistics. They offer an excellent conversational program at the main school in San José and another campus west of town in a rural setting. See their display ad in this book.

  Conversa offers some innovative programs. The first is the chance to learn on-line. Not everyone can participate in a true full immersion

Spanish program, so this is an opportunity to study on the Internet. These courses allow students to work at their own pace and meet their specific needs. The download and trial class are free. Two or more classes per week can be scheduled. Check out this one-of-a-kind program at **ConversaConmigo.com** They also offer program for retirees. Write to Apdo. 17-1007, Centro Colón, San José, Costa Rica. Tel: 2221-7649,Fax: 2233-2418, E-mail: info@conversa.com, Web: www.conversa.com.

- **Centro Cultural Costarricense Norteamericano** has eight schools in different parts of the country. Apdo. 1489-1000, San José, Costa Rica. Tel: 2207-7500, Fax: 2224-1480, Web: www.cccncr.com.
- **Centro Lingüístico Latinoamericano** teaches intensive courses, five ho**University of Costa Rica** now offers Spanish courses as a foreign language through the School of Philology, Linguistics and Literature. This program lasts four months and space is limited. The cost is about $450. Tel: 2207-5634, Fax: 2207-5089, E-mail: espanucr@cariari.ucr.ac.cr.
- **Comunucaré** is a non-profit association dedicated to teaching Spanish as a second language, to fostering a deeper understanding of Central America and to supporting community development and volunteer work. P.O Box 1383-2050 San José, Costa Rica, Tel: 2281-0432, Fax : 2224-4473, E-mail: admon@comunicare-cr.com, www.comunicare-cr.com.
- **Epifanía** is "the new kid on the block"and claims to provides students of all ages the funny and exciting experience of learning Spanish as a second language with stimulating Spanish language school teachers, interesting fellow Spanish students and Spanish language improvement. The SOS program is designed for all those who wish or need to have the necessary tools to communicate in Spanish during their stay in Costa Rica and for those on vacations or work related issues. Tel: 506-2524-1726 Address: 275 meters Northeast of Multiplaza del Este Mall in Curridabat. Fax: 506-2524-1726, E-mail: info@epifaniaschool.co www.epifaniaschool.com
- **Forester Institute International** offers a variety of classes. Prices range from $600 to $1150 depending on the program. Apdo. 6945-1000, San José, Costa Rica. Tel: 2225-1649, Fax: 2225-9236, E-mail: forester@racsa.co.cr, Web: www.fores.com

  They also offer online courses. A trial lesson is $25. The cost is $25 per 50-minute lesson with a 10-hour minimum investment. One or more lessons per week can be scheduled.
- **Intensa** has been around for twenty five years and has two-, three-, and four-week programs with home- stays available. They offer classes

Frequently Used Tiquismos (Costa Rican Expressions)

Alimentar las pulgas — To sleep
Birra — Beer
Brete — work
Pura Vida— Great, Fantastic
Caerle la peseta — To get the idea, understand.
Campo — Space (in line, on a bus etc.)
Chepe — Slang for the city of San José
Chile — A joke
Chinamo — A booth or stand where things are sold
Chuica — A rag or old clothes
Cien metros — One city block
Clavar el pico — To fall asleep
Con el moco caído — Sad
¿Diay? — What can be done about it?
Guaro — Moonshine
Harina— Slang for money
Jalado — Dissipated, pale
Jarana— A debt
Jetonear — To lie
lo duda — You said it! You're right!
Macho - Any person with fair skin or hair
Montarse en la carreta — To get drunk
Pachuco—A type of street slang
Pinche - A tight-fisted person
Platero —Money hungry person
Porta a mí — Who cares
Rajar — To brag
Tata - Father
Torta — An error or screw-up
Vieras — If you only knew; sure; would you believe
Vino — A snoopy person
Volar pico — To talk a lot

* From *Christopher Howard's Guide to Costa Rica Spanish*

in San José, Alajuela and in Heredia. Apdo. 8110-1000, San José. Tel: 2281-1818, Fax: 2253-4337, E-mail: intensa@racsa.co.cr, Web: www.intensa.com.

- **Intercultura** is located in the city of Heredia. P.O Box 1952-3000, Heredia Costa Rica. Tel/Fax: 2260- 8480 or 656- 0127. Toll-free number from the United States or Canada: 1-866-363-5421. E-mail: info@interculturacostarica.com, Web: www.interculturacostarica.com
- **Instituto de la Lengua Española** offers an excellent intensive program. Six hours daily for 15 weeks for $635. Terms begin in January, May and September. Apdo. 100-2350, San José, Costa Rica. Tel: 2227-7366, Fax: 2227-0211.
- **Istituto Guanacasteco de Idiomas** has a variety of programs. www.spanishcostarica.com
- **Instituto Universal de Idiomas** has various programs . Apdo. 751-2150, San Pedro, Moravia, Costa Rica. Ave. 2, Calle 9 Tel: 2223-9917, Fax: 2223-9917, E-mail: info@universal-edu.com, Web: www.universaledu.com.
- **Institute for Central American Development Studies** offers one-month programs, five hours a day, for $892, and includes classes, lectures, field trips, and home-stay with a Costa Rican family. Apdo. 3-2070 Sabanilla, San José, Costa Rica. Tel: 2234-1381 Fax: 2234-1337, E-mail: icads@netbox.com.
- **Centro Panamericano de Idiomas** is a school in a beautiful rural setting. The cost is about $1000 monthly and covers instruction, home-stay and excursions. Apdo. 151-3007, Heredia, Costa Rica. Tel: 2265-6866, Fax: 2265-6213.
- **IPED** has an excellent program and is located in the beautiful city of Heredia. Tel: 2238-3608 Tel:/Fax: 2237-1801 Toll-free from the United States (888)-Si Hablo or 888 744-2256, E-mail: info@learnspanishcostarica.com or ipedcr@racsa.co.cr , www.learnspanishcostarica.com
- **IPEE** Spanish Language School: Tel: 2283-7731, Fax: 506-2225-7860, E-mail: ipee@gate.net, Web: www.ipee.com.
- **ILISA,** Instituto Latinoamericano de Idiomas: Apdo. 1011, 2050 San Pedro, Costa Rica or Dept. 1420, P. O. Box 25216, Miami, FL 33102-5216. Tel: 2225-2495 Fax: 2225-4665. In United States and Canada: (800)-454-7248, E-mail: spanish@ilisa.com.
- **Lisa Tec:** Tel: 2239-2225, Fax: 2293-2894, E-mail: kisatec1@hotmail.com, www.itspanish.com.
- **La Academia de Español D'Amore** is a quality educational institution created to facilitate the learning of Spanish, in Manuel Antonio, Quepos, one of the most beautiful beaches of Costa Rica.They incorporate the

Total Spanish Immersion process of education to ensure the most efficient learning experience possible. In U.S. 4150 Arch Dr. Suite 216 , Studio City, CA 91604 , Tel: (818) 434-7290, E-mail: info@academiadamore.com www.academiadamore.com/contact_us.html

- **Mesoamerica Language Institute** gives four hours of instruction each day for $80 a week. Apdo. 1524-2050, San Pedro, Costa Rica. Tel: 2234-7682, E-mail: mesoamer@racsa.co.cr.
- **Orosi Valley Spanish School** is located in the beautiful Orosi Valley, southeast of San José. This school has a variety of packages for Spanish students starting at $815/week including classes, accomdations, breakfast and dinner, and is certified by the ICT.. Tel. 506-533-2480 E-mail: florgra30@gmail.com www.orosivalleyschool.net
- **Pura Vida Language Institute** Tel: 265-3149 Toll Free in USA and Canada: 866-490-0559, E-mail: info@puravidalanguageinstitute.com www.puravidalanguageinstitute.com
- **School of the World** began as one of the first options for studying Spanish near the beach in Costa Rica (most of the language schools are located in or around the capital city which is in the center of the country). The school's Spanish courses incorporate international Spanish teaching guidelines with Costa Rica's local variations of the language. While the program covers all aspects of Spanish, teachers place a heavy influence on developing verbal skills. Tel: 2643-2462, US phone: +1-404-935-4251, E- mail, info@schooloftheworld.org, www.schooloftheworld.org
- **University of Costa Rica School of Philology, Linguistics and Literature** offers Spanish courses as a foreign language for beginner, intermediate and advanced students. Call 2207-5632 or go to the Spanish language office located in the Facultad de Letras Building at the University of Costa Rica in San Pedro.

  There is a Spanish conversation club for foreigners wanting to improve their Spanish skills. Call 2254-1433 or 2235-7026 for details. The Instituto Universal de Idiomas (Avenida 2, Calles 7/9) has an exchange club where you can practice Spanish with a native speaker in exchange for helping with English (2257-0441). Centro Cultural also has free Spanish social- conversation classes through a program called "Simply Spanish"

You can now combine language study at **Conversa** with one of **Christopher Howard's Relocation/Retirement Tours**. Please call 800 365-2342 toll free for details.

Costa Rica's Institutions of Higher Learning

If you wish to continue your education, university-level courses are available to foreigners in subjects such as business, art, history, political science, biology, psychology, literature and Spanish, as well as all other major academic areas.

The bachillerato (bachelor's degree) takes four years of study. The school semester lasts 16 weeks. Oral public defense of studies is required for graduation. Graduate studies leading to master and doctoral degrees are available at the University of Costa Rica in a variety of fields, including biology, microbiology, philosophy, law, medicine, public administration, and education. Required standards are comparable to those in North American universities regarding requisite credits, length of study, and other requirements for graduation. Higher education is free for nearly 50 percent of the enrolled students

Foreigners can enroll directly as special students for their first two years at the University of Costa Rica. Tuition is much lower than at most U.S. universities. Students can also audit classes for a nominal fee. Contact the University of Costa Rica (UCR) at Tel: 2207-4000, fax: 2225-6950 www.ucr.ac.cr. Another excellent public university is The Nacional University (UNA) in Heredia, Tel: 506-2261-0101, Fax: 2237-7593, e-mail: webmaster@una.

The University of Costa Rica in San Pedro.

co.ac.cr, www.una.ac.cr. National Correspondence University (UNED) offers correspondence, programs, tel; 2253-2121, fax: 506-2253-4990, e-mail: cendocu@arenal.uned.ac.cr, www.uned.ac.cr.

Over the last ten years there has been a proliferation of private universities. They are mainly for students who can't qualify academically for the University of Costa Rica or National University of Heredia. These schools are more expensive than the public universities and their degrees aren't quite as prestigious. Autonomous University of Central America, or UACA as it is more commonly known here, is the oldest of these private universities and has an excellent reputation, tel: 234-0701, fax: 2224-0391, e-mail: lauaca@racsa.co.cr. See the local phone book for a listing of the many private universities found in the San José area.

Some U.S. universities offer programs in Costa Rica for which you can get university credit. Search the Internet to see what is available if you want to continue your education here and receive credits towards a degree in the United States or Canada.

Universities in Costa Rica work very differently than in the U.S. Most students don't live in campus here. Students take an admissions test which is similar to an SAT exam. A student's score on this exam will not only influence his acceptance to university, but will determine which career he is allowed to study. Unlike in the U.S. students must choose their career before enterering the university. If you don't score high enough for a particular career you will not be allowed to study it.

Affordable college education for your Children

If you are thinking about retiring here and have children or grandchildren of college age, you might consider enrolling them in a Costa Rican private or public university.

Private universities are more expensive and admission standards are not as high as those of their public counterparts. Public universities charge tuition on a sliding scale, but even the most expensive one, is very cheap when compared with a school in the U.S.

One evening I was watching the CBS Evening News on satellite and there was a story about the prohibitive cost of a university education in the United States. Apparently fifty percent of the families in the U.S. have to limit their choice of universities for their children due to a combination of the current financial crisis and the high cost of college tuition. Many are sending their children to more affordable junior colleges to save money during the first two years.

If you choose Costa Rica for living or retirement you can save a lot of money on a college education. The University of Costa Rica, the nation's best public university, charges less than a couple of hundred dollars a year for tuition. Yes, you heard right.

The author's son goes to one of the best private universities here and pays a little less the $3000 a year for tuition.

All you have to do is compare the costs of what they charge here with those in the States and you will see the obvious bargain. You can save tens of thousands of dollars a year here.

Furthermore, the quality of education is excellent. Since Costa Rican universities are recognized internationally for their academic excellence, Costa Rican students are admitted to major U.S. universities for graduate school.

Another plus is that studying a specific career in a Costa Rican university takes less time which equates to saving a lot of money on a college education. For example, students can enter law or medical school straight out of high school. They don't have to waste time spending four years as an undergraduate.

Public Universities

- University of Costa Rica (Universidad de Costa Rica)- The main campus is located in San José. There are also other campuses in Cartago, Turrialba, Puntarenas and Alajuela. Tel: 2511-000, Web: www.ucr.ac.cr.
- National University (Universidad Nacional). The main campus is in the city of Heredia. There are branches in Liberia and Pérez Zeledón. Tel: 2277-3000. Web: www.una.ac.cr.
- Institute of Technology (Instituto de Tecnología) Located in the city of Cartago. Tel: 2552-5333, www. tec.ac.cr
- The State University's Extension Program (Universidad Estatal a Distancia). The main school is in San José. There are more than 30 branches in other parts of the country. Tel: 2253-2121. Web: www.uned.ac.cr.

Private Universities

- Adventist University of Central America. Tel: 2441-5622, Fax: 2441-3465. E-mail: unadeca@racsa.co.cr.
- Escuela de Agricultura de la Región Tropical Húmedo (EARTH). Tel: 2255-2000, Fax: 2255-2726. E-mail: relext@ns.earth.acca. Web: www.earth.ac.cr.

Private "U"

- Latin American University of Science and Technology (ULACIT). Tel: 2257-5767, Fax: 2222-4542. E-mail: info@ulacit.ac.cr.
- Inter-American University of Costa Rica. Apdo. 6495-1000, San José. Tel: 2234-6262, Fax: 253-8744.
- International University of the Americas (UIA). Apdo. 1447-1002, San José. Tel: 2233-5304, Fax: 222-3216, E-mail: infomatri@uia.ac.cr. Web: www.uia.ac.cr.
- Instituto Centroamericano para la Administración de Empresa (INCAE). Apdo. 960-4050, Alajuela. Tel: 2433-0506, Fax: 2433-9101.
- University for Peace, Apdo. 138, Ciudad Colón.Tel: (506) 249-1072, Fax: (506) 2249-1929
- University Mundial. Tel: 2240-7057, Fax: 2236-6537.

Of course, certain requirements for these schools of higher learning must be met. Once again, remember that private universities are generally more expensive than public universities. See the telephone book for a more extensive list of private universities.

Outstanding Private Schools

Before I talk about Costa Rican schools, I would like to share with you what one foreign resident said motivated him to move here to educate his children:

"One of the many ills of our American society is, simply that we are TOO affluent. I know many are starving and have no shelter. I am not addressing that segment of our society. Rather, I am addressing the great masses in the middle and upper strata. We have too much house, too many cars, too many things, too much stuff. Add to this, the influence of the reactionary baby-boomer parents who wish to give their children everything they didn't have, and you end up with a population of children who have unrealistic expectations of what life is, a generation that is disenchanted, listless, confused, depressed, and seeking an out. They grow up in unstructured environments with too much stuff and not enough rules, or any kind of life ethic that would help them to grow into successful human beings. In short, they aren't optimally deprived of money, free time, privileges, etc.

Costa Rica isn't as affluent as the United States in the ways that many measure, but I'll bet the kids truly understand the principle of working to attain a goal, and I'll bet more of them have real purpose, respect, and discipline than American children. The United States has become too affluent and now complacent. We are seeing the ills of this everywhere. Costa Rica is looking pretty good."

Educational Choices

If you have small children or teenagers, you will be pleased to know that Costa Rica has a variety of schools from which to choose. There are many public schools, numerous private bilingual schools and English-language or American schools. The location of the school you choose will also determine your choice of where to live. Your educational options are much greater in the Central Valley than in rural or outlying areas. Living outside of the Central Valley will most certainly limit your choice of schools. Public schools in rural areas most often offer instruction only through the ninth grade.

Public schools tend to be crowded, but legal foreign residents are entitled to attend public schools. However, since all instruction is in Spanish, you should not even think of enrolling older children in a public school unless they speak, read and write Spanish fluently. Children younger

A group of students at a Costa Rican private school.

than 10 usually can pick up the language quickly. If your children are not Spanish speakers, you also have the option of enrolling them in a private school if there is one in your area.

All schools in Costa Rica that go beyond the ninth grade have to offer the **National Baccalaureate or Bachillerato de Educación Diversificada**. This degree is required to enroll in a university in Costa Rica. With this diploma alone, however, it is very difficult if not impossible to enter a university in the United States.

The **International Baccalaureate** is a second type of diploma offered by Costa Rica's European schools. To earn this diploma, students must complete and test in six subjects; write an extended 4,000 word essay of independent research guided by a faculty mentor; complete 150 hours of creative, action and service (CAS) activities; and participate in a critical thinking course called Theory of Knowledge. The program begins in the 11th grade and is completed in the 12th grade. Admittance to universities in the United States, Europe and Latin America is possible with this degree.

The third type of degree is the **United States Diploma**, with which students may be admitted to universities in the United States or Europe and other parts of the world. But you cannot enter a university in Costa Rica with this diploma alone. All of the American Schools in Costa Rica offer the United States Diploma. The Southern Association of Colleges and Schools, (SACS), accredits all of these schools.

Where the International Baccalaureate is not offered, in the American Schools, many students opt for two diplomas to create more opportunities when choosing a university. They work for the National Baccalaureate, then go onto the 12th grade for the United States Diploma. In the 12th grade many students take advanced placement courses, to get college credit.

It is extremely important to understand that the diplomas these schools offer is critical based on where your children want to study after high school.

All Costa Rican students whether they attend private or public schools, are required to take Public Education Ministry (MEP) testing in the sixth, ninth and 11th grades.Even if they have perfect grades, students have to pass these tests to move on to the next level.

The school week is Monday through Friday, and the day begins about 7:30 a.m. and ends about 2 p.m. in private schools. Schedules vary according to the school and age of the students. Public schools are on a similar schedule unless they are operating two shifts, in which case the second shift may not end before 5 or 6 p.m.

Most schools include pre-kinder to 12th grade. The school structure is further divided into pre-kinder, kinder, primaria (grades one to six), secundaria (seventh to 12th grades). Some private schools have a middle school (grades seven and eight) and high school (grades nine through 12). Class size in private schools ranges from 20 to 30 students, depending on the age of the students and the school. Public schools tend to have much larger classes, ranging from 40 to 60 students.

Students are graded on a scale with 100 being the highest possible score and 70 being the minimum passing grade. The grading system is not on an ABCDF system as are many schools in the United States.

Students from pre-kinder through 12th grade are required to wear uniforms established by each school. Even private schools require the use of uniforms. There is usually an emblem on the chest of each school's shirt with the name of the particular institution.

Private schools

Costa Rica's private English-language American schools are exceptional, and have high academic standards. Four are accredited in the United States: Lincoln School, Marian Baker School, Country Day School and American International School. Some follow the U.S. school year schedule with vacations in June, July and August.

Others follow the Latin American academic calendar, which begins sometime in February and ends in November or December. Changing from the U.S. calendar to one of these schools may require that your children move back half a year and start the grade over. Schools are also free to move students up a half-year if they are academically and psychologically mature enough to handle the change.

These schools are academically oriented and prepare students for admission to colleges in the United States as well as in Costa Rica. They teach English as a primary language and offer Spanish as a second language. In some ways these schools are better than similar institutions in the United States because not as many harmful distractions or bad influences exist in Costa Rica. Children also have the opportunity to learn a new language, which is of great value to them. The cost of some of these private schools can be more than $300 per month.

It is a good idea to visit a number of schools before deciding which one is right for your child. You should ask to visit a couple of classrooms as well as see all of the facilities. This way you may view the school's infrastructure.

Make a list of the pros and cons of each school before making your final decision. Do not forget to see if the school is accredited in the United States Also find out about the teacher-student ratio. Be sure to see what percentage of the students graduate and go on to universities in Costa Rica and the United States. Finally, try to talk to other foreigners who have children enrolled in private schools to see if they are satisfied with the quality of education their children receive.

A list of private schools

My son attended the Lincoln School in Moravia. He learned more there than at the private school he attended in the United States. All subjects are taught in English except for an hour a day of Spanish. There are special courses of Spanish as a second language for students new to the country and advanced classes for foreign students who have mastered the language. I have seen children who move to the country learn to speak fluent Spanish in a couple of years. Conversely, Costa Rican children are able to master English in a short period of time. If you listen to the high school students speak English, you would think they grew up in North America. It must be pointed out that, generally, the younger the student, the more quickly a second language can be learned. Junior and senior high school students take much longer to learn a new language than preschool and elementary students.

The following schools are accredited in the United States. Some follow the U.S. schedule, September to June. Others follow the Costa Rican academic year which, begins in March and ends in November:

- **Lincoln School:** Pre-kindergarten through grade 12 with classes in English. Tuition about $450 monthly: Apdo. 1919, San José, Costa Rica. Tel: 247-0800, Fax: 247-0900, E-mail: director@lincoln.ed.cr, Web: www.lincoln.ed.cr. Follows the U.S. academic year.

- **American International School:** Pre-kindergarten through grade 12. Classes taught in English, U.S.-style education. Annual tuition: $1,070 pre-kindergarten, $3,130 for kindergarten to grade 12. Apdo. 4941-1000, San José, Costa Rica. Tel: 2239-2567, Fax: 2239-0625 E-mail: ais@iscr.com, www.aiscr.com.

- **Country Day School:** (Escazú) Kindergarten through grade 12. Annual tuition: $3,245 pre-kindergarten, $6,510 grades one to 12. Apdo. 8-6170, San José, Costa Rica. Tel: 2289-8406, Fax: 2228-0919, E-mail: codasch@racsa.co.cr, Web: www.cds.ed.cr. Follows the U.S. school year.

- **Country Day School Guanacaste:** This new branch of the Country Day School offers a curriculum similar to the main campus in Escazú. Since the school is located near Flamingo, a surfing class is available for high school students. All subjects are taught in English except for Spanish language class. Future boarding facilities are being considered. Tel: 2654-5042, Fax: 654-5044, E-mail: cdsgte@costarica.net, Web: www.cds.ed.cr.

  The Country Day School in Costa Rica is an American school serving an international population. Established in 1963, the school has accreditations from Middle States Association of Colleges and Schools in the United States and the Costa Rican Ministry of Education. Each year, 100 percent of graduates are admitted to select universities and colleges, with about 90 percent going on to U.S. and Canadian universities and colleges, and 10 percent to Europe or elsewhere. Students who attend CDS receive an American high school diploma, and the curriculum also prepares students for the Costa Rican *bachillerato* examinations.

- **Marian Baker School:** Kindergarten through grade 12. U.S. curriculum with classes in English. Annual tuition: $3,550 kindergarten, $6,610 preparatory to grade six and grades seven to 12. Apdo. 4269, San José, Costa Rica, Tel: 2273-0024, Fax: 2273-4609; E-mail: mbschool@racsa.co.cr. Web: www.marianbakerschool.com. Follows the U.S. school year.

- **Blue Valley School:** Preschool to grade 12. Tel: 2215-2203,Fax: 228-8653, E-mail: bvschool@racsa.co.cr., Web: www.bluevalley.ed.cr. Follows both U.S. and Costa Rican calendars.

- **Central International School of Costa Rica (CIS):** They offer Early Childhood Center (ECC): pre-school (three year olds) to pre-kinder (four year olds), Elementary School, Kindergarten through grades five and Secondary School grades 6th and 8th , grades 9-12th . Their vision is to create a legacy of exemplary global practices in education for our friendly community of international and local families. Tel: (506) 8850-6233 or (506) 8354-7420, E-mail: rainer@cis.ed.cr or lynn@cis.ed.cr, Web: www.ciscr.com

- **The European School:** Pre-kindergarten through grade six. Apdo. 177, Heredia, Costa Rica. Tel: 2261-0717, Fax: 2237-4063, E-mail: eurschool@cafebritt.com or aaronson@racsa.co.cr, Web: www.eupeanschool.com

  The less expensive bilingual private schools below also prepare students for U.S. colleges and universities, but follow the Costa Rican academic year that begins in March and ends in November.

- **Anglo American School:** Kindergarten through grade six. Costs about $100 a month. Apdo. 3188-1000, San José, Costa Rica. Tel: 2225-1723.
- **British School:** Kindergarten through grade 12. Tel: 2200131, Fax: 506-2232-7822,E-mail:british@racsa.co.cr, Web: www.thebritishschoolof costarica.com.

- **Canadian International School:** Pre-kindergarten through grade two. About $100 monthly. Apdo. 622-2300, San José, Costa Rica. Tel: 2272-7097; Fax: 2272-6634.

- **Colegio Bilingue Santa Cecilia:** Preschool to grade 11. Tel: 2237-7733, Fax: 2237-4557, colsuper@racsa.co.

- **Colegio Humboldt:** Kindergarten through grade 12. Classes half in German, half in Spanish. Apdo. 3749, San José, Costa Rica. Tel: 2232-1455, Fax: 2232-0093, E-mail: humboldt@racsa.co.cr, Web:www.humboldt.ed.cr.

- **Colegio Internacional:** Grades seven through 10. Apdo. 963, 2050 San Pedro, Costa Rica. Tel: 224-3136 Fax: 2253-9762, E-mail: sekerdir@racsa.co.cr, Web: www.sek.net.

- **Colegio Metodista:** Kindergarten through grade 12. Classes in English and Spanish. Apdo. 931-1000, San José, Costa Rica. Tel: 2225-0655, Fax: 2225-0621.

- **Escuela Británica:** Kindergarten through grade 11, classes half in English, half in Spanish. $150 per month. Apdo. 8184-1000 San José, Costa Rica. Tel: 2220-0131 Fax: 2232-7833, E-mail: british@racsa.co.cr, Web: www.infoweb.co.cr/british.

- **Hebrew Day School:** English-based curriculum, U.S. accedited teachers, small class size and scholarships available. English, Hebrew and Spanish are taught. Tel: 2296-6565, E-mail: hds@jabadcr.com.

- **Lighthouse International School:** The most recent private school in the Guachipelín area. Apdo. 127-1255, Escazú, San José, Costa Rica. Tel: 2215-2393, E-mail: info@lighthouse.ed.cr

- **Liceo Franco-Costarricense:** Classes in French, English and Spanish. Concepción de Tres Ríos. Tel: 2273-4543, Fax: 2279-6615, E-mail: lyfrancos@racsa.co.cr, Web: www.franco.ed.cr.

- **International Christan School:** Pre-kindergarten through grade 12. Annual tuition: $990 pre-kindergarten, $1,300 preparatory and kindergarten, $2,200 grades one to six, $2,300 grades 7 - 8 , $2,500 grades 9 - 12. Apdo. 3512-1000, San José, Costa Rica. Tel: 2241-1445 Fax: 2241-4944, E-mail: intchris@racsa.co.cr, Web: wwwicscr.net.

- **Pan American School:** Pre-kinder through 12. Tel: 2293-7393, Fax: 2298-5700, E-mail: cpcrsa@racsa.co.cr, Web: www.panam.ed.cr. Located in San Antonio de Belén.

- **Saint Anthony School:** Pre-school through grade 6. Classes half in English, half in Spanish. Apdo. 29-2150, Moravia, Costa Rica. Tel: 2235-1017, Fax: 2235-2325, E-mail: santhony@racsa.co.cr.

- **Saint Francis:** Kindergarten through grade 11, classes in English and Spanish. Inquire about rates. Apdo. 4405-1000, San José Costa Rica. Tel: 2297-1704 Fax: 2240-9672, E-mail: sfc@stfrancis.ed.cr.

- **Saint Mary's:** Pre- kindergarten through grade six, about $100 monthly. Classes in English and Spanish. Apdo. 229-1250, Escazú, Costa Rica. Tel: 2228-2003.

- **Summerhill Latinoamericano:** Pre-school, elementary school and weekend camp programs. Tel: 2280-1933, Fax: 2283-0146.

- **Colegio Yurusti:** in Santo Domingo de Heredia The teaching is done in Spanish, with 14 hours a week in English. Tel. 2244 2900 , E-mail: yurusti@ice.co.cr www yurusti.ed.cr

* Go on-line or seee the yellow pages for more listings.

Home Schooling and On-Line Study

I talked with one U.S. couple who did not have the resources to afford a private school, so they opted for home schooling. They recommended several programs that you can find on the Internet: www.calvertschool.org, www.highschool.unl.edu and www.keystonehighschool.com.

The Country Day School in Costa Rica and K12International Academy have announced a partnership to offer an accredited online school program to students throughout Costa Rica. The online private school program — a first of its kind in Costa Rica — is called the CDS K12 International Academy.

Students who enroll in the CDS K12International Academy have the opportunity to receive a complete education through an internationally-accredited private school that uses a curriculum developed by K12 Inc., the U.S. leader in online school programs for students in kindergarten through high school, according to the Escazú-based school.

The CDS K12 International Academy offers students a wide variety of courses, including core subjects, honors, advanced placement, world languages, and other electives. Students living anywhere in Costa Rica – even those located in geographically remote areas – are able to earn a U.S. diploma through this cost-effective school option, said the school announcement.

The K12International Academy is a U.S.-based private school that serves students in more than 35 countries worldwide. High School students at Country Day School already have been enrolled in a wide variety of secondary K12 online courses, and educators there anticipate the enrollment in these virtual courses to increase.

12

More Useful Information

Where to Find Affordable Foods

A wide variety of delicious tropical fruits and vegetables grows in Costa Rica. It is amazing that every fruit and vegetable you can think of in addition to exotic native varieties flourish here. More common tropical fruits such as pineapples, mangoes and papayas cost about a third of what they do in the United States. Bananas can be purchased at any local fruit stand or street market for about five cents each.

Once you live in Costa Rica and get settled, you can do as many Costa Ricans do and eat a few slices of mouth-watering fruit for breakfast at one of the many sidewalk ***fruterías*** or fruit stands all over the country. For people living on a tight budget, this healthy, fresh fruit breakfast will cost about $0.75 to $1.50. There are also many ***sodas***, or small cafes, where you can eat a more typical Costa Rican breakfast for about $3 to $4.

Besides fruits and vegetables, many other bargain foods are available in Costa Rica. Bakeries sell fresh homemade breads and pastries. Other foods such as eggs, chicken, meat and honey are available at most small neighborhood grocery stores, ***pulperías***, as well as at large supermarkets.

These supermarkets are much like markets in the United States; everything is under one roof, but the selection of products is smaller. There are even 24-hour mini-markets in gas stations like the 7-Eleven and Circle-K types found in the United States.

Some imported packaged products found in Costa Rican supermarkets can be expensive. It is usual to pay more for your favorite breakfast cereal, certain canned foods and liquor. Do not worry because there are local products to substitute for your favorite U.S. brand. However, if you absolutely cannot live without your foods from the States, you can usually find them at the **AutoMercado** supermarkets, **Hipermás** or **Pricesmart** stores. You can stock-up on these hard-to-find items on shopping trips to the States and bring them back with you by plane.

Since most foods are so affordable in Costa Rica, you will be better off changing your eating habits and buying more local products so you can keep your food bill low. You can save more money by shopping at one of the central markets (*Mercado Central)* found in Heredia, in San José or in any major city or town, as many cost-conscious Costa Ricans do. The latter covers a whole city block in the heart of downtown San José, near the banking district. Under one roof are hundreds of shops where you can buy fresh fruits, vegetables, grains and much more. You can also go to an open-air street market found in most every large town, called ***feria del agricultor***, on any Saturday or Sunday morning. Farmers bring their fresh produce to these street markets each week, so you can find a variety of produce, meats

Inexpensive fruits and vegetables can be found at any of the country's weekend outdoor markets or *ferias*.

Ceviche de Corvina
(Marinated White Seabass)

1 lb. seabass, cut in small pieces
3 tablespoons omion, finely chopped
1 tablespoon celery, finely chopped
2 tablespoons fresh coriander, chopped
2 cups lemon juice
Salt, pepper and Tabasco Sauce
1/2 teaspoon Worcester Sauce

Combine all ingredients in a glass bowl.
Let it stand for at least four hours in the refrigerator.
Serve chilled in small bowls topped with catsup and soda crackers on the side. Serves 8.

TRES LECHES
(Three Milk Cake)

Cake Base
5 eggs
1 teaspoon baking powder
1 cup sugar
1/2 teaspoon vanilla
1 1/2 cups of flower

Preheat oven at 350 F. Sift baking powder. Set aside. Cream butter and sugar until fluffy. Add eggs and vanilla and beat well. Add flour to the butter mixture 2 tablespoons at a time, until well blended. Pour into greased rectangular Pyrex dish and bake at 350 F for 30 minutes. Let cool. Pierce with a fork and cover. For the filling combine 2 cups of milk, 1 can of condensed milk and one can of evaporated milk. Pour this mixture over the cool cake. To make the topping, mix 1 1/2 cups of half & half, 1 teaspoon vanilla and a cup of sugar. Whip together until thick. Spread over the top of the cake. Keep refrigerated. Serves 12.

Gallo Pinto

(Rice and Beans)
The Traditional Costa Rican Dish

Gallo Pinto is eaten nationwide.
Most people eat it for breakfast.
Others for lunch or dinner. Makes 3 to 4 servings

Preparation Time: 10 minutes

Ingredients

2 cups of cooked long grain rice
1 cup of red or black small cooked beans ("frijol criollo")
1/2 cup of finely diced white onions
3 teaspoons of vegetable oil
2 tablespoons of chopped cilantro ("Culantro de Castilla")
Salt to taste
Lizano Sauce ("Salsa Lizano" is a mild sauce used on every day cooking in Costa Rica)

Instructions

Place vegetable oil on a frying pan and heat for approximately 1 minute. Saute onions until caramelized. Add entire pot of cooked beans and its gravy into the sautéed onions. Stir over low-medium heat for a minute. Combine cooked rice to sautéed bean mix well and simmer for 5 minutes. Add salt to taste. Add cilantro. Cook on high heat and quick.Serve immediately and add the Lizano Sauce to taste.

and eggs at low prices. There is a weekly list that appears in *La Nación* newspaper listing the suggested prices of all fruits and vegetables sold at the various *ferias*.

A few words about Costa Rica's excellent seafood. With oceans on both sides, Costa Rica has a huge variety of fresh seafood. Tuna, mahi mahi and corvina, abound as do shrimp of all sizes and some crab. All of these can be purchased at any ***pescadería*** (fish market) in the country at low prices. If you haven't done so, try a heaping plate of ***ceviche*** (fish cocktail) at one of the many fish restaurants called ***marisquerías.***

Typical Costa Rican food is similar to that of Mexico and other Central American countries. Tortillas often, but not always, are eaten with a meal of rice, beans, fruit, eggs, vegetables and a little meat. The most common dish, ***gallo pinto*** (literally spotted rooster), is made with rice and black beans as a base and fried with red bell peppers and cilantro. This dish is addicting.

Some other popular Costa Rican foods include ***casado,*** the blue-plate special (fish, chicken or meat with beans and chopped cabbage), ***empanadas*** (a type of stuffed bread turnover), ***arreglados*** (a kind of sandwich) and ***palmito*** (heart of palm), which is usually eaten in salads.

The major supermarkets in the Central Valley are **Perimercados** (several locations in the San José area), **Más x Menos** (a large chain also with home delivery at 800-MASYMAS), **Auto Mercado** (upscale, also with home delivery service), **Palí** and **Megasuper**.

Modern U.S.-style supermarkets abound in Costa Rica.

For food prices on-line, see: **www.hipermas.co.cr/ofertas1.htm**, **www.masxmenos.co.cr/folleto.htm** and **www.maxibodega.co.cr/ofertas.htm**. For home delivery of groceries: **www.amidomicilio.com/servlet/catalogo** and **www.expressmart.net/version3/index.php.** For home delivered organic and natural foods see **www.NaturaStyle.com tel: 2235-7654** or **8386-0092.**

Where to Eat

Many excellent restaurants serving a wide variety of international foods are scattered all over the San José, adjoining towns and in other areas of the country. Most of these restaurants are incredible bargains when compared to similar establishments in the United States. You will be happy to know that Costa Rica's restaurants are clean, and health codes are strictly enforced by the Health Ministry *(Ministerio de Salud)*. For your convenience we have included a list of our favorite places to eat, but you are sure to discover many on your own or by word of mouth once you have lived in Costa Rica for a while.

Some of the best sea food you will ever savor may be found at **El Banco de Mariscos** in Santa Barbara de Heredia. **La Fuente de los Mariscos** behind the Hotel Irazú in the San José 2000 Shopping Center and **El Balcón de Mariscos** in Curridabat round out our list of seafood eateries. **Machu Picchu**, **Ceviche del Rey** and **the Inka Grill** serve delicious Peruvian-style seafood.

There are also many Italian restaurants. The **Balcón de Europa, Pan E Vino, L'Olivo** and **La Antigua Roma** in Heredia all serve delicious Italian food.

If you like U.S.-style food and beer served in foot-tall mugs, try **Fridays** near the university in San Pedro.

La Soda Tapia is famous for its gigantic fruit salads and typical breakfasts. **Restaurante Grano de Oro**, in the charming hotel of the same name, offers an excellent menu.

You can dine, watch TV and read an assortment of newspapers at the **News Café** in the Hotel Presidente. Their new street-side bar that is a great spot for people watching. The Hotel Balmoral's **El Patio,** is a semi-open-air restaurant across from the Hotel Presidente and another great place to obseervepasserbies. **Chelles** (Ave. Central, Calle 9) serves great sandwiches. **Café Parisien**, in the Gran Hotel Costa Rica, never closes and is one of the best locations in town to people watch and find a variety of coffee-based drinks. The **City Café** is one of many all-night restaurants and a popular North American hangout. If you get a case of the munchies and want to grab a late-night snack, there is a lot of action here with the adjacent gambling area and swinging bar. Rounding out our list of all-night eateries is **Manolo's** outdoor café in downtown San José.

Chinese restaurants abound in the San José area as well as the rest of Costa Rica. It seems as if there is one on every block. The Asian food served here is not as tasty as what you will find in San Francisco's Chinatown, but it is inexpensive.

If you want something other than chop suey, chow mein and rice dishes, try **Tin Jo** (2221-7605) restaurant. It has a wide selection including tasty Mandarin, Szechuan and even Thai food. **Saisaki** is a little restaurant which serves sushi, Korean and Philippine food.

Lovers of Mexican food should try any of the **El Fogoncito** locations, **Antojitos**.

The **Pops** ice cream parlors sell every imaginable flavor of your favorite ice cream. **Haagaen Dazs** now has stores in Escazú and Curridabat and is available in many super markets. **TCBY**, the U.S. frozen yogurt chain, even has a couple of stores here. There are several establishments that now offer Italian-style Gelato ice cream. **Spoon** pastry shops sell the best cakes and pastries in the country many locations in the San José area. The **Trigo Miel** bakery chain offers good pastries.

Bagels can even be found in Costa Rica. **Bagelmens'** in San Pedro, Curridabat, Belén and Escazú offers a wide selection of fresh baked bagels, sandwiches and excellent coffee.

Costa Rica's seafood restaurants have some of the best fish dishes you will ever savor.

We don't have Starbuck's in Costa Rica but coffee connoisseurs can savor a cup of their favorite local brew and grab a bite to eat at the **Café Parisien** in the Gran Hotel Costa Rica. The new **Port City Java** chain of gourmet Cafés in La Lindora is very similar to Starbucks. **Café Britt** offers a great coffee tour of its farm in the hills of Heredia. We recommend this excursion to tourists as well as permanent residents. They explain every step of how coffee is grown and processed and relate the history of coffee in Costa Rica. Perhaps the best Colds coffee drinks are served at one of the **Mac Cafés** found at almost any of the MacDonalds restaurants.

If you like to eat-on-the-run, you can; all of the American fast food restaurant chains operate in Costa Rica. **Pizza Hut**, **Papa John's**, **McDonald's**, **Taco Bell**, **Burger King**, **Kentucky Fried Chicken**, **Quizno's** and **Subway** sandwiches all have restaurants conveniently located in San José, the suburbs and several shopping malls.

However, the best chicken is served at the **Rosti-Pollos** restaurants in downtown San José, San Pedro, Escazú, Heredia, Alajuela, Guadalupe and many other locations. They cook their chicken over coffee branches, which gives it an incredibly delicious flavor.

Denny's has one 24-hour restaurant next to the Hotel Irazú and another by the airport with more restaurants scheduled to open in the next couple of years. The chain offers breakfast specials just as they do in the United States.

Most U.S. fast-food chains can be found in Costa Rica

Meat lovers will be pleased to know that **Tony Roma's,** famous for its ribs, opened a restaurant in Escazú. The same owners just opened the first **Wendy's** hamburger chain in Costa Rica. **Outback Steakhouse.**

Goya in downtown San José and **La Masía** in Sabana Norte offer a wide variety of Spanish and international dishes. **Olio** in Barrio Escalante features *tapas* and Mediterranean dishes.

For the best Costa Rican style cooking try **La Casa de Doña Lela** with restaurants in Escazú, Belén and in Tibás about a mile past the Saprissa Soccer Stadium. The food is delicious and a steal. **Rústico,** a local chain, also offers a wide selection of Costa Rican style dishes. They have restaurants in Multiplaza, San Pedro Mall. Paseo de las Flores and Real Cariari Mall. **La Casona del Cafetal** is a real find. This restaurant is located about 45 minutes from San José in the heart of the Orosi Valley and has a great Sunday buffet. The setting is incredible. It is located next to a lake and surrounded by a coffee plantation.

Sodas are plentiful and found all over. You can be assured that almost any small shop displaying the sign *soda* serves affordable food, since the majority of working-class *ticos* eat in these establishments. Most big towns and cities have a central market where a lot of sodas can be found. Both San Jose's and Heredia's central markets have dozens of sodas where you can find almost every imaginable dish at rock bottom prices.

The Vishnu Natural Food Restaurants offer affordable cusine.

We have eaten at the market in Heredia and many a time couldn't finish the huge amount of food that was served to us. The bill usually never runs more than three dollars.

There are a number of vegetarian restaurants all over San José and surprisingly in remote areas of the country such as Montezuma Beach. As more and more Costa Ricans become health conscious these establishments grow in popularity. Prices are generally low and the servings are huge. One establishment in San José offers soups, salad, rice, a vegetable dish, dessert and a natural fruit juice drink for around $4. **Vishnu** has over 10 branches. **Restaurante Vegetariano** of San Pedro, located near the University of Costa Rica, is one of our favorites and popular with the college crowd. **Shakti** offers a variety of vegetarian dishes.

The Tico Times carries advertisements for restaurants and feature occasional restaurant reviews. In addition, ***The Tico Times Restaurant Guide*** lists hundreds of restaurants. For a complete list of restaurants in Escazu, Santa Ana, Rohrmoser, Sabana, Pavas and Paseo Colon **www.newsletter.escazunews.com/index.php?pr=Restaurantes** or see **www.costaricaeatsguide.com/RESTAURANT_GUIDE.html**

Home delivery

Many establishments offer home delivery to metropolitan area in the United States do so in Costa Rica as well. I have listed a few below. Please consult the phone bookor information for more locations near you.

Fast Food:	
Bagelmens	2289-4616
Burger King	2257-7777
China Express	2232-2903
Dos por Uno Pizza	800-621-2121, 281-2121
McDonald's	2286-0101
Papa John's	2258-92999
Pizza Hut	2290-9595
Pollos Campero	2256-6363
RostiPollos	2218-1212
Spoon Escazú	2288-3145 (many other locations)
Subway	2290-9494

Religion

Although 90 percent of Costa Ricans are Roman Catholic, there is freedom of religion and other religious views are permitted here.

I hope the list of churches provided below will help you. Call the number of your denomination to be directed to your nearest house of worship in the San José area. Some churches in the San José area have services in English.

Baptist (San Pedro)	2253-7911
Beit Menschem	2296-6565
Bilingual Christian Fellowship	2442-3663
B'nai Israel (reformi)	2231-5243, 2257-1785
Catholic (Downtown Cathedral)	2221-3820
Catholic (Escazú)	2228-0635
Catholic (Los Yoses)	2225-6778
Catholic (Rohrmoser)	2232-2128
Catholic (Barrio San Bosco)	2221-3748
Catholic (San Rafael)	2232-6847
Christian Science	2221-0840
Episcopal	2225-0209
International Baptist Church	2253-7911

One of Costa Rica's houses of worship.

Israel Center (orthodox) 2520-1013
Jabad Lubavich (orthodox) Rohrmoser 2296-6565
Jehovah's Witness 2221-1436
Methodist 2222-0360
Mormon (Santos de Los Ultimos Días) 2234-1945
Protestant 2228-0553
Quaker 2233-6168
Seventh Day Adventists 2223-7759
Saint Mary's(Catholic) 2239-0033
Synagogue Shaare Zion 2222-5449
Unitarian .... 2228-1020 or 2228-4196
Union Church 2235-6709
Unity 2228-6051
Unity Church (Escazú) 2228-6051

Costa Rica's Holidays

Costa Ricans are very nationalistic and proudly celebrate their official holidays, called ***feriados***. During some holidays, the country virtually comes to a standstill and many banks, public institutions, government and private offices and stores close. Plan your activities around these holidays and do not count on getting business of any kind done. In fact, the whole country shuts down during *Semana Santa* (the week leading up to Easter) and the week between Christmas and New Year's Day. San José turns into a pleasantly quiet city as many Costa Rican families spend their holidays at the beach. Asterisks indicate paid holidays and days off for workers.

January 1	New Year's Day*
March 19	Saint Joseph's Day
Holy Week	Holy Thursday and Good Friday*
April 11	Juan Santamaría's Day (local hero)*
May 1	Labor Day*
May	University Week (held in San Pedro)
June	Father's Day (the third Sunday)
July 25	Annexation of Guanacaste Province*
August 2	Virgin of LosAngeles Day
August 15	Mother's Day*
September 15	Independence Day*
October 12	Columbus Day - (Discovery of America)

October 12	Limón Carnival
October 31	Halloween
November 2	Day of the Dead
December 8	Immaculate Conception
December 25	Christmas*
December 25	Feria de Zapote (December 25 to January 2)
December 25	Fiestas de Fin del Año

Bringing Your Pets in and out of Costa Rica

I did not forget those of you who have pets. There are procedures for bringing your pets into the country that require very little except patience, some paperwork and a small fee.

Dogs and cats entering Costa Rica must have a health certificate issued by a licensed veterinarian. The examination for the certificate must be conducted within two weeks prior to travel to Costa Rica.

A registered veterinarian from your hometown must certify that your pets are free of internal and external parasites. It is necessary that your pet have up-to-date vaccinations against rabies (the rabies vaccination must not be older than one year), distemper, leptospirosis, hepatitis and parvovirus

Your pets will be happy in Costa Rica

within the last three years. Remember, all of these required documents are indispensable and must be certified by the Costa Rican consulate nearest your hometown. These papers are only good for 30 days. If you do not renew them within this period of time, you will have to make another trip to the vet's office and the airline will not accept your animal. If you are bringing an exotic animal to Costa Rica —parakeet, macaw or other—you will need special permits from the Convention of International Species in Danger of Extinction and the Costa Rican Natural Resources Ministry.

If all of this paperwork is too much for you, the Association of Residents of Costa Rica (ARCR) can take care of everything, including airport pick up, for about $100. If you have no place to keep your pet, they offer boarding at $20 a day.

If you fail to comply with these regulations and do not provide the required documents, your pet(s) can be refused entry, placed in quarantine or even put to sleep. But don't worry, if worse comes to worst, there is a 30-day grace period to straighten things out.

If the animal is traveling with you as part of your luggage, the average rate is $50 from one destination to the next (i.e. Los Angeles—Miami—San José). If your pet travels alone, depending on size and weight, the average rate is $100 to $200. Please consult your airline for the actual price. Call the 800 toll-free cargo section of American Airlines and they will tell you the cost.

Whether your pet is traveling with you or separately, be aware that the weather can delay your animals arrival in Costa Rica. U.S.D.A. (Department of Agriculture) regulations on animals in flight say that you may or may not fly a pet as baggage or cargo if during any part of the trip the temperature will rise above 80 degrees or below 40 degrees at either your point of departure or a layover. Some airlines, such as Delta, will not fly any pets from May 15 to September 15. I know of several people who have arrived at the airport only to find out their animals could not travel due to a change in the weather. Call your airline the day you intend to ship your animal and again an hour or two before departure to see if your animal will be allowed to travel. This way you can avoid unpleasant surprises.

Also, make sure your dog or cat has an airline-approved portable kennel. These rules are very strict and the kennel must be the appropriate size for your animal or it will not be allowed to travel. Some airlines rent kennels. Make sure your kennel has a small tray so your pet can have food and water during the journey. Two to eight hours is a long time to go without food or water.

If there is a layover involved, the baggage handlers will give water to your pet. The operator at American Airlines told me about a special service that will walk your dog for an extra charge at some airports. Some people suggest tranquilizing dogs and cats when shipping them by plane. I talked to my vet when I was going to ship my large Siberian husky, and he did not seem to think it was a good idea. We also asked a friend who ships show dogs all over the United States and he said to use my own judgment since tranquilizers can make an animal ill.

Some airlines allow small pets to travel in kennels in the passenger cabin. You can bring one per passenger on the plane and often the airlines will only allow one pet per cabin, so reserve early. They must fit in these tiny little carriers. A few airlines have restrictions on certain breeds of dogs, including Doberman pinschers, rottweilers and pit bulls. Be sure to check with the airline if you have one of these breeds.

Here is what Continental says about prohibited dogs: "American Pit Bull Terriers (Pit Bulls , Pit Bull Terriers American and Staffordshire Terriers). Continental Airlines will accept American Pit Bull Terrier puppies which are between 8 weeks and 6 months of age provided they do not weigh more than 20 lb (9 kg). All American Pit Bull Terriers more than6 months old or weighing more than 20lb (9 kg) will be refused. Crossbreeds with American Pit Bull Terriers are also excluded from this embargo. This embargo is due to the danger presented to our aircraft and our customers.Bulldogs and other Breeds: Continental Airlines has completely embargoed French and English Bulldogs, American Bulldogs, the "American Bully" and American Staffordshire Terriers over 6 months of age or over 20 lbs/9.0 kgs.Puppies which are less than 6 months in age or under 20 lbs/9.0 kg sare permitted when the temperature along the entire route is planned to be below 85°F/(29.4° C). The purpose of this embargo is because these animals are especially susceptible to high heat, high humidity and stress and have proven difficult to move safely. Thus in the interest of these animals' safety, we have made this difficult decision."

Here is how to find information from Delta Airlines about shipping your pet. **http://www.delta.com/planning_reservations/special_travel_needs/pet_travel_information/pet_requirements_restrictions/index.jsp**

One foreigner shared the following story about when he brought his pet: "I used USAirways when I brought my small dog here last month. It was a good experience and he was with me on the plane the entire trip. The price was $100 and other than the USDA vet's certification and shot record (which must not be more than two weeks old), the pet must be cleared for import by a vet here in Costa Rica."

Another expat and animal lover hired a charter to bring her many pets to Costa Rica: "After doing major research on this, I realized that the cost of my 12 pets in cargo, renting a vehicle that could transport them, us and 20 odd pieces of luggage, driving for almost three hours to get to the airport and waiting at the airport for many hours, wasn't going to be a whole lot less expensive than doing a private charter."

There are also pet transport services such as **www.airanimal.com** and **www.pettransporter.com**, that have contracts with the airlines allowing them to make things easier for you.

If you want to take your pet out of Costa Rica, you will need a special permit, a certificate from a local veterinarian, and proof that all vaccinations are up-to-date. When you obtain these documents, take them to the Ministry of Health and your pet will be free to leave the country. The day you leave, plan on being at the airport at least two and a half hours early, since all your pet's papers must be stamped before departure. Do not for get to make sure that your papers must comply with the rules and regulations of your home country or destination.

Here is another expats take on shipping out of the country. "We have been taking our pooch back and forth to Costa Rica for years. First, you want to identify your travel date and call the airlines. Depending on where you are going there are restrictions regarding the temperatures/dates that pets can travel as baggage in the cargo section of plane. However, if you are carrying onboard (max limit 8-10 lbs in an airline authorized carry case (sold by vets everywhere) you can travel anytime of year (no temp restriction)....only 2 pets per airline trip."

"Book your flight with the airline and advise that you have a pet (to be on-board) or as cargo. When you have your reservation, etc., go to your vet and they will provide the necessary pet examination and prepare the documentation to export and import into the USA. (there is no quarantine time between the USA and Costa Rica. The veterinarians in Costa Rica take some time so be sure to allow for "*Tico* time" (2-3 weeks pre-departure) Be sure to walk your pet pre-boarding or expect a 'mess' on arrival because dogs do get nervous."

These requirements and additional information are available from the Agriculture Ministry's **Animal Sanitation Department** (2260-9046).

Veterinarians

Dr. Federico Patiño (Rohrmoser	2231-5276
Clínica Echandi	2223-3111
Dr. Adrián Molina	2228-1909
Dr. Federico Piza	2248-7166
Dr. Douglas Lutz	2225-6784
Dr. L. Starkey	2253-7142
Tecnología Veterinaria (clinic, pharmacy, and boarding)	2228-9347
Dr. Lorena Guerra (makes house calls, also boarding)	2228-9887

If you have to travel, the Clínica Echandi or one of the other places that board dog, cats or other pets will care for your animal. They charge about $7 per day for this boarding service. For additional veterinarians, look under the heading ***"Veterinaria"*** in the yellow pages. See **www.puppytravel.com.**

If you would like to adopt a pet contact the AHPPA refuge in Heredia (267-7158) where you can adopt a pet.

Services for the Disabled

Getting around in the United States or Canada is hard enough when a person is disabled, but it can be even harder in a foreign country.

Handicapped and disabled persons may find obstacles living in Costa rica. In 1998, the Costa Rican Law for the Equality of Opportunities for Persons with Disabilities went into effect. It mandated every public space in the country to be wheelchair-accessible by 2008, thus improving accessibility for the disabled. The reality, though, is that wheelchair-bound people still have mobility issues, given the lack of sidewalks and potholed streets.

However, government buildings have wheelchair access, and most buses have wheelchair entry. Several hotels such as the Hampton Inn in Alajuela and the Hotel del Sur in San Isidro, have fully equipped rooms for disabled persons.

During the rainy season, the terrain can sometimes be hard to negotiate. Recently the government increased the construction of sidewalk ramps, specially marked parking spaces and telephones for people with physical limitations.

As mention in Chapter 3, medical care is affordable in Costa Rica and should not be a problem. Also, keep in mind that taxis are inexpensive and the best way to travel for people with physical impediments. Since hired help is such a bargain, a full-time employee may be hired as a companion or as a nurse for a very reasonable price. I know several men confined to wheelchairs who have found love and married in Costa Rica. There is a social club for disabled veterans that meets once a month. Call 2443-9870 for more information.

I suggest you pick up the book, *Access to the World: A Travel Guide for the Handicapped*, by Louise Weiss, published by Chatham Square Press, 401 Broadway, New York, NY 10013. This book contains good information and suggestions for disabled travelers. Also check out **www.disabilitytravel.com/independent/accessible-costa-rica.html**.

For Our Canadian Readers

In order to escape Canada's cold winters, many Canadians live in Costa Rica on a full or part-time basis. It is therefore not surprising that many businesses and services catering to Canadians have been created.

Canadians may stay in Costa Rica for up to 90 days without a visa, however a passport is required. Extensions may be obtained from the Immigration office. If you overstay your visa or entry stamp, you will have to pay a nominal fine for each extra month you've stayed.

The **Canadian Club** helps make life easier for Canadians living or planning to live in Costa Rica. By attending club meetings people can make new friendships and establish some good contacts.

This organization provides information about acquiring residency, starting a business, transferring ownership of a vehicle, names of doctors and lawyers and will assist with purchasing medical, automobile and home insurance in Costa Rica. All Canadian visitors and residents are urged to attend. They meet at the King's Garden Restaurant above the Más x Menos supermarket in east Sabana, the third Wednesday of every month at noon. You can find a schedule of their activities and meetings in the *the Tico Times.* IN addition, the Canadian Outreach Group meets regularly to do good deeds for Costa Rican schoolchildren.

If you are a Canadian non-resident living in Costa Rica, you should think about receiving the *CRA Magazine's Canadian Expat Quarterly.* It sends out a periodic update newsletter covering topics of tax and financial interest to Canadians overseas. If you should have an expatriate-related tax or investment question, send it to them and they will try to research the answer for you. Contact Canadians Residents Abroad Inc., 305 Lakeshore Road East, Oakville, Ontario L6J 1J3, tel: (905)-842-0080, fax:(905)-842-9814, e-mail: cra@canadiansresidentabroad, **www.canadiansresidentabroad.com**.

The Canadian Embassy is now located in the Oficentro office complex, in building 5, third floor, in the Sabana Sur area of San José, behind the Contraloría. The address and phone are Apartado 351-1007 Centro Colón, San José, Costa Rica, tel: 2296-4149, fax: 2296-4270.

If you have any questions about Costa Rica or need a visa, you may contact any of the following Costa Rican Embassies and Consulates in Canada:

- **Montreal**, 1155 Dorchester Blvd. West, Suite 2902, Montreal, Quebec H3B 2L3, tel: (514) 866-8159.
- **Ottawa**, 15 Argule St., Ottawa, ON K2P 1B7, tel: (613) 234-5762 or 562-2855 fax: 230-2656.
- **Toronto**, 164 Avenue Rd., Toronto, ON M5R 2H9, tel: (416) 961-6773, fax: 961-6771.

Understanding the Metric System

If you are from the United States, you probably did not study the metric system when you were in school, as it is almost never used in the United States. If you plan to live in Costa Rica, however, it is in your best interest to understand this system. Automobile speedometers, road mileage signs, the contents of bottles, and rulers are in metric.

1. The metric system works on multiples of 10 applied to the basic measurement. The basic measurements are the gram for weight or mass, the meter for length and the liter for volume or capacity.

2. The basic metric measurements have prefixes that change the unit size by a factor of 10. Going smaller, deci is 1/10, centi is 1/100 and milli is 1/100. For example, the commonly used centimeter is 1/100th of a meter. Going larger, deka is 10 times, hecto is 100 times and a kilo is 1,000 times. Kilo is used most often as in kilometer and kilogram.

3. Learn the most commonly used metric measurements. For length, the centimeter, meter and kilometer are used in place of inches, yards and miles. For weight, the kilogram replaces pounds. Grams and milligrams are small weight measures and the metric ton is 1,000 kilograms. The liter replaces the quart for larger volumes, centiliters for ounces and milliliters for small volumes. The hectare is used to measure land and is 10,000 square meters.

4. Learn some conversion factors so you can start thinking of items in metric sizes. An inch is 2.54 centimeters, a meter is 1.09 yards and a kilometer is 0.62 miles. A liter is 1.06 quarts. A kilogram is 2.2 pounds and it takes 28.6 grams to equal 1 ounce. The hectare is equal to 2.47 acres. Start to look at objects in your world in terms of liters, kilograms and kilometers.

5. In the English system, a 1 oz. volume of water weighs 1 oz. and 1 pint (16 oz.) of water weighs 1 lb. The metric system works the same way. A liter of water weighs 1 kilogram. So a milliliter weighs 1 g and has a volume of 1 cubic centimeter.

6. Now that you understand how the metric system fits together, start looking for metric measurements. You will find them on packaging labels and on your car speedometer. When you read about grams or liters or kilometers, take time to calculate what the equal quantity is in

the English system. Soon you will understand how the metric system works for everyday life.

The conversion guide below will help you:

To Convert:	**To:**	**Multiply by:**
Centigrade	Fahrenheit	1.8, then add 32
Square km	Square miles	0.3861
Square km	Acres	247.1
Meters	Yards	1.094
Meters	Feet	3.281
Liters	Pints	2.113
Liters	Gallons	0.2642
Kilometers	Miles	0.6214
Kilograms	Pounds	2.205
Hectares	Acres	2.471
Grams	Ounces	0.03527
Centimeters	Inches	0.3937

* Here is a website you may use for metric conversion: **www.metric-conversions.org**

Special Services for Newcomers

The time-tested businesses listed in this special section provide excellent services.
The author has personally interviewed hundreds of foreigners who have utilized these services and who are extremely pleased with the quality of help they received.

ASSOCIATION OF
RESIDENTS OF COSTA RICA
"Over 20 Years Of Service"
For residency needs
• Service as your "bridge" to the government.
• Counselling and processing of residency applications.
• Renewal of residency cards and handling of periodic paperwork.
• Information on investments and banking.
And more!...
• A full range of insurance at preferred group rates.
• Contacts for real estate, buy, sell or rent.
• Orientation for importing cars, household goods and pets.
• Discount at hundreds of business for ARCR members.
• Social and cultural events.
• Seminars.
• A Corporate Service Program.
• Tour packages including: Accommodation, transportation and tours.
Newcomers:
Please call our office
to make your appointment
Free information package
ARCR
Administración S.A.
Tel.: (506) 2221-2053 / 2233-8068
Fax: (506) 2255-0061
Gte.: (506) 2667-0151
E-mail: arcr@casacanada.net
P.O. Box: 1191-1007 Centro Colón, San José, Costa Rica. www.arcr.net

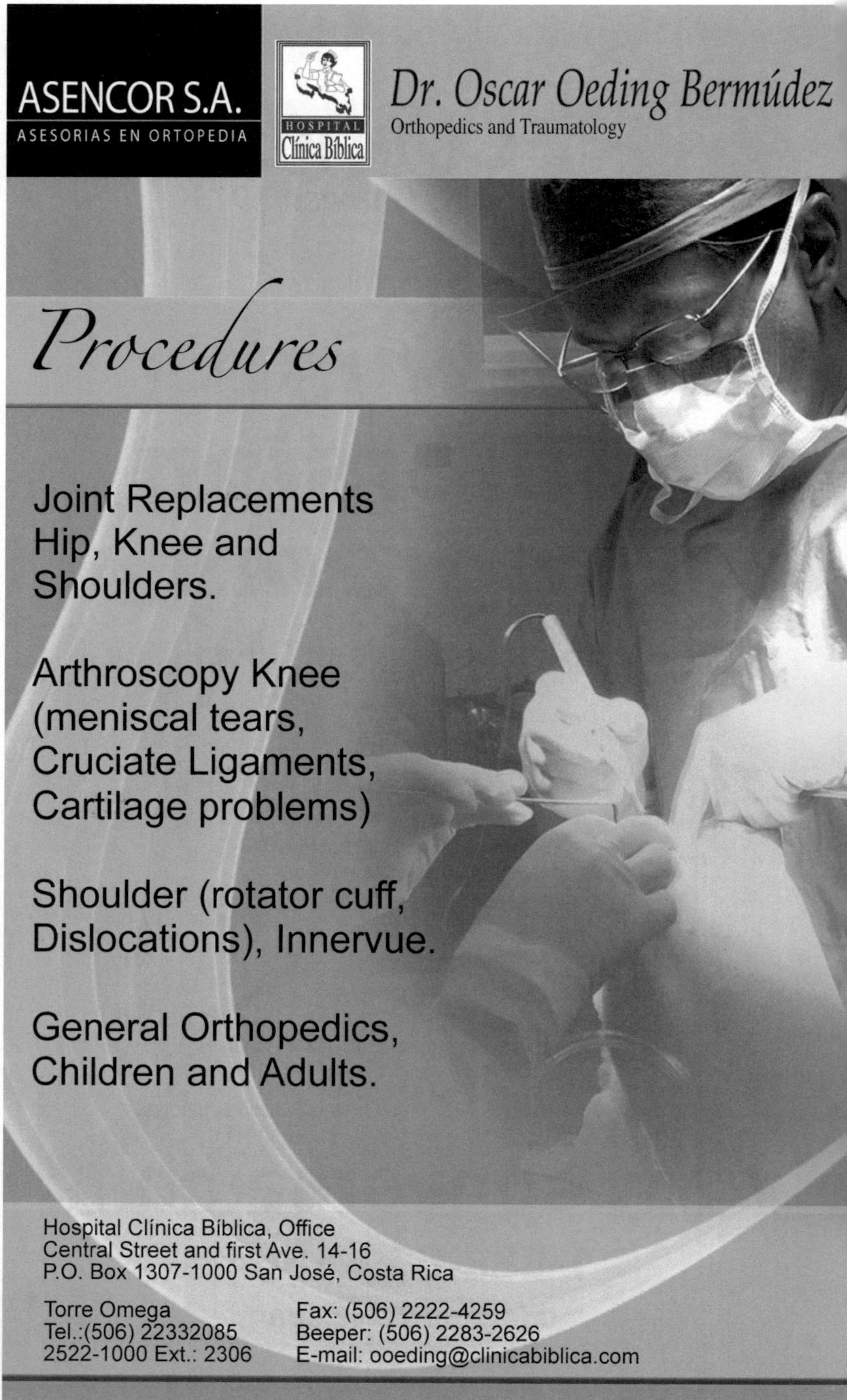
ASENCOR S.A.
ASESORIAS EN ORTOPEDIA
HOSPITAL
Clínica Bíblica
Dr. Oscar Oeding Bermúdez
Orthopedics and Traumatology
Procedures
Joint Replacements
Hip, Knee and
Shoulders.
Arthroscopy Knee
(meniscal tears,
Cruciate Ligaments,
Cartilage problems)
Shoulder (rotator cuff,
Dislocations), Innervue.
General Orthopedics,
Children and Adults.
Hospital Clínica Bíblica, Office
Central Street and first Ave. 14-16
P.O. Box 1307-1000 San José, Costa Rica
Torre Omega
Tel.:(506) 22332085
2522-1000 Ext.: 2306
Fax: (506) 2222-4259
Beeper: (506) 2283-2626
E-mail: ooeding@clinicabiblica.com

Tropical Oasis in San José
Hotel Dunn Inn
Your Home Away From Home
Whether traveling on business or pleasure it would be an honor to have you as our guest. We strive to provide the best service in San José and every effort is made to ensure an enjoyable and memorable visit. From the moment you arrive you will experience firsthand the warmth of Costa Rican hospitality and enjoy all the benefits of a full service hotel with excellent value.
For more information or reservations please contact:
Ph: (506) 2222-3232 • Fax: (506) 2221-4596
Ave. 11, Calle 5 - Barrio Amón, San José
www.hoteldunninn.com
dunninn@racsa.co.cr
Rates from $54 - Suite $104

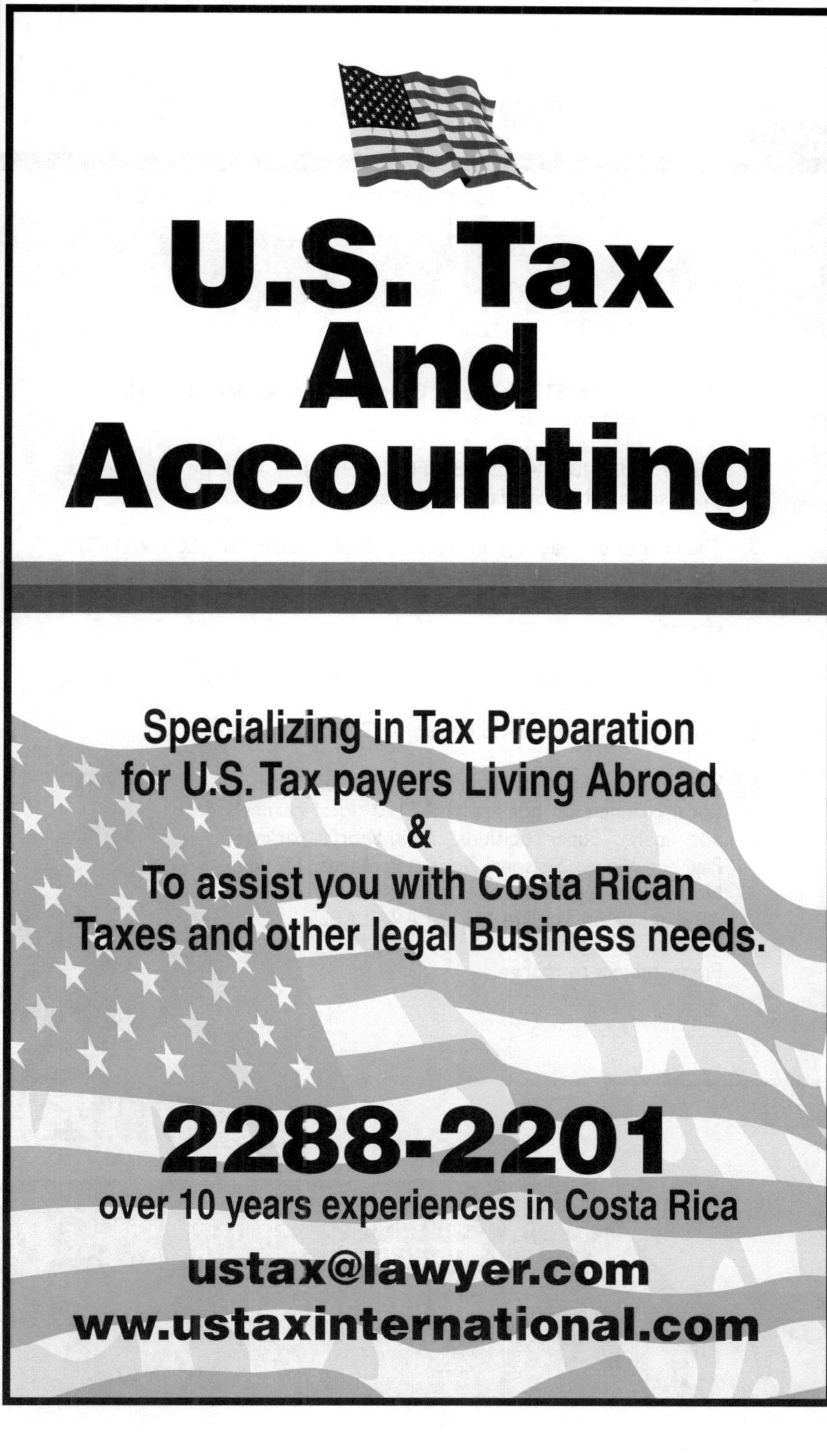
U.S. Tax
And
Accounting
Specializing in Tax Preparation
for U.S. Tax payers Living Abroad
&
To assist you with Costa Rican
Taxes and other legal Business needs.
2288-2201
over 10 years experiences in Costa Rica
ustax@lawyer.com
www.ustaxinternational.com

13

Parting Thoughts and Advice

Personal Safety in Costa Rica

Is it Safe to Live in Costa Rica?

This is a question that is frequently raised by the participants on my monthly relocation/retirement tours. There has been a lot written about crime recently in numerous on-line blogs and newspapers. To compound matters many people go on line to do their initial research about Costa Rica and come across alarmist information. Unfortunately, much of this information tends to be exaggerated.

I have lived here almost 30 years and have never been a crime victim. Furthermore I wouldn't be living here if I thought for one minute my personal safety was in jeopardy.

On the other hand, I have read about some foreigners who have been victimized several times. Most of these people fall prey to petty criminals because they don't take the right precautions. If you follow the advice in this section and use common sense you will reduce your chances of being victimized in Costa Rica.

It is comforting to know that, according to The World Bank Institute Costa Rica is #1 In Central America in fighting crime. The report also puts Costa Rica in 47th place in the world out of 209 countries. Panama is in the 104 spot and Nicaragua in the 135 position. Only Uruguay at number 43 tops Costa Rica in Latin America.

Fortunately, most violent crimes here involve revenge killings between small-time drug dealers and brawls in bars between drunks. Burglary is the most common crime in Costa Rica. Keep in mind that NO society is crime free. Costa Rica has doubled its police force and is going to pass stricter laws in an effort to get a handle on the situation. Although there has been an increase in crime here, Costa Rica is very safe when compared with some of the other countries in the region. None of the situations below exist here.

In Guatemala, El Salvador and Honduras there is a serious gang problem. There is a combined total of 70,000 violent gang members operating in those countries. To make matters worse the governments of these countries have not been able to get this situation under control.

Colombia has had a virtual civil war in some parts of the country for several decades. Thousands of innocent people, who have been caught in the crossfire, have died as a result.

In Venezuela crime, especially kidnappings, is rampant. I have talked to several Venezuelans who live in Costa Rica and almost all of them have a relative or know someone who has been abducted for for money in their country.

Mexico is whole different ball game. In Mexico City one out of ten businesses was robbed last year. Kidnappings are also out of control. Furthermore the number of murders (2,682) by organized crime in the first six months of 2008, surpassed the total for all of 2007 (2,673)according to one of Mexico's leading newspapers, *El Universal.* In the state of Chihuahua alone there were 1,026 so far in 2008. Sinaloa, Baja California, Durango, Guerrero and Michoacán are other violent areas of the country.

Who in their right mind would want to live or retire in any of these places where violent crime is endemic and out of hand?

There has been a lot of hype recently about Panama being safer than Costa Rica. Don't believe it. Panama does not report its crime statistics in an effort to protect its image and business interests. Panama's well-off classes have chosen to look the other way while pretending to ward off crime. Laying head and neck on the ground, as ostriches, will not make the hazard fade away either.

Precautions

Living in Costa Rica is much safer than residing in most large cities in the United States or Latin America, but you should take some precautions and use common sense to ensure your own safety. Remember, you should be careful in any third-world country.

In Costa Rica, the rate for violent crimes is very low, but there is a problem with theft, especially in the larger cities. If you are from a quiet rural town in the United States, you will probably find Costa Rica has more crime. On the other hand, if you come from a large city like Newark, you will think you are in heaven in Costa Rica.

Thieves tend to look for easy targets, especially foreigners, so you cannot be too cautious. Make sure your house or apartment has steel bars on both the windows and garage. The best bars are narrowly spaced because some thieves use small children as accomplices, as they can squeeze through the bars to burglarize your residence or open doors.

Make sure your neighborhood has a night watchman if you live in the city. Some male domestic employees are willing to work in this capacity. However, ask for references and closely screen any person you hire. Also, report suspicious people loitering around your premises. Thieves are very patient and often case a residence for a long time to observe your comings and goings. They can and will strike at the most opportune moment.

You should take added precautions if you live in a neighborhood where there are many foreigners. Thieves associate foreigners with wealth and look for areas where they cluster together. One possible deterrent, in addition to a night watchman, is to organize a neighborhood watch group in your area.

If you leave town, get a friend or other trustworthy person to house-sit.

Mountain areas offer some spectacular views and tranquility but are less populated and usually more isolated. This makes them prime targets for burglars and other thieves. I have a friend who moved to a beautiful home in the hills, but was burglarized a couple of times. Out of desperation he had to hire a watchman and buy guard dogs. Unfortunately, a few weeks later he was robbed while doing an errand in town. This is the down side to living off the beaten path.

If you are really concerned about protecting your valuables, you would be better off living in a condominium complex, a gated community or an apartment. These are less susceptible to burglary due to their design and the fact that, as the saying goes, there is safety in numbers.

Private home security patrols can provide an alarm system and patrol your area for a monthly fee. A few companies here specialize in security systems for the home and office. Some even offer very sophisticated monitored surveillance systems. You should contact **ADT** at 2257-7373 if interested in one of these services. I installed a complete ADT security system in my home in Heredia for less than $500.

The National Insurance Institute (INS) offers insurance policies that protect your home against burglary. However, the coverage is limited to certain items; there are stipulations, a lot of paperwork involved and there is a 10 percent deductible on the value of stolen items. All items must be listed as well as their serial numbers. Premiums run from 1 to 1.5 percent of the total on the list depending on where you live. Homes in more secure areas receive lower rates. Less protected homes in remote areas have higher rates. If your home is to be unoccupied for more than 48 hours, it must be placed under the care of a guard and you must notify the insurance company one week in advance.

According to world crime statistics the probability of losing your car in good old safe North America is a mere 750 percent greater than in Costa Rica. Nevertheless, if you own an automobile, in Costa Rica, you should be especially careful. Thieves can pop open a locked trunk and clean it out in a few minutes. Make sure your house or apartment has a garage with iron bars so your car is off the street.

When parking away from your house, always park in parking lots or where there is a watchman or *cuidacarros.* He will look after your vehicle for 100 *colones* (about 20 U.S. cents) or whatever change you have handy when you park on the street. It is not difficult to find watchmen since they usually approach and offer their services as soon as you park your car. Never park your vehicle or walk in a poorly lit area. For additional protection **Lo/Jack** is now available in Costa Rica, Tel: 2227-4227, E-mail: ventas@detektor.co.cr or see www.detektor.co.cr.

Avoid walking alone at night and during the day, and stay alert for pickpockets. Pickpockets like to hang around bus stops, parks and crowded marketplaces, especially the Central Market (between *Calles* 6 and 8, *Avenidas.* 1 and Central).

Here are some additional safety tips:

1. Dress simply.
2. The best thing you can to do to avoid being a victim is not to carry anything you can't afford to lose and keep a *low profile.*
3. Never flaunt your wealth by wearing expensive jewelry or carrying cameras loosely around your neck because they make you an easy mark on the street. Keep an eye on any valuable items you may be carrying.
4. Find a good way to conceal your money and never carry it in your back pocket. It is best to carry money in front pockets. It is also a good idea to always carry small amounts of money in several places rather than all your money in one place. If you carry large amounts of money, use traveler's checks.
5. Be very discreet with your money. Do not flash large amounts of money in public. When withdrawing cash at the bank, ask the cashier to count the money again slowly; it is not advisable to count it again in

front of others. Every time you finish a transaction in a bank or store, put away all money in your purse or wallet or money belt before going out into the street. Carry a single credit card and at least 10,000 *colones.*

6. Don't show your cellular telephone in the street. Should the cellular ring and you are walking in the street, stay close to the wall, look both ways, answer and ask the person calling to ring back later.
7. Always look at the hands and eyes of anyone walking towards you, if they have their hands in their pockets, it is possible they are carrying a weapon.
8. Avoid carrying any original documents, such as passports or visas. Make a photocopy of your passport and carry it with you at all times. The authorities will accept most photocopies as a valid form of identification, although you need to present your original passport to change money in the banks.

Avoid the dangerous parts of San José, especially the area near the Coca-Cola bus terminal and the *Zona Roja* south of Parque Central. Stay alert. Also be careful in other parts of the country including Jacó and Tamarindo. Be aware of who is around you and what they are doing. Thieves often work in teams. One will distract you while the other makes off with your valuables. Never accept help from strangers and or business propositions or other offers from people you encounter on the street. Never pick up hitchhikers.

Men should also watch out for prostitutes who are often expert pickpockets and can relieve the unsuspecting of their valuables before they realize it. Men, especially when inebriated or alone, should be careful—or avoid—the *Gringo Gulch* area in the vicinity of Morazán Park, the Holiday Inn and the Key Largo Bar. Many muggings have been reported in this area at night.

According to an August edition of *USA Today*, "Costa Rica is one of the five safest places in the world for women travelers. Only Amsterdam and Thailand are safer. However, if you are a single woman living by yourself, never walk alone at night. If you do go out at night, be sure to take a taxi or have a friend go along.

White collar crime

White-collar crime exists in Costa Rica, and a few dishonest individuals—Americans, British, Canadians, Costa Ricans and other nationalities included—are always waiting to take your money. Just because he or she speaks good English does not make the individual a good person. Over the years, many unscrupulous individuals have set up shop here. We have heard of naive foreigners losing their hard-earned savings to ingenious schemes. Con men prey on newcomers. One crook bilked countless people out of their money by selling a series of non-existent gold mines here and abroad. The guy is still walking the streets today and dreaming up new ways to make money.

One "dangerous breed of animal" you may encounter are a few foreigners between 30 and 60 years of age who are in business but do not have pensions. Most such people are struggling to survive and have to really hustle to make a living in Costa Rica. In general, they are desperate and will go to almost any means to make money. They may even have a legitimate business but most certainly try to take advantage of you to make a few extra dollars. Most complaints we hear concerning people being "ripped off" or pressured into buying real estate are about individuals who fit this description.

On your first trip to Costa Rica you will probably be besieged by con-artists anxious to help you make an investment. Be wary of blue ribbon business deals that seem too good to be true, or any other get-rich-quick schemes i.e. non-existent land, fantastic sounding real estate projects, phony high-interest bank investments or property not belonging to the person selling it. If potential profit sounds too good to be true, it probably is.

Always do your homework and talk to other expats before you make any type of investment. There seems to be something about the ambience here that causes one to trust total strangers. The secret is to be cautious without being afraid to invest. Before jumping into what seems to be a once-in-a-lifetime investment opportunity, ask yourself this question: Would I make the same investment in my hometown? Do not do anything with your money in Costa Rica that you wouldn't do at home. A friend and long-time resident here always says jokingly when referring to the business logic of foreigners who come to Costa Rica: "When they step off the plane they seem to go brain-dead."

Most people in Costa Rica are honest, hard-working individuals. However, do not assume people are honest just because they are nice. Remember, it does not hurt to be overly cautious.

What to do it you are a victim?

If you are robbed or swindled under any circumstances, contact the police or the O.I.J. *(Organización de Investigación Judicial)*, a special, highly efficient investigative unit like the FBI (Avenidas 8 and 10, Calles 15 and 17, in the middle building of the court-house complex, 2295-3271). The O.I.J. has 20 more offices around the country. All of them are open 24 hours a day.You may also want to contact the Ministry of Public Security,

How Not to Get Ripped Off in Costa Rica

by Christopher Howard M.A.

"Is it safe to invest in Costa Rica?" This is one of the most frequent questions I get asked by the guests on my monthly retirement/relocation tours. During my nearly 30 years of living in Costa Rica I have had the opportunity to observe a lot of people make money and others lose it. I have also bought and sold a lot of property here and currently have some sizeable money invested in property. Consequently, I have a good idea of what it takes to invest safely here and have seen many common denominators in cases where people have "lost their shirts" through poor investments, especially in real estate. The whole process basically boils down to perception and common sense. It is easy to overpay for something in Costa Rica if you haven't done your homework.

Because corruption and bribery in Costa Rica and most people have heard or read about the horror stories, most English speakers assume that if someone speaks English they are trustworthy. This is the BIGGEST mistake you can make. Just because someone speaks good English or is from the States, Canada or Europe does not make the individual a good person. Some people here will take advantage of naive newcomers.

Here is an example. About four years ago while conducting one of my retirement tours near Domincal I met a portly North American who called himself Gringo Mel (not his real name but similar). He owned a hotel at the time and billed himself as the best cook in Costa Rica among other things. I should have known that anyone who was so full of himself had to be a con man. Anyway he told me he wanted show me some property that he was selling because the owner was out of the country. We went there and I fell in love with the place. It had an incredible ocean view and a couple of building lots. I told him I was interested and to find out the price of the land and home on it. He told me it was $165,000 dollars. A few months passed and the property and home had not sold. On my next trip to Dominical I mentioned to a friend who lives and works in the area that I was interested in said property. She told me she had talked with the owner and the real price was around $120,000 dollars. This meant our friend *Gringo* Mel was charging a $45,000 commission as the middleman or 30 percent for his services. Needless to say, I never purchased the property but almost got taken to the cleaners by a fellow *gringo*. So, don't get *gringoed* (screwed)!

I know people who move here, and go into business and miraculously become experts overnight. Costa Rica is indeed a magical country!

Many naive newcomers have been taken advantage of by other foreigners who call themselves "experts," but are really incompetent imposters. So, be careful!

(Ministerio de Seguridad Píblica) at 2227-4866. You may not recover your money, but you may prevent others from being victimized.

If you have been a victim of any crime you should also contact the **Victim's Assistance Office,** 2295-3271, E-mail: victimadelito@poder-judicial.go.cr. The office is in charge of helping all persons (men, women and children), Costa Ricans and foreigners, who are crime victims. They provide legal counsel, psychological assistance and social work.

If you have serious security concerns you may want to contact **Executive Protection**, 2228-7750, E-mail: operations@roninpmi.com or see www.roninpmi.com.

Despite all this talk of safety and crime Costa Rica is still one of the safest countries in the world. The firm AON Corp. in its study *The Risk of Terrorism Worldwide*, ranks Costa and a handful of other countries as the safest in the world. You may find Costa Rica crime statistics at: **http://www.rohan.sdsu.edu/faculty/rwinslow/namerica/costa_rica.html.**

Handguns

Importing one

I have received numerous requests for information about Costa Rica's handgun laws. Most foreigners do not know that they can legally own a gun in Costa Rica, provided they are a legal resident.

The admission of firearms and ammunition into the territory of Costa Rica is subject to restrictions and import permits approved by Costa Rican authorities.

Applications to import non-military weapons into the country may be filed by or through a licensed importer, authorized dealer or a particular person. The Congress of Costa Rica strongly restricts the import of any military weapons into the country; therefore a military weapon in the hands of a non-authorized individual is illegal.

First check with your airline about its policy on packing guns in your luggage. If you want to bring a handgun, revolver, or pistol into Costa Rica, you must follow the required procedure:

1. Inform the airline that you are traveling with a weapon.
2. Once you arrive in Costa Rica, your weapon will remain at the Customs office until you register the weapon at the Ministry of Public Security's Department of Firearms and Ammunitions. There, you must provide the following documents:

a. Official registration of the firearm with the corresponding authorities of your state of residence (Secretary of State and or Police Department). This document must be duly certified by the Costa Rican consulate; please follow the authentication procedure.
b. Police record from the police precinct where you have legally resided for the last six months. This document must be no older than six months, and must be duly certified by the Costa Rican consulate; please follow the authentication procedure.
c. Weapon Entrance Proof of Receipt issued by the Customs/airport authorities in Costa Rica.
d. Take a psychological test in Costa Rica to evaluate your personality traits.
e. Once you obtain the required permits, bring them to the Customs office and your weapon will be released.

After reading the above, bear in mind that it is easier to buy a gun locally than to bring one from the United States.

If you are caught with a weapon without the appropriate permits and registrations in Costa Rica, your weapon will be confiscated and you will be fined, arrested or deported.

Registering a handgun

In order to legally have a handgun you must be a legal resident or a citizen of Costa Rica and it must be registered with the *Departmamento de Armas y Explosivos* (Department of Weapons and Explosives). If you bring your weapon from the United States you will have to pay taxes. They can range sometimes from 50 to 100 percent of the new value of the weapon, so expect to pay about double for a handgun in Costa Rica.

Once you have your permit, you can go and buy your gun. At most gun shops they will make you a nice offer that includes a registration (recommended). However, this registration only allows you to have your gun on your property, not to carry it as a concealed weapon.

If you don't have proof or a receipt of ownership or you want to reduce the taxes on an imported weapon , you should obtain a sworn statement (*declaración jurada*) from a lawyer saying someone gave you your weapon. This way you will not have to pay the taxes. However, if you purchase your weapon in Costa Rica, the taxes are included in the price.

If you fail to register your gun, there will be serious legal repercussions if you are caught with an unregistered weapon. To register your handgun take the proof of purchase/declaration of ownership papers and your residency *cédula* to the *Departamento de Armas y Explosivos* in Zapote.

NOTE: President Arias recently enacted a measure which prohibits any foreigner from owning a handgun. This measure was taken in response to a number of foreigners involved in violent crimes. This may not be a permanent law so be sure and check to see if it is still enforced.

Carrying a handgun

Once you have registered a handgun, it is illegal to carry it unless you have a special permit or *Permiso de Portación de Armas.* In order to get a permit you have to be a legal resident, citizen or have a Costa Rican corporation. You may register the gun through the latter. Please be aware that if your gun is in the name of a corporation and the corporation has assets in its name in addition to the gun, and you are involved in a wrongful death suite, then all of these assets may be attached if there is a judgment against you.

You have to take both the theoretical and practical exams to get your gun carry permit. The former is a psychological test in Spanish to see if you are suited to own a gun. The cost of this exam is about 10,000 *colones.* If you pass this exam, you can then take the practical exam. Finally, you take the practical exam to show a qualified instructor that you know how to use your gun by shooting at some targets. You need to score 80 percent (10 rounds fired from 10 meters). The results of both the psychological and shooting test will be filed with the *Departamento de Armas y Explosivos.*

Once you are done, they will give you a document that you need to save; wait 8 working days and then go to the **Departamento de Armas y Explosivos del Ministerio de Seguridad Pública** in San Pedro, 150 meters south of La Fuente de la Hispanidad or 100 meters south of the San Pedro Cemetery, right on the highway. Give them the document you saved and they will give you your carnet (ID permit).

There is an excellent course in combat shooting offered by Krav Maga of Costa Rica. It is the same system used by the Israeli army. They also offer self-defense courses. For more information call. 8377-1298.

Life as an Expatriate/Adapting

Getting past cultural shock

Unlike twenty years ago, the majority of people (especially travelers) know the term "culture shock." However, there still exists an "it won't happen to me" attitude in many who move overseas. The symptoms can be severe, including difficulty sleeping, loss of appetite, paranoia and depression.

Denial of the possibility of Culture Shock and ignorance of its symptoms can result in increased difficulty in adjusting to a new life overseas. A basic understanding of the reasons why it happens and what you can do about it are essential when making an international transition.

Culture shock occurs when people find that their ways of doing things just don't work in the new culture. It is a struggle to communicate, to fulfill the most basic needs, and many find that they are not as effective or efficient as before in their jobs and in their personal lives. All this loss of competence threatens a person's sense of identity.

Absent are the abilities and relationships that we relied on to tell us who we are, are absent, and we find ourselves a little lost in our new homes. To re-establish ourselves in a new context requires proactive planning in a number of different areas of life.

There are four basic areas of Culture Shock, like four legs to a chair. They are the physical, intellectual, emotional and social. To have the smoothest possible transition, one needs to employ a balanced approach in each of the areas.

After a transition such as an overseas move, the rhythms of everyday life are interrupted, including our exercise and eating habits. Often people neglect their exercise regiment because they don't know where to find a gym or they don't feel safe running or exercising in public places. Similarly, diets are neglected or some begin drinking too much alcohol. The way that our bodies feel physically directly affects our emotional health. A healthy diet and consistent exercise can help balance our emotional lives when confronting the difficulties of an international move.

The second area of concern is the intellectual dimension. When we step into a new culture we often find that we understand very little about the local customs and history. Due to our lack of understanding we sometimes assume that people think like us and value the same things we do. Reading and inquiring about the history and the culture of Costa Rica can help one to see things from a Costa Rican's perspective and develop greater empathy for their culture and ways of thinking.

Tending to emotional needs when moving overseas will help us weather the ups and downs of the adjustment period. Finding people who are in similar positions that you can talk to and confide in helps to alleviate some of the loneliness that one feels.

When a person begins to feel down, sometimes they are listening to negative "tapes" in their head. One's "tapes" consist of the things we tell ourselves or the conversations that we have in our own minds. The negative tapes need to be consciously changed to positive and hopeful messages. From "I am a failure and I hate this place" to "things are getting better every day." It may seem somewhat Pollyanna-ish, but it really works.

Finding a group of friends, learning the language, and getting involved in clubs or activities help to fill the social needs that we have when changing our latitude. This requires time and dedication, especially if one wants to meet locals. Meeting locals is essential for long-term happiness overseas, but it can take a long period of time and a great deal of proactive planning. It may sound harsh, but it's important to remember that the locals don't really need you. They have their families and friends from their entire lives. You need to insert yourselves in their lives.

In my time working with people in international transition I have seen may cases of fabulous success, but I have seen many spectacular failures. If a person develops a plan and proactively carries it out, it is very probable that you will find success and happiness in your new Latin home.

* Courtesy of Eric Liljenstolpe

Adaptation

Throughout this book I have provided the most up-to-date information available on living and retirement in Costa Rica. I have also provided many useful suggestions to make your life in Costa Rica more enjoyable and help you avoid inconveniences. Adjusting to a new culture can be difficult for some people. My aim is to make this transition easier so you can enjoy all of the marvelous things that Costa Rica offers.

Before moving permanently to Costa Rica, I highly recommend spending time here on a trial basis to see if it is the place for you. I am talking about a couple of months or longer, so you can experience Costa Rican life as it is. Remember visiting Costa Rica as a tourist is quite another thing from living here on a permanent basis. It is also good to visit for extended periods during both the wet and dry seasons, so you have an idea of what the country is like at all times of the year. During your visits, talk to many retirees and gather as much information as possible before making your final decision. Get involved in as many activities as you can during your time in the country. This will help give you an idea of what the country is really like.

It is a good idea to attend one of the monthly newcomer's seminars offered by the **Association of Residents of Costa Rica (ARCR)**. Besides gathering information, you will learn from other residents and make some good contacts. Please see Chapter 14 for more details.

The final step in deciding if you want to make Costa Rica your home is to try living here for at least a year. That's sufficient time to get an idea of what living in Costa Rica is really like and what problems may confront you while trying to adapt to living in a new culture. It may also allow you to adjust to

Survival Tips
Ten Fun and Useful Things to Know!

By Eric Liljenstolpe, M.A. Ed.

(1) The Kissing Stuff: People greet one another by touching their right cheeks and kissing into the air. People seldom actually kiss one another on the cheek. Hint! Men do not kiss men. As a foreigner, you are forgiven for not doing this, but learning this and some of the other traditions will earn you respect.

(2) At the doorway: When entering a home, it is customary to stand at the door and wait to be invited in, even if the people are good friends. When at the doorway, you might say *Con Permiso* (With your permission). Your host will then normally reply, *Adelante* or *Pase* which means come on in. This is a sign or respect and courtesy you are showing to your host.

(3) Coming and going: When entering or leaving a party or gathering, greet or say goodbye to everyone in the room with the appropriate kiss. Of course, if it is a large party that may not be possible or necessary.

(4) Bars on the windows: There are bars on the windows of many homes, but this may not mean that the neighborhood is unsafe or poor. This comes from tradition and from a different sense of private property than Anglo North American countries. However, petty theft is rampant and growing and one must be exceedingly careful of one's home and property.

(5) Business in Costa Rica: When doing business (not retail stores), it is considered good form to greet and "chat" with your customer or client before getting down to business. This can take the form of discussing the weather, the beach, an upcoming vacation or any other neutral subject.

(6) *Guachimán* (Watchman): When parking on the street there will almost always be someone who is guarding the cars. He is called

a *Guachimán* which is pronounced as one word. He or she is tipped about 200 colones (50 cents) for stays of more than half an hour. You can give less if it is a quick in-and-out trip.

7) *Ssst Ssst, Macha! Macha!* It is customary for men to compliment women in public places. These cat calls are called *piropos* and are usually harmless and should not be considered offensive unless they are vulgar. Women are advised to ignore them. Acknowledgment, even with hostility, is often interpreted as an invitation for more of the same. *Macha* refers to someone with a light complexion.

(8) However did she get into those pants? Women wear much tighter and more revealing clothes in Latin America than in many parts of the USA or Canada. This does not mean that they are sexually promiscuous.

(9) Let your yes be yes. Costa Ricans have an indirect communication style that is often misunderstood by outsiders. For a Costa Rican, it sounds harsh to come right out and say no. They will use qualified speech such as, "it is complicated" or "it will be difficult" instead of saying no. Sometimes they will even say "yes" to acknowledge that they heard you, but "yes" doesn't always mean an affirmative response.

(10) Get off my back! Costa Ricans have a smaller bubble of 'personal space' than Anglo North Americans and Western Europeans. They are quite comfortable standing closer to one another and touching more often. It is quite common that while standing in line at the bank that the person behind you will stand so close that you can feel his body heat. On a bus, you may be the only passenger, but when a *Tico* boards, he may sit next to you even when there is plenty of room elsewhere!

the climate and new foods. You can learn all the dos and don'ts, ins and outs and places to go or places to avoid before making your final decision.

You may decide to try seasonal living for a few months a year. Many people spend the summer in the United States or Canada and the winter in Costa Rica (which is its summer), so they can enjoy the best of both worlds and have an endless summer. As mentioned in Chapter 7, this is easy to do, since you can legally stay in the country up to three months as a tourist without having to get any type of permanent residency.

Whether you choose to reside in Costa Rica on a full- or part-time basis, keep in mind the cultural differences and new customs. First, life in Costa Rica is very different. If you expect all things to be exactly as they are in the United States, you will be deceiving yourself. The concept of time and punctuality are not important in Latin America. It is not unusual and not considered in bad taste for a person to arrive late for a business appointment or a dinner engagement. This custom can be incomprehensible and infuriating to North Americans but will not change since it is a deeply rooted tradition.

As previously mentioned, in most cases bureaucracy moves at a snail's pace in Costa Rica that can be maddening to a foreigner. In addition, the Latin mentality, *machismo*, seemingly illogical reasoning, traditions, different laws and ways of doing business seem incomprehensible to a newcomer.

You will notice countless other different customs and cultural idiosyncrasies after living in Costa Rica for a while. No matter how psychologically secure you are, some culture shock in the new living situation will confront you. The best thing to do is respect the different cultural values, be understanding and patient, and go with the flow. Learning Spanish will ease your way.

The fastest way to fit in with the locals is to speak the native language. You do not have to be fluent in Spanish. The locals will recognize your interest; doors will open and friendships will blossom.

Whatever you do, try to avoid being the Ugly American. I know of cases where Americans have caused themselves a lot of problems by their obnoxious behavior and by trying to impose their American ways on the locals.

Another thing: if your purpose in coming to Costa Rica is to recreate your life in the US, it is better to stay in the States. You will find it perhaps more expensive, and not like theUS. Though it might seem strange to have to say it, this is not the US but a third world nation.

If it bothers you the idea of living in a third world nation bothers you, you might want to think twice about doing so.

There are a lot of people who move here with the intention of recreating their life up north, but in a warmer, more beautiful place. Often they get very disgusted because the *Ticos* don't seem to be on board with their desires.

You might want to read *The Ticos: Culture and Social Change in Costa Rica"* by Mavis, Richard and Karen Zubris Biesanz and *Survival Kit for Overseas Living,* by L. Robert Kohls, Intercultural Press, P.O. Box 700, Yarmouth, Maine 04096. These guides are filled with useful information about adjusting to life abroad and understanding the local culture..

Costa Rica is an exciting place to live but poses many obstacles for the newcomer. Don't expect everything to go smoothly or be perfect at first. By taking the advice we offer throughout this book and adjusting to the many challenges, you should be able to enjoy all of Costa Rica's wonders.

My recommendation is not to burn your bridges or sever your ties with your home country; you may want to return home some day.

Try taking the adaptability test in this section to see if you are suited for living abroad.

Social Networks to help you adjust

Moving to a new country is not easy but new technologies like Social Media, Online Communities and Social Networks, like Boomers Abroad, can make this transition much smoother. It is impressive to be able to break distances and time. It is great to be able to do your homework from your home before you travel. It is outstanding to make friends and contact people that already live where you want to move.

Online social communities have begun popping up all over the internet. As an expatriate, these type of Social Networks can be a veru helpful resource as you transition to your new country. Whether you are looking for Information, education, alternatives, to meet new friends, locate old ones, or gain professional contacts, you are bound to find the people you are looking for online. If you haven't yet relocated to your new country yet, now is a great time to join these types of online communities. Create a profile and begin adding friends. As your network expands, you may find that your current friends already have contacts in your new country. They could introduce you, and then you would already have acquaintances there when you arrive. Already living in your new country? These types of social communities also have groups you can join to meet others with a similar interest.

There are social networks for baby boomers looking forward to traveling abroad, living abroad, retiring abroad, and of course also for those already living abroad. A social network can be the connector between those who want to live abroad and those that already live abroad. So the members of a social network who are looking forward to living abroad can ask questions to those that journeyed ahead of them. In this interactive and fun manner Baby Boomers can find information about potential countries. You can compare countries and cities within a country and neighborhoods within a city.

Members can create their own profiles, join groups of those who share their same particular interests, create their own groups, make friends, upload photos and videos, post blogs, present questions, answer questions, etc. There is no substitute for first- hand experience, and there is power in collaboration. Common wisdom is the result. We also love transparency and because every brain is a different world, in an the online community you can make your own conclusions after communicating with many persons.

Education is the Key. The education process is individual. Nobody will wake one morning and say "I'm going to Costa Rica today to retire". The truth is that deciding to do this is a gradual process that takes, normally, a lot of time. It is a process that typically includes: seminars, relocation/retirement tours, trips to different destinations, hundreds of information requests about many different issues, hundreds of conversations with friends, experts and ideally with expatriates also.

* Some excerpts are from *Boomer Abroad*

Insight from people who have moved here

Here is what my good friend Lyod Newton says about living here. "I'm from the Dallas/Ft. Worth area but I've lived in Costa Rica for four years now. On balance, it's definitely worth the move to Costa Rica. I thought I'd see if I could address the issues you mentioned. I lived many years in Arlington, Irving and my last house was up in Lewisville."

"There is regulation of real estate in Costa Rica but the laws are very different from the United States. There are a few horror stories here, but for the most part there really aren't any problems. You just have to be careful and take time to understand the laws here. Squatting can be a problem for absentee landlords, but if you plan to buy property and then not even look at it for three years, you may have a problem. If you live on the property and keep an eye on anybody trying to build on it, you won't have any problems. If buying property, it's best to get a good lawyer ; the *gringos* here can recommend many, or join the Association of Residents of Costa Rica (ARCR) and let them help."

"If you live out in the boondocks where there's never been a phone connection, you may have to wait awhile to get a phone hookup. If you live in a town where there is already a phone line, you will be able to get dial-up-quality Internet connection, depending on the condition of the phone line. Many towns have access to RDSI Internet at a minimum and ADSL Internet in a growing number of locations. I use the Internet everyday and I complain about the dial-up quality, so I decided to go get RDSI, because, as yet, ADSL isn't available in my area."

"Get a *tico* friend to help find the property you want. If you buy from a *gringo* or use a gringo real estate agent, or buy from an Internet site, you're going to pay a lot more than a *tico* would. I've always used *tico/tica* friends to help me find my rental houses and I pay about $150 to $200 less for a similar property than some of my *gringo* friends.

"Get a 4x4 or vehicle with high ground clearance. I've been all over Costa Rica in a little Dodge Colt but decided finally to buy an Isuzu Trooper 4x4. I've never had to use the 4x4, but it's nice to have. High ground clearance will get you just about anywhere. However, if you are planning to buy a property that is at the end of a long dirt uphill road, definitely go with a 4x4 for the rainy season. As for the potholes, drive a reasonable speed and learn to dodge them.

"Yep, they will try to take advantage of *gringos.* Again, get recommendations from the *gringos* who have lived here awhile. You should plan to socialize whenever you can with the gringo community here to get contacts. Fortunately, the *gringo* community here is friendly and has a lot of getogethers. Several married couples I know in the Heredia area have parties or get-togethers every couple of months, and then there are the ARCR and *Gallo Pinto* groups."

"Nothing is easy in Costa Rica when you have to deal with the government or bureaucracy, but you have to bring three things with you when do: .patience, patience and patience. It's not like the United States, and if you can adapt to it, it's not that bad. I've learned to carry a book with me whenever I have to deal with government offices. Don't expect it to function logically, though.

"Fortunately it's a small country and you learn how to get around okay. My first year here, I didn't have a car and used buses and taxis. It didn't take long to learn the area. My recommendation is to buy a cheap but good GPS and build up your knowledge of the areas before buying a car. I thought the same when I first got here watching how the people drive and the lack of directions or road signs, but I can get around as well as a *tico* these days. It helps to learn a little Spanish, too so you can ask directions if you get lost or are in doubt.

"As for me, I love it here. Great weather, beautiful country, friends both *gringo* and *tico*, low cost of living, good cheap health care, interesting culture, beaches, mountains, dancing, etc. Come on down, the water's fine."

Here is another foreign resident's observations about adapting to life here. "I have been here 15 years. I guess most people would say I have prospered here, although I sure have had my ups and downs. Nevertheless, I am still here and I love this country for many reasons. I notice and observe incoming souls because it is my business to do so. Here are some observations:

1) Culture shock can be hard the first year here. Make yourself as comfortable as you can. This is not the time to hole up in a one room cold water place after leaving your comfy nest in the United States. or elsewhere. You are dealing with language differences, cultural differences, perhaps work change. Be physically comfortable.
2) Affiliate with groups. Attend language school, church, clubs or other activities. You can be alone in a crowd, and you are far from home. Reach out to friends.
3) Have something to do. I have seen the Hammock Syndrome affect many: nothing to do, tip the rum bottle, hang out looking for women (or men), lose goals and lose focus. Volunteer, build a house, have a pet, but build a life.
4) You must learn the language. If you don't, you are not really living here; you are just existing here. Listen to people speak and copy them. It is the way a child learns his native language. Get a best friend who is *tico* and cut a deal. I teach you, you teach me. Hey, one hour a day.
5) Let yourself fall in love with this country. There are a million wonderful things about it. Avoid people who fuss and complain; it is so very boring but it reinforces negativity. Ever meet a Frenchman or a German in the United States who sits around all day talking about the potholes in Texas? I bet you would avoid that guy after a while or suggest that he go back to Stuttgart or Timbuktu. I allow myself only one tiny complaint a day. It is usually about service in public places.
6) Do what successful expatriates do. They all have created real lives here and have goals.
7) A controversial comment, but I feel I must make it: men seem to "make it" here better than women who come here from abroad. There are many reasons for this and many exceptions, I suppose. However, American women and other women: be aware of this tendency and do all you can to ameliorate it. Find a way to belong here aside from your life with mate or husband. This is probably sage advice in any country, but more so here. "

Here are some reasons why some people don't adjust to living in Costa Rica. These observations are from foreigners who already live here.

"This is not a definitive list, but in my experience the expats I've known who return to their home countries in North America or Europe do so for the following reasons, in order of frequency:

1. Need more money. I have known many who don't have the ability to make chunks of money in Costa Rica like they did in their home country, but still are able to spend large amounts of it just the same. So

they go back, make a chunk of money, return, do that a few times, then either settle down up there, or stop spending so much here and settle down here.

2. Can't adjust to the culture. Many people I know who can't adjust, get totally wiped out emotionally from a robbery and become surefire cynical. The education-by-fire regarding Napoleonic law is just too much for them. And the number of people who couldn't live without the consumer power, options and protection they were accustomed to, really, those are the quickies — in and out in a year. I've also known some who've suffered crimes and wrongs against them that were far worse than robbery, and still stayed.

   "A few I have known who have gone back to their homes were not sufficiently prepared for a different culture. I had one acquaintance who complained bitterly that Costa Ricans should speak English. She was angry all the time about banks, stores etc. She wanted an American city with Costa Rican prices and climate. Illogical and crazy, yes. Things here are done on a different time schedule and that drove another person I knew nuts. He wanted things done yesterday, which will not happen in Costa Rica.

3. Missed family and friends. Grandparents seem to fit into this category, and might repatriate after years of living here. Then there are the youngsters who were just trying out living abroad and had no intentions of leaving friends and family behind for long anyway. But the old saying around here was quite true for a very long time: 'Costa Rica is for the wanted, and the unwanted.' Most people I've known who've stayed were getting the heck away from something or someone in their home country, searching to be wanted by someone, or hoping not to be found.

4. Death of a spouse, severe health reasons and loss of income are reasons for a few folks I know going back. In a couple of instances, the move to Costa Rica was mainly the dream of only one-half of the couple, and the other half was never happy here."

5. Not realizing you are a guest, no matter how long you live here.You must be prepared to adjust to the culture, learn the language (or impr ove your ability to communicate in their tongue), realize not everything is 100 percent (is it in the United States or wherever you came from?), not treating yourself to something that reminds you of home (a trip to Denny's) and doing whatever it takes to make a life here. Not

finding a purpose for your life. Retirees, and I realize not everyone who comes here is one, haven't been trained for retirement for the most part. Time weighs heavily; some drink more, some find more things to complain about because they haven't anything to do.

6. Couples who don't see eye to eye about living here don't last. It takes unique people to move to a foreign country and couples should have a common goal to build a new life in this wonderful country.

"If he or she can't leave papa or momma or the kids, don't move to Costa Rica. If he or she doesn't want to adapt to a new culture, don't move to Costa Rica. If your marriage is on the rocks and you think a geographic cure is needed, don't move to Costa Rica."

You really need to do your homework before moving to any foreign country.

Tips from a Costa Rican on Adapting

If you're thinking of moving here, insightful Costa Rican, Guillermo Jiménez has some interesting advice about foreigners who prosper and those who fail. He states:

1. *Ticos* have disarming smiles and their accent is so sweet it is ridiculous (I know; I am a *tico*), so much so that you can't tell good from bad, so be ready for the learning curve.
2. Costa Rica is not Disneyland. Disney is fake; Costa Rica is real and much more beautiful and fun but without the liability. If you feel like jumping inside a volcano, be our guest, but then don't blame us for it. If you want to go out with that girl or guy who looks kind of suspicious, be our guest, but please leave a message for your folks saying it was not the fault of the Costa Ricans when they have to come looking for you.
3. Observe the *ticos*, then do as they do, except when driving. If you are the only *gringo* on a road in the middle of nowhere with no *tico* in sight, then try to get out of there quickly because it is either a banana plantation or a place you shouldn't be. If you see *ticos* building their roofs a certain way and using certain materials, unless you can hire a *tico* architect or an expert in tropical construction yourself, then build yours the same way.
4. Be honest always. Getting a smile from a *tico* is free; earning his trust is next to impossible. We are wired that way. Set limits and stick to them. Try to enjoy yourself. If there is one thing we *ticos* do well, it is to enjoy ourselves.

5. You are allowed to experiment all you want, but remember, we are the locals and we have the upper hand.
6. When you meet *ticos*, keep in mind you are not the only one going through culture shock. We are trying to figure you out as well.
7. Leave the S.C.C . (Second Coming of Columbus) syndrome at home. No matter what you think of us, we do not need another European-type to come save us from ourselves or to help civilize us. Get involved in the community, but avoid the rich *gringo* role."

Christopher Howard's golden rules for finding happiness and success in Costa Rica

During the 30 years that I have lived in Costa Rica I have had the opportunity to observe thousands of foreigners who have moved here. Some have been very successful while others have not. Those who found happiness and saw their dreams come true followed most of the time-tested rules below. Hopefully if you choose to live or retire here you will keep these simple principles in mind so you can take full advantage of what Costa Rica has to offer and enjoy a new exciting lifestyle or the *pura vida* (pure life/good life) which abounds everywhere.

1. Don't have false expectations.
2. Don't assume that what worked at home works here. You have to adapt to the reality of the country.
3. Don't go into business unless you want to complicate your life. Most people come here to simplify their lives. The happiest people are those with pensions or other fixed sources of income who don't have to work. If you do work, don't expect to get rich.
4. Stay busy and or find an interesting hobby Almost everyone has a hobby. If you don't have one, find a new one here. Costa Rica offers hundreds of stimulating activities from which to choose.
5. Don't hang out in bars. I have seen scores of people come down here and because they were bored they went off the deep end by drinking themselves to death.
6. Stay active and have a good exercise program.
7. Have a good doctor or team of doctors to meet your specific health needs. Costa Rica has an excellent and affordable health care system which draws retirees from all over the world.
8. Single men shouldn't get involved with low-life women or prostitutes (the easiest women to meet). Single women should watch out for younger men who are gold diggers. Take time to develop healthy relationships.
9. Don't leave your brain on the plane by forgetting to use your common sense.
10. Don't try to cut corners by thinking you can outsmart the locals by paying bribes, etc. It will all catch up to you sooner or later.
11. Don't make bad investments. If it seems too good to be true, it usually is.
12. Try not to live in isolated areas with no home security. Burglary can be a problem in some parts of Costa Rica. There is safety in numbers.
13. Don't walk around alone at night. If you have to, be sure to know the neighborhood where you are and take a friend.
14. Do your homework! Read all of the books and newspapers about Costa Rica, talk to others who have lived here for a long time, go to the ARCR's monthly seminar and in general stay informed by reading the local Spanish newspapers.

15. Learn as much as you can about the Costa Rican culture.
16. Try to always check your sources of information especially what you see on the on-line Costa Rica news groups. Something happens to people who move here. They think they are overnight experts just because they have made the move. It takes years of living here to really be considered an expert. Funny things happen to JCL's (Johnny Come Lately) minds when they come to the tropics.
17. It is VERY important to have a good BILINGUAL lawyer. Most Americans brag they have the "best lawyer". Make sure this is true by doing your homework and getting good references from other expatriates. Having a competent/honest lawyer can make the difference between success and failure.
18. LEARN Spanish! You need at least a survival level Spanish to get by here. Find a school that fits your learning style. Also read my best selling Spanish book, *Christopher Howard's Guide to Costa Rican Spanish* (amazon.com). It is designed to give you what you need to survive linguistically in Costa Rica.
19. Mix with the locals. Part of living in a foreign country is enjoying the people and culture. Don't isolate yourself in a Gringo enclave like Escazú. That's exactly why you need to learn some Spanish.
20. Form a network of friends so you can lean on them in hard times. Making friends is easy here since foreigners tend to gravitate toward each other when living abroad.
21. Don't *Jugar de vivo* as we say in Spanish. This means to not act like a WAG (a Wise Ass Know-it-all *Gringo*).
22. Don't be the Ugly American, Ugly Canadian, Ugly Englishman of ugly foreigner. This is the Costa Rica people's country, you have to live in it and you can't change it. So, DON'T wear out your welcome.
23. Obey the law here and above all, the traffic laws.
24. Travel around the country. Costa Rica is small yet very big at the same time and lots of incredibly beautiful places to see.
25. Get Skype (www.skype.com) or Vonage (www.vonage.com) to stay in contact with friends back home so as to avoid homesickness.
26. Get cable or satellite TV to get a slice of home and keep up with events there when you need it.
27. Try to leave your hang ups and serious problems at home. If you had serious issues there, you will probably have them here too.
28. Give back to the community. Try to help but don't impose the *Gringo* way of doing things.
29. Just because a person speaks English doesn't mean he or she is trustworthy.
30. The single most important thing you need to survive is a good sense of humor. Go with the flow and don't take things too seriously.

FOLLOW THIS TIME-TESTED ADVICE AND YOU WILL NEVER GO WRONG.

M.R.T.A. Overseas Living Adaptability Test

Using the figures 1 (below average), 2 (average) or 3 (above average), ask yourself the following questions and rate your answer accordingly. Couples should take the test separately. As you take the test, write your selected numbers down, then add them together. When completed, refer to the Score Comments Box at the bottom of this page.

1) Open to new adventures
select one: 1 2 3

2) Flexible in your lifestyle
select one: 1 2 3

3) Enthusiastic to new things in a new and different culture
select one: 1 2 3

4) Able to make and enjoy new friends:
select one: 1 2 3

5) Willing to learn at least basic phrases in a new language
select one: 1 2 3

6) Healthy enough mentally and physically not to see family, friends and favorite doctor for occasional visits
select one: 1 2 3

7) Confident enough to be in a "minority" position as a foreigner in a different culture

8) Independent and self-confident enough not to be influenced by negative and often ignorant comments against a possible move to a foreign country

9) Patient with a slower pace of life
select one: 1 2 3

10) Usually optimistic
select one: 1 2 3

11) Eager to travel to a new country
select one: 1 2 3

12) Open mind to dealing with a different type of bureaucracy
select one: 1 2 3

13) Understand enough to look at things in a different light without being critical and accepting the differences

14) Financially stable without needing to work
select one: 1 2 3

Score Comments:

Your Score	**Evaluation**
37-45	Great move abroad
30--35	Will have a few problems
22-32	Some problems but possible
Less than 22	Forget it, stay home!

Courtesy of Opportunities Abroad. This test taken from the book "Mexico Retirement Travel Assistance." To order wrte M.R.T.A., 6301 S. Squaw Valley Rd., Suite 23, Pahrump, NV 89648-7949

Frequently Asked Questions

Below is a list of questions often asked by people who are considering moving to Costa Rica.

1. **What is required to obtain legal residency? Can I meet these requirements? What is the cost? How often does residency have to be renewed. What are the conditions and cost of renewal?**

   Residency Requirements (see Chapter 7 for specific information): $1000 per month pension from an approved source: or investment income of $2,500 per month from an approved source or Invest between $50,000 and $200,000 in an approved sector of the economy.. According to the ARCR the approximate cost to process residency is approximately $870 per family head plus $425 for dependent spouse and $195 per dependant child. Residency renewals are usually every other year. General conditions for renewal are four months residence in Costa Rica, that the required amount of monthly income was changed into Costa Rican currency or that the terms of the investor residency are met. Renewal cost is $150 to $200. **Check with the Association of Residents of Costa Rica (ARCR) to se if there have been any changes.**

2. **What is required to visit, or while you are waiting for residency (visas, length of stay permitted, restrictions on residents on visa or in tourist or temporary resident categories)?**

   North Americans can stay in Costa Rica legally for up to three months. They must then leave for a period of 72 hours, and can then return to the country for another three months. If the three-month period is overstayed, a travel agency or ARCR can arrange payment of a small fine and prepare the travel documents required to leave the country for the required 72 hours. Tourists can own vehicles, property and businesses and generate income from self- employment.

3. **What is the political situation (dictatorship, democracy, monarchy, etc.) ?**

   Costa Rica is a democratic republic, headed by a president who is in power for one four-year term. Ministers are appointed and there is an elected Congress. There has been no military since 1948, when it was constitutionally banned.

4. How stable is the country (history of coups, potential for future unrest)?

Costa Rica has a history of stable government that stretches back to when the country was founded. It had one brief civil war in 1948, when a president wanted a second term in power. At this time, a new constitution was drawn to ensure that such a situation could not occur again.

5. What is the weather like?

Weather in Costa Rica is largely a matter of choice, unless someone is looking for snow. There is none, even on the 13,000-foot high-mountains. Weather varies from hot coastal lowlands, where rainfall depends on location and season, to very cool mountainous regions. There are plains that go months without rain, and areas where it rains daily. The average temperature in the Central Valley is ideal, with evenings of 62 F and days averaging 77 to 82 F year-round. The dry season is usually from the end of November until past Easter. The amount of rain in the rainy season depends on the climate zone, with heaviest rains usually in October. Rainfall is usually in the afternoon, if it is going to rain at all.

6. What about income taxes? Are you taxed on income brought into the country? Are you allowed to earn income in the country? If yes, how is it taxed?

There is no income tax on money earned outside of Costa Rica by residents. Personal income taxes are low compared to North America, with many personal expenses deductible from locally earned income. Corporate taxes are also low.

7. Are there other taxes (sales taxes, import duties, exit taxes, vehicle taxes, property taxes, etc.)?

- Sales tax is 13 percent
- Everyone pays an exit duty of $26.
- License plate fees are paid annually for vehicles, and depend upon the value. Fees are not excessive.
- Property taxes are very low in comparison with North America.

8. How much does it cost in fees, duties and taxes to bring personal possessions into the country? (cars, boats, appliances, electronic equipment, personal effects, artwork, etc.)?

New residents are charged import duty on cars and boats at the same rate as would be paid by a resident. Personal effects and artwork are not taxed. Electronic equipment and appliances will be valued and a duty charged.

9. **Tell me about rental property - (rental rates, laws protecting tenants, lease laws, rental taxes).**

Rental rates depend on the area. Any rental agreement is assumed to be for three years, during which time the landlord may not raise the rent if the contract says the rent is to be paid in dollars. Lease contracts are honored by the courts provided they adhere to the rental law. Landlords may not evict tenants for reasons other than non-payment of rent or illegal activities.

10. **Talk about purchasing property - (property value, taxes, restrictions on foreign ownership, purchase taxes, legal and registration fees, laws about foreign property owners, history of government respect for these laws, expropriation laws, squatters rights. If you are going to build: building regulations, how are the local construction companies, is there any guarantee on construction once finished, what are construction costs?)**

Property prices vary from area to area. There is a computerized central registry system similar to that in North America, and lawyers or others, such as the ARCR, who subscribe to the service can search titles from their office computers. Foreign residents and non-residents have the same property ownership rights as citizens, with the exception of leasing land from the municipality and purchasing land close to the-borders. Registration, taxes and legal fees will be approximately 5.5 percent of the declared value of the land on purchase. The government has an excellent history of respecting foreign ownership of land. Construction is less than that usually found in North America. A finished luxury house currently would cost about $85-$100 per square foot to build depending on the finishings. The contractor is responsible for defects in construction for five years.

11. **What communications systems are there? (Are there reliable phone and fax lines, cellular phones, connections to the Internet and other computer communication services, are there local newspapers, radio and TV in a language you understand? Is there cable TV or is satellite TV available?)**

Costa Rica has a state owned hydro/telephone company. Phone line installation can be slow, but once installed they function well. Touch-tone international dialing for phone and fax is in place, as is a well-developed cellular system. Costs are competitive. Internet was introduced in 1995 and use has become widespread. There are several Spanish language newspapers and one English- language daily newspaper, two English- and one German-language weekly, and various magazines. Foreign newspapers can be purchased readily. There are several Spanish-language television stations, and different cable TV companies offering English-language channels. Satellite TV dishes and DirecTV are readily available.

12. What is transportation like? (How are the roads? Are flights available to places you wish to go? How are the bus, train, ferry services? How costly is it to travel to and from your chosen country to frequent destinations to bring in or visit family, business interests, etc.)

Costa Rican roads are in generally poor condition. Potholes are common, and an endless chain of patching is underway. Air service from Costa Rica is well developed, with many direct flights daily to Mexico, the United States, Central and South America, and also direct flights to Europe (Italy, Spain, Germany, England, Holland), Canada and Cuba. Average return airfare to a destination in the United States is about $550. Bus service is excellent, frequent and inexpensive. Deluxe buses are operated on many runs with air conditioning and video movies. There is no passenger train service except for commuter trains near San José.

13. What time zone is your proposed country of residence in compared to areas with which you may want to be in frequent telephone communication, such as where there are family or business interests?

Costa Rica is within 2 hours of most North American cities for time zone. There is no daylight saving time, so it varies seasonally.

14. Is there good shopping? (Would you have a choice of items you wish to purchase to compare prices? In case of malfunction, are parts and service available locally? {Appliances, electronics, photographic equipment, computers, vehicles, furniture and fixtures, etc.}. Is computer software support and repair service available?)

Most things are offered for sale in and around San José, much less so in the rest of the country. The Central Valley boasts many large, enclosed malls and there is little one could want that is not readily available at competitive prices. There is a wide range of warranty, service and repair companies to choose from. Computer software sales and services are common, as are hardware repair facilities. There is a duty-free zone in Golfito in the southwest of the country, where everyone is permitted to purchase up to $500 in goods twice a year from some 80 stores offering low prices twice a year.

15. Are the types of food to which you are accustomed readily available, both in restaurants and markets?

There are thousands of restaurants in the Central Valley offering cuisine from most countries of the world. Giant supermarkets offer most familiar items. Items imported from North America are usually more expensive, however, many familiar name brands are manufactured in Central America and the prices are reasonable. Also, many items will be available inexpensively from local manufacturers with as good or better quality than the brand name you are used to.

16. If you have hobbies, are clubs, supplies and assistance available?

Almost all hobbies are represented by clubs and suppliers locally.

17. What cultural activities are available (Art, music, theater, etc.)?

There is an excellent symphony orchestra, several live theaters and many local or visiting musical, dance and entertainment groups. There is an active art community and several galleries.

18. What entertainment is available (sports, cinemas, night clubs, dancing, fiestas, etc.)?

Fútbol (soccer) is the most popular local sport. Every region, no matter how small, has a soccer field. There are dozens of cinemas, and most films are in English with Spanish sub-titles. San José never sleeps, with a large number of night clubs, discos, bars, casinos and dance halls. Fiestas are popular and frequent throughout Costa Rica.

19. What recreational facilities are available (golf courses, tennis, health clubs, recreation centers, other participatory sports)?

There are many recreation and health centers, private and public, and 18- and nine-hole golf courses. Many courses are under construction by various resort developers. Tennis and basketball are popular. White-water rafting, kayaking, horseback riding, water sports, hiking, bicycling and many other sports are popular and well provided for.

20. Will your appliances, electronics and electrical equipment work on the available power supply?

Costa Rica has 110-115 volt electricity and the NTSA television system, the same as in North America.

21. If you like the beach, are good beaches available? What is the water temperature?

There are hundreds of miles of world-class sandy beaches in various colors. The ocean temperature is warm — well over 80 F — year-round. The surfing is world-famous.

22. What is the situation with poisonous growth, insects, snakes, dangerous animals?

There are few dangerous animals. There are several varieties of poisonous snakes, but they are not usually seen. Insects are few in the Central Valley, there are more on the coasts and in the rain forests.

23. What is the violent crime rate? Sneaky crime (theft, car and house break-ins)? What support can be expected from the police department? How helpful are the police to local residents and foreign residents?

Violent crime is low. In the San José area, break-ins of unoccupied cars and buildings are common, and care is necessary to avoid this type of crime. The police do not differ in their treatment of foreigners and citizens. Generally the police will not come to a break-in until the victim goes to their office and files a report.

24. How do the local residents treat foreign visitors and residents?

Costa Ricans are a very welcoming and friendly people who welcome foreigners.

25. What are the local investment opportunities? Is there any consumer or investment protection legislation for investors? What return can you expect on investments?

There are two stock markets in Costa Rica, and all banks issue Certificates of Investment (as do many private companies and licensed finance companies). OPAB's are available (similar to money market funds) and yield about 5 percent annually. Private and national banks have savings accounts with interest rates in the two to four percent range. Mortgages, investments in private companies and investments in stock, bond and commodity markets outside of Costa Rica are easily arranged through local investment brokers. There is no consumer protection legislation.

26. Is the banking system safe and reliable? Can they transfer funds and convert foreign currency checks, drafts and transfers? Are checking, savings and other accounts you may need available to foreigners? Is there banking confidentiality? Exchange controls? Can money brought into the country be taken back out again?

There are four national (government owned) and about 23 private banks operating in Costa Rica, including Citibank from the United States and Scotiabank from Canada. All deposits in national banks are guaranteed without limit by the government of Costa Rica. Banking is both safe and reliable, although the national banks can be bureaucratic. Checking, savings and investment services are available from all of them. It is also possible to operate accounts in the United States or elsewhere through Costa Rican private banks. Banking in Costa Rica is protected by secrecy legislation. Foreigners may have bank accounts. There are no exchange controls or restrictions on removing funds from the country.

27. Are good lawyers, accountants, investment advisors and other professionals available?

There is a wide variety of professionals available in all fields. Lawyer-client relations are protected by confidentiality laws. Many of the major international accounting firms have offices in Costa Rica.

28. How is the health care system? Are there diseases that are dangerous to foreigners, and if so does the local health care system address the problem? What is the quality of hospitals, doctors, dentists? What is the availability of specialists? How is the ambulance service? Is dentistry up to the standards you are used to?

The health care system is excellent. There is a plan for citizens and residents who have work permits covering medical care, hospitalization and prescription drugs. Citizens are also covered for dental care. This is funded by employers contributing 22 percent of wages paid, and the employee contributing 9 percent. There is also private medical insurance, through the state owned insurance monopoly, which is inexpensive and covers 80 percent of medical costs. Medical services and hospitals are available on a "pay as you go" system for those without medical insurance. Medical care costs are very low compared to North America. Hospitals regularly do high-tech operations such as heart and organ transplants. There are many specialists in Costa Rica, and doctors have their home phone numbers in the yellow pages for emergencies. There is an ambulance service in almost every town in the country, operated by the Red Cross. There is also a wide choice in dental care. No special shots are required to come to Costa Rica.

29. How is sanitation? Can you drink the water? Do restaurants have good sanitation standards? Are pasteurized milk and dairy products available? Do meat, fish and vegetable markets have satisfactory sanitary standards?

Water can be drunk from the tap throughout Costa Rica. Sanitary standards are very high for a third-world country. Pasteurized milk and dairy products are normal everywhere.

30. How is the education system? If you have children, are good private schools available in the language in which you would like them to be educated? What is the school year?

There is a free education system for all children through high school. The official literacy rate is over 93 percent. There are many universities and technical training schools. Many university students have their tuition paid by grants. English is taught in the public school system but the main language is Spanish. There are excellent bilingual and trilingual schools available with a principal language of English, French or German. Some schools are on the North American school year.

31. If you are interested in having domestic staff, what is the cost of cooks, housekeepers, gardeners, etc.?

The current cost for domestic staff is about $1.80 per hour. This will varies if a if second-language ability is required, and may be dependent upon specific conditions, such as whether room and board are provided.

32. What legislation is there to protect foreign residents? What rights do foreign residents have in comparison to citizens? What is the government's past record in respecting the rights of foreign citizens?

Foreign residents are protected by the constitution, and have most of the rights of citizens. The record of the government historically has been excellent in honoring these rights. Foreign residents do not have the right to:

- Vote or participate in political activities
- Work for wages without a permit
- Own land close to national borders

33. What natural dangers are there (hurricanes, tornadoes, typhoons, volcanoes, earthquakes, droughts, floods)?

Costa Rica is in an earthquake zone. While there are many recorded earthquakes per year, only about half a dozen can be felt. There are no hurricanes, but heavy rains may cause flooding. There are several active volcanoes, the most active of which is Arenal. It erupts almost continuously, without causing damage. Loss of life and damage have been caused by volcanic eruptions in the past.

34. Where does the country stand environmentally? What are the environmental issues? What is the history in dealing with environmental concerns?

Costa Rica, in comparison with other third world countries, is very environmentally conscious. Twenty-seven percent of the area of the country has national park or protected reserve status, the 50 meters above the high-tide-line is public property and cannot be privately owned or developed and the next 150 meters inland in approximately 85 percent of the country is owned by the local municipality and cannot be sold. This land can be leased from the municipality for approved projects or residences. There are strict environmental guidelines in place for all developments and mining activity. Logging is closely monitored. Most international ecological groups are represented in Costa Rica, so even where the government overlooks an infringement of the environmental laws, the legal mechanisms are in place for concerned organizations or individuals to halt development with cause. Coastal construction is limited to low rise buildings. Attempts are being made to address pollution in rivers and streams, and vehicle emissions are now being tested anually to keep them within set standards. There are many privately funded research facilities, as may be expected in a country with more bird and insect species than all of North America, more than 200 types of hardwood trees,1,500 varieties of orchids and so on.

35. Is there controlled growth and well managed development?

Development is planned to a certain extent, although in much of the country private land can be used as the owner wishes. Subdivisions must meet government standards, including paved roads, power, water and park land, and they must be maintained by the developer for several years after being sold out. Free zones and industrial areas are well defined, and government policy has been to encourage business to take jobs providing factories to the villages to allow people to travel short distances to work and to slow the spread of large cities. All construction must meet strict earthquake standards. Most industry in Costa Rica is of a non-polluting type. Examples would be electronics, pharmaceuticals and clothing manufacturing. Agriculture is still the largest export sector, led by traditional bananas and coffee, but with non-traditional items such as ferns, flowers and tropical plants gaining rapidly. Huge refrigerated facilities are in place to encourage new agricultural exports.

36. Can pets be brought to the country?

Pets can be brought to Costa Rica. A veterinary certificate is required. Ask the ARCR office for more details on how they can assist you.

Things Every Prospective Expatriate Should Know

When moving to a foreign country, making adequate pre-departure preparations is essential. Here are some tips to make your international move easier.

1) Be sure to undergo a complete medical check-up before leaving to avoid dealing with a major health issue overseas.
2) Take one or more advance trips to your destination to familiarize yourself. It's worth the investment.
3) Take the appropriate documents on the advance trip to start the immigration paperwork. Consulate personnel in the country can secure the visa and residency permit more efficiently than those working thousands of miles away.
4) If you have dependent children, in your pre-departure research, be thorough in seeking the availability of education in your host country.
5) Make sure you and your family understand the country's culture so that they know what will be accepted in terms of volunteer and leisure activities at your new home.
6) In case of health emergencies, make sure you know good health-care providers and how to contact them.
7) Use a travel agency for booking en-route travel so you may search for low-cost fares.
8) Check into purchasing round-trip tickets for en-route travel. They may be less expensive than one-way. And the return ticket may be used for other travel.
9) Remember the sale of your Stateside home increases year-end tax costs due to lost interest deduction.
10) Cancel regular services and utilities. Pay the closing bill for garbage collecting, telephone, electricity, water, gas, cable TV, newspapers, magazines (or send them a change of address), memberships such as library and clubs, store accounts (or notify them that your account is inactive), and credit or check - cashing cards that will not be used.
11) Leave forwarding address with the Post Office or arrange for a mail forwarding service to handle all your U.S. mail.
12) Give notice to your landlord or make applicable arrangements for the sale of your home.

13) Have jewelry, art, or valuables properly appraised, especially if they will be taken abroad. Register cameras, jewelry and other similar items with customs so that there will be no problem when reentering the U.S.
14) Make sure a detailed shipping inventory of household and personal effects (including serial numbers) is in the carry-on luggage and a copy is at home with a designated representative.
15) Obtain extra prescriptions in generic terms and include a sufficient supply of essential medicine with the luggage.
16) Obtain an international driver's license for all family members who drive. Some countries do not recognize an international driver's license but they issue one of their own, provided you have a valid home country license. Bring a supply of photographs as they may be required in the overseas location for driver's licenses and other identification cards.
17) Bring a notarized copy of your marriage certificate.
18) Arrange for someone to have power of attorney in case of an emergency.
19) Close your safety deposit box or leave your key with someone authorized to open it if necessary.
20) Notify Social Security Administration or corporate accounting department (for pensions) where to deposit any U.S. income. Make sure the bank account a d routing numbers are correct.
21) Bring copies of the children's school transcripts. If they are to take correspondence courses, make arrangements prior to departure and hand-carry the course material.
22) At least learn the Language basics prior to going to a foreign country. Trying to integrate with the new culture without the ability to communicate can be frustrating if not impossible.
23) Learn about the country's people and way of life before moving there. Go to your library, call your intended destination's tourism board and read all of the travel publications (magazines and travel guidebooks) you can to educate yourself.

Though this short article only provides a brief overview of the essentials, use it as a guide to prepare yourself for a smooth transition abroad.

* Courtesy of Shannon Roxborough *Transitions Abroad Magazine, A Guide to Living Abroad*

14

Resources

NOTE: This guidebook and chapter have been well-researched. If you don't find a web site or organization mentioned that you have read about or seen on line, then there is a good chance that there may be some major issues. We have strived to list only those organizations that are time-tested or unbiased or transparent to the best of our knowledge.

- *The Publisher*

Indispensable Sources of Information About Living in Costa Rica

LIVE IN COSTA RICA is a time-proven company offering well-organized introductory trips from the United States for people interested in moving to Costa Rica. As a retirement and relocation expert, I have helped newcomers find success and happiness in Costa Rica for more than 25 years. We offer an extensive network of contacts and insider information for potential residents and investors. For more information, call toll-free at: 877-884-2502 afternoons, 1-877-322-4690 anytime or 800-365-2342, E-mail: christopher@costaricabooks.com or liveincostarica@cox.net or see www.liveincostarica.com. All trips are led by Christopher Howard, the author of this best-selling guidebook and renowned expert on living and doing business in Costa Rica. See the section in this book for sample itineraries.

ARCR SEMINARS ON LIVING IN COSTA RICA are given once a month by the Association of Residents of Costa Rica (ARCR). Do not miss the opportunity to get informed about living in Costa Rica by the experts. The topics covered are: Costa Rican Laws and Regulations, Health Care System in Costa Rica, Real Estate (buying, selling and renting), Insurance in Costa Rica, Banking in Costa Rica, Moving and Customs, and Living and Retiring in Costa Rica. Call 2221-2053 or 2233-8068 or fax 2255-0061 for more information.

EL RESIDENTE is published by the ARCR and is not for sale to the general public. If you join the association, your membership will include a bi-monthly copy of their newsletter.

TICO TRAVEL also offers trips to Costa Rica. Their trips are designed to introduce retirees, investors and entrepreneurs to the exciting opportunities that await them abroad. They remain committed to individual and high-quality service, offering un-biased information about Costa Rica. They offer shorter tailor-made tours for individuals, couples and small groups. Their trips are led by Christopher Howard. Call toll-free 800 493-8426, Fax (954) 493-8466, E-Mail: tico@gate.net or see www.ticotravel.com.

Costa Rica blogs

Reading blogs is an excellent source of information about Costa Rica. However, be forewarned that a lot of the blogs being published are nothing more then personal diaries and contain too much subjective information.

The people behind them are neophytes and have not lived in the country long enough to dole out expert advice. Just try and glean pertinent information from their experiences. We don't have the space in this guidebook to list all of the blogs containing information about Costa Rica. The two below are excellent.

- **www.liveincostarica.com/blog** is renowned author, Christopher Howard's personal blog. It contains dozens of articles related to living, retiring and investing in Costa Rica. The author shares his experiences and anecdotes about life here.

- **http://blog.costaricaretirementvacationproperties.com/** is a very informative blog about living in Costa Rica and the many aspects of purchasing and owning property. Robert Shannon is the author of most of the articles and is one of the most astute real estate experts in the country. He has spent almost twenty years as a successful developer, consultant, broker, salesman and is the principal behind **www.costaricaretirementvacationproperties.com,** which is one of the top companies in the region.

Discussion groups

With a growing number of people relocating to Costa Rica and many waiting to do so, a number of forums have sprouted up on the Internet. A wide range of information is disseminated daily through these groups.

Joining one or more of these forums is an excellent way to see what issues residents of Costa Rica face on a daily basis and to keep up with a lot of what is happening in the local expatriate community. Members can express their problems or concerns and receive a lot of constructive feedback. Many residents contribute daily while others add something occasionally or just simply read what their fellow members have to say. Another reason to follow these groups is that many friendships have been made online. Not a week goes by without numerous activities being mentioned for the group's members.

I have lived in Costa Rica for thirty years and occasionally learn something new from the many on-line forums to which I subscribe. Good information about banking, immigration matters, the cost of living, finding good doctors and moving to Costa Rica may be obtained at times from these chat groups. Unfortunately, there are a lot of trivial conversations about meaningless subjects and misinformation discussed.. Consequently, it is important to separate the wheat from the chaff.

I have witnessed on more than one occasion people talking about such meaningless topics as how to get rid of ants, complaining about the quality of butter in Costa Rica, the opinion that there is no good Mexican food in Costa Rica, lack of American products, bashing and praising the Costa Ricans and people wanting Costa Rica to be a clone of the USA etc. What you basically have is people with different opinions on life, many of whom want everything to be perfect here.

More alarming is the fact that you have many amateurs doling out advice about investments, real estate and the economy. Most of these people have only lived in the country for a short time, are still struggling to adjust to the new culture, don't even speak the language well enough to understand the country in depth and are not economists. I have noticed repeatedly that once these neophytes start to express erroneous information about the local real estate market and the economy they open a whole can of worms. The erroneous information often spreads to other chat groups, web sites and the media like wildfire, thus becoming counter productive. Foreigners who live here and chat group with members in the States then confuse distorted information with the reality of the situation. This often causes a lot of panic and anxiety, can even affect the stability of the market and above all creates confusion about living and investing here.

The obvious solution is to take a lot of what is written in these forums with a grain of salt and ONLY seek information from time-tested reliable sources and the real experts.

So, if you are thinking of moving to Costa Rica some value can be derived from the groups below. What follows is a brief description of each of the major discussion groups. Membership in all of these groups is free.

- **CostaRicaLiving@yahoogroups.com** CostaRicaLiving is an English-language e-mail group dedicated to the exchange of information about living in or visiting Costa Rica. Its approximately 5,000 members are welcome to ask questions, share tips and opinions, make recommendations, network and share experiences about retirement, travel, establishing businesses, bringing up families or virtually any other issue related to Costa Rica. Membership to the group is open. The list is moderated, non-commercial, non-religious and non-political. Promotion of personal businesses, sales, rentals and recommendations are accepted. Costa Rica Living maintains a separate bulletin board for descriptions of areas of Costa Rica, FAQs, ads, legal advice, announcements and photos.

- **Association of Residents of Costa Rica Forum (www.arcr.com)**
  This forum is for general discussion, questions, news and comments pertaining to living in Costa Rica. Posts include discussions of questions on health care, working in Costa Rica, housing, cost of living environment, social commentary or any other topic that pertains to life in Costa Rica.

- **GalloPinto@yahoogroups.com**
  Gallo Pinto translates as speckled or spotted rooster, and is the name of a flavored and garnished black bean and rice dish normally served at breakfast. *Gallo Pinto* is a different kind of Internet discussion group, one that welcomes stories, discussions and questions about Costa Rica and is open for discussion of most all other topics, as long as good taste is observed. The founder of the group states, "The prime focus is Costa Rica, by expatriates living here, those exploring doing so in the future and *ticos* (Costa Ricans). We try to dig a bit deeper into all

facets of Costa Rican life, and to break many off the old Internet rules along the way. We welcome Q and A's, stories and discussions on the history, culture, politics, religion and everything else about *Ticolandia* encouraging HTML, lucid thinking and writing and discovering "piggybacking" and short "chat room" type messages. Gallo Pinto also fosters a friendly club-like atmosphere, where members can delve into all things interesting to curious, intelligent, self-disciplined people."

- **Central Valley Living (costaricacentralvalleyliving@yahoo.com)**
  As the name indicates this group specializes in news about the Central Valley.

- **Escazú News (escazunews@yahoo.com**
  A lot of good information.
  Specializing in news about Escazú.

- **costaricaresourceguide** CostaRicaResourceGuide@gmail.com
  A good resource

- **Central America Forum (http://central-america-forum.com/)**
  Central America Forum is a community resource for old hands (locals and foreigners) and recent arrivals to share information about living in and visiting the countries of Central America: Guatemala, Belize, Honduras, El Salvador, Nicaragua, Costa Rica, and Panama. If you want to live, retire, or visit and want to talk about residency, crime, culture, or find a trip advisor, this is your place to do it.

Useful web sites

If you search online there are hundreds, if not thousands, of web sites with information about Costa Rica. The ones below are some of the more useful ones.

www.officialguidetocostaricanrealestate.com— Best Costa Rica real estateguide
www.liveincostarica.com — tours for living here
www.costaricabooks.com — books about Costa Rica
www.costaricagolfproperties.com — real estate
www.costaricaspanish.net — learning Spanish
www.costaricaretirementvacationproperties.com — good retirement homes and excellent investments

www.retireincostarica.net — tours for living here
www.aerocasillas.com — private mail service
www.arcr.net — Association of Residents of Costa Rica
www.babyboomer-magazine.com/
www.bluejeweltravel.com — more information on Costa Rica
www.clinicacatolica.com — another good private hospital
www. CostaRicaLiving@yahoogroups.com — a forum
www.drivetocentralamerica.com— making the trip by car
www.drivemeloco.com—car insurance
www.escapeartist.com — excellent information for expats
www.filetax.com/expat.hmtl — expat tax site
www.fischel.co.cr — largest pharmacy chain
www.gallopinto.com — A forum, news group
wwww.hospitalcima.com — Cima private hospital
www.interbusonline.com — bus information
www.investincentralamerica.com — investment information
www.orcag.com — Panamanian corporations
www.racsa.co.cr — telecommunications site
www.registronacional.go.cr — hall of records
www.sanborns.com — car insurance
www.ticotravel.com — tour information

Suggested Reading
Books About Costa Rica

Amcham's Guide to Investing and Doing Business in Costa Rica, by the American Chamber of Commerce of Costa Rica. AMCHAM, P.O. Box, 4946, San José, Costa Rica. An updated guide containing good information on Costa Rica's business and investment climate.

At Home in Costa Rica: Adventures in Living the Good Life, by Martin Rice. This anecdotal guide tells a fascinating tale of the trials and tribulations of learning a new way of life, a new language, making new (and unusual) friends, building two homes, rehabilitating animals and surviving the machinations of an alien institutional bureaucracy.

Bell's Walking Tour of Downtown San José, by Vernon Bell. A good guide for exploring the downtown area. P.O. Box 185, 1000, San José, Costa Rica. E-mail: home-stay@racsa.co.cr.

Butterfly in the City, by Jo Stuart. Former contributor to *The Tico Times* newspaper and current columnist for Am Costa Rica. This guide offers a great view of living in Costa Rica. To order: jostuart@amcostarica.com.

* ***Christopher Howard's Guide to Real Estate in Costa Rica***, by Christopher Howard, Peter Krupa and Lindsay Whipp. Another one-of-a-kind guide from Costa Rica books. Costa Rica's premier experts have collaborated to make this book essential reading if you plan to invest in Costa Rican real estate.

* ***Christopher Howard's Guide to Costa Rican Spanish***, by Christopher Howard. A one-of-a-kind guidebook for travelers and full-time residents of Costa Rica. A "must" if you plan to make the move and want to speak Spanish like a Costa Rican. There are translations in English of Costa Rican expressions found no where else. It may be ordered from Amazon.com or Costa Rica Books. Also see www.costaricaspanish.net for FREE Spanish lessons and tips.

****Christopher Howard's Guide to the Costa Rican Legal System***, by Adolfo Garcia. This forthcoming, easy-to-use guide promises to simplify Costa Rica's complex and often confusing legal system. Scheduled to be released in 2010.

Choose Costa Rica, by John Howells. Discovery Press. A long-time favorite and "must read" for people who want to make the move. Mr. Howells has been a part-time Costa Rican resident for many years.

Costa Rica Handbook, by Christopher D. Baker. Moon/Avalon Publications. The longest, most extensive and best guidebook for exploring the country, with more than 750 pages of invaluable information.

Diccionario de Términos Jurídicos, by Enrique Alcaraz Varó. English-Spanish, Spanish-English legal dictionary.

Living Abroad in Costa Rica, by Erin Van Rheenen. Another well-written publication from Avalon Publications. An excellent complement to this guidebook. The author has done her research.

****Driving the Pan-American Highway to Mexico and Central America***, by Raymond and Audrey Pritchard, $18.95. This is the only book available if you are planning to drive from the United States to Costa Rica via the Pan-American Highway.

McGraw-Hill's Spanish and English Legal Dictionary, by Henry Saint Dahl. Another good legal dictionary.

Shorty's Guide To the 2010 Ley de Tránsito (www.newleydetransito.com) is a complete guide for the English speaking driver so he can understand Costa Rica's complicated traffic laws.

The Costa Ricans, by Richard, Karen, and Mavis Biesanz. Waveland Press, Prospect Heights, IL. Necessary if you want to understand the people.

The Southern Costa Rica Guide, by Alexander del Sol. An excellent guidebook for the southern part of the country. To order: alexdelsol@yahoo.com or from amazon.com.

The Legal Guide to Costa Rica, by Roger Petersen, $29.95. Information about about Costa Rica's complex legal system.

Insurance in Costa Rica, by David R. Garrett. Garrett and Asociados, SJO 450, P.O. Box 025216, Miami, FL 33102-5216.

Books for Expatriates

- ***A Travelers Guide to Latin American Customs and Manners,*** by Elizabeth Devine. Published by St. Martin's Press. Helps the newcomer understand the Latin way of life.

- ***Chronicles Of The Jungle Mom***, by Michele Kohan. She came to Puerto Viejo with her two kids and immersed herself in the culture.

- ***Escape from America,*** by Roger Gallo. See http://www.escapeartist.com. This book is a must-read for anyone who wants to relocate overseas. It has the answers to all of your questions, plus profiles of the best countries in which to live. This book may be out of print.

- ***How I Found Freedom in an Unfree World,*** by Harry Browne, Liam Works — Dept. FB, P.O. Box 2165, Great Falls, MT 59403-2165, or toll- free 1-888-377-0417. This book will revolutionize your life.

- ***The World's Retirement Havens,*** by Margret J. Goldsmith. This guide briefly covers the top retirement havens in the world. Most of the material is still current since it was published in 1999. You may obtain this guide from John Muir Publications, P.O. Box 613, Santa Fe, NM 87504.

- ***Twisted Roots A Look at the Historical and Cultural Influences that Shaped Latin America Into the Most Impoverished, Unstable, and Backward Region of the Western World***, by Carlos Alberto Montaner. This book is very informative and should be read by anyone planning to move to a country in Latin America.. It is a free download at: http://www.firmaspress.com/Twisted_Roots.pdf.

Periodicals

- ***The Tico Times*** newspaper is published weekly. It is worth subscribing to if you plan to live in Costa Rica. See Chapter 8 for subscription details.

- ***Costa Rica Outdoors,*** is a magazine that covers almost all of the country's outdoor activities. To subscribe write to: Costa Rica Outdoors, Dept. SJO 2316, P.O. Box 025216, Miami, FL 33102-5216. You can also call or fax -2282-6743.

Videos

- ***Costa Rica A Travel Adventure Spectacular*** produced by Ken and Ann Creed. Order the video at www.costaricalearn.com. Ken Creed is a professional filmmaker who has done work for National Geographic and the National Audubon Society. Ann Cabezas Creed is a Travel Agent and Travel writer specializing in Costa Rica. *Costa Rica, an Adventure Travel Spectacular* takes you on a Unique Journey. This tiny country in Central America shows its magnificent natural wonders, its' rich Spanish colonial history and colorful culture. The videographers travel to pristine unspoiled beaches and primary rain forest, venture into the jungle, take the back roads through rural country towns and countrysides covered with a thousand shades of green. Visit a coffee plantation, a folkloric oxcart parade, a horse "tope", and take a peek into the lives of North Americans who choose to live and retire here. Highlights of the film: 1. History and culture 2. Pristine beaches 3. Rain forest, volcanoes, wildlife 4. Testimonial of North Americans who have made Costa Rica their home.

- ***Costa Rica Unica,*** is an informative video dealing with history, the people, archeology, ecology and touring. It provides an in-depth view of the country. This fine video may also be ordered from our company. The price is $22.95. May not be avaialable.

* **All of the titles above with an asterisk are available through Costa Rica Books by calling toll-free 800-365-2342. You may also order the same titles from www.amazon.com or www.costaricabooks.com.**

Excellent Books for Learning Spanish

- *Christopher Howard's Guide to Costa Rican Spanish*, by Christopher Howard. This book is especially designed to help you speak like a Costa Rican native. More than 25 years of research went into the preparation of this guide. It contains one section explaining Costa Rican slang. This material cannot be found anywhere else.

- *Madrigal's Magic Key to Spanish*, by Margarita Madrigal. Dell Publishing Group , 666 Fifth Avenue, New York, NY 10103. Provides an easy method of learning Spanish based on the many similarities between Spanish and English. This book is a "must" for the beginner.

- *A New Reference Grammar of Modern Spanish*, by John Butt and Carmen Benjamin. NTC Publishing Group. This is one of the best reference books ever written about Spanish grammar. It is very easy to use and understand.

- *Barron's Basic Spanish Grammar*, by Christopher Kendris. An in-depth study of Spanish grammar.

- *Barron's Spanish Idioms*, by Eugene Savaia and Lynn W. Winget. This book has more than 2,000 idiomatic words and expressions. It is a helpful handbook for students of Spanish, tourists and business people who want to increase their general comprehension of the language.

- *Barron's Spanish Vocabulary*, by Julianne Dueber. A good book for building vocabulary.

- *Household Spanish*, by William C. Harvey. Barron's Press. A user-friendly book especially for English-speakers who need to communicate with Spanish-speaking employees.

- *Nuevo Diccionario de Costarriqueñismos*, by Miguel Angel Quesada Pacheco, Editorial Tecnológica de Costa Rica. This book is a dictionary of much of the slang used in Costa Rica.

- *Open Door to Spanish* - A Conversation Course for Beginners by Margarita Madrigal. Regent Publishing Company. (books 1 and 2). Two more great books for the beginner.

- *Red-Hot Book of Spanish Slang and Idioms*, by Mary McVey Gill and Brenda Wegmann. McGraw Hill. A lot of useful idiomatic expressions.

- *Spanish for Gringos*, by William C. Harvey. Barron's Press. This is an amusing book that will help you improve your Spanish.

- Spanish for Gringos by William C. Harvey. Barron's Press. This is an amusing book that will help you improve your Spanish.

- Spanish and English Legal Dictionary by Henry Saint Dahl, McGraw Hill. One of the two best Spanish-English dictionaries.

- Spanish Slang and Colloquial Expressions by Michael Mahler, Barron's Press. A must read.

- Street Spanish by David Burke, John Wiley & Son, Inc. Good for street slang.

- *Spanish and English Legal Dictionary*, by Henry Saint Dahl. McGraw Hill. One of thr two bet Spanish-English dictionaries.

- *Spanish Slang and Colloquial Expressions*, by Michael Mahler, Barron's Press. A must read.

- *Street Spanish*, by David Burke. John Wiley & Son, Inc. Good for street slang.

- *Streetwise Spanish*, by Mary McVey Gill and Brenda Wegmann. McGraw Hill. Another good book for Spanish slang.

Useful Reference Books

Cassell's Spanish Dictionary, by Anthony Gooch and Angel García, MacMillan Publishing Co., Inc. An excellen reference book.

Dictionary of Spoken Spanish Words, Phrases and Sentences. Dover Publications Inc., New York, NY. ISBN 0-486-20495-2. This is the best of all phrase dictionaries. It contains more than 18,000 immediately usable sentences and idioms. We recommend it highly.

Latin-American Spanish Dictionary, by David Gold. Ballantine Books. A good dictionary of Spanish used in Latin America.

The New World English/Spanish Dictionary, by Salvatore Ramondino. A Signet Book. Another excellent dictionary of Latin American Spanish.

Websters New World Spanish Dictionary, by Mike González, Prentice Hall. This dictionary is essential for serious Spanish students.

Business Books

Just Enough Business Spanish, Passport Books. Full of phrases to help the businesspeople.

Talking Business in Spanish, by Bruce Fryer and Hugo J. Faria. Barron's Educational Series. Has more than 3,000 business terms and phrases. A must for any person planning to do business in the Spanish-speaking world.

Important Spanish Phrases and Vocabulary

You should know all of the vocabulary below if you plan to live in Costa Rica.

What's your name?	*¿ Cómo se llama usted?*
Hello!	*¡Hola!*
Good Morning	*Buenos días*
Good Afternoon	*Buenas tardes*
Good night	*Buenas noches*
How much is it?	*¿Cuánto es?*
How much is it worth?	*¿Cuánto vale?*
I like	*Me gusta*
You like	*Le gusta*
Where is...?	*¿Dónde está...?*
Help!	*¡Socorro!*
What's the rate of exchange	*¿Cuál es el tipo de cambio?*
I'm sick	*Estoy enfermo*

where	*dónde*	**yesterday**	*anteayer*
what	*qué*	**day after**	
when	*cuándo*	**tomorrow**	*pasado mañana*
how much	*cuánto*	**week**	*la semana*
how	*cómo*	**Sunday**	*domingo*
which	*cuál or cuáles*	**Monday**	*lunes*
why	*por qué*	**Tuesday**	*martes*
now	*ahora*	**Wednesday**	*miércoles*
later	*más tarde*	**Thursday**	*jueves*
tomorrow	*mañana*	**Friday**	*vienes*
tonight	*esta noche*	**Saturday**	*sábado*
yesterday	*ayer*	**month**	*mes*
day before		**January**	*enero*

February	*febrero*
March	*marzo*
April	*abril*
May	*mayo*
June	*junio*
July	*julio*
August	*agosto*
September	*septiembre*
October	*octubre*
November	*noviembre*
December	*diciembre*
spring	*primavera*
summer	*verano*
fall	*otoño*
winter	*invierno*
north	*norte*
south	*sur*
east	*este*
west	*oeste*
left	*izquierda*
right	*derecha*
easy	*fácil*
difficult	*difícil*
big	*grande*
small	*pequeño, chiquito*
a lot	*mucho*
a little	*poco*
there	*allí*
here	*aquí*
nice, pretty	*bonito*
ugly	*feo*
old	*viejo*
young	*joven*
fat	*gordo*
thin	*delgado*
tall	*alto*
short	*bajo*
tired	*cansado*
bored	*aburrido*
happy	*contento*
sad	*triste*

expensive	*caro*
cheap	*barato*
more	*más*
less	*menos*
inside	*adentro*
outside	*afuera*
good	*bueno*
bad	*malo*
slow	*lento*
fast	*rápido*
right	*correcto*
wrong	*equivocado*
full	*lleno*
empty	*vacío*
early	*temprano*
late	*tarde*
best	*el mejor*
worst	*el peor*
I understand	*comprendo*
I don't understand	*no comprendo*
Do you speak English?	*¿Habla usted inglés?*
hurry up!	*¡apúrese!*
O.K.	*está bien*
excuse me!	*¡perdón!*
Watch out!	*¡cuidado!*
open	*abierto*
closed	*cerrado*
occupied (in use)	*ocupado*
free (no cost)	*gratis*
against the rules or law	*prohibido*
exit	*la salida*
entrance	*la entrada*
stop	*alto*
breakfast	*el desayuno*
lunch	*el almuerzo*
dinner	*la cena*
cabin	*la cabina*
bag	*la bolsa*

sugar	*el azúcar*	**4**	*cuatro*
water	*el agua*	**5**	*cinco*
coffee	*el café*	**6**	*seis*
street	*la calle*	**7**	*siete*
avenue	*la avenida*	**8**	*ocho*
beer	*la cerveza*	**9**	*nueve*
market	*el mercado*	**10**	*diez*
ranch	*la finca*	**11**	*once*
doctor	*el médico*	**12**	*doce*
egg	*el huevo*	**13**	*trece*
bread	*el pan*	**14**	*catorce*
meat	*el carne*	**15**	*quince*
milk	*la leche*	**16**	*diez y seis*
fish	*el pescado*	**17**	*diez y siete*
ice cream	*el helado*	**18**	*diez y ocho*
salt	*la sal*	**19**	*diez y nueve*
pepper	*la pimienta*	**20**	*veinte*
post office	*el correo*	**30**	*treinta*
passport	*pasaporte*	**40**	*cuarenta*
waiter	*el salonero*	**50**	*cincuenta*
bill	*la cuenta*	**60**	*sesenta*
blue	*azul*	**70**	*setenta*
green	*verde*	**80**	*ochenta*
black	*negro*	**90**	*noventa*
white	*blanco*	**100**	*cien*
red	*rojo*	**200**	*doscientos*
yellow	*amarillo*	**300**	*trescientos*
pink	*rosado*	**400**	*cuatrocientos*
orange	*anaranjado*	**500**	*quinientos*
brown	*café, castaño*	**600**	*seiscientos*
purple	*morado,*	**700**	*setecientos*
	púrpura	**800**	*ochocientos*
0	*cero*	**900**	*novecientos*
1	*uno*	**1000**	*mil*
2	*dos*	**1,000,000**	*un millón*
3	*trés*		

* If you want to perfect your Spanish, we suggest you purchase our best-selling Spanish book, ***Christopher Howard's Guide to Costa Rican Spanish*** **see the suggested reading section in this chapter**. It is a one-of-a-kind pocket-sized course designed for people who want to learn to speak Spanish the Costa Rican way.

Tiquismos

Here are some Costa Rican expressions you should be familiar with if you plan to spend a lot of time in Costa Rica.

¡Buena Nota!	**Fantastic! Great!**
camaronear	**work an extra job**
chapa	**a coin or stupid person**
chicha	**anger**
chumeco	**dark skin**
chunche	**a thing**
color	**shame**
dar pelota	**flirt**
fila	**line**
gato	**blue-eyed person**
goma	**hangover**
harina	**money**
jalar una torta	**get in trouble**
jamar	**to eat**
¡Jale!	**Hurry up!**
maje	**pal**
pachanga	**party**
paja	**B.S.**
panga	**a small boat**
pulpería	**corner grocery store**
queque	**cake**
roco	**old person**
¡Salado!	**Too bad! Tough luck!**
soda	**a small cafe**
Tico	**a Costa Rican**
timba	**big stomach**
tiquicia	**Costa Rica**
vos	**you, informal equivalent of tú**

Important Telephone Numbers

General Emergency	911
Bilingual Tourist Information	800-343-6332
Municipality of San Jose	2223-4655, 2223-4640
Collect Calls Within Costa Rica	110
Time of Day	112
Information	113
AT&T (International Calls)	114
AT&T Collect-Credit Card Calling	0-800-011-4114
Unlisted Numbers	115
Immigration	2220-0355
INS Accident Report	800-800-8000
OIJ (Judicial Police)	2295-3271
Transit Police (Acidents)	2227-4866 Ext. 205-265
Police	117
Paramedics	118
Fire Department	118
Chamber of Commerce	2221-0005,2221-0389
International Collect Calls	116
International Information	124
Telephone out of order	119
Electric Company	126
Rural Guard	127
Ambulance	128
Bilingual Emergency Service (Like our 911)	122

Important Contact Information

Accountants

Linder, Randy 2288-2201/8839-9970

Alarms

ADT 2257-7373

Ambulance Service (private)

Emergencias Médicas (several locations) 2290-5555

Appliances

David Cohen (highly recommended
E-mail: davidcohencr@yahoo.com) 8361-0408
Gollo (www.gollotienda.com) 800-00-46556
Hogar Feliz (www.hogarfeliz.com) 2256-3321
Importadora Monge 800-222-2000
Play 2234-3586/2262-9606
Used Appliances 2282-4205

Automobile Repair
H.M.S. (English spoken, reliable and honest) 2223-0348
Taller Car-Doc (in English and Spanish) 2271-4000
Mario Alfaro (honest, knowledgeable, English
and Spanish) 8926-3229

Art Supplies
Jiménez Tanzi(several locations) 2216-1048

Banks
State-Run Banks
Banco de Costa Rica 2284-6600
www.bancobcr.com.
Banco Nacional 2212-2000
www.bncr.fi.cr

Private Banks
BAC San Jose 2295-9797, or (506) 800-SAN JOSE (800-726-5673)
www.bac.net/bacsanjose/esp/banco/index.html
Banco Cathay 2290-2233
www.bancocathay.com
Citibank (Costa Rica) S.A. 2201-0800
Formerly (Banco Cuscatlán and Banco Uno)
www.bancocmb.fi.cr
Grupo Financiero Improsa 2284-4215
www.grupoimprosa.com
HSBC Costa Rica (formerly Banco Banex) 2287-1111
www.hsbc.fi.cr/

Promerica 2519-8090
www.promerica.fi.cr/
Scotiabank 800-1SCOTIA/800-1-726842
www.scotiabankcr.com

Bottled Water
Alpina.. 2256-2020
Cristal.. 2442-5453

Building Supplies
Abonos Agro (construction and interior building supplies chain store).
Web site: www.abonosagro.com
Constru Plaza (Escazú) .... Tel: 2588-8888
Similar to Home Depot. Web site : www.construplaza.co.cr
El Lagar.. Tel: 2217-9400
Twelve locations
EPA (construction and interior supplies chain store)
Web site: www.epa.co.cr
Grupo Colono .... Tel: 2713-1029
Construction Supplies
Web site: www.grupocolono.com
Holcim (Costa Rica) S.A. .... Tel: 2552-8922
Producer and supplier cement and other products
and services for the construction industry.
Web site: www.holcim.com
Intaco
Building products including adhesives and protectorants
Web site: www.intacocr.com
Email: aalfaro@intacocr.com (general manager)

Business and Secretarial Services
BILINGUAL SECRETARIAL vvSERVICES 2228-4367
TEMPO 2222-7844

Car Dealerships
DaimlerChrysler (Mercedes) 2295-0000
AutoStar Vehicles S.A.
www.daimlerchrysler.co.cr
Ford 2523-5000

Nacional Automotriz. Nasa. S.A Honda
Franz Amrhein & Co S.A.......... 2257-6911
www.hondacostarica.com.Mazda
www.crautos.com/mazda/main.htm
Nissan.......... 2290-0505
www.nissancr.com
Toyota.......... 2287-4200
Purdy Motor
www.toyotacr.com

Car Rentals
Euurocar (our first choice).......... 2257-1158
Avis RENT-A-CAR.......... 2232-9922
Hertz.......... 2221-1818

Car Services
Emergency Autoservices.......... 2221-2053
Towing.......... 8381-6534 or 2258-4248

Chiropractors *(Quiroprácticos)*
Dra. Yolanda Camacho Alajuela.......... 2443-3276
Dr. Karl Lind Heredia.......... 2237-4268
Dr. Mark Abbott Moravia.......... 2236-3685
Dr. Ronnie Capri San José.......... 2225-3707
Dr. Juan Carlos Pozo Cartago.......... 2552-8318
Dra. Alejandra Rodriguez Atenas.......... 2446-3457
Dr. Michael Norton Liberia.......... 2666-7984
Dr. Sashe Ellison San José.......... 2231-6719
Dr. Jim Mclellan.......... Santa Ana 2282-3998
Dr. Steve Harlow Puntarenas.......... 2661-4567
Dr. Randy de Jesús San José.......... 2256-5118
Dr. Ronald Hash S. Isidro Gen. 2770-4296
Dra. Marishel Morales San Pedro.......... 2253-8997
Dr. Scott Trescott San Carlos.......... 2460-7770

Computer Repair
Marvin Bermudez (Apple/Mac.......... 8886-9711
Frank Day.......... 8396-2725
Fabio Quirós.......... 8384-5636/2228-8471
Kevin "Happy Gringo".......... 2228-1049

Credit Card Companies
American Express....2233-0044
Diner's Club....2233-0455
VISA....2223-2211

Customs Agents
Ship to Costa Rica....2258-8747

Dentists
Acebal, Mercedes....2201-7080
Acosta, Arturo....2228-9904
Arias, Tatiana....2288-5120
Fernandez, Sandra....2257-3382
Hirsch, Ronald (CHILDREN'S DENTIST)....2222-1081
Mora, Elroy....2234-6707
Seas, Adriana....2582-2100
Suárez, Carlos....2241-5652

Doctors
Aggero, Rolando....2255-4476
Arce, Luis R. (EAR, NOSE AND THROAT)....2235-5653
Arellano, Alfonso(CARDIOLOGIST)....2233-5435
Bolaños, Pedro (ACUPUNTURE)....2231-3165
Dr. Paulo Castro GYNECOLOGY)....2234-1402
Esquival, Julio(G(YNECOLOGY)....2220-1010
Gabriel,Patrick (CHIROPRACTOR)....2296-0020
Kogel, Steven
(AMERICAN PSYCHIATRIST)....2253-4502 or 2225-7149
Mario Monge (DERMATOLOGIST) Alajuela....2441-2572
Murray, Charles (PSYCHOLOGICAL COUNSELING)..2260-9902
Olman Riggioni (ALLERGIST) Heredia....2237-5912
Nuñez, Rodolfo (DERMATOLOGY)....2222-6265
Pardo, Rogelio (INTERNAL MEDICINE)....2222-1010

Electrician
Norberto Chaves....8380-3706

Errands
Rapha Nissi Multiservices....2250-5940, 2257-0305

Furniture
Akiro (www.grupoakiro com) 2588- 2020
La Artistica (www.laartisticnet 2296-2590
Searson (www.searson.co.cr) 2286-4343

Handyman Services
Maridos de Alquiler.................................. 2438-7070 or 2438-7949
Dan Schild (US trained electrician)........... 8388-5437 or 2453-2155

Hardware Stores
Brenes (Heredia) 2263-0598
El Mar 2205-2525

Home Inspections
Tom Rosenberger 8364-1989
Email: tom@costaricahomebuilder.com

Interior Shops
Altea Design 2288-2009
Escazú, San José
Web site: www.alteadesign.com/site/ing_index.shtml
Cemaco
Interiors and Household Goods
Web site: www.cemaco.co.cr
Euromobilia 2296-3050
Kitchens and Bathrooms
San José (plans for Tamarindo)
Email: euromobilia@euromobilia.com
Web site: www.euromobilia.com

Interpreters and Translators
Translation Services 2228-4367
TEMPO 2222-7844

Laundry
Dry Cleaners USA (many locations) 2220-1570, 2231-7396

Luggage Repair
Clínica de Valijas www.clinicadelasvalijas.com 2290-2107

Maids
Cinerela Domestic Services..............TEL/FAX 2262-2834, BEEPER 2256-7890 CODE 2084

Mailing Services (private)
Aerocasillas...2255--4567
Star Box 2221-9092

Massage
Mónica Bigen-Hara, Instructora de Balance Integral - HEREDIA (2-260-0960/8-393-2401/ info@BioBellaOrganics.com)
Tara Di Ponti-CMT - Heredia (Barreal [near Carriari) (8814-0763/ tara.di.ponti@gmail.com) -
Costa Rica School of Integrative Massage - Heredia (San Rafael) - One block South of the big, big church in San Rafael (2262-3444/8398-6670/ www.CRMassageSchool.com/www.LearnMassageInCostaRica.com

Medical Laboratory
Laboratorio Labin 2222-1987

Medical Recovery Center
Chetica Ranch...2268-6133

Movers Within Costa Rica
Miguel Villalobos Bolaños.............................8383-5861, 2253-2717

Pet Sitter
Adriana Núnez..2265-1251

Psychologist
Richard Stern 2280-3548

Real Estate
COSTA RICA RETIREMENT VACATION PROPERITIES
(e-mail: robert@costaricaretirement.com) ... toll-free 1-888-581-1786

Refrigerator Repair Ice Maker, Dishwashers, Dryers Etc.
Fernando .... 2225-5927 or 2294-8004
Melvin .... 2289-9565 or 8398-4614

Self-Storage

Bodega America 8392-1921,22821579, 2265-0445

Swimming Pool Supplies

Aeropuerto 2241-0333
Acuarium (Escazú) 2201-7171
Acuarium (Playa Herradura, Jacó) 2637-7148
Acuarium (Liberia) 2667-0800
Piscinas Genesis 2588-0060
Industrias Químicas Altamira S.A. 2438-4402

Supermarket Chains

Auto Mercado (many products from U.S.) .... www.automercado.com
Hipermás (U.S.-style warehouse shopping) .... www.hipermás.com
Más x Menos .... www.masmenos.com
Maxi Bodega .... www.maxibodega.co.cr
Mega Super .... www.megasuper.com
Pali (discount groceries) .... www.pali.co.cr
Perimercados .... www.perimercados.com
Pricesmart (U.S.-style discount wearhouse shopping like Costco) .... www.pricesmart.com

Taxes

U.S. tax specialist James Brohl .... 2-256-8620 (phone), 8-305-3149 (cell) Randall Linder,
U.S. Tax & Accounting Service .... 2288-2201, Cell: 011-506-8839-9970, E-mail: ustax@lawyer.com. http://www.ustaxinternational.com

Taxis

Aeropuerto 2241-0333
Coopetaxi 2235-9966
Coopetico 2224-7979
Sen Jorge 2221-3434
Taxi Alfaro 2221-8466
Taxi Coopeguaria 2226-1366
Taxis de Carga y Mudanzas(For moving) 2223-0921
Unidos 2221-6865

Television Repair
SELCTRON S.A. 2282 6176
Mario Jimenez of Electro Video 2228-0857

Translator
(Fernando E. Alvarado R) .... cell: 8318-18 98

Tours and Travel Agencies
Live in Costa Rica Tours.......... 800-365-2342
Tico Travel.......... 800-493-8426
Travel Store.......... 1-800-250-5119 or 2279-8927

Major Governmental and Autonomous Institutions

The abbreviations below represent important governmental and autonomous entities in Costa Rica. Often the abbreviation is used instead of the complete name.

AyA	(Costa Rican Institute of Aquaducts and Drains) www.aya.go.cr
BCR	(Banco de Costa Rica) - Bank of Costa Rica
BCCR	(Banco Central de Costa Rica) - Central Bank
BCAC	(Banco Crédito Agrícola de Cartago) - Bank of Cartago
BNCR	(Banco Nacional de Costa Rica) - National Bank
CCSS	(Caja Costarricense del Seguro Social) -Social Security system for medical care and retirement
CNE	(National Emergencies) Equivalent of FEMA in the U.S.
CONICIT	(Consejo Nacional de Investigaciones Científicas y Tecnológicas) - Scientific and technological research
CONAPE	(Consejo Nacional de Prestamos para la Educación) - Loans for students
DIS	(Dirección de Intelegencia y Seguridad Nacional) - Internal security
EBAIS	(local clinic) - Caja's health services in rural areas
ICAA	(Instituto Costarricense de Acueductos y Alcantarillados) -Company that supplies water to your home.

ICE	(Instituto Costarricense de Electricidad) - Telephone and electric company
INCOFER	(Instituto Costarricense de Ferrocarriles) - In charge of the railroad
INCOP	(Instituto Costarricense de Puertos del Pacífico) - In charge of the Pacific ports
ICT	(Instituto Costarricense de Turismo) - In charge of tourism
IMAS	(Instituto Mixto de Ayuda Social) - Provides a variety services and help to poor families
INA	(Instituto Nacional de Aprendizaje) - Trade schools
INEC	(Instituto Nacional de Estadística y Censos -Census Bureau
INAMU	(Instituto Nacional de las Mujeres) -Institute for Women
INS	(Instituto Nacional de Seguros) - State-run insurance company
INVU	(Instituto Nacional de Vivienda y Urbanismo) - Housing department
ITCR	(Instituto Tecnológico de Costa Rica) - Technological schools
JAPDEVA	(Junta Administrativa Portuaria y de Desarrollo Económico de la Vertiente Atlántica) - In charge of Atlantic port
JPSSJ	(Junta de Protección Social de San José) - Runs the state lottery whose profits go to social welfare
MINAE	(Ministerio de Ambiente y Energía) -Protects the environment
MCJD	(Ministerio de Cultura, Juventud y Deportes) -Ministry that promotes cultural events and sports for the youth.
MOPT	(Ministerio de Obras Públicas y Transporte) - Transportation Department
MTSS	(Ministry of Labor and Social Security) www.ministrabajo.go.cr
OIJ	(Organismo de Investigacion Judicial) - Like our F.B.I.
PANI	(Patronato Nacional de Infancia) - Child welfare association.
PROCOMER	(Promotora del Comerio Exterior de Costa Rica) - Promotes trade abroad

RECOPE	(Refinadora Costarricense de Petróleo) National Oil Refinery.
RITEVE	(Revisión Técnica Vehicular) - Place that does yearly car inspections
SENARA	(Servicio Nacional de Aguas Subterráneas, Riego y Avenamiento) - Protects and regulates country's water supplie
SETENA	www.setena.go.cr
SUGEF	(Superintendencia General de Entidades Financieras) - Regulates banks, money exchange houses and other financial businesses but not pensions or stockbrokerages.
SUGEVAL	(Superintendencia General de Valores) - Regulates, supervises and oversees Costa Rican securities markets, the activities of private individuals or corporate entities.
UCR	(Universidad de Costa Rica) - University of Costa Rica
UNED	(Universidad Estatal a Distancia) - University extension
UNA	(Universidad Nacional) - National University

Zip Codes by City

Office Name	Zip Code	Fax	Tel	Location of the Postal Office
Administración Central	1000	233-1909	233-9766	Diagonal a la Fishel, San Jose
Aeropuerto	4003	279-5418	441-1278	Aeropuerto Internacional Juan Santamaria.
Aguas Zarcas	4433	474-4062	474-4062	100 E y 25 S. De la Iglesia Catolica
Alajuela	4060	441-0122	441-9107	Avenida 5, Calle 1, Alajuela
Alajuelita	1400	254-6072	254-6826	50 Sur de la Iglesia Católica
Asamblea Legislativa	1013	233-1656	243-2528	Edificio Asamblea Legislativa
Aserri	1450	230-4115	230-4115	De la Iglesia 100 Este 125 Sur
Atenas	4013	446-5140	446-5140	Esquina sureste del mercado
B. San José, Alajuela	4030	433-9991	433-9991	Contiguo a G.A.R.
Bagaces	5750	671-1119	671-1119	De la bomba de gasolina 200 oeste
Barra del Tortuguero	7311	N/A	383-7886	Tortuguero Centro
Barranca	5460	663-2636	663-2636	Frente Bodegas del INCOP
Barrio Mexico	1005	222-2713	233-3713	Esquina Norte Plaza, 50 N 25 E
Barva de Heredia	3011	260-6622	260-6622	Avenidas 4 y 6, Calle 1
Batán	7251	718-6130	472-2075	25 Norte del Hospedaje Batáan
Boca Arenal	4407	N/A	N/A	200 Sur de la Iglesia Católica
Boca de Nosara	6233	682-0100	682-0100	Contiguo al Centro de Salud
Bribrí	7312	N/A	758-3014	Contiguo a la Municipalidad
Buenos Aires	8100	730-0003	730-0003	Contiguo a la G.A.R.
Cahuita	7302	755-0096	755-0096	Contiguo a la SubComisaria
Cañas	5700	669-0309	669-1701	Frente a Coopecompro
Cariari	7212	767-7198	767-7198	25 Este de la Escuela de Campo Kennedy
Carmona de Nandayure	5313	N/A	657-7366	Contiguo a la Municipalidad
Cartago	7050	551-0070	552-4595	Avenida 2 entre Calle 15 y 16
CATIE	7170	ext.286	556-6431	Turrialba CATIE
Centro Colón	1007	223-6674	223-6574	Calle 38 AV 0 y 1, Ed. Centro Colón
Ciudad Colón	6100	249-1966	249-1966	Costado Norte de la Casa Cural
Ciudad Quesada	4400	460-1576	460-3399	100 Norte Cruz Roja
Cobano	5361	642-0047	642-0047	Contiguo a la G.A.R.
Coco Beach (Playas del Coco)	5019	670-0418	670-0418	Frente al parque
Coronado	2200	229-1151	292-2684	200 N 50 O Iglesia
Correo Interno	2020	223-6521	223-6521	Centro Postal Zapote
Corte Suprema de Justicia	1003	223-6780	223-6780	Calle 15 y 17 AV 8 Edif. Corte
Cuidad Cortéz	8153	788-8210	788-8210	150 Oeste del Hospital Tomas Casas
Cuidad Neilly	8250	783-3140	783-3500	Costado Suroeste del Mercado
Curridabat	2300	272-0360	272-0360	300 O. Esquina suroeste Iglesia
Desamparados	2400	259-3573	259-2357	100 Sur Bomberos
El Roble	5461	663-0995	663-0995	De la entrada principal del Roble 400 norte
Escazú	1250	289-5298	289-4308	100 N. Palacio Municipal
Esparza	5500	635-5138	636-6666	100 este del Liceo Diurno Esparza
Fecosa	1009	N/A	255-1610	AV. 20 Calle E. Edif. Ferrocariles
Filadelfia	5050	688-8213	688-8213	De Coopecompro 100 sur y 25 este
Florencia	4401	475-5005	475-5005	Contiguo a la G.A.R.
Frailes	2414	N/A	544-0099	Frente Banco Nacional
Golfito	8201	775-0373	775-1911	Frente a la Plaza
Grecia	4100	444-5661	494-4501	Avenida 1, entre calles 1 y 3
Guácimo	7213	716-5028	716-5028	200 Este del Edificio Municipal
Guadalupe	2100	224-0379	253-5349	Costado Oeste Parque
Guápiles	7210	710-6161	710-7203	Costado Norte de la Municipalidad
Hatillo	1300	254-7607	254-7607	Centro Comercial Hatillo
Heredia	3000	260-6767	260-0461	Avenida Central entre Calle central y 2
Hojancha	5251	659-9186	659-9186	Costado suroeste del parque
Ipis	2110	229-0016	229-0016	Contiguo Plaza
Jaco	4023	643-3479	643-3479	Frente a la G.A.R.
Jicaral	5353	650-0114	650-0114	150 norte de la G.A.R.
Juan Viñas	7160	532-2285	532-2285	Enfrente al parque
La Cruz	5009	679-9329	679-9329	50 este del parque
La Fortuna	4417	479-9178	479-9178	50 O. De la Bomba de Gasolina
La Uruca	1150	223-0917	223-6492	100 O Lanner y Saenz
La Y Griega	1011	227-2737	227-2737	Frente Centro Comercial del Sur
Las Juntas de Abangares	5600	662-0767	662-0076	25 norte del Kinder
Liberia	5000	666-0359	666-1649	200 norte del Banco Crédito Agrícola
Limón	7300	758-1543	758-3471	Diagonal de la esquina Norte del Mercado
Los Chiles	4450	471-1061	471-1061	Local N° 06 Mercado Municipal
Miramar	5550	639-9451	639-9451	Costado norte de la iglesia principal

Moravia	2150	236-1506	235-9936	Costado Parque
Naranjo	4200	450-0644	450-0644	A la par de la estación de bomberos
Nicoya	5200	685-5004	685-5088	Diagonal al parque
Nuevo Arenal	5717	N/A	694-4310	Contiguo a la G.A.R.
Orotina	4021	428-8481	428-8481	Contiguo a la G.A.R.
Palmar Norte	8150	786-6291	786-6291	Contiguo a la G.A.R.
Palmares	4300	452-0274	453-1954	Calle Central entre calles 6 y 8
Paquera	5357	641-0060	641-0060	Contiguo a la G.A.R.
Paraíso	7100	574-7660	574-7660	Avenida 1 , Calle Central
Parque Industrial Cartago	7052	766-6242	766-6509	Parque Industrial Cartago
Parrita	6300	779-9108	779-9108	150 oeste de la Municipalidad de Parrita
Paseo Estudiantes	1002	233-0692	233-0692	Calle 9 AV. 10 y 12
Paso Canoas	8255	732-2021	732-2021	Frontera con Panamá
Pavas	1200	232-8745	232-0333	Contiguo Escuela Pavas
Pital	4437	473-3097	473-3097	Diagonal a la Plaza de Deportes
PIZFA	4002	N/A	N/A	Parque Industrial Alajuela
Plaza Mayor	1235	N/A	N/A	Pavas Centro
Puerto Jiménez	8203	735-5045	735-5045	Frente a la Plaza
Puerto Viejo de Sarapiquí	3069	766-6247	766-6509	Frente al Banco Nacional
Puntarenas	5400	661-0440	661-2156	Frente al Banco Costa Rica
Puriscal	6000	416-6073	416-7656	50 N. Esquina Noroeste Parque
Quepos	6350	777-0279	777-1471	Frente a la Plaza Rancho GDR costado Oeste
Río Claro	8200	789-9420	789-9420	200 Norte del Aserradero Impala
Río Frío	3071	764-1019	472-2075	Costado oeste del Taller Eladio
Sabanilla	2070	253-6302	253-6302	Costado Oeste Parque
Samara	5235	666-0368	656-0368	Contiguo a la G.A.R.
San Antonio Belen	4005	239-2254	293-0360	Avenida Central, Calle 6
San Francisco de Dos Ríos	2350	227-6355	227-6355	100 Sur de la Iglesia
San Francisco Guadalupe	2120	N/A	221-5041	De la Iglesia 100 Este 125 Norte
San Gerardo de Chomes	6659	N/A	N/A	Contiguo a Servicentro San Gerardo
San Ignacio de Acosta	1500	410-0095	410-0095	Costado Este Parque
San Isidro Heredia	3017	258-7692	268-7692	100 norte y 15 al este de la clínica católica.
San Isidro P.Z.	8000	771-3060	771-0346	Detrás del Colegio la Asunción.
San Joaquin de Flores	3007	265-5692	265-5692	A la par de la municipalidad
San José 2000	1017	232-3843	232-3843	Planta Baja C.C. S.J.2000
San Marcos de Tarrazú	8055	546-6325	546-6325	Contiguo a la Municipalidad
San Mateo de Alajuela	4017	N/A	N/A	Costado oeste Palacio Municipal
San Pablo de Heredia	3019	237-2269	237-2269	Esquina sur del parque
San Pablo de León Cortéz	8059	546-7679	546-7679	Fte. Parque
San Pedro de Montes de Oca	2050	225-4852	283-5138	Costado Oeste de la Plaza
San Pedro Poas	4059	448-5344	448-5344	200 sur y 25 este de la escuela.
San Rafael de Guatuso	4500	464-0132	464-0132	50 Sur de la Estación de Gasolina
San Rafael Heredia	3015	238-0461	238-0461	100 este de la iglesia
San Ramon	4250	445-5718	445-7606	Avenida 2 Calles 2 y 4
San Sebastián	1350	226-5072	226-5072	400 N. De la Iglesia
San Vito	8257	773-3130	773-3830	Contiguo a la G.A.R.
Santa Ana	6150	282-7403	282-7403	Costado Norte de la Plaza
Santa Ana 2000	6151	282-4687	282-4687	Centro Com. Sta. Ana 2000
Santa Barbara Heredia	3009	N/A	N/A	50 sur esquina noroeste del parque
Santa Cruz	5150	680-0280	N/A	Frente a la empresa Alfaro
Santa María de Dota	8051	541-1020	541-1020	Costado Norte del Parque
Santa Rosa de Pocosol	4409	477-6065	477-6065	Frente al Costado Sur del Parque
Santo Domingo	3100	244-2113	244-2113	Avenida Central, Calles 2 y 4
Sarchi Norte	4150	454-4300	454-4533	Diagonal plaza deportes costado sur
Siquirres	7200	768-8229	768-6006	Frente a la G.A.R.
Tibas	1100	235-1764	297-0767	100 E. 10 S. Parque
Tilaran	5710	695-5387	695-6230	Del estadio 150 Oeste
Tres Ríos	2250	279-5418	279-5418	Costado Oeste Escuela Central
Turrialba	7150	556-0427	556-7670	Avenida 6 Calle O
Upala	5707	470-0545	470-0174	Del parque 100 Norte
Veintisiete de Abril	5153	N/A	N/A	Contiguo a la G.A.R.
Venecia	4443	472-2075	472-2075	100 Este de la Soda Matute
Villareal	5159	653-0676	653-0676	Frente a la plaza de deportes
Zapote	2010	224-5747	283-5585	Frente Liceo de Zapote
Zarcero	4350	463-3276	463-3276	Costado Norte del Parque
Zona Franca Met. Barreal	3006	239-0236	239-0236	Zona Franca Metropolitana Barreal

INDEX

Notes

Notes

NOTES